Nakauchi

Contemporary
ECONOMICS

William A. McEachern

THOMSON

SOUTH-WESTERN

Australia · Canada · Mexico · Singapore · Spain · United Kingdom · United States

THOMSON
SOUTH-WESTERN

Contemporary Economics

William A. McEachern

VP/Editorial Director
Jack W. Calhoun

VP/Editor-in-Chief
Dave Shaut

Senior Publisher
Karen Schmohe

Executive Editor
Eve Lewis

Project Manager
Carol Sturzenberger

Consulting Editor
Jeanne Busemeyer

VP/Director Educational Marketing
Carol Volz

Senior Marketing Manager
Nancy A. Long

Marketing Coordinator
Angela Russo

Production Editor
Darrell Frye

Production Manager
Patricia Matthews Boies

Manufacturing Coordinator
Kevin Kluck

Media Developmental Editor
Matthew McKinney

Design Project Manager
Stacy Jenkins Shirley

Production House
New England Typographic Service (NETS)

Cover Designer
Grannan Graphic Design, Ltd.

Cover Images
© David Muir/Masterfile and Ian McKinnell/Getty Images

Internal Designer
Grannan Graphic Design, Ltd.

Printer
Courier, Kendallville

Username: **demand**
Password: **supply**

William A. McEachern

William A. McEachern began teaching large classes of economic principles when he joined the University of Connecticut faculty in 1973. In 1980, he started offering teaching workshops around the country and, in 1990, created *The Teaching Economist*, a newsletter that focuses on making teaching more effective and more fun.

His research has appeared in a variety of journals, including *Economic Inquiry, National Tax Journal, Journal of Industrial Economics, Public Choice,* and *Quarterly Review of Economics and Business*. His books include *Managerial Control and Performance* and *Economics: A Contemporary Introduction*, a college textbook now in its sixth edition. That textbook has also appeared in an Australian edition, a Spanish edition, and an Indonesian edition. A Chinese edition will be published shortly.

Professor McEachern has advised federal, state, and local governments on policy matters and has appeared in media such as the *New York Times, London Times, Wall Street Journal, Christian Science Monitor, Boston Globe, USA Today*, CBS MarketWatch.com, Voice of America, *Now with Bill Moyers*, and *Reader's Digest*.

In 1984, Professor McEachern won the University of Connecticut Alumni Association's Faculty Award for Distinguished Public Service and in 2000 won the Association's Faculty Excellence in Teaching Award. He is the only person in University of Connecticut history to win both awards.

He was born in Portsmouth, New Hampshire, earned an undergraduate degree in the honors program from College of the Holy Cross, served three years as an Army officer, and earned an M.A. and Ph.D. in economics from the University of Virginia.

ABOUT SOUTH-WESTERN—DEVELOPING LIFELONG LEARNING SOLUTIONS FOR ALL STUDENTS

South-Western—a Thomson business—is the leading provider of business and economics learning materials worldwide. We offer the most extensive selection in business educational materials for the K-12, higher education, corporate, and professional markets. With innovative tools and resources that engage and enhance learning, South-Western leads the way to business success. Our rich spectrum of textbooks, simulations, online courses, web sites, and software products offers the best possible learning solutions that lead students to real careers and lifetime skills.

Program Consultants

Douglas Haskell
Associate Director, Center for Economic
Education & Research
University of Cincinnati
Cincinnati, Ohio

James Martin
Teacher, Social Studies Department
Walnut Hills High School
Cincinnati, Ohio

Michael O'Bryant
Social Studies Consultant
Mason City Schools
Mason, Ohio

Alice Temnick
Economics Teacher
Cactus Shadows High School
Cave Creek, Arizona

Economics Advisory Board

James Bauer
Economics Teacher
Archbishop Moeller High School
Cincinnati, Ohio

Timothy L. Davish
Teacher, Social Studies Department
Lakota Local Schools
Liberty Township, Ohio

Dennis M. Dowling
Teacher, Social Studies Department
Lakota West High School
West Chester, Ohio

John Hamstra
Economics Teacher
Mason City Schools
Mason, Ohio

James L. Jurgens
Teacher, Social Studies Department
St. Xavier High School
Cincinnati, Ohio

Sandra L. Mangen
Teacher, Business Department
Beavercreek High School
Beavercreek, Ohio

Reviewers

Fernando Arencibia, Jr.
Social Studies Teacher
Miami Coral Park Senior High
Miami, Florida

Matthew C. Ethen
History-Social Science Teacher
Edison High School
Fresno, California

Alan Fontenot
Teacher
Pineville High School
Pineville, Louisiana

Pete A. Martinez
Microeconomics Teacher
Danbury High School
Danbury, Connecticut

Sally Meek
Economics Teacher
Plano West Senior High School
Plano, Texas

Renee K. Metcalfe
Curriculum Specialist
Springfield School District 19
Springfield, Oregon

Patti Pair
Economics Teacher
Chattahoochee High School
Alpharetta, Georgia

John Papadonis
Social Studies Department Head
Lexington High School
Lexington, Massachusetts

Carol Penland
Teacher, Business Department
South Cobb High School
Austell, Georgia

James P. Rademacher
Teacher—Economics, Business
Mainland High School
Daytona Beach, Florida

James Ragusa
Teacher, Social Studies Department
Gulf Coast High School
Naples, Florida

Alan R. Ramos
Economics Teacher
Marjory Stoneman Douglas
High School
Parkland, Florida

Paul Spegele
Economics Teacher
Pine Ridge High School
Deltona, Florida

Gail A. Tamaribuchi
Director, Center for Economic
Education
University of Hawaii
at Manoa
Honolulu, Hawaii

Shawn Prewitt Woodham
Economics Teacher
Hoover High School
Hoover, Alabama

Contents

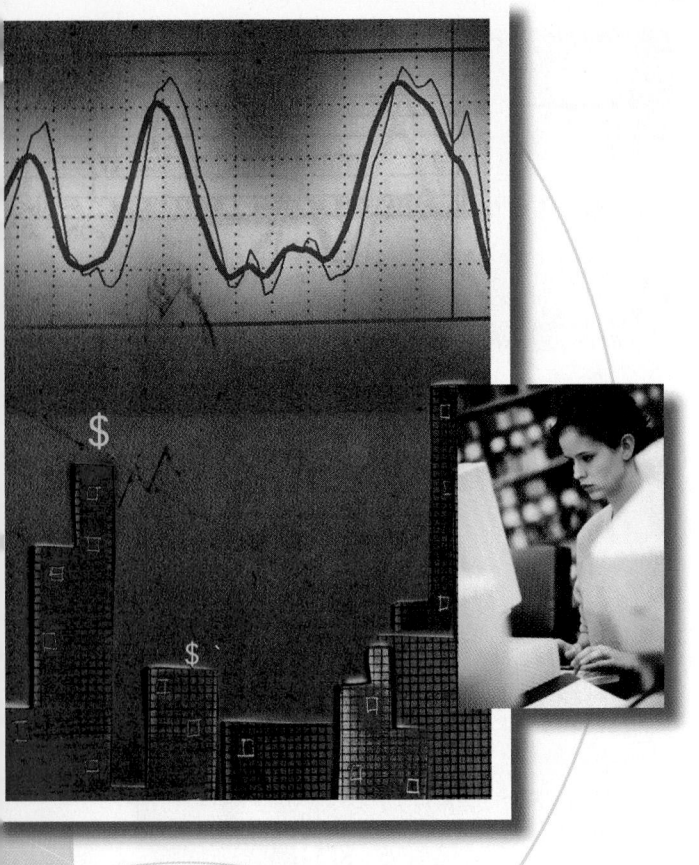

Ask the Xpert!

C O N N E C T
to History

E-CONOMICS

Ethics in Action

[In the News]

Investigate Your Local Economy

Main Idea

movers & shakers

NET Bookmark

Sharpen Your Life Skills

THE WALL STREET JOURNAL

Charts and Figures

National Content Standards in Economics

NCEE
National Council on Economic Education

Standard	Chapter Coverage in *Contemporary Economics*
1. Scarcity. Productive resources are limited. Therefore, people cannot have all the goods and services they want; as a result, they must choose some things and give up others.	Chapters 1, 2, 3, 4, 5, 8, 9, 12, 19
2. Marginal Cost/Benefit. Effective decision making requires comparing the additional costs of alternatives with the additional benefits. Most choices involve doing a little more or a little less of something: few choices are "all or nothing" decisions.	Chapters 1, 2, 3, 4, 5, 6, 8, 9, 10, 12, 14
3. Allocation of Goods and Services. Different methods can be used to allocate goods and services. People acting individually or collectively through government must choose which methods to use to allocate different kinds of goods and services.	Chapters 1, 2, 3, 19
4. Role of Incentives. People respond predictably to positive and negative incentives.	Chapters 1, 2, 3, 4, 5, 6, 7, 8, 9, 10, 12, 13, 15, 16, 17, 18, 19
5. Gain from Trade. Voluntary exchange occurs only when all participating parties expect to gain. This is true for trade among individuals or organizations within a nation, and usually among individuals or organizations in different nations.	Chapters 2, 3, 6, 10, 11, 16, 18, 19
6. Specialization and Trade. When individuals, regions, and nations specialize in what they can produce at the lowest cost and then trade with others, both production and consumption increase.	Chapters 1, 2, 3, 5, 6, 7, 16, 18, 19
7. Markets—Price and Quantity Determination. Markets exist when buyers and sellers interact. This interaction determines market prices and thereby allocates scarce goods and services.	Chapters 1, 2, 4, 5, 6, 7, 13, 18, 19
8. Role of Price in the Market System. Prices send signals and provide incentives to buyers and sellers. When supply or demand changes, market prices adjust, affecting incentives.	Chapters 4, 5, 6, 9
9. Role of Competition. Competition among sellers lowers costs and prices, and encourages producers to produce more of what consumers are willing and able to buy. Competition among buyers increases prices and allocates goods and services to those people who are willing and able to pay the most for them.	Chapters 3, 6, 7, 8, 12
10. Role of Economic Institutions. Institutions evolve in market economies to help individuals and groups accomplish their goals. Banks, labor unions, corporations, legal systems, and not-for-profit organizations are examples of important institutions. A different kind of institution—clearly defined and enforced property rights—is essential to a market economy.	Chapters 2, 3, 7, 8, 9, 10, 11, 12, 13, 15, 16, 17, 18, 19

11. Role of Money. Money makes it easier to trade, borrow, save, invest, and compare the value of goods and services.	Chapters 2, 3, 8, 10, 16, 17, 18
12. Role of Interest Rates. Interest rates, adjusted for inflation, rise and fall to balance the amount saved with the amount borrowed, which affects the allocation of scarce resources between present and future uses.	Chapters 3, 10, 11, 13, 15, 16, 17
13. Role of Resources in Determining Income. Income for most people is determined by the market value of the productive resources they sell. What workers earn depends, primarily, on the market value of what they produce and how productive they are.	Chapters 1, 3, 5, 9, 11, 12, 13, 15, 19
14. Profit and the Entrepreneur. Entrepreneurs are people who take the risks of organizing productive resources to make goods and services. Profit is an important incentive that leads entrepreneurs to accept the risks of business failure.	Chapters 1, 3, 5, 8, 10, 12, 19
15. Growth. Investment in factories, machinery, new technology, and in the health, education, and training of people can raise future standards of living.	Chapters 1, 2, 3, 8, 9, 10, 11, 12, 13, 15, 17, 19
16. Role of Government. There is an economic role for government in a market economy whenever the benefits of a government policy outweigh its costs. Governments often provide for national defense, address environmental concerns, define and protect property rights, and attempt to make markets more competitive. Most government policies also redistribute income.	Chapters 2, 3, 6, 7, 8, 12, 13, 14, 15, 16, 17, 18, 19
17. Using Cost/Benefit Analysis to Evaluate Government Programs. Costs of government policies sometimes exceed benefits. This may occur because of incentives facing voters, government officials, and government employees; because of actions by special interest groups that can impose costs on the general public; or because social goals other than economic efficiency are being pursued.	Chapters 3, 7, 13, 14, 18, 19
18. Macroeconomy—Income, Employment, Prices. A nation's overall levels of income, employment, and prices are determined by the interaction of spending and production decisions made by all households, firms, government agencies, and others in the economy.	Chapters 1, 11, 13, 15, 19
19. Unemployment and Inflation. Unemployment imposes costs on individuals and nations. Unexpected inflation imposes costs on many people and benefits some others because it arbitrarily redistributes purchasing power. Inflation can reduce the rate of growth of national living standards because individuals and organizations use resources to protect themselves against the uncertainty of future prices.	Chapters 11, 13, 15, 17, 19
20. Monetary and Fiscal Policy. Federal government budgetary policy and the Federal Reserve System's monetary policy influence the overall levels of employment, output, and prices.	Chapters 3, 13, 14, 15, 16, 17, 18

ANALYZING PRIMARY SOURCES

Analyzing something involves breaking down and looking at all of the parts of the item in order to better understand it. *Primary sources* are historical materials that were created by the people who actually participated in the historical events. Primary sources might include personal letters, diaries, memos, legal documents, photographs, artwork, or other artifacts. Some primary sources may be more valuable to one's research than others might be.

The process of analyzing primary sources can help us determine how helpful a primary source might be. For example, if someone was writing a history of an oil company that rose and fell in the 1920s, he or she might use primary sources such as diaries from the company's founders, internal company memos, or examples of advertisements for the company. The author also might come across primary sources that describe fashion trends in the 1920s, but an analysis of that information would show that it was not very useful to the study of the oil company. In analyzing primary sources, you should answer questions about it, such as what it is, who created it, when, where, how it relates to your research, and why it is important. Using a graphic organizer like the one below can help you analyze primary sources.

Graphic Organizer 1

ITEM	
What is it?	
Who created it?	
Where did it come from?	
When was it created?	
How does it relate to your research?	
Why is it important?	

IDENTIFYING POINT OF VIEW AND FRAME OF REFERENCE

Point of view is the way someone thinks about a subject. Often, point of view is influenced by a person's background or position in a situation. A consumer, for example, might have a different point of view about rising prices than a producer would.

Frame of reference is similar, but it refers to the methods by which someone develops a point of view. For example, an economist may have a different view of the effects of high unemployment than a sociologist would because each one is examining the topic from different frames of reference. An economist might look at the effects of high unemployment on other economic factors, such as consumer spending and overall economic growth. A sociologist might look at the effects of high unemployment on people's lifestyles, beliefs, and habits. Neither side is right or wrong, but they both will look at different data because of their different frames of reference. Using graphic organizers like those shown on page xxvii can help you identify points of view and frames of reference.

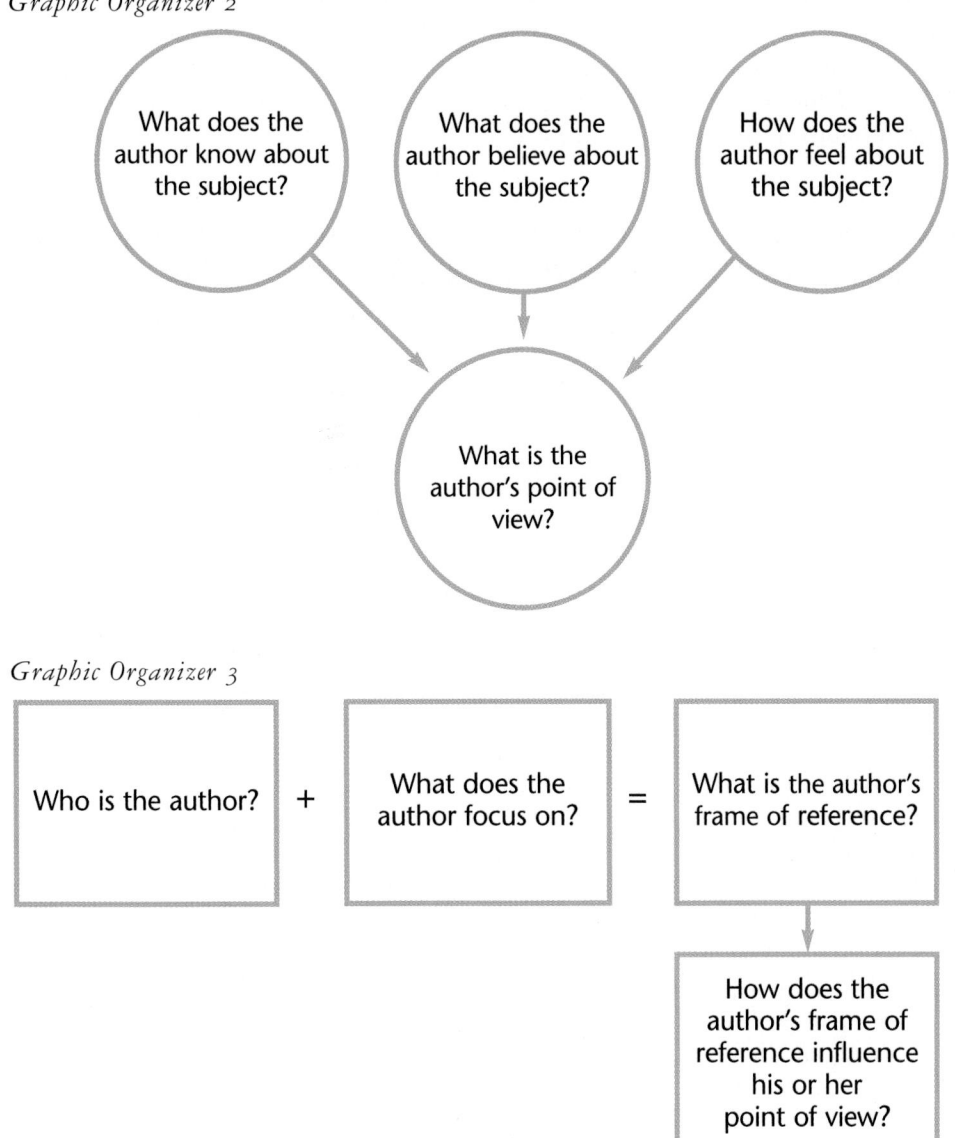

DISTINGUISHING FACT AND OPINION

When reading information about a topic, it is very important to determine if what you are reading is fact or opinion. *Facts* are statements that can be checked for accuracy, such as the amount of money that something costs. *Opinions* are statements that reflect personal feelings and cannot be verified for accuracy, such as whether or not it is worth it to pay a certain price for an item.

Many times writers will combine facts and opinions. Writers who are trying to persuade a reader that their opinion on something is correct will use facts to support the opinion. However, readers should be very clear on which parts of the argument are opinion statements and which are facts. Misuse of facts also can be a sign of *bias*, or preconceived ideas not based on true facts. A reader who confuses facts and opinions easily can be led to a false conclusion about something.

In order to distinguish facts and opinions in writing, it is helpful to break the statements down and evaluate whether they can be tested for accuracy. For example, a writer might note that a certain state has suffered from increased inflation and high unemployment for more than a year. The writer might then state that these economic problems prove that the governor of the state is a bad leader. Increased inflation and high unemployment are facts that can be verified. That the governor is a bad leader is an opinion that may be supported or weakened by the introduction of more facts.

Clue words and phrases such as *bad, good, in my opinion, poor, strong,* and *weak* can help you identify opinions. Using a graphic organizer like the one below also can help you distinguish facts from opinions.

Graphic Organizer 4

Statement	Fact	Opinion	Explain Why

USING RELIABLE INFORMATION

When conducting research, it is important to use reliable information, or information that comes from a dependable source. In analyzing the reliability of information, you need to have all of the facts about where the information is coming from and recognize any biases from the source. You usually can find a great deal of reliable information in the library. Sources that provide footnotes or other indications of where the information came from usually are more reliable that undocumented sources. The Internet often provides fast, up-to-date information, but you have to be very careful about checking the reliability of Internet sources. Some that may initially look like they have come from a reliable source actually may have come from a biased source.

You also can check the reliability of a source by comparing its information with that of other sources. For example, if the reports of five major economic groups conclude that the economy is slowly entering a period of recession, but the report by a politically interested group concludes that there are no signs of recession, you may need to question the reliability of the last report.

Whenever possible, it is best to rely on the most original version of a source that is available. For example, if you were conducting research on a controversial speech by the U.S. Secretary of Commerce, you could read news accounts of the speech or commentaries on it by various people. However, if you really wanted to verify what the secretary said, the most reliable source would be a copy of the speech itself. Most speeches by government officials and other types of government information can be obtained on government web sites. Using a graphic organizer like the one below can help you check the reliability of sources.

Graphic Organizer 5

Source	
Who is the author?	
Who is the publisher?	
Does the author or publisher have any known biases?	
Where did the author get his or her information?	
Can the information be checked against other sources?	

SOCIAL STUDIES SKILLS

IDENTIFYING CAUSE AND EFFECT AND MAKING PREDICTIONS

A *cause* is something that makes an event happen. An *effect* is the result of that cause. A *prediction* is an educated guess about what the effect of a cause might be. Understanding the relationship between causes and effects can help you understand why an event occurred. It also can help you predict what might happen when certain actions are taken. For example, the cause of an increase in gasoline prices might be a decision by OPEC to cut oil supplies. One might predict, then, that gas prices would go down if OPEC reverses this policy.

There can be more than one cause for an effect. Likewise, one cause might have many effects. Clue words and phrases such as *accordingly, as a result of, because, for this reason, in order to, since, so*, and *then* can help you identify causes as you read. In examining causes and effects of actions and events, look for logical patterns. Once you understand the patterns, you can better predict what the next action or event will probably be. Using graphic organizers like the ones below can help you in this process.

Graphic Organizer 6

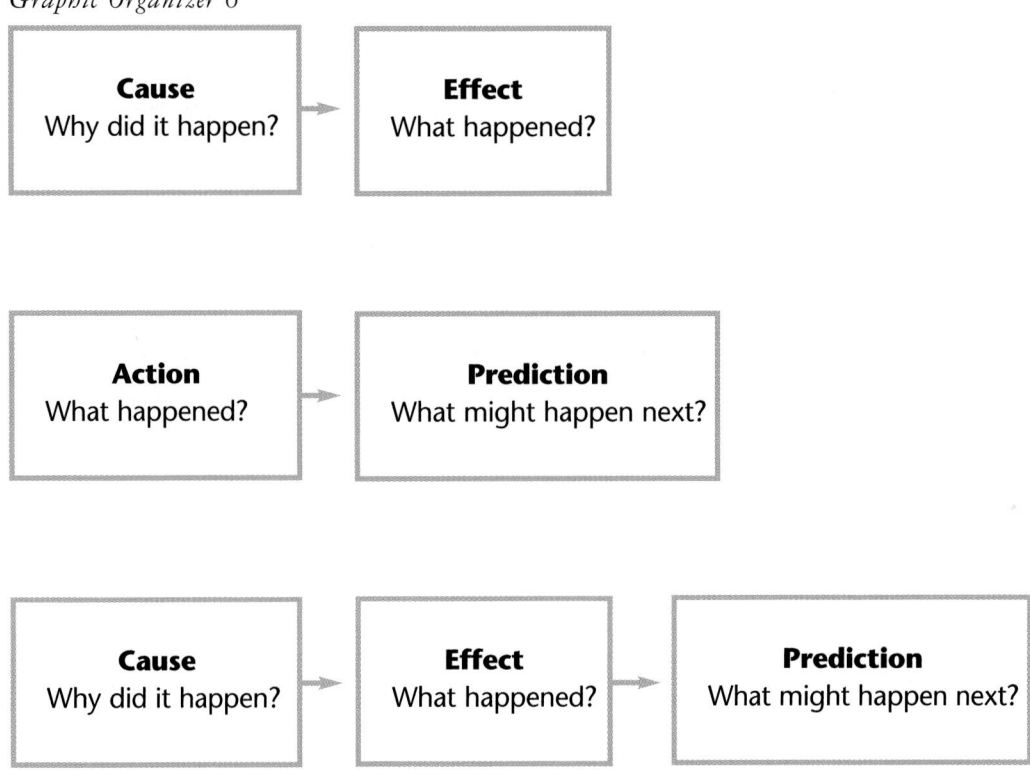

DRAWING CONCLUSIONS

Drawing conclusions is the process by which people figure something out on their own, based on observations of facts or details. Writers do not always explain everything to readers. Like a good detective, readers must piece together clues within the text, combine this information with what they already know, and draw conclusions about the topic.

For example, you might read that consumer spending in the United States dropped during a certain year. You also might read that unemployment was very high during that year, and average household incomes dropped. From these facts you might conclude that people were spending less because they had less money to spend. Using graphic organizers like the ones on page xxx can help you draw conclusions as you read.

Graphic Organizer 9

| Fact | + | Fact | + | Fact | = | Conclusion |

Graphic Organizer 10

Clues from Text	What I Already Know	My Conclusion

DECISION MAKING AND PROBLEM SOLVING

Problem solving involves gathering information to develop a solution to a dilemma. During the course of solving a problem, you also must use good decision-making skills to choose the best possible solution to the problem. The first step in solving a problem is to identify what the problem is. For example, a company might have trouble selling a product it makes. In order to come up with a solution to this problem, you would have to gather as much information as you could about the subject. For example, if a product is not selling well, market research could be conducted to find as much information as possible about where it is being marketed, who is buying it, what competitors' products are selling better, and how the competitors' products differ.

Rarely will a problem have only one solution. Often there are multiple solutions that could be chosen. This is where the decision-making process comes into play. In the course of deciding between multiple solutions, you must consider all of the positive and negative aspects of each option, including their possible consequences. For example, a company might be considering revamping its current product to compete better in the marketplace. The positive aspects of this choice might be gaining a higher market share, but the negatives might be the need for huge amounts of money to be invested in changing the product and lost revenues on the original product. Another solution might call for keeping the original product, but targeting it only to demographic groups that tend to buy the product the most. A third solution might involve a compromise between the two—the company may decide to invest in revamping the old model, while at the same time remarketing the original product to gain a larger share of a target demographic group that likes the old product.

Using a graphic organizer like the one on page xxxi can help you to solve problems and make decisions.

SOCIAL STUDIES SKILLS

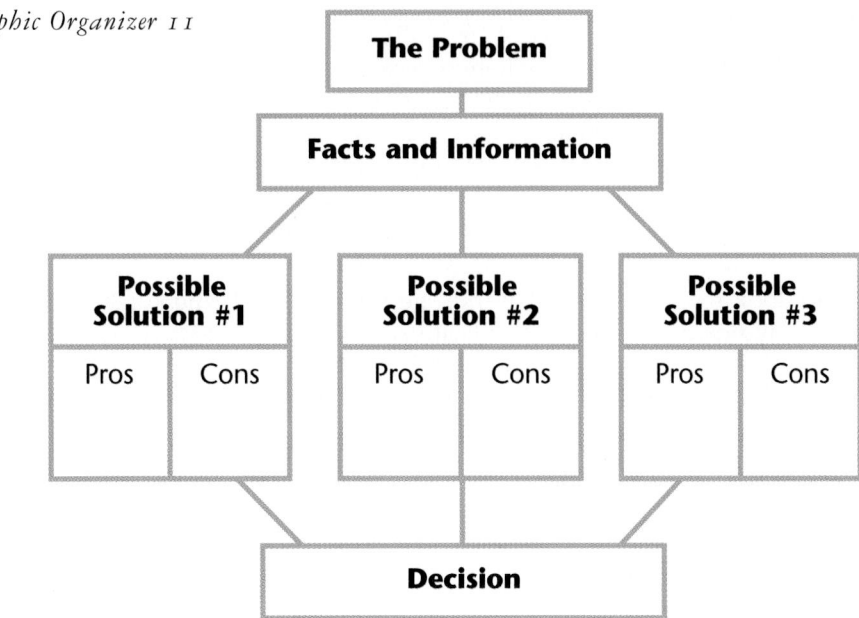

SUPPORTING A POSITION

Part of identifying a point of view and distinguishing facts from opinions involves looking at the evidence the author presents to support his or her point of view. Whenever you take a position on a subject, you must be able to support that position with persuasive arguments and well-chosen facts. A weak argument will not convince others that your position is valid. For example, if an economist took the position that lowering taxes would help boost the economy but offered no evidence that this would happen, not many people would be convinced. If, however, the economist could show that lowering taxes would increase people's incomes and encourage them to spend money and include examples of when this has happened in the past, then others might be convinced that lowering taxes would be good for the economy.

When you put together an argument in support of a position, carefully think through why you have taken the position. Once you understand your own reasoning, present the most persuasive facts that help support your position. Using a graphic organizer like the one below can help you put together an argument to support your position.

Graphic Organizer 12

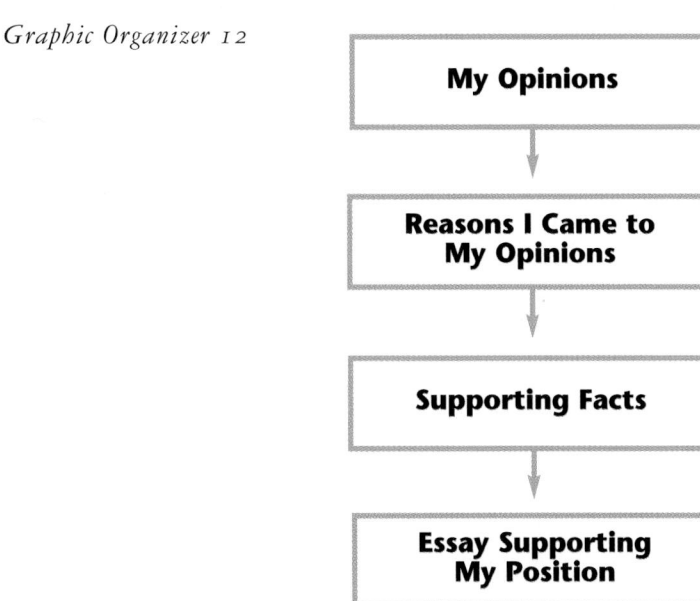

COMPARING AND CONTRASTING

Comparing involves noting similarities between two or more things. *Contrasting* involves noting differences between these things. For example, if you were to compare and contrast the economies of two countries like the United States and China, you might note that they are similar in that they both are actively involved in trade and industrial growth. You might note that they are different in that the communist government of China still has much more direct control over its economy than the U.S. government has over the U.S. economy.

As you read, look for clue words that indicate if things are being compared or contrasted. Clue words or phrases that indicate comparison include *also, as well as, like, same as*, and *similar to*. Clue words or phrases that indicate contrast include *although, as opposed to, but, different from, however, instead of, on the other hand*, and *unlike*. Using graphic organizers like the ones below can help you compare and contrast information as you read.

Graphic Organizer 13

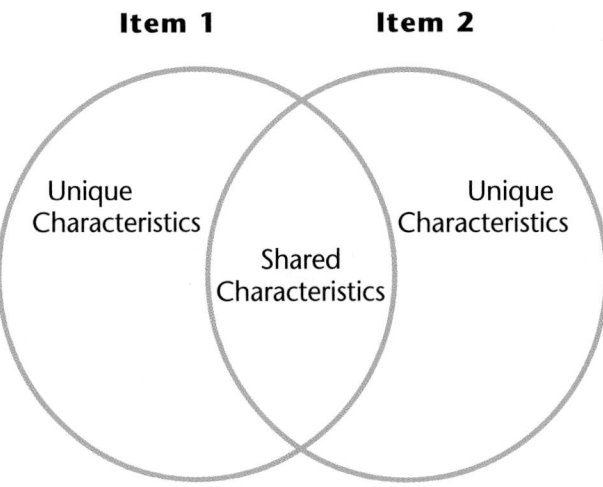

Item 1   **Item 2**

Unique Characteristics

Shared Characteristics

Unique Characteristics

Graphic Organizer 14

	Item 1	Item 2	Different or Alike?
Characteristic A			
Characteristic B			
Characteristic C			

SEQUENCING

Sequencing is the process of placing events in chronological order to better understand why and how things happen as they do. Sometimes the text will make the chronology of an event clear and may even provide time lines for clarity. At other times, it is up to the reader to figure out what the order of events really was. Timelines provide a way to sequence information in *absolute chronology*, or the exact time when something happened.

Sometimes it is not clear, nor even important to know, exactly when something happened. However, it may be very important to know the *relative chronology* of events, or when things happened in relation to one another. Relative chronology tells us what happened first, second, and last. For example, if you were trying to understand how the Federal Reserve Board works, it would be helpful to note that during a given three-month period the rate of inflation was higher than average. At the end of those three months, the Federal Reserve raised interest rates to curb inflation. Over the next three months, inflation slowed, so at the end of that three-month period the Federal Reserve left interest rates unchanged.

Some clue words that may help you identify sequence include *after, before, finally, first, following, next, then*, and *when*. Using graphic organizers like the one below also can help you sequence information.

Graphic Organizer 15

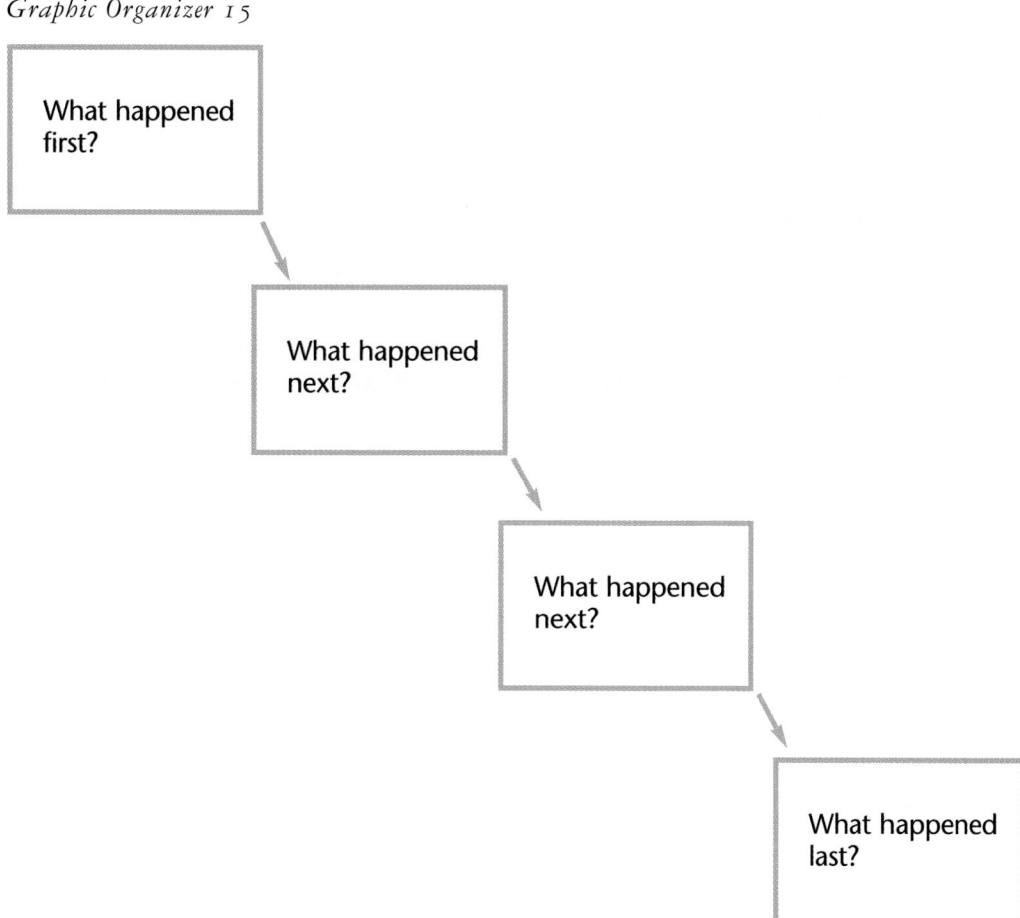

Your textbook is a guide to help you learn new information, but you cannot retain that information without reading the text effectively. The following reading skills strategies can help you get the most out of your reading.

BEFORE YOU READ

Set a Purpose for Reading
✔ Think about what you will be reading and what you hope to learn from the reading. Consider how the topic might relate to your daily life and what you already know about the topic.

Preview
✔ Look over the headings and visuals in the reading, including the chapter title, subheads, photos, graphs, charts, and maps. Look over any "preview" items the chapter provides, such as lists of bold-faced terms.

Predict
✔ Using the information you examined in your preview, predict what you will learn from it.
✔ Use the following graphic organizer to help you prepare to read new materials.

Purpose for Reading	Preview	Prediction(s)
I will be reading about _____ _____ _____. I hope to learn _____ _____ _____. The topic relates to my daily life in that _____ _____ _____. I already know _____ _____ _____.	The chapter title is _____ _____. The subheads are _____ _____ _____. Chapter visuals include ____ _____ _____ _____. Chapter preview items include _____ _____ _____.	Based on what I have previewed, I will probably learn _____ _____ _____ _____ _____ _____ _____ _____ _____ _____.

Find the Main Idea

The main idea is the most important idea in a reading passage. Sometimes the main idea of a passage is stated clearly, often in the first one or two sentences of a paragraph. But sometimes it is not stated so clearly, and you must read carefully to infer the main idea. You can test whether or not you have identified the correct main idea by offering details from the reading that support this idea. Using a graphic organizer like the one below can help you in this process.

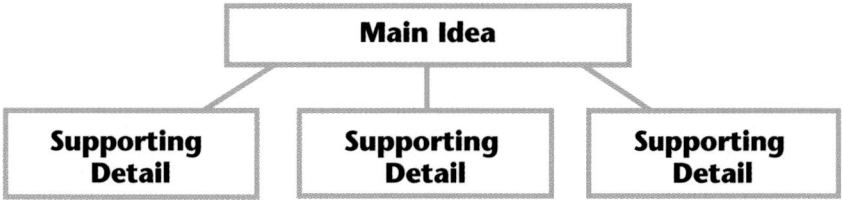

Draw Connections Between Items

As you read, pay particular attention to the relationships between people, places, events, and ideas. These relationships can include cause and effect, differences and similarities, sequencing, and problems or solutions. The Social Studies Skills section (pp. xxvi–xxxiii) contains several graphic organizers that can help you arrange this information as you read. It also contains some lists of clue words that can help you spot some relationships. Recognizing relationships between items can help you understand complicated information.

Analyze Visual Information

Pay attention to the visual information in the text. Ask yourself why it is included and what it adds to the text. Think about how your understanding of the visuals as you read may have changed from when you looked at the visuals in your preview exercise.

AFTER YOU READ

Summarize

Once you have finished your reading, try to summarize, or state in the simplest way possible, what the reading passage is all about. The process of summarizing a reading passage is very similar to finding the main idea. As you prepare to summarize a passage, look at your notes on the most important details mentioned in the reading. Use these details to state what happened in the passage in the simplest way possible. Using a graphic organizer like the one below can help you in this process.

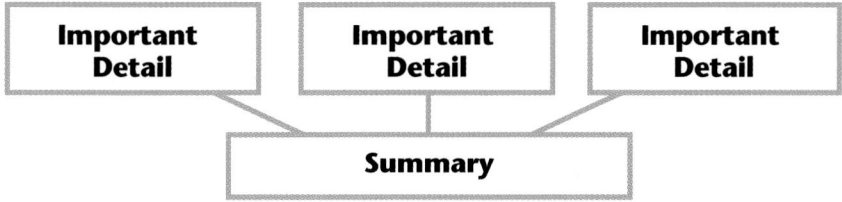

Assess

After you have finished reading and summarizing, look back at your predictions about the chapter and analyze whether you learned what you thought you were going to learn. Consider how the information you learned may be put to use in your daily life.

Economic Measurement Skills

ANALYZE VISUAL INFORMATION—TABLES

Often economic information is presented in the form of tables. *Tables* help to organize and display economic data in a clear form. Use the following steps to examine the table below.

1. Read the title of the table to understand what it is about.

2. Read all labels. They explain what information is being studied and describe the time period or range of items being compared.

3. Compare the data being presented in the columns to note changes over time or categories.

UNEMPLOYMENT RATES IN VARIOUS COUNTRIES				
Year	United States	France	Japan	United Kingdom
1970	4.9 percent	2.5 percent	1.2 percent	3.1 percent
1980	7.1 percent	6.5 percent	2.0 percent	7.0 percent
1990	5.6 percent	9.1 percent	2.1 percent	6.9 percent
2000	4.0 percent	9.1 percent	4.8 percent	5.5 percent

Source: Bureau of Labor Statistics, U.S. Department of Labor.

Use the Skill

1. What does the table show?

2. What types of information can you learn from the table?

3. What does the table tell you about trends in unemployment rates?

Apply the Skill

Create your own chart on economic data by gathering information on earnings of students in your class. Have a group of students write down how much they earn in a week from outside jobs. The information should be anonymous to maintain privacy. Once you have collected the slips of paper, organize the information into a chart that shows the distribution of income among the students. You might also use this information to create a table that shows categories of income distribution to illustrate how many students fall within certain income ranges.

ANALYZE VISUAL INFORMATION—BAR GRAPHS

A *bar graph* uses lengths of bars to show the relationship among different variables. Use the following steps to examine the bar graph below.

1. Read the title of the graph to understand what it is about.

2. Read all labels. They explain what information is being studied and how it is being measured. The labels on the vertical axis (left side) and horizontal axis (bottom) are the most important for understanding the information.

3. Compare the data being presented on the bars to note changes in measurements over time.

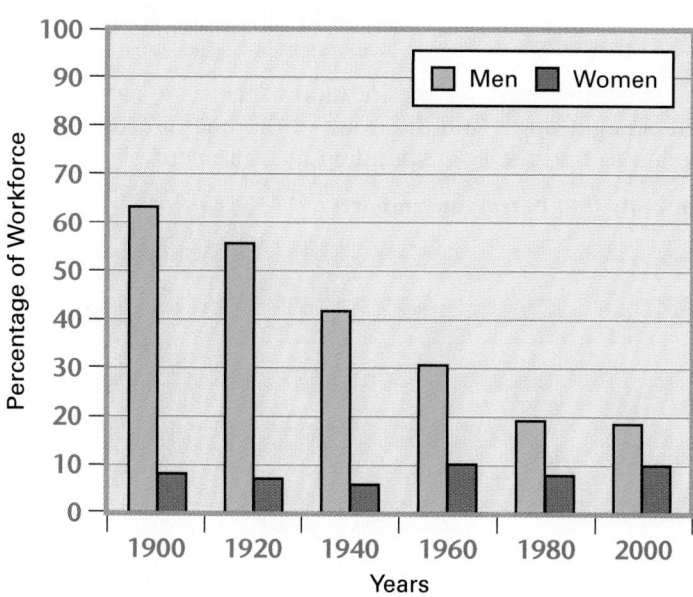

Americans Over Age 65 in the Workforce

Source: Bureau of the Census, U.S. Department of Commerce.

Use the Skill

1. What does the graph show?
2. What are the advantages of showing this information in bar graph form?
3. What does the graph tell you about changes in the workforce over time?

Apply the Skill

Take the information gathered for the "Apply the Skill" activity on the first page of this "Economic Measurement Skills" section, and use it to create a bar graph. To create the bar graph, label the vertical axis "Number of Students" and the horizontal axis "Income Categories."

ANALYZE VISUAL INFORMATION—LINE GRAPHS

A *line graph* shows the relationship among variables in the form of a line. A line graph looks simple, but it requires precise measurements along plot points to convey accurate information. A line graph is very effective for showing changes in information about the same item over time. Use the following steps to examine the line graph below.

1. Read the title of the graph to understand what it is about.

2. Read all labels. The vertical axis usually explains what is being compared. The horizontal axis usually marks periods of time.

3. Note what the lines on the graph stand for. Sometimes the lines will have labels on them. Sometimes, if there are multiple lines, there will be a legend to help you understand the lines, which will often be presented in different colors to distinguish them from one another.

4. To find information for an exact time, look for the location of that date along the horizontal axis and measure straight up to find the point of the line directly above that date. Then read to the left to find the corresponding measurement.

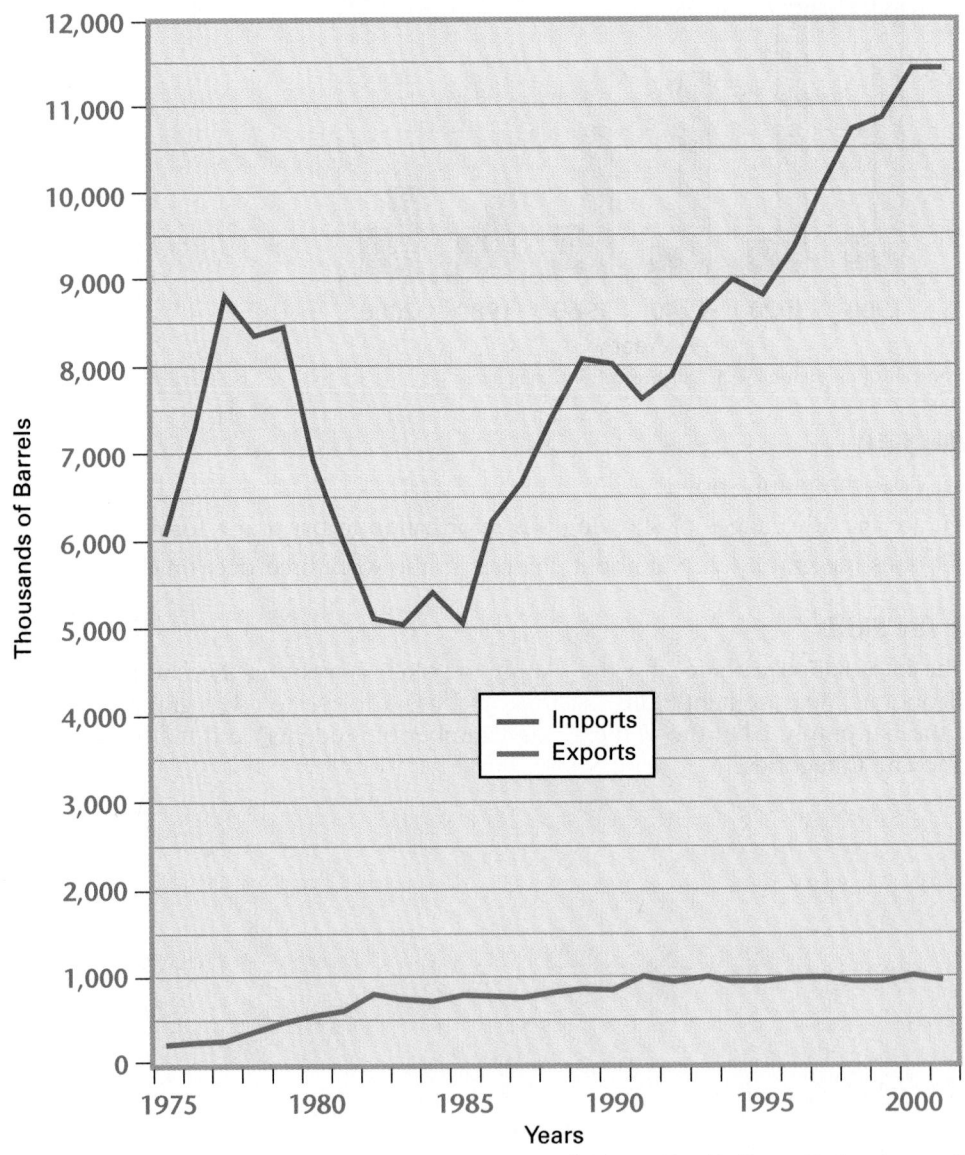

Average Daily U.S. Petroleum Imports

Source: Energy Information Administration. U.S. Department of Energy, *Monthly Energy Review*, August, 2002.

ECONOMIC MEASUREMENT SKILLS

Use the Skill

1. What does the graph show?

2. What information does the graph reveal about the relationship between U.S. imports and exports of petroleum?

3. What general trends over time does the graph reveal?

Apply the Skill

Take the bar graph that you create for the Apply the Skill activity on page xxxvii and change it into a line graph. Label the vertical axis "Number of Students" and the horizontal axis "Income Categories." Compare the different graphs and the table, and consider which is most effective at presenting the information.

ANALYZE VISUAL INFORMATION—PIE GRAPHS

Pie graphs are used to show the breakdown of something by revealing the percentages of parts to the whole. Use the following steps to examine the pie graph below.

1. Read the title of the graph to understand what it is about.

2. Read all labels or legends to understand the breakdown of the various parts.

3. Compare the sizes of the different parts of the circle to understand how they relate to one another.

Federal Budget Outlays, 2003

- National Defense 17%
- Social Security 22%
- Non-Defense Discretionary Spending 17%
- Medicare 11%
- Medicaid 7%
- Other Mandatory Spending 8%
- Debt Service 9%
- Other Entitlement Programs 6%

Source: Bureau of Industry and Security, Department of Commerce, http://www.bxa.doc.gov/DefenseIndustrialBasePrograms/OSIES/DefMarketResearchRpts/a

Use the Skill

1. What does the graph show?

2. How can a pie graph like this be useful?

3. What does the pie graph reveal about federal budget outlays?

Apply the Skill

Take the information you have gathered for the previous "Apply the Skill" activities, and convert it into a pie graph to show the percentages of students among the entire survey who fall into certain earning categories. Think about how the presentation of the information in this pie graph is different from that of your previous tables and graphs.

ANALYZE VISUAL INFORMATION—MAPS

Maps illustrate information over a geographic area. Maps you use in the study of economics are special-purpose maps. They will usually display economic information in geographic locations. In this way, you can see differences in economic data between various regions, states, and countries. Use the following steps to examine the map below.

1. Read the title of the map to understand what it is about.
2. Note what kind of geographic breakdown of information is being shown.
3. Note what kind of economic information is being shown.
4. Read all labels or legends to understand the breakdown of the various parts.

Right-to-Work States and Unionization Rates Per State

State	Rate
WA	18.6
MT	13.2
ND	7.5
MN	17.6
NH	10.1
VT	10.8
ME	12.9
OR	15.8
ID	7.6
WY	9.0
SD	5.9
WI	16.2
MI	21.8
NY	26.7
MA	14.8
RI	17.9
NV	17.0
UT	6.8
NE	7.8
IA	12.8
IL	18.3
IN	14.3
OH	17.7
PA	17.0
CT	15.8
NJ	19.6
CA	16.4
CO	8.7
KS	9.3
MO	14.2
KY	11.4
WV	14.6
VA	5.0
DE	12.2
MD	14.1
AZ	5.9
NM	8.0
OK	8.5
AR	6.3
TN	7.6
NC	3.7
DC	16.8
SC	4.5
TX	5.6
LA	7.7
MS	5.6
AL	9.5
GA	7.2
FL	6.5
AK	22.0
HI	23.9

Legend: ▢ Right to Work State   16.4 Percentage of labor force in unions

Source: National Right to Work Committee, http://www.nrtwc.org/. Unionization rates are for 2001 and right-to-work states are as of 2002.

Use the Skill

1. What does the map show?
2. How does showing this information in map form help you understand it?
3. What state has the highest percentage of union members among its labor force?

Apply the Skill

Choose an economic topic that would provide data for each state, such as unemployment rates or average income. Research the data for each state and create your own economic map, including a title, legend, and any important labels.

USE MATH SKILLS—AVERAGES AND MEDIANS

Sometimes it is useful to summarize data in general rather than specific terms. The most common method of summarizing data is to average it. The average, or *mean*, can be found by adding together the values of all variables and dividing them by the number of variables. Sometimes it is also useful to calculate the *median*, or midpoint, in a distribution of data. Use the following steps to understand how the data below was calculated.

1. Add all the numbers together.
2. Divide that sum by the total amount of numbers listed to obtain the average, or mean.
3. To locate the median, arrange the numbers in order and find the number in the middle of the list.

Costs of Food Items

1 lb bacon	$1.99
1 gal milk	$1.79
1 pt strawberries	$3.49
5 lb sugar	$1.41
1 pineapple	$2.99
1 lb tomatoes	$1.99
1 l bottled water	$ .89
1 lb ground beef	$2.99
1 bunch celery	$ .99
Total	**$18.53**

Average price is $18.53 ÷ 9 = $2.59

1 pt strawberries	$3.49
1 lb ground beef	$2.99
1 pineapple	$2.99
1 lb bacon	$1.99
1 lb tomatoes	$1.99 ← median price is $1.99
1 gal milk	$1.79
5 lb sugar	$1.41
1 bunch celery	$ .99
1 l bottled water	$ .89

Use the Skill

1. What do the lists show?
2. What are the average and median prices?
3. Are the average and median prices different? Why?
4. Which is more useful in this case, the mean or median price?

Apply the Skill

Using the data on student income you generated in Apply the Skill for "Analyze Visual Information—Bar Graphs," calculate the average and median incomes for students in your group.

USE MATH SKILLS—RATIOS AND PERCENTAGES

Sometimes it is useful to illustrate economic data in the form of ratios or percentages. *Ratios* show the relationship of one numerical value to another. *Percentages* show changes as parts of the whole, or part of 100 percent. Use the following steps to understand how the data below were calculated.

1. To find ratios, take two numbers and show them as a fraction, with the highest number on top. Reduce the fraction to its lowest terms.

2. Ratios also can be shown using more than two numbers by using colons and reducing all three numbers to their lowest terms.

3. To find the percentage relationship between two numbers, divide the smaller of the two numbers by the larger one. Then multiply the result by 100.

Banks in the United States, 2001			
Independent	**National**	**State**	**Total**
4,971	2,137	972	9,631

Source: Federal Deposit Insurance Corp., December 2000.

Ratios:

Independent to National $4{,}971/2{,}137 = 2.33/1$ For every one national bank, there are 2.33 independent banks.

Independent to State $4{,}971/972 = 5.11/1$ For every one state bank, there are 5.11 independent banks.

National to State $2{,}137/972 = 2.2/1$ For every one state bank, there are 2.2 national banks.

Independent to National to State $5.11{:}2.2{:}1$ For every one state bank, there are 2.2 national banks and 5.11 independent banks.

Percentages:

Independent $\quad 4{,}971 \div 9{,}631 = 0.52 \times 100 = 52\%$
National $\qquad 2{,}137 \div 9{,}631 = 0.22 \times 100 = 22\%$
State $\qquad\quad 972 \div 9{,}631 = 0.10 \times 100 = 10\%$

Of the nation's banks, 52 percent are independent banks, 22 percent are national banks, and 10 percent are state banks.

Use the Skill

1. What do the data show?
2. What are the advantages of showing the data as ratios or percentages?
3. The data do not include savings and loans, another type of depository institution. Based on the information above, can you calculate the ratio of savings and loans to the three types of banks? Can you calculate the percentage of savings and loans among all of these institutions?

Apply the Skill

Think about how much money you earn in an average month. Then estimate how much you spend during a month and how much you save. Calculate (1) the ratio of your spending to savings and (2) the percentages of your earnings that you spend and that you save.

ECONOMIC MEASUREMENT SKILLS

USING MATH SKILLS—RATES AND ABSOLUTE NUMBERS

In economics, information may sometimes be presented in *absolute numbers*, such as by showing that the cost of an item went from $500 to $700 in a six-month period. Economists also sometimes present information in the form of *rates*. These are percentages that are used to show how much something is rising or falling as a percentage of a whole or to reflect change. For example, economists often discuss the rate of inflation to show how quickly prices of goods are rising. You also might learn about *interest rates*, or the calculation of how much a loan will cost based on a percentage of the amount of money borrowed. Use the following steps to understand how the data below were calculated.

1. To calculate the rate of increase in the price of an item, plot the absolute price of the good over time.

2. Subtract the price you started with from the price you ended with.

3. Divide the result by the price you started with.

4. Multiply the result by 100 to get a percentage rate of change.

AVERAGE COST OF A MOVIE TICKET		
Year	Price	Annual Rate of Increase
1992	$4.15	
1993	$4.14	−0.24%
1994	$4.08	−1.45%
1995	$4.35	6.62%
1996	$4.42	1.61%
1997	$4.59	3.84%
1998	$4.69	2.18%
1999	$5.06	7.89%
2000	$5.39	6.52%
2001	$5.65	4.82%
2002	$5.80	2.65%

Source: National Association of Theater Owners, http://www.natoonline.org/statisticstickets.htm

Example: 1992 to 1993: $4.14 − 4.15/4.15 \times 100 = -0.24\%$

Use the Skill

1. What do the data show?

2. What type of unusual change in prices does the rate of increase reveal?

3. How much was the 10-year rate of increase between 1992 and 2002?

Apply the Skill

Research information about the average prices of other consumer goods for at least two years. Make a chart showing the annual rate of increase in prices for each product.

USE MATH SKILLS—INDEX NUMBERS

Economists sometimes express changes in things like prices in terms of *index numbers*. Index numbers set a *base period* and measure changes from the base period to the present. The base period has a value of 100. All other numbers are expressed as a percentage of the prices of the base period. This would mean, for example, that if an item cost $1.00 during the base period and $1.08 during another period, the second period would be shown as a price index of 108, meaning 108% of the base period. The index system allows economists to summarize a great deal of information in a simple way. Use the following steps to understand the data below.

1. Find the base period.

2. Look at the indexes for the other periods. Remember that the index is a percentage of the price for the base period.

3. Calculate the average cost of an item that was $1.00 during the base period for other periods.

CONSUMER PRICE INDEX, 1920–2002	
(base year = 1967)	
1920	60.0
1925	52.5
1930	50.0
1935	41.1
1940	42.0
1945	53.9
1950	72.1
1955	80.2
1960	88.7
1965	94.5
1970	116.3
1975	161.2
1980	248.8
1985	322.2
1990	391.4
1995	456.5
2002	535.8

Source: Bureau of Labor Statistics, U.S. Department of Labor.

ECONOMIC MEASUREMENT SKILLS

Use the Skill

1. What does the graph show?

2. What is the base year?

3. What did an item that cost $1.00 during the base year cost in 1935? In 2002?

Apply the Skill

Research the consumer price list for various consumer products. Note what year the prices were the lowest and the highest.

USE MATH SKILLS—NOMINAL AND REAL VALUES

Economists sometimes express dollar amounts in nominal and real numbers. *Nominal numbers* reflect the actual amount of money on hand. *Real numbers* reflect the nominal numbers adjusted for inflation. For example, you might earn $30,000 at your job and get a 1 percent raise of $300, raising your salary to $30,300. However, if the rate of inflation during that year was 3 percent, you will not be able to buy as much with your salary as you could the year before. Economists use price indexes to adjust nominal numbers to real ones. Use the following steps to understand how the data below were calculated.

1. Obtain the nominal numbers for an amount of money.

2. Multiply the nominal amount of money by the price index (divided by 100) for the period of time you are examining.

3. The result is the real amount of the money.

	U.S. GROSS DOMESTIC PRODUCT (in billions of dollars)		
	Nominal Dollars	**Consumer Price Index (divided by 100)**	**Real Dollars**
1990	$5,546.1 ÷	3.914 =	$1,416.99
2000	$9,824.6 ÷	5.358 =	$1,833.63

Source: Bureau of Economic Analysis, U.S. Department of Commerce.

Use the Skill

1. What do the data show?

2. What do the real dollar amounts reveal about the true value of GNP?

3. How do the data reveal the usefulness of converting nominal into real dollars?

Apply the Skill

Research to find out how much average personal income was in nominal dollars from 1990 to 2000. Then, using what you know about the Consumer Price Index, show what the real amount of average personal income was.

Unit 1

Introduction to Economics

Your aunt gives you $25 for your birthday. What will you do with that money? There are many possibilities. You could spend it on movies, pizza, CDs, gasoline, or a favorite brand of jeans. Or you could save the money toward a trip to Europe or a college education. You could even give the money to a worthy charity. Whatever you decide, you are making an economic choice. Economics focuses on how your choices and the choices of millions of others affect individual markets—such as the market for pizza—and shape the economy as a whole.

1 What Is Economics?

Consider

Why are characters in comic strips like Hagar the Horrible, Cathy, and Fox Trot missing a finger on each hand?

Why are you reading this book right now rather than doing something else?

Why is there no sense crying over spilt milk?

In what way are people who pound on vending machines relying on a theory?

POINT YOUR BROWSER

econxtra.swlearning.com

© Getty Images/PhotoDisc

The Economic Problem

Objectives

> Recognize the economic problem, and explain why it makes choice necessary.

> Identify productive resources, and list examples.

> Define goods and services, list examples, and explain why they are scarce.

Overview

Economics is always in the news. If you read a newspaper, watch television, or go online, you are bombarded with current economic information. Economic issues are reported because they are important in people's lives. People want to know the latest about jobs, housing, prices, taxes, and other matters that affect their income and spending. Economics is concerned with identifying and clarifying your choices—the range of possibilities you face now and in the future. As you learn more about economics, you will begin to think more about the choices you face.

Key Terms

scarcity

productive resources

economics

human resources

labor

entrepreneur

natural resources

capital goods

good

service

[In the News]

● Rich or Poor, It's Good To Have Money

In a market economy such as the United States, the more money you have the more options you have. Alternatively, you could say that the more money you have, the fewer choices you have to make—because you can buy more of what you want. Either way, it's hard to argue against the goal of abundance over scarcity. A recent Gallup poll shows that although few Americans now label themselves as rich, many hope to reach that status some day. One third of those polled say becoming rich is "at least somewhat likely" for them. Ten percent say it is "very likely." Only a third reject the possibility. The dream of eventual wealth is particularly alive among the young. An amazing 51 percent of those 18 to 29 say becoming rich is "a likely possibility." That's important. For a market system to work well, young people must believe in the possibility of succeeding in that system.

Think About It

Is it likely that you will become successful or even rich? Is this important to you? What choices for your future might you make differently if you thought you had little chance of success? How might you and the economy as a whole suffer as a result of your pessimism?

Economic Choices

scarcity

A condition facing all societies because there are not enough productive resources to satisfy people's unlimited wants

productive resources

The inputs used to produce the goods and services that people want

economics

The study of how people use their scarce resources to satisfy their unlimited wants

Main Idea

Scarcity

Economics is about making choices. You make economic choices every day. You make choices about whether to get a part-time job or focus on your studies, buy a car or save for college, pack a lunch or buy a Subway sandwich. You already know more about economics than you realize. You bring to the subject a rich personal experience. This experience will be tapped throughout the book to reinforce your understanding of the basic ideas.

The Economic Problem

Would you like a new car, a nicer home, better meals, more free time, more spending money, more sleep? Who wouldn't? But even if you can satisfy some of these desires, others keep popping up. Here's the economic problem: *Although your wants, or desires, are virtually unlimited, the productive resources available to help satisfy these wants are scarce.* Scarcity creates the economic problem. **Scarcity** is the condition facing all societies because there are not enough productive resources to satisfy people's unlimited wants.

Productive resources, or *factors of production,* are the inputs used to produce the goods and services that people want. *Because productive resources are scarce, goods and services are scarce too.*

A productive resource is *scarce* when it is not freely available. Because productive resources are scarce, you must choose from among your many wants. Whenever you choose, you must go without satisfying some other wants. The problem of scarce resources but unlimited wants exists for each of the six billion people on the planet.

Because you cannot have all the goods and services you would like, you must choose among them continually. Making choices means you must pass up some alternatives.

Economics Defined

Economics examines how people use their scarce resources to satisfy their unlimited wants. A taxicab driver uses the cab and other scarce resources, such as knowledge of the city, driving skills, gasoline, and time, to earn income. That income, in turn, buys housing, groceries, clothing, trips to Disney World, and other goods and services that help satisfy some of the driver's unlimited wants.

 CHECKPOINT
What is the economic problem, and why does it make choice necessary?

Because productive resources are limited, you cannot have all the goods and services you want. You must choose some things and give up others. **If you decide to attend a movie with your friends on a Saturday night, what alternatives might you have to pass up?**

© Getty Images/PhotoDisc

Productive Resources

Productive resources, also called *factors of production,* or simply *resources,* sort into three broad categories: human resources, natural resources, and capital resources.

Human Resources

The first category, **human resources**, is the broad category of human efforts, both physical and mental, used to produce goods and services. *Labor,* such as the labor of a cab driver or a brain surgeon, is the most important of the human resources. **Labor** is the physical and mental effort used to produce goods and services. Labor itself comes from a more fundamental human resource: time. Without time you can accomplish nothing. You allocate your time to alternative uses: You can sell your time as labor to earn a *wage,* or you can spend your time doing other things, such as sleeping, eating, studying, playing sports, surfing the Net, or watching TV.

Human resources also include the special skills supplied by an **entrepreneur**, who tries to earn a profit by developing a new product or finding a better way to produce an existing one. An entrepreneur seeks to discover profitable opportunities by purchasing resources and assuming the risk of business success or failure. *Profit* equals the *revenue* from sales minus the *cost* of production. If production costs exceed revenue, the entrepreneur suffers a loss. Profit provides the incentive that makes entrepreneurs willing to accept the risk of losing money. All companies in the world today began as an idea in the mind of an entrepreneur.

Natural Resources

Natural resources are so-called "gifts of nature," including land, forests, minerals, oil reserves, bodies of water, and even animals. Natural resources can be divided into renewable resources and exhaustible resources. A *renewable resource* can be drawn on indefinitely if used wisely. Thus, timber is a renewable resource if

NETBookmark

What makes a good job good? Working for a good employer might be one factor. Each year, *Fortune* magazine lists the 100 best employers. The magazine includes this list on its web site, which you can access through econxtra.swlearning.com. What factors other than compensation are cited in the report as creating a favorable work environment?

econxtra.swlearning.com

felled trees are replaced to provide a steady supply. The air and rivers are renewable resources if they can recover from a certain level of pollutants. More generally, biological resources like fish, game, livestock, forests, rivers, groundwater, grasslands, and agricultural soil are renewable if managed properly.

An *exhaustible resource*—such as oil, coal, or copper ore—does not renew itself and so is available in a limited amount. Each gallon of oil burned is gone forever. Sooner or later, all oil wells will run dry. The world's oil reserves are exhaustible.

Investigate Your Local Economy

With a partner, make a list of the natural resources found in your state. Research the impact these resources have on your local economy. Which industries use these natural resources in their production processes? How many people do these industries employ? How many dollars per year do these industries generate for the state? Report your results to the class.

human resources

The broad category of human efforts, both physical and mental, used to produce goods and services

labor

The physical and mental effort used to produce goods and services

entrepreneur

A profit-seeker who develops a new product or process and assumes the risk of profit or loss

natural resources

So-called "gifts of nature" used to produce goods and services; includes renewable and exhaustible resources

SPAN THE GLOBE

A Yen for Vending Machines

Japan has more vending machines per capita than any other country on the planet—more than twice as many as the United States, and nearly ten times as many as Europe. The reasons are both economic and cultural. A low birthrate, virtually no immigration and an aging population have created a relative scarcity of labor and driven up the cost of that labor. Therefore, to sell products Japanese retailers rely on capital, particularly vending machines, which eliminates the need for sales clerks. Research shows that Japanese consumers prefer dealing with anonymous machines rather than having to exchange greetings and pleasantries with a real person.

Think Critically

Compare the use of the vending machines in Japan with their use in the United States and Europe. Give specific reasons why you think vending machines are used relatively less in these countries as compared with Japan.

---

capital goods

All human creations used to produce goods and services; for example, factories, trucks, and machines

good

An item you can see, feel, and touch and that requires scarce resources to produce and satisfies human wants

service

Something not physical that requires scarce resources to produce and satisfies human wants

Capital Resources

Capital resources, commonly called **capital goods**, include all human creations used to produce goods and services. Capital goods consist of factories, trucks, machines, tools, buildings, airports, highways, and other manufactured items employed to produce goods and services. Capital goods include the taxi driver's cab, the farmer's tractor, the interstate highway system, and your classroom.

CHECKPOINT
Name the three categories of productive resources, and provide examples of each.

Goods and Services

Resources are combined in a variety of ways to produce goods and services.

Goods

A farmer, a tractor, 50 acres of land, seeds, and fertilizer come together to grow the good: corn. Corn is a **good** because it is tangible—something you can see, feel, and touch. It requires scarce resources to produce, and it satisfies human wants. This book, the chair you are sitting in, the clothes you are wearing, and your next meal are all goods.

Services

One hundred musicians, musical instruments, chairs, a conductor, a musical score, and a music hall combine to produce the service: Beethoven's Fifth Symphony. The performance of the Fifth Symphony is a **service** because it is intangible—that is, not physical—yet it uses scarce resources to satisfy human wants. Movies, concerts, phone calls, Internet connections, guitar lessons, dry cleaning, and your next haircut are all services.

No Free Lunch

You may have heard the expression "There is no such thing as a free lunch." This is so because all goods involve a cost to someone. The lunch may seem free to you, but it draws scarce resources away from the production of other goods. Also, whoever provides the free lunch often expects something in return. A Russian proverb makes a similar point but with a bit more bite: "The only place you find free cheese is in a mousetrap."

Because goods and services are produced using scarce resources, they are themselves scarce. A good or service is scarce if the amount people desire exceeds the amount available at a zero price. Rather than say "goods and services" every time, this book will sometimes use the term "goods" to mean both goods and services.

A few goods seem free because the amount freely available (that is, available at a zero price) exceeds the amount people want. For example, air and seawater often seem free because you can breathe all the air you want and have all the seawater you can haul away. Yet, despite the old saying, "The best things in life are free," most goods are scarce, not free. Even those that appear to be free come with strings attached. For example, clean air and clean seawater have become scarce. *Goods that are truly free are not the subject matter of economics. Without scarcity, there would be no need for prices and no economic problem.*

Sometimes you may mistakenly think of certain goods as free because they involve no apparent cost to you. Subscription cards that fall out of magazines appear to be free. At least it seems you would have no problem rounding up a pile of them if necessary. Producing the cards, however, uses scarce resources. These resources were drawn away from other uses, such as producing higher-quality magazines.

CHECKPOINT
Define goods and services, provide examples, and explain why they are scarce.

1.1 Assessment

Key Concepts

1. What is the central problem that you face when you make economic choices?

2. What are examples of productive resources you use in your life?

3. How can you tell whether the food you eat from your refrigerator is scarce?

4. Identify each of the following as a human resource, natural resource, or capital resource:

   a. a hammer used to build a wooden box

   b. the tree that was cut down to make lumber to build a wooden box

   c. the effort used to nail lumber together to make a wooden box

Xtra!
Study Tools
econxtra.swlearning.com

Graphing Exercise

5. Draw a pie chart that demonstrates how you spend the money you have (movies, CDs, clothing, food, transportation, etc). To draw a pie chart, draw a circle and divide it into slices. Label each slice with a type of spending, and identify it as either a good or a service. Each slice represents a percentage of the whole pie. The percents on the slices should add up to 100 percent.

Think Critically

6. **Government** Identify a good or service provided by the government that has no apparent cost for you. Why is this good or service not really free?

Economic Theory

1.2

Objectives

> Explain the goal of economic theory.

> Understand the role of marginal analysis in making economic choices.

> Explain how market participants interact.

Overview

An economy results from the choices that millions of individuals make in attempting to satisfy their unlimited wants. Because these choices lie at the very heart of the economic problem—coping with scarce resources but unlimited wants—they deserve a closer look. Learning about the forces that shape economic choice is the first step toward mastering economic analysis.

Key Terms

economic theory

marginal

market economics

national economics

market

[In the News]

● How Now Dow?

The stock market's Dow Jones Industrial Average, or "the Dow," measures the average stock prices of 30 major U.S. companies. The Dow is reported widely on TV news shows and cable channels and often runs along the bottom of your TV screen. The simple ups and downs of the Dow are much easier for the general public to follow and understand than the more complicated measures of economic activity favored by economists. In fact, many Americans rely on the Dow for cues about where the economy is headed. Although the Dow is only one of many economic indicators, some people adjust their spending and saving behavior based on the Dow's movements. If the Dow is rising, people think the economy is improving, so they may spend more freely. Conversely, if the Dow is falling, they may hold back on spending. In reality, movements in the Dow may be linked to the economy's performance from year to year. Day-to-day fluctuations in the Dow, however, are likely caused more by random events that may or may not have any lasting effect on the economy.

Think About It

Would you consider the Dow a useful measure of economic trends from day to day? From year to year? Why or why not?

◀ | ▶

The Role of Theory

Economists develop theories, or models, to help explain economic behavior. An **economic theory**, or *economic model,* is a simplification of economic reality that *is used to make predictions about the real world.* Thus the goal of economic theory is to make predictions about the real world, such as what happens to consumption of Pepsi when its price increases.

Simplify the Problem

A theory captures the important elements of the problem under study. It need not spell out every detail and relationship. In fact, the more detailed a theory gets, the more difficult to understand it becomes, and the less useful it may be. The world is so complex that simplifying often is necessary to make sense of things. Think of comic strip characters, for example. Cartoonists often simplify their characters, leaving out fingers or even a mouth. You might think of economic theory as a stripped-down, or streamlined, version of economic reality. One way to strip down reality is by using simplifying assumptions.

Simplifying Assumptions

To help develop a theory, economists make simplifying assumptions. One category of assumptions is the *other-things-constant assumption.* The idea is to identify the variables of interest and then focus exclusively on the relations among them, assuming that nothing else of importance changes—that other things remain constant.

Suppose you are interested in how a change in the price of Pepsi affects the number of bottles purchased. To isolate the relationship between these two variables—price and quantity purchased—you assume for purposes of the model that there are no changes in other relevant variables such as consumer income, the price of Coke, and the average outdoor temperature.

Economists also make assumptions about what motivates people—how people behave. These are called *behavioral assumptions.* Perhaps the most basic behavioral assumption is that people make choices based on their own self-interest.

Rational Self-Interest

A key assumption about behavior is that in making choices, you rationally select alternatives you perceive to be in your best interests. By *rational,* economists mean that you try to make the best choices you can, given the information available.

economic theory

A simplification of economic reality used to make predictions about the real world

E-CONOMICS

The Rational Choice Is to Stay Home from Work

Telecommuting has become a popular option for businesses and their employees. The estimated number of Americans who telecommute jumped more than 42 percent in two years, from 19.6 million in 1999 to 28 million in 2001. Most live in New England and on the East and West Coasts in areas with dense populations and a great deal of traffic congestion. Telecommuters report a great deal of satisfaction with this work arrangement. More than two-thirds of the telecommuters surveyed said they are more satisfied since they began working at home. On the corporate side, some companies that have telecommuting programs have reported 15 percent increases in productivity, lower administrative and overhead costs, a major reduction in turnover rates, and an increased ability to hire better, more qualified workers.

Think Critically

What are some reasons it might not be in a worker's rational self-interest to telecommute? Is this a work option you might enjoy? Why or why not?

In general, rational self-interest means that you try to maximize the expected benefit achieved with a given cost or to minimize the expected cost of achieving a given benefit.

Rational self-interest does not necessarily mean selfishness or greed. You probably know people who are tuned to radio station WIIFM (What's In It For Me). For most of you, however, self-interest often includes the welfare of your family, your friends, and perhaps the poor of the world. Even so, your concern for others is influenced by your personal cost of that concern. You may volunteer to drive a friend to the airport on Saturday afternoon but are less likely to offer a ride if the flight departs at 6:00 A.M. When you donate clothes to charitable organizations such as Goodwill Industries, these clothes are more likely to be old than new. People

How would choosing to volunteer at a soup kitchen that serves homeless people fit in with the concept of rational self-interest?

tend to give more to a favorite charity if contributions are tax deductible.

The assumption of rational self-interest does not rule out concern for others. It simply means that concern for others is influenced to some extent by the same economic forces that affect other economic choices. The lower your personal cost of helping others, the more help you will offer.

Rationality implies that each consumer buys the products expected to maximize

his or her level of satisfaction. Rationality also implies that each firm supplies the products expected to maximize that firm's profit. These kinds of assumptions are called behavioral assumptions because they specify how economic decision makers are expected to behave—what makes them tick, so to speak.

Everybody Uses Theories

Many people don't understand the role of theory. Perhaps you have heard, "Oh, that's fine in theory, but in practice it's another matter"—meaning that the theory provides little aid in practical matters. People who say this do not realize that they are merely substituting their own theory for a theory they either do not believe or do not understand. They really are saying, "I have my own theory that works better."

Everyone uses theories, however poorly defined or understood. Someone who pounds on a vending machine that just ate a quarter has a crude theory about how that machine works and what went wrong. One version of that theory might be, "The quarter drops through a series of whatchamacallits, but sometimes the quarter gets stuck. *If* I pound on the machine, *then* I can free up the quarter and send it on its way." This theory seems to be so widely used that many people continue to pound on vending machines that fail to perform. (This is a real problem for that industry and one reason why newer vending machines are fronted with glass.) Yet, if you asked any of these mad pounders to explain their "theory" of how the machine works, he or she would look at you as if you were crazy.

Economists Tell Stories

Economists explain their theories by telling stories about how they think the economy works. To tell a good story, an economist relies on case studies, anecdotes, parables, listener's personal experience, and supporting data.

Throughout this book, you will hear stories that shed light on the ideas under consideration. Stories, such as the one about the vending machine, breathe life into economic theory.

Normative Versus Positive Statements

Economists usually try to explain how the economy works. Sometimes they concern themselves not with how the economy *does* work but how it *should* work. Compare these two statements: "The U.S. unemployment rate is 5.8 percent" versus "The U.S. unemployment rate should be lower." The first is called a *positive economic statement* because it is a statement about economic reality that can be supported or rejected by reference to the facts. The second is called a *normative economic statement* because it reflects someone's opinion. An opinion is merely that—it cannot be shown to be true or false by reference to the facts.

Positive statements concern what *is*. Normative statements concern what, in someone's opinion, *should be*. Positive statements need not necessarily be true, but you should be able to find out whether they are true or false by referring to the facts. Economic theories are expressed as positive statements such as, "If the price increases, then the quantity purchased will decrease."

Most of the disagreement among economists involves normative debates—for example, what is the appropriate role of government—rather than statements of positive analysis. To be sure, many theoretical issues remain unresolved. However economists do agree on most basic theoretical principles—that is, about positive economic analysis.

Normative statements, or personal opinions, are relevant in debates about public policy (such as the proper role of government) provided that opinions are distinguished from facts. In such debates, you are entitled to your own opinions, but you are not entitled to your own facts.

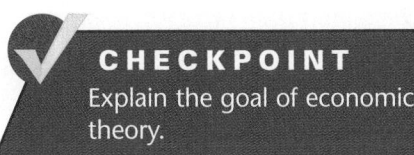

CHECKPOINT
Explain the goal of economic theory.

Marginal Analysis

Economic choice usually involves some adjustment to the existing situation, or the status quo. Your favorite jeans are on sale, and you must decide whether to buy another pair. You have just finished dinner at a restaurant and are deciding whether to eat dessert. Amazon.com must decide whether to add an additional line of products. The school superintendent must decide whether to hire another teacher.

Compare Marginal Cost with Marginal Benefit

Economic choice is based on a comparison of the expected marginal benefit and the expected marginal cost of the action under consideration. **Marginal** means incremental, additional, extra, or one more. Marginal refers to a change in an economic variable, a change in the status quo.

A rational decision maker will change the status quo as long as the expected marginal benefit from the change exceeds the expected marginal cost. For example, you compare the marginal benefit you expect from eating dessert (the added satisfaction) with its marginal cost (the added dollar cost, time, and calories). Likewise, Amazon.com compares the marginal benefit expected from adding a new product line (the added sales revenue) with the marginal cost (the added cost of resources required).

Typically, the change under consideration is small, but a marginal choice can involve a major economic adjustment, as in your decision whether or not to go to college. For a firm, a marginal choice might mean building a factory in Mexico or even filing for bankruptcy protection.

Focusing on the effect of a marginal adjustment to the status quo cuts the analysis of economic choice down to a manageable size. Rather than confront a puzzling economic reality head-on, economic analysis can begin with a marginal choice and then show how that choice affects a particular market and shapes the economy as a whole.

marginal
Incremental, additional, extra, or one more; refers to a change in an economic variable, a change in the status quo

Food for Forecasters
econxtra.swlearning.com

market economics

Study of economic behavior in particular markets, such as the market for computers or for unskilled labor

national economics

Study of the economic behavior of the economy as a whole, especially the national economy

Main Idea

Marginal Cost/Benefit

To make effective consumer decisions, you need to compare the costs and benefits of alternative choices. If you find your favorite jeans on sale, what would be the marginal benefit of purchasing another pair of these jeans? What would be the marginal cost of this decision?

© Getty Images/PhotoDisc

To the noneconomist, *marginal* usually means inferior, as in "a movie of marginal quality." Forget that meaning for this course and instead think of *marginal* as meaning incremental, additional, extra, or one more.

Choice Requires Time and Information

Rational choice takes time and requires information, but time and information are scarce and valuable. If you have any doubts about the time and information required to make choices, talk to someone who recently purchased a home, a car, or a personal computer. Talk to a corporate official deciding whether to introduce a new product, sell over the Internet, build a new factory, or buy another firm. Or consider your own decision about going to college. You already may have talked to friends, relatives, teachers, and guidance counselors about it. You might review school catalogs, college guides, and web sites. You might even visit some campuses. The decision will take time and money, and probably will involve some hassle and worry.

Because information is costly to acquire, you are often willing to pay others to gather and digest it for you. College guides, travel agents, real estate

brokers, career counselors, restaurant critics, movie reviewers, specialized web sites, and *Consumer Reports* magazine all offer information to help improve your economic choices. *Rational decision makers will continue to acquire information as long as the marginal benefit expected from that information exceeds the marginal cost of gathering it.*

Market Economics and National Economics

Although you have made thousands of economic choices, you probably have seldom thought about your own economic behavior. For example, why are you reading this book right now rather than doing something else? **Market economics**, or *microeconomics,* focuses on your economic behavior and the economic behavior of others who make choices involving what to buy and what to sell, how much to work and how much to play, how much to borrow and how much to save. Market economics examines the factors that influence individual economic choices and how markets coordinate the choices of various decision makers. For example, market economics explains how price and output are determined in the markets for breakfast cereal, sports equipment, or unskilled labor.

You probably have given little thought to what influences your own economic choices. You likely have given even less thought to how your choices link up with those made by hundreds of millions of others in the U.S. economy to determine economy-wide measures such as total production, employment, and economic growth. **National economics**, or *macroeconomics,* focuses on the performance of the economy as a whole, especially the national economy.

Thus market economics looks at the individual pieces of the economic puzzle. National economics fits all the pieces together to look at the big picture.

CHECKPOINT
Describe the role of marginal analysis in making economic choices.

Market Participants

There are four types of decision makers in the economy: households, firms, governments, and the rest of the world. Their interaction determines how an economy's resources get allocated.

Four Types of Participants

Households play the leading role in the economy. As consumers, households demand the goods and services produced. As resource owners, households supply the resources used to produce goods and services.

Firms, governments, and *the rest of the world* demand the resources that households supply, and then use these resources to supply the goods and services that households demand. The rest of the world includes foreign households, firms, and governments that supply resources and products to U.S. markets and demand resources and products from U.S. markets.

Markets

Markets are the means by which buyers and sellers carry out exchange. By bringing together the two sides of exchange, demand and supply, markets determine price and quantity. Markets may be physical places, such as super-markets, department stores, shopping malls, or flea markets. Markets also involve other ways for buyers and sellers to communicate, such as the stock market, telephones, bulletin boards, the Internet, and face-to-face bargaining.

Markets provide information about the quantity, quality, and price of products offered for sale. Goods and services are bought and sold in *product markets*. Resources are bought and sold in *resource markets*. The most important resource market is the labor, or job, market.

A Circular-Flow Model

Now that you have learned a bit about economic decision makers, consider how they interact. Such a picture is conveyed by the *circular-flow model,* which describes the flow of resources, products, income, and revenue among economic decision makers. A simple circular-flow model focuses on the interaction between households and firms in a market economy. Figure 1.1 shows households on the left and firms on the right.

Households supply human resources, natural resources, and capital goods to firms through resource markets, shown in the lower portion of the figure. In return, households demand goods and services from firms through product markets, shown on the upper portion of the figure. Viewed from the business

market
The means by which buyers and sellers carry out exchange

A shopping mall is a famil-iar type of physical market. The Internet is a communi-cations medium that enables markets to be con-ducted via computer. Compare physical markets with markets conducted via computer. How are they similar? How do they differ?

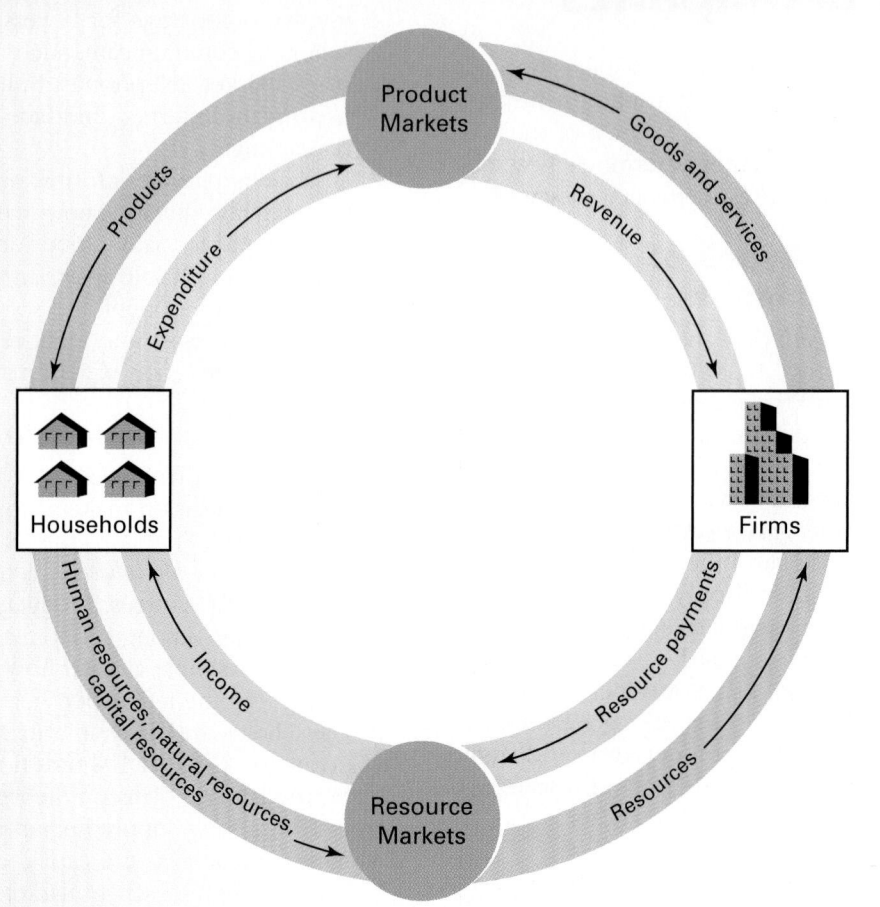

Households earn income by supplying resources to the resource markets, as shown in the lower portion of the model. Firms demand these resources to produce goods and services, which they supply to the product markets. This is shown in the upper portion of the model. Households spend their income to demand these goods and services. This spending flows through the product market to become revenue to firms.

end, firms supply goods and services to households through product markets, and firms demand human resources, natural resources, and capital resources from households through resource markets.

The flows of resources and products are supported by the flows of income and expenditure—that is, *by the flow of money.* The supply and demand for resources come together in resource markets to determine resource prices, which flow as income to the households. The supply and demand for products come together in product markets to determine the prices for goods and services, which flow as revenue to firms.

Resources and products flow in one direction—in this case, counterclockwise—and the corresponding payments flow in the other direction—clockwise.

TEAM WORK

Divide into groups of four students to study how market participants interact. One pair of students will work together to trace the flow in the circular model from households to firms. The other pair will trace the flow from firms through the product markets. Each pair of students will then explain the flow they have studied to the other pair.

✓ **CHECKPOINT**
How do market participants interact?

Key Concepts

1. How are economic theories used in the real world?

2. Why do economists often use the other-things-constant assumption when they develop economic theories?

3. What does rational self-interest suggest that people want to achieve?

4. When Anthony went to watch another school's basketball team he saw that their center was nearly seven-feet tall. He immediately decided that this person would be that team's highest scorer. What theory did he use to draw this conclusion?

5. Identify each of the following as an example of either a positive or normative statement.

    a. Drew earns $7.50 per hour at his job.

    b. $250 is too much to pay for a prom dress.

    c. Schools should hire more math teachers.

    d. The unemployment rate in 2002 was 5.7%.

    e. The minimum wage ought to be increased.

6. Tomás bought two pairs of shoes for $60 each. He chose not to purchase a third pair at this price. What do you know about the marginal value of a third pair of shoes for Tomás?

Graphing Exercise

7. Latischa works for a business that produces pocket calculators. She saves $50 from the $500 she earns each week. Yesterday she used part of her savings to make a $4,000 down payment on a new car. Draw and label a simple circular-flow model. Use the figure to the right as a guide. Place both of the transactions described on your model, and describe the flows between households and firms that result.

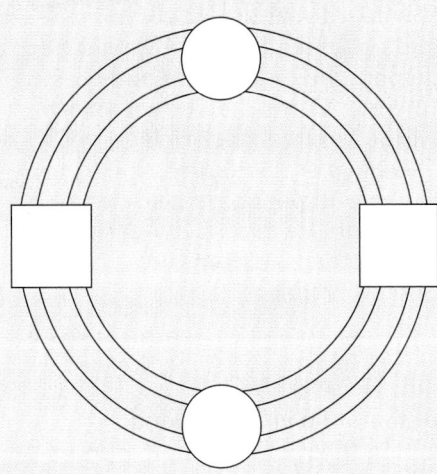

econxtra.swlearning.com

Think Critically

8. **Research** Find the number of new claims for unemployment insurance compensation filed in a recent week in your state at www.dol.gov. If you do not have Internet access, use 60,403, the number of claims filed in the second week of October 2002 in California. Explain how unemployment relates to both market economics and national economics.

9. **Marketing** Examine some of the advertising that a college or university you might choose to attend uses to try to convince new students to apply for admission. Explain how this advertising is intended to help potential students make rational choices.

movers & shakers

Christopher Curtis *Children's Book Author*

For 13 years after high school graduation, Christopher Curtis worked on an assembly line. His job was hanging doors on automobiles. It was boring, repetitive work, but he believes it helped him become a writer.

"My friend and I used to 'double up' on the assembly line. That means we would each hang 30 doors in a row instead of doing every other one, which allowed us each a half hour off every hour. I discovered that if I spent my half hour off the line writing, time would fly by for me." Writing every day helped Curtis develop the flexibility and confidence in his writing that he believes he might never have developed otherwise. Writing became his passion.

Curtis's wife, Kaysandra, knew he wanted to be a writer. Eventually, with her encouragement, he quit his job and began writing full-time. Curtis didn't own a computer, so armed with a stack of legal pads, he spent his days at the library writing his book with pen and paper. He also began attending college. He eventually earned a political science degree from the University of Michigan.

Curtis's first book, *The Watsons Go to Birmingham—1963,* is a fictional book for children. It received two honors: a Newbery Honor and a Coretta Scott King Honor. Such recognition encouraged him to begin work on his second children's book, *Bud, Not Buddy,* about a ten-year-old boy who leaves his foster home in search of his father. This book won the Newbery Medal, the most prestigious award in children's literature. It also won the Coretta Scott King Medal, given each year to a black writer for an inspirational and educational contribution to literature. His next book, to be published in 2004, is titled *Bucking the Sarge.*

Today, in addition to writing books, Curtis frequently visits schools. He meets with groups of children, explaining how he became a writer, and describing the steps he takes to write a book. He also reads to them from his books. "I tell kids that if I can do it, they can do it, too."

Aspiring writers often ask Curtis for advice. "I always tell them that the more they do it, the better they'll get. You have to be patient." He encourages everyone to look for opportunity in spite of barriers they may face. "Lack of money is a very real barrier, but it can be broken. If you are really passionate, do it for the sake of love. Plow right through."

SOURCE READING

Curtis said that if he and his friend doubled up on their job of hanging doors in the automobile factory, it "allowed us each a half hour off every hour. I discovered that if I spent my half hour off the line writing, time would fly by for me." What was the economic choice that Curtis and his friend made in the situation he describes? What were the marginal cost and the marginal benefit of their decision?

ENTREPRENEURS IN ACTION

Like everyone else, entrepreneurs make choices based on their own self-interests. Christopher Curtis chose to become a children's book author because of his passion for writing and his commitment to children. What are you passionate about? Into what type of career could you channel this passion? Write a paragraph to answer these questions.

Objectives

> Define opportunity cost.

> Evaluate guidelines for making choices.

> Analyze the opportunity cost of attending college.

Overview

Think about a decision you just made: the decision to read this chapter right now rather than study for another course, play sports, watch TV, go online, get some sleep, or do something else. Suppose your best alternative to reading this now is getting some sleep. The cost of reading this chapter is passing up the opportunity to sleep. Because of scarcity, whenever you make a choice you must pass up another opportunity—you experience an *opportunity cost*.

Key Terms

opportunity cost

sunk cost

[In the News]

● Women Continue to Move into Top Jobs

Women now hold 15.7 percent of the top-ranking executive positions at America's largest companies, compared with 12.5 percent in 2000 and 8.7 percent in 1995. According to a November 2002 Associated Press article, the number of female corporate officers at Fortune 500 companies increased 3.2 percentage points over the past two years. "It's clearly not as fast as anyone might like to see, but it's certainly measured progress, which is positive and sustainable in the right direction," said Diana Ferguson, vice president and treasurer of Sara Lee Corp. Women make up 17.9 percent of senior officers at Sara Lee. "One of the things I've been pleased to see and could be helpful in promoting more women is companies being willing to give high-potential individuals 'stretch assignments' to allow them to grow into their roles and get into the officer ranks," said Ferguson. This news is great for many women, but certainly not for all. As men have long learned, there is a heavy cost associated with the choice of aiming for the top rungs of the corporate ladder, and many opportunities lost.

Think About It

What are some of the opportunities a woman might miss out on if she aims for the top rungs of the corporate ladder?

Opportunity Cost

opportunity cost

The value of the best alternative passed up for the chosen item or activity

What do you mean when you talk about the cost of something? Isn't it what you must give up or go without to get that thing? The **opportunity cost** of the chosen item or activity is *the value of the best alternative you must pass up*. You can think of opportunity cost as the *opportunity lost*. Sometimes opportunity cost can be measured in dollar terms. However, as you shall see, money usually captures only part of opportunity cost.

Nothing Better to Do?

How many times have you heard people say they did something because they "had nothing better to do"? They actually mean they had no alternative more attractive than the one they chose. Yet, according to the idea of opportunity cost, people *always* do what they do because they had nothing better to do. The choice selected seems, at the time, preferable to any other possible choice. You are reading this page right now because you have nothing better to do.

Estimate Opportunity Cost

Only the individual decision maker can select the most attractive alternative. You, the chooser, seldom know the actual value of the best alternative you gave up, because that alternative is "the road not taken."

If you give up an evening of pizza and conversation with friends to work on a term paper, you will never know the exact value of what you gave up. You know only what you *expected*. You expected the value of working on that paper to exceed the value of the best alternative.

Opportunity Cost Varies

Your opportunity cost depends on your alternatives. This is why you are less likely to study on a Saturday night than on a Tuesday night. On Saturday night, the opportunity cost of studying is higher because your alternatives are more attractive than they are on a Tuesday night, when there's less going on.

What if you go to a movie on Saturday night? Your opportunity cost is the value of the best alternative you gave up, which might be attending a basketball

Participating in a team sport such as soccer or basketball involves many opportunity costs. If you are involved in a team sport at your school, what opportunity costs do you face? If you are not involved in a team sport, were the opportunity costs of involvement a factor in your decision not to participate? Why or why not?

Ethics in Action

game. Studying on Saturday night might rank well down the list of alternatives for you—perhaps ahead of cleaning your room but behind watching TV.

Opportunity cost is a personal thing, but in some cases, estimating a dollar cost for goods and services may work. For example, the opportunity cost of a new DVD player is the benefit of spending that $200 on the best alternative. In other cases, the dollar cost may omit some important elements, particularly the value of the time involved. For example, renting a movie costs not just the rental fee but the time and travel expense it takes to get it, watch it, and return it.

> ✓ **CHECKPOINT**
> What is opportunity cost, and why does it vary with circumstances?

Choose Among Alternatives

Now that you understand what opportunity cost is and how it can vary depending on the circumstances, consider what's involved in actually choosing among alternatives.

Calculate Opportunity Cost

Economists assume that your rational self-interest will lead you to select the most valued alternative. This does not mean you must calculate the value of all possible alternatives. Because acquiring information about alternatives is costly and time-consuming, you usually make choices based on limited or even faulty information. Indeed, some choices may turn out to be poor ones: You went for a picnic but it rained. Your new shoes pinch your toes.

Regret about lost opportunities is captured in the common expression "coulda, woulda, shoulda." At the time you made the choice, however, you believed you were making the best use of all your scarce resources, including the time required to gather information and assess your alternatives.

Time—The Ultimate Limitation

The sultan of Brunei is among the world's richest people, with wealth estimated at $16 billion based on huge oil revenues that flow into his tiny country. He has two palaces, one for each wife. The larger palace has 1,788 rooms, with walls of fine Italian marble and a throne room the size of a football field.

Supported by such wealth, the sultan appears to have overcome the economic problem caused by scarcity. However, although he can buy just about whatever he wants, his time to enjoy these goods and services is scarce. If he pursues one activity, he cannot at the same time do something else. Each activity he undertakes has an opportunity cost. Consequently, the sultan must choose from among the competing uses of his scarcest resource, time. Although your alternatives are less exotic, you too face a time constraint, especially when term papers and exams demand your time.

Ignore Sunk Cost

Suppose you have just finished shopping for groceries and are wheeling your grocery cart to the checkout. How do you decide which line to join? You pick the one you think will involve the least time. What if, after waiting ten minutes in a line that barely moves, you notice that a cashier has opened another line and invites you to check out. Do you switch to the open line, or do you think, "I've already spent ten minutes in this line. I'm staying here"?

The ten minutes you waited represents a **sunk cost**, which is a cost you have already incurred and cannot recover, regardless of what you do now. You should ignore sunk cost in making economic choices, and you should switch to the newly opened line.

Economic decision makers should consider only those costs that are affected by their choice. Sunk costs already have been incurred and are not recoverable. Therefore, sunk costs are irrelevant and should be ignored. Likewise, you should walk out on a boring movie, even one that cost you $10. The irrelevance of sunk costs is underscored by the proverb, "There's no point crying over spilt milk." The milk has already spilled. What you do now cannot change that fact.

CHECKPOINT
Evaluate guidelines for choosing among alternatives.

sunk cost
A cost you have already incurred and cannot recover, regardless of what you do now

© Getty Images/PhotoDisc

You are standing in line at a movie theater's concession stand when suddenly, a cashier opens another line. The movie is about to begin. Should you stay in the line you have been waiting in, or move to the new line? What economic concept does this situation illustrate?

CHAPTER 1   What Is Economics?

Sharpen Your Life Skills

Understand Cause and Effect

Economic events don't just happen. They almost always result from other things that happened first. One of the best ways to understand an economic event is to investigate the factors that caused it to take place. An important benefit of learning about past economic events is the insight you will gain into what might happen if similar events take place in the future.

In 1974, for example, war broke out between Israel and some of her neighboring Arab states. As a result, the flow of crude oil from the Middle East to the United States and other nations was reduced by as much as 50 percent. Oil is a basic natural resource used to produce many goods and services. In 1974, as today, the economies of the United States and most other developed nations rely on imported oil. With a reduced supply of oil these nations were faced with different sets of opportunity costs when they chose how to use the oil that they had. With this in mind, answer the following questions.

Apply Your Skill

1. Due to the shortage of oil in 1974, not enough gasoline could be produced for all the people who wanted to buy it. To try to address the problem, the government limited the amount of gasoline most people could purchase to ten gallons at one time. Later, people were allowed to buy gasoline only on every other day of the week and for a few months, no gasoline could be purchased on Sundays. Even so, some filling stations ran out of gasoline. There often were two- to three-hour waits in line to buy gasoline when it was available. Describe how events that took place nearly five thousand miles from the United States affected the economic decisions made by American consumers in 1974. How did this change the opportunity costs of their decisions?

2. Imagine that a large pipeline that carries 25 percent of the natural gas used in the Northeast is destroyed in an earthquake. It is the middle of winter and nearly half the homes in the Northeast are heated with natural gas. Further, 20 percent of the electrical power plants, and 15 percent of other businesses rely on natural gas to operate. What economic effects are likely to result from this event? How would it change the opportunity costs people face when they make decisions?

The Opportunity Cost of College

Now that you have some idea about opportunity cost and choice, you can apply these concepts in deciding whether or not to go to college.

What will be your opportunity cost of attending college full-time? What will be the most valued alternative you must give up to attend college? If you already know what kind of job you can get with a high school education, you have a fair idea of the income you must give up to attend college.

Forgone Earnings

You may think that if you do not go to college, you could find a job paying $16,000 a year, after taxes. But wait a minute. Don't many college students also work part-time during the school year and full-time during the summer? If you do the same, suppose you could earn $7,000 a year, after taxes.

Thus, by attending college you give up the $16,000 you could earn from a full-time job, yet you could still earn $7,000 from part-time and summer work. Your annual earnings would be $9,000 lower ($16,000 minus $7,000) if you attend college. One part of your opportunity cost of college is the value of what you could have purchased with that additional $9,000 in income.

Direct Costs of College

You also need to consider the direct costs of college itself. Suppose you must pay $5,000 a year for tuition, fees, and books at a public college (paying out-of-state rates would add about $5,000 to that, and attending a private college would add about $13,000). The opportunity cost of paying for tuition, fees, and books is the value of the goods and services that money could have purchased otherwise.

© Getty Images/PhotoDisc

Have you made your decision about whether or not to attend college? If not, applying this section of the textbook to your own situation will help you carefully weigh the opportunity costs of this important decision.

Other College Costs

How about room and board? Expenses for room and board are not an opportunity cost of college because, even if you did not attend college, you would still need to live somewhere and eat something, though these costs could be higher at college. Likewise, whether or not you attended college, you would still incur outlays for items such as movies, CDs, clothing, toiletries, and laundry. Such expenses are not an opportunity cost of attending college. They are personal expenses that arise regardless of what you do. So, for simplicity, assume that room, board, and personal expenses will be the same whether or not you attend college.

The forgone earnings of $9,000 plus the $5,000 for tuition, fees, and books yield an opportunity cost of $14,000 per year for a student paying in-state rates at a public college. The opportunity cost jumps to about $19,000 for those paying out-of-state rates at a public college and to about $27,000 for those at a private college. Scholarships, but not loans, would reduce your opportunity cost.

Other-Things-Constant Assumption

This analysis assumes that all other things are constant. If you expect college to be more painful than your best alternative, then the opportunity cost of attending college is even higher. In other words, if you expect to find college difficult, boring, and in most ways more unpleasant than a full-time job, then your money cost understates your opportunity cost. You not only pay the dollar cost of college, but you must also give up a more pleasant quality of life. If, however, you think college will be

To examine whether college would be a sensible investment for you, try Professor Jane Leuthold's COLLEGE CHOICE program. This program may be accessed through econxtra.swlearning.com.

econxtra.swlearning.com

more enjoyable than a full-time job, then the dollar cost overstates your opportunity cost—the next best alternative involves a less satisfying quality of life.

Evidently, most young people view college as a wise investment in their future, even though college is costly and perhaps even painful for some. College graduates on average earn about twice as much per year as high-school graduates.

Still, college is not for everyone. Some find the opportunity cost too high. For example, Tiger Woods, once an economics major at Stanford University, dropped out after two years to earn a fortune in professional golf, including a $100 million five-year endorsement contract with Nike. Some high school seniors who believe they are ready for professional basketball skip college altogether, as do most pro tennis players and many singers and actors. However, for most of you, the opportunity cost of attending college isn't nearly as high.

CHECKPOINT
How do you measure the opportunity cost of attending college?

THE WALL STREET JOURNAL

Reading It Right What's the relevance of the following statement from *The Wall Street Journal:* "With economics the most popular undergraduate major at many top colleges, demand for economics professors has led to a bidding war for the most highly regarded candidates."

Key Concepts

1. Why must there be an opportunity cost for every choice you make?

2. Why isn't the opportunity cost of using your time to do homework always the same?

3. What factor forces even people who are very wealthy to face opportunity costs?

4. Why should consumers ignore costs they have already paid when making decisions?

5. What is the greatest cost of attending college at publicly funded institutions?

Graphing Exercises

6. Harold sells snowblowers at his hardware store in North Dakota. Although he never changes his price, his sales vary throughout the year. The following table shows his sales in each month of last year. Draw a line graph that demonstrates these data.

7. Explain how your graph shows that the value of buying a snowblower changes over time. What does this have to do with the opportunity cost of other uses for limited funds?

Harold's Snowblower Sales

Month	Sales
January	13
February	11
March	3
April	0
May	0
June	0
July	0
August	0
September	8
October	32
November	38
December	21

Think Critically

8. **Entrepreneurship** Wilma owns a 200-acre farm. She could plant either beans or tomatoes. If the weather is sunny and there is enough rain, she can earn $400 per acre of tomatoes. However, if it is dry or cloudy, tomatoes may earn her no profit at all. Beans are hardy and will grow well unless the weather is truly awful. Wilma can count on earning $200 per acre from beans. Explain why Wilma cannot be sure of the opportunity cost of any decision she might make. What do you think she will choose to do? Why?

9. **Office Technology** Ms. Morra teaches introductory classes in office technology. Her school board has approved $15,000 for her to buy new computers to replace her old outdated models. For this amount she can buy 20 low-end computers that just meet her student's current needs, or she can purchase 10 computers with greater speed and capabilities that she really would like her students to learn to use. What is her opportunity cost for either of these choices?

Xtra!
Study Tools
econxtra.swlearning.com

CONNECT to History

Glassmaking in Jamestown

Despite failed attempts to establish a colony in the New World, in 1606 King James I of England granted a charter for this purpose to the Virginia Company of London. Because earlier enterprises had been expensive, the required funds were raised through a joint stock company. Colonists were instructed to settle land between the 34th and 41st parallels. The three ships arrived at the site of Jamestown Island on May 13, 1607.

Labor for the colony was provided by "colonists" hired by the company. Many of the colonists, lured by the promise of easy gold, were not prepared for the ordeal that followed. These gentlemen, often younger sons of wealthy families who were not used to hard work, struggled to survive. Still, these men perceived their opportunity cost as being small because they stood to inherit little at home. The colony seemed a way for them to gain the land and prominence they could not obtain in England. Well-to-do colonists who provided their own armor and weapons were paid in land, dividends, or additional shares of stock. Less-well-off colonists received clothes, food, and arms from the company, and then after seven years, they received land.

The Virginia Company was still recruiting colonists when Captain Christopher Newport returned to England, bringing word of a struggling colony. Although disappointed that gold and silver did not lie on the beach or grow on the trees, the entrepreneurs of the Virginia Company still saw profitable opportunities in various industries. They believed the colony could take advantage of the land's natural resources and manufacture products for sale in England. One such product was glass. Demand for glass products in England in the early seventeenth century was growing. However, scarce resources in England limited the growth of the industry. England's forests were being depleted, and it took a lot of wood—about a week of burning two to three cords per day—to get the furnaces hot enough to produce glass. The New World, with its unlimited forests, appeared an ideal spot for a glassmaking industry.

Glassmaking in England also suffered from a shortage of labor, as few people were skilled in the craft. Although some glassmakers had come from foreign countries, England could not meet its glass wants domestically. Much of it had to be imported, leading the Company to believe that a Virginia-based enterprise could produce glass more cheaply than it could be imported. Because glassmakers in England were doing very well, the opportunity cost of their leaving for the uncertainty of a new and dangerous land was too great. Countries that exported large amounts of glass were better places to recruit workers. Among the early settlers in Virginia in the summer of 1608 were eight Germans and Poles for the glassmaking industry. Some glass was produced, but the enterprise was short lived. Workers had little time to devote to their industry because they were too busy trying to survive. When the newly appointed governor of Virginia arrived on May 24, 1610, with 150 new colonists, only 60 survivors remained. Ninety percent of the colonists had died, and with them, America's first industry.

THINK CRITICALLY

Devise an economic theory that could have guided the Virginia Company's decision to begin a colony in the New World. What questions and variables might these entrepreneurs have considered? What might their assumptions have been? What might their hypotheses have been?

Chapter Assessment

Summary

1.1 The Economic Problem

a Economic choices are necessary because of our unlimited desires and the scarce supply of productive resources available to satisfy them. There are three basic types of productive resources. *Human resources* is the broad category of human efforts, both physical and mental, used to produce goods and services.

Xtra! Quiz Prep
econxtra.swlearning.com

Natural resources are so-called "gifts of nature." Natural resources can be divided into renewable resources and exhaustible resources. *Capital resources* commonly include all human creations used to produce goods and services.

b Both goods and services are able to satisfy human desires but goods can be seen, felt, and touched while services cannot. Goods and services are scarce if their price exceeds zero. Because goods and services are produced using scarce resources, they are themselves scarce. Goods or services that are truly free are not a concern of economics.

1.2 Economic Theory

a Economic models are simplifications of economic reality that are used to make predictions about the real world. When economic theories are constructed, they are based on simplifying assumptions that include *other things being equal* and *rational self-interest*.

b Some economic statements involve facts that can be proven right or wrong. These are *positive statements*. Other statements that are based on individual opinion cannot be proven right or wrong and are *normative statements*.

c Economic choice usually involves a change in the status quo. The only relevant factors are the benefits and costs of the next choice that is made. This is called *marginal analysis*. A rational decision maker will change the status quo as long as the expected marginal benefit

from the change exceeds the expected marginal cost.

d *Markets* are the means by which buyers and sellers carry out exchange. By bringing together the two sides of exchange, demand and supply, markets determine price and quantity.

e Economics can be seen from two perspectives. *Market economics* concerns how individuals make decisions. *National economics* focuses on the condition of the economy as a whole. There are four participants in the economy: *households, firms, governments,* and the *rest of the world.*

f An economic system can be represented by a circular-flow diagram that includes households, firms, resource markets, and product markets. There are flows of goods, services, and resources that move in one direction through this model, and flows of money that move in the opposite direction.

1.3 Opportunity Cost and Choice

a Whenever an economic decision is made, an *opportunity cost* is paid. Opportunity cost is the value of the best alternative to a choice that is taken. It is often impossible to know the true value of a choice that is not taken. Decisions are based on the *expected* opportunity cost of a choice.

b Opportunity costs of a decision vary with circumstances. Calculating the value of an opportunity cost requires time and information. Although opportunity costs are often seen in how you spend your limited funds, time is the ultimate limiting factor that forces even the very wealthy to make choices.

c Sunk costs have already been paid and should not be considered when you make economic decisions.

d Many choices involve both direct and indirect opportunity costs. The decision to attend college, for example, requires spending funds that could be used for other purposes as well as forgoing income that could have been earned from other uses of scarce time.

Review Economic Terms

Choose the term that best fits the definition. On a separate sheet of paper, write the letter of the answer.

_____ 1. An item you can see, feel, and touch that requires scarce resources to produce and satisfies human wants

_____ 2. The means by which buyers and sellers carry out exchange

_____ 3. The broad category of human efforts, both physical and mental, used to produce goods and services

_____ 4. The value of the best alternative passed up for the chosen item or activity

_____ 5. The study of how people use their scarce resources to satisfy their unlimited wants

_____ 6. All human creations used to produce goods and services

_____ 7. Something not physical that requires scarce resources to produce and satisfies human wants

_____ 8. A profit-seeker who develops a new product or process and assumes the risk of profit or loss

_____ 9. So-called "gifts of nature" used to produce goods and services

_____ 10. Incremental, additional, extra, or one more; refers to a change in an economic variable, a change in the status quo.

a. **capital goods**

b. **economics**

c. **entrepreneur**

d. **good**

e. **human resources**

f. **marginal**

g. **market**

h. **natural resources**

i. **opportunity cost**

j. **service**

Review Economic Concepts

11. True or False *Scarcity* exists because our supplies of *productive resources* are limited.

12. Which of the following is an example of a *natural resource*?

    a. lumber used to build a house

    b. a tree standing in a forest

    c. a carpenter who installs new cabinets

    d. gasoline you put in your car

13. A(n) __?__ is a person who tries to earn a profit by dreaming up a new product or finding a better way to produce an existing one.

14. When a firm's revenue from sales exceeds its costs of production, it will earn a(n) __?__.

15. True or False *Services* are different from *goods* because they are not able to satisfy human desires.

16. Which of the following is an exhaustible resource?

    a. crude oil in the ground

    b. corn growing in a field

    c. water in a river

    d. fish in the ocean

17. True or False When you play football in a public park you receive a *free good* because you do not pay to use the park.

18. A(n) __?__ is a simplification of economic reality that is used to make predictions about the real world.

19. When economists use the *other-things-constant assumption* they are trying to

    a. consider only variables that interest them.

    b. duplicate reality in their ideas.

    c. establish economic laws that will last indefinitely.

    d. combine several ideas into one.

20. **True or False** In general, the assumption of *rational self-interest* means that individuals try to maximize the expected benefit achieved with a given cost.

21. __?__statements concern what is.

22. **True or False** The assumption of *rational self-interest* rules out concerns for others.

23. Which of the following is a *normative statement*?

    a. On average, Rose works 30 hours a week.

    b. Rose is paid $8.00 per hour for her labor.

    c. Rose pays 7.65 percent of her earnings in Social Security tax.

    d. Rose works too many hours each week to do well in school.

24. **True or False** Most of the disagreement among economists involves debates over *positive statements.*

25. A rational decision maker will change the status quo as long as the expected __?__ benefit from the change exceeds the expected __?__ cost.

26. Which of the following is an example of *market economics*?

    a. Tyrone received a 5 percent raise in his wage from his employer last year.

    b. On average, prices increased by 2.3 percent last year.

    c. The federal government borrowed more than $100 billion last year.

    d. Businesses invested 3.1 percent more last year than in the year before.

27. **True or False** *Opportunity cost* is the value of the best alternative that you pass up whenever you make a choice.

28. Which of the following is Yo-chee's opportunity cost of spending $8 to go to a movie with her friends?

    a. the value of the $8 she spent

    b. the value of the time she worked to earn the $8

    c. the value of the enjoyment she received from seeing the movie

    d. the value of the pizza she would have bought if she had not gone to the movie

29. **True or False** If you have nothing better to do when you make a choice, you pay no opportunity cost for your decision.

30. **True or False** The value of the opportunity cost of a particular choice is the same for all people.

31. Which of the following would not be a possible opportunity cost of attending college?

    a. other uses of the money used to pay college tuition

    b. other uses of the time used to study and attend classes

    c. other uses of extra income earned because of the college education

    d. other uses of the money used to pay for room and board while attending college

32. **True or False** The opportunity cost you would incur for cleaning your room would probably be different on Saturday evening than on Tuesday afternoon.

33. Which of the following is a *sunk cost* that should be ignored when you choose whether or not to buy a new computer over the Internet?

    a. the $50 delivery charge

    b. the $30 monthly payment you already agreed to make to connect to the Internet

    c. the extra $200 you might pay to get a flat-screen monitor

    d. the $150 two-year service contract you could decide to buy

Apply Economic Concepts

34. Circular-Flow Model Sketch a copy of the circular-flow model shown below on your own paper. Place each of the following in the correct location on your model.

    a. Brad watches Monday-night football on his new TV.

b. The Sony Corporation produces a new TV.

c. Brad works at a local drugstore.

d. Brad buys a new TV from a Sears store.

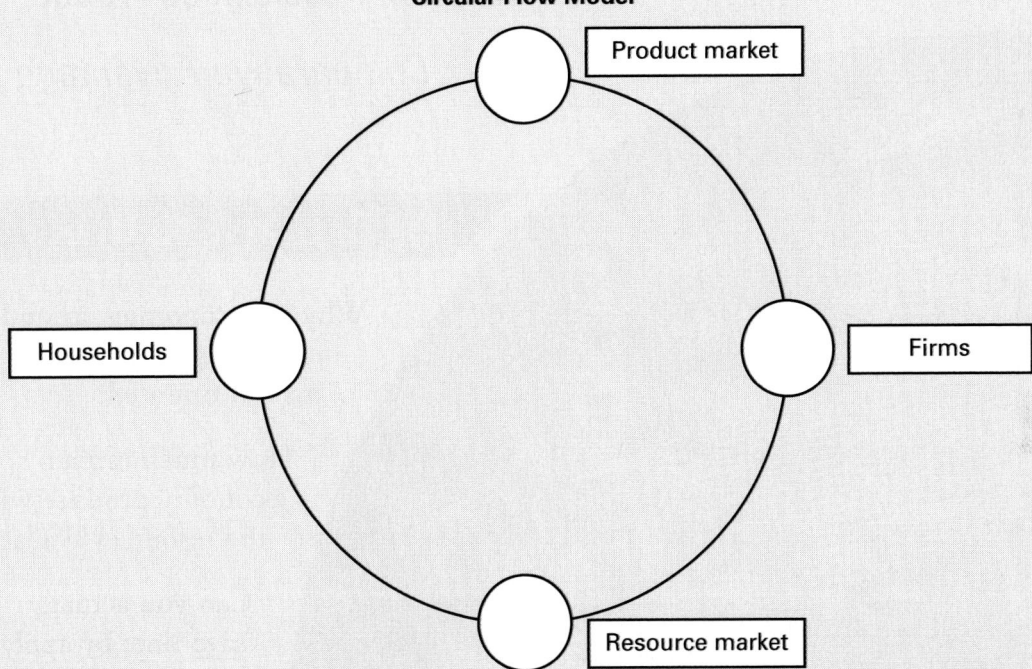

Circular-Flow Model

Product market

Households

Firms

Resource market

35. Opportunity Cost Your uncle has offered to buy either a new computer or a good-quality bicycle for you as a graduation present. The prices of both items are the same. Write an essay that identifies which gift you would choose and describes the opportunity cost that would result from your choice. Why might other people make a different choice?

36. Productive Resources List the steps that need to be taken to produce a loaf of bread. Identify examples of each type of productive resource used in this process.

37. Sharpen Your Life Skills: Cause and Effect The owners of a bakery found they had more customers who wanted to buy their bread and cakes than they could serve. As a result they decided to expand the size of their business and employ twice as many workers. How does this example demonstrate cause and effect? What additional resources would the business require in order to increase its production?

e-con @pps   econxtra.swlearning.com

38. Access **EconNews Online** at econxtra.swlearning.com. Click on e-con@pps and then click on the policy debate entitled "Are Americans Overworked?" Read the three quotations under "Issues and Background." If, as the textbook states, the fundamental human resource is "time," do you think it is a benefit or a problem for the U.S. economy that Americans are working more than ever before? Justify your answer with facts from the web site.

Economic Systems and Economic Tools

Consider

Why are economies around the world growing more market oriented?

How much can an economy produce with the resources available?

Can you actually save time by applying economic principles to your family chores?

Why is experience a good teacher?

Why is fast food so fast?

POINT YOUR BROWSER

econxtra.swlearning.com

© Getty Images/PhotoDisc

Objectives

> Identify the three questions that all economic systems must answer.

> Describe a pure market economy, and identify its problems.

> Describe a pure centrally planned economy, and identify its problems.

> Compare mixed, transitional, and traditional economies.

Overview

What should the economy produce? How should this output be produced? For whom should it be produced? More than 200 countries around the world attempt to answer these three economic questions, all using somewhat different economic systems. One way to distinguish among economic systems is to focus on the role of government. Imagine a range from the most free to the most government-controlled economic system. A *pure market economy* stands at one end of the range, and a *pure centrally planned economy* stands at the other. Although no economy in the world reflects either extreme in its purest form, knowing the features and problems of each extreme will help you understand differences around the world.

Key Terms

economic system

pure market economy

pure centrally planned economy

mixed economy

market economy

transitional economy

traditional economy

[In the News]

● Protectionism in a Free Market

Many industries in Japan have developed with the help of government protection. However, this protectionism has had a downside. A December, 2002 *Wall Street Journal* article reports that as most of the world benefited from an explosion of new drugs in the 1980s and 1990s, Japanese patients lacked access to some of the West's best-known medications. For years the Japanese government completely closed its markets to many Western drugs and intentionally delayed the introduction of other drugs. Though the government's actions obviously aided local drug producers, these actions were based mainly on the cultural prejudice that Japanese bodies differ significantly from those of Westerners. Due to this belief, pharmaceutical industry rules required that drug trials be conducted from scratch on Japanese subjects. Protectionist policies began to change in the late 1990s, when in an effort to re-energize its economy, Japan opened several of its industries to foreign competition. At the same time, patients began requesting more information from their doctors about drugs they had heard about. The new drug awareness led to increasing pressure on the government to remove the roadblocks to approval of pharmaceuticals from the West. Today the approval process for Western drug products is faster and easier. Western drug companies also have greater access to the Japanese market, and Western-style drug advertising is done through Japanese media outlets.

Think About It

Were the Japanese government's protecionist policies helping or hurting consumers with regard to pharmaceuticals? What caused Japan to change its protectionist policies in the pharmaceutical industry?

The Three Economic Questions

All economies must answer three questions:

1. What goods and services will be produced?

2. How will they be produced?

3. For whom will they be produced?

An **economic system** is the set of mechanisms and institutions that resolves the *what, how,* and *for whom* questions. Some standards used to distinguish among economic systems are

1. Who owns the resources?

2. What decision-making process is used to allocate resources and products?

3. What types of incentives guide economic decision makers?

economic system

The set of mechanisms and institutions that resolves the *what, how,* and *for whom* questions for an economy

What Goods and Services Will Be Produced?

Most people take for granted the many choices that go into deciding what gets produced—everything from which new kitchen appliances are introduced and which would-be novelists get published, to which roads are built. Although different economies resolve these and millions of other questions using different decision-making rules and mechanisms, all economies must somehow decide what gets produced.

How Will Goods and Services Be Produced?

The economic system must determine how output is to be produced. Which resources should be used, and how should they be combined to produce each product? How much labor should be used and at what skill levels? What kinds of machines should be used? What type of fertilizer should be applied to grow the best strawberries? Should a factory be built in the city or closer to the interstate highway? Millions of individual decisions determine which resources are employed and how these resources are combined.

For Whom Will Goods and Services Be Produced?

Who will actually consume the goods and services produced? The economic system must determine how to allocate the fruits of production among the population. Should equal amounts be provided to everyone? Should those willing to wait in line the longest get more? Should goods be allocated according to height? Weight? Religion? Age? Gender? Race? Looks? Strength? Political connections? The value of resources supplied?

Main Idea

Allocation of Goods and Services

An economic system determines how the three economic questions are answered *to allocate goods and services in an economy.* The *three economic questions* are closely interwoven. Why does the answer to one question depend so much on the answers to the other questions? Apply your answer to clothing products. How does what clothing is produced relate to *how it will be produced* and *for whom it will be produced?*

© Getty Images/PhotoDisc

The question "For whom will goods and services be produced?" often is referred to as the distribution question.

Interdependent Questions

The three economic questions are closely interwoven. The answer to one depends very much on the answers to the others. For example, an economy that distributes goods and services in uniform amounts to all will, no doubt, answer the what-will-be-produced question differently from an economy that allows each person to choose goods and services.

CHECKPOINT
What three questions must all economic systems answer?

Pure Market Economy

In a **pure market economy**, private firms account for all production. There is no government at all. Features of this economic system include the private ownership of all resources and the coordination of economic activity based on the prices generated in free, competitive markets. Any income derived from selling resources goes exclusively to the resource owners.

The Invisible Hand of Markets

Resource owners have *property rights* to the use of their resources and are free to supply those resources to the highest bidder. Producers are free to make and sell whatever they believe will be profitable. Consumers are free to buy whatever they can afford. All this voluntary buying and selling is coordinated by competitive markets that are free from any government regulations.

Market prices guide resources to their most productive use and channel goods to those consumers who value them the most. Markets answer the *what, how,* and *for whom* questions. Markets transmit information about relative scarcity, provide incentives to producers and consumers, and distribute income among resource owners.

No single individual or small group coordinates these activities. Rather, the voluntary choices of many buyers and sellers responding only to their individual incentives direct resources and products to those who value them the most.

According to Adam Smith (1723–1790), market forces coordinate production as if by an "invisible hand." Smith argued that *although each individual pursues his or her self-interest, the "invisible hand" of market competition promotes the general welfare.* Voluntary choices in competitive markets answer the questions *what, how,* and *for whom.*

Problems with Pure Market Economies

A pure market economy offers resource owners the freedom and the incentive to get the most from their resources. However a pure market economy has its flaws because markets do not always work on their own. The most notable *market failures* include:

1. **Difficulty Enforcing Property Rights** Market activity depends on people using their scarce resources to maximize their satisfaction. However, what if you were repeatedly robbed of your paycheck on your way home from work? What if, after you worked a week in a new job, your employer called you a fool and said you would not be paid? Why bother working? Private markets would break down if you could not safeguard your private property or if you could not enforce

Adam Smith

pure market economy

An economic system with no government involvement so that private firms account for all production

THE WALL STREET JOURNAL

Reading It Right What's the relevance of the following statement from *The Wall Street Journal:*

"Capitalism" is supposed to be the one economic system that puts consumers at the center." [Note: *Capitalism* is another term for *market economy.*]

contracts. In a pure market economy, there is no government, so there is no central authority to protect property rights, enforce contracts, and otherwise ensure that the rules of the game are followed.

2. **Some People Have Few Resources to Sell** Because of a poor education, disability, discrimination, the time demands of caring for small children, or bad luck, some people have few resources to sell in a market economy. Because markets do not guarantee even a minimum level of income, some people would have difficulty surviving.

3. **Some Firms Try to Monopolize Markets** Although the "invisible hand" of market competition usually promotes the general welfare, some producers may try to monopolize the market by either unfairly driving out competitors or by conspiring with competitors to fix prices. With less competition, firms can charge a higher price to earn more profit. Thus, firms have a profit incentive to monopolize a market.

4. **No Public Goods** Private firms do not produce so-called *public goods,* such as national defense. Once produced, public goods are available to all, regardless of who pays and who does not pay for them. Suppliers cannot easily prevent those who fail to pay for a public good from benefiting from the good. For example, reducing terrorism benefits all in the economy. Because firms cannot sell public goods profitably, they are not produced in a pure market economy.

5. **Externalities** Market prices reflect the benefits to buyers and the costs to sellers. However, some production and consumption affect third parties—those not directly involved. For example, a paper mill fouls the air breathed by local residents, but the market price of paper fails to reflect such costs. Because the pollution

Air pollution from a paper mill affects the health of local residents. Why does the market system fail to account for such problems? How can such problems be solved for a society?

© Getty Images/PhotoDisc

costs are outside—or external to—the market transaction, they are called *externalities*. Private markets fail to account for externalities. Because of this type of market failure, even market economies allow a role for government.

CHECKPOINT
What is a pure market economy, and what are its problems?

Pure Centrally Planned Economy

In a **pure centrally planned economy**, all resources are government-owned, and production is coordinated by the central plans of government. At least in theory, there is public, or *communal,* ownership of all resources. That is why central planning is sometimes called *communism.* Central planners answer the three economic questions by spelling out how many missiles, how many homes, and how much bread to produce. Central planners also decide how to produce these goods and who should get them.

The Visible Hand of Planners

Rather than rely on competitive markets, central planners direct the allocation of resources and products. Central planners may believe that market economies produce too many consumer goods and too few capital goods, especially military hardware. They also may believe that central planning yields a more even distribution of goods across households than a market economy does.

In a pure centrally planned economy, the government, or state, owns all resources, including labor. Central planners direct production through state-owned enterprises, which usually face no competition. Some goods and serv-

ices are *rationed,* meaning that each household gets a certain amount. For example, each household gets so many square feet of living space. Other products are allocated based on prices set by central planners. Prices, once set, tend to be inflexible.

In short, market economies coordinate production through the invisible hand of market competition. Centrally planned economies use the visible hands of central planners.

Problems with Centrally Planned Economies

A pure centrally planned economy ideally produces the combination of products that society desires. But this economic system has its flaws.

The most notable central planning failures include the following five failures. Because of these planning failures, countries have modified centrally planned economies to allow a greater role for private ownership and market competition.

1. **Consumers Get Low Priority**
   Central plans may reflect the preferences of central planners rather than those of consumers. Central planners decide what gets produced and who should consume the goods. When goods are rationed or offered for an inflexible price, severe shortages can result. Evidence of consumer goods shortage include empty store shelves, long waiting lines, and the "tips"—or bribes—shop operators expect for supplying scarce goods.

2. **Little Freedom of Choice** Because central planners are responsible for all production decisions, the variety of products tends to be narrower than in a market economy. Households in centrally planned economies not only have less choice about what to consume, but they also have less freedom in other economic decisions. Government planners may decide where people live and where they work.

3. **Central Planning Can Be Inefficient** Running an economy is so complicated that some resources

pure centrally planned economy

An economic system in which all resources are government-owned and production is coordinated by the central plans of government

are used inefficiently. Consider all that's involved in growing and distributing farm products. Central planners must decide what to grow, what resources to employ (who, for example, should become farmers), and who gets to consume the harvest (should it be rationed or sold for a set price?). Mistakes along the way result in inefficiencies. For example, the former Soviet Union had a centrally planned economy. About one-third of the harvest there reportedly rotted on its way to consumers.

4. **Resources Owned by the State Are Sometimes Wasted** Because resources are owned by the state, nobody in particular has an incentive to see that they are employed in their highest-valued use. Some resources are wasted. For example, Soviet workers usually had little regard for equipment that belonged to the state. New trucks or tractors might be dismantled for parts, or working equipment might be sent to a scrap plant. Stealing state-owned property, though a serious crime, also was a common practice. In contrast to the lack of regard for state property, Soviet citizens took extremely good care of their personal property. For example, personal cars were so well maintained that they lasted more than 20 years on average—twice the official projected life of an automobile.

5. **Environmental Damage** In theory, a centrally planned economy, with its focus on "the common good," should take better care of the environment than a market economy. In practice, however, state enterprises often are more concerned with meeting the goals set by the central planners. For example, in its drive for military dominance, the former Soviet government set off 125 nuclear explosions *above* ground. The resulting bomb craters filled with water, forming contaminated lakes. Thousands of barrels of nuclear waste were dumped into Soviet rivers and seas.

CHECKPOINT
What is a pure centrally planned economy, and what are its problems?

Mixed, Transitional, and Traditional Economies

No country on earth represents either a market economy or centrally planned economy in its pure form. Economic systems have grown more alike over time. The role of government has increased in market economies, and the role of markets has increased in centrally planned economies. As a result, most economies now mix central planning with competitive markets and are called **mixed economies**.

Mixed Economy

The United States is a mixed economy. Because markets play a relatively large role, it also is considered a **market economy**. Government accounts for about one-third of all U.S. economic activity.

Government also regulates the private sector in a variety of ways. For example, local zoning boards determine lot sizes, home sizes, and the types of industries allowed. Federal bodies regulate workplace safety, environmental

---

mixed economy

An economic system that mixes central planning with competitive markets

market economy

Describes the U.S. economic system, where markets play a relatively large role

NETBookmark

The CIA World Factbook provides brief descriptions of all the world's economies. Access this web site through econxtra.swlearning.com. Choose one country and identify its economy. Write a paragraph explaining the characteristics of this country's economy.

econxtra.swlearning.com

quality, competition in markets, and many other activities.

Although both ends of the economic spectrum have moved toward the center, the market system has gained more converts in recent decades. Consider countries that have been cut in two by political and economic ideology. In such cases, the economies began with similar resources and income levels right after the split. Over time the market-oriented economies produced a much higher standard of living than the centrally planned economies. For example, income per capita in Taiwan, a market-oriented economy after it split from China, averages about four times that of China, a centrally planned economy. As another example, income per capita in market-oriented South Korea is about 12 times that of North Korea, perhaps the most centrally planned economy in the world.

Recognizing the power of markets to create incentives and provide information, even some of the most diehard central planners now reluctantly accept some market activity. For example, about 20 percent of the world's population lives in China, which grows more market oriented each day. The former Soviet Union dissolved into 15 independent republics. Most are now trying

to introduce more market incentives. Even North Korea has opened a special economic zone where market forces will be allowed to operate without government interference.

Transitional Economy

More than two-dozen countries around the world are **transitional economies**, in the process of shifting orientation from central planning to competitive markets. This transition involves converting state-owned enterprises into private

TEAM WORK

The United States is a mixed economy, containing features of both a market economy and a centrally planned economy. This textbook gives many examples of the central planning role of government in the U.S. economy. In small groups, brainstorm and list evidence of how the United States is a market economy. Compare your groups' results in class.

transitional economy

An economic system in the process of shifting from central planning to competitive markets

Ethics in Action

Stealing Digital Property The U.S. government works to protect property rights, enforce contracts, and otherwise ensure the rules of the game are followed. In protecting property rights, a major issue is how to handle piracy and "bootlegging" in the software, music, and movie industries. "Stealing someone else's work is no more legal on a computer than it is with your bare hands," said Peter Chernin, CEO of Fox Group, during the 2002 Fall Comdex consumer electronics trade show. His message was supported by George Lucas, producer-director of "Star Wars," who also spoke at the show. Lucas stressed that if piracy, unauthorized copying,

and counterfeiting of big, blockbuster films is not curtailed, it might no longer make economic sense to produce them. A student in the audience argued that if the companies would lower their prices, people's desire to bootleg would decrease. His opinion was that either the prices come down or people will not stop copying from their friend's music, film, and software collections, or downloading from the Internet.

Think Critically

Explain the basic ethical problem with the college student's argument.

enterprises. This is a process called *privatization.* Altogether more than 150,000 large enterprises are trying to grow more competitive. Most of these enterprises have become more efficient and more productive. From Hungary to Mongolia, the transition now under way will shape economies for decades to come.

Traditional Economy

traditional economy
An economic system shaped largely by custom or religion

Finally, some economic systems, known as **traditional economies**, are shaped largely by custom or religion. For example, caste systems in India restrict occupational choice. Family relations also play significant roles in organizing and coordinating economic activity.

Even in the United States some occupations still are dominated by women, and others by men, largely because of tradition. Your own pattern of consumption and choice of occupation may be influenced by some of these forces.

 **CHECKPOINT**
Compare mixed, market, transitional, and traditional economies.

 **Xtra!**
Study Tools
econxtra.swlearning.com

2.1 Assessment

Key Concepts

1. Compare the answers to the three basic economic questions in a pure market economy with the answers to these questions in a pure centrally planned economy. Present your answers using a spreadsheet or grid.

2. What did Adam Smith mean when he talked about an "invisible hand" that guides production in market economies?

3. Why are property rights important to the efficient working of a market economy?

4. What problems are likely to occur in centrally planned economic systems?

5. Why is the U.S. economic system sometimes called a "mixed market economy"?

Graphing Exercise

6. Draw a horizontal line. Label the left side of the line "Pure Market Economy" and the right side, "Pure Centrally Planned Economy." Place each of the following nations on your line at a place that you think accurately represents the current state of its economy: United States, Mainland China, North Korea, Sweden, Russia, Mexico. Research the economies of the countries not familiar to you. Be prepared to explain your placements.

Think Critically

7. **Government** When governments decide how to spend money, they often behave in a way similar to centrally planned economies. Investigate an important spending decision that was made by your local government. Write a one-page paper that identifies problems that were encountered that have been common in centrally planned economies.

Objectives

> Describe the production possibilities frontier and explain its shape.

> Explain what causes the production possibilities frontier to shift.

Overview

How much can the economy produce in a particular period if resources are used fully and efficiently? In reality, an economy, such as the U.S. economy, has millions of different resources that can be combined in all kinds of ways to produce millions of possible goods and services. A simple model is used to describe the economy's production possibilities.

Key Terms

production possibilities frontier (PPF)

efficiency

law of increasing opportunity cost

economic growth

[In the News]

● Sometimes Frozen Possibilities Are a Good Thing

Starting with a small dairy herd, Lecherias Loncomilla Ltda. has expanded to become the leading producer of frozen desserts in Chile. However, in Chile, a country with 15 million consumers, the company's sales were beginning to top out at about $3 million a year. Owner Francisco Mac-Clure says, "Give us the U.S. and we'll grow and be twice as profitable." He is referring to the recently negotiated, first free-trade pact between the United States and Latin America since 1993. This United States–Chile trade pact can only help specialists like the frozen dessert maker Mac-Clure. Once the United States drops the imposed duties on ice cream and many other Chilean raw materials and products, Mr. Mac-Clure and his fellow producers will be free to sell the raw materials Chile has in greatly expandable supply. Chile's enormous crop of fresh fruit and huge dairy herds that produce rich cream and butterfat also will add to the price and quality competition in the market. Mac-Clure has another big reason to smile about the trade pact: Chile's summer is the opposite of that in the United States, and so the pact virtually doubles Chile's selling season for frozen desserts.

Think About It

What effect, if any, do you think an increase in ice cream production in Chile will have on the country's production of capital goods?

Efficiency and the Production Possibilities Frontier

How much can an economy produce with the resources available? What are the economy's production capabilities? To help consider these questions, you need a simple model of the economy, beginning with some simplifying assumptions.

Simplifying Assumptions

Here are the model's simplifying assumptions:

1. To reduce the analysis to manageable proportions, the model limits the output to two broad classes of products: consumer goods, such as pizzas and haircuts, and capital goods, such as pizza ovens and hair clippers.

2. The focus is on production during a given period—in this case, a year.

3. The resources available in the economy are fixed in both quantity and quality during the period.

4. Society's knowledge about how best to combine these resources to produce output—that is, the available *technology*—does not change during the year.

The point of these assumptions is to freeze the economy's resources and technology for a period of time to focus on what possibly can be produced during that time.

PPF Model

Given the resources and the technology available in the economy, the **production possibilities frontier (PPF)** shows the possible combinations of the two types of goods that can be produced when available resources are employed fully and efficiently. **Efficiency** means producing the maximum possible output from available resources.

The economy's PPF for consumer goods and capital goods is shown by the curve *AF* in Figure 2.1. Point *A* identifies the amount of consumer goods produced per year if all the economy's resources are used efficiently to produce consumer goods. Point *F* identifies the amount of capital goods produced per year if all the economy's

---

production possibilities frontier (PPF)
Shows the possible combinations of the two types of goods that can be produced when available resources are employed fully and efficiently

efficiency
Producing the maximum possible output from available resources

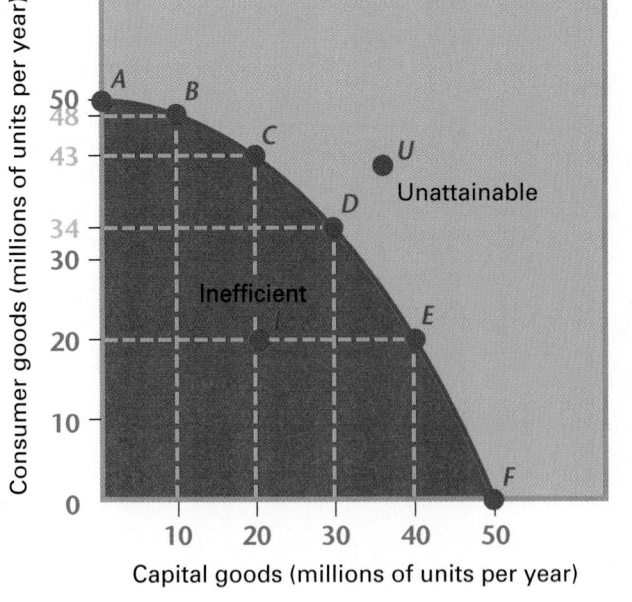

Production Possibilities Frontier (PPF) | **Figure 2.1**

econxtra.swlearning.com

The Graphing Workshop

If the economy uses its available resources and technology fully and efficiently in producing consumer goods and capital goods, it will be on its production possibilities frontier curve *AF*. The PPF is bowed out to illustrate the law of increasing opportunity cost: Additional units of capital goods require the economy to sacrifice more and more units of consumer goods. More consumer goods must be given up in moving from *D* to *E* than in moving from *A* to *B*, although in each case the gain in capital goods is 10 million units. Points inside the PPF, such as *I*, represent inefficient use of resources. Points outside the PPF, such as *U*, represent unattainable combinations.

resources are used efficiently to produce capital goods.

Points along the curve between *A* and *F* identify possible combinations of the two goods that can be produced when the economy's resources are used efficiently. Resources are employed fully and efficiently when there is no change that could increase the production of one good without decreasing the production of the other good.

Inefficient and Unattainable Production

Points inside the PPF, including *I* in Figure 2.1, represent combinations that do not employ resources fully, employ them inefficiently, or both. Note that point *C* yields more consumer goods and no fewer capital goods than point *I.* Point *E* yields more capital goods and no fewer consumer goods than point *I.* In fact, any point along the PPF between *C* and *E,* such as point *D,* yields both more consumer goods and more capital goods than *I.* So point *I* is *inefficient.* By using resources more efficiently or by using previously idle resources, the economy can produce more of at least one good without reducing the production of the other good.

Points outside the PPF, such as *U* in Figure 2.1, represent unattainable combinations, given the resources and the technology available. Thus the PPF not only shows efficient combinations of production but also serves as the border between inefficient combinations inside the frontier and unattainable combinations outside the frontier.

The Shape of the PPF

Any movement along the PPF involves giving up some of one good to get more of the other. Movement down the curve indicates that the opportunity cost of more capital goods is fewer consumer goods. For example, moving from point *A* to point *B* increases the amount of capital goods produced from none to 10 million units and reduces production of consumer goods from 50 million to 48 million units, a decline of only 2 million units. Increasing production of capital goods to 10 million units causes the production of consumer goods to fall only a little. Capital production initially employs resources (such as road graders used to build highways) that add little or nothing to production of consumer goods but are quite productive in making capital goods.

Study the two images and decide which one represents capital goods and which one represents consumer goods. If these goods were represented on a PPF, what would happen to the production of one type of good if the production of the other good increased?

A Growing Web
"The Internet is a total reversal of what Wall Street expected," says analyst Steven Vonder Haar of Interactive Media Strategies. "It delivers tailored and personalized services instead of entertainment and broadcast programming. In a word, it's practical." During the "dot-gone" era ending the 1990s, nearly 1,000 Internet companies that promised to greatly simplify our lives—such as Webvan, Furniture.com, and Pets.com—went belly-up and folded. However similar ideas live on in web sites that draw thousands, saving consumers time and money every day. These include health-related sites, grocery sites, map sites, stock-buying sites, government-services sites, clothes-shopping sites, and many others. Ken Cassar, an online retail analyst for Jupiter Research, says early results prove the Internet is "capable of allowing mass customization, better inventory management, and major cost savings in manufacturing." Internet sales have increased from $0.7 billion in 1996 to $62 billion in 2002.

Think Critically
What effect do you think success of Internet commerce will have on the production possibilities frontier? Explain your answer.

---

law of increasing opportunity cost

Each additional increment of one good requires the economy to give up successively larger increments of the other good

As shown by the dashed lines in Figure 2.1, each additional 10 million units of capital goods reduces consumer goods by successively larger amounts. As more capital goods are produced, the resources drawn away from consumer goods are those that are increasingly better suited to making consumer goods and less suited to making capital goods. *The resources in the economy are not all perfectly adaptable to the production of both types of goods. Therefore, the opportunity cost of capital goods increases as the economy produces more capital goods and fewer consumer goods.*

The shape of the production possibilities frontier reflects the law of increasing opportunity cost. If the economy uses all resources efficiently, the **law of increasing opportunity cost** states that each additional increment of one good requires the economy to give up successively larger increments of the other good.

The PPF has a bowed-out shape due to the law of increasing opportunity cost. For example, whereas the first 10 million units of capital goods have an opportunity cost of only 2 million consumer goods, the final 10 million capital goods—that is, the increase from point E to point F—have an opportunity cost of 20 million consumer goods. As the economy moves down the curve, the curve becomes steeper, reflecting the higher opportunity cost of capital goods in terms of forgone consumer goods.

The law of increasing opportunity cost also applies when moving from the production of capital goods to the production of consumer goods. When all resources in the economy are making capital goods, as at point F, certain resources, such as cows and farmland, are of little use in making capital goods. Thus, when resources shift from making capital goods to making consumer goods, few capital goods need be given up initially. As more consumer goods are produced, however, resources that are more productive in making capital goods must be used for making consumer goods, reflecting the law of increasing opportunity cost.

If resources were perfectly adaptable to the production of both types of

The Graphing Workshop

goods, the amount of consumer goods sacrificed to make more capital goods would remain constant. In this case, the PPF would be a straight line, reflecting a constant opportunity cost along the PPF.

Shifts of the PPF

The production possibilities frontier assumes that resources available in the economy and the level of technology are fixed during the period. Over time, however, the PPF may shift as a result of changes in resource availability or in technology. An outward shift of the PPF reflects **economic growth**, which is an expansion in the economy's production possibilities or ability to produce. The economy's ability to make stuff grows.

Changes in Resource Availability

If the labor force increases, such as through immigration, the PPF shifts outward, as shown in panel (a) of Figure 2.2. If people decide to work longer hours, retire later, or if the labor force becomes more skilled, this too would shift the PPF outward. An increase in the availability of other resources, such as new oil discoveries, also would shift the PPF outward.

In contrast, a decrease in the availability or quality of resources shifts the PPF inward, as shown in panel (b). For example, in 1990 Iraq invaded Kuwait, setting oil fields on fire and destroying much of Kuwait's physical capital. As a consequence, Kuwait's PPF shifted inward. In West Africa, the sands of the Sahara spread and destroy thousands of square miles of productive farmland each year, shifting the PPF of that economy inward.

Increases in Stock of Capital Goods

An economy's PPF depends in part on its supply of the stock of capital goods. The more capital goods an economy produces during one period, the more output it can produce in the next period. Thus, producing more capital goods this period (for example, more factories) shifts the economy's PPF outward the next period.

The choice between consumer goods and capital goods is really between present consumption and future production. Again, the more capital goods produced this period, the greater the economy's production possibilities next period.

economic growth

An expansion in the economy's production possibilities or ability to produce

---

Shifts of the Production Possibilities Frontier

Figure 2.2

When the resources available to an economy change, the PPF shifts. If more resources become available, the PPF shifts outward, as in panel (a), indicating that more output can be produced. A decrease in available resources causes the PPF to shift inward, as in panel (b).

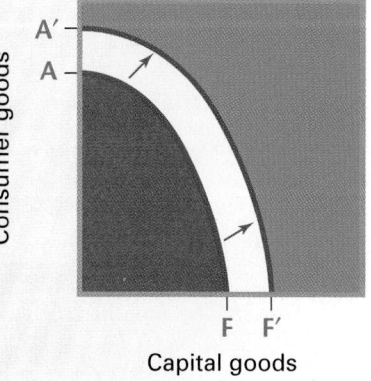

(a) Increase in available resources

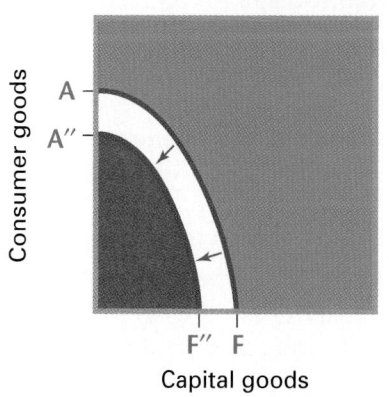

(b) Decrease in available resources

Technological Change

Another change that could shift the economy's PPF outward is a technological discovery that employs available resources more efficiently. For example, the Internet has increased the efficiency of resource markets by boosting each firm's ability to identify resource suppliers. Such an increase expands the economy's PPF, as shown in panel (a) of Figure 2.2.

Lessons from the PPF

The PPF demonstrates several concepts introduced so far. The first is *efficiency:* The PPF describes the efficient combinations of outputs that are possible, given the economy's resources and technology. The second is *scarcity.* Given the stock of resources and technology, the economy can produce only so much. The PPF slopes downward, indicating that, as the economy produces more of one good, it must produce less of the other good. This trade-off demonstrates *opportunity cost.*

The bowed-out shape of the PPF reflects the *law of increasing opportunity cost.* Not all resources are perfectly adaptable to the production of each type of good. A shift outward in the PPF reflects *economic growth.* Finally, because society must somehow choose a specific combination of output along the PPF, the PPF also emphasizes the need for *choice.* That choice will determine not only current consumption but also the capital stock available next period.

Each point along the economy's production possibilities frontier is an efficient combination of output. Whether the economy produces efficiently and how the economy selects the most preferred combination depends on the economic system.

CHECKPOINT
What causes the production possibilities frontier to shift?

Economic decision makers play a key role in determining the PPF for an economy's consumer and capital goods. What types of decision makers are suggested in this image? (Hint: The buildings in the image house businesses, governments, and citizens.) How does each type of decision maker affect the PPF for consumer and capital goods?

© Getty Images/PhotoDisc

Key Concepts

1. Explain why each of the following assumptions is made when a production possibilities frontier (PPF) is constructed.
   a. Only two goods or services are considered.
   b. The time considered is limited.
   c. The available resources are fixed in terms of quality and quantity.
   d. The available technology does not change in the time considered.

2. What does a production possibilities frontier for plastic tables and bowling balls identify?

3. What does it mean to say that a firm produces bowling balls efficiently?

4. If a firm that produces bowling balls and plastic tables is operating at a point inside its PPF, how efficiently is it using its resources?

5. Explain why the law of increasing opportunity cost causes PPFs to be bowed-out from the origin (corner) of their graphs.

6. Using consumer goods and capital goods in a production possibilities frontier, what combination would produce a straight-line PPF? What does this indicate about opportunity cost along the PPF, and why?

Graphing Exercise

7. ABC Electronics Inc. can produce either digital cameras or DVD players in its factory. The more it makes of one product, the less it is able to make of the other. The table to the right shows different combinations of the two products it could manufacture next month. Use these data to construct a production possibilities frontier for this firm. Why isn't there a one-for-one trade-off between production of these two products?

Combinations of Digital Cameras and DVD Players ABC Electronics Could Produce

Combination	Digital Cameras	DVD Players
A	0	5,000
B	2,000	4,500
C	3,400	3,400
D	4,500	2,000
E	5,000	0

Think Critically

8. **Math** Consider the table in graphing exercise 7 above. Suppose digital cameras generate $50 in profit per sale, while DVD players only earn $40 each. How much profit would ABC earn from each of the combinations of production indicated on the table? Which combination should it choose to produce?

9. **Government** Why has the federal government passed laws that are intended to encourage businesses to buy more capital goods? Given time, what should this do to the location of PPFs in the economy?

Xtra!
Study Tools
econxtra.swlearning.com

Sharpen Your Life Skills

Interpret a Graph

Apex Industries is able to produce either product A or product B from a fixed amount of resources it has each month. It also can produce different combinations of these products. However, for each additional amount of one of these products it produces, it must give up some of the other. Study the graph of Apex's production possibilities frontier, and then answer the following questions.

Apply Your Skill

1. If Apex produces 800 units of product A, how many units of product B can it make?

2. If Apex chooses to produce 400 units of product A instead of 800, roughly how many more units of product B can it make?

3. If Apex chooses to produce 500 units of product B instead of 460 of them, why must it give up the production of 400 units of product A?

4. If Apex is producing at point *D* on the graph, what can you say about the efficiency of its production?

5. Why isn't Apex able to produce at point *E* given the current situation?

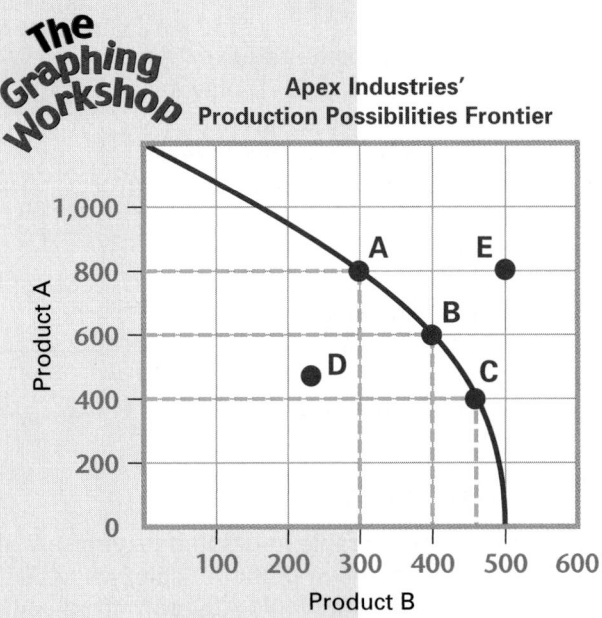

The Graphing Workshop

Apex Industries' Production Possibilities Frontier

Jamestown
and the English Mercantile System

In 1612, John Rolfe began growing tobacco in Jamestown from seeds he obtained from the Spanish colonies. Rolfe acquired the seeds despite the Spaniards' threat of death to anyone selling tobacco seeds to a non-Spaniard. The local Indians may have aided Rolfe's acquisition of the seeds, as he was engaged to marry the chief's daughter, Pocahontas. By 1614, the first tobacco from Virginia was sold in London. Despite the disapproval of King James I, this "stinking weed" came into high demand in England and throughout Europe. With tobacco as a cash crop, the Virginia colony had the basis for its economic success in place.

With the success of tobacco, the demand for labor in the colony increased. Labor was first supplied by indentured servants, who sold their labor for passage to Virginia, food, clothing, and other necessities—but no wages. After filling the terms of the contract, usually three to seven years, the indentured servant would be given land, tools, and perhaps a small amount of money. A 20 percent death rate on the voyage over, and further exposure to hard work and disease, made it difficult to recruit indentured laborers. As time passed and the survival rate increased, more were willing to come. After indentured servants proved finally to be an unsatisfactory labor resource, slavery developed. Initially more expensive to purchase than indentured servants, slaves proved to be a cheaper form of labor, as their work was bought for life.

Although crops other than tobacco, such as wheat, could be grown in the South, the opportunity cost was high. By specializing in growing tobacco, a farmer could maximize his profits over what could be made from growing other crops. As planting tobacco became more profitable, laws had to be passed to require planters to devote some portion of their land to producing food. Tobacco was profitable on any size of farm. However, by specializing in tobacco, the soil was worn out every four to seven years. Consequently, maintenance of soil fertility favored large-scale producers. From this the plantation system developed, and with it the *specialization* of labor. With this success, Virginia's *comparative advantage* lay in growing tobacco.

Virginia tobacco farmers were part of the English mercantile system. The object of the system was to increase a nation's wealth, as defined by the amount of gold it possessed. Gold could be acquired by a nation possessing a territory that produced gold. It also could be acquired by developing a positive balance of trade that brought in gold payments. For England, tobacco was an ideal mercantilist product. It was easy to ship and could replace the imports of tobacco from Spain. England did not allow Virginia tobacco to be shipped or sold anywhere but back to England, where it became a large source of import duties growing the English treasury. By 1639, at least 750 tons of Virginia tobacco had been shipped to England. After a profit was taken, it could be re-exported to Europe. Adam Smith criticized the mercantilist system. England's enforcing it became a contributing factor to the American Revolution.

THINK CRITICALLY

The colonists in Jamestown were faced with the choice of producing food for consumption or producing tobacco for sale. Draw a *production possibilities frontier* for producing food and tobacco. Label the points where the PPF intersects the axes, as well as several other points along the frontier. What would it mean for the colonists to move upward and to the left along the PPF? Under what circumstances would the PPF shift outward?

Objectives

> Explain the law of comparative advantage.

> Understand the gains from specialization and exchange.

Overview

The law of comparative advantage helps explain why even a person talented at many things can get more done by specializing. Division of labor allows firms to increase production by having each worker specialize. Specialization occurs not only among individual workers, but also among firms, regions, and entire countries.

Key Terms

absolute advantage

law of comparative advantage

specialization

barter

money

division of labor

[In the News]

● Live Longer with Specialized Care

Research has shown that people who have had a heart attack do better and recuperate faster if they are attended by a cardiac specialist rather than a general practitioner. As reported in the *New England Journal of Medicine,* a Boston research group studied Medicare data from 35,520 patients across the country. Studying a post-hospital time period of two years for the heart attack patients, the researchers found that 14.6 percent of patients with outpatient care from a cardiologist had died. In the same time period, 18.3 percent died while being treated solely by a family doctor, general practitioner, or internist. Reasons suggested for the greater success through specialization include: the patients treated by a cardiac specialist were likely to have received more focused attention, they underwent more medical procedures, and they were provided greater access to rehabilitation techniques.

Think About It

Suggest two gains from specialization for cardiologists providing medical services to their patients.

Comparative Advantage

You probably face some chores at home that your family expects you to do regularly. What if it is your responsibility to wash the two family cars and mow the lawn each week? It takes you 45 minutes to wash a car and an hour to mow the lawn. Altogether, you spend two and a half hours a week washing two cars and mowing the lawn.

Your high school friend David lives next door. He happens to face the same weekly chores—washing two family cars identical to yours and mowing a lawn identical to yours. David, however, is not nearly as quick as you. It takes him one hour to wash a car and three hours to mow the lawn. Altogether, David spends five hours a week on these chores.

Absolute Advantage

Compared to David, you have an absolute advantage in both tasks, because you can do each using fewer resources. The resource here is your labor time. More generally, having an **absolute advantage** means being able to do something using fewer resources than other producers require.

If you and David each do your own weekly chores, you take two-and-a-half hours and he takes five hours. Because you can complete each task in less time than David can, you see no point in cooperating with him to save time. However, is this the best you can do?

The Law of Comparative Advantage

It turns out that absolute advantage is not the best guide for deciding who should do what. A better guide is comparative advantage. According to the **law of comparative advantage**, the worker with the lower opportunity cost of producing a particular output should specialize in that output. **Specialization**, then, occurs when individual workers focus on single tasks, enabling each one to be more efficient and productive. Note that for the definitions of both the law of comparative advantage and specialization, the term *worker* may be replaced by the terms *firm, region,* or *country.*

What is your *opportunity cost* of washing each car? In the 45 minutes you take to wash a car, you could instead mow three-fourths of the lawn. So your opportunity cost of washing a car is mowing three-fourths of a lawn.

The Graphing Workshop

law of comparative advantage

The worker, firm, region, or country with the lowest opportunity cost of producing an output should specialize in that output

specialization

Occurs when individual workers focus on single tasks, enabling each one to be more efficient and productive

absolute advantage

To be able to make something using fewer resources than other producers require

Study the two images and decide what the comparative advantages of the areas shown might be. (Hint: The locations in the images are New York City and Hawaii.)

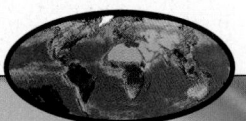

SPAN THE GLOBE

Prison Labor

The United States has a number of laws designed to prevent importing products manufactured using prison labor. Despite the laws, prisoner-produced products from a number of nations continue to make their way into the U.S. market. Prison officials in northern Mexico have for years put their inmates to work manufacturing furniture. The furniture then finds its way into Texas. In general, Mexican inmates are paid the "minimum wage" of 45 pesos ($4.50) a day, which is about half the wage free workers across the border in Texas and Arizona are paid. The reason the use of prison labor is strongly criticized around the globe is because it undercuts union pay scales, steals jobs from law-abiding workers, and poses risks of human rights abuses.

Think Critically

The law of comparative advantage states that whoever has the lower opportunity cost of producing a particular output should specialize in that output. In light of this, do you agree with the U.S. ban on imports of prisoner-made products? Why or why not?

Investigate Your Local Economy

In small groups, brainstorm a list of possible resources that provide your local economy with a comparative advantage. After five minutes of brainstorming, each group will present its results to the class.

---

barter

A system of exchange in which products are traded directly for other products

In the hour David takes to wash a car, he could instead mow one-third of the lawn. So his opportunity cost of washing a car is mowing one-third of a lawn. Because your opportunity cost of washing a car is mowing three-fourths of a lawn and David's is mowing one-third of a lawn, he faces the lower opportunity cost of washing cars.

Again, the law of comparative advantage says that the person with the lower opportunity cost should specialize in producing that output. In this example, David should specialize in washing cars.

Because David has a lower opportunity cost for washing cars, you must have a lower opportunity cost for mowing lawns. So you should specialize in mowing lawns.

Gains from Specialization

If you each specialize, David will wash your family cars, and you will mow his lawn. David washes the four cars in four hours, saving himself an hour. You cut both lawns in two hours, saving yourself a half hour. Through specialization and exchange, each of you saves time. Even though you can complete each task in less time than David can, your comparative advantage is mowing lawns. Put another way, David, although not as good as you at either task, is not as bad at washing cars as he is at mowing lawns. He has a comparative advantage in washing cars. You each specialize based on comparative advantage, and you each save time.

Absolute advantage focuses on which of you uses the fewest resources, but comparative advantage focuses on what else those resources could have produced—that is, on the opportunity cost of those resources. The law of comparative advantage indicates who should do what.

Exchange

In this example, you and David specialize and exchange your output. No money is involved. In other words, you two engage in **barter**, a system of exchange in which products are traded directly for other products. Barter works

---

best in simple economies where there is little specialization and few types of goods to trade. For economies with greater specialization, *money* plays an important role in facilitating exchange.

Money—coins, bills, and checks—serves as a *medium of exchange* because it is the one thing that everyone is willing to accept in exchange for all goods and services.

Wider Application

Due to such factors as climate, an abundance of labor, workforce skills, natural resources, and capital stock, certain parts of the country and certain parts of the world have a comparative advantage in producing particular goods. From Apple computers in California's Silicon Valley to oranges in Florida, from DVD players in Taiwan to bananas in Honduras—*resources are allocated most efficiently across the country and around the world when production and trade conform to the law of comparative advantage.*

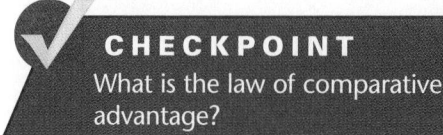

CHECKPOINT
What is the law of comparative advantage?

Specialization

Because of specialization based on comparative advantage, most people consume little of what they produce and produce little of what they consume. People specialize in particular activities, such as plumbing or carpentry, and then exchange their products for money, which in turn is exchanged for goods and services.

Did you make anything you are wearing? Probably not. Think about the degree of specialization that went into your cotton shirt. Some farmer in a warm climate grew the cotton and sold it to someone who spun it into thread, who sold it to someone who wove it into fabric, who sold it to someone who sewed the shirt, who sold it to a whole-

NET Bookmark

To learn more about how barter works in the economy, see the web site of the International Reciprocal Trade Association (IRTA). IRTA's mission is to "advance the barter industry worldwide and raise the value of barter." Access this group's web site through econxtra.swlearning.com and press "Visitors Click Here." After reading the material on the web site, write a paragraph answering the following question: Do you think barter is an effective means of exchange in a market economy? Why or why not?

econxtra.swlearning.com

saler, who sold it to a retailer, who sold it to you. Many specialists produced your shirt.

Division of Labor

Picture a visit to McDonald's: "Let's see, I'll have a Big Mac, an order of fries, and a chocolate shake." Less than a minute later, your order is ready. It would take you much longer to make a homemade version of this meal. Why is the McDonald's meal faster, cheaper, and—for some people—tastier than one you could make yourself? Why is fast food so fast?

McDonald's takes advantage of the gains resulting from the division of labor. The **division of labor** sorts the production process into separate tasks to be carried out by separate workers. Each worker specializes in a separate task. This division of labor allows the group to produce much more.

How is this increase in productivity possible? First, the manager can assign tasks according to individual preferences and abilities—that is, according to the law of comparative advantage. The worker with the nice smile and good personality can handle the customers up front. The muscle-bound worker with few social graces can do the heavy lifting in the back room.

money
Anything that everyone is willing to accept in exchange for goods and services

division of labor
An action that sorts the production process into separate tasks to be carried out by separate workers

Second, a worker who performs the same task again and again gets better at it: Experience is a good teacher. The worker filling orders at the drive-through, for example, learns how to deal with special problems that arise there. Third, there is no time lost in moving from one task to another.

Finally, and perhaps most important, the division of labor allows for the introduction of more sophisticated production techniques—techniques that would not make sense on a smaller scale. For example, McDonald's large milkshake machine would be impractical in your home. The division of labor allows for the introduction of specialized machines, and these machines make each worker more productive.

To review, the division of labor takes advantage of individual preferences and natural abilities. It allows workers to develop more experience at a particular task. It reduces the time required to shift between different tasks. Finally, it permits the introduction of labor-saving machinery. The specialization that results with the division of labor does not occur among individuals only. It also occurs among firms, regions, and entire countries.

CHECKPOINT
What are the gains from specialization and exchange?

2.3 Assessment

Key Concepts

1. Why does specialization require people to complete exchanges?

2. How does money help people complete exchanges?

3. How is a division of labor accomplished?

4. What advantages may be offered by a division of labor in addition to allowing workers to become more accomplished at the tasks they complete?

Graphing Exercise

5. Joel and Jamal work together at a bakery. In one hour Joel can ice ten cakes or prepare 5 pies. In the same time Jamal can ice eight cakes or prepare only one pie. Draw bar graphs to represent production of iced cakes and prepared pies for each of the following situations. Explain how your graphs demonstrate the law of comparative advantage.

   Situation A—Joel spends one hour icing cakes and three hours preparing pies. Jamal does the same. **Situation B**—Joel spends four hours preparing pies, while Jamal spends four hours icing cakes.

Think Critically

6. **Research** Investigate the division of labor and specialization on a high-school sports team, such as basketball, football, or field hockey. Write a paragraph explaining the different positions, and how each one contributes to the team effort.

Xtra!
Study Tools
econxtra.swlearning.com

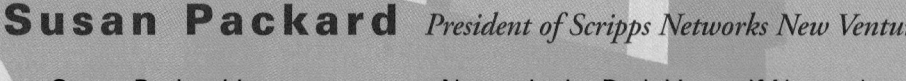

movers & shakers

Susan Packard *President of Scripps Networks New Ventures*

Susan Packard began working in cable television at an exciting time. It was 1980, cable television was new, and cable operators were still developing their programs. Their salespeople were busy selling networks into viewer's homes while at the same time finding advertisers who wanted to reach each network's audience.

Packard worked for HBO at that time. She was part of a team that eventually made HBO available to every cable-ready home in the United States. To do her job well, Packard needed to be technically literate, so she climbed poles and learned to distinguish a receiver from a modulator and a head-end. Her willingness to learn kept her career on the fast track in the rapidly growing cable industry.

After eight years at HBO and then six years at CNBC, Packard took her knowledge of the cable industry to oversee the launch of HGTV—one of the most successful and fastest-growing new cable networks. She served as chief operating officer of HGTV, and then executive vice president of Scripps Networks, owner of HGTV. Today she is president of Scripps Networks New Ventures where her responsibilities include the development of new networks. Packard also is an officer of Scripps Networks, Inc., which includes Home & Garden Television, the Food

Network, the Do It Yourself Network, and the Fine Living Network.

Each of these cable networks covers a different category of subjects, but they follow the same model. They package attractive visuals with how-to information aimed at the baby boomer and those with unique lifestyle interests and hobbies. These are audiences that advertisers often find difficult to reach. The networks are successful not only because of the programs they deliver, but because advertisers are eager to spend their money in order to reach these audiences.

Packard credits the meteoric success of these cable networks to the unique categories of programming they deliver to viewers. "We're nonviolent family fare. Everything on our air is TV-G. We appeal to specialized, passionate interests—gardeners, do-it-yourself types, hobbyists, cooks, and decorators, to name a few." Packard's knowledge and decision-making skills also deserve credit. Together they have earned her numerous awards including recognition as one of the "12 Most Powerful Women in Cable" by *Cablevision* magazine, as "One of 12 to Watch" by *Electronic Media*, and as one of the "Top 100" in the cable industry by *CableFax* magazine. Packard is the recipient of the 1998 Woman of the Year Award presented by Women in Cable & Telecommunications and in 1999 was profiled in *Modern Visionaries,* a book chronicling the contributions of pioneering women in the cable and telecommunications industry.

SOURCE READING
Packard states, "We appeal to so many interests—gardeners, do-it-yourself types, hobbyists, and those with special interests." How are these networks incorporating the idea of specialization in ways that major television networks like ABC, NBC, and CBS are not?

ENTREPRENEURS IN ACTION
Working in small groups, create a division of labor among five people producing a show about flower gardens. Could this same division of labor be used to produce a show about landscaping a home? Is it more efficient for a cable television network to produce shows about gardening and landscaping, or to produce shows about gardening and scuba diving?

Chapter Assessment

Summary

2.1 Economic Questions and Economic Systems

a All economic systems must answer three basic questions: (1) What goods will be produced? (2) How will these goods be produced? (3) For whom will these goods be produced?

b In a pure market economy, all resources are privately owned and controlled. Competition forces businesses to serve the interest of consumers when they work to earn a profit. Property rights must be protected for a pure market economy to work. Owners would not operate firms if they were not sure they could use their profits to buy more resources or satisfy their personal desires.

c Pure market economies have some problems. These include the difficulty in enforcing property rights, the possibility that people who produce little of value will fall into poverty, the possibility of businesses monopolizing markets, and a lack of public goods. Externalities may cause costs or benefits of production to flow to individuals who are neither producers nor consumers.

d In a pure centrally planned economy, all resources are publicly owned and controlled. Government planners answer the three basic economic questions according to their own priorities or those of government leaders. Problems associated with these economies include consumer desires being given a low priority in production, little consumer freedom of choice, and inefficient use of resources.

e The problems of market and centrally planned economies have caused some nations to reorient their economies. Many nations have moved toward a market economy while other nations have increased the role of their governments. Nations moving from central planning to markets have *transitional economies*.

f Some nations have *traditional economies* in which resources are allocated and used to produce goods according to traditions that are passed from one generation to the next.

2.2 Production Possibilities Frontier

a Economists construct graphs called *production possibility frontiers* (PPFs) to demonstrate different combinations of two products that can be produced from a fixed amount of resources. Assumptions made to simplify PPFs include a time limitation, a fixed technology, and an inability to add more resources.

b The PPF for two products bows out from the corner of their graph because the trade-off in production between the two goods is not one-for-one. The *law of increasing opportunity cost* states that each additional unit of one good produced requires successively larger sacrifices of the other good. This happens because resources are not perfectly adaptable to the production of both goods.

c Any point below a PPF indicates inefficient production because more goods could be produced from the same resources. Any point above a PPF indicates a level of production that cannot be achieved without additional resources. A PPF will shift out if new resources are added, technology changes, or more time becomes available.

2.3 Comparative Advantage

a According to the law of comparative advantage, people should specialize in the type of production where their opportunity cost is the lowest.

b Specialization allows workers to become more efficient through practice. When people specialize, they must exchange what they produce for other goods they desire. These exchanges are easier when they are carried out through the use of money.

c There are many steps that must be completed to produce most goods. When individual workers specialize in specific steps in this process there is a division of labor. A division of labor results in greater efficiency because workers become more skilled in their tasks and are able to use more sophisticated production techniques.

Review Economic Terms

Choose the term that best fits the definition. On a separate sheet of paper, write the letter of the answer. Some terms may not be used.

_____ 1. The set of mechanisms and institutions that resolve the what, how, and for whom questions for an economy

_____ 2. Organizing the production of goods into separate tasks to be carried out by separate workers

_____ 3. Ability to make something using fewer resources than other producers require

_____ 4. Anything that everyone is willing to accept in exchange for goods and services

_____ 5. The worker, firm, region, or country with the lowest opportunity cost of producing a particular output should specialize in that output

_____ 6. Producing the maximum possible output from available resources

_____ 7. An economic system with no government so that firms account for all production

_____ 8. Shows the possible combinations of two types of goods that can be produced when available resources are employed fully and efficiently

_____ 9. An economic system combining aspects of central planning and competitive markets

_____ 10. An expansion in the economy's ability to produce

a. absolute advantage

b. barter

c. division of labor

d. economic growth

e. economic system

f. efficiency

g. law of comparative advantage

h. law of increasing opportunity cost

i. market economy

j. mixed economy

k. money

l. production possibilities frontier (PPF)

m. pure centrally planned economy

n. pure market economy

o. specialization

p. traditional economy

q. transitional economy

Review Economic Concepts

11. **True or False** According to the *law of comparative advantage,* only people who are the most efficient producers of a product can benefit from specialization.

12. _?_ is a system of exchange in which products are traded directly for other products.

13. Which of the following is the best example of a *division of labor?*

    a. Todd lives in a cabin in the woods where he does most things for himself.

    b. Julia works as a doctor, while her husband Ted is an automobile mechanic.

    c. Benito washes dishes after lunch, while his wife dries and puts them away.

    d. Brenda reads the front page of the newspaper while her husband studies the comics.

14. **True or False** The *law of comparative advantage* applies not only to individuals, but also to firms, regions of countries, and entire nations.

15. **True or False** All economic systems must decide what goods will be produced from the resources they have.

16. The economic question _?_ often is referred to as the *distribution question.*

17. Points _?_ the PPF represent unattainable combinations given the resources and technology available.

18. Which of the following is *not* a simplifying assumption made when a *production possibilities frontier* (PPF) is created?

    a. Only two goods are considered.

    b. The prices of the goods produced do not change.

    c. Production is limited to a fixed period of time.

    d. There is a set amount of resources that may be used.

19. Movement down the PPF curve indicates that the _?_ of more capital goods is fewer consumer goods.

20. According to the *law of increasing opportunity cost,* each additional increment of one good requires the sacrifice of

    a. successively larger increments of the other good.

    b. equal increments of the other good.

    c. successively smaller increments of the other good.

    d. the level of productive efficiency.

21. **True or False** In a *pure market economy,* resources are publicly owned and controlled.

22. Adam Smith argued that although each individual pursues his or her self-interest in a market economy, the "invisible hand" of _?_ promotes the general welfare.

23. **True or False** One problem with *centrally planned economies* is too much focus on consumer needs and wants.

24. **True or False** In *centrally planned economies,* state enterprises often are more concerned with meeting the goals set by the central planners than they are about the environment.

25. _?_ is a process that involves converting state-owned enterprises into private enterprises.

26. An economic system in which the means and methods of production are passed from one generation to the next is a definition of a

    a. pure market economy.

    b. pure centrally planned economy.

    c. transitional economy.

    d. traditional economy.

Apply Economic Concepts

27. **Create a Division of Labor** Make a list of five friends who you know well. Assume that the six of you have decided to open a small restaurant. Assign each of your friends, and yourself, to one of the following job descriptions in the way that you believe would result in the most efficient operation of your restaurant. Briefly explain the reasons for each of your assignments. How does this demonstrate the advantages of specialization and a division of labor?

    a. Greet customers and take them to their tables

    b. Take customer's orders and bring food to their tables

    c. Be the chief cook in the kitchen

    d. Clear tables and wash dishes

    e. Keep the books, accept payments, order supplies, and pay the bills

    f. Be the chief cook's assistant

28. **Apply Production Possibilities** Imagine an economy that uses two resources, labor and capital, to produce two goods, wheat and cloth. Capital is relatively more useful in producing cloth, and labor is relatively more useful in producing wheat. If the supply of capital falls by 10 percent and the supply of labor increases by 10 percent, how will the PPF for wheat and cloth change?

29. **Apply Shifts of Production Possibilities** Determine whether each of the following would cause the economy's PPF to shift inward, outward, or not at all.

    a. Increase in average vacation length

    b. Increase in immigration

    c. Decrease in the average retirement age

    d. Migration of workers to other countries

30. Measure the Benefit of Specialization Both Marcy and Gloria work eight-hour days at a public library. At present, neither worker has assigned tasks, they just do what needs to be done. They never seem to finish all their work. Last Monday, Marcy spent two hours reshelving 200 returned books. Then she catalogued 150 new books during the remaining six hours of her shift. Gloria used her first six hours shelving 540 returned books and then cataloged 20 new books before she went home.

Copy and complete the following table to show Marcy and Gloria's production last Monday. Create another table that demonstrates how they could increase their total production through specialization. How much more could they produce if they each specialized in the type of production that has their lowest possible opportunity cost?

Marcy and Gloria's Production Last Monday

Marcy's Production			Gloria's Production		
Time used	# books catalogued	# books shelved	Time used	# books catalogued	# books shelved
2 hours			2 hours		
6 hours			6 hours		
Total books catalogued:					
Total books shelved:					

Marcy and Gloria's Possible Production with Specialization

Marcy's Production		Gloria's Production	
Time used	# books catalogued or shelved	Time Used	# books catalogued or shelved
hours		hours	
hours		hours	
Total books catalogued:			
Total books shelved:			
Additional books catalogued:			
Additional books shelved:			

 *econxtra.swlearning.com*

31. Access **EconNews Online** at econxtra.swlearning.com. Read the article entitled "Trade Wars in the U.S." According to the article, what percent of the population believes that foreign trade is bad for the U.S. economy? What, according to the article, is the basis for this belief? Do you agree or disagree? Justify your answer with facts from the article.

3

U.S. Private and Public Sectors

C o n s i d e r

Why did households go from self-sufficiency to relying on markets?

How did firms evolve to take advantage of large-scale production?

Why do countries trade?

If the "invisible hand" of competitive markets is so great, why do governments get into the act?

Why are some people poor even in the world's most productive economy?

© Getty Images/PhotoDisc

POINT YOUR BROWSER

econxtra.swlearning.com

Objectives

> Describe the evolution of households.

> Explain the evolution of the firm with respect to the changes in production processes.

> Demonstrate your understanding of why international trade occurs.

Overview

The U.S. private sector includes three groups of economic decision makers: households, firms, and the rest of the world. To develop a better feel for how the economy works, you must become more acquainted with these key players. You already know more about them than you may realize. You grew up as a member of a household. You have interacted with firms all your life, from Wal-Mart to Subway. You have a growing awareness of the rest of the world, from imported cars to international web sites.

Key Terms

household

utility

firm

Industrial Revolution

[In the News]

● Mom and Pop Missing in Action

In 1950 only about 15 percent of married women with children under 18 years old were employed outside the home. Now, according to data from the 2000 U.S. Census, more young children are growing up with both parents working. A wide range of socioeconomic forces during the 1990s expanded child-rearing options for many working parents. Some won more flexible schedules from their employers or arranged for job sharing with another parent. Others decided to open Internet-based businesses at home. The 1996 welfare law, which pushed more people from public-assistance rolls into the work force, also played a part in the 1990s trend.

Think About It

In Connecticut, nearly 62 percent of children under age 6 had both parents working, up from 56 percent in 1990. In Nebraska, nearly 70 percent of young children had both parents in the labor force. Connecticut has a relatively affluent population. Nebraska has a large farm economy. What might be explanations for each of those states having such a high percentage of dual working parents?

Households

Households play the starring role in a market economy. All those who live under one roof are considered part of the same **household**. Households' demand for goods and services determines what gets produced. The human resources, natural resources, and capital goods they sell help to produce that output. As buyers of goods and services and sellers of resources, households make all kinds of economic choices. These choices include what to buy, how much to save, where to live, and where to work.

Evolution of the Household

In 1850 about two-thirds of America's labor force worked on farms. The economy was primarily agricultural, and each farm household was largely self-sufficient. Individual family members specialized in specific farm tasks—preparing meals, sewing clothes, tending livestock, growing crops, and so on. These households produced most of what they consumed and consumed most of what they produced.

With the introduction of labor-saving machinery, disease-resistant seeds, and better fertilizers, farm productivity increased sharply. Because each farmer produced much more, fewer farmers were needed to grow enough food to feed the nation. At the same time, the growth of urban factories increased the need to hire factory labor. As a result, many workers and their families moved from farms to cities, where they became less self-sufficient. Now, only about 2 percent of the U.S. labor force works on farms.

Investigate Your Local Economy

Research to find how many households there are in your community. How many of those are two-earner families? How many are headed by a single parent? What is the average annual income of households in the community? What conclusions can you draw from your research?

household

The most important economic decision maker, consisting of all those who live under one roof

© Getty Images/PhotoDisc

© Getty Images/PhotoDisc

Although the makeup of households differs, each one makes a variety of economic choices. What types of choices must all households make?

U.S. households have evolved in other important ways. For example, in 1950 only about 15 percent of married women with children under 18 years old were in the labor force. Since then, higher education levels among married women and a growing need for workers increased women's earnings, raising their opportunity cost of not working. Today, more than half of married women with young children are in the labor force.

The rise of two-earner households has affected the family as an economic unit. Less production occurs in the home. More goods and services are purchased in markets. Reduced household production has led to increased availability of child-care services and greater varieties of restaurants to meet these needs. The rise of two-earner families has reduced the significance of specialization within the household.

Households Maximize Utility

There are more than 110 million U.S. households. Economists consider each household as acting like a single decision maker. Households, like other economic decision makers, are assumed to pursue their rational self-interest. This means they try to act in their best interests by selecting products and services that are intended to make them better off.

But what exactly do households attempt to accomplish in making decisions? Economists assume that households attempt to maximize their **utility**—their level of satisfaction or sense of well-being. Utility maximization depends on each household's personal goals, not on some objective standard. For example, some households maintain neat homes with well-groomed lawns. Other households pay little attention to their homes and yards.

CHECKPOINT
In what ways has the household evolved over time?

Firms

Household members once built their own homes, made their own clothes and furniture, grew their own food, and entertained themselves. Over time, however, the efficiency arising from comparative advantage resulted in a greater specialization among resource providers. Resource providers often organize as firms. A **firm** is an economic unit formed by a profit-seeking entrepreneur who combines resources to produce goods and services and accepts the risk of profit and loss. What led to the development of the firm as we know it today?

Evolution of the Firm

Specialization and comparative advantage help explain why households are no longer self-sufficient. But why is a firm the natural outgrowth? For example, rather than make a woolen sweater from scratch, couldn't a consumer take advantage of specialization by hiring someone to produce the wool, another person to spin the wool into yarn, and a third to knit the yarn into a sweater? Why is a firm even necessary?

Here's the problem with that model: If the consumer had to visit and make agreements with each of these specialists, the resulting *transaction costs*—the cost of time and information required for exchange—could easily cancel out the efficiency gained from specialization. Instead of visiting and dealing with each specialist, the consumer can pay someone else to do this. The consumer can pay an entrepreneur to purchase all the resources necessary to make the sweater. *An entrepreneur, by hiring specialists to make many sweaters rather than just one, is able to reduce the transaction costs per sweater.*

During the seventeenth and eighteenth centuries, entrepreneurs provided raw material, such as wool and cotton, to rural households. The entrepreneur hired households to turn this raw

firm
A business unit or enterprise formed by a profit-seeking entrepreneur who combines resources to produce goods and services

utility
The level of satisfaction from consumption or sense of well-being

material into finished products, such as woolen goods made from yarn. The system developed in the British Isles, where workers' rural cottages served as tiny factories. Production usually occurred during the months when farming tasks were few—when the opportunity cost for farm workers was lower.

This approach, which came to be known as the *cottage industry system*, still exists in some parts of the world. You can view this system as the bridge between the self-sufficient farm household and the modern firm that depends on trade.

The Industrial Revolution

As the economy expanded in the eighteenth century, entrepreneurs began organizing the stages of production under one roof. Technological developments, such as water power and later steam power, increased the productivity of each worker and contributed to the shift of employment from rural farm to urban factory.

Work, therefore, became organized in large, centrally powered factories that

1. promoted more efficient division of labor

2. allowed for the direct supervision of production

3. reduced transportation costs

4. facilitated the use of specialized machines far larger than anything that had been used in the home

The development of large-scale factory production, known as the **Industrial Revolution**, began in Great Britain around 1750. The Industrial Revolution quickly spread to the rest of Europe, North America, and Australia. Production evolved from self-sufficient rural households to the cottage industry system, where specialized production occurred in the household, to the Industrial Revolution of handling most production under one roof. Figure 3.1 shows this evolution.

Today, entrepreneurs combine resources in firms such as factories, mills, offices, stores, and restaurants. The entrepreneurs accept the risk of profit and loss from the enterprise. Just as households attempt

Industrial Revolution
Development of large-scale production during the eighteenth century

Evolution of Production

Figure 3.1

The production process evolved from self-sufficient rural households to the cottage industry system, where specialized production occurred in the household. From there, the Industrial Revolution saw the organization of the various stages of production under one roof with the development of large-scale factory production.

to maximize utility, firms attempt to maximize profit. Profit is the entrepreneur's reward for accepting the risks involved. Profit equals revenue—the money made from the sales of the firm's goods and services—minus the cost of production.

Profit = Revenue − Cost of Production

There are more than 25 million profit-seeking firms in the United States. Two-thirds of these are small retail businesses, small service operations, part-time home-based businesses, and small farms. Each year more than a million new businesses start up and nearly as many fail. Despite the challenges, the lure of profit provides entrepreneurs with the incentive to keep trying.

CHECKPOINT
How have production processes changed over time?

The Rest of the World

So far, the focus has been on private-sector institutions within the United States—that is, U.S. households and firms. This initial focus has been appropriate because the primary objective is to understand the workings of the U.S. economy, by far the largest in the world.

The rest of the world affects what U.S. households consume and what U.S. firms produce. For example, firms in Japan and South Korea supply U.S. markets with autos, electronic equipment, and other goods, thereby affecting U.S. prices, employment, wages, and profit. Political unrest in the Persian Gulf can drive up the price of oil, increasing U.S. production costs.

Foreign decision makers have a significant effect on the U.S. economy—on what Americans consume and on what they produce. The *rest of the world* consists of the households, firms, and governments in the more than 200 sovereign nations throughout the world.

International Trade

The gains from comparative advantage and specialization explain why households stopped trying to do everything for themselves and began to sell their resources to specialized firms. International trade arises for the same reasons. *Gains from international trade occur because the opportunity cost of producing specific goods differs across countries.*

Trade allows the countries involved to specialize and thereby increase production. Americans buy raw materials such as crude oil, diamonds, and coffee beans and finished goods such as cameras, DVD players, and automobiles

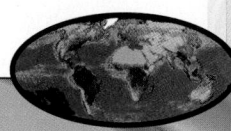

SPAN THE GLOBE

Chinese Food for Thought

December 2004 marks the third anniversary of China's membership in the World Trade Organization (WTO), the rules-making body of modern global commerce. China became a member of this group because it is moving from a planned economy to a more market-driven system. Thus far, exports and imports are rising. Economic growth remains around 8 percent per year, though growth in 2003 was slowed by the SARS virus. Economists credit WTO membership with convincing foreign investors that the Chinese marketplace will treat them according to international practices. At the same time, the government is wary of creating instability by opening markets too quickly. As China overhauls its state firms, millions of people have been put out of work in heavy industry, migrants are streaming into cities, and farmers are jittery about an invasion of cheap foreign food. The Communist Party is concerned with keeping progress moving, yet retaining its monopoly on power.

Think Critically

Compare current-day China's economic situation to that of the United States during the Industrial Revolution. What are the similarities and differences?

from other countries. U.S. producers sell to other countries sophisticated products such as computer hardware and software, aircraft, movies, and agricultural products.

International trade between the United States and the rest of the world has increased in recent decades. In 1970, only about 6 percent of U.S. production was sold to other countries. That figure has now increased to 14 percent.

Trade in Raw Materials

To give you some idea of how international trade works, consider the trade in raw materials. Figure 3.2 shows U.S.

production as a percentage of U.S. consumption for 12 key commodities. If production exceeds consumption, the United States sells the difference to other countries. If production falls short of consumption, the United States purchases the difference from other countries. For example, because the United States grows little coffee, nearly all coffee is purchased from other countries. U.S. production of coffee is only 1 percent of U.S. consumption.

The figure also shows that U.S. production falls short of consumption for oil and for metals such as lead, zinc, copper, and aluminum. At the other extreme, U.S.-grown wheat is nearly double U.S. wheat consumption. Nearly half of the U.S. wheat crop is exported. When it comes to raw materials, the United States is a net importer of oil and metals and a net exporter of crops.

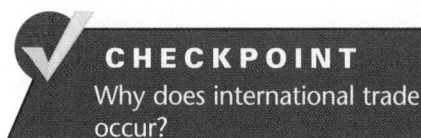

CHECKPOINT
Why does international trade occur?

U.S. Production as a Percentage of U.S. Consumption

Figure 3.2

If production exceeds consumption, the United States sells the difference to other countries. If production falls short of consumption, the United States buys the difference from other countries. For example, because the United States produces only 1 percent of its coffee consumption, 99 percent is purchased from other countries. Because U.S.-grown wheat amounts to 184 percent of U.S. wheat consumption, the 84 percent in excess of 100 percent is sold to other countries.

Source: Based on annual figures from *The Economist World in Figures: 2001 Edition* (London: Profile Books, 2001).

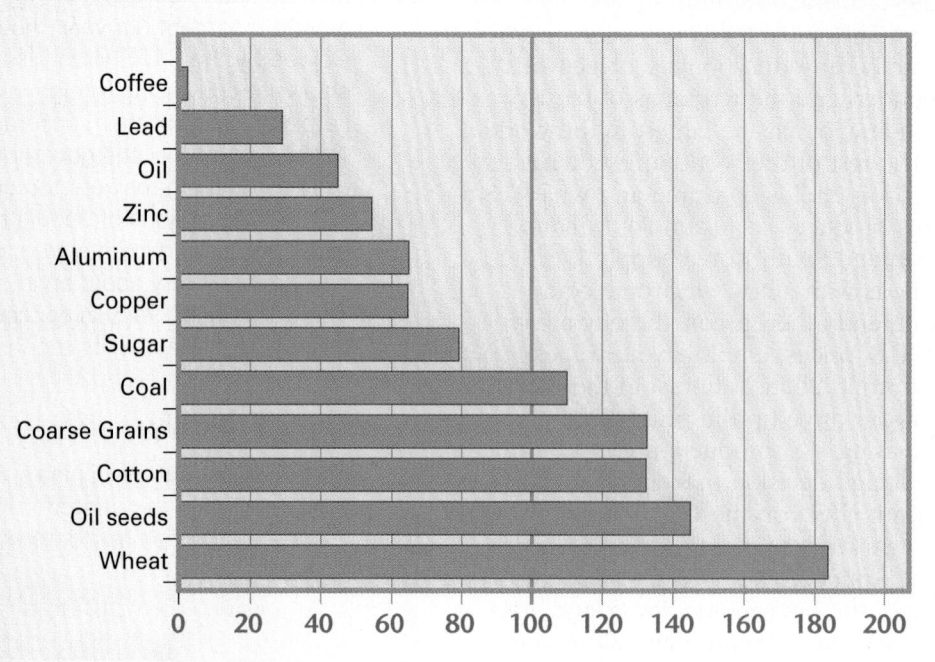

Key Concepts

1. Describe three tasks that would probably have been done within most households 100 years ago that your family now pays others to do.

2. Identify a product that you often buy and use. Describe the steps that are taken to produce this good. Explain why you do not produce this product for yourself.

3. What are several advantages that a large automobile repair shop would have over a small one?

4. In what ways is working at home on a computer today similar to, and different from, the cottage industry system that existed in the eighteenth century?

5. Think of a recent event that took place in a different part of the world that had an impact on the U.S. economy. Explain how the event affected the U.S. economy.

Xtra! Study Tools
econxtra.swlearning.com

Graphing Exercise

6. Draw a bar graph that demonstrates the declining size of the average U.S. household, based on the data in the table below. Explain why smaller households might encourage people to purchase more of the goods and services they use.

Year	Average Size of U. S. Household
1975	3.14 members
1980	2.94
1985	2.76
1990	2.63
1995	2.65
2000	2.62

Source: *Statistical Abstract of the United States 1999*, p. 60, and *2001*, p. 49.

Think Critically

7. **Research** Choose a foreign country that one of your ancestors came from or a country that interests you. Investigate this nation's economy and identify products it trades. Explain how this nation benefits from trade by using its comparative advantage.

8. **History** In 1825, Robert Owen bought a community called New Harmony in Indiana. He told people who lived in New Harmony to contribute whatever they produced to a community storehouse. They could also take whatever they needed from this storehouse for free. Look up New Harmony and find out how Owen's experiment worked out. Why weren't residents of New Harmony able to benefit from their comparative advantages?

Objectives

> Explain how government, by establishing laws and regulations, can improve operation of the private sector.

> Distinguish between regulations that promote competition and those that control natural monopolies.

> Describe how fiscal policy and monetary policy reduce the ups and downs of the business cycle.

Overview

The private sector would not run smoothly on its own in a pure market economy. With no government, there would be no laws protecting your life and property. People could rob you of your earnings and possessions. They also could steal your inventions and ideas. Business contracts would have no binding force without laws and the authority to enforce those laws. Some firms could drive competitors out of the market. Firms also could sell unsafe or defective products or otherwise cheat consumers. These actions could bring about reduced economic activity and result in high unemployment. Government regulations address these market shortcomings.

Key Terms

private property rights

antitrust laws

natural monopoly

fiscal policy

monetary policy

[In the News]

● Ball-Bearing Bonanza

Some government regulations are created to protect U.S. interests in international trade. One new law, the Continued Dumping and Subsidy Offset Act of 2000, affects the prices that foreign trading partners can charge for products they export to the United States. The law allows U.S. manufacturers to inform the government if they believe imports in their market are being "dumped"—or sold at less than fair-market value—by foreign competitors. If the government agrees, it will impose tariffs (taxes) on those imports. The manufacturers then receive the proceeds of those tariffs. The law's chief beneficiaries for 2001 were two ball-bearing companies whose lawyers helped to write the legislation. One New Jersey company, Torrington Co., took in $63 million, and Timken Co. in Ohio took in $31 million. The $94 million was collected from ball-bearing makers in Japan, the United Kingdom, Romania, Sweden, and six other countries. U.S. trading partners have criticized the law as violating international trade rules by unfairly favoring U.S. companies. The World Trade Organization (WTO) agrees. More than a few U.S. companies also agree. They say the law "promotes litigation, violates our WTO commitments, and undercuts U.S. competitiveness."

Think About It

Do you think the U.S. government should step in to prevent "dumping" of foreign goods in such a way? Why or why not?

Rules for a Market Economy

The effects of government regulations are all around you. Government-required labels that provide washing instructions are stitched into the clothes you wear. The condition of the vehicle you drive to school is regulated by the government. The government also regulates how fast you can drive and prohibits you from driving under the influence of alcohol. Government has a pervasive influence on many aspects of your life as well as on the economy.

Establishing Property Rights

In a market system, specific individuals usually own the rights to resources. **Private property rights** guarantee individuals the right to use their resources as they choose or to charge others for the use. Owners therefore have a strong incentive to get the most value from their resources. This ensures that resources will find their most productive use.

However if people could not safeguard their property, they would have less incentive to work, to save, to invest, to buy things, or to pursue other market activity. Markets could break down. For example, less investment would occur if potential investors believed their capital goods might be stolen by thieves, damaged by civil unrest, destroyed by war, or blown up by terrorists. You would have less incentive to work if your employer refused to pay you or if you were repeatedly robbed of your earnings.

Governments play a role in safeguarding private property by establishing legal rights of ownership. They then enforce these rights through national defense, police protection, legal contracts, and the judicial system.

Intellectual Property Rights

Laws also grant property rights to the creators of new ideas and new inventions. Inventors reap the rewards of

private property rights
Legal claim that guarantees an owner the right to use a resource or to charge others for its use

E-CONOMICS

Digital Crackers
Due to the lightning speed of advancements in Internet and e-commerce technology, the government is working fast to enact laws to regulate this new area. One law enacted was the 1998 Digital Millennium Copyright Act. This law covered a variety of issues including the lawful uses of copyrighted works in the electronic environment. The law had strong support from Silicon Valley companies who were trying to protect their lucrative software programs. The first criminal prosecution under this law was the case against Elcomsoft Co. Ltd. Elcomsoft was charged with selling software that allows users to disable security features in the "eBook." The eBook is reader software made by Adobe Systems. It is used to access digital publications like novels and nonfiction works. Adobe's software allows publishers to sell books online in formats that prevent the content from being copied, printed, or transferred. The Elcomsoft product, called the Advanced eBook Processor Program, *cracks* the security protections in eBook software and allows the removal of publisher-imposed usage restrictions. Elcomsoft says its program simply lets users make backup copies or transfer content to other devices, something permitted under the "fair use" concept of copyright law. When Elcomsoft began selling its product on the Internet, Adobe Systems complained to the FBI.

Think Critically
A federal jury found Elcomsoft not guilty on all counts in the case, which ended December 17, 2002. What effect, if any, do you think this decision will have on the software market?

NETBookmark

To learn more about patents, go to the U.S. Patent and Trademark Office's web page on General Information Concerning Patents. Access this web site through econxtra.swlearning.com. In your own words, describe who may apply for a patent.

econxtra.swlearning.com

their creations so they have more incentives to create.

Patent laws encourage inventors to invest the time and money required to discover and develop new products and processes. If others could simply copy successful products, inventors would be less willing to incur the up-front costs of invention. Patents also provide the stimulus to turn inventions into marketable products, a process called *innovation.*

Thus, the patent system establishes property rights to inventions and other technical advances. Likewise, a *copyright* assigns property rights to original expressions of an author, artist, composer, or computer programmer. A *trademark* establishes property rights to unique commercial marks and symbols, such as McDonald's golden arches and Nike's swoosh.

Measurement and Safety

Much market exchange involves products sold by weight, such as a pound of hamburger, or by volume, such as a gallon of gasoline. To ensure buyers don't get cheated, governments test and certify the accuracy of various measuring devices. For example, the U.S. Bureau of Weights and Measures is responsible for the annual inspection and testing of all commercial devices used to buy, sell, and ship products.

Consumers also want to be confident that the products they buy are safe. The U.S. Food and Drug Administration (FDA) regulates the safety of foods, prescription and over-the-counter drugs, and medical devices. The U.S. Department of Agriculture helps the FDA by inspecting and grading meat and poultry for freshness and quality. The Consumer Product Safety Commission, a federal agency, monitors the safety of all consumer products, from baby cribs to dishwashers.

CHECKPOINT
How can laws and regulations improve the operation of the private sector?

The FDA requires that labels appear on packages of most prepared foods, such as breads, cereals, canned and frozen foods, snacks, desserts, and drinks. How do consumers benefit from nutrition information on labels of food products?

© Getty Images/PhotoDisc

Market Competition and Natural Monopolies

It's been said that businesspeople praise competition, but they love monopoly. Their praise of competition echoes Adam Smith's argument that the invisible hand of market competition harnesses self-interest to promote the general good. However, competition imposes a discipline that most businesses would rather avoid. A business owner would prefer to be a monopolist—that is, to be the only seller of a product. As an only seller, a monopolist can usually charge a higher price and earn a greater profit than would be possible with greater competitive pressure.

Promoting Market Competition

Although competition typically ensures the most efficient use of resources, an individual firm would prefer the higher price and higher profit of monopoly. Here's the problem. When a few firms account for most of the sales in a market, such as the market for steel, those firms may join together to fix a price that is higher than one that would result from greater market competition. These firms try to act like a monopolist to boost the price and profits. An individual firm also may try to become a monopolist by driving competitors out of business or by merging with competitors.

Thus, a monopoly or a group of firms acting like a monopoly tries to charge a higher price than would result through competition. This higher price hurts consumers more than it benefits producers, making society worse off. Monopoly may harm social welfare in other ways as well. If a monopoly is insulated from market competition, it may be less innovative than aggressive competitors would be. Worse still, monopolies may try to influence the political system to protect and enhance their monopoly power.

Antitrust laws attempt to promote competition and reduce anticompetitive behavior. These laws prohibit efforts to create a monopoly in a market in which competition is desirable. Antitrust laws are enforced in the courts by government attorneys. They also are enforced by individual firms bringing lawsuits against other firms for violating these laws.

Regulating Natural Monopolies

Competition usually forces the product price lower than it would be if the product were sold by a monopoly. In rare instances, however, a monopoly can produce and sell the product for less than could several competing firms. For example, electricity is delivered more efficiently by a single firm that wires the community than by competing firms each stringing their own sets of wires. A city's subway service is delivered more efficiently by a single firm digging one tunnel system than by competing firms each digging their own. The cost per customer of delivering electricity or subway service is lower if each of these markets is served by a single firm.

When it is cheaper for one firm to serve the market than for two or more firms to do so, that firm is called a **natural monopoly**. But a natural monopoly, if unregulated by government, maximizes profit by charging a higher price than is optimal from society's point of view.

Government can increase social welfare by forcing the monopolist to lower its price. To do this, the government can either operate the monopoly itself, as it does with most urban transit systems, or regulate a privately owned monopoly, as it does with local phone services and electricity transmission. Government-owned and government-regulated monopolies are called *public utilities*.

> ## ✓ CHECKPOINT
> Why does government promote competition in some markets and control natural monopolies in others?

antitrust laws
Laws that prohibit anticompetitive behavior and promote competition in markets where competition is desirable

natural monopoly
One firm that can serve the entire market at a lower per-unit cost than two or more firms

Growth and Stability of the U.S. Economy

The U.S. economy and other market economies experience alternating periods of growth and decline in their level of economic activity, especially employment and production. *Business cycles* reflect the rise and fall of economic activity relative to the long-term growth trend of the economy. Governments try to reduce these fluctuations, making the bad times not so bad and the good times not quite so good. Pursuing these objectives through taxing and spending is called *fiscal policy.* Pursuing them by regulating the money supply is called *monetary policy.*

Fiscal Policy

Fiscal policy uses taxing and public spending to influence national economic variables such as how much is produced, how many people have jobs, and how fast the economy grows. The idea behind fiscal policy is that when economic activity in the private sector slows down, the government should offset this by cutting taxes to stimulate consumption and investment. The government also may increase its own spending to offset a weak private sector.

If, on the other hand, the economy is growing so fast as to cause higher *inflation,* which is an increase in the economy's average price level, the government should increase taxes and reduce its own spending to cool down the economy. This will keep inflation from getting too high.

When economists study fiscal policy, they usually focus on the federal government, although governments at all levels affect the economy. The federal, state, and local governments in the United States spend about $3.5 trillion per year, making the public sector a significant part of the country's $11 trillion economy.

Monetary Policy

Just as oil makes the gears in a car move more smoothly, money reduces the friction—the transaction costs—of market exchange. Too little money can leave parts creaking. Too much money can gum up the works.

Monetary policy tries to supply the appropriate amount of money to help stabilize the business cycle and promote healthy economic growth. In the United States, monetary policy is the responsibility of the Board of Governors of the Federal Reserve System, the U.S. central bank established by Congress in 1913. The Federal Reserve System, or Fed, used monetary policy in 2001 and 2002 to try to revive the nation's stalled economy. By putting more money into circulation, the Fed pushed interest rates to their lowest levels in more than 40 years. This action was intended to encourage more borrowing and spending that would lead to economic recovery.

Too much money in circulation results in higher inflation. For example, in 1994 huge increases in Brazil's money supply resulted in wild inflation. Prices in Brazil were on average about 3.6 million times higher in 1994 than in 1988.

At the other extreme, too little money in an economy can make market exchange more difficult. For example, people tried to cope with a severe money shortage in the early American colonies by maintaining very careful records, showing who owed what to whom. However, the transaction costs of all this record keeping used up scarce resources and reduced output in the economy.

CHECKPOINT

How do fiscal policy and monetary policy reduce the ups and downs of the business cycle?

Key Concepts

1. Describe one way your life might be different if the government did not protect individual property rights.

2. Study the contents label of a cereal box. Explain how the government attempts to protect consumers when it requires manufacturers to place these labels on food products.

3. In 2001 the government passed laws that reduced many federal taxes. Explain why this could be seen as an example of *fiscal policy* that was intended to cause the economy to produce more goods and services.

4. During the economic expansion of the late 1990s, the Federal Reserve System took steps to reduce the rate of growth of money in the U.S. economy. Was this an example of monetary policy that was intended to slow the growth of production? Why or why not?

Graphing Exercise

5. Draw a double line graph of changes in the money supply and interest rates charged to large businesses in the U.S. economy, based on the data at the right. Describe how these two sets of data appear to be related to each other.

Think Critically

6. **Math** Calculate the amount of the federal government's surplus or deficit in different years, using data in the table at the right. Are you concerned about the government spending more than it receives in taxes? Explain your point of view.

7. **Research** In the 1970s, American Telephone and Telegraph (AT&T) was a good example of a natural monopoly. At that time, AT&T provided almost all of the local and long-distance telephone service in the country. To prevent AT&T from setting high prices, the government told the company how much it could charge its customers. Research the history of AT&T. Describe what has taken place in the past 30 years to reduce this firm's monopoly power and the government's need to set its prices.

Xtra!
Study Tools
econxtra.swlearning.com

Changes in the Money Supply and Interest Rates, 1993–2001

Year	% change in money [M1]	% interest charged to businesses [prime]
1993	+ 10.3%	6.0%
1994	+ 1.8	7.2
1995	− 2.0	8.8
1996	− 4.2	8.3
1997	− 0.6	8.4
1998	+ 2.3	8.4
1999	+ 2.5	8.0
2000	− 3.2	9.2
2001	+ 8.3	6.9

Source: *Economic Indicators,* October, 2002, pp. 26 & 30.

Federal Spending and Tax Revenue, 1996–2002
Amounts in billions of dollars, 2002 values estimated

Year	Spending	Tax Revenue	Difference
1996	1,560	1,453	_____
1997	1,601	1,579	_____
1998	1,652	1,722	_____
1999	1,702	1,828	_____
2000	1,789	2,025	_____
2001	1,863	1,991	_____
2002	2,012	1,853	_____

Source: *Economic Indicators,* October, 2002, p. 32.

movers & shakers

George Herrera *President and CEO, United States Hispanic Chamber of Commerce*

George Herrera has always been interested in helping Hispanic businesses grow. For 17 years he worked at Burgos and Associates, Inc., a company that provides management and technical help to minority businesses throughout the United States. This work was the ideal training ground for his next job as president and chief executive officer of the United States Hispanic Chamber of Commerce (USHCC). Herrera has held this job since 1998.

The USHCC, headquartered in Washington, D.C., promotes the interests of more than 1.2 million Hispanic-owned businesses in the United States and Puerto Rico. Herrera's goal is to help these businesses and their owners succeed. As the number of U.S. Hispanic residents grows, so too does the number of Hispanic businesses grow. According to the 2000 U.S. Census, 12.5 percent of the U.S. population, more than 35 million, are Hispanic or Latino. Herrera believes it is important to help this growing segment of the U.S. population succeed.

Herrera has been instrumental in encouraging President George W. Bush to recognize the Hispanic community. He has called President Bush "a tremendous asset, not only to Hispanic businesses, but also to the Hispanic people." President Bush placed Hispanics in key positions in his administration. He appointed Mel Martinez as Secretary of Housing and Urban Development and Hector V. Barreto, Jr., as Administrator of the Small Business Administration. In a recent address to the USHCC, President Bush stated, "Small businesses are the pathway to advancement and success for many Americans, especially women and new arrivals to our country, and to minorities. I believe in small business because I know that two-thirds of all new jobs created in America every year come from small businesses. More than one million small businesses are owned by Hispanic Americans. And this is good news for America."

Herrera has been recognized by *Hispanic Business Magazine* as one of the 100 Most Influential Hispanics in the United States. *Black Enterprise Magazine* has named him one of the 30 future leaders for economic empowerment of minority communities. One of Herrera's most significant accomplishments was the creation of the first-ever national Hispanic television show, *Hispanics Today,* which is syndicated across the United States.

SOURCE READING
Analyze the quotation from President Bush's address to the USHCC. Explain why you think he said, "More than one million small businesses are owned by Hispanic Americans. And this is good news for America."

ENTREPRENEURS IN ACTION
Working with a partner, choose a minority group, such as African Americans, Asian Americans, Native Americans, Hispanic Americans, etc. Research the number of small businesses in the United States owned by members of this minority. Interview a successful small business owner who is a member of this minority group. Ask about his or her education and work background. Also ask what advice he or she has for students thinking about becoming small business owners. Present your findings in class.

Objectives

> Describe and provide examples of four types of goods.

> Define negative externalities and positive externalities, and discuss why government intervenes in such markets.

Overview

Government focuses on improving the performance of the private sector—enforcing property rights, promoting competition, regulating natural monopolies, and smoothing out the economy's ups and downs. However the private sector can't profitably supply some goods that people want. The government is in a better position to supply goods such as national defense or a highway system. What's more, the private sector sometimes affects people not involved in the market transaction, such as the factory that pollutes the air breathed by nearby residents. In such cases, the government often intervenes to improve the market's performance.

Key Terms

private goods

public goods

quasi-public goods

open-access goods

negative externalities

positive externalities

[In the News]

● The Healthcare Dilemma

Should a country's healthcare system be a private good or a public good? With the exception of Medicare and Medicaid, the United States currently has a private healthcare system. If the United States had a national health system, like its national defense system, health services would be available to all in an equal amount. The following issue in the news highlights one problem with the private U.S. healthcare system. Lobbying interests in Washington are pressing for limitations on when, where, and how consumers can file healthcare-related lawsuits. They argue that lawsuit limitations will help save struggling medical-related businesses, preserve jobs in the health field, and protect the public's access to healthcare. The American Medical Association (AMA), a group representing the nation's doctors, contends that limits on consumers' right to sue would benefit consumers. The group points to statistics showing that physicians have left some parts of the country because of costly malpractice lawsuits and the expensive insurance they must carry to protect themselves. The AMA also is lobbying for a federal law limiting damage awards in medical lawsuits, such as those for pain and suffering, to $250,000. Opponents of further limits, particularly the American Trial Lawyers Association (ATLA) are gearing up for battle.

Think About It

Do you think limitations on lawsuits would protect the public's access to healthcare and reduce costs, or would these limitations likely only protect bad doctors and insurance companies? Explain your answer. Do you think healthcare should be available to everyone in an equal amount, regardless of an individual's ability to pay? Why or why not?

Private Goods, Public Goods, and In Between

So far this book has been talking mostly about private goods, such as tacos, toasters, and telephone service. Other categories of goods exist as well. At the other extreme are public goods, with various categories in between, including quasi-public goods and open-access goods.

Private Goods

Private goods have two important features. First, they are *rival in consumption*. This means that the amount consumed by one person is unavailable for others to consume. For example, when you and some friends share a pizza, each slice they eat is one less available for you. A second key feature of a private good is that suppliers can easily exclude those who don't pay, so a private good is said to be *exclusive*. Thus a private good is both *rival* and *exclusive*.

Public Goods

In contrast to private goods, **public goods**, such as national defense, the Centers for Disease Control, or a neighborhood mosquito-control program, is nonrival in consumption. One person's benefit does not reduce the amount available to others. Such goods are available to all in equal amount. The marginal cost of providing the good to an additional consumer is zero.

Public goods cannot be provided through the market system because of the problem of who would pay for them. Public goods are both nonrival and nonexclusive. Once produced, public goods are available for all to consume, regardless of who pays and who doesn't. As a consequence, for-profit firms cannot profitably sell public goods. For example, if a private firm were to spray a neighborhood for mosquitoes, all of the households in the neighborhood would benefit. However, some households might not pay, figuring that they would still benefit from the spraying. These households would be called *free riders*. If this service is provided by a local government, all the households would pay for it with their tax money.

The government provides public goods and funds them through enforced taxation. Sometimes nonprofit agencies also provide public goods, funding them through charitable contributions and other revenue sources.

Quasi-Public Goods

The economy consists of more than just private goods and public goods. Some goods are nonrival but exclusive. For example, additional households can tune to a TV show without harming the TV reception of other viewers. Television signals are nonrival in consumption. Yet the program's producer can make viewers "pay" for the show, either by adding commercials or by charging each household for the show, as with cable TV. So the TV signal is nonrival but exclusive. Goods that are nonrival but exclusive are called **quasi-public goods**.

Open-Access Goods

Finally, some other goods are *rival* but *nonexclusive*. The fish in the ocean are rival because every fish caught is not available for others to catch. The same goes for migratory game, like wild geese. Ocean fish and migratory game are nonexclusive in that it would be costly or impossible for a private firm to prevent access to these goods. Goods that are rival but nonexclusive are

---

private goods

Goods with two features: (1) the amount consumed by one person is unavailable to others and (2) nonpayers can easily be excluded

public goods

Goods that, once produced, are available to all, but nonpayers are not easily excluded

quasi-public goods

Goods that, once produced, are available to all, but nonpayers are easily excluded

---

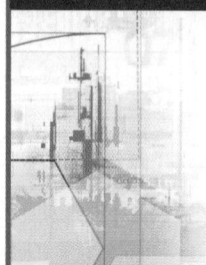

TEAM WORK

In small groups, brainstorm a list of public goods that you and your families consume. Make sure that each good you list is both nonrival and nonexclusive.

Some households receive television signals through satellite-dish technology. What type of good is the television signal that is received this way? Explain your answer.

called **open-access goods** because it would be difficult and costly to block access to these goods.

In the absence of any regulations, open-access goods are overfished, over-hunted, and overused. For example, the United Nations reports that 11 of the world's 15 primary fishing grounds are seriously depleted.

By imposing restrictions on open-access resource use, governments try to keep renewable resources from becoming depleted. Output restrictions are aimed at reducing resource use to a sustainable rate. For example, in the face of the tendency to overfish, governments now impose a variety of restrictions on the fishing industry.

Summary Table

Figure 3.3 summarizes the four types of goods in the economy. Across the top, goods are either *rival* or *nonrival,* and along the left margin, goods are either *exclusive* or *nonexclusive.* Private goods usually are provided by the private sector. Quasi-public goods are sometimes provided by government, as with a municipal golf course, and sometimes provided by the private sector, as with a private golf course. Government usually regulates open-access goods, such as with fishing licenses. Government usually provides public goods, funding them with enforced taxation.

 CHECKPOINT
Name the four categories of goods, and provide an example of each.

Externalities

The rivers in Jakarta, Indonesia, are dead—killed by acid, alcohol, and oil. Some coral reefs in the South Pacific have been ripped apart by dynamite fishing. The air in some U.S. cities does not meet health standards. These are all examples of *negative externalities,* which are by-products of production and consumption. Some externalities are

open-access goods

Goods that are rival in consumption but exclusion is costly

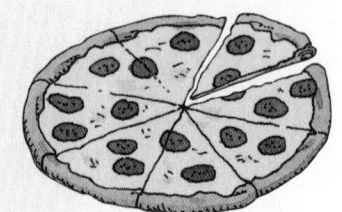

Private

Quasi-public

The four types of goods—private, quasi-public, open-access, and public—are characterized as being either rival or nonrival in consumption and either exclusive or nonexclusive. Can you think of two more examples for each type of good?

Open-access

Public

negative externalities

By-products of production or consumption that impose costs on third parties, neither buyers nor sellers

positive. For example, if you get vaccinated, you reduce your chances of contracting that disease. However you also reduce the chances that others will catch it from you, so they benefit too. The private sector, operating on its own, produces too many negative externalities and too few positive externalities. Government intervenes in the market to improve the outcome.

Negative Externalities

A renewable resource can be used indefinitely if used conservatively. Some renewable resources also are open-access resources, and this creates a special problem for the environment. The atmosphere and waterways are renewable resources to the extent they can absorb and neutralize a certain level of pollutants yet still remain relatively clean.

Negative externalities generally are by-products of production or consumption that impose costs on third parties (those who are neither buyer nor seller in the transaction). For example, some spray cans once released chlorofluorocarbons into the atmosphere, affecting those not directly involved in the purchase or sale of the spray cans. These gases were suspected of causing a thinning of the ozone layer that protects people from the sun's ultraviolet rays. The use of chlorofluorocarbons as a propellant in aerosol cans now is outlawed in the United States.

NETBookmark

Federal efforts to address negative externalities that harm the air, water, and soil are coordinated by the Environmental Protection Agency (EPA). Access the EPA web site through econxtra.swlearning.com. Identify four of the major U.S. environmental laws.

econxtra.swlearning.com

Correcting for Negative Externalities

Polluters of the atmosphere, waterways, and other open-access resources tend to ignore the impact of their pollution on other people and on the resource's ability to renew itself. Therefore, the quality and quantity of an open-access resource tends to deteriorate over time.

Government restrictions can improve the allocation of open-access resources. For example, antipollution laws limit the kind and amount of gases that can be released into the atmosphere from factories, automobiles, and other pollution sources. Restrictions aimed at maintaining water quality limit what can be dumped into the rivers, lakes, and oceans. Noise restrictions aim at maintaining the peace and quiet. Local zoning laws limit where firms can locate and in what condition homes must be maintained. In short, government restrictions try to reduce negative externalities.

Market prices can direct the allocation of resources as long as property rights are well defined and can be enforced at a reasonable cost. Pollution of air, land, water, peace and quiet, scenery, and so on arises not so much from the misdeeds of producers or consumers as from the fact that open-access resources are overused.

Positive Externalities

Some externalities are positive, or beneficial. **Positive externalities** occur when the by-products of consumption or production benefit third parties—those who are neither buyers nor sellers in the transaction. For example, people who get inoculated against a disease reduce their own likelihood of contracting the disease. In the process they also reduce the risk of transmitting the disease to others. Inoculations thus provide external benefits on others.

Education also generates positive externalities. Society as a whole receives external benefits from education because those who acquire more education become better citizens, can read road signs, and become more productive workers who are better able to support themselves and their families. Educated people also are less likely to require public assistance or to resort to

positive externalities

By-products of consumption or production that benefit third parties, who are not buyers or sellers

Ethics in Action

Wildlife Refuge at Stake Soaring energy prices and uncertainty about the availability of Persian Gulf oil are increasing the chances Congress will approve oil drilling in the Arctic National Wildlife Refuge. Millions of barrels of oil are thought to be under the coastal plain of the refuge in the far northeastern corner of Alaska. Extraction of this oil for domestic use has been at the heart of President Bush's energy agenda. Many Democrats are determined to protect the 100-mile sliver of tundra. Such protection has been an obsession among some environmentalists who insist that drilling will destroy its value as a sanctuary for polar bears, musk oxen, caribou, and migratory birds. While Bush has argued that the refuge's oil should be tapped to reduce U.S. dependence on foreign crude, the refuge oil won't be available for at least three to four years, even if Congress gives the go-ahead. Though drilling in the refuge may increase oil production and thus reduce the price of fuel, the unintended side effects may cause irreversible problems for animals and the environment.

Think Critically

Draw conclusions regarding the specific positive and negative externalities that you think could result from drilling oil in the Arctic National Wildlife Refuge. What do you think the government should do in this situation?

Government plays an economic role in a market economy whenever the benefits of a government policy outweigh its costs. Governments often provide for national defense, address environmental concerns, define and protect property rights, make markets more competitive, and redistribute income. In each of these cases, how do the benefits of the government policies outweigh their costs?

crime for income. Thus, education benefits those getting the education, but it also confers benefits on others.

When there are positive externalities, governments aim to increase the level of production beyond what would be chosen privately. For example, governments try to increase the level of education by providing free primary and secondary education, by requiring students to stay in school until they reach 16

years of age, by subsidizing public higher education, and by offering tax breaks for some education expenditures.

 CHECKPOINT
What are negative externalities and positive externalities, and why does government intervene to regulate them?

Key Concepts

1. In 2002, there was a debate over whether smallpox vaccinations should be given to the general public. Would vaccinations be an example of a *public good*. Why or why not?

2. Identify and describe an example of each of the following types of goods that you encounter in your life.

   a. Private good

   b. Quasi-public good

   c. Open-access good

   d. Public goods

3. Describe an example of a negative externality that has been a problem in your community.

4. Describe steps that have been taken in your community to try to eliminate or reduce the negative externality you identified in exercise 3 above.

Graphing Exercise

5. Construct a pie chart for 1990 and another for 2000 that show federal spending on natural resources and the environment. Base your charts on the data in the table. What parts of this spending may have been dedicated to trying to reduce negative externalities?

Federal Spending for Natural Resources and the Environment 1990–2000
Amounts in Billions of Dollars

Type of Spending	1990	% of total	2000	% of total
Water Resources	$ 4.4	25.7%	$5.1	21.3%
Conservation	3.6	21.1	5.9	24.6
Recreation	1.9	11.1	3.4	14.2
Pollution control	5.2	30.1	7.4	30.8
Other	2.0	11.7	3.0	12.1
Total	$17.1	100.0	$24.8	100.0

Source: *Statistical Abstract of the United States*, 2001, p. 307.

Think Critically

6. **Government** Determine the open-access goods that exist in your county or state. Investigate whether the county or state government regulates these goods. If they do, what are the regulations? If not, why do you think these goods are not regulated?

7. **Business Management** Although trucks powered by natural gas are expensive to purchase, they create little pollution when they are operated. Why do you think some states have passed laws that give tax reductions to businesses that use natural gas-powered trucks? Explain how this is an effort by these states to reduce a negative externality. Do you think this is a good idea?

Objectives

> Determine why incomes differ across households, and identify the main source of poverty in the United States.

> Describe government programs that provide a safety net for poor people.

Overview

Operating on its own, the private sector offers no guarantee that people will earn enough to survive. Some people may have few resources that are valued in the market. Because markets do not assure even a minimum level of income, society has made the political choice that poor families should receive short-term public assistance, or welfare. This assistance reflects society's attempt to provide a social safety net. However public assistance could reduce incentives to work, because welfare benefits decrease as earnings from work increase.

Key Terms

median income

social insurance

income-assistance programs

[In the News]

● Good News/Bad News for U.S. Kids

In July 2002, the Federal Interagency Forum on Child and Family Statistics reported encouraging news on the health, economics, and education of some 70 million children in the United States. The best news was a drop in the infant mortality rate—from 7.2 deaths per 1,000 babies under age one in 1998, down to 6.9 deaths per 1,000 babies in 2000. Other positive trends: More children were covered by health insurance; fewer eighth and tenth graders smoked; more children were read to every day by a family member; and more youngsters ages two to five had a good diet. However, numerous measures did not change: In 2000, 16 percent of children lived in poverty; only 76 percent of toddlers got the recommended immunizations; and only 87 percent of young adults finished high school. Drug and alcohol use among junior high and high school students held steady. The report also found that in 2001, 19 percent of children had at least one parent born outside the United States, up from 14 percent in 1994.

Think About It

What do the above statistics say about the social safety net in the United States?

Income and Poverty

In a market economy, income depends primarily on earnings, which depend on the value of each person's contribution to production. The problem with allocating income according to productivity is that some people are not able to contribute much value to production. Individuals born with mental or physical disabilities tend to be less productive and may be unable to earn a living. Others may face limited job choices and reduced wages because of advanced age, poor health, little education, discrimination, bad luck, or the demands of caring for small children. Consider first why incomes differ across households.

Why Household Incomes Differ

The **median income** of households is the middle income when incomes are ranked from lowest to highest. In any given year, half the households are above the median income and half are below it.

The main reason household incomes differ is that the number of household members who are working differs. For example, the median income for households with two earners is nearly double that for households with only one earner and about four times that for households with no earners. Household incomes also differ for all the reasons that labor earnings differ, such as differences in education, ability, job experience, and so on.

At every age, people with more education earn more on average. For example, those with a professional degree earn about four times as much as those with only a high school education. Age itself has an important effect on income. As workers mature, they typically

NETBookmark

Data and reports about income distribution can be found at the U.S. Census Bureau's web site. Access this web site through econxtra.swlearning.com.

Click on the link to Frequently Asked Questions CPS. Write down five income statistics you learned about income in the United States.

econxtra.swlearning.com

median income
The middle income when a group of incomes is ranked from lowest to highest

Ask the Xpert!
econxtra.swlearning.com

Will there always be poverty?

Main Idea

💡 **Role of Resources in Determining Income**

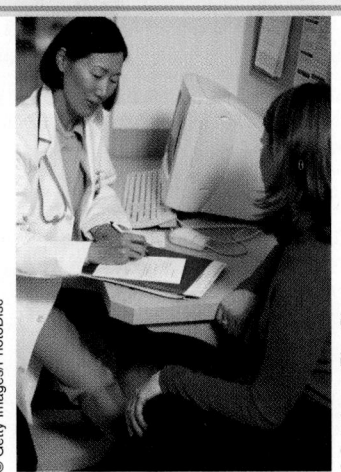

Income for most people is determined by the market value of the productive resources they sell. What they earn depends on the market value of what they produce and how productive they are. **What are the products of the two people shown in the photos? Which one do you think should earn more than the other, and why?**

© Getty Images/PhotoDisc

© Getty Images/PhotoDisc

acquire valuable job experience, get promoted, and earn more.

Differences in earnings based on age and education reflect a normal life-cycle pattern of income. In fact, most income differences across households reflect the normal workings of resource markets, whereby workers are rewarded according to their productivity. Because of these lifetime patterns, it is not necessarily the same households that remain rich or poor over time. There is much income mobility among households.

Despite this mobility over time, generalizations can be made about rich and poor households at a point in time. High-income households typically consist of well-educated couples with both spouses employed. Low-income households typically are headed by a single mother who is young, poorly educated, and unemployed.

Young, single motherhood is a recipe for poverty. Often the young mother drops out of school, which reduces her future earning possibilities when and if she seeks work outside the home. Even a strong economy is little aid to households with nobody in the labor force.

Official Poverty Rate

Because poverty is such a relative concept, how can it be measured objectively over time? The federal government determines the official poverty level and adjusts this benchmark over time to account for inflation. For example, the official poverty level for a family of four was $18,104 in 2001.

U.S. poverty since 1959 is presented in Figure 3.4. Poverty is measured both in millions of people living below the official poverty level and the percentage of the U.S. population below that level. Periods of U.S. recession are shaded. A *recession* is defined as a decline in the nation's total production that lasts at least six months. Note that poverty increases during recessions.

The biggest decline in U.S. poverty occurred before 1970. The poverty rate dropped from 22 percent in 1959 to 12 percent in 1969. During that period, the number of poor people decreased from about 40 million to 24 million. More recently, the rate declined from 15 percent in 1993 to 12 percent in 2001, one of the lowest rates since 1973. The 33 million people in poverty in 2001 was 6 million below the 1993 level.

Number and Percentage of U.S. Population in Poverty: 1959–2001　　**Figure 3.4**

On the line graph, the "number in poverty" line shows how many millions of people were living below the official poverty level. The "poverty rate" line shows the percentage of the U.S. population below that level. Periods of U.S. recession are shaded. What happens to the number in poverty and the poverty rate during a recession?

Source: U.S. Census Bureau, *Poverty in the United States: 2001,* Current Population Reports, September 2002, Figure 3, www.census.gov/hhes/www/poverty01.html.

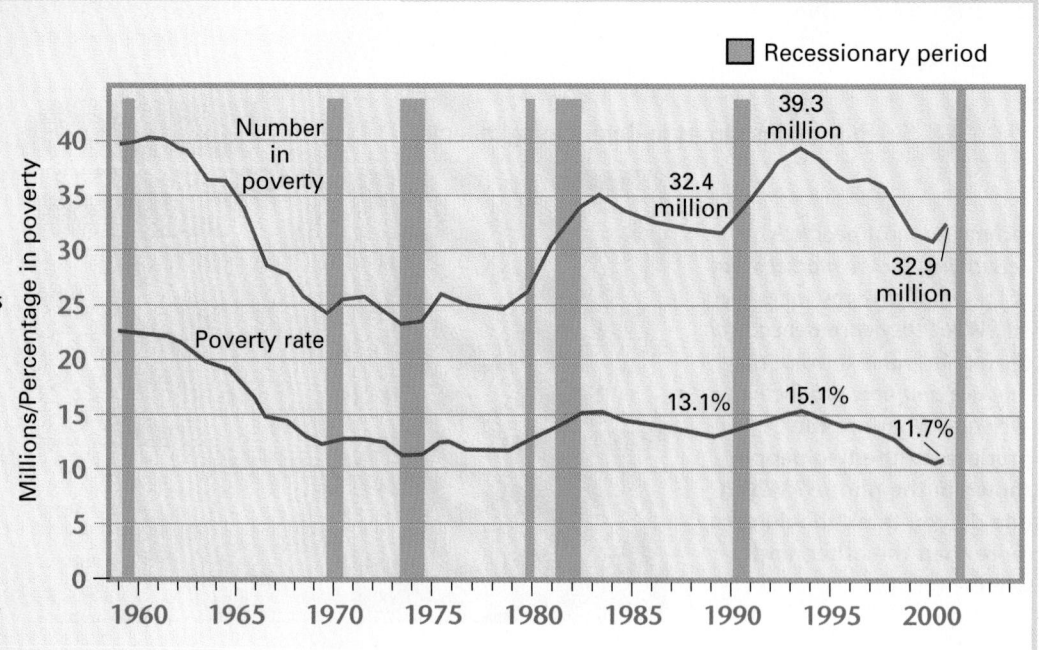

Poverty is a relative term. If you examined income differences across countries, you would find huge gaps between rich and poor nations. The U.S. official poverty level of income is many times greater than the average income for most of the world's population. Many other countries set a much lower income level as their poverty level. For example, the poverty level for a family of four in the United States in 2001 worked out to be about $12 per person per day. China uses a poverty level of only $0.30 per person per day. In China, $0.30 can purchase more goods and services than it can in the United States.

Poverty and Marital Status

One way of measuring poverty is based on the marital status of the household head. Figure 3.5 compares poverty rates during the last three decades for

1. families headed by females with no husband present

2. families headed by males with no wife present

3. married couples

Three trends are clear. First, poverty rates among female-headed families are five to six times greater than rates among married couples. Second, poverty rates among female-headed families are two to three times greater than those for male-headed families. And third, since the mid-1990s poverty rates have trended down for all types of families, before rising slightly in the recession year of 2001.

The percentage of births to unmarried mothers is five times greater today than in 1960. Many of these births are to teenage mothers. The United States has the highest teenage pregnancy rate in the developed world—twice the rate of Great Britain and more that 12 times that of Japan. Because the father in such cases typically assumes little responsibility for child support, children born outside marriage are much more likely to be poor than other children. Births to single mothers make up the primary source of poverty in the United States.

CHECKPOINT
Why do incomes differ across households, and what is the main source of poverty in the U.S. economy?

U.S. Poverty Rates and Types of Households

Figure 3.5

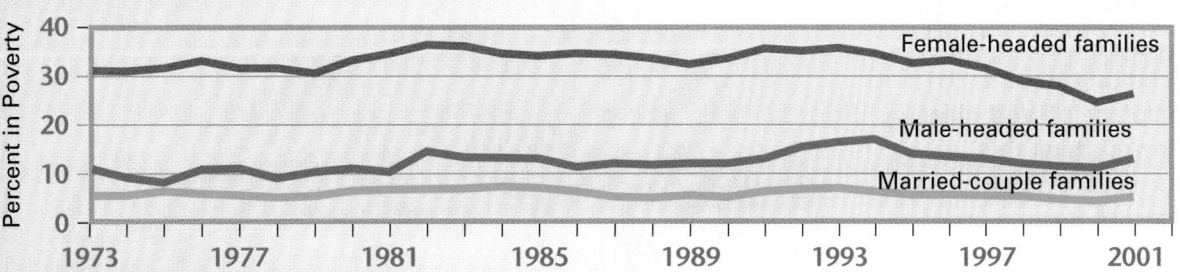

Female-headed families have the highest poverty rate in the United States, followed by male-headed families and married couples.

Source: Developed from U.S. Census Bureau, *Poverty in the United States: 2001,* Current Population Reports, September 2002, Table A-3.

Programs to Help the Poor

What should be society's response to poverty? Families with a full-time worker are nine times more likely to escape poverty than are families with no workers. Thus, the government's first line of defense in fighting poverty is to promote job opportunities. Yet even when the unemployment rate is low, some people still remain poor.

Since the 1960s, spending for income redistribution at all levels of government has increased significantly. These programs divide into two broad categories: social insurance and income assistance.

Social Insurance

Social insurance programs are designed to help make up for the lost income of people who worked but are now retired, temporarily unemployed, or unable to work because of disability or work-related injury. The federal government funds all these programs. The major social insurance program is Social Security, established during the Great Depression of the 1930s. *Social Security*

provides retirement income for those with a work history and a record of making payments to the program.

Medicare, another social insurance program, provides health insurance for short-term medical care, mostly to those age 65 and older, regardless of income. There were about 40 million Social Security and Medicare beneficiaries in 2001.

The social insurance system tends to redistribute income from rich to poor and from young to old. Most current Social Security beneficiaries receive far more in benefits than they paid into the program, especially those with a brief work history or a record of low wages.

Other social insurance programs include unemployment insurance and workers' compensation, which supports workers injured on the job. Both programs require that beneficiaries have a prior record of employment.

Income-Assistance Programs

Income-assistance programs—typically called *welfare programs*—provide money and in-kind assistance to poor people. In-kind assistance is help in the form of goods and services. Programs

social insurance

Cash transfers for retirees, the unemployed, and others with a work history and a record of contributions to the program

income-assistance programs

Government programs that provide money and in-kind assistance to poor people

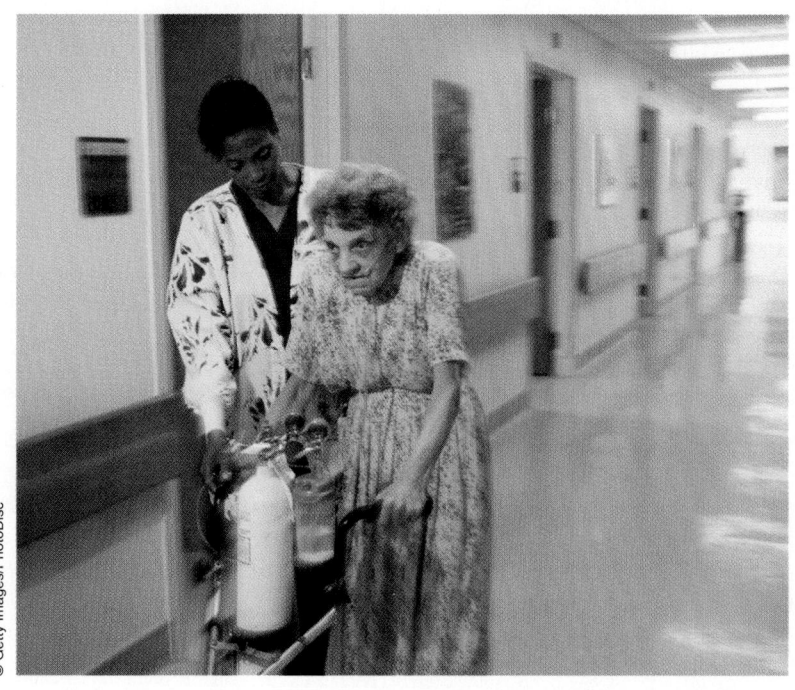

© Getty Images/PhotoDisc

Medicare is a social insurance program that provides health insurance for short-term medical care, mostly to people age 65 and older. Why do you think this insurance is provided regardless of income level?

that pay money directly to recipients are called cash transfer programs. Other forms of assistance, such as housing and healthcare, are provided through in-kind transfer programs.

Unlike social insurance programs, income-assistance programs do not require a work history or a record of contributions. Instead, income-assistance programs are means tested. In a *means-tested program,* a household's income and assets must fall below a certain level to qualify for benefits. The federal government funds two-thirds of welfare spending, and state and local governments fund one-third.

Cash Transfer Programs

The two main cash transfer programs are *Temporary Assistance for Needy Families (TANF),* which provides cash to poor families with dependent children, and *Supplemental Security Income (SSI),* which provides cash to the elderly poor and the disabled. Cash transfers vary inversely with family income from other sources. The federal government gives each state a fixed grant to help fund TANF programs. Each state determines eligibility standards.

The SSI program provides support for the elderly and disabled poor, including people addicted to drugs and alcohol, children with learning disabilities, and, in some cases, the homeless. SSI is the fastest-growing cash-transfer program, with outlays of $33 billion in 2001, double the TANF outlays that year.

In-Kind Transfer Programs

A variety of *in-kind transfer programs* provide goods and services such as food stamps, healthcare, housing assistance, and school lunches to the poor. *Medicaid* funds medical care for those with incomes below a certain level who are elderly, blind, disabled, or are living in families with dependent children. Medicaid is the largest welfare program, costing nearly twice as much as all cash transfer programs combined. It has grown more than any other poverty program, quadrupling in the last decade and accounting for nearly a quarter of the typical state's

budget. States get federal grants covering half or more of their Medicaid budget.

The qualifying level of income is set by each state. Some states are quite strict. Therefore, the proportion of poor covered by Medicaid varies greatly across states. In 2001, more than 36 million people received free medical care under Medicaid at a total cost of more than $200 billion. Outlays averaged about $5,600 per recipient. In all, there are about 75 means-tested federal welfare programs.

To get some idea of how much the federal government spends on programs to help the poor, also called *income redistribution programs,* look at Figure 3.6. This figure shows the composition of federal outlays since 1960. As you can see, income redistribution, including Social Security, Medicare, and various welfare programs, increased from about one-fifth of federal outlays in 1960 to about half by 2000. Conversely, defense spending fell from more than half of federal outlays in 1960 to less than one-fifth by 2000. Thus, income redistribution claims a growing share of the federal budget.

Earned-Income Tax Credit

The *earned-income tax credit* supplements wages of the working poor. For example, a family with two children and earning $13,000 in 2001 would not pay federal income tax and would receive a cash transfer of about $4,000. The idea is to increase income and to provide incentives for people to work. More than 18 million working families received such transfers in 2001, requiring federal outlays exceeding $30 billion.

Welfare Reform

The biggest reform of the welfare system in the last 60 years came with 1996 legislation that created the current system, Temporary Assistance for Needy Families (TANF). The earlier program established eligibility rules that guaranteed the federal government would pay most of the cost. Families could stay

THE WALL STREET JOURNAL

Reading It Right What's the relevance of the following statement from *The Wall Street Journal*? "Family households maintained by women without a husband present saw incomes rise 4.0 percent to $28,116 from 1999 to 2000, the Census Department said. Other types of households had no significant change in their median household income."

on welfare for a decade or more. Under the new system, states get a fixed amount of aid from the federal government and can run their own welfare programs. The system requires welfare recipients to look for jobs and limits cash transfers to five years.

About half the states impose time limits shorter than five years. Some observers fear that states now have an incentive to keep welfare costs down by cutting benefits. To avoid becoming destinations for poor people—that is, to avoid becoming "welfare magnets"—

states may be tempted to offer relatively low levels of benefits.

Welfare reform has reduced welfare rolls and increased employment. However, because most people on welfare are poorly educated and have few job skills, wages for those who find jobs remain low. Part-time work also is common, as is job loss among those who initially find jobs.

On the plus side, however, the earned-income tax credit provided up to $4,000 in 2001 in additional income to low-income workers. Most of those going to work also can receive food stamps, child care, and Medicaid. All this has helped reduce the overall poverty rate.

CHECKPOINT

What are the main government programs that try to offer a safety net?

Income Redistribution—Composition of Federal Outlays

Figure 3.6

Since 1960, spending on income redistribution has increased and spending on defense has decreased as a share of federal outlays.

Source: Computed based on figures from the *Economic Report of the President*, January 2001, Table B-80. Access the most current report through econxtra.swlearning.com.

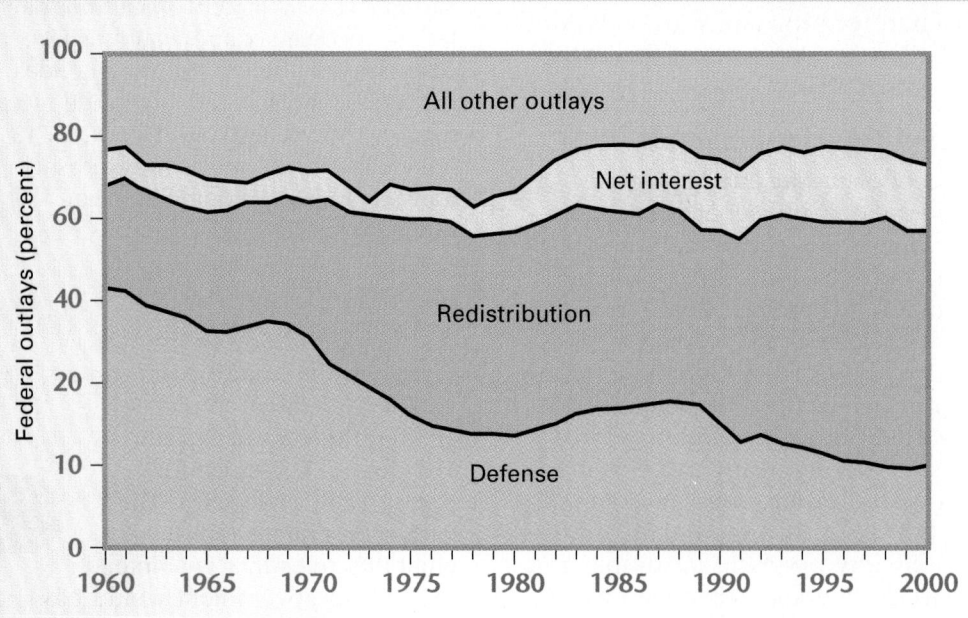

Sharpen Your Life Skills

Use Mathematics to Draw Conclusions

Federal, state, and local governments receive a large part of the income that is generated from production in the U.S. economy through taxes, fees, and borrowing. Some of the government's revenue is used to purchase goods or services while other parts become transfer payments. Welfare, Social Security, and unemployment compensation payments are examples of government transfers of income to individuals. Use data in the table below to calculate the percent of total income earned from production that has flowed through the government in recent years. What conclusions could you draw from these data about the importance of government in deciding how income in our nation will be used?

Apply Your Skill

1. Assume that all people currently alive will live to an age of at least 67. Use the *Statistical Abstract of the United States* to find the approximate number of people who will become eligible for Social Security benefits (67 years of age) in the 2010s, 2020s, and 2030s. Do this by finding the number of people who are currently in age groups that will reach 67 in each of these decades. Explain why these data indicate that government spending for Social Security and Medicare insurance is likely to grow as a share of total income in the future.

2. In 2000, the federal government's spending for national defense totaled $294.5 billion, or about 3 percent of the value of all production in the U.S. economy during that year. If spending for defense had grown by 5 percent in each of the following five years, how much would it total by 2005? If the value of total U.S. production increased by 3 percent in each of these years, what would happen to the share of that production that would have been devoted to our national defense?

Government Spending and Transfers as a Percent of Total Production, 1980–2000 Values in Billions of Dollars

Year	Government Spending and Transfers	Value of Total Production	Government Spending & Transfers as a Percent of Total Production
1980	$ 812.0	$2,795.8	
1990	$1,778.0	$5,803.2	
2000	$2,772.5	$9,963.1	

Key Concepts

1. Explain why a pure market economy would not work well if all people were guaranteed the same income by the government.

2. Why is *poverty* a relative term?

3. Think of a person you know who you think lives in poverty. What steps could the government take to help this person escape poverty? Do you think the government should do these things? Would you be willing to pay more taxes to support this type of help?

4. Why do you think that spending for Medicare is the most rapidly growing part of the social insurance program?

5. Between 1996 and 2002 the number of welfare cases in the United States fell by more than half. Explain why this does not mean that the number of people living in poverty was also cut in half during these years.

Graphing Exercise

6. Draw a double line graph of the percent of U.S. residents and children who were officially designated as living in poverty from 1991 through 1999, based on the data in the table to the right. As a percent, why do more children live in poverty than adults? What do you think happened to these percentages during the downturn in the U.S. economy after 2000?

Percent of U.S. Residents and Children Living in Poverty, 1991–1999

Year	% of total population living in poverty	% of children living in poverty
1991	14.2%	21.1%
1993	15.1%	22.0%
1995	13.8%	20.2%
1997	13.3%	19.2%
1999	11.6%	16.3%

Source: *Statistical Abstract of the United States*, 2001, p. 442.

Think Critically

7. **English** Read *The Grapes of Wrath* by John Steinbeck or a summary of this novel. This book describes what it was like for poor people to live through the Great Depression of the 1930s. Describe why these conditions led the government to create many of the programs that help people living in poverty today.

8. **Research** Find current data concerning poverty as it relates to education, race, and age by searching the Internet for the *Statistical Abstract of the United States*. Look for useful data in a table titled "Families Below Poverty Level by Selected Characteristics" in the *Income, Expenditures, and Wealth* section of the *Abstract*. What relationships can you draw see in these data?

to History

The Commerce Clause

In September, 1786, at a meeting held in Annapolis, Maryland, delegates from five states met to discuss the problems of interstate commerce. Realizing that the problems were beyond their power to resolve, the Virginia delegation and Alexander Hamilton called for a general convention to be held in Philadelphia the next year. When the convention met on May 25, it was with the purpose of revising the Articles of Confederation. The delegates decided to abandon the Articles and write a new plan of government. By September 17, the 55 delegates representing 12 of the 13 states had drafted the U.S. Constitution. Although inspired by economic circumstances, the U.S. Constitution is not just an economic document. Even so, the Constitution contains the basis of the country's economic success.

Much of the federal government's regulatory power comes from Article 1, Section 8, the Commerce Clause, of the U.S. Constitution. This section states that Congress shall have the power to "regulate commerce with foreign nations, and among the several states, and with Indian tribes." The first major case involving the Commerce Clause was *Gibbons v. Ogden*. In its decision the U.S. Supreme Court, led by Chief Justice John Marshall, established the government's right to regulate interstate commerce. However, Marshall didn't stop there. He used the case as an opportunity to expand the power of the federal government by broadening the definition of commerce. Reading the phrase "to regulate commerce . . . among the several states," Marshall rejected the notion that "commerce" meant only the transportation of goods across state lines for sale. In his opinion, the term "commerce" came to include nearly every commercial activity that sooner or later will include the transportation of persons, things, services or power across state lines. This opinion was confirmed by subsequent Court rulings.

The 1887 Interstate Commerce Act, which created the Interstate Commerce Commission (ICC), and the Sherman Antitrust Act (1890) were the federal government's first major use of the Commerce Clause as the authority for its regulation of the economy. This introduced the Progressive Era of the early twentieth century, which saw the government increase its regulatory power with the Hepburn Act (1906), the Mann-Elkins Act (1910), and the creation of the Federal Trade Commission (1914). The Commerce Clause has been used as justification to expand government into many aspects of the national life and economy. For example, it has been used to justify laws prohibiting child labor, to regulate business-labor relations, to create a federal minimum wage, and to prosecute gangsters.

The Commerce Clause has been the subject of more Supreme Court cases between 1789 and 1950 than any other Constitutional clause. The Court's actions have made it an important, if not *the most* important, source of government power over the economy. President Ronald Reagan tried to roll back some of that power in the 1980s, when he attempted to abolish the Interstate Commerce Commission (ICC). He argued that deregulation had made the agency unnecessary. Congress refused to go along. Today the power of the federal government to regulate any business activity that even remotely affects interstate commerce seems well established.

THINK CRITICALLY

Read and analyze the Fifth Amendment and the rest of the Commerce Clause of the U.S. Constitution. What parts of these affect the U.S. economic system and how?

3 Chapter Assessment

Summary

3.1 The U.S. Private Sector

a There are four groups of decision makers in the U.S. economy: *households, firms, government,* and *the rest of the world.*

b Firms expanded their importance in the economy during the Industrial Revolution. By gathering factors of production into one location, businesses are able to create a more efficient *division of labor.*

Xtra! Quiz Prep
econxtra.swlearning.com

c Decisions made by the rest of the world affect the consumption and production of U.S. households. The United States buys goods from other nations that have lower opportunity costs of production and sells goods that have lower opportunity costs to U.S. producers.

3.2 Regulating the Private Sector

a The private sector of the U.S. economy would not run smoothly without government regulation. Economic rules created and enforced by the government set standards for quality and weights and measures, and protect property rights and consumer safety.

b The federal government promotes competition in the market and limits monopoly power through enforcing *antitrust laws* and regulating *natural monopolies.*

c The government promotes economic growth and stability through *fiscal* and *monetary policies.* Fiscal policy uses taxes and public spending to influence economic conditions. Monetary policy adjusts the amount of money in the economy to influence interest rates, borrowing, spending, and production.

3.3 Public Goods and Externalities

a All goods can be classified as *private goods, public goods, quasi-public goods,* or *open-access goods.*

b Public goods are nonrival and nonexclusive. If a public good is used by one person that does not prevent another from benefiting from using it.

c Quasi-public goods are nonrival but exclusive. The use of a public park by one person does not prevent others from enjoying it, too, unless it is very crowded. The government, however, may impose a fee to enter the park, which makes it exclusive for those who choose to pay.

d Open-access goods are rival but nonexclusive. If you collect seashells at the beach, the shells you gather cannot be collected by others, but you are free to collect as many as you can find.

e *Negative externalities* are costs of production that are imposed on people who are neither the producer nor the consumer of the product.

3.4 Providing a Safety Net

a In a pure market economy, people would receive income in proportion to the value of their contribution to production. Individuals unable to work could fall into poverty and starve. The U.S. government provides social services for those who otherwise might live in poverty.

b The official poverty rate in the United States declined in most years since the government began to measure poverty. Poverty is most common among households headed by single mothers.

c The government has established many programs to help specific groups of people. Among these are *social insurance programs, income-assistance programs, the earned-income credit for federal income tax,* and *in-kind transfers.*

d The nation's *welfare programs* were reformed in 1996, when the Temporary Assistance for Needy Families Program was created.

Review Economic Terms

Choose the term that best fits the definition. On a separate sheet of paper, write the letter of the answer. Some terms will not be used.

_____ 1. The satisfaction received from consumption

_____ 2. Laws that prohibit anticompetitive behavior and promote competition

_____ 3. Legal claims that guarantee an owner the right to use a good or resource exclusively or to charge others for its use

_____ 4. The federal government's use of taxing and public spending to influence the national economy

_____ 5. The Federal Reserve System's attempts to control the money supply to influence the national economy

_____ 6. One firm that can serve an entire market at a lower per-unit cost than can two or more firms

_____ 7. A good with two features: (1) the amount consumed by one person is unavailable to others and (2) nonpayers can easily be excluded

_____ 8. A good that, once produced, is available for all to consume, but the producer cannot easily exclude nonpayers

_____ 9. A good that is rival in consumption but exclusion is costly

_____ 10. The most important economic decision maker, consisting of all those who live under one roof.

a. antitrust laws

b. firm

c. fiscal policy

d. household

e income-assistance programs

f. Industrial Revolution

g. median income

h. monetary policy

i. natural monopoly

j. negative externalities

k. open-access good

l. positive externalities

m. private good

n. private property rights

o. public good

p. quasi-public good

q. social insurance

r. utility

Review Economic Concepts

11. All those who live under one roof are considered to be part of the same _?_.

12. Firms organizing production in large, centrally powered factories did all of the following except

    a. promote a more efficient division of labor.

    b. reduce transportation costs.

    c. reduce consumer reliance on trade.

    d. enable the use of specialized machines.

13. In the evolution of the firm, the _?_ was the bridge between the self-sufficient farm household and the modern firm.

14. Which of the following is correct?

    a. Revenue = Profit – Cost of Production

    b. Profit = Cost of Production – Revenue

    c. Profit = Revenue – Cost of Production

    d. Cost of Production = Revenue + Profit

15. **True or False** International trade occurs because the opportunity cost of producing specific goods differs among countries.

16. A(n) _?_ awards an inventor the exclusive right to produce a good for a specific period of time.

17. Which of the following is *not* a true statement about monoplies?

    a. Monopolies try to charge higher prices than would result through competition.

    b. By maximizing profits, monopolies ultimately benefit social welfare.

    c. Antitrust laws attempt to reduce monopoly power.

    d. Monopolies may try to influence the political system in order to protect and enhance their power.

18. Which of the following is the *best* example of the government regulating a *natural monopoly*?

    a. emission standards for automobiles

    b. required testing and approval to market new drugs

    c. rules for selling new shares of corporate stock

    d. set prices for distributing natural gas to homes

19. **True or False** *Public goods* can be used by all consumers and have no economic cost.

20. _?_ are nonrival but exclusive, such as cable TV signals.

21. **True or False** *Poverty* is a relative term that has different meanings at different times and in different locations.

22. Which of the following would be an example of an attempt by the Federal Reserve System to stimulate the economy through *monetary policy*?

    a. a 5 percent reduction in federal income tax rates

    b. an increase in government spending for road construction

    c. an increase in the amount of money in the economy

    d. an increase in the tax on goods purchased from other countries

23. Another term for *welfare* is

    a. job-placement program.

    b. income-assistance program.

    c. social insurance program.

    d. tax rebate program.

Apply Economic Concepts

24. **Identifying Goods** Copy the figure below. Place the letter of each of the following in the correct box of the figure.

    A. Police protection

    B. Shrimp in the ocean

    C. Public vaccinations

    D. Picnic tables in a national park

    E. Your television set

    F. An unused public tennis court

    G. Seashells on a beach

    H. Your uncle's fishing boat

	Rival	Nonrival
Exclusive		
Nonexclusive		

25. **Examples in Your Community** Make a second copy of the figure in Exercise 24. Place two examples of each type of good that exist in your community in the appropriate boxes. Use examples that are different from those in exercise 24.

26. **Your Share of the Cost** In 2001, the cost of national defense for the United States was just over $300 billion. At that time, there were approximately 280 million people living in this country. Calculate the cost of national defense per person in 2001. Explain why it is difficult to charge individuals their "fair share" of the cost of national defense.

27. **Sharpen Your Life Skills—Use Mathematics to Draw Conclusions** In 2001, the value of total production in the United States was $10.442 trillion. In that year, the federal government spent or transferred $1.864 trillion. What percent of the nation's total income flowed through federal government in 2001? The table below shows the experience over a longer period. On a separate sheet, fill in the right-hand column. What has been the trend over the period? What do these data show about the importance of federal government spending and transfers in the economy in these years? Considering recent history, would you expect this trend to continue in the future?

Government Spending and Transfers as a Percent of Total Production, 1980–2000
Values in Billions of Dollars

Year	Federal Government Spending and Transfers	Value of Total Production	Federal Spending & Transfers as a Percent of Total Production
1980	$ 812.0	$2,795.8	_____
1990	$1,778.0	$5,803.2	_____
2000	$3,012.4	$9,963.1	_____
Source: *Statistical Abstract of the United States,* 2002, p. 305.			

 econxtra.swlearning.com

28. Access **EconData Online** at econxtra. swlearning.com. Click on "Microeconomics," "Income Distribution and Poverty," and then "Civilian Unemployment Rate." After analyz- ing the information available, write a paragraph to explain why the unemployment rate is inversely related to the growth rate of real GDP over the business cycle.

Investing In Your Future

The Situation

Aleesha Johnson had a big decision to make. For years, animals had fascinated her. She devoured every television program, book, and movie she could find about the animal kingdom. Now, the metropolitan area's new zoo was opening, and there were jobs available for interns. However, the new zoo was some 12 miles away, located even outside the ring of suburbs that surrounded the city. Aleesha's guidance counselor said that with her excellent grades and level of interest, she was a shoe-in for one of the positions. Unfortunately, however, Aleesha had no way to get there. Of course, she just turned 16 and, if her parents would co-sign a loan for her as they promised, she could buy a car and drive to work. Her parents made it clear that she would need to make the car payments and pay for the maintenance and insurance herself.

The Decision

Thanks to a long-term grant received by the zoo, an intern's pay was $1 an hour above the minimum wage. That would probably pay for her car expenses, but Aleesha wasn't sure. She was convinced, however, that with working 20 hours a week as an intern after school and on some weekends, she would lose her positions on the school's track and basketball teams. Her honor-roll GPA also might suffer. Then there was her social life, which was just starting to get interesting.... Still, the intern position appealed to her. It wasn't just animals that Aleesha had observed and learned about in her life. She recognized that some of the really successful people in the world took special steps early in their lives to follow their dreams. The internship would be a chance to learn the nuts and bolts of how a state-of-the-art zoo operates. Who knew what doors would open as a result?

⊚ Activities

Divide into teams or work individually, as directed by your teacher, to perform the following tasks.

Apply the steps in the following decision-making process to Aleesha's situation:

1. *Define the problem.* Define Aleesha's problem in a way that will allow a clear solution.

2. *Identify the choices.* List the various alternatives among which she must choose.

3. *Evaluate the pluses and minuses of each choice.* Carefully weigh the value Aleesha puts on each alternative and the opportunity cost(s) for each.

4. *Make a choice.* Which course of action should she choose? Be prepared to present and defend your choice in class.

5. *Provide "action" steps that are appropriate to the decision.* Make sure these are realistic and timely to ensure the necessary actions are taken to resolve the problem.

6. *Critique the decision.* The class will assist in the review and evaluation of your plan of action. In real life, you should review not only the decision and its result, but also the process by which you make it. Set a time to initiate reviewing the decision or identify an event that would trigger its review.

⊚ Research

Research for the information you need to effectively make the decision, such as how much it would cost to operate her car, the level of the minimum wage, the career opportunities for zookeepers, etc.

⊚ Present

Arrive at a decision. Then prepare a presentation for the class on the six steps you took to achieve this decision. Be ready for questions and criticisms.

Unit 2

OPEN

The Market Economy

In 1962, Sam Walton opened his first store in Rogers, Arkansas, with a sign that read: "Wal-Mart Discount City. We sell for less." Wal-Mart now sells more than any other retailer in the world because prices there are the lowest around. As a consumer, you understand why people buy more at a lower price. Wal-Mart, for example, sells on average more than 20,000 pairs of shoes *an hour*. Buyers love a bargain, but sellers must make sure their prices cover the costs of supplying the goods. Differences between the desires of buyers and sellers are sorted out by competitive pressures in a market economy.

4 Demand

Consider

Why are newspapers sold in vending machines that allow you to take more than one copy?

How much do you eat when you can eat all you want?

What cures spring fever?

What economic principle is behind the saying, "Been there, done that"?

Why do higher cigarette taxes cut smoking by teenagers more than by other age groups?

POINT YOUR BROWSER

econxtra.swlearning.com

© Getty Images/PhotoDisc

Objectives

> Explain the law of demand.

> Interpret a demand schedule and a demand curve.

Overview

The primary building blocks of a market economy are demand and supply. Consumers demand goods and services that maximize their utility, and producers supply goods and services that maximize their profit. As a consumer in the United States' market economy, you demand all kinds of goods and services. You buy less of a good when its price increases and more of it when the price decreases. This section draws on your experience as a consumer to help you understand demand, particularly the demand curve.

Key Terms

demand

law of demand

marginal utility

law of diminishing marginal utility

demand curve

quantity demanded

individual demand

market demand

[In the News]

● Demand Rising Slowly For Digital HDTV

Officials at the most recent National Association of Broadcasters Exposition (NAB) say that sales of digital, high-definition television (HDTV) sets are slowly gaining momentum. Little by little, consumers are learning about the new technology's clearer picture and better sound quality versus standard analog TV. However, there are a few obstacles to demand for this product. One obstacle is the limited availability of digital programming for HDTVs. Another is the relatively high cost. Although a small number of consumers will buy the newest technologies regardless of price, most people have learned that if you wait a bit for new electronics products, the prices will come down. For example, big-screen TVs started out selling at $4,000 to $5,000, and then a year later sold for less than half that price. A 27-inch set that cost $700 to $800 five years ago sells for $180 today. Because they know the law of demand, consumer electronics marketers plan their strategies to sell to the early adopters at a higher price, and then begin lowering the price to increase the quantity demanded.

Think About It

Why do most consumers wait to purchase new consumer electronics products such as HDTVs?

Law of Demand

How many 12-inch pizzas will people buy each week if the price is $12? What if the price is $9? What if it's $6? The answers reveal the relationship between the price of pizza and the quantity purchased. Such a relationship is called the *demand* for pizza.

Demand indicates how much of a product consumers are both *willing* and *able* to buy at each possible price during a given period, other things remaining constant. Because demand pertains to a specific period—a day, a week, a month—you should think of demand as the desired *rate of purchase per time period* at each possible price. Also, notice the emphasis on *willing* and *able*. You may be *able* to buy a rock concert ticket for $30 because you can afford one. However

you may not be *willing* to buy one if the performers do not interest you.

This relation between the price and the quantity demanded is an economic law. The **law of demand** says that quantity demanded varies inversely with price, other things constant. Thus, the higher the price, the smaller the quantity demanded. The lower the price, the greater the quantity demanded.

Demand, Wants, and Needs

Consumer demand and consumer wants are not the same thing. You know that wants are unlimited. You may want a new Mercedes-Benz SL500 roadster convertible, but the $95,000 price tag is likely beyond your budget. (The quantity you demand at that price is zero.) Nor is demand the same as need. You may have outgrown your winter coat and so need a new one. But if the price is $200, you may decide your old coat will do for now. If the price drops enough—say, to $100—then you become both willing and able to buy a new coat.

Substitution Effect

What explains the law of demand? Why, for example, is more of a product demanded when the price falls? The explanation begins with unlimited wants meeting scarce resources. Many goods and services are capable of satisfying your particular wants. For example, you can satisfy your hunger by eating pizza, tacos, burgers, chicken, sandwiches, salads, or hundreds of other items. Similarly, you can satisfy your desire for warmth in the winter with warm clothing, a home-heating system, a trip to Hawaii, or in other ways.

Some ways of satisfying your wants will be more appealing than others. A trip to Hawaii is more fun than wearing warm clothing. In a world without scarcity, everything would be free, so you would always choose the most attractive alternative. Scarcity, however, is a reality, and the degree of scarcity of one good relative to another helps determine each good's relative price.

Notice that the definition of *demand* includes the other-things-constant assumption. (A Latin phrase you may

© Getty Images/PhotoDisc

The law of demand applies even to personal choices, such as whether or not to own a pet. For example, after New York City passed an anti-dog-litter law, owners had to follow their dogs around the city with scoopers and plastic bags. The law raised the cost, or price, of owning a dog. What do you think happened to the quantity of dogs demanded as a result of this law, and why?

hear for "other things constant" is *ceteris paribus*.) Among the "other things" assumed to remain constant are the prices of other goods. For example, if the price of pizza declines while other prices remain constant, pizza becomes relatively cheaper. Consumers are more *willing* to purchase pizza when its relative price falls. People tend to substitute pizza for other goods. This is called the *substitution effect of a price change*. On the other hand, an increase in the price of pizza, other things constant, causes consumers to substitute other goods for the now higher-priced pizza, thus reducing their quantity demanded.

Remember that *the change in the relative price—the price of one good relative to the prices of other goods—causes the substitution effect*. If all prices changed by the same percentage, there would be no change in relative prices and no substitution effect.

Income Effect

A fall in the price of a product increases the quantity demanded for a second reason. What if you take home $36 a week from a Saturday job, and your money income is $36 per week. Your *money income* is simply the number of dollars you receive per period, in this case $36 per week. Suppose you spend all your income on pizza, buying four a week at $9 each. What if the price drops to $6? At that price you can now afford six pizzas a week.

Your money income remains at $36 per week, but the decrease in the price has increased your *real income*—that is, your income measured in terms of how many goods and services it can buy. The price reduction, other things constant, increases the purchasing power of your income, thereby increasing your *ability* to buy pizza and, indirectly, other goods. The quantity of pizza you demand likely will increase because of this *income effect of a price change*. You may not increase your quantity demanded to six pizzas, but you can now afford six. If you purchase five pizzas a week when the price drops to $6, you would have $6 left to buy other goods.

Thus, the income effect of a lower price increases your real income and

thereby increases your *ability* to purchase pizza and other goods. Because of the income effect of a price decrease, other things constant, consumers typically increase their quantity demanded as the price decreases. Conversely, an increase in the price of pizza, other things constant, reduces real income, thereby reducing the ability to purchase pizza. Because of the income effect of a price increase, consumers typically reduce their quantity demanded as the price increases.

Diminishing Marginal Utility

After a long day of school, studies, and sports, you are starved, and so you visit a local pizzeria. That first slice tastes great and puts a serious dent in your hunger. The second is not quite as good as the first. A third is just fair. You don't even consider a fourth slice. The satisfaction you derive from an additional unit of a product is called your **marginal utility**. For example, the additional satisfaction you get from a second slice of pizza is your marginal utility of that slice.

The marginal utility you derive from each additional slice of pizza declines as your consumption increases. Your experience with pizza reflects the **law of diminishing marginal utility**. This law states that the more of a good an individual consumes per period, other things constant, the smaller the marginal utility of each additional unit consumed.

Diminishing marginal utility is a feature of all consumption. A second foot-long submarine sandwich at one meal would probably yield little or no marginal utility. You might still enjoy a second movie on Friday night, but a third one is probably too much to take.

Consumers make purchases to increase their satisfaction, or utility. In deciding what to buy, people make rough estimates about the marginal utility, or marginal benefit, they expect from the good or service. Based on this marginal benefit, people then decide how much they are willing and able to pay. Because of diminishing marginal

Ask the Xpert!

econxtra.swlearning.com

Why do consumers buy less of an item when its price rises?

marginal utility

The change in total utility resulting in a one-unit change in consumption of a good

law of diminishing marginal utility

The more of a good a person consumes per period, the smaller the increase in total utility from consuming one more unit, other things constant

NET Bookmark

For an example of pricing that uses the law of diminishing marginal utility, visit the Universal Studios Orlando web site. Access this web site through econxtra.swlearning.com. Click on "Tickets and Vacations." Which offer or offers demonstrate the theme park's understanding of the law of diminishing marginal utility? Explain your answer.

econxtra.swlearning.com

increase consumption as long as the marginal benefit you expect from another slice exceeds the price. You stop buying more when your expected marginal benefit is less than the price. Simply put, you aren't willing to pay $2 for something that's worth less to you.

What if the price of pizza drops from $2 to $1 a slice? You buy more if the marginal benefit of another slice exceeds $1. *The law of diminishing marginal utility helps explain why people buy more when the price decreases.*

Diminishing marginal utility has wide applications. Restaurants depend on the law of diminishing marginal utility when they offer all-you-can-eat specials—and no doggie bags. The deal is all you can eat now, not all you can eat now and for as long as the doggie bag holds out.

After a long winter, that first warm day of spring is something special and is the cause of "spring fever." The fever is cured by many warm days like the first. By the time August rolls around, most people get much less marginal utility from yet another warm day.

utility, you would not be willing to pay as much for a second slice of pizza as for the first. This is why it takes a decrease in price for you to increase your quantity demanded.

Suppose pizza sells for $2 a slice. How many slices will you buy? You will

How does the law of diminishing marginal utility apply to pizza consumption?

For some goods, the drop in marginal utility after the first unit is dramatic. For example, a second copy of the same daily newspaper would likely provide you with no marginal utility. In fact, the design of newspaper vending machines relies on the fact that you will not want to take more than one.

More generally, the expressions "Been there, done that" and "Same old, same old" convey the idea that, for many activities, things start to get old after the first time. Your marginal utility, or marginal benefit, declines.

CHECKPOINT
Explain the law of demand in your own words.

TEAM WORK

In small groups, brainstorm a list of products that most members of the group consume in a typical week. Then, working on your own, apply the law of diminishing marginal utility to each item. How many units of each item would you consume before the marginal benefit is less than the price of each unit? Compare your answers with those of other group members.

Demand Schedule and Demand Curve

Demand can be expressed as a *demand schedule* and as a *demand curve.* Panel (a) of Figure 4.1 shows a hypothetical demand schedule for pizza. When you

describe demand, you must specify the units being measured and the period considered. In this example, the price is for a 12-inch regular pizza and the period is a week. The schedule lists possible prices, along with the quantity demanded at each price.

At a price of $15, for example, consumers demand 8 million pizzas per week. As you can see, the lower the price the greater the quantity demanded, other things constant. If the

The Graphing Workshop
econxtra.swlearning.com

Demand Schedule and Demand Curve for Pizza

Figure 4.1

Market demand curve *D* shows the quantity of pizza demanded, at various prices, by all consumers.

(a) Demand schedule

	Price per Pizza	Quantity Demanded per Week (millions)
a	$15	8
b	12	14
c	9	20
d	6	26
e	3	32

(b) Demand curve

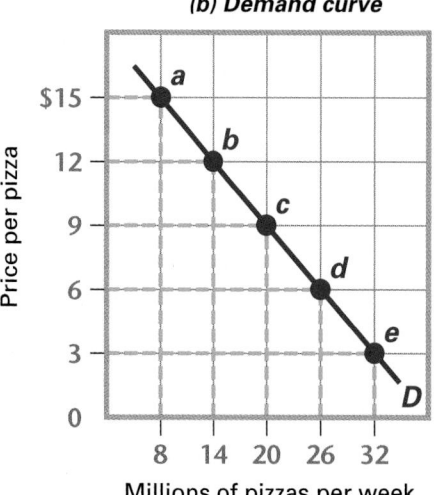

demand curve

A curve or line showing the quantities of a particular good demanded at various prices during a given time period, other things constant

quantity demanded

The amount demanded at a particular price

price drops as low as $3, consumers demand 32 million per week. As the price falls, consumers substitute pizza for other goods. As the price falls, the real income of consumers increases, causing them to increase the quantity of pizza they demand. As pizza consumption increases, the marginal utility of pizza declines, so quantity demanded will increase only if the price falls.

The *demand schedule* in panel (a) of Figure 4.1 appears as a **demand curve** in panel (b), with price on the vertical axis and the quantity demanded per week on the horizontal axis. Each combination of price and quantity listed in the demand schedule in the left panel becomes a point in the right panel. Point *a*, for example, indicates that if the price is $15, consumers demand 8 million pizzas per week. These points connect to form the demand curve for

pizza, labeled *D*. Note that some demand curves are straight lines and some are curved lines, but all of them are called demand *curves.*

The demand curve slopes downward, reflecting the *law of demand*—that is, price and quantity demanded are inversely, or negatively, related, other things constant. Several things are assumed to remain constant along the demand curve, including the prices of other goods. Thus, along the demand curve for pizza, the price of pizza changes *relative to the prices of other goods.* The demand curve shows the effect of a change in the *relative price* of pizza—that is, relative to other prices, which do not change.

Demand Versus Quantity Demanded

Be sure to distinguish between *demand* and *quantity demanded*. An individual point on the demand curve shows the **quantity demanded** at a particular price. For example, point *b* on the demand curve in Figure 4.1 indicates that 14 million pizzas are demanded when the price is $12. The *demand* for pizza is not a specific quantity, but the *entire relation* between price and quantity

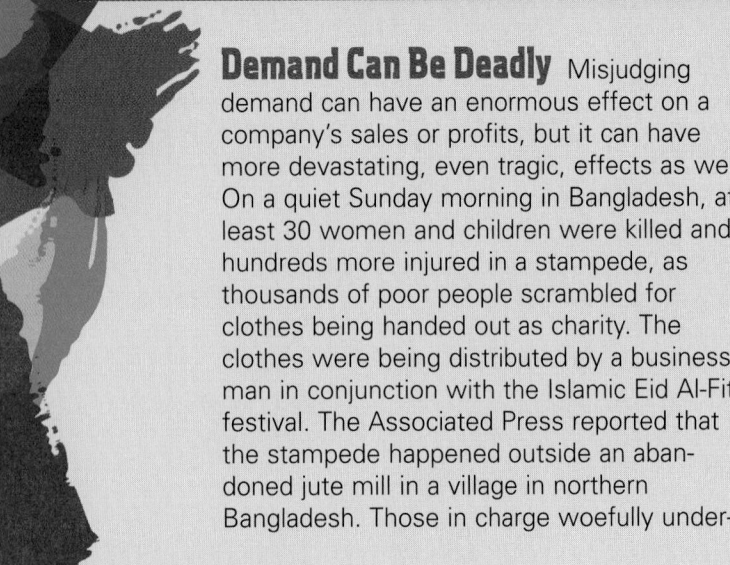

Ethics in Action

Demand Can Be Deadly Misjudging demand can have an enormous effect on a company's sales or profits, but it can have more devastating, even tragic, effects as well. On a quiet Sunday morning in Bangladesh, at least 30 women and children were killed and hundreds more injured in a stampede, as thousands of poor people scrambled for clothes being handed out as charity. The clothes were being distributed by a businessman in conjunction with the Islamic Eid Al-Fitr festival. The Associated Press reported that the stampede happened outside an abandoned jute mill in a village in northern Bangladesh. Those in charge woefully under-estimated the response to the news of the giveaway—they failed to predict what the demand for the clothing would be at a price of $0. Consequently, they were totally unprepared for the more than 10,000 people who showed up to get the free clothes. Two men in charge of distributing the clothes were arrested for possible negligence.

Think Critically

Analyze this situation. Do you think the two men, attempting to be charitable, should be punished for underestimating the demand and not preparing for the crowds? Why or why not?

demanded. This relation is represented by the demand schedule or the demand curve. To recap, quantity demanded is represented by one point on the demand curve or schedule, whereas demand is represented by the entire demand curve or schedule.

Individual Demand and Market Demand

It is useful to distinguish between **individual demand**, which is the demand of an individual consumer, and **market demand**, which sums the individual demands of all consumers in the market. *The market demand curve shows the total quantity demanded per period by all consumers at various prices.*

In most markets, there are many consumers, sometimes millions. To give you some feel for how individual demand curves sum to the market demand curve, assume that there are only three consumers in the market for pizza: Hector, Brianna, and Chris.

Figure 4.2 shows how three individual demand curves are added together to get the market demand curve. When the price of pizzas is $8, for example, Hector demands two pizzas a week, Brianna demands one, and Chris demands none. The market demand at a price of $8 is therefore three pizzas. At a price of $4, Hector demands three per week, Brianna two, and Chris one, for a market demand of six. Panel (d) sums across each individual's demand curve to arrive at the market demand curve.

The market demand curve is simply the sum of the individual demand curves for all consumers in the market. Unless otherwise noted, this book will focus on market demand.

individual demand
The demand of an individual consumer

market demand
The sum of the individual demands of all consumers in the market

> ✓ **CHECKPOINT**
> What do a demand schedule and demand curve show?

 Main Idea

Role of Price in Market System: Market Demand for Pizzas Figure **4.2**

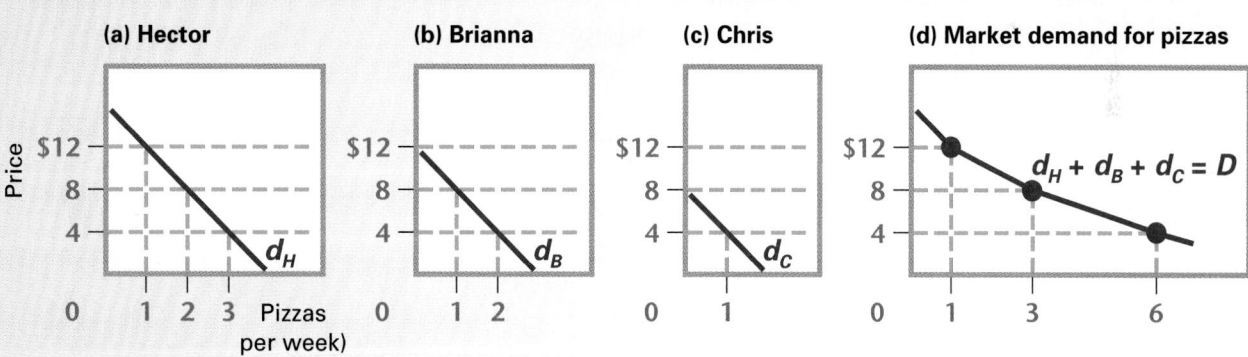

Prices send signals and provide incentives to buyers. When demand changes, market prices adjust, affecting buyers' incentives. For example, at a price of $8 per pizza, Hector demands 2 per week, Brianna demands 1, and Chris demands none. Market demand at a price of $8 is 2 + 1 + 0 = 3 pizzas per week. At a lower price of $4, Hector demands 3, Brianna demands 2, and Chris demands 1. Market demand at a price of $4 is 6 pizzas. The market demand curve D is the horizontal sum of individual demand curves d_H, d_B, and d_C.

Key Concepts

1. Many students would like to own an expensive sports car. Is this considered demand? Why or why not?

2. Why would demand for one fast food restaurant's hamburgers grow if the price of the hamburgers at the fast food restaurant across the street increased by $0.50?

3. How would the *income effect of a price change* be demonstrated by a $10 reduction in the price of tickets to a concert that resulted in a sell-out crowd?

4. Joe is willing to pay $1.50 for one taco after basketball practice but chooses not to purchase a second taco for the same price. How does this illustrate the *law of diminishing marginal utility*?

5. On Saturday nights, lots of people attend movies at the State Theater. The number who attend depends at least in part on the price of tickets. At the current price of $8 per ticket, an average of 285 tickets are sold each Saturday night. What is the *demand* and what is the *quantity demanded* in this example?

6. What is the market demand per day for lunches in the cafeteria at your school?

Graphing Exercise

7. The owners of a local shoe store surveyed their customers to determine how many pairs of running shoes they would buy each month at different prices. The results of the survey appear in the demand schedule below. Use these data to construct a demand curve for running shoes. Explain how your graph demonstrates the law of diminishing marginal utility.

Demand for Running Shoes

Price	Quantity Demanded
$70	40
$60	50
$50	60
$40	70
$30	80

Think Critically

8. **Marketing** Nancy is the sales manager of the shoe store. The owner has told her that she must set a price that allows the store to sell at least 50 pairs of running shoes next month. What price should she set? If another local store has a big sale and lowers its price for running shoes by 25 percent, will Nancy's employer reach the sales goal? Why or why not?

9. **History** When television sets first became available to consumers in the late 1940s, many people wanted one. Still, very few sets were sold at first. Explain why people's desire to own televisions did not result in a great demand for this product.

Objectives

> Compute the elasticity of demand, and explain its relevance.

> Discuss the factors that influence elasticity of demand.

Overview

Knowing the law of demand is useful, but a demand curve can provide even more information. It can tell how sensitive quantity demanded is to a change in price. For example, a fast-food restaurant would like to know what will happen to its total revenue if it introduces a dollar menu. The law of demand indicates that a lower price increases quantity demanded, but by how much? A firm's success or failure depends on how much it knows about the demand for its product. This section measures how sensitive quantity demanded is to a change in price.

Key Terms

elasticity of demand

total revenue

[In the News]

● Super Bowl of Avocados

Super Bowl Sunday is the biggest single day of avocado consumption in the United States, thanks to the serving up of bowls and bowls of the zesty green dip known as guacamole. More than 40 million pounds of avocados are smashed, mashed, whipped, and eaten with blue and white corn chips, flour tortillas, tacos, and chunks of bread during Super Bowl festivities, according to the California Avocado Commission. California growers sold a record 400 million pounds of avocados for a very profitable $398 million (nearly a dollar a pound) in the 2001–2002 season. California is home to 86 percent of the nation's crop, and 46 percent of the state's avocados come from San Diego County. The more than 6,000 avocado growers see a huge potential for growth in the market. Until fairly recently, the avocado, originally from southern Mexico, was either unknown or considered odd and exotic in most of the United States. But the expanding popularity of California cuisine and the spread of Hispanic populations over the years have opened a host of new markets for avocado growers. Today only 18 percent of the population, mainly in the Southwest, eat nearly half of all avocados sold in the United States. Avocados are consumed in nearly 45 percent of U.S. homes, but in the West the portion is 80 percent.

Think About It

What if in the following season the growers reduce the price of avocados from approximately $1 a pound to 90 cents a pound? Based on the expanding market predictions, would the total revenue probably be less than $398 million, remain the same, or be more than $398 million? Explain your answer.

Computing the Elasticity of Demand

Figure 4.3 shows the downward sloping demand curve for pizza developed earlier. As you can see, if the price of pizzas falls from $12 to $9, the quantity demanded increases from 14 million to 20 million. Is such a response in quantity demanded a little or a lot? The demand elasticity measures consumer responsiveness to the price change. *Elasticity* is another word for *responsiveness*. Specifically, the **elasticity of demand** measures the percentage change in quantity demanded divided by the percentage change in price, or

Elasticity of demand =

$$\frac{\text{Percentage change in}}{\text{Percentage change in price}}$$

What's the demand elasticity when the price of pizza falls from $12 to $9? The percentage increase in quantity demanded is the change in quantity demanded, 6 million, divided by 14 million. So, quantity demanded increases by 43 percent. The percentage change in price is the price change of $3 divided by $12, which is 25 percent.

The elasticity of demand is the percentage increase in quantity demanded, 43 percent, divided by the percentage decrease in price, 25 percent, which equals 1.7.

Elasticity Values

Does an elasticity of 1.7 indicate that consumers are sensitive to the price change? To offer some perspective, economists sort elasticity into three general categories. If the percentage change in quantity demanded exceeds the percentage change in price, the resulting elasticity exceeds 1.0. Such a demand is said to be *elastic*, meaning that a percentage change in price will result in a larger percentage change in the quantity demanded. Thus quantity demanded is considered relatively *responsive* to a change in price. The demand for pizza is elastic when the price falls from $12 to $9.

If the percentage change in quantity demanded just equals the percentage change in price, the resulting elasticity is 1.0, and this demand is called *unit-elastic*. Finally, if the percentage change in quantity demanded is less than the percentage change in price, the resulting

The Demand for Pizza

Figure 4.3

If the price falls from $12 to $9, the quantity of pizza demanded increases from 14 million to 20 million per week.

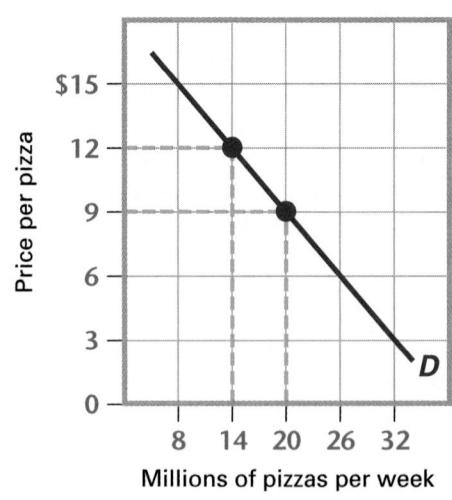

---

elasticity of demand

Measures how responsive quantity demanded is to a price change; the percentage change in quantity demanded divided by the percentage change in price

CHAPTER 4 Demand

elasticity lies between 0 and 1.0, and this demand is said to be *inelastic*.

In summary, *demand is elastic if greater than 1.0, unit elastic if equal to 1.0, and inelastic if between 0 and 1.0.* Also, the measure of the price elasticity of demand usually is different at different points on a demand curve. Demand is almost always more elastic at higher prices and less elastic at lower prices. This is particularly true when the demand curve is a straight line that slopes down from left to right.

Elasticity expresses a relationship between two amounts: the percentage change in price and the resulting percentage change in quantity demanded. Because the focus is on the percentage change, you need not be concerned with how output or price is measured. For example, suppose the good in question is apples. It makes no difference in the elasticity formula whether you measure apples in pounds, bushels, or even tons. All that matters is the percentage change in quantity demanded. Nor does it matter whether you measure price in U.S. dollars, Mexican pesos, French francs, or Zambian kwacha. All that matters is the percentage change in price.

Elasticity and Total Revenue

Knowledge of elasticity is especially valuable to producers, because it indicates the effect a price change will have on how much consumers spend on this product. **Total revenue** is price multiplied by the quantity demanded at that price. What happens to total revenue when price decreases? A lower price means producers are paid less for each unit sold, which tends to decrease total revenue. However, according to the law of demand, a lower price increases quantity demanded, which tends to increase total revenue.

The impact of a lower price on total revenue can be estimated using the product's price elasticity of demand. When the elasticity is greater than 1.0, or *elastic,* reducing the price by 5 percent will cause sales to grow by more than 5 percent. Thus the total

revenue will increase. When the elasticity is equal to 1.0, or *unit elastic,* reducing the price by 5 percent will cause sales to grow by 5 percent. In this

total revenue
Price multiplied by the quantity demanded at that price

SPAN THE GLOBE

We Ate All the Big Fish

"Fisherman used to go out and catch these phenomenally big fish," said a fisheries biologist in Nova Scotia. "But they cannot find them anymore. They're not there. We ate them." He adds that about 90 percent of big fish—such as giant tuna, swordfish, and Chilean sea bass—are gone from the world's oceans. In fact, at a UN summit meeting in 2002, 192 nations signed a declaration to try to restore fish to healthy levels by 2015. Chilean sea bass is a good example of what happened to the big fish. Eight to ten years ago, very few people had heard of this fish. There wasn't much demand, and it was selling at $3 or $4 a pound. After several years of word-of-mouth and magazine advertising, and strong recommendations from food critics and TV chefs, Chilean sea bass became "the hot new fish." All the publicity increased the demand, and the low price increased the quantity demanded. Suddenly, Chilean sea bass was featured on thousands of restaurant menus and sold in every supermarket. Fishermen couldn't catch enough sea bass to keep up with the rising demand, though they tried. They were overfishing and not giving the fish enough time to replenish their populations. Today, Chilean sea bass sells for $18 to $20 a pound, and is on the menu of only upscale, "trendy" restaurants. The once inexpensive, great-tasting fish is now gone from most supermarkets. At $20 per pound, the quantity demanded has decreased considerably. Unfortunately, the species also is nearly gone from our oceans.

Think Critically

Suppose that at a price of $3 a pound, the quantity of Chilean sea bass demanded is 500,000 pounds, and at a price of $18 a pound, the quantity demanded is 100,000 pounds. At these prices and quantities, is the demand elastic, unit elastic, or inelastic?

case the total revenue will remain unchanged. When the elasticity is less than 1.0, or *inelastic,* reducing the price by 5 percent will cause the sales to grow, but by less than 5 percent. So, total revenue will fall.

Knowing a product's elasticity can help businesses when they set their prices. If demand is inelastic, producers will never willingly cut the price since doing so would reduce total revenue. The percentage increase in quantity demanded would be less than the percentage decrease in price. Why cut the price if selling more reduces total revenue?

CHECKPOINT
What does the elasticity of demand measure?

Determinants of Demand Elasticity

So far you have explored the link between elasticity of demand and what happens to total revenue when the price changes. However, you have not yet considered why elasticity differs for different goods. Several characteristics influence the elasticity of demand.

Availability of Substitutes

As noted earlier, your individual wants can be satisfied in a variety of ways. A rise in the price of pizza makes other foods relatively cheaper. If close substitutes are available, an increase in the price of pizza will prompt some consumers to switch to substitutes. But if nothing else satisfies like pizza, the quantity of pizza demanded will not decline as much. *The greater the availability of substitutes for a good and the more similar the substitutes are to the good in question, the greater that good's elasticity of demand.*

The number and similarity of substitutes depend on the definition of the good. *The more broadly a good is defined, the fewer substitutes there are and the less elastic the demand.* For example, everyone needs some sort of shoes, so the demand for shoes as a general category of product is quite inelastic. If the price of all shoes goes up 20 percent, most people will still buy shoes. If you consider one particular brand of shoes, however, the demand is sure to be elastic because there are many other brands of shoes you could buy instead. For example, if only one shoe manufacturer raises the price of its shoes by 20 percent, most consumers will substitute a different brand of shoes that have not increased in price.

Certain goods—many prescription drugs, for instance—have no close substitutes. The demand for such goods tends to be less elastic than for goods with close substitutes, such as Bayer aspirin. Much advertising is aimed at establishing in the consumer's mind the uniqueness of a particular product—an effort to convince consumers "to accept no substitutes."

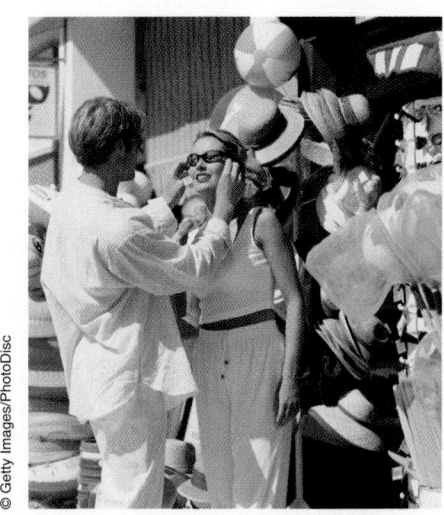

© Getty Images/PhotoDisc

Do you think demand for sunglasses is elastic or inelastic? Identify the determinant of demand that supports your answer.

Share of Consumer's Budget Spent on the Good

Recall that a higher price reduces quantity demanded in part because a higher price reduces the real spending power of consumer income. A demand curve reflects both the *willingness* and *ability* to purchase a good at alternative prices. Because spending on some goods represents a large share of the consumer's budget, a change in the price of such a good has a substantial impact on the amount consumers are *able* to purchase.

An increase in the price of housing, for example, reduces consumers' ability to purchase housing. The income effect of a higher price reduces the quantity demanded. In contrast, the income effect of an increase in the price of, say, paper towels is less significant because paper towels represent such a tiny share of any budget. *The more important the item is as a share of the consumer's budget, other things constant, the greater is the income effect of a change in price, so the more price elastic is the demand for the item.* This explains why the quantity of housing demanded is more responsive to a given percentage change in price than is the quantity of paper towels demanded.

A Matter of Time

Consumers can substitute lower-priced goods for higher-priced goods, but finding substitutes usually takes time. For example, between 1973 and 1974, the OPEC oil cartel raised the price of oil sharply. The result was a 45-percent increase in the price of gasoline, but the quantity demanded decreased only 8 percent. As more time passed, however, people purchased smaller cars and made greater use of public transportation. Because the price of oil used to generate electricity and to heat homes increased as well, people bought more energy-efficient appliances and insulated their homes better. As a result, the change in the amount of oil demanded was greater over time as consumers adjusted to the price hike.

The longer the adjustment period, the greater the consumers' ability to substitute relatively higher-priced products with lower-priced substitutes. Thus, the longer the period of adjustment, the more responsive the change in quantity demanded is to a given change in price.

Figure 4.4 demonstrates how demand for gasoline becomes more elastic over time. Given an initial price of $1.00 a gallon, let D_w be the demand curve one week after a price change; D_m, one

CNN video

Smokers and the Bandits

econxtra.swlearning.com

© Getty Images/PhotoDisc

© Getty Images/PhotoDisc

Compare the income effect of an increase in the price of a car to the income effect of an increase in the price of a grocery store item. For which product is demand more price elastic?

D_w is the demand curve one week after a price increase from $1.00 to $1.25. Along this curve, quantity demanded per day falls from 100 to 95 million gallons. One month after the price increase, quantity demanded has fallen to 75 million gallons along D_m. One year after the price increase, quantity demanded has fallen to 50 million gallons along D_y. At any given price, D_y is more elastic than D_m, which is more elastic than D_w.

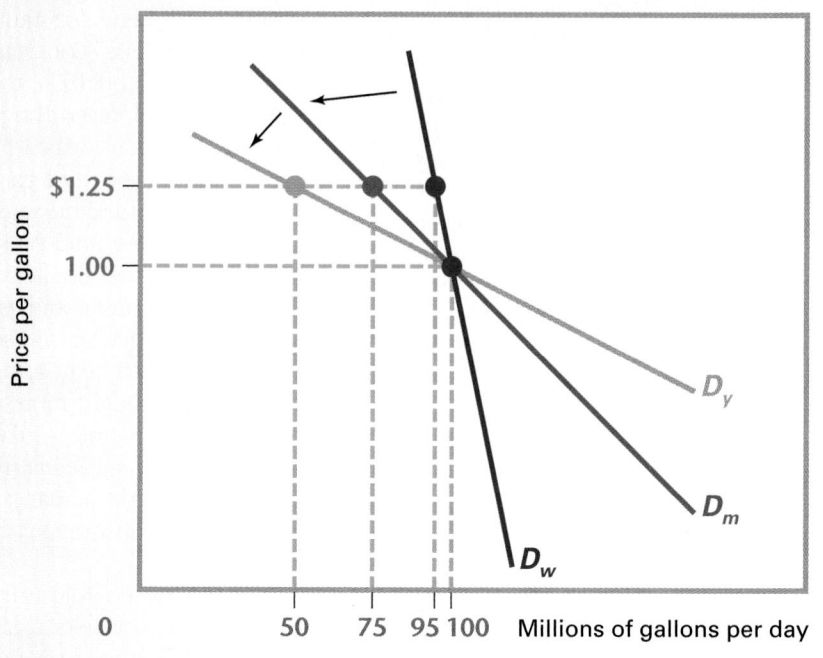

month after; and D_y, one year after. Suppose the price increases to $1.25. The more time consumers have to respond to the price increase, the greater the reduction in quantity demanded. The demand curve D_w shows that one week after the price increase, the quantity demanded has not declined much—in this case, from 100 to 95 million gallons per day. The demand curve D_m indicates a reduction to 75 million gallons per day after one month, and demand curve D_y shows a reduction to 50 million gallons per day after one year.

Some Elasticity Estimates

Let's look at some estimates of the elasticity of demand for particular goods and services. As noted earlier, the substitution of lower-priced goods for a good whose price has just increased often takes time. Thus, when estimating elasticity, economists often distinguish between a period during which consumers have little time to adjust—call it the short run—and a period during which consumers can more fully adjust to a price change—call it the long run. Figure 4.5 provides some short-run and long-run elasticity estimates for selected products.

The elasticity of demand is greater in the long run because consumers have more time to adjust. For example, if the price of electricity rose today, consumers in the short run might cut back a bit on their use of electrical appliances, and those in homes with electric heat might lower the thermostat in winter. Over time, however, consumers would switch to more energy-efficient appliances and might convert from electric heat to oil or natural gas. So the demand for electricity is more elastic in the long run than in the short run, as noted in Figure 4.5. In fact, in every instance where estimates for both the short run and the long run are available, the long run is more elastic than the short run.

When estimating elasticity, economists distinguish between the short run (a period during which consumers have little time to adjust) and the long run (a period during which consumers can more fully adjust to a price change). The elasticity of demand is greater in the long run because consumers have more time to adjust.

Product	Short Run	Long Run
Electricity (residential)	0.1	1.9
Air travel	0.1	2.4
Medical care and hospitalization	0.3	0.9
Gasoline	0.4	1.5
Movies	0.9	3.7
Natural gas (residential)	1.4	2.1

CHECKPOINT
What are the determinants of demand elasticity?

An Application: Teenage Smoking

As the U.S. Surgeon General warns on each pack of cigarettes, smoking cigarettes can be hazardous to your health. Researchers estimate that smoking causes more than 400,000 deaths a year in the United States—nearly 10 times the fatalities from all traffic accidents.

One way to reduce smoking is to raise the price of cigarettes through higher cigarette taxes. Economists estimate the demand elasticity for cigarettes among teenage smokers to be about 1.3, so a 10 percent increase in the price of cigarettes would reduce smoking by 13 percent. Among adult smokers, the estimated elasticity is only 0.4, or only about one-third that of teenagers.

Why are teenagers more sensitive to price changes than adults? First, recall that one of the factors affecting the elasticity of demand is the importance of the item in the consumer's budget. The share of income that a teenage smoker spends on cigarettes usually exceeds the share for adult smokers. Second, peer pressure is more influential in a young

person's decision to smoke than in an adult's decision to continue smoking. (If anything, adults face peer pressure not to smoke.) The effects of a higher price get multiplied among young smokers because a higher price reduces smoking by peers. With fewer peers smoking, there is less pressure to smoke. And third, because smoking is addictive, young people who are not yet hooked are more sensitive to price increases than are adult smokers, who are already hooked.

NETBookmark

For more information about the dangers of smoking, The Campaign for Tobacco Free Kids maintains a web site with a page devoted to articles on the economics of tobacco policy. Access this site through econxtra.swlearning.com. Click on Tobacco Facts. According to this article, is the total number of smokers in the world increasing or decreasing? The article states that between 80,000 and 100,000 young people around the world become addicted to tobacco every day. If this trend continues, how many children alive today will die from tobacco-related disease?

econxtra.swlearning.com

econxtra.swlearning.com

Key Concepts

1. What would a shoe store need to do to calculate the price elasticity of demand for the running shoes it sells if it decides to raise its prices by 10 percent?

2. If the shoe store found that the measure of elasticity for its running shoes is 1.3, is there elastic, unit elastic, or inelastic demand for this product at the current price?

3. If the shoe store increases its price for running shoes by 10 percent, what would happen to the store's total revenue from these products?

4. Why should you expect the demand for a particular brand of cake mix to be elastic?

Graphing Exercise

5. Consider this graph for running shoes. Note that if the store's manager increases the price for running shoes from $60 to $70 (16.7%), the store's sales would fall from 50 to 40 pairs per month (20.0%). What is the elasticity of demand? Is this price elasticity of demand elastic, unit elastic, or inelastic? Will the store's total revenue increase, decrease, or remain unchanged?

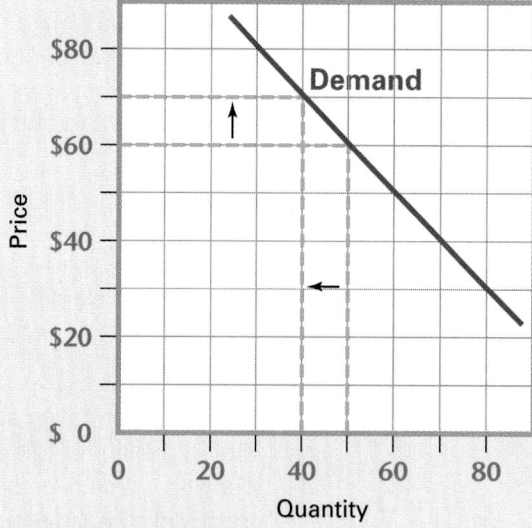

Demand Curve for Running Shoes

Think Critically

6. **Sociology** The elasticity of demand for some products is affected by the personal values of possible customers. Consider people who practice the Hindu faith. They believe it is wrong to eat meat. In Hindu communities, the price elasticity of demand for meat products is 0.0, or completely inelastic—consumers won't buy meat no matter what happens to its price. Describe several other situations where other factors are more important to the buying decision than price.

7. **Entrepreneurship** If there are 10 bakeries in a small city, why might the price elasticity of demand for the products they supply be high? Why might this not be a good location for you to open another bakery?

movers & shakers

Julie Azuma *President, Different Roads to Learning*

Finding appropriate toys for her autistic daughter was always a challenge for Julie Azuma. In 1995 she met that challenge by starting a business selling educational toys for learning disabled children via the Internet. Her first obstacle—she was not computer literate. With determination and courage, Azuma met the obstacle head-on, and within months her web site was established. Her company, Different Roads to Learning, received its first orders by December of that year.

Selling product via the Internet meant Azuma didn't need a storefront. This was something she originally wanted but quickly learned she couldn't afford. Selling via the Internet had its advantages, however. Azuma was able to reach potential customers throughout the world, and today 10 percent of her customers are from Canada, the United Kingdom, and Australia.

From the start, Different Roads to Learning's web site included a complete line of products. "But as soon as the site went up, we received requests for a printed catalog, too." Azuma responded by printing 3,000 catalogs for customers who requested them. It was a good decision. Although catalog requests typically came from parents, "we found that parents were bringing the catalog to their child's school, asking their school districts to purchase many of the items." That resulted in larger orders for more products. Today Azuma prints 50,000 to 100,000 catalogs a year.

Azuma prides herself on serving her customers the best she can. She's quick to advise parents on what materials may be appropriate for their child, as well as what toys may not be a good fit. "We try to ship all of our orders on the day we receive them if at all possible," she explains. "Parents of autistic children need to have their materials as soon as possible."

In response to the increased demand for advice on helping an autistic child to learn, in 1999 Azuma started a publishing company, DRL Books, Inc. Her first book, a comprehensive handbook for parents of autistic children, sold more than she projected. She began to look for more books that met her high standards of assisting parents and teachers. By 2002, the company had published eight books with sales of $175,000. While the first books she published were extremely popular, not every book has met Azuma's expectations. "I thought that all of our books would have the same appeal, but there are a lot of autism books available now."

In 1996, Different Roads to Learning's first year in business, gross sales were $8,000. By 2000, sales exceeded expenses and the company became profitable. Gross sales in 2002 exceeded $1,000,000, and in 2003 sales were expected to increase even more. In addition to increasing sales, Azuma also has learned how to make her business more profitable. Azuma's efforts to help parents of autistic children have earned her New York State's prestigious Martin Luther King Award for community service.

SOURCE READING

Although the first books published by DRL Books, Inc. exceeded sales goals, the books she published later were not as popular. Azuma said, "I thought that all of our books would have the same appeal, but there are a lot of autism books available now." What influenced the elasticity of demand for the company's later books?

ENTREPRENEURS IN ACTION

If Azuma's first book sold for $22 and 875 copies were sold, what was her total revenue? What would likely happen to Azuma's total revenue if she decreased the price of the book to $18? If demand is inelastic, would Azuma's decision to lower the price be a good one? Why or why not?

Objectives

> Identify the determinants of demand, and explain how a change in each will affect the demand curve.

> Distinguish between the money price of a good and the time price of a good.

Overview

So far the discussion of demand has been limited to the relationship between price and quantity demanded. That is, the focus has been on movement along a particular demand curve. A demand curve isolates the relation between the price of a good and the quantity demanded when other factors that could affect demand remain unchanged. What are these other determinants of demand, and how would changes in them affect demand?

Key Terms

tastes

movement along a given demand curve

shift of a demand curve

[In the News]

● Will Business-Fare Cuts Bring Business Flyers Back?

Major airlines have experienced a huge drop in demand that will result in roughly $4 billion in losses in a year. This loss has airlines searching for ways to generate more revenue. One way being tested is to offer business travelers lower fares. This contradicts the airlines' long-held belief that business travelers would pay whatever they had to for their necessary business trips. That belief may have been true when the economy was soaring and planes were full on the popular routes. However, it's a much harder argument in light of tighter travel budgets and lots of empty seats offering travelers more choices. Business travelers have been staying at home or in the office, buying well in advance of their trip to get the discounts, or going to "no-frills" discount airlines. The airlines have been cutting back their sky-high business-travel fares in selected markets to see if lower fares will bring these flyers back. The early test results are encouraging some carriers to believe that they can in fact cut business fares and maintain or even increase their revenues. Delta Air Lines has cut business fares by about 21 percent in more than 400 small markets with no announcement. The company was rewarded with a double-digit increase in revenue. Continental Airlines also has been quietly conducting tests of lower business fares in a number of select markets with "mixed but not discouraging" results, according to Continental officials.

Think About It

Will the airlines' tests cause a movement along the demand curve or a shift in the demand curve? Explain.

Changes That Can Shift the Demand Curve

A demand curve isolates the relation between price and quantity when other factors that could affect demand are assumed constant. These other factors, often referred to as *determinants of demand,* include

1. Consumer income

2. The prices of related goods

3. The number and composition of consumers

4. Consumer expectations

5. Consumer tastes

How does a change in each affect demand?

Changes in Consumer Income

Figure 4.6 shows the market demand curve *D* for pizza. Consumers' money income is assumed to remain constant along a demand curve. Suppose money income increases. Some consumers will then be willing and able to buy more pizza at each price, so market demand increases. The demand curve shifts to the right from *D* to *D'*. For example, at a price of $12, the amount of pizza demanded increases from 14 million to 20 million per week, as indicated by the movement from point *b* on demand curve *D* to point *f* on demand curve *D'*. In short, *an increase in demand–that is, a rightward shift of the demand curve–means that consumers are more willing and able to buy pizza at each price.*

Normal Goods

Goods are classified into two broad categories, depending on how the demand for the good responds to changes in money income. The demand for a *normal good* increases as money income increases. Because pizza is a normal good, the demand curve for pizza shifts rightward when consumer income increases. Most goods are normal.

Inferior Goods

In contrast, the demand for an *inferior good* actually decreases as money income increases. Examples of inferior

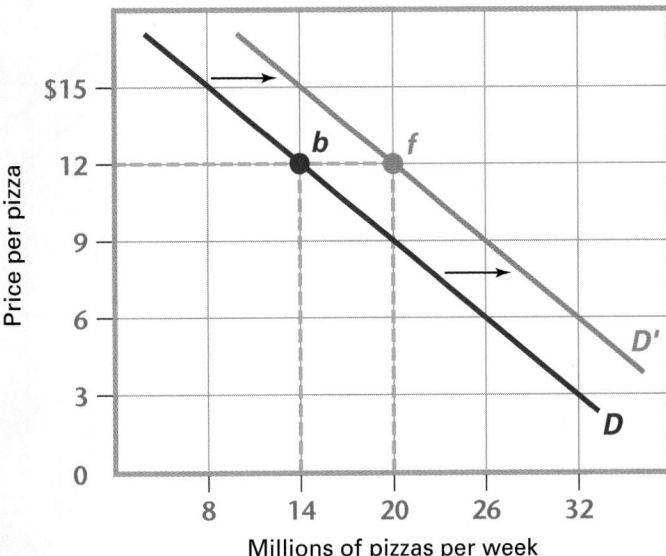

The Graphing Workshop
econxtra.swlearning.com

An Increase in the Market Demand for Pizza

Figure 4.6

An increase in the demand for pizza is reflected by a rightward shift of the demand curve. After the increase in demand, the quantity of pizza demanded at a price of $12 increases from 14 million (point *b*) to 20 million (point *f*).

goods include bologna sandwiches, used furniture, used clothing, trips to the Laundromat, and bus rides. As money income increases, consumers switch from consuming these inferior goods to consuming normal goods— like roast beef sandwiches, new furniture, new clothing, a washer and dryer, and automobile or plane rides.

Changes in the Prices of Related Goods

As you've seen, the prices of other goods are assumed to remain constant along a given demand curve. Now you are ready to consider the impact of changes in the prices of other goods.

Substitutes

Products that can be used in place of each other are called substitutes. Consumers choose among substitutes partly on the basis of their relative prices. For example, pizza and tacos are substitutes, though not perfect ones. Yet an increase in the price of tacos, other things constant, reduces the quantity of tacos demanded along a given taco demand curve and shifts the demand curve for pizza right, as shown in

Figure 4.6. Two goods are *substitutes* if an increase in the price of one shifts the demand for the other rightward and, conversely, if a decrease in the price of one shifts demand for the other leftward.

A decrease in the price of tacos would reduce the demand for pizza, as shown in Figure 4.7, where the demand curve for pizza shifts to the left from *D* to *D''*. As a result, consumers are less willing and able to buy pizza at every price. For example, at a price of $12, the amount demanded decreases from 14 million to 10 million per week, as indicated by the movement from point *b* on demand curve *D* to point *j* on demand curve *D''*.

Complements

Certain goods are often used in combination. Pizza and soft drinks, milk and cookies, computer hardware and software, and airline tickets and rental cars are complements. When two goods are complements, a decrease in the price of one shifts the demand for the other rightward. For example, a decrease in the price of soft drinks shifts the demand curve for pizza rightward.

A Decrease in the Market Demand for Pizza

Figure 4.7

A decrease in the demand for pizza is reflected by a leftward shift of the demand curve. After the decrease in demand, the quantity of pizza demanded at a price of $12 decreases from 14 million (point *b*) to 10 million (point *j*).

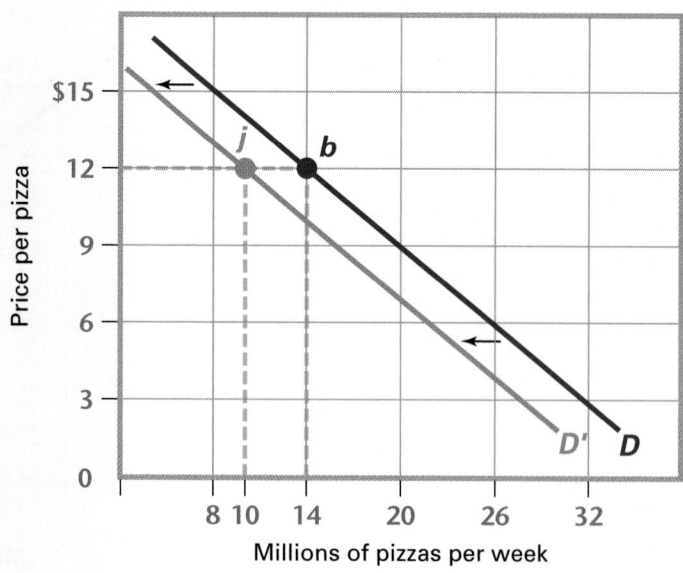

Changes in the Size or Composition of the Population

As mentioned earlier, the market demand curve is the sum of the individual demand curves of all consumers in the market. If the population grows, the number of consumers in the market increases. For example, if the population grows, the demand curve for pizza will shift rightward. Even if the total population remains unchanged, demand could shift as a result of a change in the composition of the population. For example, a bulge in the teenage population could shift pizza demand rightward. A baby boom would shift rightward the demand for car seats and baby food.

Changes in Consumer Expectations

Another factor assumed to be constant along a given demand curve is consumer expectations about factors that influence demand, such as the future income and the future price of the good. A change in

Investigate Your Local Economy

Examine changes or trends in the composition of the population of your city or town. What products or categories of products might these changes affect?

consumer expectations can shift the demand curve. For example, you may spend a little more after lining up a summer job, even before summer arrives.

Changes in price expectations also can shift demand. For example, if you expect pizza prices to jump next week, you may buy an extra one now for the freezer, thereby shifting the demand for pizza rightward. Or if consumers come to believe that home prices will climb

E-CONOMICS

Technology Is a Girl's Best Friend

Banners flying the headline "Technology Is a Girl's Best Friend" greeted attendees to the 2003 International Consumer Electronics Show (CES) in Las Vegas. The show included a product showcase devoted specifically to female-friendly products. Also featured at the annual show was a series of conferences and events concerned with understanding and promoting women's increased role in the consumer electronics world. A few years earlier, about 70 percent to 80 percent of the show's attendees were men. These days, however, the attendance ratio is down to about 60–40 in favor of men. In 2003, women's spending accounted for about $55 billion of the projected $100 billion U.S. consumer electronics market, according to a CES vice president. She also said that women initiate nearly 75 percent of such purchases on their own or with a spouse. Consumer electronics companies are realizing that female buyers are a demographic worthy of their attention. They also realize that young girls are more receptive to technology than older women, according to Ann Shoket of *Cosmo Girl* magazine. "This generation of girls is going to change everything," Shoket said. "They don't see technology as some sort of alien, strange thing they're afraid of."

Think Critically

Identify the determinant of demand this situation illustrates. Explain your answer.

next year, some will increase their demand for housing this year, shifting the demand for housing rightward.

Changes in Consumer Tastes

Do you like anchovies on a pizza? How about sauerkraut on a hot dog? Is music to your ears more likely to be rock, country, heavy metal, hip-hop, reggae, jazz, new age, or classical? Choices in food, music, clothing, reading, movies, TV shows—indeed, all consumer choices—are influenced by consumer tastes.

Tastes are your likes and dislikes as a consumer. What determines your tastes? Your desires for food when hungry and liquid when thirsty are largely biological. So is your preference for shelter, comfort, rest, personal safety, and a pleasant environment. Your family background shapes many of your tastes. Other influences include the surrounding culture and peer influence. Generally, economists claim no special expertise in understanding how tastes develop.

Economists recognize, however, that tastes are important in shaping demand. For example, although pizza is a popular food, some people just don't like it and others might be allergic to the cheese or tomatoes. Thus, some people like to eat pizza and others don't. A change in the tastes for a particular good shifts the demand curve. For example, a discovery that the combination of cheese and tomato sauce on pizza promotes overall health could affect consumer tastes, shifting the demand curve for pizza to the right.

But a change in tastes is difficult to isolate from other economic changes. That's why economists attribute a change in demand to a change in tastes only after ruling out other possible explanations.

Movement Along a Demand Curve Versus a Shift of the Curve

You should remember the distinction between a movement along a demand curve and a shift of a demand curve. A change in price, other things constant, causes a **movement along a demand curve**, changing the quantity demanded. A change in one of the determinants of demand other than price causes a **shift of a demand curve**, changing demand.

CHECKPOINT
What are the five determinants of demand, and how do changes in each shift the demand curve?

Extensions of Demand Analysis

Because consumption does not occur instantaneously, time plays an important role in demand analysis.

Role of Time in Demand

The cost of consumption has two components: the *money price* of the good and the *time price* of the good. Goods are demanded because of the benefits they provide. Thus, you are willing to pay more for medicine that works faster. Similarly, it is not the microwave oven, personal computer, or airline trip that you value but the services they provide. Other things constant, the good that provides the same benefit in less time is preferred. That's also why you are willing to pay more for ready-to-eat foods that you don't need to prepare yourself.

tastes
Consumer preferences; likes and dislikes in consumption; assumed to be constant along a given demand curve

movement along a given demand curve
Change in quantity demanded resulting from a change in the price of the good, other things constant

shift of a demand curve
Increase or decrease in demand resulting from a change in one of the determinants of demand other than the price of the good

NETBookmark

To learn more about the economics of consumption, read Jane Katz's "The Joy of Consumption: We Are What We Buy," in the Federal Reserve Bank of Boston's *Regional Review*. Access this article through econxtra.swlearning.com. What evidence does Katz cite about how the rising value of time has affected consumer spending patterns?

econxtra.swlearning.com

Your willingness to pay more for time-saving goods and services depends on the opportunity cost of your time. Differences in the value of time among consumers help explain differences in the consumption patterns observed in the economy. For example, a retired couple has more leisure time than a working couple. The retired couple may clip coupons and search the newspapers for bargains, sometimes going from store to store for particular grocery items on sale that week. The working couple usually will ignore the coupons and sales and will eat out more often and purchase more at convenience stores, where they are willing to pay extra for the convenience. The retired couple will be more inclined to drive across country on vacation, whereas the working couple will fly to a vacation destination.

The Cost of Waiting In Line

Just inside the gates at Disneyland, Disney World, and Universal Studios, visitors see signs posting the waiting times of each attraction and ride. At that point, the visitor already has paid the dollar cost of admission, so the marginal dollar cost of each ride and attraction is zero. The waiting times offer a menu of the marginal *time cost* of each ride or attraction. The opportunity cost of waiting in line is not enjoying other rides or attractions. Incidentally, people who are willing to pay up to $55 an hour at Disney World and $60 an hour at Disneyland (plus the price of admission) could until recently take VIP tours that bypass the lines.

Differences in the opportunity cost of time among consumers shape consumption patterns and add another dimension to demand analysis.

CHECKPOINT
What's the difference between the money price of a good and its time price?

Sharpen Your Life Skills

Draw Conclusions

Demand for many products can be affected by a single important event. In September 2002, for example, Hurricane Isadore plowed into the southern coast of Louisiana, leaving widespread destruction in its wake. Thousands of homes were destroyed along with many businesses, roads, and public buildings.

Consider how this disaster must have changed people's demand for goods and services in Louisiana. Divide the following businesses into two lists: one made up of firms that would have had increased demand for their products because of Isadore, the other of businesses that would have experienced reduced demand. Explain your placement of each business.

- building contractors
- swimming pool installers
- luxury hotels
- apartment buildings
- lumber yards
- amusement parks

Apply Your Skill

Imagine that the United States mobilizes its military forces to fight a war in a foreign country. It calls up 250,000 reserve soldiers and increases its purchases of military equipment. Many factories operate 24 hours a day to keep up with government orders. Describe several ways in which this would shift demand for products in the U.S. economy.

Key Concepts

1. What would happen to the demand curve for bus tickets if the price of gasoline increased to $5 per gallon? Which of the determinants of demand does this demonstrate?

2. What would happen to the demand curve for a particular brand of shampoo if a famous movie actress with beautiful hair announces that it is the best shampoo she has ever used? Which of the determinants of demand does this demonstrate?

3. What would happen to the demand curve for towels today if a large store advertises that it will have a 50 percent off sale on towels next week? Which of the determinants of demand does this demonstrate?

4. If the price of hot dogs increases by $.20 per pound when the price of substitute products remains the same, will the demand curve for hot dogs shift to the right, shift to the left, or stay in the same location? Explain your answer.

5. Why is the demand for "Quick Oats" that cook in 2.5 minutes greater than the demand for regular oats that take 5 minutes to prepare?

Graphing Exercise

6. To the right is the demand curve for running shoes at a local retailer. Make a copy of the demand curve. Draw the shift in demand on your copy that would result from each of the following events. Label each shift in the demand curve.

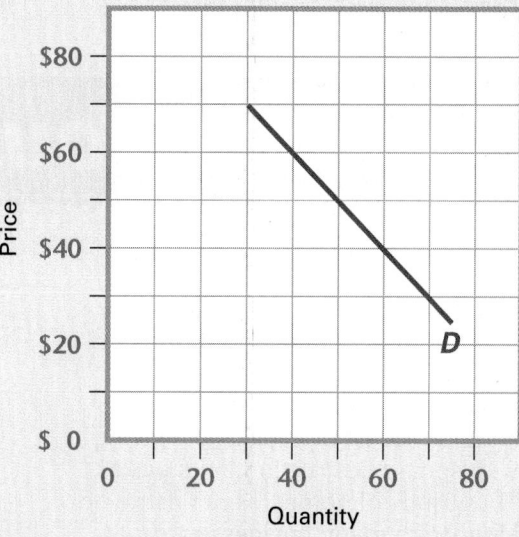
Demand Curve for Running Shoes

   a. Many people decide to buy new running shoes to run in a local marathon.

   b. Three months of almost uninterrupted rain keeps most people inside.

   c. Income tax rates for most workers are increased by 10 percent.

   d. A new housing development is built near a store.

Think Critically

7. **History** When the stock market crashed in 1929, demand for most consumer products fell. Explain why this happened and how it contributed to the causes of the Great Depression that took place during the 1930s.

8. **Health** For many years, cigarette manufacturers have been required to place health warnings on their products. What are these warnings intended to do to smokers' demand curves for cigarettes?

to History

The Industrial Revolution in England: The Demand for Cotton

The Industrial Revolution began with England's textile industry in the late 1700s. Cotton had been around since the 1630s, when it was introduced to Europe from India. Although popular, cotton was considered a threat to the British wool, linen, and silk industries. In response, Parliament restricted cotton imports. The restrictions lasted until 1736, when Great Britain changed the laws allowing the manufacture and sale of cotton. This marked the beginning of cotton manufacturing in the West.

The two basic stages of manufacturing cotton textiles were spinning and weaving. Typically these tasks were done in the home in what was called a cottage industry. Entrepreneurs supplied raw materials, such as raw cotton or thread, to a household. Then members of the household would produce thread or cloth for the entrepreneur. Of the two tasks, spinning was simpler and the spinners produced more thread than the weavers could weave. John Kay's 1733 invention, the flying shuttle, changed much of that. It allowed one weaver rather than two to operate a loom and produce more cloth. The demand for thread began to rise.

To satisfy this demand, James Hargreaves invented the spinning jenny in the 1760s. With his invention, a single worker could spin multiple threads, but it produced a relatively weak product. Richard Arkwright invented the water frame in 1769. This innovation produced a stronger, coarser thread. Finally, Samuel Crompton's 1779 spinning mule produced a strong yet fine thread. Once again spinners were producing more than what weavers could use.

Edmund Cartwright's power loom, patented in 1785, enabled the British cotton textile industry to explode. In 1796, the country manufactured 21 million yards of cotton cloth. That number increased to 347 million by 1830. The demand for cotton cloth proved to be highly elastic. The technological advances, coupled with a source supply in the United States, caused the price of cotton cloth to drop. By the early part of the century, Britain was even able to sell cotton cloth in India. With this increased technology, the demand for raw cotton increased. Great Britain found in the United States a willing and able supplier.

THINK CRITICALLY

Indicate how the demand curve for cotton would shift with each of the Industrial Revolution's technological inventions. Use D_1 for the cottage industry demand, D_2 for John Kay's flying shuttle, D_3 for Samuel Crompton's spinning mule, and D_4 for Edmund Cartwright's power loom.

Chapter Assessment

Summary

4.1 The Demand Curve

a *Demand* indicates how much of a product consumers are willing and able to buy at each possible price during a given period, other things remaining equal. The *law of demand* states that the higher the price, the smaller the quantity demanded, and vice versa.

b The *quantity demanded* of a product grows as prices fall because of the *substitution effect*, *income effect*, and *diminishing marginal utility. The law of diminishing marginal utility* states that additional units of a product normally provide smaller additional amounts of utility to a consumer within a period of time.

c Demand for a product can be expressed in a *demand schedule* or a graph called a *demand curve*. Most demand curves slope down from left to right, indicating an inverse relationship between changes in price and quantity. This means that as prices decline, the quantity demanded of the product will grow.

4.2 Elasticity of Demand

a The *price elasticity of demand* measures the responsiveness of the quantity demanded to a change in price. Elasticity is calculated by dividing the percentage change in the quantity demanded by the percentage change in price.

b The price elasticity of demand may be *elastic, unit elastic,* or *inelastic.* Elastic demand is indicated by a value greater than 1.0. When there is elastic demand, a percentage change in price will result in a larger percentage change in the quantity demanded. Unit elastic demand is indicated by a value of 1.0. When there is unit elastic demand, a percentage change in price will result in the same percentage change in the quantity demanded. Inelastic demand is indicated by a value less than 1.0. When there is inelastic demand, a percentage change in price will result in a smaller percentage change in the quantity sold.

econxtra.swlearning.com

c The price elasticity of demand can be used to predict what will happen to a firm's *total revenue* when it changes the price of its product. When there is elastic demand, an increase in price will result in reduced total revenue. When there is unit elastic demand, an increase in price will result in unchanged total revenue. When there is inelastic demand, an increase in price will result in increased total revenue.

d Products that have many substitutes tend to have elastic demand. Those that are very important and have few substitutes, or that represent a small proportion of the consumer's budget, tend to have inelastic demand. As a general rule, the more time that passes, the more elastic demand will be.

4.3 Changes in Demand and the Time Price of Goods

a There are five general classifications of events that can cause the location of a demand curve to move. These are: (1) a change in consumer income, (2) a change in the price of related goods, (3) a change in the number and composition of consumers, (4) a change in consumer expectations, and (5) a change in consumer tastes.

b *Substitute* products may be used interchangeably. An increase in the price of one will cause demand for the other to increase. *Complementary* products are normally used together. An increase in the price of one will cause the demand for the other to fall.

c The demand for products can be influenced by time. Customers who must wait in line to buy a product may choose not to wait. They are being required to pay in time as well as money to purchase the product.

Review Economic Terms

Choose the term that best fits the definition. On a separate sheet of paper, write the letter of the answer.

_____ 1. The sum of the individual demand of all consumers in the market

_____ 2. A graph that shows the quantities of a particular good that will be demanded at various prices during a given time period, other things constant

_____ 3. The demand of a single consumer in the market

_____ 4. The amount of a product that is demanded at a particular price

_____ 5. An increase or decrease in demand that results from a change in a determinant of demand

_____ 6. A change in the quantity of a product demanded that results from a change in the product's price

_____ 7. The change in total utility resulting from a one-unit increase in consumption of a particular product

_____ 8. The more of a good a person consumes per period, the smaller the increase in total utility from consuming one more unit, other things constant

_____ 9. The quantity of a good demanded per period relates inversely to its price, other things constant

_____10. Price multiplied by the quantity demanded at that price

_____11. A relation showing the quantities of a good that consumers are willing and able to buy at various prices per period, other things constant

_____12. Measures how responsive quantity demanded is to a price change

_____13. Consumer preferences; assumed to be constant along a given demand curve

a. demand

b. demand curve

c. elasticity of demand

d. individual demand

e. law of demand

f. law of diminishing marginal utility

g. marginal utility

h. market demand

i. movement along a given demand curve

j. quantity demanded

k. shift of a demand curve

l. tastes

m. total revenue

Review Economic Concepts

14. **True or False** A change in the price of a product will not cause that product's *demand curve* to shift.

15. The __?__ is demonstrated by the fact that people will buy more hot dogs and hamburgers when the price of pizza increases.

16. *Elasticity* expresses a relationship between the percentage change in __?__ and the resulting percentage change in __?__.

17. Which of the following is false about demand curves?

a. They normally slope down from left to right.

b. They show the relationship between price and the quantity demanded.

c. They can be used to calculate a product's price elasticity of demand.

d. They show how much profit is earned by businesses that sell the product.

18. **True or False** *Quantity demanded* at a particular price is represented by an individual point on the demand curve.

19. Which of the following is the correct formula for the *price elasticity of demand*?

    a. $\dfrac{\text{change in the price of the product}}{\text{change in the quantity demanded}}$

    b. $\dfrac{\text{change in the quantity demanded}}{\text{change in the price of the product}}$

    c. $\dfrac{\text{\% change in the price of the product}}{\text{\% change in the quantity demanded}}$

    d. $\dfrac{\text{\% change in the quantity demanded}}{\text{\% change in the price of the product}}$

20. **True or False** A firm's *total revenue* will increase if it raises the price of a product that has a price elasticity of demand equal to 0.73.

21. If the *total revenue* from selling a product declines when the product's price is increased, the demand for that product is __?__.

22. **True or False** A business is more likely to increase the price of its products if the demand for these products is elastic than if the demand is inelastic.

23. Which of the following does *not* influence the *elasticity of demand*?

    a. availability of substitute products

    b. availability of complementary products

    c. the share of the consumer's budget spent on the good

    d. the timeframe of the purchase

24. **True or False** *Market demand* is the demand of an individual consumer.

25. Which of these products is most likely to have very elastic demand?

    a. a cable television service

    b. a particular brand of hand soap

    c. ground black pepper

    d. taxi service in a large city

26. **True or False** When consumers earn more income, their demand for all products will increase.

27. Which of the following is *not* a determinant of demand?

    a. consumer income

    b. prices of related goods

    c. consumer expectations and tastes

    d. all of the above would affect demand when other factors are assumed constant

28. **True or False** Demand for a *normal good* decreases as money income increases.

29. The purpose of advertising is to

    a. shift a product's demand curve to the right.

    b. shift a product's demand curve to the left.

    c. make a product's demand more elastic.

    d. point out a product's substitutes to its consumers.

30. Your __?__ income is your income measured in terms of how many goods and services it can buy.

31. Which of the following pairs of products are examples of *complementary goods*?

    a. blank sheets of paper and copy machines

    b. dining room tables and floor lamps

    c. heating oil and natural gas

    d. warm gloves and trips to Florida

    e. peanut butter and jelly

    f. private and public transportation

    g. Coke and Pepsi

    h. alarm clocks and automobiles

    i. golf clubs and golf balls

32. A change in a __?__ will change demand for a product when there is no change in price.

33. **True or False** If a person's income falls to zero, he or she will still demand some products.

Apply Economic Concepts

34. Graphing Shifts in Demand The owner of Rita's Tacos bought ads in a local newspaper. As a result, the demand for her tacos increased as demonstrated in the demand schedule below.

Draw a graph of her demand as it was before the ads were printed. On the same graph, draw the new demand curve for tacos. Explain why many businesses advertise their products.

Old and New Demand Schedule for Rita's Tacos

Price Per Taco	Old Quantity Demanded	New Quantity Demanded
$2.00	25	75
$1.75	50	100
$1.50	75	125
$1.25	100	150
$1.00	125	175
$0.75	150	200

35. Price Elasticity of Demand If Rita changed the price of her tacos from $1.75 to $1.50 each, her sales would grow from 100 to 125 per day. Calculate the percentage change in price and quantity demanded and then the price elasticity of demand. Is this demand elastic, unit elastic, or inelastic?

36. Total Revenue Calculate the total revenue Rita received from the tacos when she sold them at a price of $1.75 and now that she sells them at a price of $1.50. Can you be sure that her business is more profitable at the lower price? Explain why.

37. Market Demand Working in small groups, determine your group's market demand for gasoline. Make up a chart listing a variety of prices per gallon of gasoline, such as $1.00, $1.25, $1.50, $1.75, $2.00, $2.25. Each group member should determine how many gallons *per week* they would purchase at each possible price. Then do the following:

a. Plot each group member's demand curve. Check to see whether each person's responses are consistent with the law of demand.

b. Derive the "market" demand curve by adding up the quantities demanded by all students at each possible price.

c. What do you think will happen to that market demand curve after your class graduates and your incomes rise?

 *econxtra.swlearning.com*

38. Read the Real Per Capita Disposable Income article in the **EconDataOnline** section at econxtra.swlearning.com. What happens to quantity of goods demanded when real per capita disposable income increases?

5 Supply

Consider

Why might a firm decide to store its products in a warehouse rather than offer them for sale?

What's the meaning of the old expression "Too many cooks spoil the broth"?

Can a firm shut down without going out of business?

Why do movie theaters have so many screens?

POINT YOUR BROWSER

econxtra.swlearning.com

© Getty Images/PhotoDisc

Objectives

> Understand the law of supply.

> Describe the elasticity of supply, and explain how it is measured.

Overview

Just as consumer behavior shapes the demand curve, producer behavior shapes the supply curve. When studying demand, you should think like a consumer, or a demander. When studying supply, however, you must think like a producer, or a supplier. You may feel more natural as a consumer—after all, you are a consumer. But you know more about producers than you may realize. You have been around them all your life—Wal-Mart, Sony, Blockbuster, Exxon, McDonald's, Microsoft, Kinko's, Ford, Home Depot, Sears, Gap, and hundreds more. You will draw on this knowledge to develop an understanding of supply and the supply curve.

Key Terms

supply

law of supply

supply curve

elasticity of supply

[In the News]

● Pay Phones Don't Pay Anymore

Where will Clark Kent change into his Superman outfit now that it's getting harder and harder to find a phone booth? Pay phones are being eliminated from all the familiar spots—shopping centers, gasoline stations, restaurants, and street corners. It seems they're just not profitable anymore. In the mid-1990s, there were as many as 2.7 million pay phones across the country. That number is down to about 1.9 million now, and dropping. For the most part, they have been replaced by wireless cell phones. The few small companies that collect the monies and service pay phones are leaving the business. These companies have found that even with an increased price of 50 cents a call, the majority of pay phones operate at a loss when factoring in the costs of cleaning, maintaining, and repairing them. For the time being, pay phones continue to be supplied and maintained in the low-income areas of cities. Many people who live in these areas can't afford to own any type of phone, and so pay phones are still profitable there.

Think About It

What, if anything, can suppliers of pay phones do to save their industry?

Law of Supply

With demand, the assumption is that consumers try to maximize utility, a goal that motivates their behavior. With supply, the assumption is that producers try to maximize profit. Profit is the goal that motivates the behavior of suppliers.

Role of Profit

In trying to earn a profit, firms transform productive resources into products. Profit equals total revenue minus total cost. Total revenue is the total sales, or total dollars, received from consumers for the day, week, or year. Total cost includes the cost of all resources used by a firm in producing goods or services, including the entrepreneur's opportunity cost.

supply

A relation showing the quantities of a good producers are willing and able to sell at various prices during a given period, other things constant

law of supply

The quantity of a good supplied during a given time period is usually directly related to its price, other things constant

supply curve

A curve or line showing the quantities of a particular good supplied at various prices during a given time period, other things constant

© Getty Images/PhotoDisc

Entrepreneurs take the risks of organizing productive resources to make goods and services. A restaurant venture is an especially risky business that uses the productive resources of people and food to prepare and serve meals to customers. The profit incentive leads restaurant entrepreneurs to accept the risks of business failure.

$$\text{Profit} = \text{Total revenue} - \text{Total Cost}$$

When a firm *breaks even,* total revenue just covers total cost. Over time, total revenue must cover total cost for the firm to survive. If total revenue falls short of total cost year after year, entrepreneurs will find more attractive uses for resources, and the firm will fail.

Each year, millions of new firms enter the U.S. marketplace and nearly as many leave. The firms must decide what goods and services to produce and what resources to employ. Firms must make plans while facing uncertainty about consumer demand, resource availability, and the intentions of other firms in the market. The lure of profit is so strong that entrepreneurs are always eager to pursue their dreams.

Supply

Just as demand is a relation between price and quantity demanded, supply is a relation between price and quantity supplied. **Supply** indicates how much of a good producers are *willing* and *able* to offer for sale per period at each possible price, other things constant. The **law of supply** says that the quantity supplied is usually directly related to its price, other things constant. Thus, the lower the price, the smaller the quantity supplied. The higher the price, the greater the quantity supplied.

Figure 5.1 presents the market *supply schedule* and market **supply curve** *S* for pizza. Both show the quantities of 12-inch pizzas supplied per week at various possible prices by the many pizza makers in the market. As you can see, price and quantity supplied are directly (or positively) related, other things constant. The supply curve shows, for example, that at a price of $6 per pizza, the quantity supplied is 16 million per week. At a price of $9 per pizza, the quantity supplied increases to 20 million.

Like the demand curve, the supply curve represents a particular period of time. It shows quantity supplied per period. For any supply curve, it is assumed that the prices of other goods

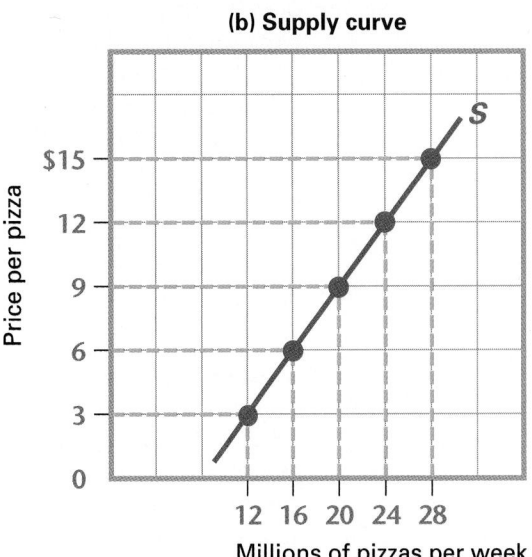

(a) Supply schedule

Price per Pizza	Quantity Supplied per Week (millions)
$15	28
12	24
9	20
6	16
3	12

Market supply curve *S* shows the quantity of pizza supplied, at various prices, by all pizza makers.

(b) Supply curve

the business could produce remain unchanged. Thus, along the supply curve for pizza, the price of pizza changes *relative to other prices,* which do not change. The supply curve shows the effect of a change in the *relative price* of pizza—that is, relative to the prices of other goods the resources could supply. Producers supply more pizza at a higher price than at a lower price, so the supply curve slopes upward.

More Willing to Supply

Producers offer more for sale when the price rises for two reasons. First, as the price increases, other things constant, a producer becomes more *willing* to supply the good. Prices act as signals to existing and potential suppliers about the rewards for producing various goods. An increase in the price of pizza, with other prices remaining constant, creates an incentive to shift some resources out of producing other goods, whose prices are now relatively lower, and into pizza, whose price is now relatively higher. *A higher pizza price makes pizza production more profitable and attracts resources from lower-valued uses.*

More Able to Supply

Higher prices also increase the producer's *ability* to supply the good. The cost of producing an additional unit of a good usually rises as output increases—that is, the *marginal cost* of production increases as output increases. (You will learn more about marginal cost in Lesson 5.3.) Because suppliers face a higher marginal cost for producing the good, they must receive a higher price to be *able* to increase the quantity supplied. *A higher price makes producers more able to increase quantity supplied.*

For example, a higher price for gasoline in recent decades increased producers' ability to explore for oil in less-accessible areas, such as the remote jungles of the Amazon, the stormy waters of the North Sea, and the frozen tundra above the Arctic Circle. Thus, the quantity of oil supplied increased as the price increased. On the other hand, a two-decade long slide in the price of gold means producers are no longer able to mine gold in less-accessible regions or where each ton of ore holds less gold. As the price declined, the quantity supplied decreased.

In short, a higher price makes producers more *willing* and better *able* to increase quantity supplied. Suppliers are more *willing* because production of the higher-priced good now is more profitable than the alternative uses of the resources involved. Suppliers are better *able* because the higher price allows them to cover the higher marginal cost that typically results from increasing production.

Supply Versus Quantity Supplied

As with demand, economists distinguish between *supply* and *quantity supplied*. *Supply* is the entire relation between the price and quantity supplied, as reflected by the supply schedule or supply curve. *Quantity supplied* refers to a particular amount offered for sale at a particular price, as reflected by a point on a given supply curve. Thus, it is the *quantity supplied* that increases with a higher price, not *supply*. The term *supply* by itself refers to the entire supply schedule or supply curve.

Individual Supply and Market Supply

Economists also distinguish between *individual supply* (the supply of an individual producer) and *market supply* (the supply of all producers in the market). *The market supply curve shows the total quantity supplied by all producers at various prices.*

In most markets, there are many suppliers, sometimes thousands. Assume for simplicity, however, that there are just two suppliers in the market for pizza: Pizza Palace and Pizza Castle. Figure 5.2 shows how the supply curves for two producers in the market are added together to yield the market supply curve. Individual supply curves are summed across to get a market supply curve.

For example, at a price of $9, Pizza Palace supplies 400 pizzas per week and Pizza Castle supplies 300. Thus, the quantity supplied in the market for pizza at a price of $9 is 700. At a price of $12, Pizza Palace supplies 500 and Pizza Castle supplies 400, for a market supply of 900 pizzas per week. The market supply curve in panel (c) of Figure 5.2 shows the horizontal sums of the individual supply curves in panels (a) and (b).

The market supply curve is simply the horizontal sum of the individual supply curves for all producers in the market. Unless otherwise noted, when this book talks about supply, you can take that to mean market supply.

Summing Individual Supply Curves to Find the Market Supply Curve

Figure 5.2

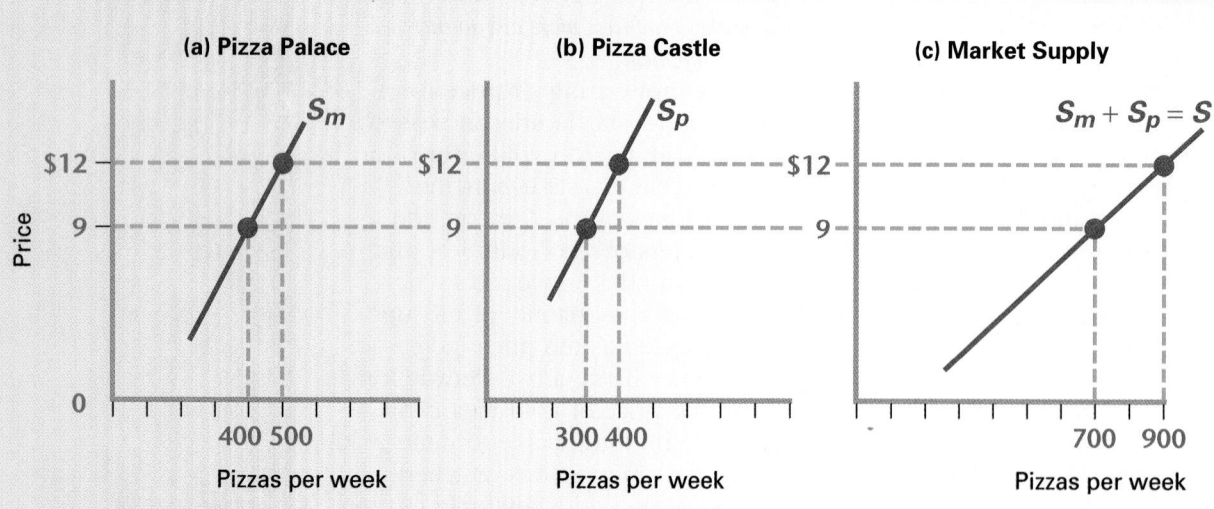

The market supply curve is the horizontal sum of each individual supply curve.

CHAPTER 5 Supply

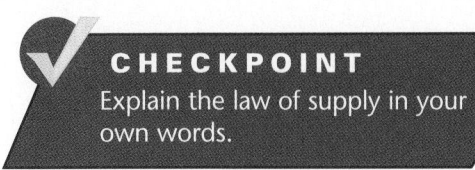

CHECKPOINT

Explain the law of supply in your own words.

Elasticity of Supply

Prices are signals to both sides of the market about the relative scarcity of products. High prices discourage consumption but encourage production. The elasticity of demand measures how responsive consumers are to a price change. Likewise, the elasticity of supply measures how responsive producers are to a price change.

Measurement

The elasticity of supply is calculated in the same way as the elasticity of demand. The **elasticity of supply** equals the percentage change in quantity supplied divided by the percentage change in price.

Elasticity of supply =

$$\frac{\text{Percentage change in quantity supplied}}{\text{Percentage change in price}}$$

Suppose the price increases. Because a higher price usually results in an increased quantity supplied, the percentage change in price and the percentage change in quantity supplied move in the same direction. So, the price elasticity of supply usually is a positive number.

Figure 5.3 depicts the typical upward-sloping supply curve presented earlier. As you can see, if the price of pizza increases from $9 to $12, the quantity supplied increases from 20 million to 24 million. What's the elasticity of supply? The percentage change in quantity supplied is the change in quantity supplied—4 million—divided by 20 million. So quantity supplied increases by 20 percent. The percentage change in price is the change in price—$3—divided by $9, which is 33 percent.

The elasticity of supply is, therefore, the percentage increase in quantity

elasticity of supply

A measure of the responsiveness of quantity supplied to a price change; the percentage change in quantity supplied divided by the percentage change in price

The Graphing Workshop **The Supply of Pizza**   **Figure 5.3**

econxtra.swlearning.com

If the price increases from $9 to $12, the quantity of pizza supplied increases from 20 million to 24 million per week.

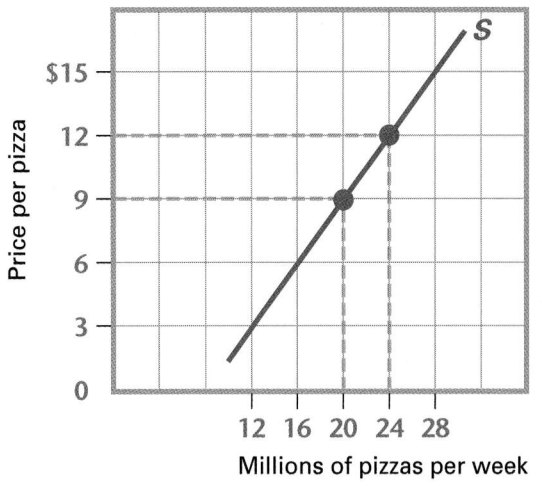

supplied—20 percent—divided by the percentage increase in price—33 percent—which equals 0.6.

Categories of Supply Elasticity

The terminology for supply elasticity is the same as for demand elasticity. If supply *elasticity* exceeds 1.0, supply is *elastic.* If it equals 1.0, supply is *unit elastic.* If supply is less than 1.0, it is *inelastic.* Because 0.6 is less than 1.0, the supply of pizza is inelastic when the price increases from $9 to $12. Note that elasticity usually varies along a supply curve.

Determinants of Supply Elasticity

The elasticity of supply indicates how responsive producers are to a change in price. Their responsiveness depends on how costly it is to alter output when the price changes. If the marginal cost of supplying additional units rises sharply as output expands, then a higher price will generate little increase in quantity supplied, so supply will tend to be inelastic. However, if the marginal cost rises slowly as output expands, the profit lure of a higher price will prompt a relatively large boost in output. In this case, supply will be more elastic.

One important determinant of supply elasticity is the length of the adjustment period under consideration. Just as demand becomes more elastic over time as consumers adjust to price changes, supply also becomes more elastic over time as producers adjust to price changes. The longer the time period under consideration, the more easily producers can adjust. For example, a higher oil price will prompt suppliers to pump more from existing wells in the short run. However, in the long run, suppliers can explore for more oil.

Figure 5.4 demonstrates how the supply of gasoline becomes more elastic over time, with a different supply curve for each of three periods. S_w is the supply curve when the period of adjustment is a week. As you can see, a higher gasoline price will not prompt much of a response in quantity supplied because firms have little time to adjust. This supply curve is inelastic if the price increases from $1.00 to $1.25 per gallon.

S_m is the supply curve when the adjustment period under consideration is a month. Firms have a greater ability to

SPAN THE GLOBE

Mongolian Goats and the Price of Cashmere Sweaters

Think there's a connection? Cashmere comes from the hair of cashmere goats, the majority of which (some 10 million) are raised primarily in Mongolia and northern China. Although that's a lot of goats, each one yields only about $2\frac{1}{2}$ pounds of fleece per shearing. That $2\frac{1}{2}$ pounds, in turn, produces only about 5 ounces of usable cashmere fiber after the labor-intensive job of cleaning and de-hairing. Consequently, the price of the warmer, softer cashmere usually is far higher than its competitor, wool. In past years, Mongolia's exports of this unique product have grown dramatically and, up until 2003, totaled around 2,000 tons with its internal usage of the product between 1,600 and 2,000 tons annually. Unfortunately for the Mongolian producers, the price of cashmere currently is down from a high of almost $20 per pound in 2002 to $9 a pound. This price decline has caused the Mongolian herdsmen to stockpile more than 3,000 tons of the material.

Think Critically

In the short run (over the next few months), is Mongolia's supply of cashmere elastic or inelastic along the supply curve at the price of $9 per pound? Mongolia barely raises enough food for its people, much less its animals, and more than a million of the goats recently have starved to death. In view of this, would you consider the longer-term response to the $9 price to be elastic or inelastic? Explain your answer.

vary output in a month than they do in a week. Thus, supply is more elastic when the adjustment period is a month than when it's a week. Supply is even more elastic when the adjustment period is a year, as is shown by S_y. A given price increase in gasoline prompts a greater quantity supplied as the adjustment period lengthens. Research confirms the positive link between the elasticity of supply and the length of the adjustment period. *The elasticity of supply is typically greater the longer the period of adjustment.*

The ease of increasing quantity supplied in response to a higher price differs across industries. The long run will be longer for producers of electricity and timber (where expansion may take years) than for window washing and hot-dog vending (where expansion may take only days).

CHECKPOINT
What does the elasticity of supply measure, and what factors influence its numerical value?

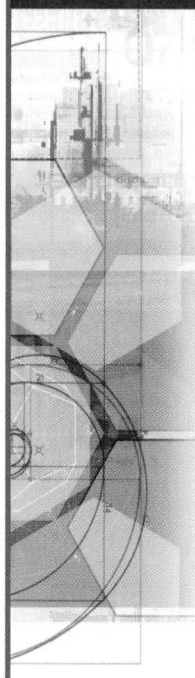
Market Supply Becomes More Elastic Over Time

Figure 5.4

The supply curve one week after a price increase, S_w, is less elastic, at a given price, than the curve one month later, S_m, which is less elastic than the curve one year later, S_y. Given a price increase from $1.00 to $1.25, quantity supplied per day increases to 110 million gallons after one week, to 140 gallons after one month, and to 200 million gallons after one year.

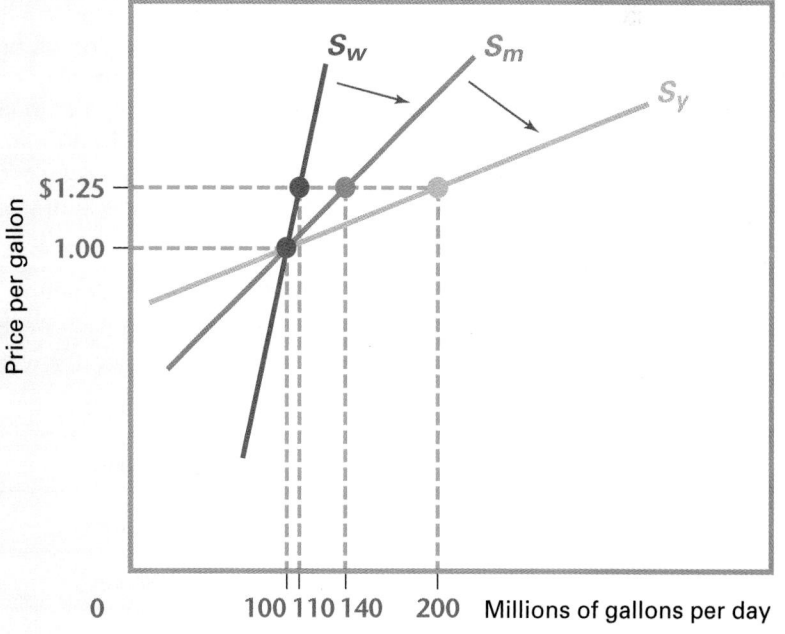

Xtra!
Study Tools
econxtra.swlearning.com

Key Concepts

1. In what ways are the motives of a pizza restaurant owner different from the motives of customers who buy the restaurant's pizza?

2. Why should the quantity of winter jackets supplied increase when there is an increase in the price of these jackets?

3. There are three restaurants that open at 7:00 A.M. to serve breakfast in a small community. Each one charges $4.00 for two eggs, bacon, toast and a cup of coffee. Together they sell 220 breakfasts on an average weekday morning. What is the individual and market supply in this situation?

4. When the market price of kitchen chairs increases by 10 percent, producers of these chairs increase the quantity supplied by 20 percent. Is supply elastic, unit elastic, or inelastic? Explain how you know your answer is correct. What is the measure of elasticity in this situation?

5. Why is the price elasticity of supply likely to be greater for wooden bowls than for natural pearls?

Graphing Exercise

6. The owner of a shoe store reviewed her costs to determine how many pairs of running shoes she would be willing to supply each month at different prices. The results of her research appear in the supply schedule at the right. Use this data to construct her supply curve for running shoes. Explain how the graph demonstrates the law of supply.

Supply of Running Shoes

Price	Quantity Supplied
$70	100
$60	80
$50	60
$40	40
$30	20

Think Critically

7. **Mathematics** The table below shows how much cheese three dairies in a small community supply each month at the current price of $3.00 per pound. It also shows how much each one would supply if the price increased to $4.00. Calculate the percentage change in price and quantity supplied that would result from this price increase. What is the price elasticity of supply for cheese in this market? Is the supply elastic, unit elastic, or inelastic?

Supply of Cheese at $3.00 and $4.00 per pound

Dairy	Quantity Supplied at $3.00	Quantity Supplied at $4.00
A	1,000 pounds	1,300 pounds
B	1,700 pounds	2,600 pounds
C	2,300 pounds	3,100 pounds
Total Production	5,000 pounds	7,000 pounds

Sharpen Your Life Skills

Understand Cause and Effect

In economics, as in most other fields of study, things don't "just happen." There is a logical reason, or a cause, for almost every economic event. One goal of studying economic events that have taken place in the past is to learn about their causes so we can predict what will happen when similar events take place in the future. Consider each of the following events from American history and their results. What can you learn that could help you better understand future economic events?

In 1892, workers at the Carnegie Steel Plant in Homestead, Pennsylvania, went on strike, closing down this factory. This reduced the supply of steel and may have contributed to workers at other factories that used steel being laid off.

In 1903, the Wright brothers were credited with having made the first powered flight. This led to a new mode of transportation that millions of Americans now use each year. With a few exceptions, the supply curve of air transportation has steadily moved to the right over time.

In 1929, the stock market crash contributed to the failure of thousands of U.S. businesses and the onset of the Great Depression of the 1930s. The supply of many products fell during the early years of the Great Depression.

In 1938, the Fair Labor Standards Act was passed that established the 40-hour workweek. This caused some businesses to hire additional workers to avoid paying workers overtime wages and may have increased their cost of production. If this was true, the supply curve for these firms' products would have shifted to the left.

Apply Your Skill

1. At the beginning of 2003, President George W. Bush suggested reducing taxes for businesses that purchased new machinery or hired additional workers. Describe the effect that this suggested policy was intended to cause. How would it affect the supply of many products in the U.S. economy?

2. In 2003, farmers in central California were told that they were taking more than their share of water from the Colorado River. They were ordered to plan to reduce the amount of water they took for irrigation. Nearly a third of the lettuce and many other vegetables grown in the United States are produced in central California. If this ruling were enforced, what might happen to the supply of vegetables American consumers could buy?

Objectives

> Identify the determinants of supply, and explain how a change in each will affect the supply curve.

> Contrast a movement along the supply curve with a shift of the supply curve.

Overview

The supply curve illustrates the relation between the price of a good and the quantity supplied, other things constant. Assumed constant along a supply curve are the determinants of supply other than the good's price. There are five such determinants of supply. A change in one of these determinants of supply causes a shift of the supply curve. This contrasts with a change in price, other things constant, that causes a movement along a supply curve.

Key Terms

movement along a supply curve

shift of a supply curve

[In the News]

● Conflict vs. Clean Diamonds

In 2003, President George W. Bush signed the Clean Diamond Trade Act. The Act should decrease markedly the importation and sale of diamonds from several nations where brutal regimes control their production. The Act institutionalizes the Kimberley Process Certification Scheme. This scheme or plan is intended to insure that diamonds entering the United States are certified as not being "conflict diamonds." These are diamonds that have been mined and sold to finance decades-long wars and atrocities in Africa and have reportedly financed al-Qaeda as well. More than 50 countries, both producing and importing nations, have agreed to participate in the plan. In addition, the diamond industry has agreed to establish a system of warranties under which dealers purchase stones only from sellers who can prove the merchandise's legitimacy.

Think About It

What effect(s) do you think this Act will have on the supply curve of diamonds in the United States?

Determinants of Supply

Because each firm's supply curve is based on the cost of production and profit opportunities in the market, anything that affects production costs and profit opportunities helps shape the supply curve. Following are the five determinants of market supply other than the price of the good:

1. The cost of resources used to make the good

2. The price of other goods these resources could make

3. The technology used to make the good

4. Producer expectations

5. The number of sellers in the market

Changes in the Price of Resources

Any change in the costs of resources used to make a good will affect the supply of the good. For example, suppose the price of mozzarella cheese falls. This reduces the cost of making pizza. Producers are therefore more willing and able to supply pizza at each price, as reflected by a rightward shift of the supply curve from S to S' in Figure 5.5. After the shift, the quantity supplied increases at each price level. For example, at a price of $12, the quantity supplied is higher from 24 million to 28 million pizzas a week, as shown by the movement from point g to point h. In short, *an increase in supply—that is, a rightward shift of the supply curve—means that producers are more willing and able to supply more pizzas at each price.*

What if there is an increase in the price of a resource used to make pizza? This means that at every level of output, the cost of supplying pizza increases. An increase in the price of a resource will reduce supply, meaning a leftward shift of the supply curve. For example, if the wage of pizza workers increases, the higher labor cost would increase the cost of making pizza.

Higher production costs decrease supply, so pizza supply shifts leftward, as from S to S'' in Figure 5.6. After the decrease in supply, producers offer less for sale at each price. For example, at a price of $12 per pizza, the quantity supplied falls from 24 million to 20 million

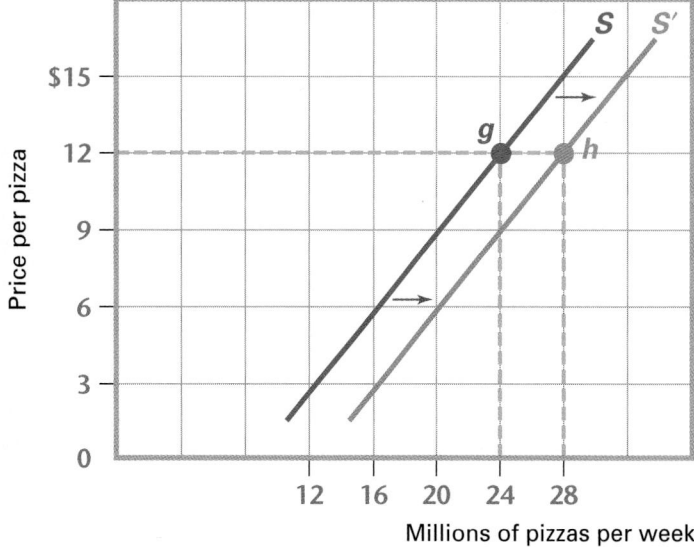

The Graphing Workshop

econxtra.swlearning.com

An Increase in the Supply of Pizza

Figure 5.5

An increase in the supply of pizza is reflected by a rightward shift of the supply curve, from S to S'. After the increase in supply, the quantity of pizza supplied at a price of $12 increases from 24 million pizzas (point g) to 28 million pizzas (point h).

per week. This is shown in Figure 5.6 by the movement from point *g* to point *i*.

Changes in the Prices of Other Goods

Nearly all resources have alternative uses. The labor, building, machinery, ingredients, and knowledge needed to make pizza could produce other products, such as bread sticks, rolls, and other baked goods.

A change in the price of another good these resources could make affects the opportunity cost of making pizza. For example, if the price of rolls falls, the opportunity cost of making pizza declines. These resources are not as profitable in their best alternative use, which is making rolls. So pizza production becomes relatively more attractive. As resources shift from baking rolls to making pizza, the supply of pizza increases, or shifts to the right, as shown in Figure 5.5.

On the other hand, if the price of rolls increases, so does the opportunity cost of making pizza. Some pizza makers may bake more rolls and less pizza, so the supply of pizza decreases, or shifts to the left, as in Figure 5.6. A change in the price of another good these resources

could produce affects the profit opportunities available to producers.

Changes in Technology

The state of technology represents the economy's stock of knowledge about how to combine resources efficiently. Discoveries in chemistry, biology, electronics, and many other fields have created new products, improved existing products, and lowered the cost of production. For example, the first microprocessor, the Intel 4004, could execute about 400 computations per second when it hit the market in 1971. Today a standard PC often can handle more than 2 billion computations per second, *or 5 million* times what the 1971 Intel 4004 could handle. Technological change—in this case, faster computers—lowers the cost of producing goods whose production involves computers, from automobile manufacturing to document processing.

Along a given market supply curve, technological know-how about how this good can be manufactured is assumed to remain unchanged. If a more efficient technology is discovered, the cost of production will fall, making this market more profitable. Improvements in technology make firms more willing and

A Decrease in the Supply of Pizza

Figure 5.6

A decrease in the supply of pizza is reflected by a leftward shift of the supply curve, from *S* to *S″*. After the decrease in supply, the quantity of pizza supplied at a price of $12 decreases from 24 million pizzas (point *g*) to 20 million pizzas (point *i*).

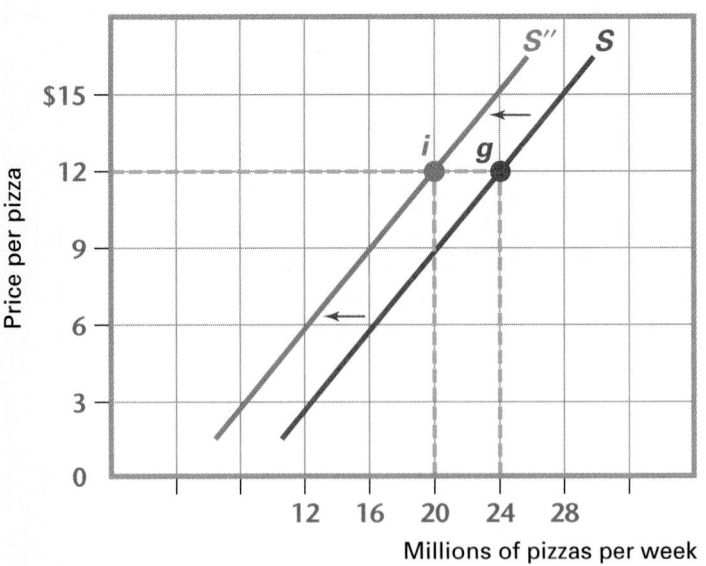

able to supply the good at each price. Consequently, supply will increase, as reflected by a rightward shift of the supply curve. For example, suppose a new high-tech oven bakes pizza in half the time. Such a breakthrough would shift the supply curve rightward, as from S to S' in Figure 5.5, so that more is supplied at each possible price.

Changes in Producer Expectations

Producers transform resources into goods they hope can be sold for a profit. Any change that affects producer expectations about profitability can affect market supply. For example, if pizza prices are expected to increase in the future, some pizza makers may expand production capacity now. This would shift the supply of pizza rightward, as shown in Figure 5.5.

Some goods can be stored easily. For example, crude oil can be left in the ground and grain can be stored in a silo. Expecting higher prices in the future might prompt some producers of these goods to *reduce* their current supply while awaiting the higher price. This would shift the supply curve to the left, as shown in Figure 5.6. Thus, an expectation of higher prices in the future could either increase or decrease current supply, depending on the good.

Changes in the Number of Sellers in the Market

General changes in the market environment also can affect the number of sellers in the market. For example, government regulations may influence market supply. As a case in point, for decades government strictly regulated the prices and entry of new firms in a variety of industries including airlines, trucking, and telecommunications. During that period, the number of firms in the market was artificially limited by these government restrictions. When these restrictions were eliminated, more firms entered these markets, increasing supply.

Any government action that affects a market's profitability, such as a change in business taxes, could shift the supply curve. Lower business taxes will increase supply and higher business taxes will reduce supply.

The increase in the number of firms is not simply a response to a price change. Along a given market supply curve, there usually are fewer suppliers at lower prices than higher prices. Higher prices attract producers and increase the quantity supplied along the supply curve.

Businesses generally pay income taxes to local, state, and the federal government. Contact your local government's bureau of taxation. Find out the current tax rate for businesses. Also find the rate for the past five years. Has an increase or decrease in the tax rate affected supply in your area? Write a paragraph to explain your findings.

 CHECKPOINT
What are the five determinants of supply, and how do changes in each affect the supply of a good?

Movements Along a Supply Curve Versus Shifts of a Supply Curve

Note again the distinction between a *movement along a supply curve* and a *shift of a supply curve*. A change in *price*, other things constant, causes a **movement along a supply curve** from one price-

movement along a supply curve

Change in quantity supplied resulting from a change in the price of the good, other things constant

shift of a supply curve

Increase or decrease in supply resulting from a change in one of the determinants of supply other than the price of the good

quantity combination to another. A change in one of the determinants of supply other than the price causes a **shift of a supply curve**, changing supply. A shift of the supply curve means a change in the quantity supplied at each price.

A change in price, other things constant, changes quantity supplied along a given supply curve. A change in a determinant of supply other than the price of the good—such as the prices of resources used to make the good, technology used to make the good, the price of other goods these resources could produce, producer expectations, and the number of firms in the market—shifts the entire supply curve to the right or left.

NETBookmark

Read the E-conomics feature, below, about the use of credit-card technology at fast-food restaurants. McDonald's Corporation is working with eMac Digital in developing its new point-of-sale (POS) software system. To learn more about the relationship between McDonald's and eMac, access two press releases through econxtra.swlearning.com. Why did McDonald's sell its ownership interest in eMac? How is this consistent with McDonald's focus on specialization and division of labor? What determinant of supply does the POS system represent?

econxtra.swlearning.com

CHECKPOINT

Explain the difference between a movement along a supply curve and a shift of a supply curve.

E-CONOMICS

Faster Fast Food

Pay for your Big Mac with a credit card? McDonald's has been testing the system and says customers soon will be able to pay for their burgers and fries with credit cards. In a world of charging everything on plastic cards, fast-food chains have been slow to get with the program. But customers want to be able to put just about everything they buy on a credit card. According to a market research firm, if credit-card use really takes hold, service at fast-food outlets will become even faster. The lines will move more quickly because the latest high-speed technologies and fiber-optic networks are making credit-card transactions even faster than paying with cash. Current technologies enable a customer to call out an order at the drive-through, or at the counter, and then swipe a credit card and have it approved in less than 5 seconds. On the other hand, cash transactions take an average of 8 to 10 seconds. With widespread use of credit cards, fast-food outlets will be able to supply more hungry customers in the same amount of time.

Think Critically

Will the use of credit-card technology at fast-food restaurants be likely to cause a movement along the supply curve or a shift of the supply for fast food? Explain your answer.

Key Concepts

1. One year a farmer grows corn on his 200 acres of land. He sells his corn in September for $3.00 per bushel. Early the next spring he notices that the price of soybeans has gone up 50 percent while the price of corn has remained the same. What will probably happen to his supply curve for corn? Explain your answer.

2. The Apex Plastics Corp. finds a new way to produce plastic outdoor furniture from recycled milk bottles at very low cost. What will happen to the supply curve for plastic furniture? Explain your answer.

3. A big storm destroys most of the sugarcane crop in Louisiana. Most people expect this to cause a large increase in the price of sugar in the next few months. What will happen to the supply curve for sugar?

4. The cost of crude oil increases by 25 percent. Crude oil is the basic raw material used to produce plastic. What will this do to the supply curve for plastic toys?

5. How might an increase in the minimum wage shift both the demand curve and supply curve for pizza?

Graphing Exercise

6. Make a copy of the supply curve. Draw and explain the shifts of the market supply on your copy that would result from each of the following events. Label each shift of the supply curve.

    a. There is an increase in the cost of rubber used to produce the soles of running shoes.

    Supply Curve for Running Shoes

    (Graph: Price on vertical axis marked $20, $40, $60, $80; Quantity on horizontal axis marked 0, 20, 40, 60, 80, 100, 120. Upward-sloping line labeled "Supply.")

    b. There is a decrease in the market price of rubber tires.

    c. A new machine is invented that produces running shoes with only one-third as many workers.

    d. A new mall is built in town with three stores that offer running shoes for sale.

Think Critically

7. **Research** Use newspapers, magazines, or the Internet to research a world event that could have an impact of the supply of a product consumed in the United States. Describe this event and explain how it might shift the U.S. supply curve.

8. **Technology** Choose a single product many consumers buy, and write a paragraph that discusses whether the creation of the Internet has shifted the supply curve for this product.

movers & shakers

John Schnatter *Founder, Papa John's Pizza*

During high school and college, John Schnatter earned spending money by working part-time in national-chain pizzerias. He noticed something missing from every one of them: No one was making a superior-quality pizza that could be delivered directly to the customer. He dreamed of one day opening his own pizza restaurant, doing everything right.

In 1984, Schnatter graduated from Ball State University with a degree in business administration and then returned home to Jeffersonville, Indiana. There he took the first step to introduce the world to his own superior pizza. First he knocked out a broom closet in the rear of his father's business. Then he sold his beloved 1972 Camaro in order to purchase $1,600 worth of used restaurant equipment, including his first pizza oven. The first Papa John's restaurant opened in 1985. Less than twenty years later 3,000 Papa John's restaurants operate in 49 states and 12 international markets.

Schnatter's successful business philosophy is to focus on one thing and do it better than anyone else. He keeps the menu simple and uses only superior-quality ingredients. He insists on using fresh (never frozen) water-purified traditional dough, vine-ripened fresh-packed tomato sauce, and 100 percent mozzarella cheese.

For four consecutive years, Papa John's was rated number one in customer satisfaction among all national fast-food restaurants in the American Customer Satisfaction Index. Papa John's also was rated number one in product quality in the Restaurants & Institutions' Choice in Chains consumer survey for seven consecutive years. In 2000, Papa John's become the third-largest pizza company in the world.

Schnatter established his company headquarters in Louisville, Kentucky, and is one of Louisville's most successful business leaders. Now in his early forties, this young entrepreneur is generous with his annual earnings, which exceed $1 million a year.

The pizza market has presented Papa John's with some obstacles. In 2001, the industry became stagnant, partly because of increasingly strong competition from frozen grocery pizzas. When things didn't change in 2002, Papa John's largest rivals, Pizza Hut and Dominos, focused on offering deep discounts to customers to increase sales. Instead of following suit, Schnatter decided his company would focus on product quality and manager retention. He spent between $6 million and $7 million on these two efforts alone. Schnatter said he believes that "consistently getting a better product out the door" will result in improved sales, adding that one way to enhance quality is to reduce staff turnover. The company also has begun online ordering.

As Papa John's founder, Chairman of the Board, President, and Chief Executive Officer, Schnatter continues to be enthusiastic about making superior-quality pizzas that can be delivered directly to the customer. "I love the product, I like the people, I love the business. You've got to understand I've been doing this since I was 15...It's all I know."

SOURCE READING
Analyze the quotations attributed to John Schnatter. From these statements, what qualities do you think he possesses that make him a successful entrepreneur?

ENTREPRENEURS IN ACTION
In small groups, role-play Papa John's Board of Directors, with one student portraying Schnatter. The company is faced with stiff competition from frozen grocery pizzas and deep discounting from its direct competitors. Discuss the steps management needs to take in order to keep the company growing.

Objectives

> Understand how marginal product varies as a firm employs more labor in the short run.

> Explain the shape of the firm's marginal cost curve and identify what part of that is the firm's supply curve.

> Distinguish between economies of scale and diseconomies of scale in the long run.

Overview

How much will a firm supply in order to maximize profit? The answer to this question requires a brief introduction to how a firm converts productive resources into outputs. In general, a profit-maximizing firm will supply more output to the market as long as the marginal revenue from each unit sold exceeds its marginal cost.

Key Terms

short run
long run
total product
marginal product
law of diminishing returns
fixed cost
variable cost
total cost
marginal cost
marginal revenue
competitive firm's supply curve
economies of scale
long-run average curve cost

[In the News]

● At the Local Megaplex

Have you ever wondered why movie theaters seem to be offering moviegoers more and more screens? Think about it in this way: A theater with one screen needs someone to sell tickets, someone to sell popcorn, and someone to operate the projector. If another screen is added, the same staff can perform these tasks for both screens. Thus, the ticket seller becomes more productive by selling tickets to both movies. Also, construction costs per screen are reduced because only one lobby and one set of rest rooms are required. The theater can run bigger, more noticeable newspaper ads and can spread the cost over more films. From 1990 to 2000, the number of screens in the United States grew faster than the number of theaters, so the average number of screens per theater increased.

Think About It

As you read this section, look for the economic principle this situation illustrates. What do economists call this principle?

short run

A period during which at least one of a firm's resources is fixed

long run

A period during which all resources can be varied

total product

The total output of the firm

marginal product

The change in total product resulting from a one-unit change in a particular resource, all other resources constant

law of diminishing returns

As more of a variable resource is added to a given amount of fixed resources, marginal product eventually declines and could become negative

Production in the Short Run

A firm tries to earn a profit by converting productive resources, or *inputs,* into goods and services, or *outputs.* Consider production at a hypothetical moving company called Hercules at Your Service.

Fixed and Variable Resources

All producers, like Hercules, use two categories of resources: fixed and variable. Resources that cannot be altered easily—the size of the building, for example—are called *fixed resources.* Hercules' fixed resources consist of a warehouse, a moving van, and some moving equipment. Resources that can be varied quickly to change output are called *variable resources.* In this example, assume that labor is the only variable resource.

When considering the time required to change the quantity of resources employed, economists distinguish between the short run and the long run. In the **short run**, at least one resource is fixed. In the **long run**, no resources are fixed. Hercules is operating in the short run because some resources are fixed. In this example, labor is the only resource that varies in the short run. A firm can enter or leave a market in the long run but not in the short run.

Figure 5.7 relates the amount of labor employed to the amount of furnishings moved. Labor is measured in worker-days, which is one worker for one day, and output is measured in tons of furnishings moved per day. The first column shows the total product per day, measured in tons of furniture moved. **Total product** is the total output of the firm. The second column shows the number of workers required for that total product. The third column shows the **marginal product** of each worker—that is, the amount by which the total product changes with each additional worker, assuming other resources remain unchanged.

Increasing Returns

Without labor, nothing gets moved, so total product is zero when no workers are hired. If one worker is hired, that person must do all the driving, packing, and moving. A single worker cannot easily move some of the larger items. Still, one worker manages to move 2 tons per day. When a second worker is hired, some division of labor occurs, and two can move the big stuff more easily, so production more than doubles to 5 tons per day. The marginal product of the second worker is 3 tons per day.

Adding a third worker allows for an even better division of labor, which contributes to increased production. For example, one worker can specialize in packing fragile items while the other two do the heavy lifting. The total product of three workers is 9 tons per day, 4 tons more than with two workers. The firm experiences *increasing returns* from labor as each of the first three workers is hired, meaning that marginal product increases as more labor is hired.

Law of Diminishing Returns

Hiring a fourth worker adds to the total product but not as much as was added by a third. Hiring still more workers increases total product by successively smaller amounts, so the marginal product in Figure 5.7 declines after three workers. Beginning with the fourth worker, the **law of diminishing returns** takes hold. This law states that as more units of one resource are added to all other resources, marginal product eventually declines. *The law of diminishing returns is the most important feature of production in the short run.*

As long as marginal product is positive, total product continues to increase. However, as additional workers are hired, total product may eventually decline. For example, an eighth worker would crowd the work area so much that people get in each other's way. As a result, total output would drop, meaning a negative

Total Product (tons moved per day)	Units of the Variable Resource (worker-days)	Marginal Product (tons moved per day)
0	0	—
2	1	2
5	2	3
9	3	4
12	4	3
14	5	2
15	6	1
15	7	0
14	8	−1

As each of the first three workers is hired, the firm experiences increasing returns from labor. Marginal product increases as more labor is hired. Beginning with the fourth worker, the law of diminishing returns takes hold. This law states that as more units of one resource are added to all other resources, marginal product eventually declines.

marginal product. Likewise, a restaurant can hire only so many workers before congestion and confusion cut total product. "Too many cooks spoil the broth."

Marginal Product Curve

Figure 5.8 shows the marginal product of labor, using data from Figure 5.7. Note that because of increasing returns, marginal product increases with each of the first three workers. Beginning with the fourth worker, diminishing returns cut marginal product. Marginal product turns negative if an eighth worker is hired. Figure 5.8 identifies three ranges of marginal product:

1. Increasing marginal returns

2. Diminishing but positive marginal returns

3. Negative marginal returns.

As you will soon learn, firms normally produce in the range of diminishing but positive marginal returns.

© Getty Images/PhotoDisc

When Hercules at Your Service hires a second worker, division of labor occurs, and production more than doubles. What is total product and marginal product with two workers? With three workers? What happens when a fourth worker is hired?

The Marginal Product of Labor

Figure 5.8

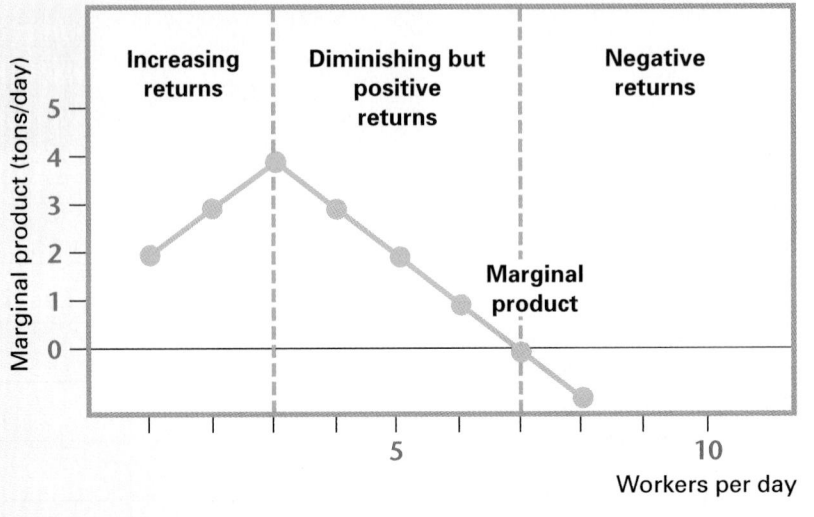

The marginal product of the first three workers shows increasing returns. The next four workers show diminishing but positive returns, and the eighth worker shows negative returns.

 CHECKPOINT
How does marginal product vary as a firm employs more labor in the short run?

Costs in the Short Run

Now that you have some idea about production in the short run, consider how the firm's costs vary with output. A firm faces two kinds of costs in the short run: fixed cost and variable cost.

Fixed and Variable Costs

A **fixed cost** is one that does not change in the short run, no matter how much output is produced. A firm must pay a fixed cost even when nothing gets produced. Even if Hercules hires no labor and moves no furniture, the firm must pay for the warehouse, property taxes, insurance, vehicle registration, and equipment. By definition, fixed cost is just that—fixed. It does not vary with output in the short run. Fixed cost is sometimes called *overhead*. Hercules's fixed cost is $200 per day.

Variable cost varies with the amount produced. With Hercules, only labor

varies in the short run, so labor is the only variable cost. For example, if Hercules hires no labor, output is zero, so variable cost is zero. As more labor is employed, output increases, as does variable cost. Variable cost depends on the amount of labor employed and on the wage. If the firm can hire each worker for $100 a day, variable cost equals $100 times the number of workers hired.

Total Cost

Figure 5.9 offers cost information for Hercules. The table lists the daily cost of different output totals. Column 1 shows the number of tons of furniture moved per day. Column 2 indicates the fixed cost for each output total. By definition, fixed cost remains at $200 per day regardless of output. Column 3 shows the quantity of labor needed to produce each level of output. For example, moving 2 tons a day requires one worker, 5 tons requires two workers, and so on. Only the first six workers are listed, because more workers add nothing to total product.

Column 4 lists variable cost, which equals $100 times the number of workers employed. For example, the variable cost of moving 9 tons of furniture per day is $300 because this output requires three workers. Column 5 lists the **total cost**, which sums fixed cost

fixed cost
Any production cost that is independent of the firm's output

variable cost
Any production cost that changes as output changes

total cost
The sum of fixed cost and variable cost

and variable cost. As you can see, when output is zero, variable cost is zero, so total cost consists entirely of the fixed cost of $200.

Marginal Cost

Of special interest to the firm is how much total cost changes with output. In particular, what is the marginal cost of moving another ton? As shown in columns 6 and 7, the **marginal cost** of production is simply the change in total cost divided by the change in quantity, or

$$\frac{\text{Change in total cost}}{\text{Change in quantity}}$$

= Marginal cost

For example, increasing output from 0 to 2 tons increases total cost by $100. The marginal cost of each of the first 2 tons is the change in total cost, $100, divided by the change in output, 2 tons, or $100/2, which equals $50. The marginal cost of each of the next 3 tons is the change in total cost, $100, divided by the change in output, 3 tons, or $100/3, which equals $33.33.

Unit labor cost is the term used to describe the cost of labor per unit of output. Because labor costs generally represent the largest share of costs, this value is closely watched by businesspeople and analysts at the Federal Reserve. Look at the most recent data on unit labor costs at the Bureau of Labor Statistics web site. Access this web site through econxtra.swlearning.com. What is the current trend? What forces may be pushing unit labor costs downward? What does this mean for the profitability of firms?

econxtra.swlearning.com

Notice in column 7 that marginal cost first decreases and then increases. Changes in marginal cost reflect changes in the productivity of the variable resource, labor. The first three workers show increasing returns. This rising marginal product of labor reduces

marginal cost

The change in total cost resulting from a one-unit change in output; the change in total cost divided by the change in output

Short-Run Cost Data for Hercules at Your Service

Figure 5.9

1 Tons Moved per Day	2 Fixed Cost	3 Workers per Day	4 Variable Cost	5 Total Cost	6 Change in total cost ÷ Change in tons moved =	7 Marginal Cost
0	$200	0	$ 0	$200	—	
2	200	1	100	300	$100 ÷ 2	$ 50.00
5	200	2	200	400	$100 ÷ 3	33.33
9	200	3	300	500	$100 ÷ 4	25.00
12	200	4	400	600	$100 ÷ 3	33.33
14	200	5	500	700	$100 ÷ 2	50.00
15	200	6	600	800	$100 ÷ 1	100.00

Column 7 shows the marginal cost of moving another ton of furnishings. It is the change in total cost divided by the change in tons moved.

marginal cost for the first 9 tons moved. Beginning with the fourth worker, the firm experiences diminishing returns from labor, so the marginal cost of output increases. Thus, marginal cost in Figure 5.9 first falls and then rises, because returns from labor first increase and then decrease.

Marginal Cost Curve

Figure 5.10 shows the marginal cost curve for moving furniture based on the data in Figure 5.9. Because of increasing returns from labor, the marginal cost curve at first slopes down. Because of diminishing marginal returns from labor, the marginal cost curve slopes up after 9 tons. Keep in mind that economic analysis is marginal analysis. Marginal cost is one key to the firm's production decision.

Marginal Revenue

To understand how firms work, it may help to draw on your knowledge of demand. Remember that demand is based on the marginal benefit that consumers get from buying each additional unit of the good. Likewise, supply is based on the marginal benefit that producers get from selling each additional unit of a good. The marginal benefit that producers get from supplying another unit is the **marginal revenue** they receive. This is the change in total revenue from selling that unit. In competitive markets, the firm's marginal revenue is the market price. A competitive firm receives the market price for selling one more unit.

Short-Run Losses and Shutting Down

In general, producers sell additional units as long as the marginal revenue they receive exceeds the marginal cost. In competitive markets, the firm supplies additional units as long as the price exceeds marginal cost. The firm settles on the level of output where *marginal revenue equals marginal cost.*

There is one qualification to this output rule. Sometimes the market price may be so low that production makes no economic sense. At the level of output where marginal revenue equals marginal cost, the firm's total revenue must at least cover its variable cost. A firm that can't cover variable cost will lose less in the short run by shutting down.

Here's the logic behind the shutdown decision. Even if the firm produces nothing in the short run, it must still pay fixed cost. If nothing is produced, the firm's loss equals fixed cost. For example, Hercules would lose $200 a day if no furniture gets moved.

What if the market price is really low, but the firm decides to produce anyway and hires two workers for $200? Because the price is so low, the total revenue received from selling that output is only $150. That amount pays none of the fixed cost and only a portion of the variable cost. The firm would not only lose its fixed cost of $200, but it also would lose $50 of variable cost. The firm would lose less—only $200—by shutting down. Why produce when doing so only increases any loss?

marginal revenue

The change in total revenue from selling another unit of the good

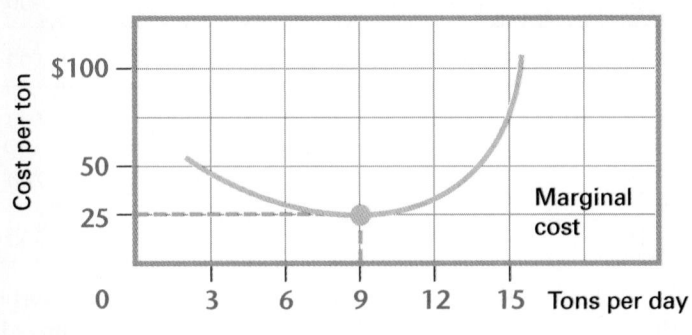

The Graphing Workshop

econxtra.swlearning.com

Marginal Cost Curve for Hercules At Your Service

Figure 5.10

Marginal cost first declines, reflecting increasing marginal returns, and then increases, reflecting diminishing marginal returns.

A firm's *minimum acceptable price* is a price high enough to ensure that total revenue at least covers variable cost. If the market price is below that minimum, the firm will shut down. Note that shutting down is not the same as going out of business. A firm that shuts down keeps its productive capacity intact—paying the rent, fire insurance, and property taxes, keeping water pipes from freezing in the winter, and so on. For example, auto factories sometimes shut down for a while when sales are soft. Businesses in summer resorts often close for the winter. These firms do not escape fixed cost by shutting down, because fixed cost by definition is not affected by changes in output.

If in the future the price increases enough, the firm will resume production. If market conditions look grim and are not expected to improve, the firm may decide to leave the market. But that's a long-run decision. The short run is defined as a period during which some resources and some costs are fixed. A firm cannot escape those costs in the short run, no matter what it does. The firm cannot enter or leave the market in the short run.

The Firm's Supply Curve

To produce in the short run, the price must be high enough to ensure that total revenue covers variable cost. The **competitive firm's supply curve** is the upward sloping portion of its marginal cost curve at and above the minimum acceptable price. This supply curve shows how much the firm will supply at each price.

In the Hercules example, a price of $33.33 allows the firm to at least cover variable cost. Hercules's short-run supply curve is presented in Figure 5.11 as the upward-sloping portion of the marginal cost curve starting at $33.33. At that price, Hercules will supply 12 tons of moving a day. At a price of $50 per ton, the company will move 14 tons, and at a price of $100 per ton, the company will move 15 tons. The market supply curve sums individual supply curves for firms in the market.

> ✓ **CHECKPOINT**
> Why does the firm's marginal cost curve slope upward in the short run?

Production and Costs in the Long Run

So far, the analysis has focused on how short-run costs vary with output for a firm of a given size. In the long run, all

competitive firm's supply curve

The rising portion of a firm's marginal cost curve at or above the price that will allow the firm to cover variable cost

The Graphing Workshop

Supply Curve for Hercules at Your Service   **Figure 5.11**

A competitive firm's supply curve shows the quantity supplied at each price. The supply curve is the upward-sloping portion of its marginal cost curve, beginning at the firm's minimum acceptable price. The minimum acceptable price, in this case $33.33, is the price that allows the firm's total revenue to cover its variable cost.

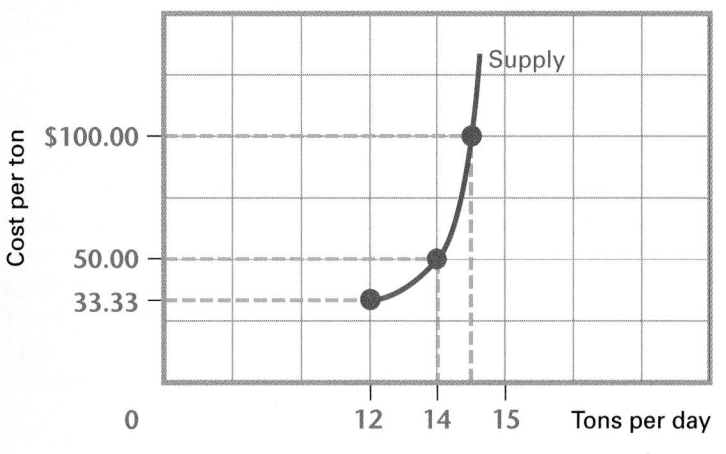

inputs can be varied, so there are no fixed costs. What should be the size of the firm?

Economies of Scale

long-run average cost curve

A curve that indicates the lowest average cost of production at each rate of output when the firm's size is allowed to vary

economies of scale

Forces that reduce a firm's average cost as the firm's size, or scale, increases in the long run

Because all resources can vary in the long run, the focus is on the average cost of production, not the marginal cost. *Average cost* equals total cost divided by output. The firm's owner would like to know how the average cost of production varies as the size, or scale, of the firm increases. A firm's *long-run average cost* indicates the lowest average cost of producing each output when the firm's size is allowed to vary.

If the firm's long-run average cost declines as the firm size increases, this reflects **economies of scale**. Consider some reasons for economies of scale. *A larger-size firm often allows for larger, more specialized machines and greater specialization of labor.* Typically, as the scale of the firm increases, capital substitutes for labor. Production techniques such as the assembly line can be introduced only if the firm is sufficiently large.

Diseconomies of Scale

As the scale of the firm continues to increase, however, another force may eventually take hold. If the firm's long-run average cost increases as production increases, this reflects *diseconomies of scale.* As the amount and variety of resources employed increase, so does the *task of coordinating all these inputs.* As the workforce grows, additional layers of management are needed to monitor production. Information may not be correctly passed up or down the chain of command.

It is possible for long-run average cost to neither increase nor decrease with changes in firm size. If neither economies of scale nor diseconomies of scale occur as the scale of the firm expands, a firm experiences *constant returns to scale* over some range of production.

Long-Run Average Cost Curve

Figure 5.12 presents a firm's **long-run average cost curve**, showing the lowest average cost of producing each level of output. The curve is marked into segments reflecting economies of scale, constant returns to scale, and diseconomies of scale. Production must reach quantity *A* for the firm to achieve the *minimum efficient scale,* which is the smallest scale, or size, that allows the firm to take full advantage of economies of scale. At the minimum efficient scale, long-run average cost is at a minimum. From output *A* to output *B,* the firm experiences constant returns to scale. Beyond output rate *B,* diseconomies of scale increase long-run average cost.

Firms try to avoid diseconomies of scale. Competition weeds out firms that grow too large. To avoid diseconomies of scale, IBM divided into six smaller decision-making groups. Other large corporations have spun off parts of their operations to create new companies. HP started Agilent Technologies, and AT&T started Lucent Technologies.

The long-run average cost curve guides the firm toward the most efficient plant size for a given level of output. However, once a plant of that scale is built, the firm has fixed costs and is operating in the short run. A firm in the short run chooses the output rate where marginal revenue equals marginal cost. Firms plan for the long run, but they produce in the short run.

CNN video
Economic Health
econxtra.swlearning.com

THE WALL STREET JOURNAL

Reading It Right What's the relevance of the following statement from *The Wall Street Journal:* "As with any new technology, the early OLED (organic light-emitting diode) display screens are expensive, perhaps six times more than liquid-crystal-display screens. But OLED backers say that problem will in part be addressed once mass production gears up and economies of scale are reached."

✓ **CHECKPOINT**
How are economies of scale and diseconomies of scale reflected in a firm's long-run average cost curve?

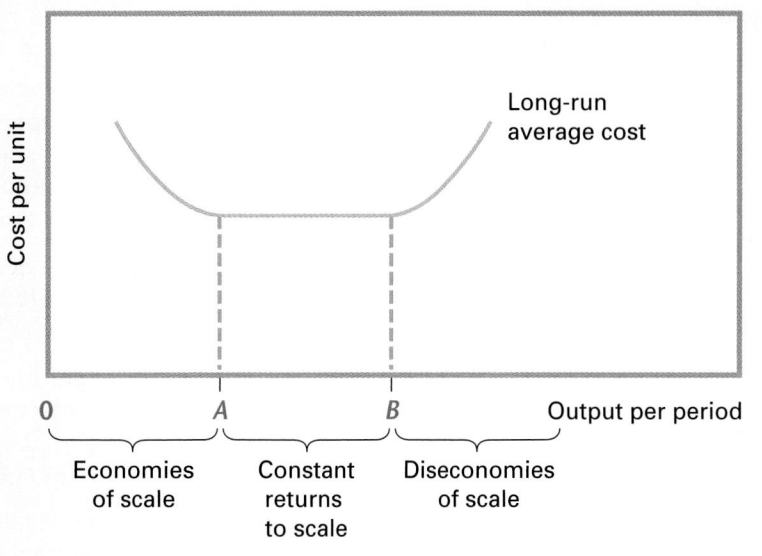

Average cost declines until production reaches output level *A*. The firm is experiencing economies of scale. Output level *A* is the minimum efficient scale—the lowest rate of output at which the firm takes full advantage of economies of scale. Between *A* and *B*, the economy has constant returns to scale. Beyond output level *B*, the long-run average cost curve reflects diseconomies of scale.

Ethics in Action

Worker's Compensation

All across the nation, the cost of worker's compensation insurance has been spiking upward at a frightening rate. A seafood wholesaler in Los Angeles saw its rates climb 68 percent in one year to almost $7,000 per employee. Most insurance costs have risen for companies in the past few years, but "worker's comp," as it is often called, is a major problem because firms have no control over cost increases. By law, companies must provide worker's comp insurance, which pays for medical treatment for job-related injuries and for wages lost as a result of those injuries. Because every employee must have worker's comp insurance, the only way a company can reduce this cost is to eliminate employees. Increased insurance costs have caused both large and small companies to lay off workers, and—in many cases—it has forced them out of business. The main reasons for the sharp increases in worker's comp costs are soaring medical and legal costs, and fraud. Workers fake injuries and stay out of work longer than necessary. Doctors, chiropractors, and lawyers work together to cheat the system. Companies also manipulate their employee reports and downplay the dangers involved in the work that's being done in order to pay less than they should.

Think Critically

What are the ethical issues involved with worker's compensation insurance? How does the increase in worker's compensation insurance affect a firm's long-run average cost curve?

Key Concepts

1. Tanya runs a computer repair business in a small room in her basement. Many people wanted her to fix their computers so she hired another worker, who doubled the number of computers she could fix each day. But when she hired a third worker, she found that the number of computers she could service hardly changed at all. Explain how this demonstrates the law of diminishing returns.

2. Tanya has borrowed more than $10,000 to buy special equipment she needs in order to repair computers. Is the $750 she pays each month to repay her loan a fixed or a variable cost? Explain your answer.

3. Tanya pays her worker $15.00 per hour. If, on average, he can repair one computer in two hours, what is the marginal cost of fixing one more computer? What other information does she need to have before she can decide how much to charge her customers for computer repairs?

4. Tanya's monthly fixed costs total $1,000. She pays her assistant $2,500 each month. She could take a job with a different business that would pay her $3,000 each month. Her total revenue from sales last month amounted to $6,000. Should she continue to operate the business or shut it down?

Graphing Exercise

5. Construct a graph of fixed cost, variable cost, and total cost, and then a second graph of marginal cost for Tony's Pizza, using the data in the cost table below. What other information does Tony need in order to determine how many pizzas he should produce per week? Explain your answer.

Weekly Cost Data for Tony's Pizza

Output	Fixed Cost	Variable Cost	Total Cost	Marginal Cost
0	$500	0	$ 500	- - -
10	$500	$1,000	$1,500	$100
20	$500	$1,500	$2,000	$ 50
30	$500	$1,800	$2,300	$ 30
40	$500	$2,100	$2,600	$ 30
50	$500	$2,600	$3,100	$ 50
60	$500	$3,600	$4,100	$100

Think Critically

6. **Entrepreneurship** You own a gasoline station. You have found that the cost of keeping your store open is $35 per hour for labor and power. Between midnight and 5:00 A.M., sales are not that great. On average, during this time you sell only 100 gallons of gasoline per hour. At the current price of $1.50 per gallon, your markup on gasoline is $.25 per gallon. Should you keep your business open all night?

CONNECT *to History*

The
Industrial Revolution in the United States: The Supply of Cotton

The increases in the production of cotton textiles in the late 1700s brought about the Industrial Revolution. As production became more industrialized, suppliers of raw cotton were faced with heavy demand. In the United States, growing cotton was profitable only along a narrow strip along the coast of Georgia and the Carolinas. It was the only place Sea Island cotton could be grown. Another strain, which could be grown in the interior, was unprofitable because it produced a lot of seeds, which could be removed only by hand. It took a day's work to separate the seeds from the lint, making it too slow and too expensive to satisfy the demands of the industry.

Eli Whitney changed all this in 1793 with his invention of the cotton gin. Whitney's invention allowed one man to produce what it had previously taken 50 men, mostly slaves, to produce. Cotton now could be grown where it formerly had been cost prohibitive, enabling the American South to supply Great Britain's growing demand for raw cotton. Within two years, cotton exports from the United States to Great Britain rose from 487,000 pounds to 6,276,300. Because Great Britain's textile mills were demanding ever-increasing amounts of cotton, Southern planters were willing to move inland and devote more land and resources to producing cotton. The quantity of cotton supplied increased rapidly, keeping pace with the growing British cotton textile industry.

The British government, protective of its textile industry, passed laws preventing anyone with knowledge of the workings of a textile mill from leaving the country. Despite that prohibition, an English textile mechanic, Samuel Slater, was attracted by a prize being offered for information about the English textile industry. He disguised himself as a farm laborer and came to the United States. Slater established a mill at Pawtucket, Rhode Island. Building its machinery entirely from memory, he started the American textile industry on December 20, 1790. Still, American mills had a difficult time competing with British imports and could afford only cheaper cotton imported from the West Indies. Southern states sold all of their cotton at a better price to English mills.

THINK CRITICALLY

What variable cost did the invention of the cotton gin allow Southern cotton producers to lower? How were the growers able to create "economies of scale"? Why do you think the American cotton mills, using essentially the same equipment, had difficulty competing with the British cotton imports?

Summary

5.1 The Supply Curve

a Firms are motivated to produce products out of their desire to earn profit. *Supply* indicates how much of a good producers are willing and able to offer for sale per period at each possible price, other things constant. The *law of supply* states that the quantity of a product supplied will be greater at a higher price than at a lower price, other things constant.

b Businesses supply more products at higher prices because they can shift resources from the production of other products that have lower prices. Further, higher prices encourage producers to find new sources of resources, or more efficient means of production. *Individual supply* is the quantity of product supplied by one firm in a market. *Market supply* is the total quantity of product supplied by all firms in a market.

c The *price elasticity of supply* is the relationship between a percentage change in the price of a product and the resulting percentage change in the quantity supplied. Supply may be elastic, unit elastic, or inelastic. As a general rule, the more difficult or costly it is to change the quantity of a product produced, the less elastic supply will be.

5.2 Shifts of the Supply Curve

a There are five determinants of supply that shift the location of a supply curve when they change. They are (1) changes in the cost of resources used to make the good, (2) changes in the price of other goods these resources could make, (3) changes in the technology used to make the good, (4) changes in the producers' expectations, and (5) changes in the number of sellers in the market.

b A change in the price of a product will cause movement along a supply curve that is called a change in the quantity supplied. A change in a determinant of supply will cause a supply curve to move or shift to the left or right.

5.3 Production and Cost

a Production in the *short run* takes place in a period during which at least one productive resource cannot be changed or is fixed. Variable resources may be changed in the short run. In the *long run*, all resources are variable.

b The *marginal product* of an additional worker is the change in total production that results from employing one more worker. When production of a product is increased, there are typically first increasing returns and then diminishing returns.

c *Fixed cost* must be paid in the short run and does not change with the quantity produced. *Variable cost* is zero when output is zero and increases when output increases.

d *Marginal cost* equals the change in total cost divided by the change in total quantity. *Marginal revenue* is the additional revenue resulting from selling one more unit of output. Businesses will sell more output as long as the marginal revenue exceeds the marginal cost. In the short run, a firm's supply curve is that portion of its marginal cost curve rising above the minimum acceptable price.

e In the short run, firms that are losing money will continue to produce as long as their total revenue is greater than their variable cost. If they shut down, they would lose more than they would if they continued to make products.

f In the long run, firms face *economies* and *diseconomies of scale*. The *long-run average cost curve* first slopes downward as the scale of the firm expands, reflecting economies of scale. At some point it may flatten out, reflecting constant returns to scale. As the scale of the firm increases, the long-run average cost curve may begin to slope upward, reflecting diseconomies of scale.

Review Economic Terms

Choose the term that best fits the definition. On a separate sheet of paper, write the letter of the answer. Some terms may not be used.

_____ 1. A period of time during which at least one of a firm's resources is fixed

_____ 2. The change in total revenue from selling another unit of a product

_____ 3. Any cost that does not change with the amount of production in the short run

_____ 4. A period of time during which all of a firm's resources can be varied

_____ 5. The change in total cost resulting from producing one more unit of output.

_____ 6. Any production cost that changes as output changes

_____ 7. A measure of the responsiveness of the quantity of a product supplied to a change in price

_____ 8. The change in total product that results from an increase of one unit of resource input

_____ 9. As more of a variable resource is added to a given amount of fixed resources, marginal product eventually declines and could become negative

_____ 10. Forces that reduce a firm's average cost as the firm's size grows

_____ 11. The total output of the firm

a. competitive firm's supply curve

b. economies of scale

c. elasticity of supply

d. fixed cost

e. law of diminishing returns

f. law of supply

g. long run

h. long-run average cost curve

i. marginal cost

j. marginal product

k. marginal revenue

l. short run

m. supply

n. supply curve

o. total cost

p. total product

q. variable cost

Review Economic Concepts

12. A shift of a product's *supply curve* will be caused by each of the following *except*

    a. an increase in the cost of the resources used to produce the product.

    b. an improvement in the technology used to produce the product.

    c. an increase in consumer demand for the product.

    d. a decrease in the price of other products that resources could be used to produce.

13. **True or False** If a product's *elasticity of supply* is 0.8, a 2 percent increase in price will cause a greater than 2 percent increase in the quantity supplied.

14. Typically, the longer the period of time, the __?__ a product's *elasticity of supply* will be.

15. Which of the following events would cause the supply curve to shift to the left?

    a. A firm's employees negotiate a 5 percent increase in their wages.

    b. A firm's managers buy new, more efficient machinery for workers to use.

    c. A firm provides its workers with training to better use their tools.

    d. A firm finds a new, less expensive source of raw materials.

16. An increase in the price of a firm's product will cause __?__ the firm's supply curve.

17. **True or False** In the long run, all costs of production are variable.

18. An increase in the price of a product will cause __?__ the supply curve for that product.

19. If a firm experiences diminishing returns, it finds that

    a. there will be no increase in production when it hires another worker.

    b. the next worker hired will add less to production than the last worker hired.

    c. it will earn no profit if it hires additional workers.

    d. it must lay off workers to earn a profit.

20. Which of the following is an example of a variable cost?

    a. the cost or wages for night security guards

    b. the cost of fire insurance for a firm's factory

    c. the cost of raw materials used to produce goods

    d. the cost of renting a computer for a firm's accounting office

21. In the short run, __?__ cost does not change as a firm produces additional output.

22. **True or False** A firm's *marginal cost* of production decreases as output increases.

23. __?__ are forces that reduce a firm's average cost of production as the firm grows in size.

24. If a 1 percent change in price results in a 2 percent change in the quantity of the product that is supplied, the supply of that product is

    a. elastic.

    b. unit elastic.

    c. inelastic.

    d. perfectly elastic.

25. A producer's __?__ is the change in its total revenue that results from selling one more unit of a product.

26. **True or False** The *law of supply* states that the quantity of a product that is supplied will grow as the price of that product increases.

27. In the long run, a firm will

    a. face economies of scale as its long-run average cost curve slopes up.

    b. face diseconomies of scale as its long-run average cost curve slopes down.

    c. face diseconomies of scale as its long-run average cost curve slopes up.

    d. face economies of scale after its long-run average cost curve reaches its lowest point.

28. **True or False** On the left side of a firm's long run average cost curve, its average costs decline as production increases.

Apply Economic Concepts

29. A firm has the following marginal costs at different levels of production. If it is able to sell all the products it can produce at $5 each, how many will it produce? Explain your answer.

Units	Marginal Cost Per Unit
100	$6
200	$4
300	$3
400	$4
500	$5
600	$6

30. The lowest long-run average cost for whatsits is $50 per unit. To take advantage of economies of scale and produce whatsits at this low cost, a firm would need to build a factory that could produce 5,000,000 whatsits per year. There are only 20,000 people who are willing to pay anything to buy a whatsit per year. Why won't a large whatsits factory be built?

31. Calculating the Price Elasticity of Supply Complete the table below by calculating each missing elasticity of supply value. Is the supply elastic or inelastic?

Price Elasticity of Supply for Dozens of Bagels

Price	Percentage Change	Quantity Supplied	Percentage Change	Elasticity	Elastic/Inelastic
$8	- - -	100	- - -	- - -	- - -
$7	12.5%	90	10.0%	_____	_____
$6	14.3%	80	11.1%	_____	_____
$5	16.6%	70	12.5%	_____	_____
$4	20.0%	60	14.3%	_____	_____
$3	25.0%	50	16.6%	_____	_____

32. Sharpen Your Life Skills: Cause and Effect During the summer of 2003, Americans were warned that shortages of natural gas could cause its price to increase by as much as 50 percent or more during the following winter. Natural gas is a primary ingredient used in the production of artificial fertilizer. Much of the fertilizer used by U.S. farmers during the spring of 2004 was produced during the preceding winter. If the cost of producing this fertilizer increased as predicted, what would have happened to the location of the supply curve for agricultural products in 2004? Explain your answer.

33. Accounting Classify each of the following costs as variable or fixed. Explain your decision for each cost.

- The cost of a leased delivery truck
- The cost of a night security service
- The cost of delivering finished products
- The cost of fire insurance
- The cost of electricity used to run production machinery

 econxtra.swlearning.com

34. Access EconData Online at econxtra .swlearning.com. Read the article entitled "Labor Cost Per Unit of Output." Find the answers to the following questions from the article: (1) What is the relationship between labor productivity and worker's compensation insurance? (2) Why is labor cost an important indicator of trends in production costs? Write your answers in complete sentences on a sheet of paper.

6 Market Forces

Consider

How is market competition different from competition in sports and in games?

Why do car dealers usually locate together on the outskirts of town?

What's the difference between making stuff right and making the right stuff?

Why do government efforts to keep rents low usually lead to a housing shortage?

Why do consumers benefit nearly as much from a low price as from a zero price?

CLEARANCE

© Getty Images/PhotoDisc

POINT YOUR BROWSER

econxtra.swlearning.com

Objectives

> Understand how markets reach equilibrium.

> Explain how markets reduce transaction costs.

Overview

Markets allow you to buy and sell for a price. Price is the amount you pay when you buy a good and the amount you receive when you sell it. As a buyer, or demander, you have a different view of the price than a seller, or supplier, does. That's because demanders pay the price and suppliers receive it. As the price rises, consumers reduce their quantity demanded along their demand curve, and producers increase their quantity supplied along their supply curve. How is this conflict between producers and consumers resolved? Market forces resolve the differences.

Key Terms

equilibrium

surplus

shortage

transaction cost

[In the News]

The Toy Business Is Not Child's Play

U.S. toy sales exceeded $25 billion a year in 2001, but the business is not much fun for toy makers. Most toys don't make it from one season to the next, turning out to be costly duds. A few have staying power—like G.I. Joe, who could retire after more than 30 years of military service; Barbie, who is pushing 40; and the Wiffle Ball, still a hit after 40 years. Most store buyers must order in February for Christmas delivery. Can you imagine the uncertainty of this market? Who, for example, could have anticipated the phenomenal success of Tickle Me Elmo, Beanie Babies, Teletubbies, Furbies, Pokemon, or PlayStation 2? A few years ago, the Mighty Morphin Power Rangers were hot. Within a year, the manufacturer increased production tenfold, with 11 new factories churning out nearly $1 billion worth of Rangers. Still, at a selling price of $13, quantity demanded exceeded quantity supplied. Why don't toy manufacturers simply let the price find equilibrium? Suppose, for example, that the market-clearing price for Power Rangers was $26, twice the actual selling price. Consumers might have resented paying so much for such a small toy. Toy manufacturers usually make a variety of toys and may not want to be viewed as price gougers. After all, a firm's reputation is important, and surveys indicate that consumers consider some price hikes to be unfair. Suppliers who hope to retain customers over the long haul may want to avoid appearing greedy.

Think About It

What other factors can you think of that would lead a company to set the price for its product rather than letting supply and demand determine the price?

Investigate Your Local Economy

Go to a local shopping center. Look for evidence of specific goods that seem to be experiencing a surplus and those that seem to be experiencing a shortage. Make a list of at least four examples of each. Share your list of goods in class, and discuss the evidence that led you to choose each one.

equilibrium

The quantity consumers are willing and able to buy equals the quantity producers are willing and able to sell

surplus

At a given price, the amount by which quantity supplied exceeds quantity demanded; a surplus usually forces the price down

Market Equilibrium

When the quantity that consumers are willing and able to buy equals the quantity that producers are willing and able to sell, that market reaches **equilibrium**. In equilibrium, the independent plans of buyers and sellers exactly match, and there is no incentive for change. Therefore, market forces exert no further pressure to change price or quantity.

Surplus Forces the Price Down

To understand how a particular market reaches equilibrium, you need to consider demand *and* supply. Figure 6.1 shows the market for pizza, using schedules in panel (a) and curves in panel (b). What if the price initially is $12 per pizza? At that price, producers supply 24 million pizzas per week, but consumers demand only 14 million, resulting in an *excess quantity supplied,* or a **surplus**, of 10 million pizzas per week. This surplus means that suppliers are stuck with 10 million pizzas they can't sell at $12.

Suppliers' desire to eliminate the surplus puts downward pressure on the price. The arrow pointing down in the graph represents this pressure. As the price falls, producers reduce their quantity supplied and consumers increase their quantity demanded. As long as quantity supplied exceeds quantity demanded, the surplus forces the price lower.

Shortage Forces the Price Up

What if the initial price is $6 per pizza? Figure 6.1 shows that at that price, consumers demand 26 million pizzas a week, but producers supply only 16 million. This results in an *excess quantity demanded,* or a **shortage**, of 10 million pizzas per week. Producers soon notice that the quantity supplied has sold out and the consumers unable to buy pizza for $6 are frustrated. Profit-maximizing producers and frustrated consumers create market pressure for a higher price. The arrow pointing up in the graph represents this pressure. As the price rises, producers increase their quantity supplied and consumers reduce their quantity demanded. The price continues to rise as long as quantity demanded exceeds quantity supplied.

Thus, *a surplus puts downward pressure on the price, and a shortage puts upward pressure.* As long as quantity demanded and quantity supplied differ, this difference forces a price change. Note that a shortage or a surplus is always measured at a particular

Main Idea

Role of Incentives

Suppliers and consumers respond predictably to positive and negative incentives. Suppliers view a surplus as a negative incentive, and they act to eliminate it by lowering the price of the good. Consumers, on the other hand, view a surplus as a positive incentive, and increase the quantity they buy due to the lower price. If a fruit market had an excess supply of bananas, what would the manager probably do with the price? How would consumers likely respond?

© Getty Images/PhotoDisc

price. There is no such thing as a general shortage or a general surplus.

Market Forces Lead to Equilibrium Price and Quantity

In Figure 6.1, the demand and supply curves intersect at the *equilibrium point*, identified as point *c*. The *equilibrium price*, which equates quantity demanded with quantity supplied, is $9 per pizza. The *equilibrium quantity* is 20 million per week. At that price and quantity, the market is said to *clear*. That's why the equilibrium price also is called the *market-clearing price*. Because there is no shortage and no surplus, there is no longer any pressure for the price to change. The equilibrium price will remain at $9 unless there is some shift in demand or supply.

A market finds equilibrium through the independent and voluntary actions of thousands, or even millions, of buyers and sellers. In one sense, the market is personal because each consumer and each producer makes a personal decision regarding how much to buy or sell at a given price. In another sense, the market is impersonal because it requires no conscious coordination among consumers or producers. *The independent decisions of many individual buyers and many individual sellers cause the price to move to reach equilibrium in competitive markets.*

CHECKPOINT
How do markets reach equilibrium?

Market Exchange

Buyers and sellers have different attitudes about the price of a particular good. Markets help sort out those differences. Markets answer the questions of *what to produce, how to produce it,* and *for whom to produce it.*

Adam Smith's Invisible Hand

Market prices guide resources to their most productive uses and channel goods to those consumers who value

Ask the Xpert!
econxtra.swlearning.com

Why do some prices adjust more slowly?

shortage
At a given price, the amount by which quantity demanded exceeds quantity supplied; a shortage usually forces the price up

---

The Graphing Workshop
econxtra.swlearning.com

Equilibrium in the Pizza Market

Figure 6.1

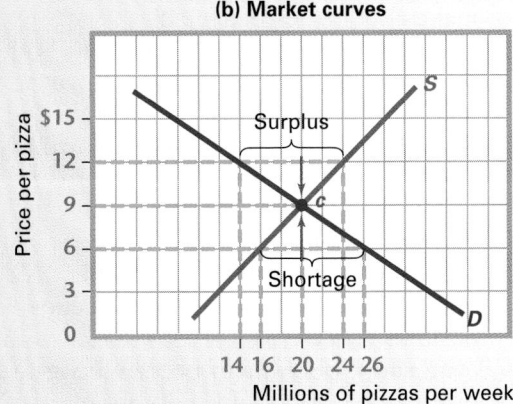

(b) Market curves

(a) Market schedules

Millions of Pizzas per Week

Price per Pizza	Quantity Demanded	Quantity Supplied	Surplus or Shortage	Effect on Price
$15	8	28	Surplus of 20	Falls
12	14	24	Surplus of 10	Falls
9	20	20	Equilibrium	Remains the same
6	26	16	Shortage of 10	Rises
3	32	12	Shortage of 20	Rises

Market equilibrium occurs at a price at which the quantity demanded by consumers is equal to the quantity supplied by producers. This is shown at point c. At prices above the equilibrium price, the quantity supplied exceeds the quantity demanded. At these prices there is a surplus, and a downward pressure on the price. At prices below equilibrium, quantity demanded exceeds quantity supplied. The resulting shortage puts upward pressure on the price.

Shortage of Internet Access Creates Hot Spots

You're grabbing a quick bite at McDonald's and use your laptop's Internet connection to check the price of a stock you bought earlier today. You're flying to Santa Fe and are on a layover in Dallas. You check your e-mail using your hand-held game device's Internet connection. A few years ago none of these functions would have been possible due to the shortage or non-availability of hard-wired access points to an Internet service provider (ISP). Today, the widespread demand for Internet access has a new type of supplier creating "hot spots" or zones where wireless connectors can stream information at an incredible speed. Access to wireless hot spots is available for about $20 per month for nationwide service. Compare this to phone dial-up ISPs' flat rates of around $10 per month. As wireless Internet coverage expands, you may find such hot spots just about anywhere.

Think Critically

How is the demand for such wireless service reflected in the relative pricing of wireless versus hard-wired ISPs?

them the most. Market prices transmit information about relative scarcity and provide incentives to producers and consumers. Markets also distribute earnings among resource owners.

The coordination that occurs through markets takes place not because of some central plan but because of Adam Smith's "invisible hand." No individual or small group coordinates market activities. Rather, it is the voluntary choices of many buyers and sellers responding only to their individual incentives. Buyers and sellers direct resources and products to those who value them the most. Although each individual pursues his or her own self-interest, the "invisible hand" of market competition promotes the general welfare.

Market Exchange Is Voluntary

Your experience with competition likely comes from sports, games, and the like, where one side wins and the other side loses. Market exchange is not like that. Market exchange is a voluntary activity in which both sides of the market expect to benefit and usually do. Neither buyers nor sellers would participate in the market unless they expected to be better off. A buyer values the product purchased at least as much as the money paid for it. A seller values the money received at least as much as the product sold.

For example, a consumer will pay $9 for a pizza only if he or she thinks the marginal benefit of that pizza is worth at least $9. The pizza maker will supply a pizza for $9 only if he or she thinks its marginal cost will be no more than $9. Again, voluntary exchange usually makes both sides better off.

Market prices serve as signals to both buyers and sellers about the relative scarcity of the good. A higher price encourages consumers to economize by finding substitutes for the good or even going without it. A higher price also encourages producers to allocate more resources to the production of this good and fewer resources to the production of other goods.

In short, prices help people recognize market opportunities to make better choices as consumers and as producers. The beneficial effects of market exchange include trade between people or organizations in different parts of the country, and among people and organizations in different countries.

Markets Reduce Transaction Costs

A market sorts out the conflicting views of price between demanders and suppliers. Markets reduce **transaction costs**, or the cost of time and information needed to carry out market exchange. The higher the transaction cost, the less likely the exchange will actually take place. For example, imagine you are looking for a summer job. One approach might be to go from employer to employer looking for openings. This would be time consuming and could have you running around for days. A more efficient strategy would be to read the help-wanted ads in the local paper or go online to look for job openings. Classified ads and web sites, which are elements of the job market, reduce the transaction costs required to bring workers and employers together. Thus, *markets reduce transaction costs*.

transaction cost

The cost of time and information needed to carry out market exchange

CHECKPOINT
How do markets reduce transaction costs?

6.1 Assessment

Key Concepts

1. How would the owner of a dress shop react if she found she had 30 extra prom dresses that she could not sell at the current price?

2. How would the owners of a nursery react if hundreds of customers wanted to buy yucca plants at the current price of $15 when they have only 25 plants to sell?

3. How is it possible for both you and the owner of a fast-food restaurant to benefit when you choose to buy a hamburger for $2.00?

4. What are the transaction costs involved in shopping for shoes at your local mall?

Graphing Exercise

5. Construct a graph of the demand and supply for running shoes from the data in the demand and supply schedule. What is the equilibrium price? What would happen to the price and quantity demanded and supplied if the current price was $60?

Demand and Supply for Running Shoes

Price	Quantity Demanded	Quantity Supplied
$70	40	100
$60	50	80
$50	60	60
$40	70	40
$30	80	20

Think Critically

6. **Science** Scientists have created tomatoes through genetic engineering that are resistant to many diseases. Over time this has caused the equilibrium price of tomatoes to fall. Explain why this has happened.

movers & shakers

Mary Engelbreit *Artist and Entrepreneur*

When Mary Engelbreit was 11 years old, she moved into her first art studio—a closet in her home in St. Louis, Missouri. After high school graduation, Engelbreit went to work in an art supply store and then in a small advertising agency. She accepted freelance art projects, held independent showings of her work, and for a short time worked as an editorial cartoonist for the St. Louis Post-Dispatch. Although she learned a lot, Engelbreit felt she did her best work when it came from her imagination.

In 1977, newly married and with encouragement from her husband, Engelbreit took her portfolio to New York City and called on some well-known publishing houses. One New York art director suggested she try greeting cards. "I was kind of crushed," she recalls, but then she saw how suitable the suggestion might be. Engelbreit's open-mindedness toward new possibilities became one of the keys to her success.

Engelbreit sold her first three greeting-card designs for $150. But she didn't like depending on the whims of the card companies. So in 1983 Engelbreit began her own greeting-card company. While some may have thought the timing was not right to start her own company—she was due to have a baby in just one month—Engelbreit said, "There's always a reason not to do things; it's too expensive, or it's not the best time, or this, or that; but I believe there are always wonderful oppor-

tunities sailing by, and you have to be ready to grab them."

Engelbreit has been grabbing opportunities ever since. In just a few years, her greeting cards blossomed into a million dollar business. Today she is the leader of three companies:

- Mary Engelbreit Studios develops licensed products—including greeting cards, books, calendars, gifts, frames, dinnerware, and fabrics—sold by thousands of retailers throughout the United States and in many foreign countries.

- The Mary Engelbreit Store in St. Louis, Missouri, carries more than 1,000 products, including the exclusive ME products that are available only in her store.

- *Mary Engelbreit's Home Companion* magazine has a readership of more than two million and covers topics including family life, food, home décor, crafts, gardening, and collectibles. Today, most of Engelbreit's products are sold through specialty stores and major retailers, as well as through online stores, including her own, which opened in July 2003.

Each of Engelbreit's products reaches a similar audience, and she clearly is a success. In 2000, she was named by *Giftware Business* magazine as the second best-selling licensed property (a close second to Winnie the Pooh). In 2001 and 2003, the International Licensing Industry Merchandisers' Association honored Mary Engelbreit with the prestigious Best Art License of the Year award.

SOURCE READING
Mary Engelbreit was not thrilled with the idea of illustrating greeting cards. After some thought, however, she reconsidered. What were some of the market forces that would have helped Mary determine the price of her greeting cards and the quantity she should produce?

ENTREPRENEURS IN ACTION
In small groups, discuss the similarities in the markets for Mary Engelbreit's three companies. Think of one or more companies that Engelbreit might consider starting, based on these similarities.

Objectives

> Explain how a shift of the demand curve affects equilibrium price and quantity.

> Explain how a shift of the supply curve affects equilibrium price and quantity.

> Explain what happens to equilibrium price and quantity if both curves shift.

Overview

When a market reaches equilibrium, the quantity of products demanded and supplied are the same. The equilibrium price and quantity will continue until one of the determinants of demand or supply changes. This section examines how a change in any one of these determinants will shift the demand curve or the supply curve, and in the process change equilibrium price and quantity. The adjustment to a new equilibrium is usually swift. At times, however, often because of government intervention, markets fail to achieve equilibrium.

Key Terms

increase in demand

decrease in demand

increase in supply

decrease in supply

[In the News]

● A Cold Slap in the Face

In February 2003, a cold snap and a quick rise in natural gas prices drove up monthly heating costs for some U.S. homeowners to nearly twice what they had been in February 2002. A retired Long Island, N.Y., executive reported a gas bill of $425, which was 107 percent more than he paid the year earlier. The unexpected cold snap drove up demand for the limited supply of gas. Adding to the problem was that the price of oil also was high at that time. (Because oil and natural gas are interchangeable for many industrial uses, their prices often rise together.) The 2003 supply of gas in the United States was less than half of what it had been the year before. Experts foresee continued increases in the demand for gas, while available resources will remain in decline. "All the big, easy-to-get gas got pulled out to provide for us in the [19]90s," said a spokesperson for the American Gas Association. "For the next three to five years, this is what we're going to be seeing." Oddly enough, homebuilders say the high heating costs don't seem to bother many of today's home buyers, who keep demanding bigger and bigger homes. A home-building industry spokesperson estimates that improved construction and insulation in the last decade has cut the amount of gas required to heat a new house by more than 30 percent.

Think About It

Which curve for natural gas—supply or demand—was affected by the cold snap, and which way did it shift? What was the effect on price and quantity?

169

Shifts of the Demand Curve

In Figure 6.2, demand curve D and supply curve S intersect at the equilibrium price of $9 and the initial equilibrium quantity of 20 million 12-inch pizzas per week. What happens to equilibrium price and quantity when the demand curve shifts? A shift of the demand curve means that quantity demanded changes at each price.

What Could Shift the Demand Curve?

If one of the factors that determine the demand for pizza changes in a way that increases demand, this would shift the demand curve to the right from D to D'. Any of the following could shift the demand for pizza rightward:

1. An increase in the money income of consumers (because pizza is a normal good)

2. An increase in the price of a substitute, such as tacos, or a decrease in the price of a complement, such as beverages

3. A change in expectations that encourages consumers to buy more pizza now

4. A growth in the population of pizza consumers

5. A change in consumer tastes in favor of pizza

An Increase in Demand

Any one of those five changes could increase the demand for pizza. An **increase in demand** means that consumers are now more willing and able to buy the product at every price. Note that none of these changes will shift the supply curve.

After the demand curve shifts rightward to D' in Figure 6.2, the amount demanded at the initial price of $9 increases to 30 million pizzas. Because producers supply only 20 million pizzas at that price, there is a shortage of 10 million pizzas. Many consumers are frustrated because they can't find pizza at that price. Producers realize that they could charge more for pizza. This shortage puts upward pressure on the price.

As the price increases, the quantity demanded decreases along the new demand curve, D', and the quantity supplied increases along the existing supply curve, S, until the two quantities are once again equal. The new equilibrium price is $12, and the new equilib-

increase in demand
Consumers are more willing and able to buy the product at every price

Effects of an Increase in Demand

Figure 6.2

After an increase in demand shifts the demand curve from D to D', quantity demanded exceeds quantity supplied at the old price of $9 per pizza. As the price rises, quantity supplied increases along supply curve S, and quantity demanded falls along demand curve D'. When the new equilibrium price of $12 is reached, the quantity demanded once again equals the quantity supplied. Both price and quantity are higher following the increase in demand.

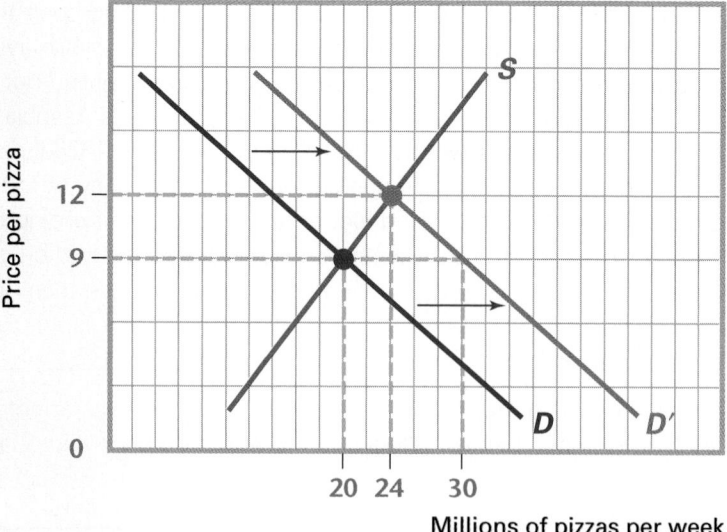

rium quantity is 24 million pizzas per week. *As long as the supply curve slopes upward, a rightward shift of the demand curve increases both price and quantity.*

A Decrease in Demand

What if one of the determinants of demand changed in a way that reduced demand—such as a decrease in consumer income, a decrease in the price of a substitute, or a reduction in the number of consumers? This results in a **decrease in demand** and consumers are now less willing and able to buy the product, pizza, at every price.

The effect of a decrease in demand is shown in Figure 6.3. The demand for pizza shifts leftward from *D* to *D″*. The amount demanded at the initial price of $9 is now 10 million pizzas. Because producers supply 20 million at that price, there is a surplus of 10 million pizzas. To eliminate the surplus, the price must fall. Thus, this surplus puts downward pressure on the price.

As the price falls, the quantity demanded increases along the new demand curve *D″* and the quantity supplied decreases along the existing supply curve *S* until the two quantities are equal once again. The new equilibrium price is $6, and the new equilibrium quantity is 16 million pizzas per week.

week. *As long as the supply curve slopes upward, a leftward shift of the demand curve reduces both price and quantity.*

Summary of Demand Shifts

Given an upward-sloping supply curve, a rightward shift of the demand curve increases both price and quantity and a leftward shift of the demand curve decreases both price and quantity. One way to remember this is to picture the demand curve shifting along a given upward-sloping supply curve. If the demand curve shifts rightward, price and quantity increase. If the demand curve shifts leftward, price and quantity decrease.

CHECKPOINT
How does a shift of the demand curve affect equilibrium price and quantity?

Shifts of the Supply Curve

What happens to equilibrium price and quantity when there is a shift of the supply curve? A shift of the supply curve

decrease in demand
Consumers are less willing and able to buy the product at every price

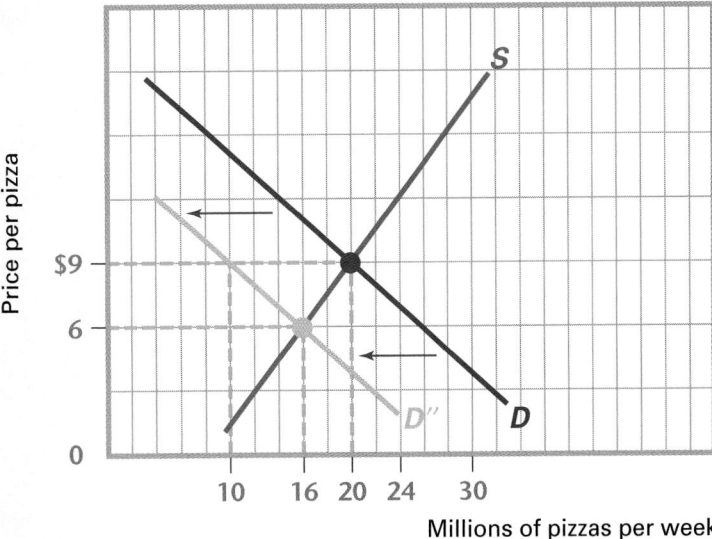

The Graphing Workshop
econxtra.swlearning.com

Effects of a Decrease in Demand

Figure 6.3

After a decrease in demand shifts the demand curve from *D* to *D″*, quantity supplied exceeds quantity demanded at the old price of $9 per pizza. As the price falls, quantity supplied decreases along supply curve *S*, and quantity demanded increases along demand curve *D″*. When the new equilibrium price of $6 is reached, the quantity demanded once again equals the quantity supplied. Both price and quantity are lower following the decrease in demand.

means that quantity supplied changes at each price. In Figure 6.4, demand curve *D* and supply curve *S* intersect to yield the initial equilibrium price of $9 and the initial equilibrium quantity of 20 million 12-inch pizzas per week.

What Could Shift the Supply Curve?

If one of the factors that determine supply changes in a way that increases supply, this would shift the supply curve to the right from *S* to *S'*. Any of the following could shift the pizza supply curve rightward:

1. A reduction in the price of a resource used to make pizza, such as mozzarella cheese

2. A decline in the price of another good these resources could make, such as Italian bread

3. A technological breakthrough in pizza ovens

4. A change in expectations that encourages pizza makers to expand production

5. An increase in the number of pizzerias

An Increase In Supply

Any of the above changes will shift the supply curve, but none will shift the demand curve. An **increase in supply** means that producers are more willing and able to supply pizza at every price. After the supply curve shifts rightward to *S'* in Figure 6.4, the amount supplied

increase in supply

Producers are more willing and able to supply the product at every price

What would happen to the supply curve for pizza in your area if many of the pizza restaurants invested in a new type of pizza oven?

The Graphing Workshop

Effects of an Increase in Supply

econxtra.swlearning.com

Figure 6.4

An increase in supply is depicted as a shift to the right of the supply curve, from *S* to *S'*. At the new equilibrium, quantity is greater and price is lower than before the increase in supply.

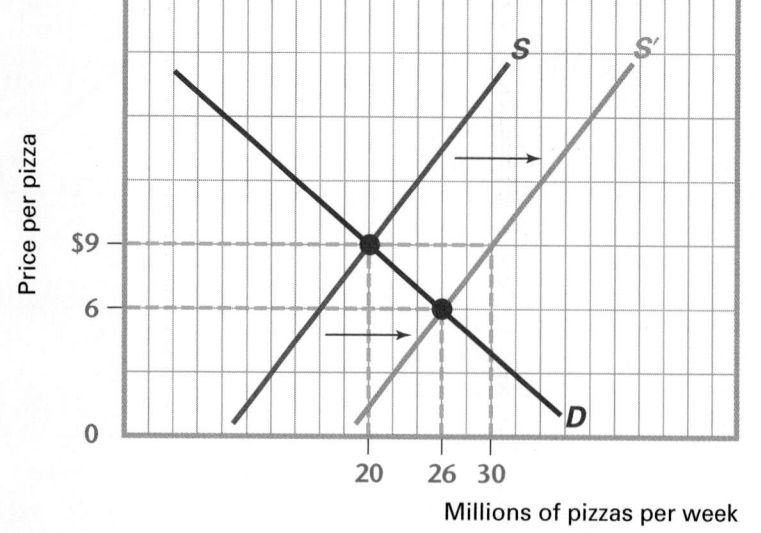

at the initial price of $9 increases from 20 million to 30 million. Producers supply 10 million more pizzas than consumers demand. The build up of unsold pizzas frustrates producers stuck with pizzas they can't sell for $9 each. This surplus forces the price down.

As the price falls, the quantity supplied declines along the new supply curve and the quantity demanded increases along the existing demand curve until a new equilibrium point is reached. The new equilibrium price is $6, and the new equilibrium quantity is 26 million pizzas per week. *As long as the demand curve slopes downward, a rightward shift of the supply curve reduces the price but increases the quantity.*

A Decrease In Supply

What if one of the determinants of supply changed in a way that reduced supply—such as an increase in the price of a resource used to make pizza, an increase in the price of another good these resources could make, or an decrease in the number of pizzerias?

A **decrease in supply** means that producers are less willing and able to supply pizza at every price. After the supply curve shifts leftward to *S″* in Figure 6.5, the amount supplied at the initial price of $9 decreases from 20 million to 10 million. Producers supply 10 million

fewer pizzas than consumers demand. This shortage forces the price up.

As the price rises the quantity supplied increases along the new supply curve and the quantity demanded decreases along the existing demand curve until a new equilibrium point is reached. The new equilibrium price is $12, and the new equilibrium quantity is 14 million pizzas per week. *As long as the demand curve slopes downward, a leftward shift of the supply curve increases the price but reduces the quantity.*

Summary of Supply Shifts

Thus, *given a downward-sloping demand curve, a rightward shift of the supply curve decreases price but increases quantity, and a leftward shift of the supply curve increases price but decreases quantity.* Picture the supply curve shifting along a given downward-sloping demand curve. If the supply curve shifts rightward, price decreases but quantity increases. If supply shifts to the left, price increases but quantity decreases.

CHECKPOINT
How does a shift of the supply curve affect equilibrium price and quantity?

Oil Creates Troubled Waters
econxtra.swlearning.com

decrease in supply
Producers are less willing and able to supply the product at every price

---

Effects of a Decrease in Supply

Figure 6.5

A decrease in supply is depicted as a shift to the left of the supply curve, from *S* to *S″*. At the new equilibrium, quantity is lower and price is higher than before the increase in supply.

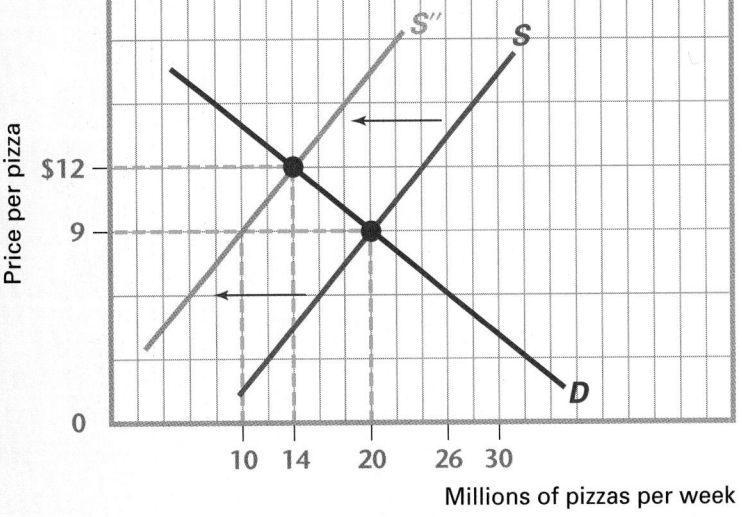

Millions of pizzas per week

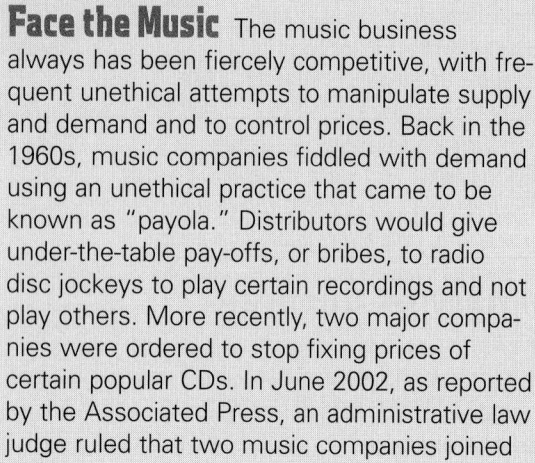

Ethics in Action

Face the Music The music business always has been fiercely competitive, with frequent unethical attempts to manipulate supply and demand and to control prices. Back in the 1960s, music companies fiddled with demand using an unethical practice that came to be known as "payola." Distributors would give under-the-table pay-offs, or bribes, to radio disc jockeys to play certain recordings and not play others. More recently, two major companies were ordered to stop fixing prices of certain popular CDs. In June 2002, as reported by the Associated Press, an administrative law judge ruled that two music companies joined forces to sell recordings of the opera stars known as the Three Tenors and illegally fixed prices. The illegal "piracy" of music recordings and films has for years created chaos on the supply side of the business. Also, the Internet continues to create ethical and legal issues surrounding the duplicating and distribution of music and other copyrighted art forms.

Think Critically

The music industry is not alone in its attempts to manipulate supply, demand, and prices. Can you think of how other industries might apply similar unethical or illegal practices?

Both Curves Shift

As long as only one curve shifts, you can determine what will happen to equilibrium price and quantity. If both curves shift, the outcome is less certain.

If Curves Shift in the Same Direction

If both demand and supply increase, buyers are more willing and able to demand the good at every price and sellers are more willing and able to sell it at every price. All you can say for sure is that equilibrium quantity will

Main Idea

Market—Price and Quantity Determination

The housing market exists when people who want to purchase a home interact with people who have a house for sale. How are prices in the housing market determined? If the demand for housing increases more than the supply, what happens to the price and quantity of homes on the market?

© Getty Images/PhotoDisc

increase. What happens to price depends on which curve shifts more.

If the demand curve increases more than the supply curve, equilibrium price will increase. For example, in the last decade, the demand for housing has increased more than the supply, so both price and quantity have increased.

If the supply curve increases more than the demand curve, equilibrium price will decrease. For example, in the last decade, the supply of personal computers has increased more than the demand, so price has decreased and quantity has increased.

Conversely, if both the demand and supply curves decrease, or shift to the left, this means that buyers are less willing and able to demand the good and sellers are less willing and able to supply it. So equilibrium quantity decreases. But again, you cannot determine what will happen to equilibrium price unless you examine the relative shifts. If the demand curve shifts more than the supply curve, the price will fall. If the supply curve shifts more, the price will rise.

If Curves Shift in Opposite Directions

If demand and supply shift in opposite directions, you can determine what will happen to equilibrium price.

THE WALL STREET JOURNAL

● **Reading It Right** What's the relevance of the following statement from *The Wall Street Journal*?

"California officials attribute generally lower electricity prices to relatively mild weather in recent days, conservation efforts in the state, and the return of some power plants to full operation."

Equilibrium price will increase if demand increases and supply decreases. Equilibrium price will decrease if demand decreases and supply increases. Without knowledge of particular shifts, however, you cannot say what will happen to equilibrium quantity.

Figure 6.6 summarizes the four possible combinations of changes. Keep in mind that demand curves shift due to factors that determine demand, and supply curves shift due to factors that determine supply.

CNN video
Exploring Higher Gas Prices
econxtra.swlearning.com

 CHECKPOINT
What happens to equilibrium price and quantity if both curves shift in the same direction?

Effects of Changes in Both Supply and Demand   Figure 6.6

When the supply and demand curves shift in the same direction, equilibrium quantity also shifts in that direction. The effect on equilibrium price depends on which curve shifts more. If the curves shift in opposite directions, equilibrium price will move in the same direction as demand. The effect on equilibrium quantity depends on which curve shifts more.

		Change in Demand	
		Demand increases	Demand decreases
Change in Supply	Supply increases	Equilibrium price change is indeterminate. Equilibrium quantity increases.	Equilibrium price falls. Equilibrium price change is indeterminate.
	Supply decreases	Equilibrium price rises. Equilibrium quantity change is indeterminate.	Equilibrium price change is indeterminate. Equilibrium quantity decreases.

Sharpen Your Life Skills

Analyze Visuals

The demand, supply, and equilibrium price for a product are unlikely to stay the same over long periods of time. Economists often demonstrate changes on graphs of demand and supply with arrows. Horizontal arrows that point to the right (→) indicate an increase in either demand or supply that shifts a curve to the right. Horizontal arrows that point to the left (←) indicate a decrease in either demand or supply that shifts a curve to the left. When the demand or supply curve for a product shifts, there will be a shortage or surplus of the product. When there is a surplus of a product, the producer will have an incentive to lower the price to a new equilibrium price. This change often is demonstrated on a graph of demand and supply with a vertical arrow that points down (↓). When there is a shortage of a product, the producer will have an incentive to increase the price to a new equilibrium price. This change often is demonstrated on a graph of demand and supply with a vertical arrow that points up (↑).

Apply Your Skill

Consider the graph of demand and supply for disposable cameras below. Redraw the graph to show what would happen as a result of each of the following events. Use arrows to show the shift in demand or supply, the resulting shortage or surplus, and the change in the price that would eliminate these amounts. Explain what you have done in each case.

Demand and Supply for Disposable Cameras

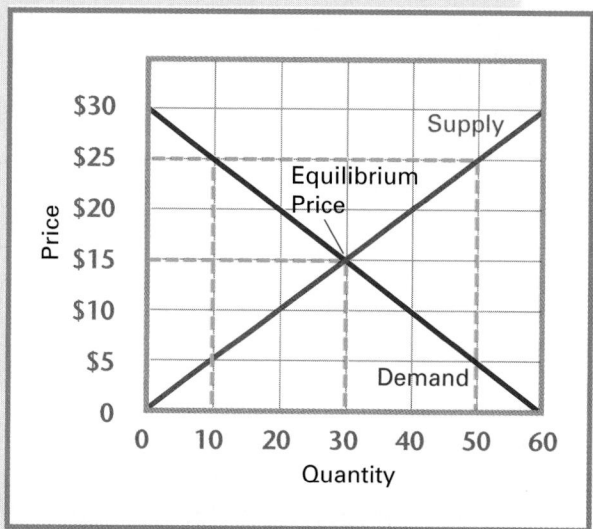

1. Travel increases during the summer months. This leads many more people to take vacation photographs.

2. There is an increase in the cost of film that causes the cost of producing a disposable camera to grow by 10 percent.

3. A new type of digital camera is marketed that is inexpensive and takes excellent photographs. Many people who used to buy disposable cameras choose to purchase these new digital cameras instead.

4. A new process is invented that allows the producer to assemble disposable cameras with half as many workers. This causes the firm to be willing to offer more cameras for sale at each possible price.

6.2 Assessment

Key Concepts

1. What would happen to a student's demand curve for movie tickets if she lost her after-school job?

2. What would happen to a student's demand curve for movie tickets if the price of DVD movies rentals increased by $4.00 each?

3. What would happen to the equilibrium price and demand curve for New York Yankee baseball caps if the Yankees had just won the World Series?

4. What would happen to the equilibrium price and location of a bakery's supply curve for loaves of bread if it agreed to give its workers a 10 percent raise in pay?

5. What would happen to the locations of a bowling alley's demand and supply curves if the Social Security rate of taxation was increased from 7.65 percent to 9.0 percent for both workers and employers? What would happen to the equilibrium price per game of bowling?

econxtra.swlearning.com

Graphing Exercise

6. Suppose that running becomes much more popular. As a result, consumers are willing to purchase 30 more pairs of running shoes at each possible price. The demand and supply schedule below shows this increase in demand. Construct a graph showing this shift of demand and the unchanged supply for running shoes. What is the new equilibrium price? Explain why the equilibrium price changed from $50.

Demand and Supply for Running Shoes

Price	Quantity Demanded		Quantity Supplied
	Old	New	
$70	40	70	100
$60	50	80	80
$50	60	90	60
$40	70	100	40
$30	80	110	20

Think Critically

7. **Advertising** Find an advertisement for a well-known brand of candy. Explain what the firm is trying to do to the location of its product's demand curve. If the firm is successful, what will probably happen to its profits?

8. **History** During 1974, there was a war in the Middle East that caused many petroleum-exporting nations to stop shipping oil to the United States. Explain what this did to the location of the supply curve and price for gasoline in the United States.

Objectives

> Distinguish between productive efficiency and allocative efficiency.

> Explain what happens when government imposes price floors and ceilings.

> Identify the benefits that consumers and producers get from market exchange.

Overview

Demand and supply are the foundation of a competitive market economy. Although a market usually involves the interaction of many buyers and sellers, few markets are consciously designed. Just as the law of gravity works whether or not you understand Newton's principles, market forces operate whether or not buyers and sellers understand the laws of demand and supply. Market forces arise naturally, much the way car dealers gather together in the city's outskirts.

Key Terms

productive efficiency

allocative efficiency

disequilibrium

price floor

price ceiling

consumer surplus

[In the News]

● Blood Pressure

In June 2002, the United States blood supply reached its lowest level in decades. America's Blood Centers (the federation that provides half the U.S. public blood supply) and the blood-collection centers of the American Red Cross both reported huge shortfalls. The shortages had a direct and measurable impact on healthcare across the nation. Hospitals were forced to cancel scheduled surgeries, and sur-charges were imposed on blood usage. The problem was a surprise. Just one year earlier, after the tragic 9-11 terrorist attacks, there was a surge in the number of Americans who rolled up their sleeves to bolster the blood supply. In fact, the Red Cross tripled its supply in the weeks following the attacks. One explanation for the drop in the number of donors was that, after the public's burst of generosity in 2001, people were just plain drained of giving, regardless of the need. The phenomenon was termed "compassion fatigue." But, most doctors said that even compassion fatigue doesn't fully explain the apathy toward donating blood.

Think About It

What are some ideas that might ensure that the nation's supply of blood keeps up with demand?

Competition and Efficiency

How do competitive markets stack up in terms of efficiency? To judge market performance, economists employ two measures of efficiency. The first, called *productive efficiency,* refers to producing output at the lowest possible cost. The second, called *allocative efficiency,* refers to producing the output that consumers value the most. Market competition promotes both productive efficiency and allocative efficiency.

Productive Efficiency: Making Stuff Right

Productive efficiency occurs when a firm produces at the lowest possible cost per unit. The firms that survive and thrive in a competitive market are those that supply the product at their lowest price. *Competition ensures that firms produce at the lowest possible cost per unit.* Firms that are not efficient must either shape up or leave the industry.

Allocative Efficiency: Making the Right Stuff

Producing at the lowest possible cost per unit is no guarantee that firms are producing what consumers most prefer. This situation is like the airline pilot who announces to passengers that there's some good news and some bad news: "The good news is that we're making record time. The bad news is that we're lost!" Likewise, firms may be producing efficiently but producing the wrong goods—that is, making stuff right but making the wrong stuff.

Allocative efficiency occurs when firms produce the output that is most valued by consumers. How do economists know that market competition guarantees allocative efficiency? The answer lies with the market demand and supply curves. The demand curve reflects the marginal benefit that consumers attach to each unit of the good, so the market price is the amount of money people are willing and able to pay for the final unit they purchase.

You also know that the equilibrium price equals the marginal cost of supplying the final unit sold. Marginal cost measures the opportunity cost of resources employed by the firm to produce that final unit sold. Thus the supply curve reflects the opportunity cost of producing the good.

The supply and demand curves intersect at the combination of price and quantity at which *the marginal benefit that consumers attach to the final unit purchased just equals the marginal cost of the resources employed to produce that unit.*

As long as marginal benefit equals marginal cost, that last unit purchased is worth as much as, or more than, any other good that could have been produced using those same resources. There is no way to reallocate resources to increase the total value of output to society. Thus, there is no way to reallocate resources to increase the total benefit consumers reap from production.

When the marginal benefit that consumers derive from a good equals the marginal cost of producing that good, that market is said to be allocatively efficient. Competition among sellers encourages producers to supply more of what consumers value the

productive efficiency

Occurs when a firm produces at the lowest possible cost per unit

allocative efficiency

Occurs when a firm produces the output most valued by consumers

Competition among running shoe brands encourages shoe producers to supply the types of shoes that consumers want to buy. What type of efficiency does this statement suggest?

most. Firms not only are making stuff right, they are making the right stuff.

CHECKPOINT
Distringuish between allocative efficiency and productive efficiency.

Disequilibrium

disequilibrium

A mismatch between quantity demanded and quantity supplied as the market seeks equilibrium; usually temporary, except where government intervenes and sets the price

price floor

A minimum legal price below which a product cannot be sold

price ceiling

A maximum legal selling price above which a product cannot be sold

One way to appreciate markets is to examine instances when they are slow to adjust or where they are not free to work. A surplus of goods exerts downward pressure on the price, and a shortage of goods exerts upward pressure. But markets do not always reach equilibrium quickly. During the time required for adjustment, the market is said to be in disequilibrium. **Disequilibrium** is usually a temporary condition when the plans of buyers do not match the plans of sellers. Sometimes, usually as a result of government intervention in markets, disequilibrium can last a while.

Price Floor

At times public officials set the price above its equilibrium level. For example, the federal government often regulates the prices of agricultural products in an attempt to ensure farmers a higher and more stable income than they would earn otherwise. To achieve higher prices, the federal government establishes a price floor for a product, making it illegal to sell below the floor price. A **price floor** is a minimum selling price that is above the equilibrium price.

Panel (a) of Figure 6.7 shows the effect of a $2.50 per gallon price floor for milk. At that price, farmers supply 24 million gallons per week, but consumers demand only 14 million gallons. Thus, the price floor results in a surplus of 10 million gallons. This surplus milk will accumulate on store shelves and eventually sour. So, as part of the price-support program, the government usually agrees to buy up the surplus milk to take it off the market. The federal government, in

NET Bookmark

The *minimum wage* is a price floor in the market for labor. The government sets a minimum price per hour of labor in certain markets, and no employer is permitted to pay a wage lower than that. Access the Department of Labor web site through econxtra.swlearning.com to learn more about the mechanics of the program. Then use a supply and demand graph to illustrate the effect of a minimum wage above equilibrium on a particular labor market. What happens to quantity demanded and quantity supplied as a result?

econxtra.swlearning.com

fact, has spent billions buying and storing surplus agricultural products.

Price Ceiling

Sometimes public officials try to keep prices below their equilibrium levels by establishing a **price ceiling**, or a *maximum* selling price. For example, concern about the rising cost of rental housing in some cities prompted public officials to impose rent ceilings, making it illegal to charge more than the ceiling price. Panel (b) of Figure 6.7 represents the demand and supply for rental housing in a hypothetical city. The vertical axis shows the monthly rent, and the horizontal axis shows the quantity of units rented. The equilibrium, or market-clearing, rent is $1,000 per month. The equilibrium quantity is 50,000 housing units.

Suppose government officials are concerned that rents of $1,000 per month are not affordable to enough households. They pass a law that sets a maximum rent of $600 per month. At that ceiling price, 60,000 rental units are demanded, but only 40,000 are supplied, resulting in a housing shortage of 20,000 units.

Because of the price ceiling, the rental price no longer allocates housing to those who value it the most. Other devices emerge to ration housing, such as waiting lists, personal connections, and

(a) Price floor for milk

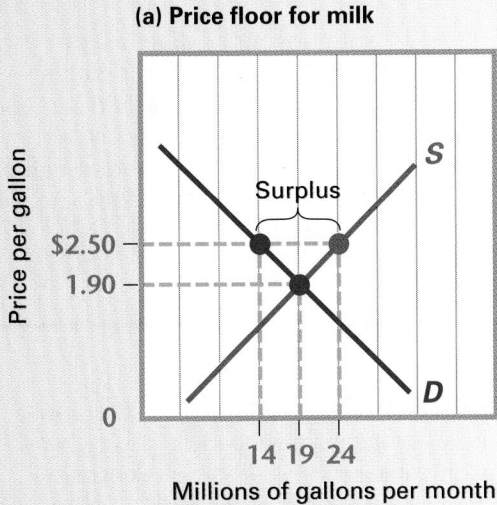

(b) Price ceiling for rent

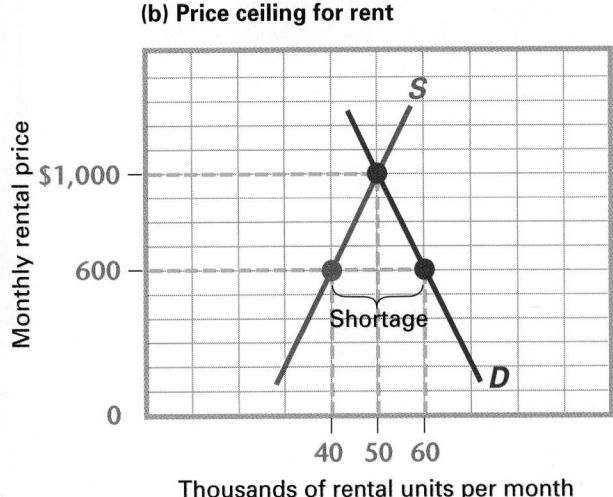

If a price floor is established above the equilibrium price, a permanent surplus results. A price floor established at or below the equilibrium price has no effect. If a price ceiling is established below the equilibrium price, a permanent shortage results. A price ceiling established at or above the equilibrium price has no effect.

the willingness to make under-the-table payments, such as "key fees," "finder's fees," high security deposits, and the like.

To have an impact, a price floor must be set above the equilibrium price, and a price ceiling must be set below the equilibrium price. A floor price above the equilibrium price creates a surplus, and a ceiling price below the equilibrium price creates a shortage. Various nonprice devices emerge to cope with the disequilibrium resulting from the market interference.

Price controls distort market prices and interfere with the market's ability to allocate resources efficiently. Prices no longer provide consumers and producers accurate information about the relative scarcity of goods. The good intentions of government officials create shortages and surpluses that often are economically wasteful.

Other Sources of Disequilibrium

Government intervention in the market is not the only source of disequilibrium. Sometimes, when new products are intro-

duced or when demand or supply changes suddenly, the market takes a while to adjust. For example, popular toys, best-selling books, and chart-busting CDs often sell out and are unavailable while suppliers produce more. In these cases, there is a temporary shortage.

On the other hand, some new products attract few customers and pile up unsold on store shelves, awaiting a "clearance sale." In this case, there is a temporary surplus.

CHECKPOINT
What happens when governments impose price floors and price ceilings?

Consumer Surplus

In equilibrium, the marginal benefit of pizza just equals its marginal cost. The cost to the economy of bringing that final pizza onto the market just equals the marginal benefit that consumers get from that pizza. Does this mean that consumers get no net benefit from the good? No. Market exchange usually benefits both consumers and producers.

Market Demand and Consumer Surplus

A demand curve shows the marginal benefit consumers attach to each unit of the good. For example, based on the demand curve for pizza presented earlier, consumers demanded 8 million pizzas at a

consumer surplus

The difference between the total amount consumers are willing and able to pay for a given quantity of a good and what they actually pay

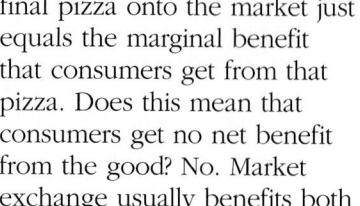

TEAM WORK

In small groups, discuss the pros and cons of "clearance sales" with regard to consumers and suppliers. Who wins? Who loses? What impact do you think these sales have on the prices of other goods the store sells?

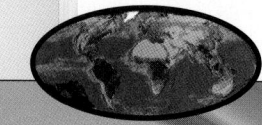

SPAN THE GLOBE

Oil for One and One for Oil

The Organization of Petroleum Exporting Countries (OPEC) is an 11-member, international group that works together to control the output and price of oil. OPEC pumps about a third of the world's crude oil. Its production policies can have a profound effect on the price consumers pay to drive their cars and heat their homes. Representatives of the 11 countries meet periodically and agree to increase or decrease the number of barrels of crude oil they supply in order to maintain the price levels they want. If the price drops, OPEC will cut back production (lower the ceiling). If the price rises, OPEC increases its oil output. OPEC has no control over the demand for oil. However, by using its control over supply, OPEC's goal is to artificially create an equilibrium and maintain the price of oil at the level it wants.

Think Critically

What are some safeguards the United States could employ to keep OPEC from raising petroleum prices unreasonably in the future?

price of $15. Apparently, those consumers believed the marginal benefit of pizza was worth at least $15. Consumers demanded 14 million pizzas at a price of $12. At a price of $9, consumers demanded 20 million pizzas, even though some were willing to pay $15 each for 8 million pizzas and $12 each for 14 million pizzas.

Consumers enjoy a consumer surplus because they get to buy all 20 million pizzas for $9 each even though they would have been willing to pay more for lesser amounts. At a given price, **consumer surplus** is the difference between the total amount consumers would have been willing and able to pay for that quantity and the total amount they actually do pay.

To get a clearer idea of consumer surplus, refer to the demand curve in Figure 6.8. If the price is $2 per unit, each person adjusts his or her quantity demanded until the marginal benefit of the final unit he or she purchases equals at least $2. Each consumer gets to buy all other units for $2 each as well. The dark-shaded area bounded above by the demand curve and below by the price of $2 depicts the consumer surplus when the price is $2.

The light-shaded area shows the increase in consumer surplus if the price drops to $1. If this good were free, the consumer surplus would be the entire area under the demand curve. Notice that at a price of zero, the consumer surplus is not that much greater than when the price is $1. Competitive markets maximize the amount of consumer surplus in the economy.

An Application of Consumer Surplus: Free Medical Care

Certain Americans, such as the elderly and those receiving public assistance, are provided government-subsidized medical care. Taxpayers spent more than $420 billion in 2000 to provide medical care to 75 million Medicare and Medicaid recipients, for an average annual cost of about $5,600 per beneficiary. The dollar cost to most beneficiaries was usually little or nothing. The problem with giving something away is that beneficiaries consume it to the point where their marginal benefit from the final unit is zero. However, the marginal cost to taxpayers can be substantial.

This is not to say that beneficiaries derive no benefit from free medical care. Although they may not value the final unit consumed very much, most derive a large consumer surplus from the other units they consume. For example, suppose that Figure 6.8 represents the demand for medical care by Medicaid beneficiaries. Because the dollar price to them is zero, they consume medical care up to the point where the demand curve intersects the horizontal axis. Their consumer surplus is the entire area under the demand curve.

The cost to taxpayers of providing that final unit of medical care may be $100 or more. One way to reduce the total cost to taxpayers of such programs without really harming beneficiaries is to charge a small price—say, $1 per physician visit. Beneficiaries would eliminate visits they value less than $1. This would yield significant savings to taxpayers but would still leave beneficiaries with good health care and a substantial consumer surplus. This is measured in Figure 6.8 as the area under the demand curve but above the $1 price.

As a case in point, one Medicaid experiment in California required some beneficiaries to pay $1 per visit for their first two office visits per month (after two visits, the price of additional visits went back to zero). A cost of at most $2 per month would not impose much of a

The Graphing Workshop
Market Demand and Consumer Surplus
Figure 6.8

econxtra.swlearning.com

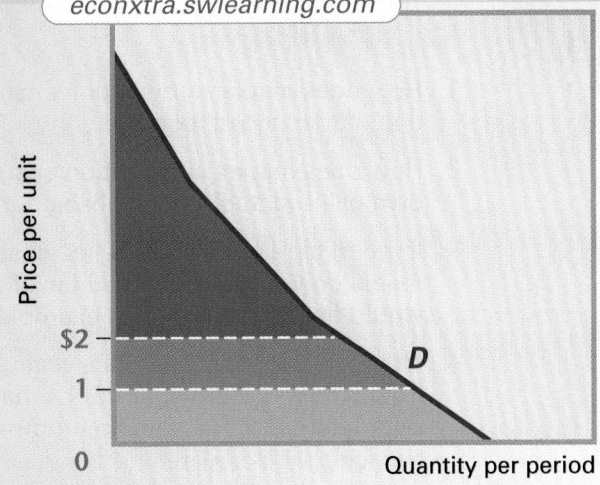

Consumer surplus at a price of $2 is shown by the darker area. If the price falls to $1, consumer surplus increases to include the lighter area.

burden on recipients. As a means of comparison, another group continued to receive completely free medical care. The $1 charge reduced office visits by 8 percent compared to the group not charged.

Medical care, like other goods and services, is also sensitive to a time price. For example, a 10 percent increase in the average travel time required to visit a free outpatient clinic reduced visits by 10 percent. Similarly, when the relocation of a free clinic at one college campus increased students' walking time by 10 minutes, student visits dropped by 40 percent.

These findings do not mean that certain groups shouldn't receive low-cost medical care. The point is that when something is provided for free, people consume it until their marginal benefit is zero. Even a modest money cost or time cost would reduce program costs yet still leave beneficiaries with a substantial consumer surplus.

✓ CHECKPOINT
How do consumers benefit from market exchange?

Key Concepts

1. How does market competition ensure that consumers will be offered a selection of low-priced foods?

2. How does market competition ensure that a new type of camera you want to own will eventually be available for you to purchase?

3. If the minimum wage were increased to $20 per hour, how many of your classmates do you believe would look for a job? How many jobs do you expect they would find? How is this an example of a price floor?

4. If the government set a price ceiling of $5 per month to subscribe to an Internet Service Provider (ISP), what would happen to the number of ISPs that offer Internet access and the number of people who wished to purchase their service?

5. Suppose you buy a salad for lunch every day for $2.75. This is the most you would be willing to pay for your salad. One week there is a special on salads and the price is reduced to $2.00. What is the value of the consumer surplus you will receive if you buy five salads during that week?

6. Most students pay no direct cost in terms of money for public education. To them the value of their education is a consumer surplus. Why doesn't this result in lots of students demanding extra homework and remedial classes after school?

Graphing Exercise

7. Suppose the government became concerned about the high price of running shoes and imposed a price ceiling of $40 per pair. Given the data in the demand and supply schedule at the right, what would the results of such a regulation be? Why would many consumers and producers be upset with this result? Construct a graph that demonstrates the result of such a regulation.

Demand and Supply for Running Shoes

Price	Quantity Demanded	Quantity Supplied
$70	40	100
$60	50	80
$50	60	60
$40*	70	40
$30	80	20

*(government price ceiling)

Think Critically

8. **History** In the early 1900s, many businesses produced horse-drawn wagons at very low cost. Still, many of these firms were forced out of business due to a lack of consumer demand. Many people chose to purchase automobiles instead of wagons. Explain how this fact demonstrates the importance of allocative efficiency.

CONNECT *to History*

The Rocky Mountain Fur Company

On March 20, 1823, an ad appeared in the *Missouri Republican*:

> "... to enterprising young men. The subscriber wishes to engage one hundred young men to ascend the Missouri River to its source, there to be employed for one, two, or three years. For particulars enquire of Major Henry, near the lead mines in the country of Washington, who will ascend with, and command, the party of the subscriber near St. Louis."
>
> *William H. Ashley*

This call for young men began the era of the Mountain Men and the fur trade in the American Far West. To the north, the French and the British had long established a profitable fur trade in North America, but Americans did not reach the Far West until after the Lewis and Clark expedition. The trade was driven by the demand of the markets in the eastern United States and Europe for furs, but the Napoleonic Wars and the War of 1812 closed many of these markets. Following the peace, the demand once again rose in the United States and Europe.

With the establishment of trading posts, most furs were obtained by trading with the Native Americans. Some were obtained by company-employed hunters and trappers. The average take was 120 beaver skins a season. A third method was by purchasing them from independent hunters and trappers. Ashley and Henry's company, the Rocky Mountain Fur Company, cut costs by taking an innovative approach that would send groups of trappers into the wilderness. Each would trade or trap furs and then would meet at the end of the season at a predetermined location, where a rendezvous was held. At the rendezvous, the Mountain Men would sell their furs and obtain more supplies for the next season. This method allowed the company to cut costs by avoiding the building and maintaining of expensive trading posts.

THINK CRITICALLY

Using supply and demand curves, demonstrate the following situations:
1. The effects of the end of the War of 1812 on the market for fur
2. The effects of the depletion of the supplies of fur
3. The effect of the substitute of silk for fur in men's hats

Chapter Assessment

 6.1 *Price, Quantity, and Market Equilibrium*

a In a competitive market, the forces of demand and supply push prices to their *equilibrium* level where the quantity demanded and supplied are the same.

b Any price above the equilibrium price will cause a *surplus* that will force producers to lower their price to the equilibrium price. Any price below the equilibrium price will cause a *shortage* that will encourage producers to increase their price to the equilibrium price.

c In competitive markets, buyers and sellers are free to exchange goods or services for money voluntarily. When there is a voluntary exchange, both parties gain because of the different values they place on goods, services, or money.

d *Transaction costs* are costs that are necessary to carry out market exchanges. Markets encourage exchanges by reducing transaction costs. Similar businesses often choose to be located in the same area to reduce the transaction costs of shopping.

 6.2 *Shifts of Demand and Supply Curves*

a There are five types of factors that can shift the demand curve for a product. These are (1) changes in consumer money income, (2) changes in the price of substitute or complementary products, (3) changes in consumer expectations, (4) changes in consumer population, and (5) changes in consumer tastes.

b There also are five types of factors that can shift the supply curve for a product. These are (1) changes in the cost of a resource used to make the product, (2) changes in the price of other goods that these resources could be used to produce, (3) changes in technology that reduce the cost of making the product, (4) changes in producer expectations, and (5) a change in the number of producers.

c When either the demand or supply curve for a product shifts, there will be a corresponding change in the equilibrium price and the quantity of the product.

 6.3 *Market Efficiency and Gains from Exchange*

a Competitive markets exhibit productive and allocative efficiency. *Productive efficiency* occurs when products are manufactured at the lowest possible cost. *Allocative efficiency* occurs when firms produce the products that are most valued by consumers.

b *Disequilibrium* occurs when the quantity of a product consumers demand is not equal to the quantity producers supply. It is usually a temporary condition, but can continue over time, particularly when government intervenes in the market. Government-imposed *price floors* are likely to result in surpluses of a product, while government *price ceilings* usually cause shortages.

c A *consumer surplus* is the difference between the amount of money consumers would have been willing to pay for a product and what they actually pay for it. Government price regulations or subsidized services often result in consumer surpluses. Free or low-cost medical care provided by the government to the poor and elderly are examples of this type of situation.

Review Economic Terms

Choose the term that best fits the definition. On a separate sheet of paper, write the letter of the answer. Some terms may not be used.

_____ 1. The quantity of a product demanded is not equal to the quantity supplied

_____ 2. Quantity demanded equals quantity supplied and the market clears

_____ 3. A situation achieved when a firm produces output most desired by consumers

_____ 4. A minimum legal price below which a product cannot be sold

_____ 5. The amount of a product that cannot be sold at a given price

_____ 6. Consumers are more willing and able to buy a product at every price

_____ 7. A maximum legal price above which a product cannot be sold

_____ 8. A situation achieved when a firm produces output at the lowest possible cost

_____ 9. The amount by which the amount of a product demanded exceeds the amount supplied at a particular price

_____ 10. The cost of time and information needed to carry out market exchange

_____ 11. Producers are less willing and able to supply a product at every price

a. **allocative efficiency**

b. **consumer surplus**

c. **equilibrium**

d. **decrease in demand**

e. **decrease in supply**

f. **disequilibrium**

g. **increase in demand**

h. **increase in supply**

i. **price ceiling**

j. **price floor**

k. **productive efficiency**

l. **shortage**

m. **surplus**

n. **transaction cost**

Review Economic Concepts

12. **True or False** A price below a product's *equilibrium* price will result in a surplus of the product.

13. When there is a voluntary exchange, it is reasonable to believe

    a. both the buyer and seller gained.

    b. neither buyer nor seller gained.

    c. the buyer gained more than the seller.

    d. the seller gained more than the buyer.

14. **True or False** A market is always in a state of equilibrium.

15. **True or False** Government regulations affect equilibrium in the markets for some goods and services.

16. Given an upward sloping supply curve, a rightward shift of the demand curve

    a. decreases both equilibrium price and quantity.

    b. increases both equilibrium price and quantity.

    c. decreases equilibrium price only.

    d. increases equilibrium price only.

17. **True or False** A shift of the supply curve results from a change in quantity demanded at all prices.

18. A market will stay in equilibrium until

    a. one of the factors that determines demand changes.

    b. one of the factors that determines supply changes.

    c. all the suppliers go out of business.

    d. both a and b

19. __?__ are costs that must be paid to complete a market exchange.

20. Each of the following will cause the demand for butter to increase *except*

    a. an increase in the price of margarine.

    b. a scientific study that shows butter is good for people's health.

    c. an increase in the number of people who are unemployed.

    d. an increase in the number of people who might purchase butter.

21. **True or False** An increase in a firm's cost of production will cause its supply curve to move to the left.

22. Each of the following will cause a firm's supply to increase *except*

    a. the firm's workers are trained to be more efficient.

    b. the firm finds a new, lower-cost source of electric power.

    c. the firm invests in new technology that reduces its costs of production.

    d. a number of experienced workers retire and are replaced by new workers.

23. **True or False** If a firm's costs of production fall while the demand for its product grows, you can be sure the equilibrium price for its product will fall.

24. There is __?__ when a firm produces products at the lowest possible cost.

25. Suppose the current equilibrium price for natural gas is $1.05 per thousand cubic feet. The government decides to impose a price ceiling of $.90. This will cause

    a. the quantity demanded to fall and the quantity supplied to fall.

    b. the quantity demanded to fall and the quantity supplied to grow.

    c. the quantity demanded to grow and the quantity supplied to fall.

    d. the quantity demanded to grow and the quantity supplied to grow.

26. __?__ is the difference between the total amount consumers would be willing and able to pay for a product and what they actually had to pay.

Apply Economic Concepts

27. **Equilibrium** On a separate sheet of paper, complete the table below:

Demand and Supply Schedule for Tacos

Price Per Taco	Quantity Demanded	Quantity Supplied	Surplus/ Shortage	Will the price rise or fall?
$2.00	25	175	_____	_____
$1.75	50	150	_____	_____
$1.50	75	125	_____	_____
$1.25	100	100	_____	_____
$1.00	125	75	_____	_____
$0.75	150	50	_____	_____

28. **Graphing Demand and Supply** Construct a graph of the demand and supply for tacos from the data provided in the table in exercise 27.

29. **Graphing Shifts in Demand and Supply** On your graph, draw and label the shifts in demand and supply curves for tacos that would result from each of the following events.

   a. The cost of corn meal increases 50 percent.

   b. The price of pizza goes down 25 percent.

   c. The number of people who like tacos increases by 30 percent.

   d. A new machine is invented that makes tacos automatically.

30. **Sharpen Your Life Skills: Analyze Supply and Demand Graphs** Between 2000 and June of 2003, the unemployment rate in the United States grew from 4.0 percent to 6.4 percent. This 2.4 percent increase added more than 3.6 million workers to the ranks of the unemployed in this country. People who are out of work may receive unemployment compensation payments from the government. These payments, however, replace only a portion of the income they had been earning. After unemployed people pay for food, clothing, and shelter for their families, they often have little left over to purchase other goods or services. Increased unemployment in the United States between 2000 and June of 2003 contributed to a decline in demand for many household appliances. Sketch a graph similar to the one to the right that shows what happened to the demand and supply for refrigerators in these years. Place arrows on your graph to show shifts in demand, the surplus of products, and change in the equilibrium price. Label the changes that took place and explain what happened.

Demand and Supply for Home Refrigerators, 2000

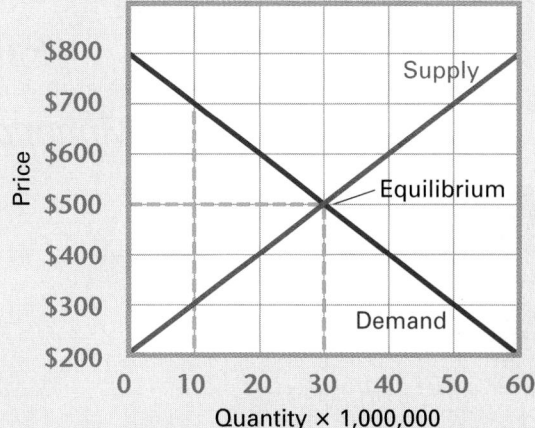

31. **Make Predictions** Predict how the equilibrium price of coffee would be affected by the following changes:

   a. Poor growing conditions for coffee beans (demand remains constant)

   b. Major advertising campaign in the United States by a group of the world's coffee growers (supply remains constant)

   c. The publication of a new medical study warning against coffee consumption in excess of one cup per week (supply remains constant)

   d. Trade prohibition against a country in South America that produces a significant share of the U.S. coffee supply (demand remains constant)

 econxtra.swlearning.com

32. Access **EconNews Online** at econxtra. swlearning.com. Read the article entitled "PC Price Cuts."

   a. Draw a graph showing the price and quantity of personal computers. Then show the effects of the recession on the demand curve and the quantity at a given price.

   b. Draw a second graph of the demand for computers. Assume computer suppliers responded by offering price discounts on new computers. Illustrate what happened on your graph.

7 Market Structure

Perfect Competition and Monopoly **7.1**

Monopolistic Competition and Oligopoly **7.2**

Antitrust, Economic Regulation,
and Competition **7.3**

C o n s i d e r

What does a bushel of wheat
have in common with a share
of Microsoft stock?

What's so perfect about
perfect competition?

Why don't most
monopolies last?

Why are some panty
hose sold in egg-shaped
cartons?

Why was OPEC
created?

Is the U.S. economy
more competitive now
than it used to be?

POINT YOUR BROWSER

econxtra.swlearning.com

© Getty Images/PhotoDisc

Objectives

> Distinguish the features of perfect competition.

> Describe the barriers to entry that can create a monopoly.

> Compare the market structures of monopoly and perfect competition in terms of efficiency.

Overview

A firm's decision about how much to supply depends on the structure of the market. Market structure describes the important features of a market, including the number of buyers and sellers, the product's uniformity across suppliers, the ease of entry into the market, and the forms of competition among firms. All firms that supply output to a particular market—such as the market for cars, shoes, or wheat—are referred to as an *industry*. Therefore, the terms *industry* and *market* are used interchangeably. The first two market structures you will examine are perfect competition and monopoly.

Key Terms

market structure

perfect competition

commodity

monopoly

barriers to entry

market power

[In the News]

All that Glitters

At the start of 2003, economists who specialize in precious metals and jewels were predicting that the price of gold was going to rise dramatically. The predictions were based on three factors: a rocky U.S. economy, the unsettling war on terrorism, and a worldwide decrease in the production of gold. International events and the uncertainties they create often cause the price of an ounce of gold to rise. When people don't trust their national currencies, they often invest in precious metals and jewels as an alternative. Since the start of the millennium, worldwide demand for gold has been growing at a steady 2 percent to 3 percent a year. Yet, while demand increased, production remained the same or was cut back. Some observers suggest that the rising price might be just the spark that motivates mining companies to invest heavily and quickly in gold exploration. Others remind us that world economic conditions that could decrease the demand for gold also might arise, such as a great improvement in the U.S. economy or an easing of tensions in the Middle East and Asia. The decrease in demand would then drive down the price of gold.

Think About It

Read the first section of this lesson on perfect competition. Assuming that the market for gold is perfectly competitive, what effect would each of the following have on the supply and demand graph: (1) growing mistrust of national currencies, (2) an easing of international tensions, and (3) the opening of new gold mines?

Perfect Competition

market structure

Important features of a market, including the number of buyers and sellers, product uniformity across sellers, ease of entering the market, and forms of competition

perfect competition

A market structure with many fully informed buyers and sellers of an identical product and ease of entry

commodity

A product that is identical across sellers, such as a bushel of wheat

To begin your study of different **market structures**, familiarize yourself with the descriptions of market features shown in Figure 7.1. The first market structure to consider is **perfect competition**. Perfectly competitive markets are assumed to have the following features:

1. There are many buyers and sellers—so many that each buys or sells only a tiny fraction of the total market output. This assumption ensures that no individual buyer or seller can influence the price.

2. Firms produce a standardized product, or a **commodity**. A commodity is a product that is identical across producers, such as a bushel of wheat or a share of Microsoft stock. A buyer is not willing to pay more for one particular supplier's product. Buyers are concerned only with the price.

3. Buyers are fully informed about the price, quality, and availability of products, and sellers are fully informed about all resources and technology.

4. Firms can easily enter or leave the industry. There are no obstacles preventing new firms from entering profitable markets.

If these conditions exist in a market, individual buyers and sellers have no control over the price. Price is determined by market demand and supply. Once the market establishes the price, each firm is free to produce whatever quantity maximizes its profit or minimizes its loss. *A perfectly competitive firm is so small relative to the size of the market that the firm's choice about how much to produce has no effect on the market price.*

Example Markets

Examples of perfect competition include markets for the shares of large corporations such as Microsoft or General Electric; foreign exchange, such as yen, euros, and pounds; and those for most agricultural products, such as livestock, corn, and wheat. In these markets, there are so many buyers and sellers that the actions of any one cannot influence the market price.

In the perfectly competitive market for wheat, for example, a single firm in this market is a wheat farm. In the world market for wheat, there are tens of thousands of farms, so any one supplies just a tiny fraction of market output. For example, the thousands of wheat farmers in Kansas together produce less than 3 percent of the world's supply of wheat. No single wheat farmer can influence the market price for a bushel of wheat.

Market Price

In Figure 7.2, the market price of wheat of $5 per bushel is determined in panel (a) by the intersection of the market demand curve *D* and the market supply curve *S*. Once the market price is established, farmers can sell all they want at that market price.

Market Structure — Figure 7.1

Market structure describes the important features of a market.

Market Feature	Questions to Ask
1. Number of buyers and sellers	Are there many, only a few, or just one?
2. Product's uniformity across suppliers	Do firms in the market supply identical products, or are products differentiated across firms?
3. Ease of entry into the market	Can new firms enter easily, or do natural or artificial barriers block them?
4. Forms of competition among firms	Do firms compete based only on prices, or are advertising and product differences also important?

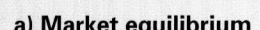
a) Market equilibrium

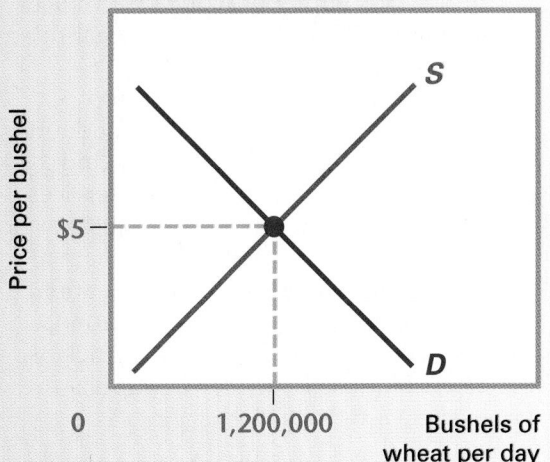

b) Firm's demand

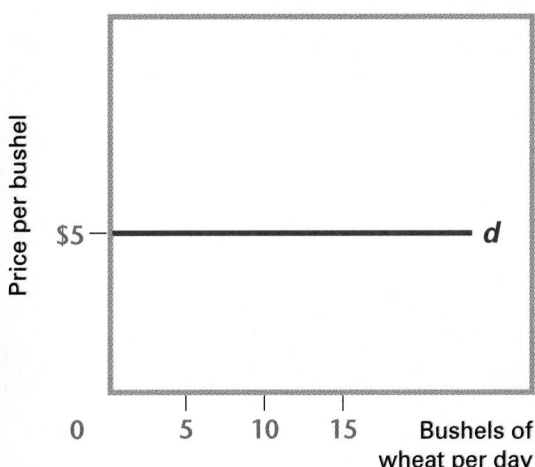

In panel (a), the market price of $5 is determined by the intersection of the market demand and supply curves. The individual perfectly competitive firm can sell any amount at that price. The demand curve facing the perfectly competitive firm is horizontal at the market price, as shown by demand curve *d* in panel (b).

Each farm is so small relative to the market that each has no impact on the market price. Because all farmers produce an identical product—bushels of wheat—anyone who charges more than the market price will sell no wheat. For example, if a farmer charged $5.25 per bushel, wheat buyers would simply turn to other sellers.

Of course, any farmer is free to charge less than the market price. But why do that when all wheat can be sold at the market price? *The demand curve facing an individual farmer is, therefore, a horizontal line drawn at the market price.* In this example, the demand curve in panel (b) is drawn at the market price of $5 per bushel.

It has been said, "In perfect competition there is no competition." Two neighboring wheat farmers in perfect competition are not really rivals. They both can sell all they want at the market price. The amount one sells has no effect on the market price or on the amount the other can sell. Likewise, no two buyers compete for the product because they both can buy all they

want at the market price. Each farm, or firm, tries to maximize profit. Firms that ignore this strategy don't survive.

CHECKPOINT
What are the features of perfect competition?

Monopoly

The monopoly market structure is the extreme opposite of the perfect competition structure. **Monopoly** is the sole supplier of a product with no close substitutes. *Monopoly* is from a Greek word meaning "one seller." A monopolist has more market power than does a business in any other market structure. **Market power** is the ability of a firm to raise its price without losing all sales to rivals. A perfect competitor has no market power.

monopoly

A sole supplier of a product with no close substitutes

market power

The ability of a firm to raise its price without losing all sales to rivals

Barriers to Entry

barriers to entry
Restrictions on the entry of new firms into an industry

A monopolized market has high **barriers to entry**, which are restrictions on the entry of new firms into an industry. Barriers to entry allow a monopolist to charge a price above the competitive price. There are three types of entry barriers: legal restrictions, economies of scale, and control of an essential resource.

Legal Restrictions

One way to prevent new firms from entering a market is to make entry illegal. Patents, licenses, and other legal restrictions imposed by the government provide some producers with legal protection against competition.

Governments confer monopoly rights to sell hot dogs at civic auditoriums, collect garbage, offer bus and taxi service, and supply other services ranging from electricity to cable TV. The government itself may become a monopolist by outlawing competition. For example, many states are monopoly sellers of liquor and lottery tickets. The U.S. Postal Service (USPS) has the exclusive right to deliver first-class mail.

Economies of Scale

A monopoly sometimes emerges naturally when a firm experiences substantial economies of scale, as reflected by the downward-sloping, long-run average cost curve shown in Figure 7.3. A single firm can sometimes satisfy market demand at a lower average cost per unit than could two or more smaller firms. Put another way, market demand is not great enough to allow more than one firm to achieve sufficient economies of scale.

Thus, a single firm will emerge from the competitive process as the sole supplier in the market. The transmission of electricity involves economies of scale. Once wires are run throughout a community, the marginal cost of linking additional households to the power grid is relatively small. Consequently, the average cost per household declines as more and more households are wired into the system.

A monopoly that emerges from the nature of costs is called a *natural monopoly*. A new entrant cannot sell enough output to experience the economies of scale enjoyed by an established natural monopolist. Therefore, entry into the market is naturally blocked.

In less-populated areas, natural monopolies include the only grocery store, movie theater, or restaurant for miles around. These are *geographic*

SPAN THE GLOBE

Flower Auction Holland

Five days a week in a huge building 10 miles outside Amsterdam, some 2,500 buyers gather to participate in Flower Auction Holland. At this auction, more than 14 million flowers from 5,600 growers around the globe are auctioned off each day. The auction is held in the world's largest commercial building, and it is spread across the equivalent of 100 football fields. Flowers are grouped and auctioned off by type—long-stemmed roses, tulips, and so on. Hundreds of buyers are seated in theater settings with their fingers on buttons. Once the flowers are presented, a clock-like instrument starts ticking off descending prices until a buyer stops it by pushing a button. The winning bidder gets to choose how many and which items to take. The clock starts again until another buyer stops it, and so on, until all flowers are sold. Buyers also can bid from remote locations. Flower auctions occur swiftly—on average one transaction occurs every four seconds. This is an example of a *Dutch auction,* which starts at a high price and works down. Dutch auctions are common where multiple lots of similar, though not identical, items are sold, such as flowers in Amsterdam, tobacco in Canada, and fish in seaports around the world.

Think Critically

Is Flower Auction Holland a perfect example of a perfectly competitive market? Why or why not?

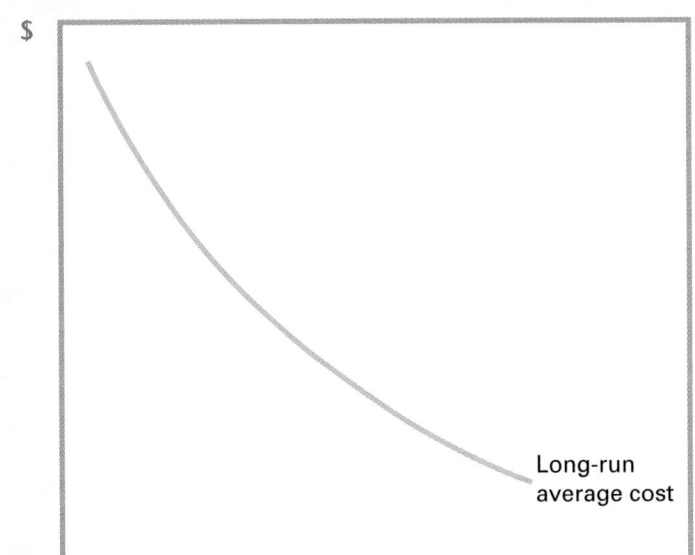

A monopoly sometimes emerges naturally when a firm experiences economies of scale as reflected by a downward-sloping, long-run average cost curve. An individual firm can satisfy market demand at a lower average cost per unit than could two or more firms operating at smaller rates of output.

monopolies for products sold in local markets.

Control of Essential Resources

Sometimes the source of monopoly power is a firm's control over some resource critical to production. Following are some examples of the control of essential resources barrier to entry.

- For decades Alcoa controlled the world's supply of bauxite, the key raw material in aluminum.

- China is a monopoly supplier of pandas to the world's zoos. The zoo in Washington, D.C., for example, rents a pair of pandas from China for $1 million a year. As a way of controlling the panda supply, China stipulates that any offspring from the Washington pair become China's property.

- Since the 1930s, the world's diamond trade has been controlled primarily by De Beers Consolidated Mines. De Beers mines diamonds and also buys most of the world's supply of rough diamonds.

© Getty Images/PhotoDisc

De Beers's advertising slogan is "A diamond is forever." What results do you think the company hopes to achieve with this slogan?

The Graphing Workshop

Monopolists May Not Earn a Profit

Because a monopoly, by definition, supplies the entire market, the demand curve for a monopolist's output also is the market demand curve. That demand curve, therefore, slopes downward, reflecting the law of demand. Price and quantity demanded are inversely related.

Even a monopolist with iron-clad barriers to entry may go broke. Although a monopolist is the sole producer of a good with no close substitutes, the demand for that good may not be great enough to keep the firm in business. After all, many inventions are protected from direct competition by patents, yet most patented products never get produced and many that are produced fail to attract enough customers to survive.

True Monopolies Are Rare

Long-lasting monopolies are rare because a profitable monopoly attracts competitors and substitutes. Even where barriers to entry are initially strong, technological change tends to create substitutes. For example, railroads at one time enjoyed a natural monopoly in shipping goods across country. The monopoly ended when the trucking industry was born.

The development of wireless transmission of long-distance telephone calls created competitors for the monopolist AT&T and may soon erase the monopoly held by some local cable TV

providers and some local phone services. Likewise, fax machines, e-mail, the Internet, and firms such as FedEx have all cut into the U.S. Postal Service's monopoly on first-class mail.

 CHECKPOINT
Name and describe the three barriers to entry into a market.

Monopoly and Efficiency

Monopolists are not guaranteed a profit. Monopolies can lose money. Monopolies are relatively rare. So, then, what's the problem?

Monopoly Versus Perfect Competition

One way to understand the problem is to compare monopoly to perfect competition. Competition forces firms to be *efficient*—that is, to produce the maximum possible output from available resources—and to supply the product at the lowest possible price. Consumers get a substantial consumer surplus from this low price. However, a successful monopolist typically will charge a higher price than would competitive firms. Thus, fewer consumers will be able to afford to buy the product.

To compare monopoly and perfect competition, suppose D in Figure 7.4 is the *market demand* for a product sold in perfect competition. The market price is P_c and the market quantity is Q_c. Consumer surplus for the perfectly competitive price is the triangular area below the demand curve and above the price, measured by acp_c. (Recall that *consumer surplus* is the difference between the total amount consumers are willing to pay for a given quantity of a good and what they actually pay.)

What if one firm buys up all the individual firms in the perfectly competitive market, creating a giant

Access the rate page of the USPS web site through econxtra.swlearning.com. Describe the process by which the USPS sets its postage rates. What role, if any, do the forces of competition play in rate setting?

econxtra.swlearning.com

A perfectly competitive industry would produce output Q_c and sell at a price p_c. A monopoly that could produce at that same minimum average cost would produce output Q_m and sell at price p_m. Thus, output is lower and price is higher under monopoly than under perfect competition. With perfect competition, the consumer surplus is the entire triangle acp_c, reflected by the shaded area. With monopoly, consumer surplus shrinks to the blue-shaded triangle.

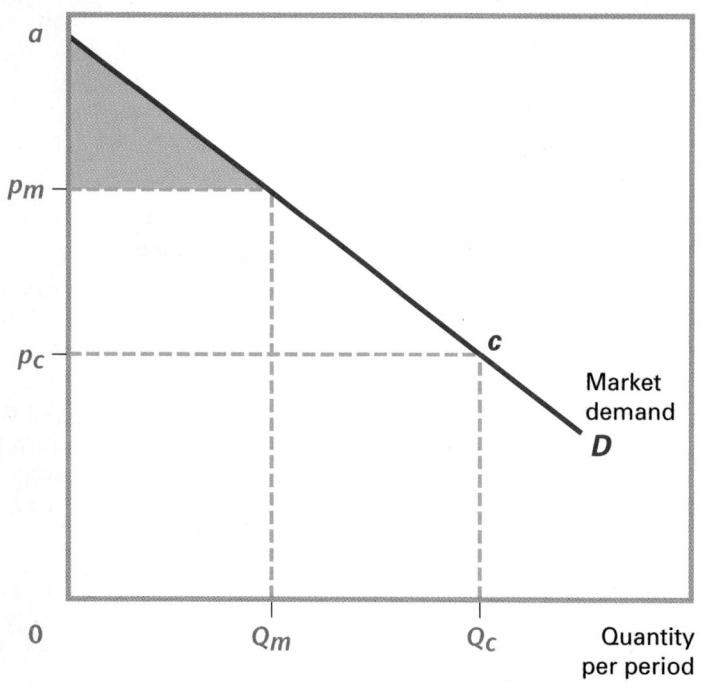

monopoly? In this case, the market demand curve becomes the monopolist's demand curve. What if average cost per unit is the same with monopoly as with perfect competition? The monopolist will restrict quantity to Q_m and will increase the price to p_m. With monopoly, consumer surplus shrinks to the blue triangle, which is much smaller than consumer surplus with perfect competition.

Other Problems with Monopoly

Monopolies may reduce social welfare for other reasons besides higher prices to consumers. These include a possible waste of resources and inefficiencies that may develop in their operation.

Resources Wasted Securing Monopoly Privilege

Because of their size and economic importance, monopolies may have too much influence on the political system, which they use to protect and strengthen their monopoly power. Lawyers' fees,

lobbying expenses, and other costs associated with gaining a special privilege from government are largely a social waste because they use up scarce resources but add not one unit to output.

Monopolies May Grow Inefficient

The monopolist, insulated from the rigors of market competition, could grow fat and lazy, and thus become inefficient. Corporate executives might waste resources by creating a more comfortable life for themselves. Lavish salaries and corporate perks boost the average cost of production above the competitive level. Monopolists also have been criticized for being slow to adopt the latest production techniques, reluctant to develop new products, and generally lacking in innovation.

Monopoly Might Not Be So Bad

For several reasons, some monopolies may not be as socially wasteful as was just described.

Ask the Xpert!

econxtra.swlearning.com

Why are cable rates so high?

Economies of Scale

If economies of scale are substantial, a monopolist might be able to produce output at a lower average cost than could competitive firms. Therefore, the price, or at least the cost of production, could be lower with monopoly than with perfect competition.

Government Regulation

Government intervention can increase social welfare by forcing the monopolist to lower price and increase output. The government can either operate the monopoly itself, as it does with most urban transit systems, or it can regulate a privately owned monopoly, as it does with local phone services and electricity transmission. You will read more about government regulation later in the chapter.

Keeping Prices Low to Avoid Regulation

A monopolist might keep prices below the profit-maximizing level to avoid government regulation. For example, the prices and profits of drug companies, which individually are monopoly producers of patented medicines, come under scrutiny from time to time by public officials who threaten to regulate drug prices. Drug firms might try to avoid such treatment by keeping prices below the level that would maximize profit.

Keeping Prices Low to Avoid Competition

Finally, a monopolist might keep the price below the profit-maximizing level to avoid attracting competitors. For example, at one time Alcoa was the only U.S. producer of aluminum. Industry observers claimed that the company kept prices and profits below their maximum to discourage competition.

CHECKPOINT

How does monopoly compare to perfect competition in terms of efficiency?

Ethics in Action

Price-Control Program Challenged

The state of Maine recently enacted legislation designed to make prescription medicine less expensive for the neediest of its citizens. This legislation currently is being challenged in the U.S. Supreme Court. In recent years, the cost of prescription drugs has jumped by more than 15 percent annually. In addition to Maine, a dozen other states have indicated they would like to enact similar laws. Maine's approach is to use the combined buying power of citizens in an entire state to bargain for savings of 25 percent or more on prescription drugs. Sponsors of Maine's legislation have stated that their program does for its citizens what a number of other nations have done for theirs: put pressure on the drug companies to bargain. The pharmaceutical companies take the point of view that Maine is illegally strong-arming them into reducing prices. These firms argue that they have spent hundreds of millions of dollars developing and testing each drug, and they should be allowed to recover those costs. They claim that if they are forced to lower prices in one state, the rest of the country would get stuck with the bill to make up the difference.

Think Critically

The pharmaceutical industry has market power—that is, the ability to raise price without losing all sales. Is it ethical for a state to try to force these firms to lower their prices?

7.1 Assessment

Key Concepts

1. What characteristics of farms demonstrate that these firms operate in perfectly competitive markets?

2. Three years ago, the town of Mt. Utopia had three fast-food restaurants. The town's population has grown rapidly in the past two years. As the town grew, the sales and profits of these restaurants increased. There now are seven fast-food restaurants in Mt. Utopia. None of them earns a large profit. What feature of competitive markets does this demonstrate? Explain your answer.

3. Identify a firm that operates in your community that you think has a significant amount of monopoly power. Explain why you chose this firm.

4. At one time, the American Telephone and Telegraph Corp. (AT&T) had a great deal of monopoly power and earned large profits. In recent years AT&T has lost money, and it could be purchased by another firm. What happened to AT&T's monopoly power?

Graphing Exercise

5. Use data in the table to construct two graphs: the market demand and supply curve, and the individual demand curve for the Apex Coal Mine. Apex is able to produce a maximum of 1,000 tons of coal per month. What is the market equilibrium price? Explain how you were able to construct the individual demand curve for Apex Coal.

Market Coal Demand and Supply Schedule Per Month

Price per Ton	Market Demand (tons)	Market Supply (tons)
$200	4,000,000	8,000,000
$175	5,000,000	7,000,000
$150	6,000,000	6,000,000
$125	7,000,000	5,000,000
$100	8,000,000	4,000,000

Think Critically

6. **Advertising** Although individual farmers do not purchase advertising for their products, it is common for groups of farmers to join together to do this. In New York, for example, the Upstate Milk Cooperative collects funds from thousands of dairy farmers and uses the money to buy advertisements for milk products. Explain why this makes sense. What are the farmers trying to accomplish?

7. **History** Between 1880 and 1900, the Standard Oil Company came to control almost 90 percent of the production of oil products in the United States. It did this by buying up or driving other firms out of business. With this monopoly power, the firm's owners were able to earn as much as a 20 percent profit on the value of the firm's assets, such as its refineries, pipelines, etc. Much of the firm's profit was used to develop new technologies that, according to the owners, contributed to lower prices. In your opinion, is it possible for monopolies to be good for consumers? Explain your answer.

Sharpen Your Life Skills

Read Pie Graphs

Study the pie graphs to the right that show the approximate percentage of motor vehicle sales in this country made by each of the three largest U.S. producers, foreign-owned producers, and other U.S.-owned producers in 1980 and 2002. Summarize the changes in the U.S. automobile market that these graphs show.

Apply Your Skill

1. If U.S. producers wanted to regain a larger share of the U.S. motor vehicle market, how might they achieve their goal?

2. How might the U.S. government help U.S. producers regain their share of the U.S. motor vehicle market? Do you think the U.S. government should do these things? Explain your answer.

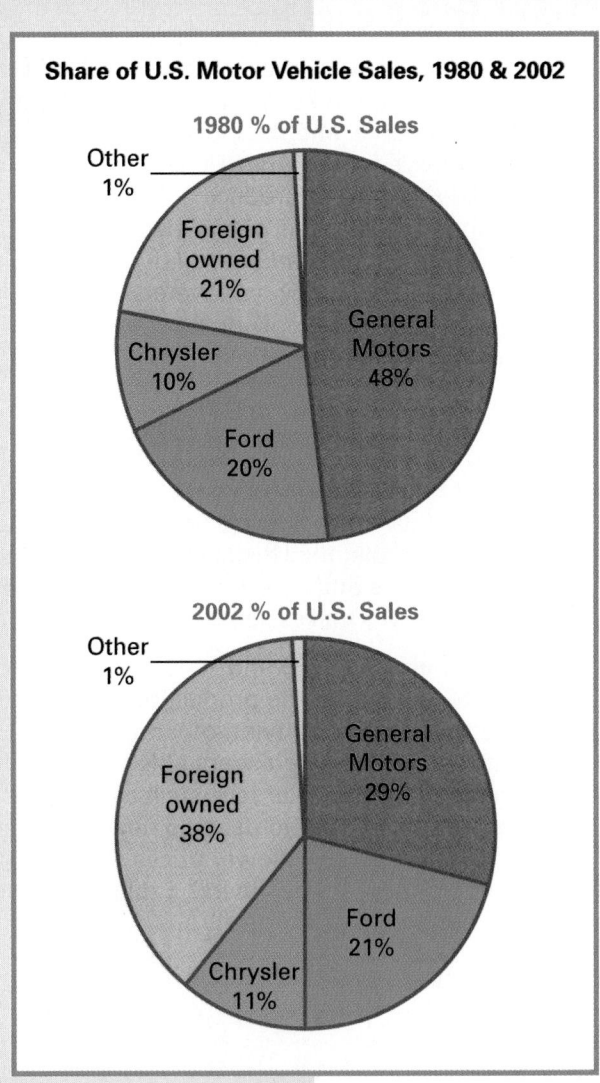

Share of U.S. Motor Vehicle Sales, 1980 & 2002

1980 % of U.S. Sales

Other 1%
Foreign owned 21%
Chrysler 10%
General Motors 48%
Ford 20%

2002 % of U.S. Sales

Other 1%
Foreign owned 38%
General Motors 29%
Ford 21%
Chrysler 11%

Objectives

> Identify the features of monopolistic competition.

> Identify the features of oligopoly, and analyze firm behavior when these firms cooperate and when they compete.

Overview

You are now aware of the two extreme market structures of perfect competition and monopoly. Now you will learn about monopolistic competition and oligopoly, the two structures that exist in between. These are the market structures in which most firms operate. Firms in each of these market structures face downward-sloping demand curves for their products, so each has some control over the price. Monopolistic competition is like a golf tournament in which each player strives for a personal best. Firms in oligopoly are more like players in a tennis match, where each player's actions depend on how and where the opponent hits the ball.

Key Terms

monopolistic competition

oligopoly

cartel

[In the News]

The Unfriendly Skies

At one time, airline routes were straight lines from one city to another. Now they radiate like the spokes of a wagon wheel from a "hub" city. From 29 hub airports across the country, the airlines send out planes along the spokes to about 400 commercial airports and then quickly bring them back to the hubs. Major airlines dominate hub airports. For example, United Airlines accounts for half the passengers at the Dallas-Fort Worth airport. A new airline trying to enter the industry must secure a hub airport as well as landing slots at crowded airports around the country. This is not an easy task because all the viable hubs are taken, and landing slots are scarce. Another trend in the airline industry is the offering of frequent-flyer mileage programs. The biggest airlines fly more national and international routes, and so they offer greater opportunities for fliers to both accumulate frequent-flyer miles and to use the mileage for free flights. Thus, the biggest airlines have the most attractive programs.

Think About It

What are the barriers to entry in the airline industry discussed in this feature?

Monopolistic Competition

In monopolistic competition, many firms offer products that differ slightly. As the expression **monopolistic competition** suggests, this structure contains elements of both monopoly and competition. The "monopolistic" element is that each firm has some control over its price. Because the products of different suppliers differ slightly, each firm's demand curve slopes downward. The "competition" element of monopolistic competition is that barriers to entry are so low that any short-run profit will attract new competitors, erasing profit in the long run.

Market Characteristics

Because barriers to entry are low, firms in monopolistic competition can, in the long run, enter or leave the market with ease. Consequently, there are enough sellers that they behave competitively. There also are enough sellers that each tends to get lost in the crowd. A particular firm, in deciding on a price, does not worry about how other firms in the market will react. For example, in a large city, an individual restaurant, gas station, drugstore, dry cleaner, or convenience store tends to act *independently* from its competitors.

Product Differentiation

In perfect competition, the product is identical across suppliers, such as a bushel of wheat. In monopolistic competition, the product differs slightly among sellers, as with the difference between one rock radio station and another. Sellers differentiate their products in four basic ways.

Physical Differences

The most obvious way products differ is in their physical appearance and their qualities. The differences among products are seemingly endless. Shampoos, for example, differ in color, scent, thickness, lathering ability, and bottle design. Packaging also is designed to make a product stand out in a crowded field, such as panty hose in a plastic eggshell and yogurt in a tube.

Location

The number and variety of locations where a product is available also are means of differentiation. Some products seem to be available everywhere, including the Internet. Finding other products requires some search and travel.

Services

Products also differ in their accompanying services. For example, some take-out restaurants deliver. Others don't. Some retailers offer product demonstrations by a well-trained staff. Others are mostly self-service.

Product Image

A final way products differ is in the image the producer tries to foster in the consumer's mind. For example, some products use celebrity endorsements to boost sales.

© Getty Images/PhotoDisc

Monopolistic competition may result in higher costs for firms, but it also provides more choices for consumers, such as a choice among many restaurants. Would you be willing to pay more for food if it means you would have more restaurants to choose from?

Costs of Product Differentiation

Firms in monopolistic competition spend more on advertising and other promotional expenses to differentiate their products. This increases average cost. Some economists argue that monopolistic competition results in too many firms and in product differentiation that is artificial. Others argue that consumers are willing to pay a higher price for a wider choice.

Excess Capacity

Firms in monopolistic competition are said to operate with excess capacity. *Excess capacity* means that a firm could lower its average cost by selling more. Such excess capacity exists, for example, with gas stations, drugstores, banks, convenience stores, restaurants, motels, bookstores, and flower shops.

As a specific example, industry analysts argue that the nation's 22,000 funeral homes could efficiently handle 4 million funerals a year, but only about 2.4 million people die. So the industry operates at 60 percent capacity. This results in a higher average cost per funeral because resources remain idle much of the time.

> **✓ CHECKPOINT**
> What are the important features of monopolistic competition?

Investigate Your Local Economy

In small groups, brainstorm a list of markets in your area in which firms seem to be operating with excess capacity. Then for each market listed, cite evidence of the excess capacity.

Oligopoly

Oligopoly is a Greek word meaning "few sellers." When you think of "big business," you are thinking of **oligopoly**, a market dominated by just a few firms. Perhaps three or four firms account for three-quarters of market output. Because an oligopoly has only a few firms, each must consider the effect of its own actions on competitors' behavior. Oligopolistic industries include the markets for steel, oil, automobiles, breakfast cereals, and tobacco.

In some oligopolies, such as steel or oil, the product is identical, or undifferentiated, across producers. Thus, an *undifferentiated oligopoly* sells a commodity, such as an ingot of steel or a barrel of oil. In other oligopolies, such as automobiles or breakfast cereals, the product is differentiated across producers. A *differentiated oligopoly* sells products that differ across producers, such as Ford versus Toyota or General Food's Wheaties versus Kellogg's Corn Flakes.

Firms in an oligopoly are interdependent. Therefore, each firm knows that any changes in its price, output, or advertising may prompt a reaction from its rivals. Each firm may react if another firm alters any of these features.

Barriers to Entry

Why have some industries evolved into an oligopolistic market structure, dominated by only a few firms, whereas other industries have not? Although the reasons are not always clear, *an oligopoly often can be traced to some barrier to entry, such as economies of scale or brand names built up by years of advertising.* Most of the barriers that applied to monopoly also apply to oligopoly.

Economies of Scale

Perhaps the most significant barrier to entry is economies of scale. The *minimum efficient scale* is the lowest rate of output at which the firm takes full advantage of economies of scale. If a firm's minimum efficient scale is relatively large compared to industry output, then only a few firms are needed to produce the total amount

oligopoly
A market structure with a small number of firms whose behavior is interdependent

CNN video
Consumers Creamed
econxtra.swlearning.com

demanded in the market. For example, an automobile factory of minimum-efficient scale could make enough vehicles to supply nearly 10 percent of the U.S. market. To compete with existing producers, a new entrant must sell enough automobiles to reach a competitive scale of operation.

The High Cost of Entry

The total investment needed to reach the minimum-efficient size often is huge. A new auto factory or new computer chip plant can cost more than $1 billion. The average cost of developing and testing a new drug exceeds $300 million. Advertising a new product enough to compete with established brands also could require enormous outlays. A failed attempt at securing a place in the market could cripple a new firm. That's why most new products usually come from existing firms, which can better withstand the possible loss. For example, McDonald's spent $100 million in its unsuccessful attempt to introduce the Arch Deluxe. Unilever lost $160 million when its new detergent, Power, failed to catch on.

Product Differentiation Costs

Oligopolists often spend millions and sometimes billions trying to differentiate their products. Some of these expenditures provide valuable information to consumers and offer them a wider array of products. However, some forms of product differentiation appear to be of little value. Slogans such as "Generation Next" or "Always Cola-Cola" convey little information, yet Pepsi and Coke spend huge sums on such messages. In 2000, Coke spent nearly $2 billion on advertising. Product differentiation expenditures create barriers to entry.

cartel

A group of firms that agree to act as a single monopolist to increase the market price and maximize the group's profits

When Oligopolists Collude

To decrease competition and increase profit, oligopolistic firms, particularly those that offer identical products, may try to *collude,* or agree on a price. *Collusion* is an agreement among firms in the industry to divide the market and fix the price. A **cartel** is a group of firms that agree to act as a single monopolist to increase the market price and maximize the group's profits.

Compared with competing firms, colluding firms usually produce less, charge higher prices, earn more profit, and try to block the entry of new firms. Consumers lose consumer surplus because of the higher prices, and potential entrants suffer from being denied the chance to compete.

Collusion and cartels are illegal in the United States. However, monopoly profit can be so tempting that some U.S. firms break the law. Some other countries are more tolerant of cartels. Some even promote them, as with the 11 nations of OPEC, the world oil cartel. If OPEC members were ever to meet in the United States, those officials could be arrested for price fixing. Even though they are outlawed in some countries, cartels can operate worldwide because there are no international laws banning them.

The biggest obstacle to maintaining a profitable cartel is the powerful temptation to cheat on the agreement. By offering a price slightly below the established price, individual firms in the cartel usually can increase their own sales and profit. A cartel collapses when cheating becomes widespread.

A second obstacle to cartel success is the entry of rival firms. The profit of the cartel attracts entry, entry increases market supply, and increased supply forces down the market price. A cartel's continued success therefore depends on the ability to block the entry of new firms or to get new firms to join the cartel.

Finally, cartels, like monopolists, must be concerned that technological change can erode their market power. For example, hydrogen-powered

THE WALL STREET JOURNAL

Reading It Right What's the relevance of the following statement from *The Wall Street Journal:* "Few OPEC members other than Saudi Arabia have had significant spare production. That means quota-busting, the usual foil to OPEC unity, has been minimal."

fuel cells may replace gasoline in automobiles.

OPEC's initial success attracted so many other oil suppliers that OPEC now accounts for less than half the world's oil output. As a result, OPEC has lost much of its market power. Efforts to form cartels in the world markets for bauxite, copper, coffee, and some other products have failed so far.

✓ CHECKPOINT
What are the important features of oligopoly, and how do oligopolists that cooperate compare to those that compete?

When Oligopolists Compete

Because oligopolists are interdependent, analyzing their behavior is complicated. At one extreme, the firms in the industry may try to coordinate their behavior so they act collectively as a single monopolist, forming a cartel, as was just discussed. At the other extreme, oligopolists may compete so fiercely that price wars erupt, such as those that flare up in markets for cigarettes, computers, airline fares, and long-distance phone service.

You have now worked through the four market structures, including perfect competition, monopolistic competition, monopoly, and oligopoly. Features of the four are compared in Figure 7.5.

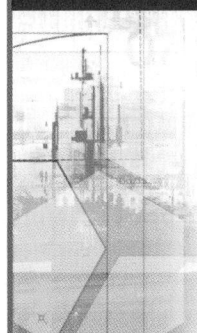

TEAM WORK

In small groups, brainstorm five additional examples to those given in Figure 7.5 of industries that compete in each of the four market structures (perfect competition, monopolistic competition, oligopoly, and monopoly).

Ask the Xpert!
econxtra.swlearning.com

What are the major differences among the four market structures?

Comparison of Market Structures

Figure 7.5

	Perfect Competition	Monopolistic Competition	Oligopoly	Monopoly
Number of firms	most	many	few	one
Control over price	none	limited	some	complete
Product differences	none	some	none or some	none
Barriers to entry	none	low	substantial	insurmountable
Examples	wheat, shares of stock	convenience stores, books	automobiles, cigarettes	local electricity and phone service

Key Concepts

1. There are probably 20 or more brands of laundry detergent in the grocery store where your family shops. Make a list of different ways in which producers try to differentiate one detergent brand from another. Why can some brands have prices that are much higher than the price of others and still sell well?

2. Why can't most oil producers compete successfully with large oil refiners such as Texaco, Shell Oil, or Mobil Oil?

3. In the 1990s, many nations that grew coffee beans tried to set up a cartel that would have limited coffee production and stabilized prices at a higher level. This effort failed. Explain why it is so hard to create a successful cartel when there are many members.

Graphing Exercise

4. The graph below shows the current demand and long-run average cost curves (discussed in Chapter 5) for Sleepwell Mattresses, one of more than 50 firms that manufacture mattresses. At the present, the firm is just breaking even—its total costs equal its total revenue. The firm's owners want to differentiate their product by convincing consumers that their mattresses are better than those offered by other firms. This would increase demand for their products and decrease their average cost by taking advantage of economies of scale. To do this, they undertake a major advertising campaign. If it is successful, what will happen to the location of the firm's demand curve and the location of the inter-section between the demand curve and the firm's long-run average cost curve? Make a copy of the graph and sketch in the new demand curve. Assuming the firm continues to sell mattresses for $150 each, what happens to the firm's average cost and profit?

Demand and Long-Run Average Cost for Sleepwell Mattresses

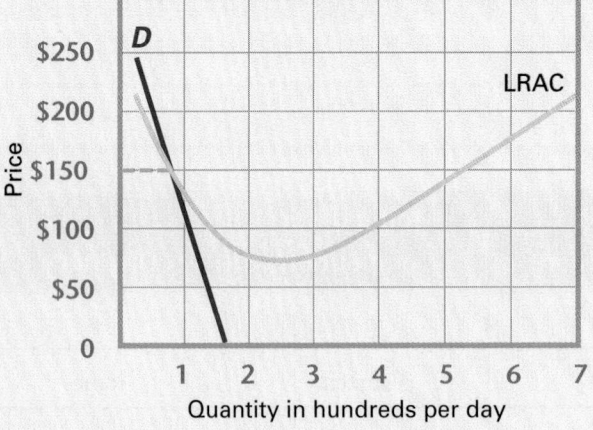

Think Critically

5. **Research** In 2003, the American Broadcasting Company (ABC) charged $2.2 million for a 30-second advertisement on television during the Super Bowl. Investigate the cost of this type of advertising during the latest Super Bowl. Why are businesses willing to spend this amount for a 30-second advertisement? What are they trying to accomplish?

movers & shakers

Dwight Cooper *Co-Owner, Professional Placement Resources*

Dwight Cooper met his friend and business partner, Keith Frein, when the two attended Florida State University. After graduating, they became co-workers at a medical staffing company. Each man dreamed of one day running his own business. In 1996, their dreams became reality when they invested their combined savings of $10,000 to found Professional Placement Resources (PPR). The company placed physical therapists, occupational therapists, and speech language pathologists into jobs. Because a shortage of workers in these fields had left organizations desperate for such qualified workers, PPR grew quickly.

Within a year, the company settled into offices in Jacksonville Beach, Florida, and employed five people. They added a travel service, allowing the therapists to work for 13 weeks in one city and then either move to a new assignment in a new city, remain in the same assignment for another 13 weeks, or take some time off before accepting a new assignment. The lure of travel, combined with attractive salaries and benefits (including free housing), helped PPR triple in size in just two years. When the therapist shortage ended in 1998, PPR began placing nurses instead. The nursing field continues to face a severe shortage throughout the United States. For the next two years, PPR recorded average annual growth of 244 percent.

Although PPR was founded when the market was expanding, "start-up was not easy," Cooper says. He credits the company's initial success to a lot of hard work and a little bit of luck. Although the

company's growth was welcome, it also presented challenges. "We grew really fast from early on," Cooper explains. "And as we grew, our business became more complex. We had so many more relationships to manage, and we no longer had the luxury or the time to discuss every issue among ourselves."

Cooper found the challenge of quickly building systems and processes suitable for the company to be "a bit overwhelming." He compares it to "living in a society with no laws and rules...imagine having to establish laws and rules for that first time."

Today PPR competes with more than 200 companies that also provide traveling nurses to hospitals across the United States. For PPR, "this healthy marketplace lets the customer decide what is a fair price for a nurse, and lets the nurse ultimately decide what is a fair wage," Cooper explains. "The market keeps all companies in this industry honest."

PPR's revenues will exceed $30 million in 2003. Its oceanfront headquarters have grown to 6,000 square feet. The company employs a staff of 65 dedicated employees who place more than 300 nurses in positions throughout the United States. Recognizing the need to expand its search for qualified nurses, PPR now recruits from as far away as Australia, India, and the Philippines to fill jobs in the United States.

In recognition of their accomplishments, Cooper and Frein were selected as finalists for Ernst and Young's Entrepreneur of the Year Award in 2000 and 2001. PPR twice was named one of the fastest-growing companies in north Florida by the *Jacksonville Business Journal.* Further, *Inc. Magazine* included PPR on its list of fastest-growing privately held companies in 2001 and 2002.

SOURCE READING
Dwight Cooper said, "The market keeps all companies in this industry honest." What do you think he means by this?

ENTREPRENEURS IN ACTION
As the company grew, Cooper said it was a challenge to establish rules quickly, without the time to discuss every issue with his partner. In small groups, discuss how you might handle this situation.

Objectives

> Explain the goal of U.S. antitrust laws.

> Distinguish between the two views of government regulation.

> Discuss why U.S. markets have grown more competitive in recent decades.

Overview

More than 225 years ago, Adam Smith remarked, "People of the same trade seldom meet together, even for merriment or diversion, but the conversation ends in a conspiracy against the public, or in some contrivance to raise prices." The tendency of firms to seek monopolistic advantage is understandable in light of their drive to maximize profit. But monopoly often harms the economy. Public policy can promote competition in markets where competition seems desirable. It can reduce the harmful effects of monopoly in markets where the output can be most efficiently produced by one or a few firms.

Key Terms

antitrust activity

merger

deregulation

[In the News]

Foot-Tingling Deregulation

When the power industry's natural monopoly was deregulated at the federal level, experts hoped the action would create competition in power generation throughout the country. The same experts warned, however, that deregulation also could lead to neglect of the transmission grids that delivered the generated power to the customers. The accuracy of this warning was made obvious when testimony before a federal panel pinpointed the triggering incident for the great northeastern blackout of mid-August, 2003: an overheated, melting electrical transmission line outside Cleveland that eventually sagged enough to touch a tree and short-circuit. The utility responsible for that part of the transmission grid already had a bad enough summer. Its New Jersey operation had been under fire for rolling blackouts that injured shore businesses and for inadequate maintenance that allowed stray electricity to run through the ground. This neglect left residents of Brick, N.J., tingling when they stepped into pools and Jacuzzis. In addition, one of its nuclear power plants had been shut down to prevent an accident when an acid leak had eaten through the steel lid of a reactor. A federal judge ruled it had violated the Clean Air Act by not installing pollution-control equipment at a coal-fired plant.

Think About It

What do you think this says about deregulation of some natural monopolies? What would you recommend to a government panel trying to correct the situation in the power industry?

Antitrust

Although competition typically promotes the most efficient use of the nation's resources, an individual firm would prefer to operate as a monopoly. If left alone, a firm might try to create a monopoly by driving competitors out of business, by merging with competitors, or by colluding with competitors to rig prices and increase profits. **Antitrust activity** attempts to prohibit efforts to monopolize markets in which competition is desirable.

U.S. Antitrust Activity

Antitrust activity tries to

1. Promote the market structure that will lead to greater competition, and

2. Reduce anticompetitive behavior.

Antitrust Laws

Antitrust laws attempt to promote socially desirable market performance. Three early laws dealt with the growing problem of antitrust activity. These included the Sherman Antitrust Act, the Clayton Act, and the Federal Trade Commision Act.

The Sherman Antitrust Act of 1890 outlawed the creation of trusts, restraint of trade, and monopolization. A *trust* is any firm or group of firms that tries to monopolize a market. The Clayton Act of 1914 was passed to outlaw certain practices not prohibited by the Sherman Act and to help government stop a monopoly before it developed. The Federal Trade Commission (FTC) Act of 1914 established a federal body to help enforce antitrust laws. The FTC has five full-time commissioners assisted by a staff of mostly economists and lawyers.

These three laws provide the U.S. antitrust framework. This framework has been clarified and enhanced by amendments and court decisions over the years.

Mergers and Antitrust

One way that firms may try to reduce competition is by merging with competing firms. A **merger** is the combination of two or more firms to form a single firm. Much of what federal antitrust officials do today is to approve or deny proposed mergers. These officials consider the merger's impact on the share of sales by the largest firms in the industry. If a few firms account for a relatively large share of sales in the market (say, more than half), any merger that increases that share may be challenged.

Federal guidelines sort all mergers into two categories. *Horizontal mergers* involve firms in the same market, such as a merger between competing oil companies. *Nonhorizontal mergers* include all other types of mergers. Horizontal mergers currently hold greater interest for antitrust officials. When determining whether to challenge a particular merger, officials consider factors such as the ease of entry into the market and possible efficiency gains from the merger. They would ask, for example, can the merger increase the resulting firm's economies of scale?

Flexible Merger Policy

In recent years, the government has shifted from rules that restrict big mergers to a more flexible approach. This new approach allows big companies to merge if the combination is more efficient or more competitive with other big firms in the market. For example, the government approved Boeing's $15 billion acquisition of McDonnell Douglas, another aircraft manufacturer, because Boeing still competes fiercely with Airbus, a European rival, in the world market for aircraft. As one antitrust official put it, "I do not believe that size alone is a basis to challenge a merger." However, just the threat of a legal challenge has stopped many potentially anticompetitive mergers.

> ✓ **CHECKPOINT**
> What is the goal of antitrust laws?

antitrust activity
Government efforts aimed at preventing monopoly and promoting competition in markets where competition is desirable

merger
The combination of two or more firms to form a single firm

Regulation of Natural Monopolies

Antitrust laws try to prevent monopoly in those markets where competition seems desirable. On the other hand, the *regulation of natural monopolies* tries to control price, output, the entry of new firms, and the quality of service in industries in which monopoly appears inevitable or even desirable. *Natural monopolies,* such as local electricity transmission, local phone service, or a city subway system, are regulated. Several other industries, such as land and air transportation, were regulated in the past based on the same idea.

Two Views of Government Regulation

Why do governments regulate the price and output of certain markets? There are two views of regulation. The first view has been the one discussed so far—namely, such regulation is in the *public interest.* Regulation promotes social welfare by reducing the price and increasing the output when a market is served most efficiently by one or just a few firms.

A second view is that such regulation is not in the public interest but is in the *special interest* of producers. According to this view, well-organized producer groups expect to profit from government regulation by persuading public officials to impose restrictions that these groups find attractive. Such restrictions include limiting entry into the industry and preventing competition among existing firms.

Producer groups may argue that competition in their industry would hurt consumers. For example, the alleged problem of "cutthroat" competition among taxi drivers has led to regulations that eliminated price competition and restricted the number of taxis in most large metropolitan areas. The problem is that regulation has made taxis more expensive and harder to find.

The special-interest theory may be valid even when the initial intent of the legislation was in the consumer interest. Over time, the regulators may start acting more in the special interests of producers.

Why do you think it is desirable for local phone service to be regulated by government?

CHECKPOINT
Compare the two views of government regulation of monopoly.

© Getty Images/PhotoDisc

Competitive Trends in the U.S. Economy

The U.S. economy has grown more competitive in the last half century. The number of industries judged to be competitive increased from about half of all industries in 1960 to more than three-fourths of all industries today. Causes of increased competition include antitrust activity, deregulation, international trade, and technological change. Consider the impact of each.

Antitrust Activity

Antitrust officials now spend most of their time evaluating the impact of proposed mergers on market competition. Although not many mergers ultimately are challenged by government, just the threat of a legal challenge has deterred many potentially anticompetitive mergers.

Perhaps the most significant antitrust case in recent years not involving a merger was the agreement antitrust officials reached with Microsoft. Microsoft was charged with having a monopoly in operating-system software and with attempting to extend this monopoly to the Web browser market. Among other

Judge Offers Windows
econxtra.swlearning.com

E-CONOMICS

Microsoft on Trial

The most significant antitrust case in the last decade was the U.S. Justice Department's (DOJ's) case against Microsoft Corporation. The DOJ accused Microsoft of engaging in a pattern of "predatory conduct" to protect its operating-system monopoly and to extend that monopoly into Internet software. Microsoft disputed the charges and said the government was interfering with its right to create new products that benefit consumers. After 78 days of testimony and months of deliberation, Judge Thomas Penfield Jackson ruled that Microsoft maintained a monopoly in operating-system software by anticompetitive means. He also found that Microsoft attempted to monopolize the Web browser market by unlawfully "tying" Internet Explorer with Windows. As a remedy, Judge Jackson proposed restricting Microsoft's business practices and dividing the firm into a Windows-based operating-system company and an applications-software company. Microsoft appealed the decision to the U.S. Court of Appeals. This court upheld the finding that Microsoft violated antitrust laws and acted illegally in maintaining a monopoly in

its operating system. However, they also found that Judge Jackson had engaged in "serious judicial misconduct" in making negative comments about Microsoft to the media. The court ordered a new judge to decide on the punishment. In September 2001, however, the DOJ announced it would not seek a breakup of Microsoft, but would ask the court for a series of tough restrictions. In November 2001, Microsoft reached a settlement with the DOJ and with most of the state attorneys general. The settlement gave personal-computer makers greater freedom to install non-Microsoft software on new machines and to remove access to competing Microsoft features, such as Internet browsers. It also banned exclusive contracts and prohibited Microsoft from acting against companies that take advantage of these freedoms. Further, it required Microsoft to disclose design information to hardware and software makers, so they can build competing products that will run smoothly with Windows.

Think Critically

Who benefits from the settlement Microsoft reached with the Justice Department?

things, the settlement with Microsoft gives personal-computer makers greater freedom to install non-Microsoft software on new machines. Read more about this important antitrust case in the E-conomics feature on page 211.

Deregulation

deregulation

A reduction in government control over prices and firm entry in previously regulated markets, such as airlines and trucking

For most of the twentieth century, industries such as trucking, airlines, securities trading, banking, and telecommunications were regulated by the government to limit price competition and restrict entry. The trend in recent decades has been toward **deregulation**, which reduces or eliminates government regulations. For the most part, deregulation has increased competition and benefited consumers.

Take, for example, the regulation and deregulation of airlines. The Civil Aeronautics Board (CAB), established in 1938, once strictly regulated the U.S. interstate airline business. Any potential entrant interested in serving an interstate route had to persuade the CAB that the route needed another airline, a task that proved impossible. During the 40 years of regulation, potential entrants submitted more than 150 applications for long-distance routes, *but not a single new interstate airline was allowed.* The CAB also forced strict compliance with regulated prices. A request to lower prices on any route would result in a rate hearing, during which both the CAB and competitors scrutinized the request. In effect, the CAB created a cartel that fixed prices among the 10 existing major airlines and blocked new entry.

In 1978, despite opposition from the existing airlines and their labor unions, Congress passed the Airline Deregulation Act, which allowed price competition and new entry. By 2000, airfares averaged 27 percent below previously regulated prices. Passenger miles nearly tripled. Airlines became more productive by filling a greater percentage of seats. The net benefits of deregulation to consumers now exceed $20 billion a year, or about $75 per U.S. resident.

Regulations that limited competition also have been repealed in trucking, securities trading, banking, and telecommunications. For the most part, these industries have become more competitive as a result of deregulation. Consumers benefit from lower prices and better products.

International Trade

Foreign imports increased competition in many industries, including autos, tires, and steel. Many imported goods were attractive to U.S. consumers because of their superior quality and lower prices. Finding themselves at a cost and technological disadvantage, U.S. producers initially asked for government protection from foreign competitors through trade barriers, such as quotas and tariffs. Despite their efforts to block foreign goods, U.S. producers still lost market share to imports.

For example, General Motors dominates U.S. auto manufacturing. GM's sales account for half of U.S. automobile sales by U.S. firms. However, when sales by Japanese and European producers are included, GM's share of the U.S. auto market falls to less than one third. To survive in the market, U.S. producers improved quality and offered products at more competitive prices.

Technological Change

Some industries are growing more competitive as a result of technological change. Here are some examples: In the last two decades, the prime-time audience share of the three major television networks (NBC, CBS, and ABC)

NET Bookmark

A review of the history of airline deregulation from a conservative viewpoint is available online from the Heritage Foundation's magazine. Access this web site through econxtra.swlearning.com. What actions was the Department of Transportation considering at the time this review was written? What nonregulatory alternatives does the author suggest?

econxtra.swlearning.com

dropped from 91 percent to 46 percent as satellite and cable technology delivered many more channels.

Despite Microsoft's dominance in operating systems, the packaged software market for personal computers barely existed in 1980. It now thrives in a technology-rich environment populated by thousands of software makers. Also, the Internet has opened possibilities for greater competition in a number of industries, from online stock trading to all manner of electronic commerce.

Some web sites offer consumers ready information about the price and availability of products. This makes comparison shopping easier and lowers the transaction costs of buying and selling.

CHECKPOINT
Why have U.S. markets grown more competitive in recent decades?

Main Idea

Role of Competition

The trend toward e-commerce has led to greater competition in the U.S. economy. For example, *competition among online sellers lowers costs and prices and encourages producers to make more of the products buyers want. Competition among online buyers increases price and allocates goods and services to people who are willing and able to pay for them.*

© Getty Images/PhotoDisc

Key Concepts

1. Imagine there are two large discount stores in a small town. Describe one way in which consumers might be harmed if these stores merged and one way they might benefit.

2. The basic antitrust laws in the United States have not changed very much in many years. Still, over time, there has been a significant difference in the way these laws have been enforced. What could explain this situation?

3. Fifty years ago, the vast majority of shoes sold in the United States were manufactured in this country. In recent years, U.S.-made shoes have accounted for less than 10 percent of this market. How has foreign competition reduced the monopoly power of U.S. shoe producers?

4. What would happen to the market power of a firm that found, patented, and received FDA approval to market a drug that prevents HIV infections? Why might such a firm not charge an extremely high price for this drug?

Graphing Exercise

5. Study the two demand curves below. One is for a drug manufactured by Acme Pharmaceuticals that thousands of people need in order to stay healthy. The other is for a particular brand of shampoo. In which case is demand elastic and in which case is it inelastic? Which of these products is Product A and which is Product B? How did you make this determination? Which of these firms has greater monopoly power? In general, do firms with elastic or inelastic demand have more monopoly power?

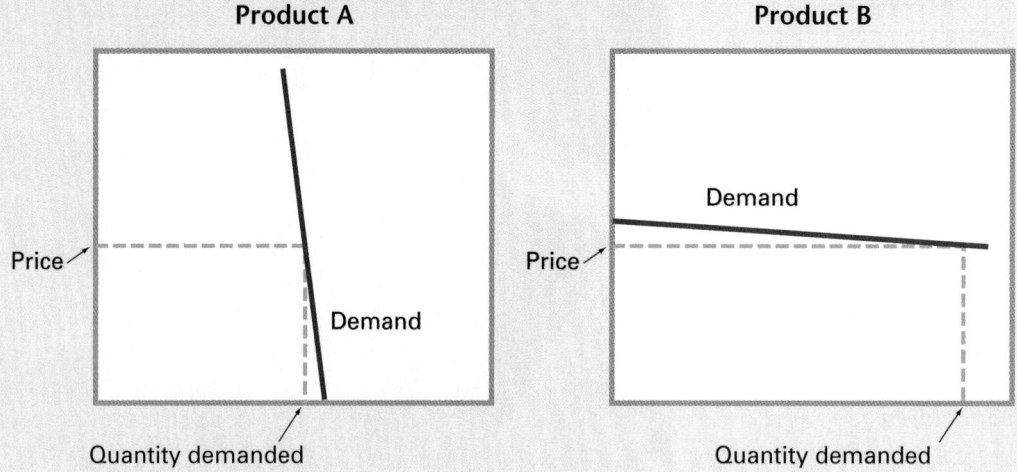

Think Critically

6. **Government** The U.S. Postal Service (USPS) lost billions of dollars in the decade between 1992 and 2002. In 2003, some people argued that the USPS should be privatized or sold to private businesses to be run. What has happened to the USPS since then? Has its monopoly power been increased or decreased? Does it remain as a government monopoly or has it been sold? Do you think the situation has improved or worsened for consumers?

CONNECT *to History*

The North American Fur Trade

From 1804 to 1816, two companies—the Hudson Bay Company (HBC) headquartered in London, and the Northwestern Company (NWC) of Montreal—dominated the North American fur trade. Both companies operated over large areas of the Canadian wilderness. For the most part, each company respected the other's territory and business operation without a formal market-sharing agreement.

With the start of the Napoleonic War in Europe, the demand for furs in Britain declined 50 percent as the European markets were closed off from British trade. The HBC suffered greater losses than its rival, because the HBC's charter prohibited it from trading anywhere but England. The NWC, on the other hand, was able to find markets in China, the United States, and even Europe. Despite the drop in demand, the HBC refused to slow down its operations in the hope that the war would be short. It also did not want to jeopardize its business relations with the Native Americans, from whom it purchased the pelts. Instead, in an attempt to control supply and maintain prices, it chose to store the furs it collected.

However, where the two companies previously had respected each other's territory, the HBC's financial problems led it to end their informal agreement. It began to move into the area in which the NWC had been trapping exclusively. The cost of obtaining furs rose as competition between the companies drove up the price each had to pay the Native Americans. Both companies also engaged in attempts to disrupt the other's operation by employing "bully boys." This harmful competition ended in 1821, when the companies agreed to merge and form a monopoly. The new company brought an end to the destructive practices and lowered costs by taking advantage of the economies of scale. The combined company also provided a unified front in purchasing from the Native Americans.

THINK CRITICALLY

Referring to the characteristics of monopolistic competition and oligopoly, analyze the behavior of the Hudson Bay Company and the Northwest Company during the period from 1804 to 1821. What effect do you think the merger of the two companies had on the price of fur?

7 Chapter Assessment

Summary

 Perfect Competition and Monopoly

a *Perfectly competitive* markets share four features: (1) they have many buyers and sellers; (2) producers sell the same standard product; (3) buyers are fully informed about the price, quality, and availability of products and sellers are fully informed about all resources and technology used to make them; and (4) firms and resources are free to enter or leave the market.

Xtra! Quiz Prep
econxtra.swlearning.com

b The price that individual producers in perfect competition charge is determined by market supply and market demand. A firm that charged more than the prevailing market price would have no customers.

c A *monopoly* is the only supplier of a product that has no close substitutes. For monopolies to exist in the long run, there must be *barriers to entry*. These may include legal restrictions such as patents, economies of scale that make established firms more efficient than new firms, and control of essential resources not available to other firms.

d The demand curve for a monopoly slopes down from left to right. This means that the firm must lower its price on all products to sell additional products.

e Many people believe that monopolies harm the general welfare because they may waste resources, exert undue influence on the government, or grow lazy and inefficient. Others believe that monopolies may have lower costs and prices because of economies of scale and that government regulation can prevent them from exploiting consumers.

7.2 Monopolistic Competition and Oligopoly

a *Monopolistic competition* is a market structure with many firms offering similar but not identical products. Each monopolisticcom-

petitor tries to attract customers by differentiating its product. Forms of product differentiation include physical differences, sales locations, services offered with the product, and the product's image.

b *Oligopoly* is a market structure in which a few businesses dominate production in the market and are interdependent. Oligopolies typically exist in markets where there are economies of scale and high costs of entry.

c Oligopolists sometimes cooperate with each other in pricing their products. When they actually agree to set prices, they collude. Internationally, some nations have worked together to establish *cartels* that are intended to increase or stabilize prices by controlling supply.

7.3 Antitrust, Economic Regulation, and Competition

a The federal government has passed three basic *antitrust* laws intended to limit the monopoly power of large businesses: (1) the Sherman Antitrust Act, (2) the Clayton Act, and (3) the Federal Trade Commission Act.

b Many of the firms that became monopolies gained their power through merger. Mergers are either horizontal—when firms supplying the same market join—or nonhorizontal—when firms not supplying the same product join. Much of the federal antitrust activity today is directed toward limiting the ability of firms to merge if doing so would result in businesses with significant monopoly power.

c An alternative to limiting the ability of firms to merge is to regulate those that have a significant amount of monopoly power. The federal government and all states have regulatory agencies that are designed to protect the public's interests.

d In recent years there has been a trend toward *deregulation* of many parts of the economy. The monopoly power of many U.S. businesses has been reduced as a result of new technologies and foreign competition.

Review Economic Terms

Choose the term that best fits the definition. On a separate sheet of paper, write the letter of the answer.

_____ 1. A market structure with many fully informed buyers and sellers of an identical product with no barriers to entry

_____ 2. A sole supplier of a product with no close substitutes

_____ 3. Restrictions on the entry of new firms into an industry

_____ 4. The ability of a firm to raise its price without losing all its sales

_____ 5. A market structure with no entry barriers and many firms selling products differentiated enough that each firm's demand curve slopes downward

_____ 6. A market structure with a small number of firms whose behavior is interdependent

_____ 7. A group of firms that agree to act as a monopolist to increase the market price and maximize the group's profits

_____ 8. Government efforts aimed at preventing monopoly and promoting competition in markets where competition is desirable

_____ 9. The combination of two or more firms into a single firm

_____10. A product that is identical across sellers

_____11. A reduction in government control over prices and firm entry in previously regulated markets

_____12. Important features of a market, including the number of buyers and sellers and the product's uniformity across sellers.

a. **antitrust activity**

b. **barriers to entry**

c. **cartel**

d. **commodity**

e. **deregulation**

f. **market power**

g. **market structure**

h. **merger**

i. **monopolistic competition**

j. **monopoly**

k. **oligopoly**

l. **perfect competition**

Review Economic Concepts

13. Which of the following statements is *not* true of firms in *perfect competition*?

   a. All producers charge the same price.

   b. All producers make the same product.

   c. Each firm tries to sell more by reducing its price.

   d. There are no barriers to entry.

14. **True or False** The demand curve for a single firm in competition is a horizontal line.

15. A firm operating in the __?__ market structure has no market power.

16. **True or False** *Monopolies* may emerge naturally when a firm has substantial economies of scale.

17. *Monopolies* must lower the price of the products they sell to

   a. sell more output.

   b. earn a profit.

   c. shift the demand curve.

   d. meet their competition.

18. **True or False** By definition, all *monopolies* earn substantial profits.

19. **True or False** Most *monopolies* tend to last for a long time.

20. Suppose a giant *monoply* is created when one firm buys up all the individual firms in a perfectly competitive market. In this case, the __?__ curve becomes the monopolist's demand curve.

21. Firms in *monopolistic competition*

    a. all produce exactly the same product.

    b. all charge the same price.

    c. all earn the same profit.

    d. all work to differentiate their products.

22. **True or False** One problem for society resulting from *monopoly* is that the monopoly may have too much influence on the political system.

23. Which of the following is not a way in which sellers in *monopolistic competition* differentiate their products?

    a. physical differences

    b. location and services

    c. collusion

    d. product image

24. A firm that has __?__ can lower its average cost by selling more of the good.

25. The demand curve facing an individual firm operating in perfect competition

    a. is a vertical line drawn at the number of units.

    b. is a horizontal line drawn at the market price.

    c. slopes down from left to right.

    d. slopes up from left to right.

26. In a(n) __?__ *oligopoly,* the product is identical across producers.

27. Firms in an *oligopoly*

    a. are totally independent from each other.

    b. are interdependent.

    c. always have excess capacity.

    d. none of the above is true.

28. **True or False** The minimum efficient scale is the highest rate of output at which a firm takes full advantage of economies of scale.

29. Which of the following industries is most likely to be regulated by government?

    a. consumer products

    b. electrical service

    c. dry-cleaning service

    d. precious jewels

30. **True or False** Government regulatory agencies are designed to protect the public's interests.

31. Each of the following is a basic federal antitrust law in the United States *except*

    a. the Fair Labor Standards Act of 1938.

    b. the Clayton Act of 1914.

    c. the Sherman Act of 1890.

    d. the Federal Trade Commission Act of 1914.

32. **True or False** Consumers usually benefit from *deregulation* because of the resulting lower prices.

Apply Economic Concepts

33. **Analyze Pricing in Oligopoly** The two largest producers of commercial aircraft in the world are Airbus of Europe and the Boeing Corporation of the United States. Most economists regard the market for large commercial aircraft as a good example of an oligopoly. Describe what you think Boeing would do if Airbus increased the price of its airplanes by 20 percent. How does this show the interdependency of these firms?

34. **Business Law** An important question today is whether limits should be placed on what consumers may download from the Internet. According to copyright law, those who produce literature, music, films or works of art should be able to profit from what they create. They should, in effect, have a monopoly on their work. Indeed, if their work is placed on the Internet for others to copy for free, they may choose not to produce anything at all. Investigate the current status of this issue, and state your opinion of what should be done.

35. **History** There was a time when Nabisco, Post Cereals, Kellogg's, and General Mills sold nearly 75 percent of the breakfast cereal purchased in the United States. These firms were part of an oligopoly, but those days are now gone. Describe what has happened to reduce the monopoly power of these firms in the market. Think about the breakfast cereal shelves in your grocery store.

36. **Sharpen Your Life Skills: Auto Industry** Review changes in the distribution of sales in the U.S. automobile market that were presented in the Sharpen Your Life Skills activity on page 200 of this chapter. Assume that the trend in sales between 1980 and 2002 demonstrated by the pie graphs continues for another 22 years to 2024. How would the U.S. economy be affected? Would U.S. consumers benefit or be harmed? What would happen to businesses and people employed in the U.S. auto industry?

37. **Problems with Monopoly** During the 1960s the three largest U.S. producers of automobiles (Ford, General Motors, and Chrysler) sold nearly 90 percent of the cars purchased by U.S. consumers. During the 30 years between 1970 and 2000 these firms lost about one-third of their market to foreign competition that was more technologically advanced. What problem common to monopolies does this situation demonstrate?

38. **Distinguish Between Competition and Monopoly** The graph below provides demand curves for two different firms. One of them is for a competitive firm and the other is for a firm with monopoly power. Identify the firm that is competitive and the one that is a monopoly. Explain how you know which is which. What would happen to the sales of the competitive firm if it tried to raise its price? What would happen to the firm that is a monopoly? Why do businesses prefer to have monopoly power?

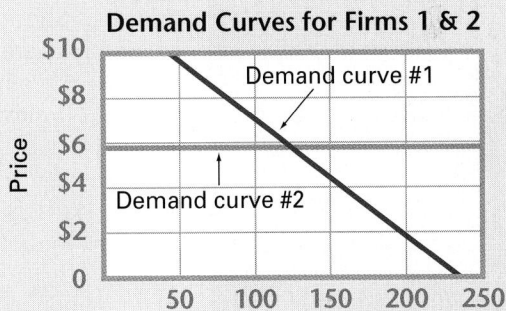

Demand Curves for Firms 1 & 2

econxtra.swlearning.com

39. Access **EconDebate Online** at econxtra.swlearning.com. Read the policy debate entitled "Should the antititrust exemption for baseball be eliminated?" Analyze this issue from both points of view, and write a paragraph summarizing each side.

Investing In Your Future

❂ The Situation

Graduation from high school was just around the corner for Aleesha. She had worked for the zoo as an intern for almost two years now, and had become a trusted and valued employee. The zoo manager had offered her a full-time position as his administrative assistant upon her graduation. The used car her father helped her pick out had held up well, but it was just about worn out. Aleesha had managed to keep her grades high, but she had let her participation in sports drop away. Of course, even though she had lots of opportunities, her social life had suffered, at least up until the last few months. Then she had met Charles, an associate manager at the local convenience store. He had been persistent in his invitations, and they had been dating on weekends for about two months. He was even talking about their getting married after she graduated, and starting a family.

❂ The Decision

However, Aleesha's basic love for the zoo and its animals remained strong. She cared for them, kept a personal set of records on the ones she tended, read articles about them in professional zoo journals, and did her own research in the field. She was filled with ideas about better ways to provide for their well-being and improve the relationship between the animals and the public. Aleesha knew that to develop her ideas and someday have a position where they could be applied, she would have to go to college. However, the nearest college with an appropriate degree program was a long distance away. She would have to live near campus rather than at home. On the positive side, the zoo manager was confident that she could get a scholarship from the zoological society. The award would cover tuition and books for a year, and it could be renewed as long as Aleesha maintained a B average.

Activities

Divide into teams or work individually, as directed by your teacher, to perform the following tasks.

Apply the steps in the following decision-making process to Aleesha's situation:

1. *Define the problem.* Define Aleesha's problem in a way that will allow a clear solution.

2. *Identify her choices.* List the various alternatives among which she must choose. Develop budgets and project the quality of life for each of the following choices. See econxtra.swlearning.com for links to tools of analysis that will help you to perform this step.

a. Aleesha takes the assistant's position and marries Charles.

b. Aleesha takes the assistant's position at the zoo but does not marry. Due to the needs of her brothers and sisters, she has to move out of the home within a year of graduation.

c. Aleesha applies for and receives the scholarship to college. Her parents are unable to help her financially but she is eligible for loans and grants.

3. *Evaluate the pluses and minuses of each choice.* Carefully weigh the value Aleesha puts on each alternative and the opportunity costs for each.

a. Project Aleesha's lifetime income level for each choice. See econxtra.swlearning.com for links to tools of analysis that will help you to perform these steps.

b. What personal, emotional, and psychological factors do you think will affect Aleesha's choice?

4. *Make a choice.* Which course of action should she choose? Be prepared to present and defend your choice in class.

5. *Provide "action" steps that are appropriate to the decision.* Make sure these are realistic and timely to ensure the necessary actions are taken to resolve the problem.

6. *Critique the decision.* The class will assist in the review and evaluation of your plan of action. In real life, you should review not only the decision and its result, but also the process by which you make it. Set a time to initiate reviewing the decision or identify an event that would trigger its review.

Research

Research for the information you need to effectively make the decision, such as the lifetime income levels Aleesha could expect for each choice.

Present

Arrive at a decision. Then prepare a presentation for the class on the six steps you took to achieve this decision. Be ready for questions and criticisms.

6/24

1/5

5/14

Unit 3

Market Institutions

One important decision maker in a market economy is you. Your consumption choices and those of other consumers determine what gets produced. To help supply the products that you and others demand, several institutions have developed to nurture a market economy. Among the most important are businesses, labor markets, and financial markets. You already have some acquaintance with all three. You have interacted with businesses all your life. Most of you have observed labor markets first hand. You are even familiar with financial markets—from credit cards to bank accounts.

8 Businesses

© Getty Images/PhotoDisc

Consider

Why do some people want to call themselves "boss"?

Why start a business if most new businesses don't last five years?

What does your summer lawn-mowing operation have in common with General Motors?

What do *Corp.* or *Inc.* in a company's name tell you about how the owners treat debt?

How could it be possible that most U.S. businesses have no paid employees?

POINT YOUR BROWSER

econxtra.swlearning.com

Objectives

> Understand the role of the entrepreneur in a market economy.

> Differentiate entrepreneurs from people who perform a limited entrepreneurial role.

Overview

In a market economy, people are free to risk their time and their savings to start a business. If the business succeeds, they are rewarded with profit. If the business fails, they could lose a bundle. Chances of success are not great. Most new businesses fail in the first five years. On the other hand, some businesses survive, a few thrive, and a tiny few make their founders wealthy. Despite the high rate of business failure, the promise of profit attracts many prospective entrepreneurs. By putting their ideas into action, entrepreneurs drive the economy forward.

Key Terms

financial capital

innovation

[In the News]

Hip-Hop's Surprise Entrepreneur

From its first downbeat, hip-hop music has been dominated by urban and inner-city African-American artists—with a few exceptions like the white artists Eminem and the Beastie Boys. Now there's another white face gaining prominence in the rap and hip-hop music scene. His name is Devin Lazerine, and he's from a suburban town outside Los Angeles. Just 19 years old, Lazerine began his career with a web site. Then, with financial backing and other assistance from media giant Time Warner, he started a "fan 'zine" called *Rap-Up.* The glossy publication is targeted to a new market referred to as "Generation Y" —hip-hop's rapidly growing base of fans. *Rap-Up*'s first issue sold an amazing 200,000 copies. In March 2003, Lazerine made *Fast Company* magazine's list of top 50 "Champions of Innovation," entrepreneurs whose achievements are having a major impact on both the business world and our culture. Lazerine's first celebrity interview for *Rap-Up* was with the group Destiny's Child. He hooked their agent's interest with a phone call talking up the new magazine, and she called back the next day. When Lazerine's mom answered the phone and told the agent he was in school, the agent thought it was a joke. Lazerine persisted and ultimately did get the interview. In his own interview with *USA Weekend* magazine, Lazerine talked about how difficult it was getting respect at such a young age. However, he also said, ". . . if you have a love for something, I don't think age or color or anything should make a difference."

Think About It

How do you think Devin Lazerine overcame the obstacle of age to become a successful entrepreneur? How big a part did creativity play in his success?

Role of Entrepreneurs

An *entrepreneur* is a profit-seeker who develops a new product or process and assumes the risk of profit or loss. The entrepreneur is the prime mover in the market economy—a visionary, someone who can see what others can't. The entrepreneur's role is to discover and introduce new and better products and more efficient ways of doing things. Because new products often involve long and costly development, they are risky. Entrepreneurs must have the confidence to accept that risk and must inspire confidence in others, such as resource suppliers and lenders. In short, *an entrepreneur comes up with an idea, turns that idea into a marketable product, accepts the risk of success or failure, and claims any resulting profit or loss.*

An entrepreneur goes into business to earn a profit by satisfying consumer wants. A business can consist simply of one self-employed person earning a few thousand dollars by mowing lawns during the summer. Or, a business can be as complex as General Motors, with 365,000 employees, factories around the world, and annual revenue of $200 billion. The lawn-mowing operation and General Motors are both businesses. There are about 25 million businesses in the United States. Most of these businesses consist of just one self-employed person. Most of these self-employed enterprises will remain tiny. A handful will become the largest businesses in the world.

Entrepreneurs and Creative Change

The introduction of new or better products and new production methods are sources of technological progress and economic growth in the economy. Entrepreneurs initiate four types of creative changes in a market economy.

1. **Introduce New Products** Some entrepreneurs try to come up with new products, opening up markets that had not existed. For example, the Segway™ Human Transporter, a personal transport device, was developed by Dean Kamen and introduced in 2003. The product is marketed as an alternative to walking or riding a bicycle.

NETBookmark

To learn more about the Segway™ Human Transporter, access the company's web site through

econxtra.swlearning.com

© Rick Friedman/CORBIS

With some new products, entrepreneurs invent a whole new market, like the market for the Segway™ Human Transporter. Do you think this new product will succeed in the marketplace? Why or why not?

2. Improve Quality of Existing Products
Some entrepreneurs begin with an existing product and make it better. For example, Howard Schultz took the simple cup of coffee and turned it into liquid gold by offering higher quality and greater variety in a more inviting atmosphere. Founded by Schultz in 1985, Starbucks Coffee now is a multibillion-dollar operation with more than 70,000 employees in thousands of locations around the world.

3. Introduce New Production Methods
Some entrepreneurs combine resources more efficiently to reduce production costs. They use less costly materials, employ better technology, or combine resources in more economical ways. Henry Ford, for example, introduced the assembly line, where automobiles move along a conveyer and the workers stay put. Ford didn't invent the automobile, but his assembly line made owning one affordable to millions of households.

4. Introduce New Ways of Doing Business
Some entrepreneurs step outside existing business models to create a new way of doing business. For example, Michael Dell began in 1984 with $1,000 and the idea to sell computers directly to customers rather than through retailers. His made-to-order computers are sold by phone and over the Internet. Dell is now the largest computer seller in the world, with sales exceeding $50 million *a day*. Mary Kay Ash did the same for skin care products and cosmetics, selling $2 billion a year directly to consumers around the world through independent Mary Kay consultants.

Financing the Business

A good idea in itself does not guarantee profit. To succeed, entrepreneurs must figure out how best to transform their ideas into reality. They must acquire the necessary resources, including hiring employees and buying supplies. They also must obtain **financial capital**, that is, the money needed to start or expand the business.

Financial capital may be obtained through bank loans or from *venture capitalists*—individuals or companies that specialize in financing start-up firms. Entrepreneurs also often draw from their own savings to invest in the new enterprise. Some even sell all they own to get the business off the ground. For example, the filmmaker Michael Moore sold all his possessions to finance his first documentary film, *Roger and Me*. To accept such risks, entrepreneurs must have confidence in their ideas.

Ask the Xpert!

econxtra.swlearning.com

How do businesses raise cash to finance startups and expansions?

financial capital
Money needed to start or expand a business

© Getty Images/PhotoDisc

Describe the ways in which entrepreneurs may obtain financial capital for their business.

Profit Attracts Competitors

If an innovation succeeds in the market, many people benefit. The entrepreneur is rewarded with profit and the satisfaction of creating something of value. Workers are rewarded with more and better jobs. Consumers are rewarded with new and better products. The government benefits from higher tax revenue, which can be used to fund public goods and services or to lower other taxes. Overall the economy reaches a higher level of business activity. This translates into a higher standard of living for the people who live in the economy.

Entrepreneurs may earn profit in the short run. However, it is profit in the long run that attracts competitors and substitutes. Other businesses will enter the market and try to duplicate the success of the original entrepreneur. Competitors try to offer a better product or a lower price. Because these copycats must be creative and take risks, they, too, are entrepreneurs.

The original entrepreneur must fight to remain profitable in the long run.

Ultimately, the pursuit of profit can lead to a chain of events that creates new and better products, more competition, more production, higher quality, and lower prices. Entrepreneurs are the key players in a market economy. They supply the creative sparks that drive the economy forward.

If the new business loses money and has no prospects for a turnaround, this tells the entrepreneur to find a better use for the resources. Profits tell entrepreneurs they are on the right track. Losses tell them to change tracks. You could think of profits as a way of keeping score, a way of telling entrepreneurs whether they are winning or losing. When an entrepreneur wins, many others in the economy win as well. When an entrepreneur loses, it's mostly the entrepreneur who suffers.

CHECKPOINT
Explain the role of entrepreneurs in a market economy.

Main Idea

Growth

An entrepreneur's investment in a new business venture benefits the economy as a whole. The *investment leads to* a higher level of business activity, and ultimately to a *higher standard of living* for the people who live in the economy.

© Getty Images/PhotoDisc

© Getty Images/PhotoDisc

© Getty Images/PhotoDisc

Who Isn't an Entrepreneur?

Some people may carry out just one of the functions of an entrepreneur. For example, they may dream up a new product or process, they may manage resources, or they may assume the risk of success or failure. Carrying out just one of the roles alone does not make you an entrepreneur, however. A way of determining more about who is an entrepreneur is to learn more about people in business who are not entrepreneurs.

Invention, Innovation, and Entrepreneurs

Innovation is the process of turning an invention into a marketable product. Inventors are entrepreneurs if they bear the risk of success or failure. Most inventors work for firms as paid employees. For example, corporations such as Pfizer, Dow Chemical, or Intel employ thousands of scientists to improve existing products and develop new ones. These corporate inventors, sometimes referred to as *intrapreneurs,* are paid even in years when their creative juices slow down. Because these

hired inventors take no more risks than most other employees, they are not considered to be entrepreneurs.

Figure 8.1 shows the source of inventions since 1980 as measured by U.S. patents awarded. The number of patents more than doubled from 1980 to 2000. The number of patents awarded to individuals fell from 22 percent to only 14 percent, however. Some of these individual inventors are in the business of inventing new products and selling the idea to others. These inventors accept risks in a way that the inventors working for corporations do not. Therefore, individual inventors usually are entrepreneurs.

Managers and Entrepreneurs

Most entrepreneurs do more than simply sell their good ideas to others. They try to bring their ideas to the market by paying resource owners for the right to control these resources in the businesses. Then they claim any profit or loss that results. This right to control resources does not necessarily mean the entrepreneur must manage the firm. The entrepreneur does have the power to hire and fire the manager.

For example, Dean Kamen, inventor

innovation

The process of turning an invention into a marketable product

---

Source of U.S. Patents Awarded for Inventions by Year

Figure **8.1**

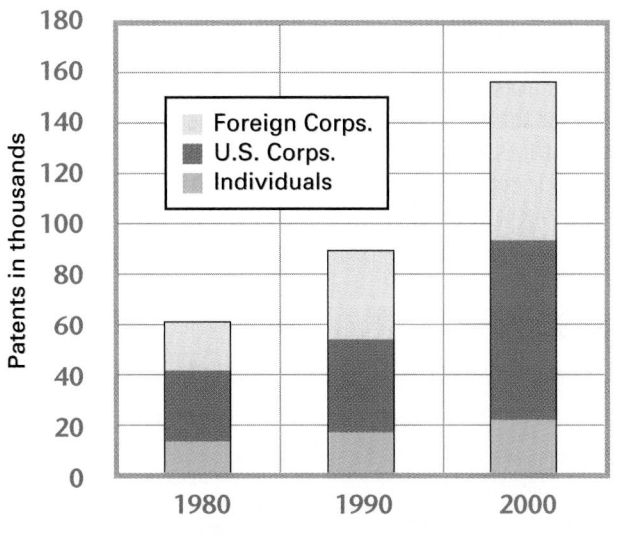

The number of patents grew from 61,800 in 1980 to 157,500 in 2000. In 1980, 22 percent of all patents were awarded to individuals. By 2000, only 14 percent went to individuals.

Source: U.S. Bureau of the Census, *Statistical Abstract of the United States,* 2001.

of the Segway personal transporter, created a company to make and sell his invention. Kamen also hired a chief executive officer to run the business. Even though he doesn't run the business himself, Kamen still is an entrepreneur because he has the power to hire and fire the manager. Kamen's chief executive officer is a well-paid employee, but he is not an entrepreneur.

Stockholders and Entrepreneurs

More than half of all households in the United States—over 50,000,000 of them—now own corporate stock. If a corporation fails, stockholders could lose the amount they paid for that particular stock. If the corporation thrives, the stock value will increase and stockholders will benefit.

People buy a corporation's stock because they believe in the managers' ability to increase the value of the business. They think the managers can make more profitable use of their funds than they themselves can. At the same time, the stockholders assume the risk of the company's success or failure. Does this make the stockholders entrepreneurs? No, it does not. True entrepreneurs do more than take the risk of success or failure. They decide what to produce and usually figure out how to produce it profitably. Stockholders, on the other hand, usually have little say in the firm's operation.

SPAN THE GLOBE

Are We Deporting Our Future?

Have events since the September 11, 2001, terrorist attacks made the United States hostile to newcomers? By withdrawing the welcome mat, will we suffer the loss of much-needed skills and energetic entrepreneurial spirit? Both the public and the government have overreacted in some cases: A Sikh gas-station owner from India was murdered by a crazed revenge seeker. A high-tech company executive was yanked from a routine commercial flight and questioned because, though he was actually a peaceful Hindu from India wearing $500 shoes and a $4,000 suit, he looked suspicious. More than a third of Silicon Valley's software engineers have emigrated from India. If the United States discourages the influx of professionals from this area, will the Valley and the nation as a whole suffer as a result? For many years, the United States was a haven for talented people seeking a safe and inviting home to pursue their professional passions. However, the professional climate for immigrants has changed dramatically. Entrepreneurs around the world are getting the message that foreigners who even remotely fit the terrorist profile no longer are welcome in the United States, no matter how talented they are. Paul Saffo, Director of the Institute for the Future, says, "We can't afford to deport our future. Our country cannot sustain the technology sector without brilliant minds from all over the planet. If we stay on our current path, we will enjoy an illusory sense of security, but it will come at the cost of strangling the nation's technological and economic future."

Think Critically

Do you think Mr. Saffo's concern is justified? Why or why not?

CHECKPOINT
What groups perform part of the entrepreneur's role but are not considered entrepreneurs?

Key Concepts

1. Which of the following describes an entrepreneur? (a) a person employed to mow lawns by a landscaping firm or (b) a person who buys a lawn mower to cut her neighbor's lawn for $20. Explain your answer.

2. What creative changes have fast-food restaurant owners used to distinguish their products from similar products offered by other firms?

3. Why aren't entrepreneurs likely to earn large profits from their businesses for many years?

4. Why wasn't the Bell Labs employee who invented the first transistor an entrepreneur?

5. What role do entrepreneurs play in the U.S. economy?

Graphing Exercise

6. Many entrepreneurs begin their businesses by inventing a product and then patenting it. Construct a bar graph from the data in the table that concerns patents granted by the federal government. What does your graph show about the number of inventions that are being made by individuals and corporations? Why are only some of these inventions examples of entrepreneurship?

Patents Granted by the Federal Government, 1980–2000

Year	Patents Granted to Individuals	Patents Granted to U.S. Corporations
1980	13,800	27,700
1985	12,900	31,200
1990	17,300	36,100
1995	17,400	44,000
2000	22,400	70,900

Source: U.S. Bureau of the Census, *Statistical Abstract of the United States*, 2001, p. 494.

Think Critically

7. **History** Review an American history textbook to identify a historical figure who was an important entrepreneur. Explain what this person did and the influence he or she had on the development of the United States.

8. **Marketing** Entrepreneurship may involve finding a new way to market an existing product. For example, Wal-Mart sells the same products as many other discount stores, but it is much more successful than most. What did Sam Walton do differently that made him a successful entrepreneur?

movers & shakers

Roxanne Quimby, *Burt's Bees*

Roxanne Quimby learned at a young age that hard work pays off. As a child, she worked with her grandmother selling sandwiches at a Boston beach. An immigrant from Siberia, her grandmother "demonstrated to me what it was like to start from nothing and make a living," Roxanne remembers. Roxanne tried her own hand at business early on. She began by selling homemade cookies, and later made and sold yarn dolls in her Massachusetts neighborhood.

By the early 1980s, Roxanne was the divorced mother of twins living in a cabin she built herself in Maine. She raised chickens and rabbits, and waited tables to support her family. That's when she met Burt Shavitz, her town's local beekeeper. Burt agreed to teach Roxanne about beekeeping if she would help him sell his honey. Before long, in addition to selling honey, Roxanne put her degree from the San Francisco Art Institute to use by making candles and furniture polish from the discarded beeswax. She traveled to flea markets and crafts fairs selling the products she and Burt created. In addition to selling, however, Roxanne spent a lot of time listening to her customers. She heard over and over that what they wanted was personal-care products made from natural ingredients.

Soon Roxanne stopped selling furniture polish and began to make and sell new personal-care items. To accommodate the changes, she and Burt moved their operation from Roxanne's kitchen to an old bowling alley. Within a year their small company needed more room, and they relocated again. By 1992, Burt's Bees was manufacturing about half a million beeswax candles a year along with personal-care items. By 1994, Burt's Bees' sales totaled $3 million.

As their business once again outgrew its walls, Burt and Roxanne decided to move the company to North Carolina, home to numerous cosmetics manufacturers. Although in favor of moving the company, Burt opted to remain in Maine, taking a lesser role in the company. A few years later he sold his share of Burt's Bees to Roxanne, leaving Roxanne solely in charge of the ever-growing company.

Today 120 employees work at Burt's Bees headquarters in Raleigh, North Carolina. They make more than 150 products, including lip color, facial creams, hair products, natural remedies, and specialty items for men and for babies. Most of Burt's Bees' products are 100 percent natural, harvested from nature. All of the products contain only natural colors and natural preservatives. They are sold in retail stores, online, and through the mail.

Roxanne keeps her business growing by setting daily, weekly, and monthly goals. "Sometimes I don't know how I'm going to reach them, but it's important to set them. People tend to get bogged down in the process [of setting goals], but that's backwards," she states. Her first goal was sales of $10,000 a year. In 2002, her goal was sales of $50 million. Keeping a focus on the customer is her means of reaching her goals. "I call myself a media junkie. Keeping abreast of what's happening gives you a clear understanding of what your customer is all about," she says.

SOURCE READING
Re-read Roxanne Quimby's comments about setting goals. How important do you think her focus on goal setting was to the success of Burt's Bees? Explain your answer.

ENTREPRENEURS IN ACTION
Imagine you are Roxanne Quimby and selling beeswax candles at flea markets. Write a business plan that would incorporate each of the steps she took from that point forward to become a successful entrepreneur. Include plans for product development and ideas for handling growth.

Objectives

> Describe the advantages and disadvantages of sole proprietorships.

> Describe the advantages and disadvantages of partnerships.

Overview

Entrepreneurs make all kinds of decisions when they start a business. One of the first is to decide how to organize the firm. What form of business would work best? Entrepreneurs may organize their firm in one of three ways: as a sole proprietorship, a partnership, or a corporation. Each type has its advantages and disadvantages. Sole proprietorships and partnerships are the easiest business forms to start, but they each also present a great deal of risk for the business owner.

Key Terms

sole proprietorship

liability

partnership

general partnership

limited partnership

[In the News]

Tougher Bankruptcy Laws

A major disadvantage of the sole proprietorship form of business is unlimited personal liability for any loss. If a business goes bankrupt, the owner may have to draw on personal savings or sell personal assets in order to pay the business's debts. Under a measure recently approved by the U.S. House of Representatives, debtors who file for bankruptcy would not be protected from as many bills as they are under current law. The new legislation would make it much more difficult for bankruptcy filers to completely eliminate unpaid balances, even after liquidating their assets. The new law also would require bankruptcy filers to take a means test. They might also be subjected to an in-depth investigation to determine if they have additional resources that could be used to pay off more of their debt. Credit card companies, banks, and retailers have applied their top lobbyists to push for this new legislation. The legislation's supporters argue that there are widespread abuses under the former bankruptcy laws. They also argue that these abuses are the main reason for rising interest rates on both business and consumer credit. Opponents argue that the bill will only serve to make people and businesses in trouble even more desperate, especially in a weak economy. They say it will provide greater profits to the credit industry without reducing the interest rates charged.

Think About It

How would the new legislation and its harsher treatment of bankruptcy filers affect owners of small businesses, and the economy itself?

Sole Proprietorship

sole proprietorship

The simplest form of business organization; a firm that is owned and managed by one person, but sometimes hires other workers

The simplest form of business organization is the **sole proprietorship**, where a firm is owned and managed by a single individual. That person, the sole proprietor, earns all the firm's profits and is responsible for all the firm's losses. Although some sole proprietorships have many employees, most do not. Most have just one self-employed individual. *A self-employed person is not considered to be a paid employee.*

Who Is a Sole Proprietor?

The majority of businesses in your community are owned by sole proprietors. These include self-employed plumbers, farmers, hair stylists, truckers, lawyers, doctors, and dentists. Most sole proprietorships consist of just one self-employed person. A self-employed person may work at the business all the time throughout the year, or only part of the year, or part-time. For example, most self-employed farmers hold other jobs that are their primary occupations.

About three quarters of all businesses in the United States are owned by sole

proprietors. There were about 19 million sole proprietorships in 2000. Because this type of business is typically small, however, sole proprietorships generate only 5 percent of all U.S. business sales.

Figure 8.2 shows the distribution of sole proprietorships based on firm revenue and based on the industry in which the business operates. You can see in the pie chart on the left that nearly all sole proprietorships are small. About two thirds reported annual sales, or revenue, of less than $25,000. Only 0.4 percent had sales of $1 million or more.

The pie chart on the right in Figure 8.2 shows the industry breakdown of sole proprietors. Nearly half provide services, such as health services and business services. About one in ten works in agriculture.

Advantages of Sole Proprietorships

The sole proprietorship is the most common type of business for a reason. It offers several advantages.

1. **Easy to Start** A sole proprietorship is easy to start. This form involves minimum red tape and legal expense.

Distribution of Sole Proprietorships Based on Annual Sales and by Industry   **Figure 8.2**

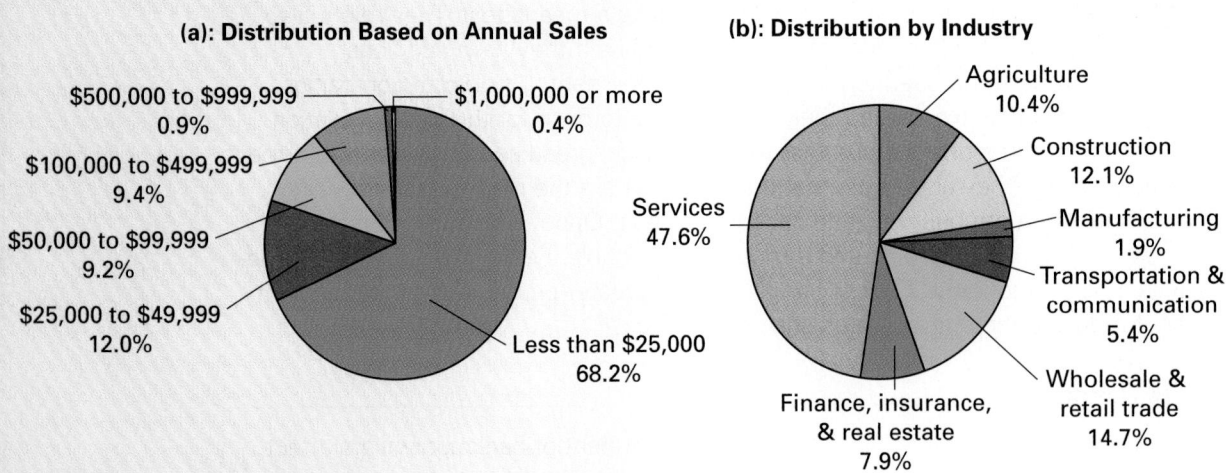

(a): Distribution Based on Annual Sales

- $500,000 to $999,999 — 0.9%
- $1,000,000 or more — 0.4%
- $100,000 to $499,999 — 9.4%
- $50,000 to $99,999 — 9.2%
- $25,000 to $49,999 — 12.0%
- Less than $25,000 — 68.2%

(b): Distribution by Industry

- Agriculture 10.4%
- Construction 12.1%
- Manufacturing 1.9%
- Transportation & communication 5.4%
- Wholesale & retail trade 14.7%
- Finance, insurance, & real estate 7.9%
- Services 47.6%

More than half of all sole proprietors earn $25,000 or less a year. Most sole proprietorships are service businesses.

Source: U.S. Bureau of the Census, *Statistical Abstract of the United States,* 2002.

A sole proprietor might need to secure a local business license and a permit to collect state or local sales taxes.

2. **Few Government Regulations** Once established, a sole proprietorship faces relatively few government regulations beyond maintaining accurate tax records and complying with employment laws. As noted, most sole proprietors have no employees.

3. **Complete Control** The sole proprietor is the boss, with complete authority over all business decisions, such as what to produce, what resources to hire, and how to combine these resources.

4. **Owner Keeps All Profit** The sole proprietor does not have to share profits with anyone.

5. **Lower Taxes** Income from a sole proprietorship is taxed only once as the owner's personal income. As you will learn later, corporate income is taxed twice.

6. **Pride of Ownership** Creating a successful business and watching it grow can provide a sole proprietor tremendous satisfaction.

Disadvantages of Sole Proprietorships

There are also some significant disadvantages of sole proprietorships, when compared to other forms of business.

1. **Unlimited Personal Liability** A sole proprietor faces unlimited personal liability for any loss. **Liability** is the legal obligation to pay any debts of the business. Sole proprietors are personally responsible for paying all their business debts. If the business goes bankrupt or is sued, the owner is personally responsible. He or she may have to draw from personal savings or sell personal assets, such as a home or automobile.

2. **Difficulty Raising Financial Capital** Because the sole proprietor has no partners or other financial backers, raising enough money to get the business going can be a problem. Banks

© Getty Images/PhotoDisc

Only about 2 percent of sole proprietorships are manufacturing companies. Why do you think this number is so small?

are reluctant to lend money to a new business with no track record and few assets. Even a sole proprietorship that's been around for a while may seem risky to lenders.

3. **Limited Life** With a sole proprietorship, the business and the owner are one and the same. The business ends when the owner dies or leaves the business. The firm's assets can be sold or turned over to someone else, who may restart the business. The result is a new firm with new ownership.

liability
The legal obligation to pay any debts of the business

4. **Difficulty Finding and Keeping Good Workers** Because of its lack of permanence and difficulty raising financial capital, sole proprietors have trouble offering workers the job security and opportunity for advancement available in larger businesses. Therefore, a sole proprietorship may have difficulty attracting and retaining talented employees.

5. **Unlimited Responsiblity** Sole proprietors shoulder a great deal of responsibility. They must manage the firm, maintain financial records, oversee production, market the product, keep up with competition, and perform dozens of other tasks. It is not likely that one person can do all of these things well. However, small firms typically cannot afford to hire experts to carry out these functions. This may lead to long work days—and a lot of stress—for the sole proprietor.

partnership

Two or more people agree to contribute resources to the business in return for a share of the profit

> ✔ **CHECKPOINT**
> What are the advantages and disadvantages of sole proprietorships?

Partnerships

Another relatively simple form of business organization is the **partnership**, which involves two or more individuals who agree to contribute resources to the business in return for a share of the profit. A partnership sometimes consists of one person who is talented at running the business and one or more who supply the money needed to get the business going. In 2000, there were about 2 million partnerships in the United States. They accounted for about 8 percent of all businesses and about 8 percent of all business sales.

Law, accounting, real estate, and medical partnerships typify this business form. Figure 8.3 shows the distribution of partnerships by annual revenue on the left, and by industry on the right. More than half of all partnerships had annual sales of less than $25,000. Only 5.6 percent had sales of $1 million or more. About half of all partnerships are in finance, insurance, or real estate. Though not shown in the pie chart, real-estate firms alone

---

Distribution of Partnerships Based on Annual Sales and Industry   **Figure 8.3**

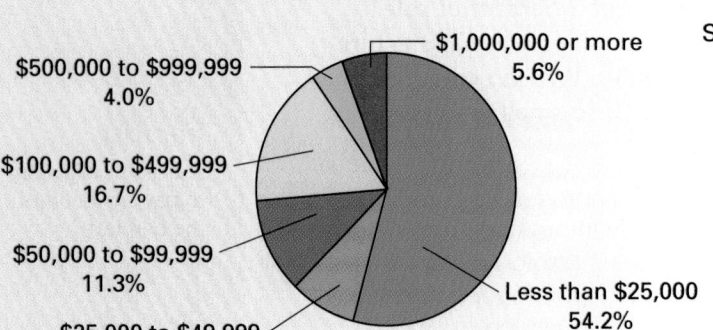

(a): Distribution Based on Annual Sales

- $1,000,000 or more 5.6%
- $500,000 to $999,999 4.0%
- $100,000 to $499,999 16.7%
- $50,000 to $99,999 11.3%
- $25,000 to $49,999 8.2%
- Less than $25,000 54.2%

(b): Distribution by Industry

- Services 17.6%
- Agriculture 15.1%
- Construction 6.3%
- Manufacturing 1.7%
- Transportation & communication 6.5%
- Wholesale & retail trade 2.0%
- Finance, insurance, & real estate 50.8%

Most partnerships had annual sales of less than $25,000. About half of all partnerships are in finance, insurance, or real estate.

Source: U.S. Bureau of the Census, *Statistical Abstract of the United States,* 2002.

account for about 40 percent of all partnerships.

Types of Partnerships

There are two broad categories of partnerships: general partnerships and limited partnerships. Each divides responsibilities and liabilities differently.

General Partnerships

The most common type of partnership is the **general partnership**, where partners share both in the responsibility for running the business and in any liability from its operation. Professional groups such as doctors, lawyers, and accountants often form general partnerships.

Limited Partnerships

With a **limited partnership**, at least one partner is required to be a general partner. General partners manage the business and have unlimited personal liability for the partnership. The other partners don't manage the business. Their contribution is strictly financial. The most they can lose is the amount they have invested in the firm. Because their liability is limited, they are called *limited* partners. A limited partnership can have any number of limited partners.

Advantages of Partnerships

Partnerships offer several advantages.

1. **Easy to Start** As with the sole proprietorship, partnerships are easy to start. The partners need only agree on how they will share business responsibilities, rewards, and losses. Some partnerships are formed with articles of partnership, a legal agree-

general partnership

Partners share both in the responsibility of running the business and in any liability from its operation

limited partnership

At least one general partner runs the business and bears unlimited personal liability; other partners provide financial capital but have limited liability

© Getty Images/PhotoDisc

In a general partnership with two partners, both are responsible for running the business and for any liability that results from its operation. If you were to start a business, would you rather be a partner or a sole proprietor? Give reasons for your answer.

ment spelling out each partner's rights and responsibilities. In most states, partnerships that do not have their own agreement are governed by the Uniform Partnership Act (UPA), which established partnership rules.

2. **Few Government Regulations** Once the partnership has begun operating, it faces relatively few government regulations. Like the sole proprietorship, the partnership must maintain accurate tax records and comply with employment laws.

3. **Shared Decision Making and Increased Specialization** A sole proprietor makes all key business decisions. But general partners usually share decision-making responsibilities. On average there were about 8 partners per partnership in 2000. By discussing important decisions, partners may make better decisions than a sole proprietor can make alone. By relying on the different skills of each partner, general partnerships also may be more efficient than sole proprietors. For example, one partner may be good at dealing with the public while another excels at record keeping and paperwork.

4. **Greater Ability to Raise Financial Capital** Partnerships often find it easier than sole proprietors to raise the financial capital needed to get a business going. First, the partners themselves can come up with money from their own sources, such as a savings account. Second, banks may be more willing to lend money to a partnership than to a sole proprietor. With a partnership, the loans are backed by the promise and property of each partner.

5. **More Able to Attract and Retain Workers** Compared to sole proprietors, partnerships offer employees more opportunities for advancement. For example, a partnership can make a key employee, such as a promising lawyer or accountant, a partner. A partnership typically is more able to attract and retain talented workers than is a sole proprietorship.

6. **Lower Taxes** Partners pay personal income taxes on their share of partnership income. The partnership itself does not have to pay a separate tax, as does the corporation.

Disadvantages of Partnerships

There also are disadvantages to partnerships. Some of these drawbacks are the same as for sole proprietorships.

1. **Unlimited Personal Liability** In a general partnership, each partner is personally responsible for paying all business debts. If the business fails or is sued, the partners may have to draw from personal savings or sell personal assets, such as a home, to pay debts. This means one partner could lose it all because of another's blunder. In a limited partnership, the limited partners have less liability than the general partners. Their liability for the firm's debts and losses is limited to the amount of capital they have invested.

2. **Limited Life of the Business** A partnership has no life of its own, independent of the partners. The partnership ends when one partner dies or leaves the business. A new partnership can be formed to continue the business, but the transition could be tricky. A partnership might end even if remaining partners would like it to continue.

TEAM WORK

Divide into small groups. Your group is starting a general partnership. Decide the type of business your partnership will run. Then decide the area of responsibility each team member will handle. Match each member's strengths and interests with the tasks to be done.

3. **Partners May Disagree** Partners may not always agree on important decisions. Unlike a sole proprietorship, where the one owner makes all the decisions, partners must reach a consensus. Disagreements and disputes may hamper operations and could end the partnership.

4. **Profits Must Be Shared** Partners must share any profits according to the original partnership agreement. This may seem unfair to a partner who accounts for most of the profit. Unless the sharing agreement is revised, the most productive partner may look for a better deal elsewhere. This could end the partnership. Some major law partnerships have dissolved recently because of this.

© Getty Images/PhotoDisc

 CHECKPOINT
What are the advantages and disadvantages of the partnership form of business?

Partners may not always agree on all business matters. What advice do you have for potential partners to help them avoid arguments?

E-CONOMICS

Partnering for Start-Ups

Although Silicon Valley in California continues to lose thousands of jobs, some potential entrepreneurs think the time has never been better for creating a start-up company. One software designer wants to introduce a new service she says will permanently end spam for e-mail users. "Computers are incredibly inexpensive now, network bandwidth is essentially free, and there is surplus equipment," she said. Her business premise is that consumers will pay a small annual fee for a solution to spam. Coming from a creative background, this entrepreneur has decided to form a limited partnership to finance her venture. She knows that many feature film and Broadway show producers get financing without giving up creative control under this form of organization. She also is aware of many e-commerce start-ups that began as limited partnerships. In the new venture, this entrepreneur and her close associates will be the general partners, manage the business, and make all the creative decisions. The investors will be limited partners, and their contribution will be strictly financial.

Think Critically

What is the major disadvantage to the entrepreneur and her close associates of their role as general partners?

Key Concepts

1. Why are more restaurants organized as sole proprietorships than are industrial construction firms?

2. Why do many sole proprietorships become less efficient as they grow?

3. Why are many sole proprietorships run by part-time entrepreneurs who earn most of their income by being employed by another firm?

4. Why do most partnerships last for only a few years or less?

5. Why do many new lawyers seek to become partners in established law firms?

Graphing Exercise

6. In 1998, all U.S. partnerships had a total of $1.5 trillion in sales. The federal government classified partnerships into 20 categories. However, the bulk of the sales were made by partnerships in seven of the federal classifications, as listed in the table to the right. Use the data in this table to construct a pie graph showing partnerships' sales. Why do you think some types of businesses lend themselves to being organized as partnerships?

Gross Sales by Partnerships in 1998
Values in Millions of Dollars

Business Classification	Sales	Percent of Total
Manufacturing	$247,489	16.1%
Finance and insurance	184,489	12.0
Retail trade	170,809	11.1
Professional, scientific, and technical services	147,765	9.6
Wholesale trade	133,261	8.7
Real estate and rental and leasing	110,831	7.2
Construction	106,321	6.9
All other	432,788	28.4

Source: U.S. Bureau of the Census, *Statistical Abstract of the United States,* 2001, p. 476

Think Critically

7. **Management** Make a list of all the management functions a sole proprietor must perform to be successful. What types of courses should a person who wants to own a business take? What types of experience should such a person look for in a job he or she might work in while going to school?

8. **Research** Review listings for physicians in your local Yellow Pages. How many of them are partners in a group and how many of them practice independently? Why do you think so many physicians prefer to participate in partnerships with other physicians?

Objectives

> Describe how a corporation is established.

> Understand why the corporate form is favored by large businesses.

> Recognize other types of organizations businesspeople use to accomplish their goals.

Overview

Sole proprietorships and partnerships may suit small businesses, but they are not appropriate for larger, more complex businesses. They need a more flexible business organization that allows the firm to raise a sufficient amount of financial capital and cope with a changing business environment. The corporation is the favored type of business organization for large businesses. Additionally, business owners may choose to organize as a limited liability company, limited liability partnership, cooperative, or not-for-profit organization.

Key Terms

corporation

articles of incorporation

private corporation

publicly traded corporation

S corporation

limited liability company (LLC)

limited liability partnership (LLP)

cooperative

not-for-profit organizations

[In the News]

• Open Season on CEOs

The widespread corporate scandals shaking the United States have corporate CEOs (Chief Executive Officers) feeling less than proud of their titles. "Clearly it's open season on CEOs," said the CEO of Ford Motor Company. "But the broad brush with which everyone is tainted isn't really justified." Most CEOs resent having to spend time defending their reputations and distancing themselves from the ugly shadow cast by executives at Enron, WorldCom, and other companies. Most assert that their companies' accounting records are accurate and that their employees are honest and ethical. They're angry that the negative attitudes towards corporate America are destroying their companies' reputations, stock prices, and overall value. Congress is calling for more independent directors on corporate boards. It also is asking for closer scrutiny of the hiring and firing of CEOs—including their salaries, bonuses, expense accounts, and termination packages.

Think About It

Do you think the public outrage against CEOs is justified? Do CEOs who receive multi-million dollar salaries deserve to earn that much money? Why or why not?

Incorporating

By far the most influential and most complex form of business organization is the corporation. A **corporation** is a legal entity with an existence that is distinct from the people who organize it, own it, and run it. The corporation can earn a profit, lose money, be sued, and even be found guilty of a crime.

There were about five million corporations in the United States in 2000, accounting for about one fifth of all businesses. Because they tend to be much larger than the other two business types, however, corporations account for 86.5 percent of all business sales. Figure 8.4 summarizes the three types of businesses in terms of business type and business sales. Even though sole proprietors rep-

resent the largest share of businesses by type, corporations are much more important, based on business sales.

Figure 8.5 shows the distribution of corporations based on sales and on the industry. Whereas the median-sized sole proprietorship or partnership had annual sales of less than $25,000, the median-sized corporation had sales of $100,000 to $499,999. Virtually all the nation's large businesses are corporations. Compared with the other types of businesses, a smaller share of corporations is in agriculture and a larger share is in manufacturing.

Articles of Incorporation

A corporation is established through **articles of incorporation**, a written application to a state seeking permission

---

Comparing Corporations with Sole Proprietorships and Partnerships — Figure 8.4

(a): As a Share of All Businesses

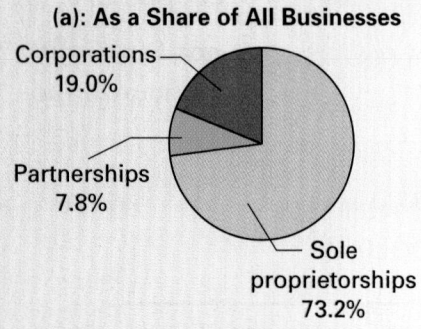

Corporations 19.0%
Partnerships 7.8%
Sole proprietorships 73.2%

(b): As a Share of Business Sales

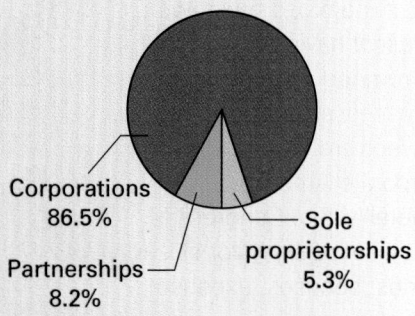

Corporations 86.5%
Partnerships 8.2%
Sole proprietorships 5.3%

Sole proprietorships account for nearly three quarters of all U.S. businesses, but corporations account for most business sales.

Source: U.S. Bureau of the Census, *Statistical Abstract of the United States,* 2002.

Distribution of Corporations by Annual Sales and by Industry — Figure 8.5

(a): By Annual Sales

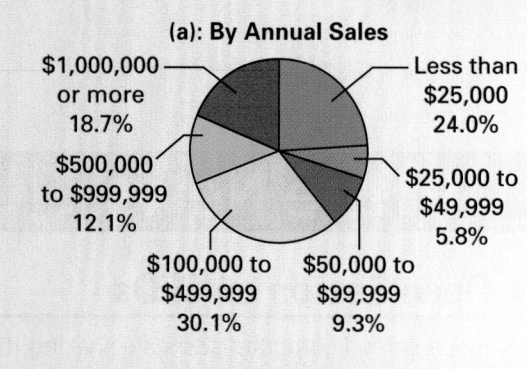

$1,000,000 or more 18.7%
$500,000 to $999,999 12.1%
Less than $25,000 24.0%
$25,000 to $49,999 5.8%
$50,000 to $99,999 9.3%
$100,000 to $499,999 30.1%

(b): By Industry

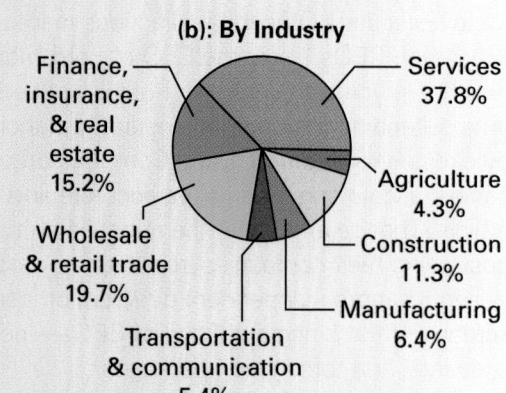

Finance, insurance, & real estate 15.2%
Wholesale & retail trade 19.7%
Transportation & communication 5.4%
Services 37.8%
Agriculture 4.3%
Construction 11.3%
Manufacturing 6.4%

Nearly one in five corporations had annual sales of $1 million or more. About four in ten corporations are in services, such as health care.

Source: U.S. Bureau of the Census, *Statistical Abstract of the United States,* 2002.

---

to form a corporation. If these articles comply with state and federal laws, a charter is issued and the corporation becomes a legal entity. A *charter* offers the legal authorization to organize a business as a corporation.

A board of directors is elected by stockholders to oversee the firm's operation. The board sets major goals and decides major policy issues, and it appoints and sets salaries of top officers. Day-to-day duties of running the business are delegated to the corporate executives the board hires.

The owners of a corporation are issued *shares of stock,* entitling them to corporate profits and to vote for members of the board of directors and on various other issues in proportion to their stock ownership. For example, a stockholder who owns 1 percent of the stock has a right to 1 percent of the firm's profit paid in dividends and can vote 1 percent of the shares. *Dividends* are a share of a corporation's profits paid to its stockholders.

Types of Corporations

A **private corporation** issues stock to just a few people, sometimes only family members. Such stockholders rarely sell their stock. Instead they pass it on within the family. Private corporations account for the overwhelming share of corporations in the United States.

In contrast, a **publicly traded corporation** has many shareholders—sometimes numbering in the millions—who can buy or sell shares. Stocks are bought and sold in financial markets called stock exchanges. You will read more about these in a later chapter.

By any measure of size, whether it be sales or employment, publicly traded corporations are larger than private corporations. Publicly traded corporations account for less than 1 percent of all corporations.

CHECKPOINT
How is a corporation established?

Advantages and Disadvantages

Here are the advantages and disadvantages of establishing of corporation.

Advantages of Incorporation

The corporate form offers advantages to the stockholders and to the business itself.

1. **Easier to Raise Financial Capital** The corporate form is the most effective structure for raising financial capital. This is especially true if large sums are needed to start or expand a business. Many investors—hundreds, thousands, even millions—can exchange their money for company shares, giving the firm a huge pool of funds. Corporations have more ways to raise money than either sole proprietors or partnerships.

2. **Limited Liability** In most cases, stockholders, the owners of the corporation, are responsible for the firm's debts only up to the amount they paid for their shares. Stockholders are said to have limited liability. Their personal assets cannot be seized to pay the debts of the business. Use of the abbreviations "Inc." or "Corp." in the company name serves as a warning that stockholders will not accept personal liability for corporate debts.

3. **Unlimited Life** Unlike sole proprietorships and partnerships, a corporation does not cease to exist if a major stockholder dies or leaves the business. In fact, even if all stockholders die, the shares would pass on to others and the corporation would continue. Because stock is transferable—that is, it can be bought and sold or given to someone else—corporations can exist indefinitely, independently of its owners.

4. **Specialized Management** In sole proprietorships and general partnerships, the firms' owners and

private corporation

Ownership limited to just a few people, sometimes only family members; shares are not publicly traded

publicly traded corporation

Owned by many shareholders; shares can be bought or sold

managers often are one and the same. Therefore, owners usually must possess management skills. However, the owners of a corporation—the stockholders—need no special management skills. Because ownership is separated from management, a corporation can hire experts to run the firm.

Disadvantages of Incorporation

The U.S. economy depends heavily on the corporate form. However, this business type also has some disadvantages when compared to sole proprietors and partnerships.

1. **Difficult and Costly to Start** Compared to the two other business forms, a corporation is more complicated to start. Articles of incorporation can be difficult and costly to draw up and get approved by government.

2. **More Regulated** Corporations, especially those publicly traded, face more regulations and red tape than other forms of business. For example, pub-licly traded corporations must issue financial reports every three months and issue annual reports prepared by an outside accounting firm. These reports must be filed with the Securities and Exchange Commission (SEC), a federal agency that regulates trading of corporate stocks.

3. **Owners Have Less Control** Owners of large, publicly traded corporations usually are far removed from the day-to-day operations of the business. The firm's owners have little direct control over the firm they own. Professional managers run the business, but they may not always act in the owners' best interests, as evidenced by some management failures in large corporations such as Enron and WorldCom.

4. **Double Taxation** In the eyes of the law, a corporation is a legal entity separate from its owners. The corporation therefore pays taxes on any earnings. Stockholders must then pay personal income taxes on any earnings they receive from the corporation. Thus, each dollar of corporate

Ethics in Action

Execs Corrupted by Corporate Culture?

According to a 2002 Gallup Poll taken in the aftermath of the Enron and WorldCom scandals, the only people less trusted than corporate CEOs were health maintenance organization managers and car dealers. Curiously, while only 23 percent of Americans said they trusted heads of big businesses, 75 percent believed that most people who run small businesses can be trusted. Responding to the scandals and subsequent outrage against corporations, 120 top executives met to brainstorm the subject of how to restore public confidence in corporate America. Warren Buffett, one of the richest men in America, was the keynote speaker at the meeting titled "The Forum for Corporate Conscience." Buffett said that the need to restore corporate integrity was "vital to this country." He argued that, for the most part, the scandals were not created by absolute crooks. Rather, he said the problem was that basically good people got caught up in a corporate culture that blurred the lines and led them to do bad things.

Think Critically

In view of Buffett's remarks, do you think a "bad-guy" executive corrupted by the corporate culture should get a lighter sentence than a bank robber who claims he was corrupted by a poor upbringing? Why or why not?

earnings gets taxed twice—first by the corporate income tax and then by the personal income tax.

CHECKPOINT
Why is the corporation the preferred business form for large businesses?

Other Organizations

So far you have considered the three basic business forms: sole proprietorships, partnerships, and corporations. Other ways of doing business have developed that combine attractive features of the basic forms.

Hybrid Businesses

A big advantage of sole proprietorships and partnerships is that business earnings are taxed only once—as income to the business owners. A big advantage of the corporation is that all owners are protected by limited liability. Some new business hybrids have developed that offer the protection of limited liability while avoiding the double taxation of business income. Here are the most important new business types.

S Corporation

The **S corporation** was introduced about two decades ago to combine the limited liability protection of the corporate form with the single taxation feature of a partnership. To qualify as an S corporation, a business must be incorporated in the United States, must have no more than 75 stockholders, and must not have foreign stockholders. Because of these restrictions, S corporations tend to be smaller than other corporations. About half of all U.S. corporations are S corporations.

Limited Liability Company (LLC)

Like an S corporation, a **limited liability company (LLC)** combines the limited liability feature of the corporation with the single-tax provisions of a partnership. An LLC does not have the ownership restrictions of the S corporation, making it ideal for a business with foreign investors. An LLC must have at least two members, and a member can personally guarantee certain obligations of the LLC. This gives a new business more financial flexibility. For example, a prospective landlord about to lease office space to a new business most likely will require a personal guarantee from a business owner. The LLC structure would allow one or more company members to make such a guarantee. Because of its more flexible management structure, the LLC has become a common way to own and operate a business.

Limited Liability Partnership (LLP)

An existing partnership may find it difficult to convert to an LLC. This is the reason the **limited liability partnership (LLP)**, a newer type of organization, was created. An LLP has the advantages of an LLC and is easier to establish, especially if a business needs to convert from a partnership. An existing partnership usually can be converted to an LLP simply by changing the partnership agreement and registering as an LLP. Both LLPs and LLCs are taxed as partnerships.

Cooperatives

A **cooperative** is a group of people who pool their resources to buy and sell more efficiently than they could independently. The government grants most cooperatives tax-exempt status.

limited liability company (LLC)
Business with limited liability for some owners, single taxation of business income, and no ownership restrictions

limited liability partnership (LLP)
Like a limited liability company but more easily converted from an existing partnership

S corporation
Organization that offers limited liability combined with the single taxation of business income; must have no more than 75 stockholders with no foreign stockholders

cooperative
An organization consisting of people who pool their resources to buy and sell more efficiently than they could independently

NETBookmark

LLPs are governed by the Revised Uniform Partnership Act (RUPA). Access the text of this Act through econxtra.swlearning.com. The LLP amendments to RUPA deal with four major issues. List these issues, and write a sentence summarizing each one.

econxtra.swlearning.com

There are two types: consumer cooperatives and producer cooperatives.

Consumer Cooperative

A *consumer cooperative* is a retail business owned and operated by some or all of its customers in order to reduce costs. Some cooperatives require members to pay an annual fee and others require them to work a certain number of hours each year. Members sometimes pay lower prices than other customers or may share in any revenues that exceed costs. In the United States, consumer cooperatives operate credit unions, electric-power facilities, health plans, and grocery stores, among others. If you go to college, your college bookstore may be a cooperative.

Producer Cooperative

In a *producer cooperative,* producers join forces to buy supplies and equipment and to market their output. Each producer's objective is to reduce costs and increase profits. For example, farmers pool their funds to purchase machinery and supplies. Farm cooperatives also provide storage facilities, processing, and transportation to market, thereby eliminating wholesalers. Federal legislation allows farmers to cooperate in this way without violating antitrust laws.

Firms in other industries could not do this legally.

Not-for-Profit Organizations

So far, you have learned about organizations that try to maximize profits or, in the case of cooperatives, minimize costs. Some organizations have neither as a goal. **Not-for-profit organizations** engage in charitable, educational, humanitarian, cultural, professional, and other activities, often with a social purpose.

Like businesses, not-for-profit organizations evolved to help people accomplish their goals. Examples include nonprofit hospitals, private schools and colleges, religious organizations, the Red Cross, charitable foundations, orchestras, museums, labor unions, and professional organizations such as the National Education Association. There are about 300,000 not-for-profit organizations in the United States. They employ about nine million workers, with hospitals accounting for about half of these jobs.

Even not-for-profit organizations must somehow pay the bills. Revenues typically include some combination of voluntary contributions and service charges, such as college tuition and hospital charges. In the United States, not-for-profit organizations usually are exempt from taxes.

Investigate Your Local Economy

Identify a not-for-profit organization in your area. Research to discover how this organization affects your local economy. For example, find out what services the organization provides and how many paid employees and volunteers work for the organization. Share your findings in class.

CHECKPOINT

Name and describe other types of organizations businesspeople may choose.

not-for-profit organizations

Groups that do not pursue profit as a goal; they engage in charitable, educational, humanitarian, cultural, professional, or other activities, often with a social purpose

Key Concepts

1. Why would most people not invest in corporations if there were no limited liability for stock owners?

2. Why might a family business organize as a private corporation rather than as a sole proprietorship?

3. Although stockholders do not need to be professional managers, they should stay aware of decisions made by the people who run the firm. Why is this true?

4. If publicly traded corporations account for only 1 percent of all corporations, why should society care what they do?

5. Identify a local not-for-profit organization that operates in your community. In what ways is this firm different from other businesses?

Graphing Exercise

6. In the years between 1995 and 2000, many publicly held corporations in the United States reported large and growing profits. Although some of their profits were paid to stockholders in dividends, a large part was kept as retained earnings. Use the data in the table to construct a double line graph that shows the change in corporate profits and dividends in these years. Why do you think these firms chose not to pay a larger share of their profits in dividends?

Corporate After-Tax Profits and Dividends, 1995–2000
Values in Billions of Dollars

Year	After-Tax Profits	Dividends	Dividends as a Percent Of After-Tax Profits
1995	$458	$254	55.5%
1996	503	298	59.1
1997	555	335	60.4
1998	514	352	68.5
1999	567	371	65.4
2000	641	397	61.9

Source: U.S. Bureau of the Census, *Statistical Abstract of the United States,* 2001, p. 501.

Think Critically

7. **History** Investigate the history of a major U.S. corporation. How did it begin? What factors led to its growth? What impact has it had on the lives of American consumers?

Sharpen Your Life Skills

Draw Conclusions

In drawing a conclusion, you first must gather information about the issue at hand. Then you must consider all aspects of the information before reaching your conclusion. Consider Rita, who for many years has made brightly colored glass Christmas ornaments for her friends and relatives. Everyone who has received one of Rita's ornaments has been thrilled. She has decided to go into business manufacturing and selling ornaments.

Rita has asked you to help her translate her ideas into a successful business. Here's the information she has gathered so far. The materials in each ornament cost $1.00, and it takes 20 minutes to produce one by hand. In addition, Rita has determined that she will need to do the following:

- Invest $10,000 in equipment and supplies and have $40,000 to cover her costs until her products begin to sell

- Hire and train one full-time or two part-time employees

- Manufacture and sell 12,000 ornaments each year

- Receive $9 for each ornament

- Keep track of the business's income and expenditures

Apply Your Skill

1. Rita has $25,000 to invest in the business. How much more does she need to start her business? What method would you advise her to use to raise the rest of the money? Explain the reasons for your advice.

2. Rita doesn't know very much about marketing. She could hire someone to market her ornaments and pay that person a 25 percent commission. Or, she might try to convince a mail-order firm to sell her ornaments. If she makes this choice, the firm will keep half the revenue from her sales. So, she would have to charge a higher price.

3. What sort of organization should Rita use to start her business—a sole proprietorship, a partnership, or a corporation? Explain the reasons for your choice.

to History

Andrew Carnegie—
Entrepreneur and Philanthropist

When he was 12, Andrew Carnegie moved with his family from Scotland to the United States. Soon after arriving in this country, he got a job working in a cotton mill for $1.20 a week. At age 18, he took a job as a telegrapher for the Pennsylvania Railroad. While working there, he won the favor of Thomas A. Scott, a top official in the company. With Scott's help, Carnegie rose quickly through the company ranks. By age 24, he had become the superintendent of the western division of the railroad. He invested much of his earnings in stocks.

By age 30, Carnegie was earning $50,000 a year—a fortune at the time—and turned all his efforts and investments to the steel industry. This industry would make him the richest man in America. He believed that the new Bessemer process would cause the industry to grow. He hired good managers and reinvested the profits back into his companies. He used what he learned from his railroad experience to lower costs and keep prices low. By controlling costs and reinvesting profits, he was able to take advantage of economies of scale. Smaller companies unable to undertake all the phases of production were at a disadvantage. He was able to increase his market share and expand his holdings. Carnegie purchased iron ore deposits and coke fields. Adding these to his steel mills, ships, and railroads, Carnegie was able to control the entire steel-making process, from ore to finished products.

When he sold his company to J.P. Morgan in 1901, Carnegie received $250 million—worth $4.5 billion today. He then set out to give away much of his fortune. In 1889, Carnegie wrote in an essay for the *American Review* that the man who dies rich, dies disgraced. Although at his death in 1919 he was worth more than $22 million, Carnegie did not die disgraced. He had given away 90 percent of his fortune—$350 million—to libraries, concert halls, and other public institutions across the nation and the world.

© Hulton-Deutsch Collection/CORBIS

© Richard Cummins/CORBIS

THINK CRITICALLY

Research the life of another successful American entrepreneur. What were the keys to his or her success, and what lessons can be learned from that success?

8 Chapter Assessment

Summary

Xtra! Quiz Prep
econxtra.swlearning.com

8.1 *Entrepreneurs*

a *Entrepreneurs* are the prime movers in our market economy. They bring about creative change through their effort to earn profits.

b Entrepreneurs take risks when they operate businesses. They must obtain and risk *financial capital* to get their businesses off the ground. When entrepreneurs are successful, their success attracts other entrepreneurs to the same type of production. This creates competition that improves the quality of products and lowers prices for consumers.

c Not all businesspeople are entrepreneurs. Many employees are paid to be innovative or to manage businesses. If they are not risking their own funds, they are not entrepreneurs. Stockholders are not entrepreneurs because they do not generally participate in day-to-day management.

8.2 *Sole Proprietorships and Partnerships*

a The three basic types of business organization in the United States are sole proprietorships, partnerships, and corporations.

b *Sole proprietorships* are the most common type of business organization. A sole proprietorship is owned by a single person who is totally responsible for its operation, receives all of its profits, or incurs all its losses. It exists only as long as the owner lives. Sole proprietorships are relatively easy to start, enjoy a lower level of government regulation, and are taxed only once on the profits they earn.

c *General partnerships* are created when two or more owners form a business by agreeing to share responsibilities for the firm and any resulting profits or losses. *Limited partnerships* are formed when at least one owner is a general partner and other owners contribute funds to become limited partners.

d Partnerships also are relatively easy to start, and general partners have unlimited *liability* for the debts of the firm. Partnerships are better able to raise financial capital than sole proprietorships, and their profits are taxed only once. The lives of partnerships are limited to the lives of the partners.

8.3 *Corporations and Other Organizations*

a *Corporations* are able to raise large amounts of financial capital by selling stock. Almost all large firms in the United States are corporations. They may either be private or publicly traded. *Private corporations* issue stock to a limited number of people, who often are members of a family. *Publicly traded corporations* raise funds by selling stock to anyone who is willing to buy it. Stockholders receive a vote for each share owned for important business decisions that are made. They also have a claim to a share of the firm's profits.

b Corporations are established through *articles of incorporation.* Corporations are legal entities separate from the individual owners of their stock. The owners of corporate stock enjoy limited liability. They risk no more than the funds they use to purchase stock. Corporations have unlimited life. If an owner dies, the remaining owners may make decisions for the firm without the participation of the deceased owner.

c Corporations are more difficult and costly to start than other forms of business organizations. They are more closely regulated by the government, and their profits are taxed twice—once when they are earned by the firm and again when they are paid to the stockholders in dividends or when shareholders gain by selling shares.

d Some special forms of business organizations are called hybrid businesses. These include *S corporations, limited liability companies,* and *limited liability partnerships.* Other ways of organizing production that help people accomplish their goals include *cooperatives* and *not-for-profit organizations.* Each of these forms of organization was created to fill the specific needs of a particular group of people.

Review Economic Terms

Choose the term that best fits the definition. On a separate sheet of paper, write the letter of the answer. Some terms may not be used.

_____ 1. The process of turning an invention into a marketable product

_____ 2. Two or more people agree to contribute resources to a business in return for a share of the profit

_____ 3. Ownership is limited to just a few people, sometimes only family members; shares are not publicly traded

_____ 4. An organization consisting of people who pool their resources to buy and sell more efficiently than they could independently

_____ 5. The legal obligation to pay any debts of a business

_____ 6. The simplest form of business organization; a firm that is owned and run by one person

_____ 7. A legal entity with an existence that is distinct from the people who organize, own, and run it

_____ 8. Owned by many shareholders; shares can be bought and sold

_____ 9. Limited liability combined with the single taxation of business income; must have no more than 75 stockholders and no foreign stockholders

_____ 10. Money needed to start or expand a business

_____ 11. Partners share both in the responsibility of running the business and in any liability from its operation

_____ 12. At least one general partner runs the business and bears unlimited personal liability; other partners provide financial capital but have limited liability

_____ 13. A written application to the state seeking permission to form a corporation

_____ 14. Business with limited liability for some owners, single taxation of business income, and no ownership restriction

_____ 15. Groups that do not pursue profit as a goal and often engage in activities with a social purpose

a. articles of incorporation

b. cooperative

c. corporation

d. financial capital

e. general partnership

f. innovation

g. liability

h. limited liability company (LLC)

i. limited liablility partnership (LLP)

j. limited partnership

k. not-for-profit organization

l. partnership

m. private corporation

n. publicly traded corporation

o. S corporation

p. sole proprietorship

Review Economic Concepts

16. _Entrepreneurs_ bring about creative change in each of the following ways _except_

   a. they improve the quality of existing products.

   b. they introduce new products.

   c. they find ways to eliminate competition.

   d. they introduce new production methods.

17. **True or False** Once established, most _entrepreneurs_ are able to maintain a substantial profit margin on the products they produce and sell.

18. Competitors are attracted to a market that yields

   a. profit in the short run.

   b. unlimited liability.

   c. lower prices for consumers.

   d. higher tax revenues.

19. Which of the following examples demonstrates *entrepreneurship*?

   a. A scientist invents a long-lasting paint and sells it to a large manufacturer.

   b. A government official creates a new tax form that is easier to complete.

   c. A technician discovers a new type of wax that is used by the firm that employs her.

   d. A student cuts his elderly neighbor's lawn for free.

20. **True or False** *Sole proprietorships* are the most common form of business organization in the United States.

21. *Sole proprietors* enjoy each of the following advantages *except*

   a. they receive all the profit their businesses earn.

   b. it is easy for them to gather large amounts of financial capital.

   c. they can make business decisions quickly.

   d. it is easy for them to form their business.

22. Owners of *sole proprietorships* and *partners* both have __?__ for the firm's debts if the firm fails to pay its bills.

23. *Corporations* are

   a. the most common type of business organization.

   b. the easiest form of business to start.

   c. the type of business organization that is best able to raise funds.

   b. the least-regulated form of business organization.

24. **True or False** Most large businesses in the United States are *corporations*.

25. **True or False** A *corporation's* stockholders are held responsible to pay off all the firm's debts if the firm files for bankruptcy.

26. A *consumer cooperative* generally is formed to

   a. earn a profit for its owners.

   b. reduce costs of buying goods or services for its members.

   c. avoid paying income tax on its profits.

   d. limit the type of people who can shop at specific stores.

27. **True or False** Almost all corporations in the United States are *publicly traded corporations*.

28. Which of the following types of business organizations cannot have a foreign owner?

   a. S corporation

   b. limited liability company

   c. limited liability partnership

   d. not-for-profit organization

29. *Publicly traded corporations* must issue financial reports and file them with the __?__, a federal agency that regulates trading of corporate stocks.

30. **True or False** An important disadvantage of *corporations* is the fact that their profits are taxed twice.

31. Which of the following does not describe a disadvantage of a *corporation*?

   a. difficult to start

   b. less regulated

   c. owners have little control

   d. earnings are taxed twice

32. Which of the following is not true of *private corporations*?

   a. They exist to earn a profit.

   b. They must reorganize when an owner dies.

   c. Their income is taxed more than employee earnings.

   d. They are treated as an individual separate from their owners by the law.

33. **True or False** Use of the abbreviations "Inc." or "Corp." in a company name indicates that the owners are personally liable for the company's debts.

Apply Economic Concepts

34. **Entrepreneurship** Gretchen has invented a new lubricant that reduces friction between moving parts in an engine to almost nothing. This product should increase automobile gas mileage by at least 50 percent and make automobile engines last almost forever. Explain how Gretchen could become an entrepreneur through her invention.

35. **Assess Limitations of Sole Proprietorships** Paul opened a florist business that marketed tropical flowers as a sole proprietorship. His idea was that by offering flowers that no other local store sold, he could charge high prices and earn a good profit. This may have been a good idea, but his business failed. First, he had only $30,000 to get started, so he was never able to keep many flowers in stock. Although he knew flowers, he didn't know much about advertising, accounting, or how to direct employees. Even when he put in 80-hour weeks, things didn't get done on time. When the business failed, he owed $40,000. The bankruptcy court took his house and car to pay his debts. Explain why Paul's business might have been more successful if it had been organized as a corporation.

36. **Limited Liability** Gretchen has successfully tested her lubricant on small engines. She has not tried to use it in large engines or for extended periods of time. To complete these tests, she needs many thousands of dollars to buy equipment and run the tests. If the tests are successful, Gretchen thinks her product could earn many millions of dollars in profit every year. If they fail, all the funds invested in the tests could be lost. Why would Gretchen want to limit her liability when she starts her business?

37. **Forms of Business Organization** Identify the type of business organization Gretchen should form to be able to produce and market 10,000,000 gallons of her lubricant each year.

38. **Sharpen Your Life Skills: Draw Conclusions** After five years, Rita's business has become very successful. Her annual sales have reached $450,000 and she employs three full-time workers. She is convinced she could double her sales if she employed three more workers and spent $500,000 to purchase additional equipment. Rita has saved only $100,000 that she could invest. She spends almost all of her time working. She never takes a day off, and still, some orders can't be filled on time. Rita once again has come to you for advice. Her business is still organized as it was when she started out. (See your answer to Question 3 for *Sharpen Your Life Skills* on page 248.) What are the issues and the possible solutions?

 econxtra.swlearning.com

What would you advise Rita to do?

39. Access **EconLinks Online** through econxtra.swlearning.com. In the Government listing, click on Federal Independent Agencies and Organizations. Then click on the link to the Securities and Exchange Commission web site. Under "About the SEC," click on "Laws and Regulations." Read the information about the Sarbanes-Oxley Act of 2002. Write a paragraph explaining the purpose of this Act.

9 Labor Markets

Demand and Supply of Resources **9.1**

Wage Determination **9.2**

Labor Unions **9.3**

Consider

Why do truck drivers in the United States earn at least 20 times more than rickshaw drivers in Asia?

Why do some professional basketball players earn 50 times more than others?

Among physicians, why do surgeons earn twice as much as general practitioners?

What's the payoff for a college education?

POINT YOUR BROWSER

econxtra.swlearning.com

Objectives

> Determine the shape of a resource demand curve and a resource supply curve.

> Identify what can shift a labor demand curve.

> Identify what can shift a labor supply curve.

Overview

As with all prices, prices of productive resources—the inputs used to produce goods and services—are determined by the interaction of demand and supply. Demand and supply in resource markets determine the price and quantity of resources employed. The distribution of resource ownership determines the distribution of income throughout the economy. Your earnings will depend on the market value of the resources you supply. In deciding upon your career—the labor market in which you will work—you should consider the income you could expect from alternative occupations.

Key Terms

derived demand

productivity

equilibrium wage

resource substitutes

resource complements

[In the News]

● Higher Productivity, Fewer Workers

In 2003, figures from the U.S. Department of Labor reflected trends that suggested both the good news and the bad news about the current state of the American economy. The good news was that productivity—one of the most important indicators of a dynamic and growing economy—increased by a seasonally adjusted 7.2%. This information was provided in the Labor Department's report on the economy's performance in the second quarter of 2003. However, this strong showing on the part of American workers was offset by the fact that the gains were accomplished using fewer employees. By restructuring and tightening management controls, businesses are able to get maximum production out of their workers. At the same time, the rise in productivity helps to lower unit labor costs and hold off inflationary price increases. Though it hurts the job market in the short run, many economists argue that in the long run, gains in productivity are not only good for the economy, but help workers as well. Gains in productivity allow businesses to increase workers' pay without increasing prices.

Think About It

What do you think would happen to prices if worker productivity fell?

Demand and Supply of Resources

In the market for goods and services—the *product market*—households are demanders and firms are suppliers. Households demand the goods and services that maximize utility. Firms supply the goods and services that maximize profit. In the *resource market,* roles are reversed. Households are suppliers and firms are demanders. Households supply resources to maximize utility. Firms demand resources to maximize profit. Any differences between the utility-maximizing goals of households and the profit-maximizing goals of firms are sorted out through voluntary exchange in markets.

Market Demand for Resources

Why do firms employ productive resources? Firms use resources to produce goods and services. They try to sell the goods and services to earn a profit. A firm values not the resource itself but the resource's ability to produce goods and services. Because the value of any resource depends on the value of what it produces, the demand for a resource is said to be a *derived demand.* Another term for "derive" is "arise from." Thus, **derived demand** arises from the demand for the good or service produced by the resource. For example, demand for a carpenter arises, or derives, from the demand for the carpenter's output, such as a cabinet or a new deck. Demand for professional baseball players derives from the demand for ballgames. Demand for truck drivers derives from the demand for transporting goods.

The derived nature of resource demand helps explain why professional baseball players usually earn more than professional hockey players, why brain surgeons earn more than tree surgeons, and why tractor-trailer drivers earn more than delivery-van drivers. *The more a worker produces and the higher the price of that product, the more valuable that worker is to a firm.* Thus the demand for a

Main Idea

Role of Resources in Determining Income

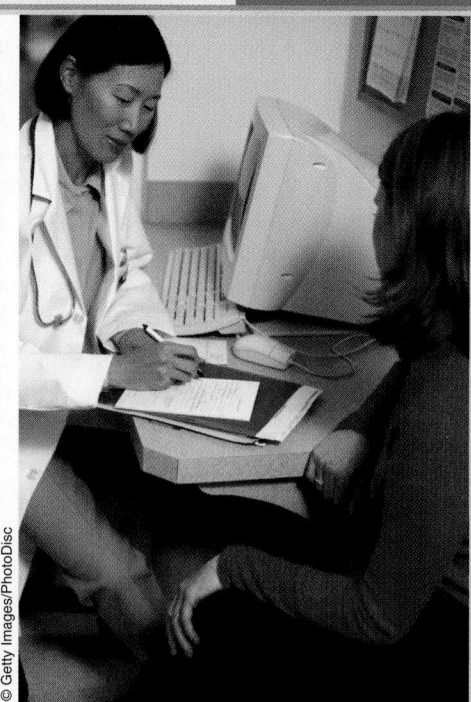

Income for most people is determined by the market value of the productive resources they sell. What they earn depends on the market value of what they produce and how productive they are. What outputs do the two people shown in the photos produce? Which one do you think should earn more than the other, and why?

resource is tied to the value of the output produced by that resource, or its **productivity**. The more productive a resource, the more a firm is willing to pay for it.

The market demand for a particular resource is the sum of demands for that resource in all its different uses. For example, the market demand for carpenters adds together the demand for carpenters in residential and commercial construction, remodeling, cabinetmaking, and so on. Similarly, the market demand for the resource, timber, sums the demand for timber as lumber, railway ties, furniture, pencils, toothpicks, paper products, firewood, and so on. The demand curve for a resource, like the demand curves for the goods produced by that resource, slopes downward. This is depicted by the demand curve for carpenters, *D*, in Figure 9.1.

As the price of a resource falls, firms are more willing and more able to employ that resource. Consider first the firm's greater *willingness* to hire resources as the resource price falls. In developing the demand curve for a particular resource, the prices of other resources are assumed to remain constant. If the wage of carpenters falls, this type of labor becomes relatively cheaper com-

pared with other resources the firm could employ to produce the same output. Firms, therefore, are more willing to hire carpenters rather than hire other, now relatively more costly, resources.

Firms may make *substitutions in production.* For example, a homebuilder can employ more carpenters and fewer prefabricated sections made at a factory. Likewise firms can substitute coal for oil

NETBookmark

The demand for architects is derived from the demand for new construction, particularly commercial buildings. The American Institute of Architects maintains a career center with a job board. Access this web site through econxtra.swlearning.com. You can find analysis and forecasts for many jobs in the Bureau of Labor Statistics' *Occupational Outlook Handbook (OOH)*. Access the prospectus for architects in the OOH through econxtra.swlearning.com. What is the future employment outlook for professional architects?

econxtra.swlearning.com

The Graphing Workshop

productivity
The value of output produced by a resource

Labor Market for Carpenters

Figure 9.1

The intersection of the upward-sloping supply curve of carpenters with the downward-sloping demand curve determines the equilibrium wage rate, *W*, and the level of employment, *E*.

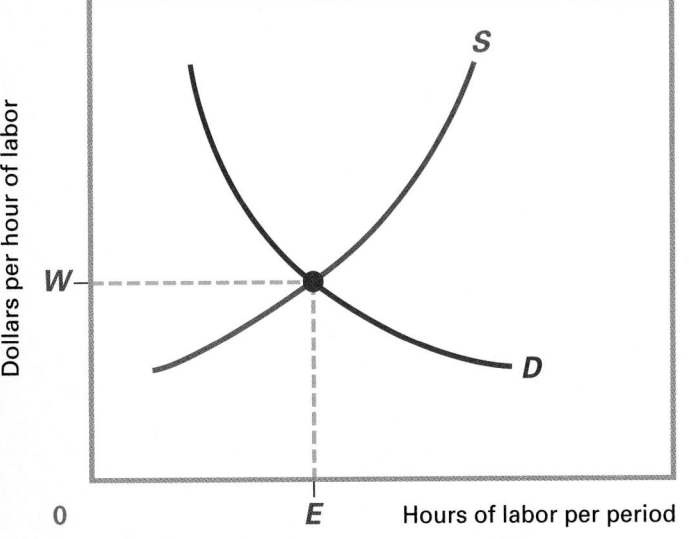

The Graphing Workshop

equilibrium wage
The wage at which the quantity of labor firms want to hire exactly matches the quantity workers want to supply

or security alarms for security guards, as the relative price of coal or security alarms declines.

A lower price for a resource also increases a firm's *ability* to hire that resource. For example, if the wage for carpenters falls, homebuilders can hire more carpenters for the same total cost. The lower resource price means the firm is *more able* to buy the resource. Because producers are more willing and more able to employ a resource when the price of the resource declines, the demand curve for a resource slopes downward, as shown in Figure 9.1.

Market Supply of Resources

On the other side of the market, resource suppliers tend to be both more *willing* and more *able* to supply the resource as its price increases. This explains the upward-sloping market supply curve, as shown in Figure 9.1 by the supply curve of carpenters, *S*. Resource suppliers are more *willing* because a higher resource price, other things constant, means more goods and services can be purchased with the earnings from each unit of the resource supplied.

Resource prices are signals about the rewards for supplying resources to alternative activities. A high resource price tells the resource owner, "The market really values your resource and is willing to pay you well for what you supply." Higher prices will draw resources from lower-valued uses. For example, as the wage for carpenters increases, the quantity of labor supplied will increase. Some carpenters will give up leisure time to work more hours. Also, people in other lines of work will be attracted to carpentry.

The second reason a resource supply curve slopes upward is that resource owners are more *able* to supply the resource at a higher price. For example, a higher carpenter's wage means more apprentices will choose to undergo training to become carpenters. The higher wage *enables* resource suppliers to increase their quantity supplied. Similarly, a higher timber price enables loggers to harvest trees in more remote regions. A higher oil price enables drillers to explore more remote parts of the world.

The interaction in Figure 9.1 of the labor demand curve, *D*, and the labor supply curve, *S*, determines the equilibrium wage for carpenters, *W*, and the equilibrium employment of carpenters, *E*. At the **equilibrium wage**, the quantity of labor firms want to hire exactly

SPAN THE GLOBE

The Immigration Issue

According to recent polls, the U.S. public is more opposed to any kind of immigration than their elected officials realize. Whether legal or illegal, the public seems to be canceling America's invitation engraved on the Statue of Liberty: "Give me your tired, your poor, your huddled masses yearning to breathe free...." However, it seems legislators and other national leaders charged with shaping legal policy on the issue haven't heard the news. According to a poll by the Chicago Council on Foreign Relations, 70 percent of 2,862 people interviewed said that "controlling and reducing illegal immigration" should be a "very important" policy goal. Only 22 percent of 400 of leaders from Congress, business, the media, labor, and religious and academic groups agreed. Moreover, 55 percent of the general public also wants to reduce quotas and legal immigration, compared to only 18 percent of the country's leaders. Many suggest the reason for the opinion gap between the public and its leaders is that a great many Americans are afraid of immigrants taking their jobs. The nation's leaders, on the other hand, have little fear of job competition from immigrants.

Think Critically

What if Congress eliminated immigration into the United States? In the short run, what would happen to the wage rate and level of employment in the United States? What might happen in the long run?

matches the quantity carpenters want to supply. At the equilibrium wage, there is neither an excess quantity of carpenters demanded nor an excess quantity supplied. The interaction of labor demand and labor supply determines the market wages and thereby allocates the scarce resource, labor.

> ✔ **CHECKPOINT**
> Describe the shape of a resource demand curve and a resource supply curve.

Nonwage Determinants of Labor Demand

The quantity of labor demanded increases as the wage decreases, other things constant, because a lower wage makes employers more willing and more able to hire workers. Thus the labor demand curve slopes downward, other things constant, as you saw in Figure 9.1. What are the other things that are assumed to remain constant along a given demand curve? In other words, what are the nonwage factors that help shape the labor demand curve?

Demand for the Final Product

Labor demand is derived from the demand for the output produced by that labor. For example, the demand for carpenters derives from the demand for what they produce. Because the demand for labor is *derived* from the demand for that labor's output, any change in the demand for that output affects resource demand. For example, an increase in the demand for housing will increase the demand for carpenters. As shown in Figure 9.2, this causes the demand curve for that labor to shift to the right, from *D* to *D'*. A rightward shift of the demand for carpenters will increase the market wage and employment.

Prices of Other Resources

The prices of other resources are assumed to remain constant along the downward sloping demand curve for labor. A change in the price of other resources could shift the demand for labor. Some resources substitute for each other in production. For example, as mentioned already, prefabricated

The Graphing Workshop

An Increase in the Demand for Carpenters

Figure 9.2

An increase in the demand for carpenters is shown by a rightward shift of that labor demand curve. This will increase the market wage and increase employment of carpenters.

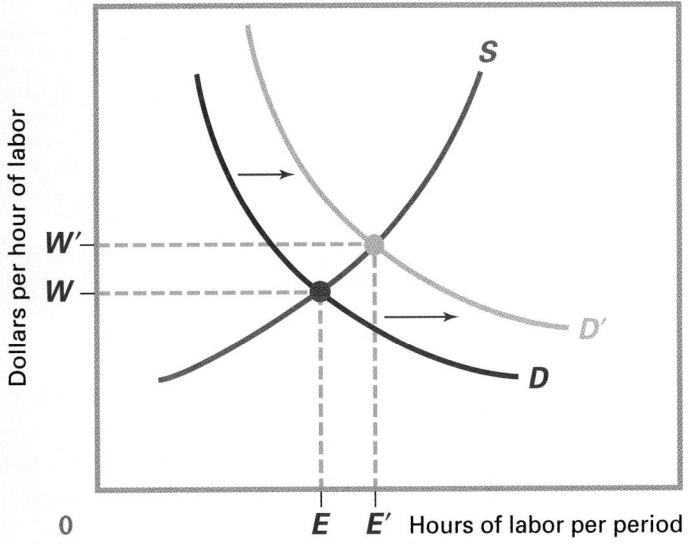

resource substitutes

One resource can replace another in production; an increase in the price of one resource increases the demand for the other

resource complements

One resource works with the other in production; a decrease in the price of one increases the demand for the other

home sections built mostly by machine at the factory substitute for on-site home construction by carpenters. Substitutes can replace each other in production. With **resource substitutes**, an increase in the price of one increases the demand for the other. For example, an increase in the price of prefabricated home sections will increase the demand for carpenters. This will shift the demand for carpenters to the right, as in Figure 9.2.

Some resources are complements in production—carpenters and lumber, for example. Complements go together in production. With **resource complements**, a decrease in the price of one leads to an increase in the demand for the other. If the price of lumber decreases, the quantity of lumber demanded increases, which increases the demand for carpenters, shifting the demand for carpenters to the right.

As another example, trucks and truck drivers are complements. Any increase in the quantity or quality of a complementary resource, such as trucks, boosts the productivity of the resource in question, such as truck drivers. This, in turn, increases the demand for truck drivers. Bigger and better trucks make truck drivers more productive.

Technology

A labor demand curve assumes a given level of technology in that market. Thus, technology is assumed to be constant along a labor demand curve. A change in technology can shift the labor demand curve. More technologically sophisticated capital can increase the productivity of labor, thus increasing the demand for labor. For example, better power tools, such as a pneumatic nail driver, enable carpenters to be more productive, thus shifting the demand for carpenters to the right. Alternatively, improved technology could make some workers unnecessary, thus shifting the demand for carpenters to the left. An example of this would be a factory

© Getty Images/PhotoDisc

One reason truck drivers in the United States earns at least 20 times more than rickshaw drivers in Asia is the nature of the vehicles themselves. Compare the photograph of a rickshaw on the first page of this chapter to the tractor-trailer shown here. What specific characteristics of the tractor-trailer would make it a more productive resource than the rickshaw?

using a robot to perform a delicate task once performed by a human worker.

Sometimes a technological improvement can boost the productivity of some resources but reduce the demand for others. For example, the development of computer-generated animated movies increased the demand for computer programmers with that skill. At the same time, it decreased the demand for animators who drew each frame by hand.

CHECKPOINT
What are the nonwage factors that help shape the labor demand curve?

Nonwage Determinants of Labor Supply

The quantity of labor supplied increases with the wage, other things constant, so the labor supply curve slopes upward, as shown in Figure 9.1. What are the other things that are assumed to remain constant along a given supply curve? In other words, what are the nonwage factors that help shape the labor supply curve?

Worker Wealth

Although some jobs are rewarding in a variety of nonmonetary ways, the main reason people work is to earn money to buy goods and services. The wealthier people are, the less they need to work for a living. Thus, a person's supply of labor depends, among other things, on his or her wealth, including homes, cars, savings, stock holdings, and other assets. A person's wealth is assumed to remain constant along the labor supply curve.

A decrease in wealth would prompt people to work more, thus increasing their supply of labor. For example, the stock market decline between 2000 and 2003 reduced significantly the wealth that many people planned to draw on during retirement. As a result, they had to put retirement plans on hold and instead work more and longer to rebuild their retirement nest egg. This increased the supply of labor, as shown by the rightward shift of the labor supply curve from S to S' in Figure 9.3. This will reduce the wage and increase employment.

An Increase in the Supply of Carpenters

Figure 9.3

An increase in the supply of carpenters is shown by a rightward shift of the labor supply curve. This will reduce the market wage and increase employment of carpenters.

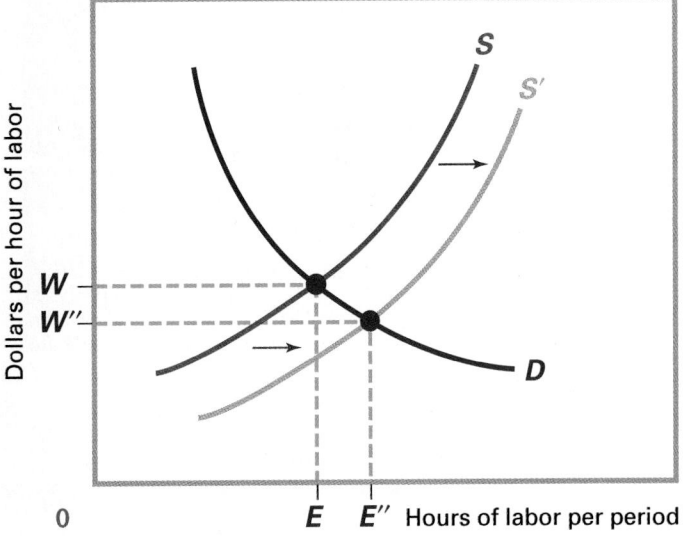

As an example of the opposite effect, winners of multimillion-dollar lotteries often announce they plan to quit their jobs. This would reduce their supply of labor in response to the increase in their wealth. In your own life, if you were to inherit some money from a relative, you might decide not to work next summer. This would decrease your labor supply.

Working Conditions

Labor supply to a particular market depends on the working conditions, such as the difficulty of the job and the attractiveness of the work environment. Working conditions are assumed to remain constant along a given labor supply curve. Any improvement in working conditions would shift the labor supply curve rightward. For example, if employers offer carpenters more flexible hours, many will find this more attractive than a rigid work schedule. These carpenters will increase their supply of labor, shifting the labor supply curve to the right. More generally, people supply less labor to jobs that are dirty, dangerous, dull, exhausting, illegal, low status,

CNN video
French Desert France
econxtra.swlearning.com

Investigate Your Local Economy

In small groups, discuss job tastes among students at your high school. Do you see any trends? Are some jobs more desirable than others? Why do you think this is so?

dead-end, and involve inconvenient hours. They choose to supply more labor to jobs that are clean, safe, interesting, energizing, legal, high status, have advancement potential, and involve convenient hours.

Tastes for Work

Just as consumer tastes for goods and services are assumed to remain constant along a demand curve, worker tastes for jobs are assumed to remain constant along a given labor supply curve. Job tastes are relatively stable. They don't change overnight. Still, over time the supply of labor could change because of a change in the tastes for a particular job. For example, suppose carpentry becomes more appealing because people become more attracted to jobs that provide exercise, fresh air, and the satisfaction of building something. In this case, the supply of labor to carpentry would shift rightward, as in Figure 9.3.

As another example of how worker tastes can change over time, most teenagers a decade ago found jobs at fast-food restaurants relatively attractive. Teenagers today seem to prefer upscale employers such as Starbucks and the Gap.

© Getty Images/PhotoDisc

Based on working conditions, do you think that the job of steel worker would have a large supply of labor? Why or why not?

CHECKPOINT

What are the nonwage factors that help shape the labor supply curve?

Key Concepts

1. What is the demand for workers in your school cafeteria derived from?

2. Why would the demand for roofers increase if the price of shingles falls by 50 percent?

3. Why would an increase in the price of heating oil increase the quantity of heating oil supplied to the market?

4. What would happen to the demand for technicians who produce computer chips if a new chip-manufacturing process using only half as much raw material was introduced?

5. Why might the supply of high-school students who are willing to work in fast-food restaurants decrease if there was an economic boom and a large increase in stock values?

Graphing Exercise

6. Draw a labor supply curve for students who are willing to work, based on the data in the table. Explain what would happen to the location of this labor supply curve as a result of each of the listed events.

Hourly Wage Rate	Number of Students Willing to Work
$6	5
$7	10
$8	15
$9	20
$10	25

a. A large employer in town closes and thousands of workers are laid off.

b. Wearing old clothes becomes popular among students. This style causes many young people to stop buying new clothing.

c. The state board of education raises the grade requirement to graduate.

Think Critically

7. **Management** Make a list of nonwage determinants of labor supply that managers could use to increase the number of workers who are willing to be employed.

8. **Science** Identify scientific developments that have taken place in the last 50 years that have changed the demand for labor in the marketplace.

Sharpen Your Life Skills

Working with Percentages

Raw economic data can be difficult to interpret. It often is more meaningful if expressed in terms of percentages. For example, your father might have said something like this in December 2002: "In 1980, when I was 16 years old, I earned only $3.10 an hour." You might believe that what he said was true. However, would this information give you an accurate idea of how well he was paid? Probably not. In order to compare values over time, many economists adjust them for inflation and then express the values as percentages. The most common tool they use for comparing values is the Consumer Price Index (CPI). In 1980, the CPI was 82.4. At the end of 2002, it was 180.9. But again, what do these values mean? You can answer this question by finding the percentage change in the CPI and using it to adjust the value of your father's 1980 income.

To calculate the percentage change in the CPI, you need to find the change in the index (180.9 − 82.4 = 98.5) and divide this change by the original index (98.5 ÷ 82.4 = 1.20 or 120%). According to the CPI, prices increased by 120% between 1980 and 2002.

To find the purchasing power of the 1980 wage in 2002, you need to multiply $3.10 times the percentage increase in the CPI and then add the result to the 1980 wage of $3.10:

$$\$3.10 \times 1.2 = \$3.72$$

$$\$3.72 + \$3.10 = \$6.82$$

Knowing that the purchasing power of your father's 1980 wage was $6.82 is more meaningful to you than simply knowing he earned $3.10 at that time.

Apply Your Skill

1. In 1990, the CPI was 130.7 and the average price for an eight-foot 2-by-4 used to construct houses was $1.59. In December 2002, the same 2-by-4 cost $2.29. Use the method demonstrated above to calculate whether the price of 2-by-4s increased more or less rapidly than the CPI.

2. Suppose you earned $10.00 per hour in December 2002. Further, suppose that by December 2005, the CPI is 196.7. If you earn $14.00 per hour at that time, what will the real value of your wage be in terms of December 2002 dollars? Will you be better off or worse off than you are now?

movers & shakers

Dr. Tim Kremchek *Orthopedic Surgeon*

Tim Kremchek started college with two goals in mind—to play baseball and to have fun. Academics were not high on his priority list, and after two years of college his grade-point average was 2.2.

During a holiday break, Tim's father, an orthopedic surgeon, invited Tim to join him at work. "He knew I was clueless about my future, but he didn't pressure me to make a decision about life after college." While watching his father work, Tim observed how much his father loved what he was doing. It seemed more like fun than work. After the break Tim returned to college knowing he wanted to become an orthopedic surgeon. From that point on, he earned a 4.0 grade-point average.

After four years of college, Tim attended four more years of medical school, followed by a two-year residency in general surgery. Wanting to specialize in orthopedics meant an additional four years of training. Then, because he wanted to specialize in treating athletes, Tim opted to participate in an orthopedic sports-medicine fellowship for a year. Finally, at the age of 34—after 15 years of schooling beyond high school—this highly trained surgeon began his life's work.

Today Tim Kremchek, M.D., is not only the director of sports medicine and chief orthopedic surgeon for the TriHealth hospital system in Cincinnati, Ohio. He also is the medical director and chief orthopedic surgeon for the Cincinnati Reds major league baseball team. He provides the team with medical advice and has performed multiple surgeries on such major league players as Ken Griffey, Jr., and Barry Larkin. Because of his expertise, out-of-town athletes now regularly travel to Dr. Kremchek for surgery and physical therapy. Asked why he thinks athletes opt to travel to Cincinnati instead of larger cities for their medical care, he said, "I think they trust me and appreciate my straightforward approach to diagnosing their problem. I offer a team approach to care and have surrounded myself with expert personnel to assist in that care." High school and college athletes also routinely seek his expertise in their desire to overcome injuries and return to the playing field.

In addition to his busy practice, Dr. Kremchek's role with the Cincinnati Reds has meant his attendance at every Reds home game. Of 81 home games played each year, Kremchek has missed only one in the last seven years. Although it's not a requirement for the job, Dr. Kremchek attends each game because "by being there and getting to know each athlete, I'm able to develop relationships with them and understand them. It builds my credibility not only with the Reds players but with visiting players as well, some who come to me for treatment from other parts of the world."

Married with five children, Dr. Kremchek bases his success on his love for his work. He proudly states that in addition to his family, "I love baseball. I like the challenge of taking care of baseball players. I'm very good at it, and I'm so lucky to be able to say that."

SOURCE READING

Dr. Kremchek admits that after two years of college, he "was clueless" about his future. However, he made some decisions that drastically altered his career course. What were those decisions? How did his decisions affect his life as it is now?

ENTREPRENEURS IN ACTION

Dr. Kremchek found a career that combined his love of baseball with his desire to be successful in business. What special interests do you have? What career will enable you to use those interests? What training do you need for this goal?

Objectives

> Explain why wages differ across labor markets.

> Describe minimum wage legislation, and discuss its impact on employment and nonwage compensation.

Overview

Because of the division of labor and comparative advantage, the U.S. work force is becoming more specialized. For example, the U.S. Census of 1850 identified 322 job titles. In the 2000 Census, there were 31,000 job titles—about 100 times the number in 1850. The pay for each of these specialties is determined by the intersection of a labor demand curve and a labor supply curve. The resulting differences in pay across job specialties can be huge.

Key Terms

minimum wage law

[In the News]

• Winner-Take-All Labor Markets

Each year *Forbes* magazine reports on the multimillion-dollar earnings of top entertainers and professional athletes. Entertainment and sports have come to be called "winner-take-all" labor markets because a few key people critical to the overall success of an enterprise are richly rewarded. For example, the credits at the end of a movie list the dozens of people involved in its production. Hundreds, sometimes thousands, more are employed behind the scenes. Despite a huge cast and crew, the difference between a movie's financial success and its failure depends on the performance of just a few people—the lead actors, the director, and the screenwriter. These are the people who are compensated the most. The same happens in sports. Although thousands of players compete each year in professional tennis, for example, the value of television time, ticket sales, and endorsements is based on the drawing power of just the top players. In professional golf, attendance and TV ratings are significantly higher for tournaments in which Tiger Woods is in the running. Compensation for top performers is determined through open competition for their talents. The competition bids up their pay to extremely high levels, such as the $20 million per movie earned by some top stars. This is more than 1,000 times the average annual earnings of Screen Actors Guild members.

Think About It

Do you think it is fair that top entertainers and sports figures earn as much money as they do? Why or why not?

Why Wages Differ

Wages differ substantially across labor markets. Figure 9.4 shows the average hourly wages for the 128 million U.S. workers in 2001. Workers are sorted into 22 occupations from the highest to the lowest average wage. Management earns the highest wage, at $34 an hour, and food workers earn the lowest, at $8 an hour. Wage differences across labor markets can be attributed to differences in labor demand, labor supply, or both.

Differences in Training, Education, Age, and Experience

Some jobs pay more because they require a long and expensive training period. Costly training reduces market supply because fewer individuals are willing to undergo the time and expense required. However, extensive training increases the productivity of labor. This in turn increases the demand for workers with those skills. For example, certified public accountants (CPAs) earn more than file clerks because the extensive training for CPAs limits the supply to this field and because this training increases the productivity of CPAs compared to file clerks. Reduced supply and increased demand both increase the market wage. Even among physicians, some specialties earn more than others because of a longer training period. This is why, for example, surgeons on average earn twice as much as general practitioners.

Figure 9.5 shows how education and experience affect earnings. Age groups are shown on the horizontal axis and

Ask the Xpert!

econxtra.swlearning.com

What would happen if everyone were paid the same?

Average Hourly Wage by Occupation

Figure 9.4

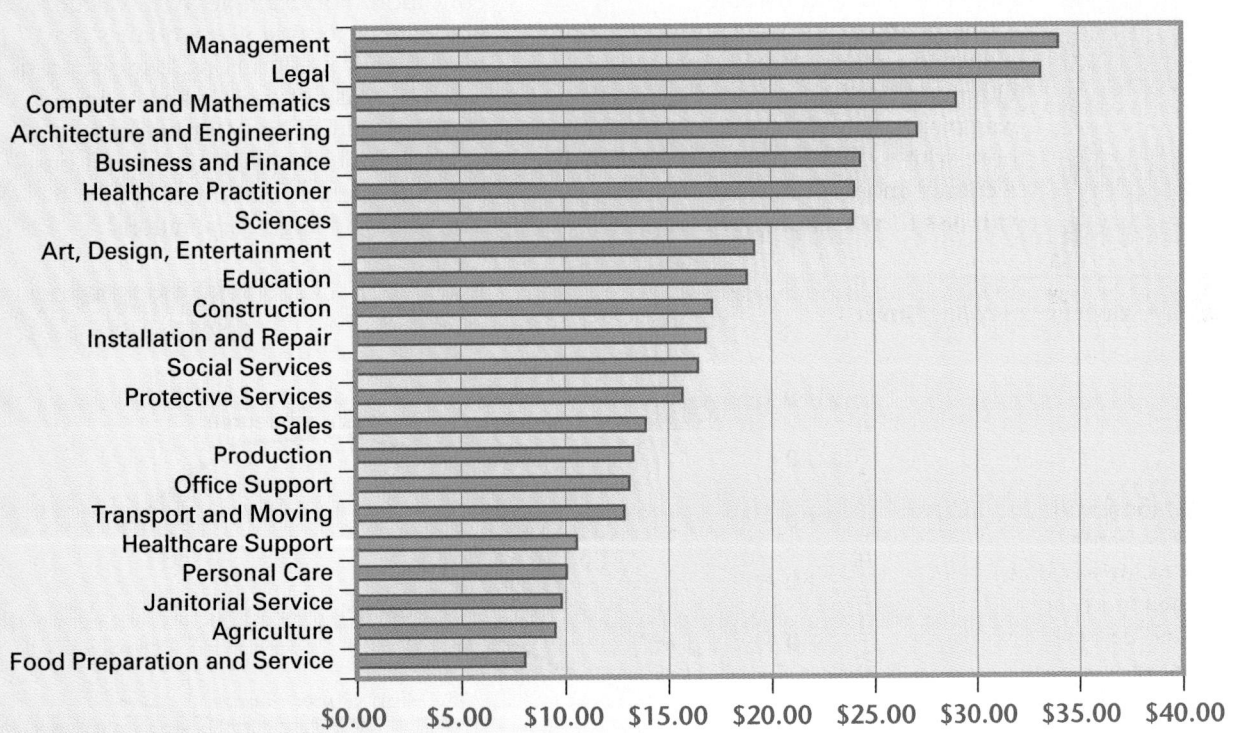

The average hourly wages for the 128 million U.S. workers in 2001 are sorted from the highest to the lowest in this graph. Wage differences across labor markets can be attributed to differences in labor demand, labor supply, or both.

Source: U.S. Bureau of Labor Statistics. Figures are for 2001.

TEAM WORK

Divide into groups of four. Each group member should choose one of the occupation categories shown in Figure 9.4. Make sure that each member chooses a different occupation. As a group, discuss the reasons for the wage differences among the four occupations.

average annual earnings, on the vertical axis. Earnings are for all full-time, year-round workers in 2001. The lines are labeled to reflect the highest level of education achieved and range from "Less Than Ninth Grade" (bottom line) up to "Professional Degree" (top line). Professional degrees include graduate degrees in law, medicine, business administration, and the like.

The relationship between income and education is clear. At every age, those with more education earned more. For example, in the 35-to-44 age group, those with a professional degree earned five times more on average than those with less than a ninth-grade education.

Age itself also has an important effect on income. Earnings increased as workers gained more job experience and became more productive.

Notice that the pay increase with age is greater for more-educated workers. For example, among those with less than a ninth-grade education, workers in the 45-to-54 age group earned on average only 8 percent more than those in the 25-to-34 age group. But among those with a professional degree, workers in the 45-to-54 age group earned on average 86 percent more than those in the 25-to-34 age group.

These earnings differences reflect the normal operation of labor markets. More education and more job experience increase labor productivity, and more productive workers earn more.

Differences in Ability

Because they are more able and more productive, some workers earn more than others with the same training and education. For example, two college graduates majoring in economics may have identical educations, but one earns more because of greater ability and higher productivity. Most business executives have extensive training and business experience, but few become chief executives of large corporations.

Education Pays More for Every Age Group

Figure 9.5

At every age, those with more education earned more. Earnings increased as workers gained more job experience and became more productive.

Source: U.S. Bureau of Labor Statistics. Figures are average earnings for all full-time, year-round workers in 2001.

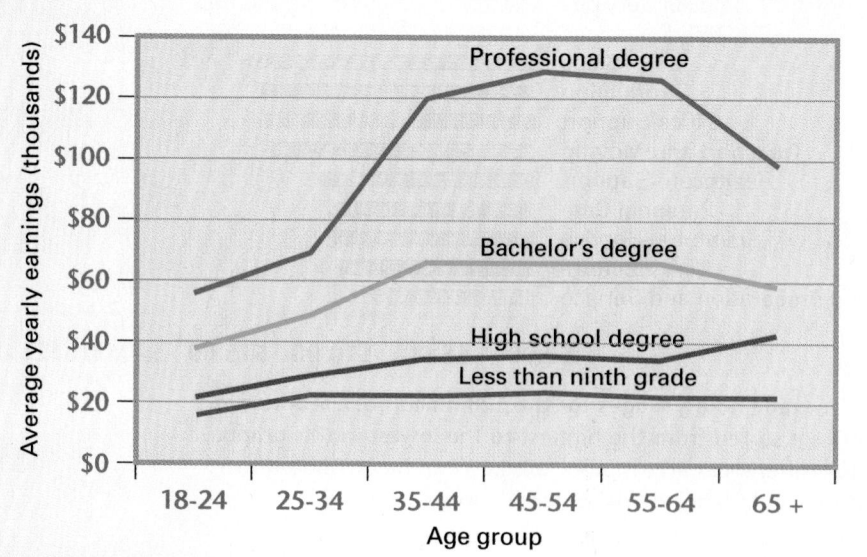

The same goes for professional athletes. In the National Basketball Association, for example, Kevin Garnet of Minnesota was paid $25.2 million in 2002, which was about 50 times that of the lowest-paid player. Being tall helps boost productivity and pay. Nine of the ten highest-paid players were at least 6 feet 9 inches tall.

Differences in Risk

Jobs with a higher probability of injury or death, such as coal mining and fishing, pay more than safer jobs, other things constant. Workers also earn more, other things constant, in seasonal jobs such as construction and fishing. This is due to the higher risk of unemployment at certain times of the year.

Some jobs are both dangerous and seasonal. For example, deckhands on fishing boats in the winter waters of the Bering Sea off Alaska earn more than $4,000 for five days of work. The temperature on the boats is seldom above zero and daily shifts allow only three hours for sleep.

Geographic Differences

People have a strong incentive to supply their resources in the market where they earn the most, other things constant. For example, place kickers in the National Football League come from around the world for the attractive salaries available. Likewise, because physicians earn more in the United States than elsewhere, thousands of foreign-trained physicians migrate here each year. The flow of labor is not all one way. Some Americans seek their fortune abroad, with basketball players going to Europe and baseball players headed to Japan.

Job Discrimination

Some people earn lower wages because of discrimination in the job market based on race, ethnicity, or gender. Although such discrimination is illegal, history shows that certain groups—including African Americans, Hispanics, and women—have systematically earned less than others of apparently equal ability.

Job-market discrimination can take many forms. An employer may fail to

© Getty Images/PhotoDisc

hire a minority job applicant because the applicant lacks training. But this lack of training can arise from discrimination in the schools, in union apprenticeship programs, or in employer-run training programs. For example, evidence suggests that black workers receive less on-the-job training than otherwise similar white workers.

The Equal Employment Opportunity Commission, established by the Civil Rights Act of 1964, monitors cases involving unequal pay for equal work and unequal access to promotion. Research suggests that civil rights legislation has helped narrow the black-white earnings gap.

The gap between male and female pay also has narrowed. For example, among all full-time, year-round U.S. workers, females in 1980 earned only 60 percent of what males earned. By 2002, females earned 77.5 percent of male pay. In addition to discrimination as a source of the pay gap, women do more housework and childcare than men do. This tends to reduce female job experience. It also causes some to seek more flexible positions, which often pay less.

Union Membership

Finally, workers represented by labor unions earn more on average than other workers. The final section of this chapter discusses the effects of labor unions on the market for labor.

The Graphing Workshop

 **CHECKPOINT**
Why do wages differ across labor markets?

Ethics in Action

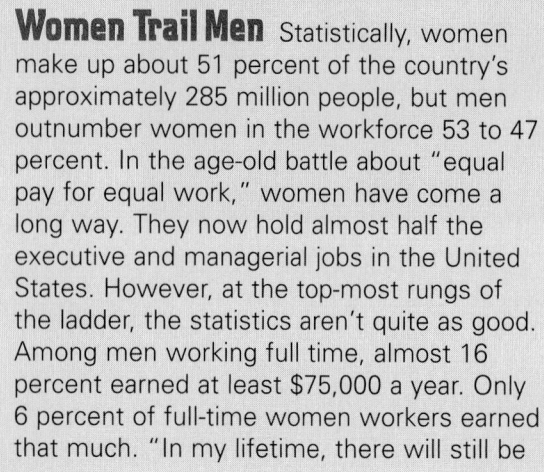

Women Trail Men Statistically, women make up about 51 percent of the country's approximately 285 million people, but men outnumber women in the workforce 53 to 47 percent. In the age-old battle about "equal pay for equal work," women have come a long way. They now hold almost half the executive and managerial jobs in the United States. However, at the top-most rungs of the ladder, the statistics aren't quite as good. Among men working full time, almost 16 percent earned at least $75,000 a year. Only 6 percent of full-time women workers earned that much. "In my lifetime, there will still be a wage gap," said the president of the National Association of Female Executives. "It's up to women in senior positions to bring other women up, or else it's not going to happen." Women's leaders say that discrimination is at least partly to blame for differences between men's and women's compensation.

Think Critically

What are the social factors behind gender discrimination? Do you think it should be up to the government to correct this wage gap? Why or why not?

---

minimum wage law

Establishes a minimum amount that an employer can pay a worker for an hour of labor

The Minimum Wage

In March 2000, Congress sent the president a measure to increase the U.S. minimum wage by $1.00 to $6.15. The legislation was vetoed. The **minimum wage law** establishes a minimum amount that an employer can pay a worker for an hour of labor.

Coverage of the Law

When the legislation was vetoed, about 7 percent of the U.S. workforce earned between $5.15 and $6.15 an hour and thus could have been affected by an increased minimum wage. This group included workers with few job skills. Most were young, the majority worked only part time, and they were employed primarily in service and sales occupations. For example, while 8 of 10 working teenagers earned less than a dollar above the minimum wage, fewer than 1 in 10 workers in their mid-40s earned that little.

Effects of the Minimum Wage

Advocates of minimum-wage legislation argue that it increases the income of the poorest workers at little or no cost to overall employment. Critics argue that a minimum wage established above the equilibrium wage causes employers either to reduce the quantity of labor employed or change something else about the job.

Most research on the effects of the minimum wage finds either no effect on employment or a negative effect, particularly among teenage workers. Employers often react to a minimum wage increase by

- substituting part-time jobs for full-time jobs

NET Bookmark

The U.S. Department of Labor maintains a Minimum Wage web page. Access this page through econxtra.swlearning.com. What is the current federal minimum wage? Which groups of workers are exempt from minimum wage laws?

econxtra.swlearning.com

- substituting more-qualified minimum-wage workers (such as high school graduates) for less-qualified workers (such as high school dropouts)

- adjusting some nonwage features of the job to reduce employer costs or increase worker productivity.

Nonwage Job Features

Congress may be able to legislate a minimum wage, but employers can still adjust many other conditions of the employment. Here are some of the nonwage job components that an employer could alter to offset the added cost of a higher minimum wage: the convenience of work hours, expected work effort, on-the-job training, time allowed for meals and breaks, wage premiums for night shifts and weekends, paid vacation days, paid holidays, sick leave policy, health-care benefits, and so on. For example, one study found that restaurants responded to a higher minimum wage by reducing fringe benefits, particularly vacation time, and reducing the higher wages offered for less-desirable shifts.

Higher Opportunity Cost of School

A higher minimum wage also raises the opportunity cost of staying in

THE WALL STREET JOURNAL

Reading It Right What's the relevance of the following statement from *The Wall Street Journal:* "'I'm afraid you are going to unemploy more people,' Sen. Don Nickles, R-Oklahoma, said of what would happen if a minimum wage increase is included."

school. According to one study, an increase in the minimum wage encouraged some 16- to 19-year-olds to quit school and look for work, though many failed to find jobs. Those who had already dropped out of school were more likely to become unemployed because of a higher minimum wage. Thus, an increase in the minimum wage may have the unintended consequence of encouraging some students to drop out of school. The unemployment rate is highest for high-school dropouts. In 2003, 11 states had a minimum wage higher than the federal level.

CHECKPOINT
How might an increase in the minimum wage affect nonwage compensation for low-wage workers?

© Getty Images/PhotoDisc

Jobs high school students find, such as waitressing, often pay minimum wage. One study found that if the minimum wage were increased, some students would drop out of high school to pursue full-time work. What is your opinion on this issue? Should government keep the minimum wage lower so the dropout rate won't increase?

Key Concepts

1. Why are people who are trained to repair computers paid more than people who are trained to mend clothing?

2. Why is the earning power of a college liberal arts major less than that of an electrical engineering major?

3. Why does job discrimination harm not only the people who are discriminated against but also society in general?

4. Why might an increase in the minimum wage cause greater unemployment among low-skill workers?

Graphing Exercise

5. When data are gathered about the labor supply in the United States, people are divided into several categories. Some people are not considered because they are too young or unable to work for other reasons. The remaining people comprise the *civilian noninstitutional population (CNP)*. Of this group, some people do not choose to seek employment and so are not considered to be in the labor force. The remaining people are in the labor force and are either employed or unemployed. Use the data in the table to construct a multiple line graph that illustrates the data given below. What does your graph tell you about the growth in the labor supply available to U.S. employers during the 1990s?

Labor Force Data, 1990–2000
Values in Millions of People

Year	CNP	Not in Labor Force	In Labor Force	Employed	Unemployed
1990	189.2	63.5	125.8	118.8	7.0
1992	192.8	64.7	128.1	118.4	9.7
1994	196.8	65.8	131.0	123.1	7.9
1996	200.6	66.6	134.0	126.7	7.3
1998	205.2	67.5	137.7	131.5	6.2
2000	209.7	68.8	140.9	135.2	5.7

Think Critically

6. **Government** In 1968, the federal minimum wage was $1.60 per hour. This might seem to be a small amount. However, when adjusted for inflation it had the same purchasing power as $7.92 per hour in 2000 dollars. In 2000, the federal minimum wage was $5.15 per hour. Therefore, the real (adjusted for inflation) value of the minimum wage fell by about 35 percent between 1968 and 2000. Why do you think the federal government did not increase the minimum wage at the same rate as inflation? How might this have affected the number of minimum-wage jobs offered to workers?

Objectives

> Describe the history and tools of U.S. labor unions.

> Analyze how labor unions try to increase wages.

> Discuss recent trends in union membership.

Overview

The aspect of labor markets that makes the most news headlines is the activity of labor unions. Labor negotiations, strikes, picket lines, and heated confrontations between workers and employers all fit neatly into TV's "action news" format. But despite all the media attention, only about one in seven U.S. workers belongs to a labor union. What's more, the overwhelming share of union contracts are reached without a strike. The typical union member is more likely to be a government employee than a steelworker or autoworker. Labor unions focus on negotiating higher pay and more benefits for members.

Key Terms

labor union

right-to-work law

collective bargaining

mediator

binding arbitration

strike

featherbedding

[In the News]

• Union Activity at Amazon.com

Labor unions made minor efforts toward organizing at Amazon.com as early as 1998. A serious organizing campaign began nearly four years later when about 50 employees from the company's 400-person customer service center in Seattle gathered to strategize. The employees had many concerns, including job security, mandatory overtime shifts, and erratic schedules. About the same time, the United Food and Commercial Workers (UFCW) began a drive to unionize workers in eight of the company's distribution centers. The UFCW drive has focused on educating workers about what unions can do for them. They're taking it slow and waiting for the right time to ask workers to sign union cards and prompt a formal election for union representation. To counter the union's moves, Amazon has started its own campaign. The company has staged mandatory employee meetings to respond to union arguments. They've coached managers on the best ways to deal with organizing efforts. They also continually post responses to employees' frequently asked questions. It's a gentle battle of education and persuasion but a very serious battle nonetheless. Amazon has devoted its best people to the issue as well as significant resources to combat the union. For now, it remains a war of words and ideas.

Think About It

Do you think it would be easier to unionize high-tech workers today than it was at the beginning of the "Dot-Com" revolution? Why or why not?

Organized Labor

right-to-work law

State law that says a worker at a union company does not have to join the union or pay union dues to hold a job there

labor union

A group of workers who join together to seek higher pay and better working conditions by negotiating a labor contract with their employers

collective bargaining

The process by which representatives of the union and the employer negotiate wages, employee benefits, and working conditions

mediator

An impartial observer brought in when labor negotiations break down, to suggest how to resolve differences

binding arbitration

When labor negotiations break down and the public interest is involved, a neutral third party is brought in to impose a settlement that both sides must accept

strike

A labor union's attempt to withhold labor from the firm

In the late nineteenth century, factory workers averaged 11-hour days, 6 days a week. Those in steel mills, paper mills, and breweries averaged 12-hour days, 7 days a week. Child labor was common, and working conditions often were dangerous. For example, according to one estimate, fatal accidents in the steel mills of Pittsburgh accounted for one-fifth of all male deaths in that city during the 1880s. Despite the long hours and dreadful working conditions, millions of immigrants entered the work force, increasing the supply of labor and keeping wages low.

History of Labor Unions

Through a **labor union**, workers join together to improve their pay and working conditions by negotiating a labor contract with their employers. The first labor unions in the United States were *craft unions,* where membership was limited to workers with a particular skill, or craft—such as carpenters, shoemakers, or printers. Craft unions eventually formed their own national organization, the *American Federation of Labor (AFL),* in 1886. The AFL was not a union itself but rather an organization of national unions, each retaining its own independence.

The Clayton Act of 1914 exempted labor unions from antitrust laws, meaning that *union members at competing companies could join forces legally in an effort to raise wages and improve working conditions.* Unions also were exempt from taxation. This favorable legislation encouraged the union movement.

The *Congress of Industrial Organizations (CIO)* was formed in 1935 to serve as a national organization of unions in mass-production industries. Whereas the AFL organized workers in particular crafts, the CIO organized all workers in a particular industry. These *industrial unions* organized all workers in an industry, such as all autoworkers or all steelworkers. They still had to organize workers company by company, however. Workers at a company became unionized if a majority of them voted for union representation.

After World War II, economic conditions and public sentiment seemed to turn against unions. In 1947, Congress passed the *Taft-Hartley Act,* which authorized states to approve right-to-work laws. A **right-to-work law** says that a worker at a union company does not have to join the union or pay union dues to hold a job there. Twenty-two states have passed right-to-work laws. These states are mostly in the South, the Plains, and the Mountain states. Union membership rates in the right-to-work states average only half the rates in other states. For more information on the history of labor unions, see the Connect to History feature on page 281.

Collective Bargaining

Collective bargaining is the process by which representatives of a union and an employer negotiate wages, employee benefits, and working conditions. Once a preliminary agreement is reached, union representatives present it to the membership for a vote. If the agreement is accepted, union representatives and the employer sign a labor contract. If the agreement is rejected, the union can strike or can continue negotiations.

If the negotiators cannot reach a decision, and if the public interest is involved, government officials may ask a mediator to step in. A **mediator** is an impartial observer who listens to both sides separately and then suggests a solution. The mediator has no power to impose a settlement on the parties.

In the provision of certain vital services such as police and fire protection, a strike could harm the public. The government may impose **binding arbitration** in these cases. This means that a neutral third party evaluates both sides of the dispute and issues a ruling that both sides must accept. Some disputes skip the mediation and arbitration steps and go directly to a strike.

The Strike

A major source of union power in the bargaining relationship is the threat of a **strike**. This is a union's attempt to withhold labor from the firm. The purpose of a strike is to stop production so as to force the firm to accept the union's position. Strikes also can hurt union members, who suffer a drop in income and who may lose their jobs permanently. The threat of a strike hangs over labor negotiations and can encourage an agreement. *Although neither party usually wants a strike, rather than give in on key points, both sides act as if they could and would go through one.*

If a strike is called, unions usually picket the targeted employer to prevent or discourage so-called strikebreakers from "crossing the picket lines." With non-striking employees and temporary workers, a firm sometimes can maintain production during a strike. That's bad news for the union.

CHECKPOINT
What are the tools used by U.S. labor unions?

Union Wages and Employment

The union's focus usually is on higher wages. Here are two approaches unions employ to increase the wages of their members: (1) reduce the supply of labor and (2) increase the demand for union labor.

Reduce the Supply of Labor

One way to increase wages is for the union to somehow reduce the supply of labor. This occurs with craft unions, such as unions of carpenters or plumbers. The effect of a supply restriction is shown as a leftward shift of the labor supply curve from S to S'' in panel (a) of Figure 9.6. The result is a higher wage and reduced employment.

Successful supply restrictions of this type require the union first to limit its membership and second to force all employers in the market to hire only union members. The union can restrict membership with high initiation fees,

long apprenticeship periods, difficult qualification exams, restrictive licensing requirements, and other devices aimed at slowing down or discouraging new membership. But, even if unions can restrict membership, they have difficulty requiring all firms in the market to hire only union workers. In right-to-work states, for example, workers do not have to belong to a union even if the company is unionized.

Professional groups—doctors, lawyers, and accountants, for example—also impose entry restrictions through education and examination requirements. These restrictions usually are defended by the professions on the grounds that they protect the public. Some observers, however, see the restrictions as attempts to increase pay among existing professionals by limiting the labor supply.

Increase the Demand for Union Labor

Another way to increase the wage is to increase the demand for union labor. This strategy is reflected by a rightward shift of the labor demand curve from D to D' in panel (b) of Figure 9.6. This is an attractive alternative because *it increases both the wage and employment.* Here are some ways unions try to increase the demand for union labor.

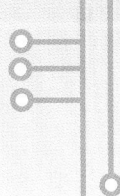

NETBookmark

Does it make a difference to the quality of a job if the workplace is unionized? The AFL-CIO, an umbrella organization for most of the nations' unions, certainly believes it makes a difference. Access the AFL-CIO web site through econxtra.swlearning.com to read about how and why people join unions. In your opinion, what would be the biggest benefit of union membership? Are there any benefits cited that you do not think would be helpful? If so, what are they?

econxtra.swlearning.com

Increase Demand for Union-Made Products

The demand for union labor may be increased through a direct appeal to consumers to buy only union-made products. Increasing the demand for union-made products increases the demand for union labor.

Restrict Supply of Nonunion-Made Products

Another way to increase the demand for union labor is to restrict the supply of products that compete with union-made products. The United Auto Workers, for example, supports restrictions on imported cars. Fewer imported cars means greater demand for cars produced by U.S. workers, who are mostly union members.

Increase Productivity of Union Labor

In the absence of a union, a dissatisfied worker may simply look for another job. Losing workers in this way is costly to the firm because the departing worker often leaves with abundant on-the-job experience that makes the worker more productive. Unions sometimes try to keep workers from quitting or goofing off. This increases worker productivity, thereby increasing the demand for union labor.

Featherbedding

Another way unions try to increase the demand for union labor is by **featherbedding**. This is an attempt to ensure that more union labor is hired than employers would prefer. For example, union rules require that each Broadway theater hire a permanent "house" carpenter, electrician, and property manager. Once the play begins, these workers appear only on payday. In addition, the theater's box office must be staffed by at least three people. With featherbedding, the union tries to set not only the wage but also the number of workers that must be hired at that wage.

featherbedding

Union efforts to force employers to hire more workers than demanded for the task

---

The Graphing Workshop

Effect of Reducing Supply or Increasing Labor Demand

Figure 9.6

(a) Reducing labor supply

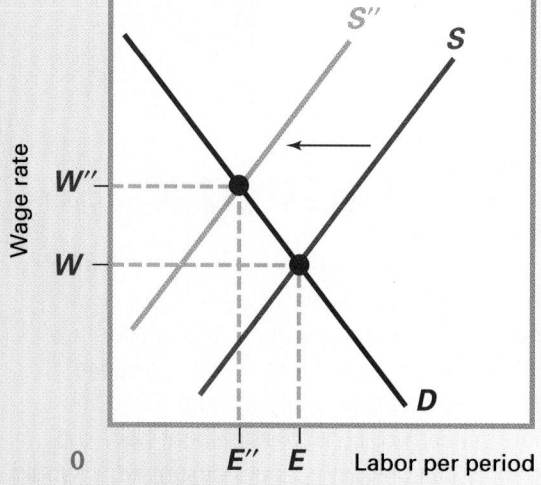

(b) Increasing labor demand

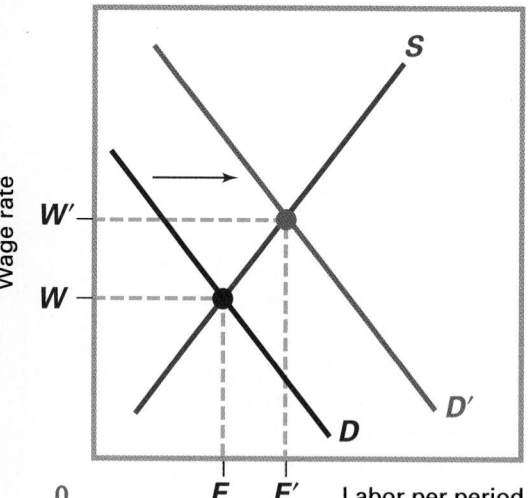

If a union can restrict labor supply to an industry, the supply curve shifts to the left from *S* to *S"*, as in panel (a). The wage rate rises from *W* to *W"*, but at the cost of a reduction in employment from *E* to *E"*. In panel (b), an increase in labor demand from *D* to *D'* raises both the wage and the level of employment.

Union Pay Is Higher

Studies have shown that unions increased members' wages by an average of about 15 percent above the wages of similarly qualified nonunion workers. Figure 9.7 compares the median weekly earnings of union and nonunion workers. Unions are more successful at raising wages in less-competitive industries. For example, unions have less impact on service industries, where product markets tend to be competitive. Unions have greater impact on wages in government, transportation, and construction, which tend to be less competitive.

When there is more competition in the product market, employers cannot easily pass along higher union wages as higher product prices. New firms can enter the industry, pay lower wages, and sell the product for less.

CHECKPOINT
How do unions try to increase the wages of union workers?

Trends in Union Membership

In 1955, about one-third of workers in the United States belonged to unions. Union membership as a fraction of the workforce has since declined. Now only about one-seventh of all workers belong to a union. Government workers now make up nearly half of all union members, even though they account for just one-sixth of U.S. workers. Compared with other advanced economies, the United States ranks relatively low in the number of workers who belong to a union. However, rates abroad have declined as well.

Median Weekly Earnings: Union vs. Nonunion

Figure 9.7

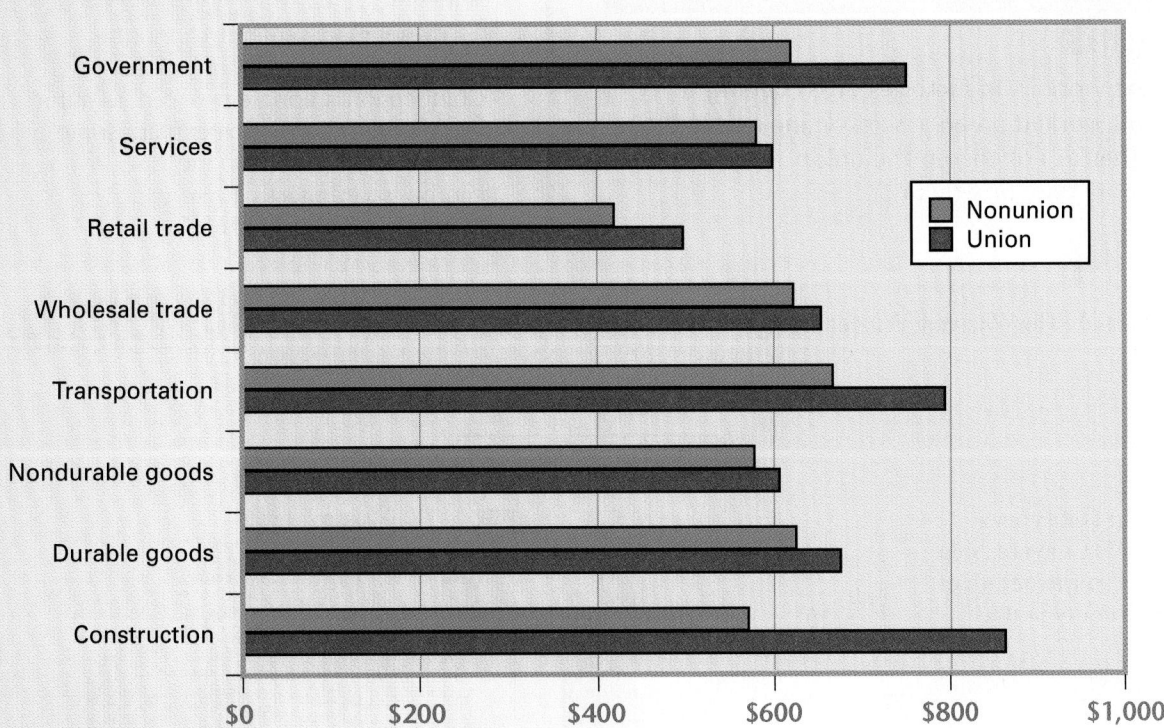

Median weekly earnings are higher for union workers than for nonunion workers.

Source: U.S. Bureau of Labor Statistics. Figures are for full-time workers in 2001.

Membership by Gender, Age, and Geography

The bar graph in Figure 9.8 indicates U.S. union membership rates by age and gender. The rates for men, shown by the green bars, are higher than the rates for women. This, in part, is due to the fact that men are employed more in manufacturing. Women are employed more in the service sector, where union membership historically has been lower. The highest membership rates are for middle-aged males.

Membership Across States

Union membership rates also vary across states. Figure 9.9 shows union membership as a percent of those employed by state. The figure also shades right-to-work states, where workers in unionized companies do not have to join the union or pay union dues. As noted earlier, unionization rates in right-to-work states average only half the rates in other states. New York has the highest unionization rate at 26.7 percent. North Carolina has the lowest, at 3.7 percent.

Reasons for Declining Membership

Improvements in the conditions of the average worker since the late nineteenth century have been remarkable. The average workweek in some industries has been cut in half. The workplace now is monitored more closely for health and safety hazards. Child labor was outlawed decades ago. Wages have increased substantially.

These improvements cannot be entirely credited to labor unions. Competition among employers to attract qualified workers helps explain some of the improvements. The increase in wages can be traced mostly to an increase in labor productivity. This is because

Assembly-line workers in factories often belong to unions. If you worked on an assembly line and had to decide whether or not to join the union, do you think you would join? Why or why not?

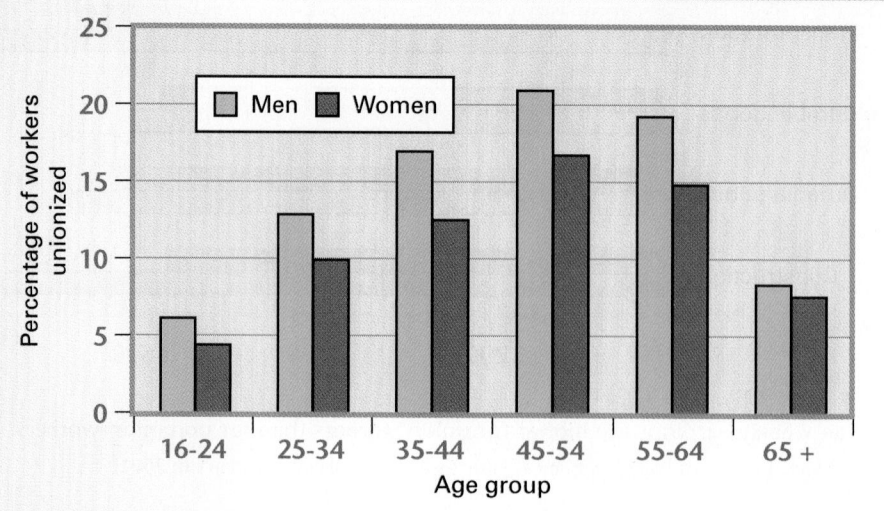

U.S. Union Membership for Men and Women by Age

Figure 9.8

Men in the United States have higher rates of union membership than women, due to the nature of the work each group typically performs.

Source: U.S. Bureau of Labor Statistics. Percentages are for 2001.

Shaded areas show right-to-work states, where workers in unionized companies do not have to join the union or pay union dues. Percentages indicate union membership as a fraction of those employed by state. States that have right-to-work laws have only about half the unionization rates (percent of workers who belong to unions) of other states.

Source: National Right to Work Committee, http://www.nrtwc.org/. Unionization rates are for 2001 and right-to-work states are as of 2002.

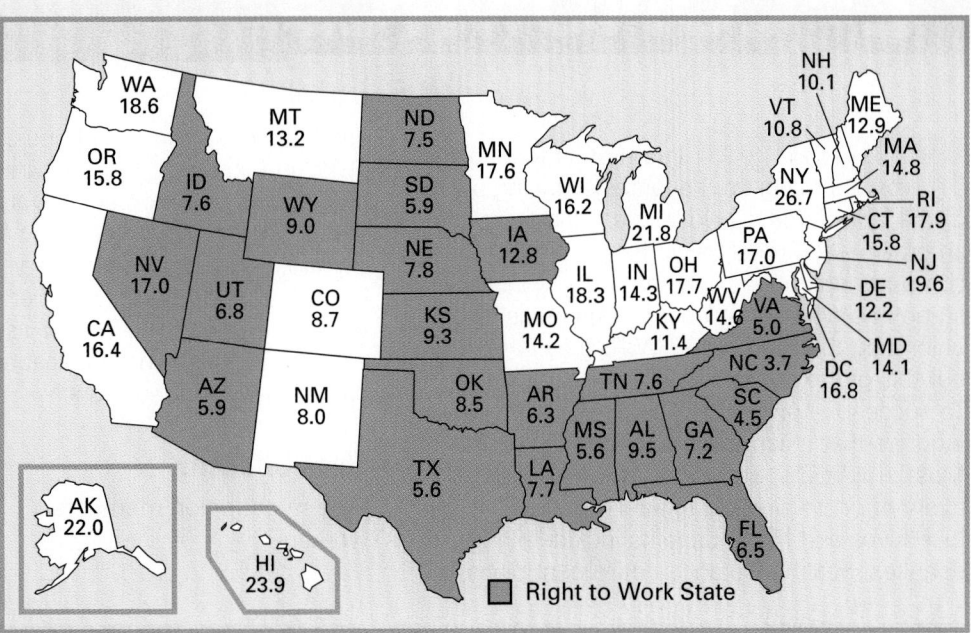

WA 18.6 | MT 13.2 | ND 7.5 | MN 17.6 | NH 10.1 | VT 10.8 | ME 12.9 | MA 14.8 | NY 26.7 | RI 17.9 | CT 15.8 | NJ 19.6 | DE 12.2 | MD 14.1 | DC 16.8 | OR 15.8 | ID 7.6 | WY 9.0 | SD 5.9 | WI 16.2 | MI 21.8 | PA 17.0 | NV 17.0 | UT 6.8 | CO 8.7 | NE 7.8 | IA 12.8 | IL 18.3 | IN 14.3 | OH 17.7 | WV 14.6 | VA 5.0 | CA 16.4 | KS 9.3 | MO 14.2 | KY 11.4 | NC 3.7 | AZ 5.9 | NM 8.0 | OK 8.5 | AR 6.3 | TN 7.6 | SC 4.5 | MS 5.6 | AL 9.5 | GA 7.2 | TX 5.6 | LA 7.7 | FL 6.5 | AK 22.0 | HI 23.9

 Right to Work State

workers now have more education and training and benefit more from physical capital. However, unions played a crucial role in improving wages and working conditions and in calling public attention to labor problems.

Because working conditions and wages are now much better, workers today feel less inclined to join a union, especially in those states where they don't need to join to enjoy union benefits. Fewer union members mean fewer voters who belong to unions, so unions also have lost some political clout. Unions have, in a sense, become the victims of their own success. Here are some other reasons why union membership has declined.

Changes in the Economy

The decline in union membership is due partly to changes in the industrial structure of the U.S. economy. Unions have long been more important in the goods-producing sector than in the service-producing sector. But employment in the goods-producing sector, which includes manufacturing and construction, has fallen in recent decades as a share of all jobs.

Competition from Nonunion Firms

Another factor in the decline of union membership is the growth in market competition, particularly from imports. Increased competition from nonunion employers, both foreign and domestic, has reduced the ability of unionized firms to pass higher labor costs on as higher prices.

Strikes Are Fewer and Less Effective

Finally, the near disappearance of the strike has reduced union power. The 1970s averaged nearly 300 strikes a year involving 1,000 or more workers in the United States. Since 1995, there have been only about 30 such strikes a year. Many recent strikes ended badly for union workers because companies hired permanent replacements. Union members now are more reluctant to strike because of the increased willingness of employers to hire replacements and the increased willingness of workers—both union and nonunion—to cross picket lines.

✓ CHECKPOINT

In what sense is the union movement a victim of its own success?

E-CONOMICS

Unionizing IT

Information technology (IT) workers make up the fastest-growing sector of the labor force. IT workers are the people in an organization responsible for keeping all the computer operations and networks running smoothly. Why aren't labor unions focusing on unionizing these workers? Well, they have tried, but this group poses some special challenges. To succeed, a union must be able to convince workers that it can make a difference for them. Most employers, on the other hand, make every effort to hire and retain IT workers. Incentives and fringe benefits include hiring bonuses, health insurance, retirement plans, stock options, free cell phones, laptops, flextime, and a relaxed work environment. Another problem for union organizers is that IT workers are a collection of full-time workers, telecommuters, part-timers, temporary workers, freelancers, and a growing number of foreign workers on short-term work visas. Unions have a hard time even communicating with such a diverse, independent bunch.

Think Critically

Why might union membership not appeal to IT workers?

9.3 Assessment

Key Concepts

1. What are the potential costs and benefits for striking union members?

2. Why are unions more often successful in negotiating for higher wages with firms that have monopoly power than with firms that are in strong competition?

3. Why is union membership often lower in states that passed right-to-work laws? How did this affect the effectiveness of unions in these states?

Graphing Exercise

4. In the late 1950s, nearly one-third of workers in the United States belonged to a labor union. Since then the share of organized workers has declined steadily. Use data in the table to construct a line graph to show this decline since 1985.

Think Critically

5. **Research** Investigate a recent strike in your state. What issues were involved? What was the result of the strike?

Union Membership as a Percent of the Labor Force, 1985–2000

Year	% of Labor Force Organized
1985	18.0%
1990	16.1
1995	14.9
2000	13.5

to History

Labor
Unions

The United States labor movement had its roots in craft industries and skilled workers. The National Trades Union, the country's first national labor union, did not survive the panic of 1837. Only after the Civil War and the great boom in industrial growth in the United States did the union movement grow, as labor organizers realized the bargaining power of national organizations. The first major union to attempt a national reach was the National Labor Union. Started in 1866 in Baltimore, it grew to 60,000 members by 1872. Unwieldy with a diverse membership drawn from many industries, it failed to survive an economic downturn—the panic of 1873.

A third attempt at a national union was the Knights of Labor. Founded in 1869 in Philadelphia, the Knights had a goal of organizing all workers, skilled and unskilled, men and women. The union took a long-term view of labor reform with issues such as pay equity, the eight-hour workday and the abolition of child labor. The Knights of Labor shied away from using the strike as a tool and played down higher wages as a goal. The broad reforms it sought, and its attempts to unite all segments of the work force, proved difficult, as its members wanted more immediate results. Still, by 1886 it had grown to 750,000 members. In that year, the union was unjustly accused of the bombing of Haymarket Square in Chicago. This led to a public backlash against it and, ultimately, its demise.

Studies show that, unlike those of today, strikes of the 1880s rarely ended in compromise. Only about 10 percent led to something other than total victory for management or labor. The successful strikes for labor—about 50 percent of the total—occurred if the union was supported and the strikes were short. If strikebreakers were employed, the strike likely would fail.

National unions of skilled trades created the American Federation of Labor (AFL), the nation's oldest large-scale labor organization. Unlike the Knights, the AFL wanted to organize skilled workers by craft. Skilled workers were more difficult to replace, giving the unions more bargaining power. It concentrated on small companies that were less likely to be able to bust the unions. Led by Samuel Gompers, the AFL emphasized basic issues such as higher wages, shorter hours, and better working conditions. It pressed for the "closed shop," a workplace where only union members could be hired. Although it questioned the effectiveness of strikes and boycotts, it did use those methods to force employers to engage in collective bargaining. Mediation also came into more common use to settle labor disputes.

THINK CRITICALLY
Using the concepts of supply and demand, explain how a closed shop could be used to control the labor market within an industry.

9 Chapter Assessment

Summary

 Demand and Supply of Resources

a The demand for resources is a *derived demand* that arises from the demand for final goods and services.

b A firm's willingness to hire workers depends on the wage rate and the cost of other resources it needs to produce the products it sells. If the cost of one type of resource increases, the firm will try to substitute a less costly resource. If wage rates fall, the firm will hire more workers because they are relatively less expensive than other resources.

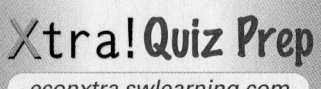
econxtra.swlearning.com

c The quantity of resources available for a firm to purchase depends on the price businesses are willing and able to pay and the alternative uses of those resources. When a wage rate results in the same number of workers seeking employment as there are job openings, the labor market is at the *equilibrium wage.*

d There are many nonwage determinants of labor demand and supply. Nonwage determinants of labor demand include demand for the final product, prices of other resources, and the technology used in production. Nonwage determinants of supply include workers' wealth and working conditions as well as current tastes for work.

9.2 Wage Determination

a Wages differ across labor markets for a variety of reasons, including differences in education, training, and experience. People who contribute labor that has greater value to production tend to be better paid.

b There are many factors related to jobs that result in different levels of compensation for workers. Those who have jobs that involve significant levels of risk, unpleasant locations, or disagreeable tasks often are paid more for their labor. Discrimination also can cause some workers to be paid more or less for their labor.

c The purpose of *minimum wage* legislation is to increase levels of compensation for the nation's lowest-paid workers. Supporters of higher minimum wages say the laws can help low-paid workers improve their standards of living. Opponents suggest that higher minimum wages will reduce the number of jobs offered to low-skill workers.

9.3 Labor Unions

a *Labor unions* are formed when workers join together to improve their pay and working conditions by negotiating labor contracts with their employers. Labor unions fall into two general classifications—craft unions and industrial unions. Craft unions limit membership to workers with a particular skill. Industrial unions are formed by workers in a particular industry who join together.

b Union and management negotiations are carried out through a process called *collective bargaining.* Once a preliminary agreement is reached between the union bargaining team and management, union members vote to either ratify or reject the proposal. Negotiations can be assisted through *mediation* or *binding arbitration,* which involve a neutral third party.

c Unions work to improve wages and working conditions for their members by reducing the supply of labor available to employers or by increasing the demand for labor. This may be accomplished by limiting union membership, increasing demand for union-made products, restricting the supply of non-union-made products, or increasing the productivity of union workers. *Featherbedding* takes place when contracts are negotiated that require employers to hire more workers than they think are needed.

d In recent years union membership has declined. There are many possible reasons for this, including improved wages and working conditions, a reduction in the number of industrial jobs in the U.S. economy, competition from nonunion businesses either within or outside the United States, and the apparent ineffectiveness of *strikes* in recent history.

Review Economic Terms

Choose the term that best fits the definition. On a separate sheet of paper, write the letter of the answer. Some terms may not be used.

_____ 1. A labor union's attempt to withhold labor from a firm

_____ 2. An impartial observer brought in when labor negotiations break down, to suggest how to resolve differences

_____ 3. The process by which representatives of the union and the employer negotiate wages, employee benefits, and working conditions

_____ 4. A state law that says workers do not have to join a union or pay union dues to hold a job

_____ 5. When labor negotiations break down and the public interest is involved, a neutral third party is brought in to impose a settlement both sides must accept

_____ 6. The demand for a resource that arises from the demand for the product that resource produces

_____ 7. One resource works with the other in production; a decrease in the price of one resource increases the demand for the other

_____ 8. One resource can replace another in production; an increase in the price of one resource increases the demand for the other

_____ 9. The wage at which the quantity of labor firms want to hire exactly matches the quantity workers want to supply

_____ 10. The value of output produced by a resource

_____ 11. Establishes a minimum amount that an employer can pay a worker for an hour of labor

_____ 12. A group of workers who join together to seek higher pay and better working conditions by negotiating a labor contract with their employers

_____ 13. Union efforts to force employers to hire more workers than demanded for a task

a. binding arbitration
b. collective bargaining
c. derived demand
d. equilibrium wage
e. featherbedding
f. labor union
g. mediator
h. minimum wage law
i. productivity
j. resource complements
k. resource substitutes
l. right-to-work law
m. strike

Review Economic Concepts

14. The demand for resources is derived from
    a. the demand for products the resources are used to produce.
    b. the demand for higher wages for workers.
    c. the demand for profits by business owners.
    d. the demand for taxes to pay for government services.

15. **True or False** Resource prices provide information to producers that allow them to use resources in a way that maximizes their value.

16. If two resources are __?__, an increase in the price of one will cause businesses to demand less of the other.

17. The market supply of labor will change as a result of each of the following *except*
    a. a change in the amount of wealth workers hold.
    b. a change in the conditions in which employees are expected to work.
    c. a change in the demand for products workers produce.
    d. a change in workers' tastes for being employed in a particular career.

18. **True or False** Some workers are better paid because they have acquired special training that makes their labor more valuable to employers.

19. Which of the following workers would be best paid?

    a. a worker who has not graduated from high school

    b. a worker who just completed a master's degree in English literature

    c. a worker who is willing to stay up all night to guard a bank's deposit box

    d. a worker who helped design Microsoft's Windows 2000 software

20. __?__ takes place when a person is not employed because of his or her race, ethnicity, or gender.

21. **True or False** Membership in industrial unions is limited to workers with a particular skill.

22. When a labor settlement is imposed on management and a union by a neutral third party,

    a. there is a right-to-work law.

    b. binding arbitration has taken place.

    c. there has been mediation.

    d. there is likely to be a strike.

23. __?__ takes place when a contract requires management to hire more workers than it feels are necessary.

24. A craft union is formed when workers who all __?__ join together to form a union.

    a. have the same employer

    b. work in the same area

    c. work in a particular industry

    d. have the same skill

25. __?__ takes place when unions and management negotiate to reach a labor contract.

26. **True or False** In recent years, union membership has declined.

Apply Economic Concepts

27. **Resource Substitutes** The Apex Pot company manufactures high-quality kitchen pans. Currently it employs 500 workers, who produce stainless steel pans one at a time on individual machines. It takes a worker six minutes to produce each item. The workers are paid $12 per hour for their labor. Apex managers have found that they can purchase machines that will produce products with equal quality automatically. One machine costs $200,000 but can produce one pan per minute. So far, management has chosen not to purchase any of the machines. The workers' contract is due to expire next month. Their union has asked to have the wage rate increased to $14 per hour. Apex management has stated that the firm cannot afford to pay them any more than they currently receive. What factors should each side consider during collective bargaining?

28. **Minimum Wage Laws** Imagine that you own a fast-food restaurant. The restaurant employs 20 workers, who are paid the minimum wage of $5.15 per hour. Next month, Congress passes a law that will increase the minimum wage you must pay your workers to $6.15 per hour. What steps could you take to control your production costs and protect your profits?

29. **Labor Unions** Interview a friend or relative who is a member of a labor union. Ask why this person joined a union. Ask what the biggest benefit is of union membership. Write a paragraph summarizing your interview.

30. **Binding Arbitration** You are the president of a fire fighter's union in a large city. There is a law that provides for binding arbitration for vital public employees in your state. The current contract between your union and the

city is about to expire. Your members want at least a 4 percent increase in their wages in each of the next three years. The city has offered a 2 percent raise per year. Negotiators have not been able to reach a decision. The city has said it will call for binding arbitration unless the union accepts its "final offer." If an arbitrator is called in, he or she might award the union more than the city's 2 percent offer. But, you know the city is in a financial bind. The arbitrator could award less than the 2 percent. What recommendation would you make to your members? Explain your reasons for this recommendation.

31. **History** Investigate the Knights of Labor organization after the Civil War. Why was this industrial union largely unsuccessful? What led to its end after 1886? How were the problems it faced different from those labor organizations face today?

32. **Dealing with a Labor Shortage** Consider Marcy, who owns a wedding photography business. She currently employs four photographers, whom she pays $25 per hour. She has more customers than she can serve and would hire another employee if she could find a qualified worker. Unfortunately, few photographers meet her standards. She could hire a photographer away from one of her competitors if she were willing to pay this person $30 per hour. Her current employees then would expect to be paid more, too. Assume that each of her photographers works a 40-hour week. How much more would Marcy have to pay each week to employ this fifth worker? Why might an employer choose not to hire a worker away from a competitor when there is a labor shortage?

33. **Assess a Strike** Garbage collectors in several cities in a state went on strike for better wages and a continuation of their employer-paid medical insurance coverage. At that time, the state and many of its local governments had large budget deficits. They argued that they could not afford to pay the garbage collectors more and demanded that these workers contribute to the cost of their medical coverage. Write an essay that addresses two issues: (1) Should garbage collectors be allowed to strike? Why or why not? (2) Should the garbage collectors be forced to pay all or part of the cost for their medical insurance when it has been totally paid by their employers in the past?

34. **Sharpen Your Life Skills: Working with Percentages** Every month the Bureau of Labor Statistics calculates the *labor force participation rate (LFPR)* This is the percentage of the *civilian noninstitutional population (CNP)* that is either employed or looking for work. Economists believe that this value provides insight into workers' attitudes about the economy by showing how interested they are in working. It is found by dividing the labor force (the total of employed workers and those looking for work) by the CNP. In 2000, the CNP was 209.7 million people. In that same year, there were 135.2 million employed workers and 5.7 million unemployed workers who were actively seeking employment. Calculate the LFPR for 2000. If the LFPR was 67.0% in 2001, what might it show about the economy?

 econxtra.swlearning.com

35. Access **EconDebate Online** at econxtra.swlearning.com. Click on the following policy debate: "Does an increase in the minimum wage result in a higher unemployment rate?" Choose one article that argues in support of increasing the minimum wage and one that argues against it. Summarize each article in a paragraph. Then write a paragraph explaining your opinion on this issue.

10 Financial Markets and Business Growth

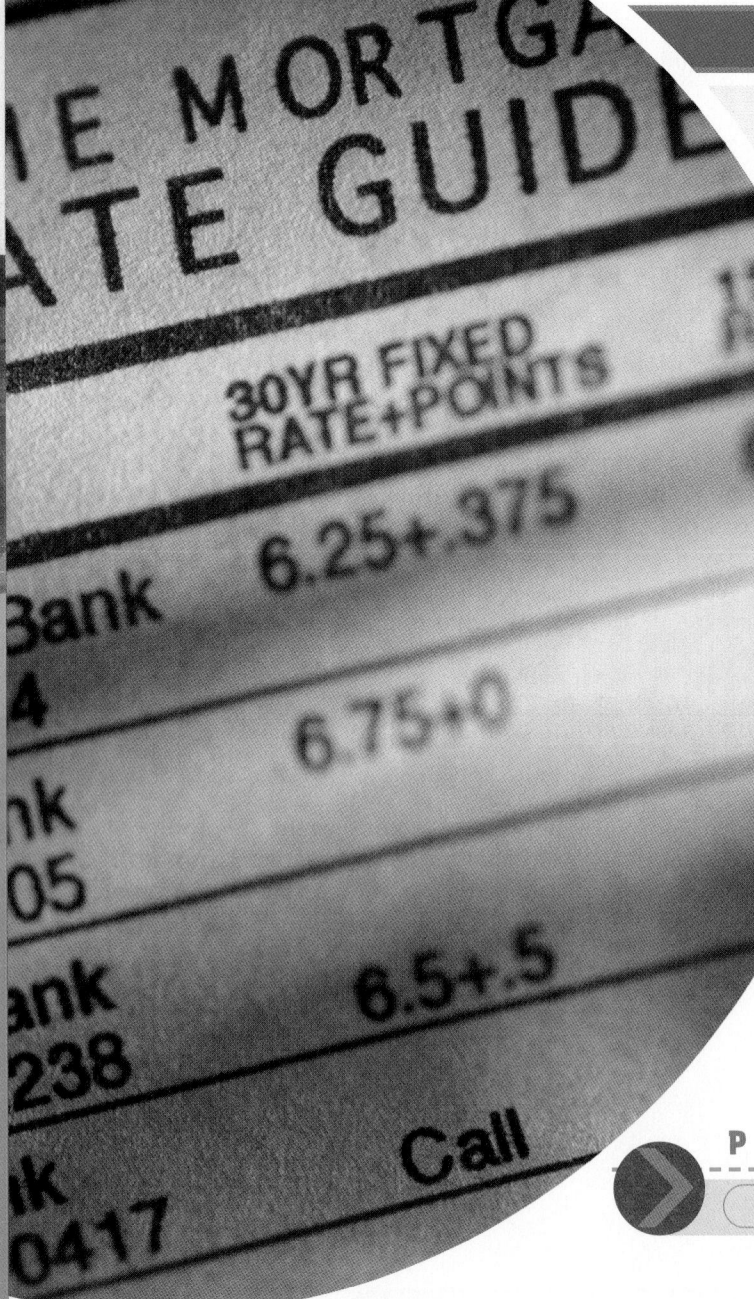

© Getty Images/PhotoDisc

Consider

What's seed money, and why can't Farmer Jones grow anything without it?

Why are you willing to pay more at a first-run movie theater than at other theaters?

Why do you repeatedly burn your mouth eating pizza, despite knowing the risk?

Why is a bank more likely to be called Security Trust than Benny's Bank?

Why do banks charge more interest on car loans than on home loans?

POINT YOUR BROWSER

econxtra.swlearning.com

Objectives

> Explain why production requires savings.

> Explain why people often pay more to consume now.

> Apply demand and supply analysis to the market for loans.

Overview

Time plays an important role in both production and consumption. From an entrepreneur's bright idea for a new product to its delivery to market, production takes time. For example, consider the textbook you are now reading. This book was years in the making and required dozens of specialists, including an author, a project manager, editors, supplement writers, designers, photographers, reviewers, typesetters, paper makers, printers, binders, and marketers. All this effort was made before a single copy was sold, so no revenue was coming in. During the long production process, how did these resource suppliers survive?

Key Terms

interest rate

demand for loans curve

supply of loans curve

market for loans

equilibrium interest rate

[In the News]

● Current Trends in the Mortgage Market

You are sitting quietly in front of your computer monitor, surfing the Internet. Suddenly a pop-up ad appears: "Obtain a 4.25% mortgage. Credit problems are not problems. Approvals on same day of application. Cash Outs. Lender Does Battle for Your Business." Roadside billboards, some with flashing electronic signs, also greet you with current mortgage rates and invitations to visit nearby lenders. Well-known entertainment and sports figures assure you on television that now is the time to refinance your home. Whether you are a 55-year-old suburban dweller or a 15-year-old high-school student, you suddenly are aware that the once-conservative mortgage industry is changing. The industry has evolved overnight into an aggressive, customer-pursuing, market-creating force. Why is this happening now? After all, interest rates were quite low in the late 1990s, but this marketing approach was not in use then. The answer is that vast numbers of homeowners today see refinancing as a way not only to lower the payments on their home mortgage, but also to consolidate all forms of high-interest debt into one low-interest loan. According to mortgage companies, refinancing once made up about 10 to 15 percent of their business. It now makes up about 40 percent. The refinancing homeowners increase the size of their loans by an average of more than $40,000.

Think About It

What do you think has caused the change in approach among mortgage companies? Why are so many homeowners choosing to refinance their homes? What long-term effects do you think this will have on home ownership?

Production and Time

Jones is a primitive farmer in a simple economy. Isolated from any neighbors or markets, he literally scratches out a living on a plot of land, using only crude sticks. While a crop is growing, none of it is available for current consumption.

© Getty Images/PhotoDisc

Farmer Jones must decide whether to invest his time in making a plow. Does adding 50 more bushels a year outweigh the one-time cost of 200 bushels? If you were Farmer Jones, how would you decide?

Production Takes Time

None of the crop is ready for consumption until it grows, so to survive, Jones must rely on food saved from prior harvests while the new crop comes in. The longer the growing season, the more Jones must have saved during prior periods. In this simple example, it is clear that *production cannot occur without savings from prior periods.*

Investment Takes Time

With his current resources of land, labor, seed corn, fertilizer, and some crude sticks, Jones grows about 200 bushels of corn a year. He soon realizes that if he had a plow—*a capital good*—his productivity would increase. Making a plow in such a primitive setting, however, would take time and keep him away from his fields for a year. Thus, the plow has an opportunity cost of 200 bushels of corn. Jones would be unable to survive this drop in production unless he has saved enough from prior harvests. The question is: Should he invest his time in the plow? The answer depends on the costs and benefits of the plow. You already know that the plow's opportunity cost is 200 bushels—the forgone output. The benefit depends on how much the plow will increase production and how long the plow will last. Jones figures that the plow will boost his yield by 50 bushels a year and will last his lifetime. In making the investment decision, he compares current costs to the future stream of benefits.

Capital Increases Labor Productivity

Rather than work the soil with his crude sticks, Jones produces capital to increase his future productivity. Making the plow is an investment of his time. For the economy as a whole, more investment means more capital goods, increasing the economy's ability to produce in the future. This growth can be shown by an expansion of the economy's production possibilities frontier. Advanced industrial economies invest more than other economies.

These additions to capital accumulate over time. Figure 10.1 shows the value of capital goods in the United States in recent years. The combined value of business equipment and business structures, such as factories and buildings, increased from $7.5 trillion in 1991 to $10.2 trillion in 2001. This increase in capital makes U.S. workers more productive.

You can see from the Farmer Jones example why most production cannot occur without prior saving. *Production depends on savings because production of both consumer goods and capital goods takes time. This is time during which consumer goods are not available for current consumption.*

Financial Intermediaries

To modernize the example, suppose Farmer Jones can borrow money. Many farmers visit the bank each spring to borrow enough "seed money" to survive until the crops come in. Likewise, other businesses often borrow at least a portion of the financial capital needed until output gets sold.

The **interest rate** is the price of borrowing—the annual interest expressed as a percentage of the amount borrowed. For example, if the interest rate is 5 percent, the interest

NETBookmark

Bloomberg.com's financial news network provides quick links to the latest key interest rates at its markets web site. Access this site through econxtra.swlearning.com. Click on "Rates and Bonds" under "Market Data." Analyze the trends in the key rates and mortgage rates over the one-year period.

econxtra.swlearning.com

charged is $5 per year for each $100 borrowed. The lower the interest rate, the lower the price of borrowing. The lower the price of borrowing, the more Farmer Jones and other producers are willing and able to borrow.

In a modern economy, producers need not rely exclusively on their own savings. They can borrow the funds needed to help finance a business.

Ask the Xpert!
econxtra.swlearning.com

Why are some rates of interest so much higher than others?

CHECKPOINT
Why does production require savings?

interest rate
Annual interest expressed as a percentage of the amount borrowed or saved

---

Value of Business Structures and Equipment in the United States

Figure 10.1

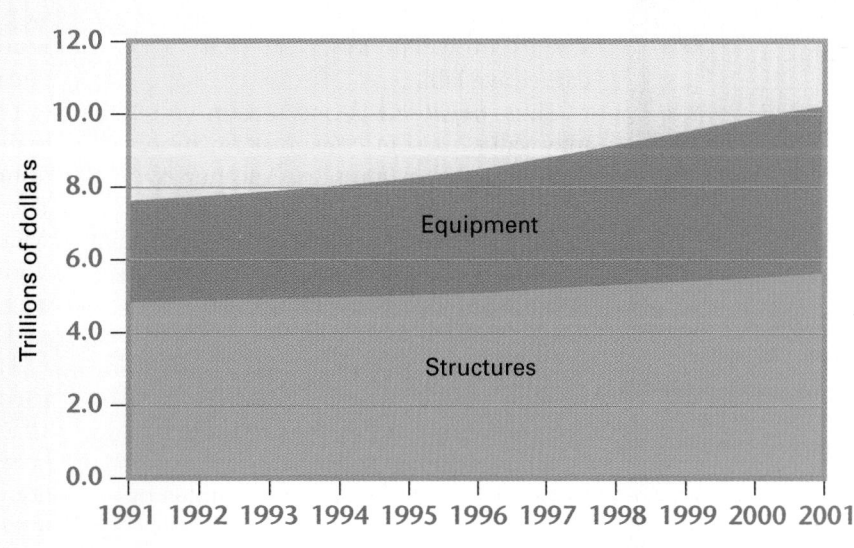

The combined value of business equipment and business structures increased nearly $3 trillion from 1991 to 2001.

Source: Developed from estimates in the U.S. Department of Commerce, *Survey of Current Business,* September 2002, Table 15. Structures include factories, buildings, and other permanent business fixtures. Figures are adjusted to eliminate the effects of inflation.

Consumption and Time

Did you ever burn the roof of your mouth biting into a slice of pizza that hadn't sufficiently cooled? Have you done this more than once? Why do you continue to do this when you know what is likely to happen? You continue because that bite of pizza is worth more to you now than the same bite two minutes from now. You are so anxious to eat that pizza that you are willing to risk burning your mouth rather than wait until it can no longer harm you. In a small way, this reflects the fact that you and other consumers often value *present* consumption more than *future* consumption.

Paying More to Consume Now

When you value present consumption more than future consumption you are willing to pay more to consume now rather than wait. Prices often reflect your greater willingness to pay to consume sooner. Consider the movies. You pay more to see a movie at the theater rather than wait until it comes out on video or DVD. The same is true for books. By waiting for the paperback, you usually save more than half the price of the hardback. Photo developers, dry cleaners, fast-food restaurants, convenience stores, and other suppliers advertise the speed of their services. They know that consumers are willing to pay more for earlier availability.

Thus, *impatience* is one reason you may value present consumption more than future consumption. Another is *uncertainty.* If you wait, something might prevent you from consuming the good. A T-shirt slogan captures this point best: "Life is uncertain. Eat dessert first."

One way to ensure that goods and services can be consumed now is to borrow money to buy these products. Home mortgages, car loans, personal loans, and credit cards are examples of household borrowing. People borrow more when the interest rate declines,

other things constant. For example, home purchases increase when mortgage rates decline.

CHECKPOINT
Why are people often willing to pay more to consume now?

The Market for Loans

You already know that producers are willing to pay interest to borrow money: This borrowing finances the production of consumer goods and capital goods. The simple principles developed for Farmer Jones can be generalized to other producers.

The Demand for Loans

Firms borrow to help fund production and investment. Firms need money to pay for resources until output is produced and sold. Firms also need money to invest in capital, such as machines, trucks, and buildings. The interest rate is the cost of borrowing. The lower the interest rate, other things constant, the more firms are willing and able to borrow. So the demand for loans is a downward-sloping curve. It shows that firms borrow more when the interest rate declines.

Firms are not the only demanders of loans. Households borrow to pay for homes, cars, college tuition, and more. The lower the interest rate, the more willing and able households are to borrow. Therefore, households, like firms, borrow more when the interest rate declines, other things constant. The downward-sloping **demand for loans curve**, labeled *D* in Figure 10.2, reflects the negative relationship between the interest rate and the quantity of loans demanded. The lower the interest rate, the greater the quantity of loans demanded, other things constant.

demand for loans curve

A downward-sloping curve showing the negative relationship between the interest rate and the quantity of loans demanded, other things constant

Role of Interest Rates: Market for Loans

Figure 10.2

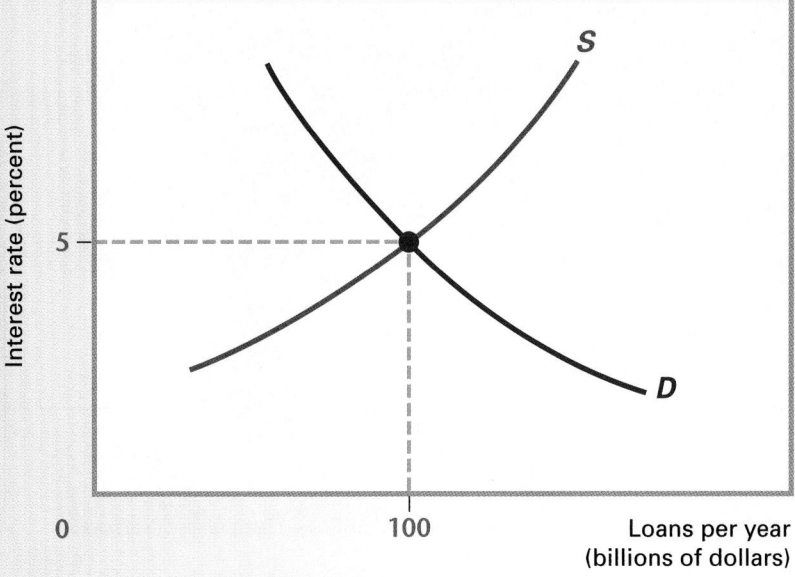

The quantity of loans demanded is inversely related to the rate of interest. The quantity of loans supplied is directly related to the interest rate. The equilibrium rate of interest, 5 percent, is determined at the intersection of the demand curve and supply curve for loans.

The interest rate rises or falls to balance the amount saved with the amount borrowed. What if the initial interest rate was 8 percent? *The equilibrium interest rate determines the allocation of scarce resources in the economy between present uses and future uses.* In the market for loans, who trades present spending for future spending, and who trades future spending for the ability to spend now?"

The Supply of Loans

What about the supply of loans? Because you and other consumers often value present consumption more than future consumption, you must be rewarded to postpone consumption. The amount saved during the year equals income minus consumption. When they save a portion of their incomes in financial institutions such as banks, households give up present consumption in return for interest. *Interest is the reward for not consuming now.*

People delay present consumption for a greater ability to consume in the future. The higher the interest rate, other things constant, the greater the reward for saving, so the more people save. Savers are the suppliers of loans.

The more saved, the greater the quantity of loans supplied.

The **supply of loans curve**, labeled *S* in Figure 10.2, shows the positive relationship between the interest rate and the quantity of loans supplied, other things constant. As you can see, this supply of loans curve slopes upward.

Market Interest Rate

The demand for loans and the supply of loans come together in the market for loans to determine the market interest rate, as in Figure 10.2. The **market for loans** brings together borrowers, or demanders of loans, and savers, or suppliers of loans, to determine the market rate of interest. The interest rate is the price of borrowing and the reward for

supply of loans curve

An upward-sloping curve showing the positive relationship between the interest rate and the quantity of loans supplied, other things constant

market for loans

The market that brings together borrowers (the demanders of loans) and savers (the suppliers of loans) to determine the market interest rate

The demand for loans and the supply of loans come together in the market for loans to determine the market interest rate. In this photograph, representatives of the bank are working with the couple on the left to fill out loan applications. Who is demanding the loans, and who is supplying the loans?

© Getty Images/PhotoDisc

equilibrium interest rate

The only interest rate at which the quantity of loans demanded equals the quantity of loans supplied

saving. In this case, the **equilibrium interest rate** of 5 percent is the only one that exactly matches the intentions of savers and borrowers. Here, the equilibrium quantity of loans is $100 billion per year.

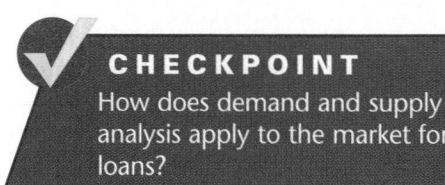

CHECKPOINT
How does demand and supply analysis apply to the market for loans?

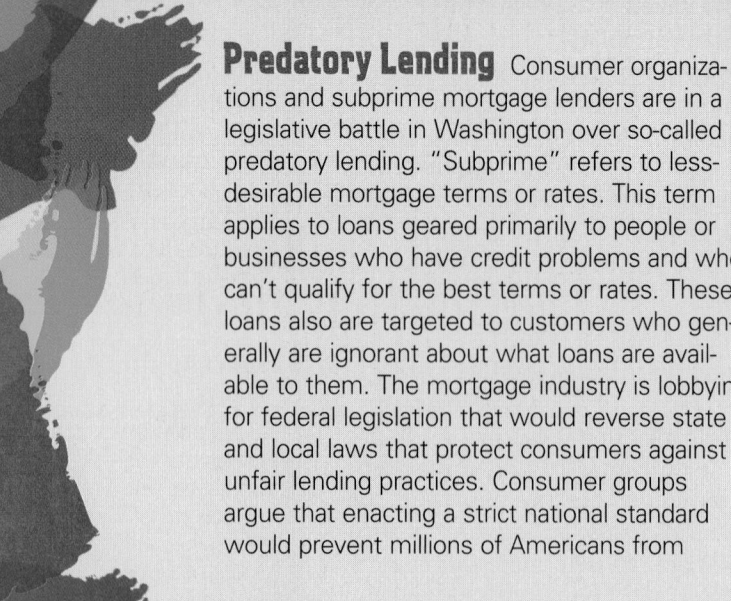

Ethics in Action

Predatory Lending Consumer organizations and subprime mortgage lenders are in a legislative battle in Washington over so-called predatory lending. "Subprime" refers to less-desirable mortgage terms or rates. This term applies to loans geared primarily to people or businesses who have credit problems and who can't qualify for the best terms or rates. These loans also are targeted to customers who generally are ignorant about what loans are available to them. The mortgage industry is lobbying for federal legislation that would reverse state and local laws that protect consumers against unfair lending practices. Consumer groups argue that enacting a strict national standard would prevent millions of Americans from

losing these protections. In the most abusive instances, predatory lending activities have destroyed the equity borrowers had built up in their homes over many years. In far too many cases, borrowers have lost their homes. Many of these people, particularly older Americans, have been persuaded or fooled by unethical salespeople into borrowing against their home equity, often to pay for unnecessary, high-priced home renovations. Still others have been charged sky-high fees and interest rates.

Think Critically

Do you think that laws against predatory lending should be at the state or local level or at the national level? Explain your answer.

Key Concepts

1. Why couldn't you open up a pizza restaurant tomorrow if you wanted to?

2. Before the 1970s there were no hand-held electronic calculators. When these products first became available, they cost about $100 each. Why were people willing to invest so much in a calculator that could only add, subtract, multiply, and divide? How did the calculator change workers' productivity?

3. Why were many more consumers willing to buy automobiles when manufacturers offered special 0 percent interest rates in 2002?

4. Why do most people borrow funds to purchase a home or an automobile rather than wait until they can afford to pay cash?

5. What happens to the demand for loans that causes the equilibrium interest rate to fall during a downturn in the economy?

Graphing Exercise

6. Home mortgage interest rates change over time with the demand and supply for loans. Use data given in the table to construct a line graph that shows the annual average for new-home mortgage interest rates from 1993 through 2002. How much did this interest rate fall from 2000 through 2002? How important is a change of 1 percent in the mortgage interest rate to a person who wants to borrow $100,000 to buy a home?

New Home Mortgage Interest Rates, 1993–2002

Year	Interest Rate	Year	Interest Rate
1993	7.20%	1998	7.07%
1994	7.49	1999	7.04
1995	7.87	2000	7.52
1996	7.80	2001	7.00
1997	7.71	2002	6.43

Think Critically

7. **Financial Management** Most businesses rely on borrowed money. In the early 1980s, interest rates were very high in the United States, reaching levels of 20 percent of more. How would such high interest rates affect businesses and, therefore, the overall economy?

8. **Advertising** Businesses that market expensive consumer products such as refrigerators, computers, and home furnishings typically include statements about "easy payment plans" in their ads. Why do they include this information? If many consumers choose to borrow to finance their purchases, what will this do to the demand for loans and interest rates?

Objectives

> Explain the role of banks in bringing borrowers and savers together.

> Understand why interest rates differ among types of loans.

> Identify and discuss a corporation's sources of financial capital.

Overview

You now understand why borrowers are willing to pay interest and why savers expect to be paid interest. Banks serve both groups. Banks are willing to pay interest on consumer savings because the banks can, in turn, charge higher rates of interest to those who need credit, such as farmers, home buyers, college students, and entrepreneurs looking to start or expand a business. Banks bring borrowers and savers together and try to earn a profit by serving both groups.

Key Terms

financial intermediaries

credit

line of credit

prime rate

collateral

initial public offering (IPO)

dividends

retained earnings

bond

securities

[In the News]

● The Bank that Never Closes

Juniper Bank never closes. It's open 24 hours a day, 365 days a year. With Internet access, bank customers can pay bills, check account balances, and borrow money from anywhere in the world. Juniper was one of the nation's first virtual banks—one of the first authorized to offer banking services on the Internet. The bank can accept deposits from customers in all 50 states. All accounts are FDIC insured. Because Internet banks don't have to spend money on buildings and bank tellers, they can offer their customers higher interest rates on savings accounts. When it comes to getting cash and making deposits, however, virtual bank customers do need a physical connection. Juniper Bank customers can get cash at thousands of ATM locations. Deposits are accepted at ATMs, through the mail, direct deposit, electronic transfers, and at any of the 4,200 Mail Boxes Etc. locations. With the easy access offered by Internet banks such as Juniper Bank, customers increasingly are shopping nationwide for the best rates for deposits, credit cards, and loans.

Think About It

What, if any, impact do you think additional competition from online banks will have on interest rates on savings accounts?

Banks as Intermediaries

Banks accumulate funds from savers and lend these funds to borrowers, thereby serving as **financial intermediaries** between the two groups. Savers need a safe place for their money. Borrowers need **credit**, which is the ability to borrow now, based on the promise of repayment in the future.

Serving Savers and Borrowers

Savers are looking for a safe place for their money. Banks try to inspire confidence among savers. Banks usually present an image of trust and assurance. For example, banks are more likely to be called First Trust or Security National than Benny's Bank or Easy Money Bank and Trust.

Banks gather various amounts from savers and repackage these funds into the amounts demanded by borrowers. Some savers need their money back next week, some next year, and others, only after retirement. Likewise, different borrowers need credit for different lengths of time. Some need credit only for a short time, such as the farmer who borrows until the crop comes in. Homebuyers need credit for up to 30 years. Banks, as intermediaries, offer desirable durations to both savers and borrowers.

Banks Specialize in Loans

As lenders, banks try to identify borrowers who are willing to pay interest and are able to repay the loans. Because of their experience and expertise, banks can judge the creditworthiness of loan applicants better than an individual saver could. Because banks have experience in drawing up and enforcing contracts with borrowers, they can do so more efficiently than an individual saver lending money directly to a borrower.

Thus, savers are better off dealing with banks than making loans directly to borrowers. The economy is more efficient because banks develop expertise in evaluating borrowers, structuring loans, and enforcing loan contracts. In short, *banks reduce the transaction costs of channeling savings to creditworthy borrowers.*

Reducing Risk Through Diversification

By lending funds to many borrowers rather than lending just to a single borrower, banks reduce the risk to each individual saver. A bank, in effect, lends a tiny fraction of each saver's deposit to each of the many borrowers. If one borrower fails to repay a loan, this failure will hardly affect a large, diversified bank. However, if someone lends his or her life's savings directly to a borrower who defaults on the loan, that would be a financial disaster for the lender.

financial intermediaries
Banks and other institutions that serve as go-betweens, accepting funds from savers and lending them to borrowers

credit
The ability to borrow now, based on the promise of repayment in the future

© PHOTO CREDIT/STONE

What are the benefits of saving your money in a bank?

E-CONOMICS

Identity Theft

The Federal Trade Commission (FTC) reports that more than 40 percent of all consumer complaints it receives involve identity theft. Identity theft basically is someone assuming your identity for the purpose of stealing your money or obtaining and using credit in your name. Many experts expect this problem to grow, due to easy access to personal information via the Internet and the minimal penalties given to identity thieves who are caught. One identity-theft ring stole the personal data and complete credit histories of more than 30,000 people, generating $2.7 million in fraud. The theft was traced to a credit bureau employee who used the Internet and stolen passwords in the scheme. To obtain a new credit card in your name, all an identity thief needs is your Social Security number and a birth date. With a few additional bits of your personal data, the thief is able to get loans, start up utility accounts—even wipe out your bank accounts.

Not only do you end up in debt with no money in the bank, but your credit is destroyed as well. Businesses are doing what they can to stop the thieves. Some banks now include photos and special holograms on credit cards. Many restaurants are installing a new wireless device that allows customers to swipe their own credit cards at the table. Individuals also must take personal responsibility to avoid becoming victims. The experts' best advice is to avoid revealing any part of your Social Security number to anyone. Shredding papers with personal information and destroying your credit card receipts also is strongly advised. Once targeted, experts estimate that the victim of identity theft can expect to spend more than 175 hours and more than $1,100 on setting things right.

Think Critically

How does identity theft affect interest rates on the credit cards you have?

---

line of credit
An arrangement with a bank through which a business can quickly borrow needed cash

Line of Credit

Businesses often need to borrow during the year to fund those stretches when sales are low. For example, many retail businesses sell most of their output during the Christmas shopping season. These firms may need to borrow to get through those months when little is sold. Because of these fluctuations in cash needs, many businesses negotiate a **line of credit** with a bank. This allows the business to access cash as needed during the year. For example, the business applies for a line of credit of, say, $200,000. If the application is approved, the business can draw on that line of credit as needed without having to fill out a loan application each time. This line of credit is equivalent to a consumer's credit-card limit.

NET Bookmark

Access tips for safe Internet banking from the Federal Deposit Insurance Corporation (FDIC) web site through econxtra.swlearning.com. What can you do to protect your privacy if you choose to do your banking online? Write a paragraph explaining your answer.

econxtra.swlearning.com

CHECKPOINT
How do banks serve as financial intermediaries between borrowers and savers?

Why Interest Rates Differ

So far, the discussion has focused on the market rate of interest, as if there were only one interest rate in the economy. At any particular time, however, a range of interest rates coexists. For example, there are different interest rates applied to home mortgages, car loans, personal loans, business loans, and credit card balances. Figure 10.3 shows interest rates for loans in various markets. The lowest is the so-called **prime rate**, the interest rate lenders charge the most trustworthy business borrowers. The highest is the rate charged on credit card balances. Why do interest rates differ?

Risk

Some borrowers are more likely than others to *default* on their loans—that is, to not pay them back. Before a bank lends money, it usually requires that a borrower put up **collateral**. This is an asset owned by the borrower that can be sold to repay the loan in the event of a default. With business loans, any valuable assets owned by the firm serve as collateral. With a home mortgage, the home itself becomes collateral. With car loans, the car becomes collateral.

Investigate Your Local Economy

Identify three banks in your area. Contact the banks or access their web sites to find the interest rates they currently apply to home mortgages, car loans, personal loans, business loans, and credit card balances. Compare the results in spreadsheet format. Share your results in class. Are the interest rates consistent among banks for each of the categories?

The more valuable the collateral backing up the loan, the lower the interest rate charged on that loan. The interest rate charged on car loans is higher than on home loans. A car loses its value more quickly than a home, and it can be driven away by a defaulting borrower. Thus, a car is not as good collateral as a home. Interest rates are

prime rate

The interest rate lenders charge for loans to their most trustworthy business borrowers

collateral

An asset owned by the borrower that can be sold to pay off the loan in the event the loan is not repaid

---

Interest Rates Charged for Different Types of Loans

Figure 10.3

Generally, the less collateral associated with a loan, the higher the interest rate will be.

Source: Federal Reserve Board. Interest rates are annual averages during 2002, except for prime rate, which is for December 2002.

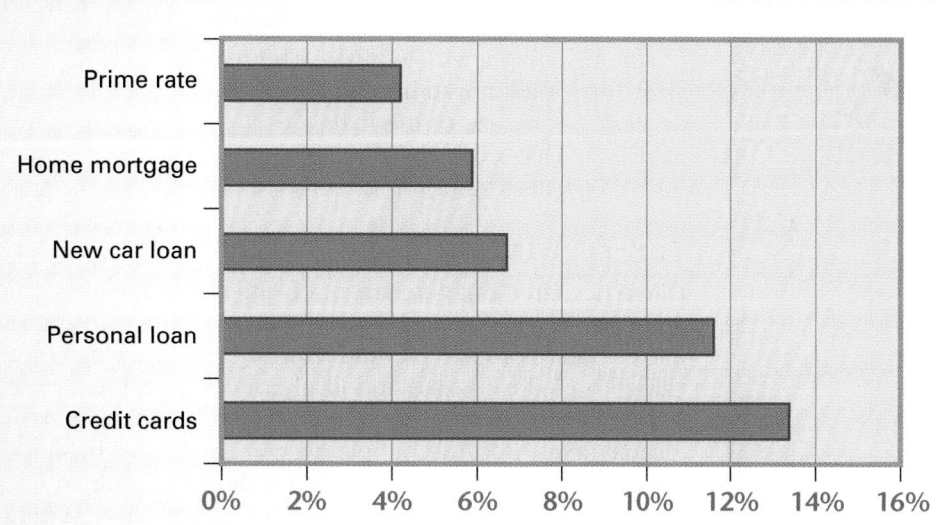

CHECKPOINT
Why do interest rates differ for
different types of loans?

Reading It Right What's the relevance of the following statement from *The Wall Street Journal:* "The Mortgage Bankers Association of America said the percentage of borrowers who fell behind on their mortgage loans rose to a seasonally adjusted 4.62% in the second quarter, from 4.52% the previous quarter. The delinquency rate for loans insured by the Federal Housing Administration, a government program that helps first-time home buyers, rose more sharply to a record 12.59%, from 11.65% in the first quarter."

higher still for personal loans and credit cards, because there usually is no collateral at all with these loans.

Duration of the Loan

The future is uncertain, and the further into the future a loan is to be repaid, the more uncertain that repayment becomes. Thus, under normal circumstances, as the duration of a loan increases, the interest rate charged increases to compensate for the greater risk. For example, the annual interest rate on a 10-year loan typically is higher than on a 1-year loan.

Cost of Administration

The costs of executing the loan agreement, monitoring the loan, and collecting payments are called the *administration costs* of the loan. These costs, as a proportion of the loan, decrease as the size of the loan increases. For example, the cost of administering a $100,000 loan is not much greater than the cost of administering a $10,000 loan. The relative cost of administering the loan declines as the size of the loan increases. This reduces the interest rate for larger loans, other things constant.

Tax Treatment

Differences in the tax treatment of different types of loans also will affect the interest rate. For example, the interest earned on loans to state and local governments is not subject to federal income taxes. Because people do not have to pay federal income taxes on this interest, they are more willing to lend money to state and local governments.

Corporate Finance

During the Industrial Revolution, labor-saving machinery made large-scale production more profitable. However, building huge factories filled with heavy machinery required substantial sums—more money than any single bank would lend. The corporate structure became the easiest way to finance such investments, and by 1920, corporations accounted for most employment and output in the U.S. economy.

You know that a corporation is a legal entity, distinct from its shareholders. The corporation may own property, earn a profit, borrow, and sue or be sued. Stockholders, the owners of the corporation, are liable for company debts up to the amount of their investment in the firm.

Corporate Stock

Suppose you have developed a recipe for a spicy chili that your friends have convinced you will be a best seller. You start a sole proprietorship called Six-Alarm Chili. As the founder, you are that firm's entrepreneur. Recall that entrepreneurs are profit-seeking decision makers. They begin with a good idea, organize a business to make that idea happen, and assume the risk of its operation.

Your chili company meets with early success. You believe, however, that you need to achieve economies of scale to remain competitive. To do that, you need to grow faster than your own savings or company profits would allow. To obtain the funds you need for expansion, you decide to incorporate the business. The newly incorporated company issues 1,000,000 shares of stock. You award yourself 100,000 shares. You, in effect, pay for your shares with "sweat equity," or all the hard work you did to get the company rolling. The remaining shares are sold to the public for $10 per share. This raises $9 million for the company.

Corporations issue and sell stock to fund operations and to pay for new plants and equipment. The initial sale of stock to the public is called an **initial public offering (IPO)**. A share of corporate stock represents a claim on the net income and assets of a corporation. Each share gives the shareholder one vote on corporate issues.

Corporations must pay corporate income taxes on any profit. After-tax profit is either paid as **dividends** to shareholders or reinvested in the corporation. Reinvested profit, or **retained earnings**, allows the firm to grow more. The corporation is not required to pay dividends. Young firms usually pay no dividends. They prefer instead to put any profit back into the firm so it can grow faster. For example, Six-Alarm Chili might use its retained earnings to enter additional geographic markets.

Once shares of stock are issued, their price tends to fluctuate directly with the firm's potential for earning a profit. People buy stock because of the dividends they hope to receive. They also hope the value of the stock will increase over time.

Corporate Borrowing

Your corporation can acquire financial capital by issuing stock, retaining earnings, or borrowing. To borrow money, the corporation can go to a bank for a loan. Such loans usually are for short durations—from a matter of months to two or three years. For longer-term borrowing, corporations will usually issue bonds. A **bond** is the corporation's promise to pay back the holder a fixed sum of money on the designated *maturity date* plus make annual interest payments until that date. For example, a corporation might sell bonds of $1,000 each, which promise the bond buyer annual interest of, say, $50 plus the $1,000 back at the end of 20 years. Corporate bonds have maturity dates as short as two years and as long as 30 years.

The payment stream to those who own bonds is more predictable than that for those who own stocks. Unless the corporation goes bankrupt, it must pay bondholders the promised amounts. On the other hand, stockholders are last in line when resource holders get paid. Because bondholders get paid before stockholders, bonds are considered less risky than stocks. Less risk means lower returns. Stocks have outperformed bonds in all decades.

Securities Exchanges

Both stocks and bonds are called **securities**. Securities are represented on pieces of paper. In the case of a share of stock, the security shows how much of the corporation the stockholder owns. In the case of a bond, it shows how much the corporation owes the bondholder.

Once corporations have issued stocks and bonds, owners of these securities are usually free to resell them on *security exchanges*. In the United States, there are seven security exchanges registered with the Securities and Exchange

© Getty Images/PhotoDisc

Stock certificates show how much of the corporation a shareholder owns. How does the information on a stock certificate differ from the information on a bond certificate?

Commission (SEC), the federal body that regulates securities markets. The two largest are the New York Stock Exchange, which trades the stock of more than 3,300 major corporations, and the NASDAQ, which trades more than 4,000 corporate stocks, many of them technology companies.

Nearly all the securities traded each day are *secondhand securities* in the sense that they have already been sold by the corporation. Therefore, the bulk of daily transactions do not finance firms in need of investment funds. The money goes from a securities buyer to a securities seller. By providing a *secondary market* for securities, exchanges enhance the *liquidity* of these securities—that is, the exchanges make the securities more easily sold for cash. This ready conversion into cash makes securities more attractive.

More than half the trading volume on major exchanges is done by *institutional investors*, such as banks, insurance com-panies, and mutual funds. A *mutual fund* issues stock to individual investors and with the proceeds buys a portfolio of securities.

The secondary market for stocks also determines the current market value of a corporation. The market value of a firm at any given time can be found by multiplying the share price by the number of shares outstanding. The share price reflects the current value of the expected profit. For example, General Electric, one of the most valu-able U.S. corporations, had a market value of $315.9 billion at the close of business on September 16, 2003. At that time, the market value of all publicly traded U.S corporations was more than $15 trillion.

CHECKPOINT

What are the sources of financial capital for a corporation?

© Getty Images/PhotoDisc

Buyers and sellers of securities come together through their representatives in the trading room of stock exchanges. Why are most securities transactions said to take place in the secondary market for securities?

Key Concepts

1. Why are banks often unwilling to provide mortgage loans to people who want to purchase homes in urban neighborhoods with high crime rates and decreasing home values?

2. Would you rather lend a friend $50 until she gets paid tomorrow or until the end of the school year when she hopes to find a summer job? What does this tell you about the interest rates that are charged for short- and long-term loans?

3. Why might a corporation prefer to raise funds by selling stock than by borrowing money from a bank?

4. Why are stock exchanges necessary for corporations to successfully market stocks to the public?

Graphing Exercise

5. Corporations sell new issues of stock to the public to finance expansion and to obtain operating funds. The amount of new stock sold is one indicator of how much business activity is taking place in the economy. Construct a bar graph from the data in the table that shows the value of new stock sold by U.S. corporations between 1992 and 2000. What does your graph tell you about the U.S. economy during these years?

New Public Stock Issues, 1992–2002
Values in Billions of Dollars

Year	New Stock Issues
1992	$ 88.3
1993	122.5
1994	84.6
1995	99.7
1996	149.6
1997	154.4
1998	176.6
1999	217.4
2000	291.2

Think Critically

6. **History** Investigate the development of the NASDAQ market. Why have many high-tech corporations chosen to be listed on the NASDAQ rather than on a centralized exchange, such as the New York Stock Exchange?

7. **Communication** Identify a publicly traded corporation that does business in your community. Imagine that this firm wants to raise funds by issuing new stock. Write a letter that could be sent to potential investors that explains why they should consider buying shares of this firm's newly issued stock.

Sharpen Your Life Skills

Make Inferences

One of the most important factors businesses consider when they decide whether to make an investment is the interest rate they must pay to borrow funds. Large businesses pay the *prime rate.* Smaller firms usually pay prime plus one or two percent. The prime interest rate often is influenced by the Federal Reserve System (the Fed). If the Fed wants to encourage businesses to borrow and invest more money, it can push the prime interest rate down. If it wants businesses to invest fewer dollars, the Fed can pull the prime rate up. The table indicates the average prime interest rates charged by banks from 1993 through 2002. What do these data show about the Fed's interest-rate policies in these years?

Apply Your Skill

1. Suppose that economic conditions improve by 2005 and the economy is booming. What would this do to the demand for loans, the supply of loans, and the level of interest rates that the Fed would like to have banks change? Considering all of these factors, what would you expect to happen to interest rates under these conditions? Explain your reasons.

2. Suppose Congress passes a law that eliminates the federal income tax on interest income. As a result, individuals and banks are able to keep all the interest income they receive. What would this do to the supply of loans available and the prevailing interest rates charged to those who borrow?

Prime Interest Rates Charged by U.S. Banks, 1993–2002

Year	Prime Interest Rate	Year	Prime Interest Rate
1993	6.00%	1998	8.35
1994	7.15	1999	8.00
1995	8.83	2000	9.23
1996	8.27	2001	6.91
1997	8.44	2002	4.67

Objectives

> Recognize the role of profit and franchising in business growth.

> Identify the types of corporate mergers and the four merger waves that occurred during the last century.

> Examine the multinational corporation as a source of corporate growth.

Overview

Some owners of small businesses, such as grocers, plumbers, or pizza makers, are quite content running a small operation. They have no plans for expanding their businesses. However, many entrepreneurs who develop a profitable business want to see the business grow. Perhaps the business needs to grow to achieve economies of scale or to become more competitive in its market. Maybe the owner believes the product could be profitably sold across the country or around the world. Whatever the reason, owners often believe that growth is desirable to maximize profits. Several growth strategies are available for business owners. These include franchising the business, merging with other firms, and operating globally with a multinational corporation.

Key Terms

vertical merger

conglomerate merger

multinational corporation (MNC)

[In the News]

● Banks Are Changing the Combination

In the 1990s, banks began a merger spree, making new and bigger combinations to provide consumers with one-stop shopping for insurance, stocks, bonds, credit cards, checking accounts, and every other kind of financial service. Why the change? In the past, banks would lend you money, charge some interest, and wait for you to repay it. Today, that simple approach has changed. Banks continue to make loans and charge interest on car loans, mortgages, credit cards, and the like. However, instead of handling the loans themselves, they now package loans together and sell them to pension funds or insurance companies that have huge sums of money to invest. Banks no longer hold your mortgage for the money it would make on the interest charged. Rather, the bank now makes money from you by charging upfront fees for selling you the loan. It then charges the group that bought the loan package fees for collecting the payments from you. Banks are merging into bigger and more diverse institutions to maximize their assets and expand their fee-based services.

Think About It

What do you think are the advantages and disadvantages to consumers of the growth of banks through mergers and acquisitions?

Profit and Growth

Profitability is the surest path to firm growth, regardless of the type of business. A profitable firm can reinvest earnings, and the more profit, the faster that firm can grow. This is true whether the firm is a sole proprietorship, partnership, or corporation. Firm owners are more willing to invest their own savings in a business if it is profitable. Profitable firms also find it easier to borrow the financial capital needed for expansion. Banks are more willing to lend to businesses that are profitable, because such firms are more able to pay back their loans.

To summarize, more profitable firms can grow faster because

1. more profits can be reinvested into the firm

2. owners are willing to invest more of their own money in such firms

3. banks are more willing to lend to such firms.

Corporate Profits and Growth

Corporate profitability opens up paths of growth that are not available to sole proprietorships or partnerships. The greater a corporation's profit, other things constant, the higher the value of shares on the stock market. The higher the value of the shares, the more money a corporation can raise by issuing new shares. Unprofitable corporations cannot sell new shares easily. More profitable corporations also find it easier to borrow from banks or to sell bonds. The more profitable the corporation, the lower the interest charged on bank loans and on corporate bonds.

Thus, financial markets allocate funds more readily to profitable corporations than to corporations in financial difficulty. Some corporations may be in such poor shape that they cannot issue stocks or bonds. *Securities markets promote the survival of the fittest by lending financial capital to those firms that seem able to make the most profitable use of those funds.*

Franchises

One way a business with a successful product can grow quickly is by franchising that product. A *franchise* is a contract between a parent company (franchiser) and another business or individual (franchisee). For a fee, the parent company grants the franchisee the exclusive right to sell a certain product in a given region.

The franchiser supplies the retailer with a brand name, production and marketing experience, and other expertise. The parent firm can achieve economies of scale in research and development, building design, business practices, and promoting the brand name.

Franchises allow people with limited experience to enter a business. They are guided by the franchise plan, which can reduce their risk of failure. Most important is the brand name and reputation that comes with a franchise. Popular franchise programs also increase customer awareness of the business because many businesses operate in different locations using the same franchise name and promotions.

The franchise has been common for decades with gas stations and auto dealers. Of growing importance are franchise structures for hotels, fast-food outlets, and restaurants. There are now more than 4,000 franchisers in the United States.

NETBookmark

McDonald's maintains a web page devoted to information about obtaining a franchise. Access this web page through econxtra.swlearning.com. Look over the FAQ file. How much cash does a potential franchisee currently need to qualify? How many partners can be involved in a McDonald's franchise? Who selects the sites? Who constructs the building?

econxtra.swlearning.com

CHECKPOINT
Why do more profitable firms
usually grow faster?

Corporate Mergers

One way a firm can double its size
overnight is by merging with another
firm of equal size. Mergers represent the
quickest path to growth.

Types of Mergers

Horizontal mergers occur when one
firm combines with another firm making
the same product, such as Exxon
merging with Mobil. With a **vertical
merger**, one firm combines with
another from which it buys inputs or to
which it sells output. An example of a
vertical merger would be one between
a steel producer and an automaker.
Finally, a **conglomerate merger** is a
combination of firms in different industries, such as a merger between a plastics maker and an electronics firm.
There have been four merger waves in
this country over the last century. They
are summarized in Figure 10.4.

First Merger Wave: 1887–1904

In the last half of the nineteenth
century, two important developments
caused firms to get big quickly. First,
technological breakthroughs led to more
extensive use of capital, increasing the
minimum efficient size of manufacturing
firms. Second, transportation costs
declined as railroads increased from
9,000 miles of track in 1850 to 167,000
miles of track by 1890. *Economies of scale
and cheaper transportation costs extended the
geographical size of markets.* Firms grew
larger to reach markets over a broader
geographical area. Mergers offered an
opportunity to get bigger quicker.

Mergers during this first wave tended
to be horizontal. For example, the firm
that is U.S. Steel today was created in
1901 through a billion-dollar merger that
involved dozens of individual steel producers and two-thirds of the industry's
production capacity. During this first
wave, similar merger trends occurred in
Canada, Great Britain, and elsewhere.
This first merger wave created dominant
firms, some of which still survive today,
more than a century later.

vertical merger
One firm combines
with another from
which it buys inputs
or to which it sells
output, such as a
merger between a
steel producer and
an automaker

**conglomerate
merger**
One firm combines
with another firm in
a different industry,
such as a merger
between a plastics
maker and an
electronics firm

Merger Waves in the Past Century

Figure 10.4

Four distinct
merger waves
took place in the
United States
between 1887
and 2000.

Wave	Years	Dominant Type of Merger	Examples	Stimulus
First	1887–1904	Horizontal	U.S. Steel, Standard Oil	Span national markets
Second	1916–1929	Vertical	Copper refiners with fabricators	Stock market boom
Third	1948–1969	Conglomerate	Litton Industries	Diversification
Fourth	1982–2000	Horizontal and vertical	Banking, tele-communications, health services, insurance	Span national and global markets, stock market boom

Second Merger Wave: 1916–1929

The first merger wave cooled with the introduction of antitrust laws. Because these laws restrained horizontal mergers, vertical mergers became more common during the second merger wave. This wave of mergers took place between 1916 and 1929. A vertical merger combines firms at different stages of the production process. For example, a copper refiner merges with a copper fabricator. The stock market boom of the 1920s fueled this second wave, but the stock market crash in 1929 stopped it cold.

Third Merger Wave: 1948–1969

The Great Depression and World War II slowed merger activity for two decades. The third merger wave began after the war. More than 200 of the 1,000 largest firms in 1950 had disappeared by the early 1960s as a result of this merger wave. Between 1948 and 1969, many large firms were absorbed by other, usually larger, firms. The third merger wave peaked in a frenzy of activity between 1964 and 1969. During this time, conglomerate mergers accounted for four-fifths of all mergers.

Merging firms were looking to diversify their product mix and perhaps reduce costs by producing a variety of goods. For example, Litton Industries combined firms that made calculators, appliances, electrical equipment, and machine tools. As it turned out, this strategy didn't seem to work very well. Conglomerate mergers stretched management expertise and lost the efficiency gains that spring from specialization and comparative advantage. The firm resulting from a conglomerate merger no longer focused on producing a particular product efficiently. It tried to produce all kinds of different products efficiently, which proved too challenging for some corporate executives.

Fourth Merger Wave: 1982–2000

The fourth merger wave began in 1982 and involved both horizontal and vertical mergers. Some large conglomerate mergers of the 1960s were undone during this latest wave as firms tried to focus on what they did best and sell off unrelated operations. About one-third of mergers during the 1980s resulted from *hostile takeovers,* where one firm would buy control of another against the wishes of the target firm's management. Hostile takeovers dwindled to less than one-tenth of mergers during the 1990s.

The break up of the Soviet Union in 1991 expanded market economies around the world. Companies tried to achieve a stronger competitive position in global markets by merging with other firms here and abroad. Merger activity gained momentum during the latter half of the 1990s, with the dollar value of each new merger topping the previous record. Most mergers during this period were financed by the exchange of corporate stock and were fueled by a booming stock market.

The largest mergers in history occurred during the late 1990s and in 2000. During this time, the most merger activity took place in banking, radio and television, telecommunications, health services, and insurance. The latest merger wave ended with the stock market plunge that began in 2000.

Not all the mergers during this latest wave turned out well. Corporate scandals engulfed some companies that had used mergers aggressively to grow, such as Enron and WorldCom. A recent deal that experienced difficulties was the $103 billion merger of AOL and Time Warner. In 2002, the merged company lost $99 billion, a world record.

With a fading stock market and slumping economy, merger activity fell sharply after 2000, thus ending the fourth wave. For example, among Internet and software companies, the value of merger deals in 2002 was less than one-tenth their value in 2000.

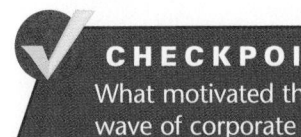

CHECKPOINT
What motivated the most recent wave of corporate mergers and what ended it?

Multinational Corporations

The developer of a successful product has a profit incentive to sell the product around the world. Because of high shipping costs and differences in labor costs, a firm often finds it more profitable to make products around the world as well. Many large corporations operate factories overseas and sell their products globally.

A corporation that operates globally is called a **multinational corporation (MNC)**. These companies also may be called transnational corporations, international corporations, or global corporations.

Running Multinationals

An MNC is usually headquartered in its native country and has affiliates in other countries. Most of the world's largest multinationals are headquartered in the United States, such as General Electric, General Motors, and Coca-Cola. Some are headquartered in Japan, such as Toyota, Honda, and Sony. Others are in Western Europe, such as Shell, BP, and Nestlé.

An MNC usually develops new products in its native country. It manufactures some or all of the goods abroad, where production costs are usually lower. For example, Whirlpool, the world's leading manufacturer of major home appliances, is headquartered in the United States but operates in more than 170 countries. The company motto is "Every home...Everywhere."

The multinational can take advantage of a successful brand by selling it around the world. Multinationals benefit consumers and workers worldwide by supplying products and creating jobs. Multinationals also spread the latest tech-nology and the best production techniques around the globe. This allows the firms located in less-developed countries to adopt cutting-edge technologies.

Problems of Multinationals

Running a multinational is more complicated than running a domestic firm. It requires coordinating far-flung operations, adapting operations and products to suit local cultures, and coping with different business regulations, different tax laws, and different currencies.

multinational corporation (MNC)
A large corporation that makes and sells its products around the world

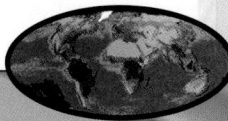

SPAN THE GLOBE

Betting Dollars to Doughnuts

Dick Clark, TV personality and producer, is betting dollars to doughnuts on a new venture in England. In the 1960s, Clark helped introduce several hot British rock bands to the United States through his *American Bandstand* program. With his new venture, he'll help introduce a hot American product to the United Kingdom—the Krispy Kreme doughnut. Mr. Clark's partnership wants to open as many as 25 Krispy Kreme stores throughout the United Kingdom. Clark and his franchise partners are betting that Krispy Kreme's assortment of sugar-powdered, glazed, and custard- or berry-filled delicacies will become a number-one hit with the British people. Their bet is a pretty good one. Each year about 25 percent of all Europe's sugar products and nearly 34 percent of its chocolate are consumed in the United Kingdom. Krispy Kreme's future franchise plans include a major international expansion. After the U.K. openings, more stores are scheduled to open in Australia, New Zealand, Japan, South Korea, Spain, and Mexico.

Think Critically

Krispy Kreme thinks its franchise stores will be a big hit in Britain. What, if any, holes do you see in that thinking?

Union leaders in the United States have claimed that multinationals are hiring workers overseas because wages there are lower. It's true that wages are lower in poorer countries. However, the wages paid there by multinationals are usually higher than wages offered by local employers for the jobs otherwise available. Some experts say workers in those poorer countries are better off because multinationals provide jobs that offer relatively good wages. U.S. multinationals export more to their foreign affiliates than they import from their foreign affiliates. As a result, foreign operations may tend to *create* U.S. jobs on balance.

Some critics also charge that multinationals have too much influence on the culture and the politics in the countries where they operate. However, foreign production by U.S. multinationals account on average for less than 4 percent of the value of all production in the countries in which they operate. Of the countries where U.S. multinationals account for the largest share of output, most are not poor countries but advanced economies such as Canada, the United Kingdom, and the Netherlands. Advanced economies would seem to be less affected by cultural or political influences by U.S. multinationals.

CHECKPOINT
Why do firms become multinational corporations?

© Getty Images/PhotoDisc

Of the countries where U.S. multinationals account for the largest share of output, most are advanced economies such as the Netherlands. What do you think would be the benefits to advanced economies of the presence of U.S. multinationals?

Key Concepts

1. Why are some people willing to invest in new firms that have not yet made any profit and do not expect to earn a profit for several years?

2. Suppose you have inherited $50,000 and want to use the money to start a business. Would you rather organize the business by yourself or purchase a franchise? Explain your reasons.

3. Do you think mergers are more often helpful or harmful for consumers? Explain your reasons.

4. When firms merge, they often lay off some workers to reduce their costs. Is it possible that this could be good for the economy?

5. Why have multinationals tended to "level the playing field" among workers and businesses in different nations?

Graphing Exercise

6. Mergers have an important impact on the U.S. economy, and they can be a sign of economic activity as well. More mergers tend to take place when the economy is booming and stock prices are high. They are less likely to occur when businesses are not earning good profits or when it is difficult to obtain funding to finance mergers. Use the data in the table to construct two bar graphs of merger activity in the U.S. economy from 1985 through 1999. One graph should show the number of mergers that took place. The other should show their value. What do your graphs show about economic conditions in the United States during these years?

Mergers With a Value in Excess of $5 Million, 1985–1999

Year	Number of Mergers	Value of Mergers in Billions of Dollars
1985	1,719	$ 149.6
1990	4,239	205.6
1995	4,981	895.8
1999	9,599	3,401.6

Think Critically

7. **Business Management** Many firms that offer franchise opportunities promote their organizations on the Internet. Identify a particular franchise business that exists in your community. Search the Internet for information about this franchise. What does the organization offer its members? What is the cost of becoming a franchisee? Would you consider ever starting this type of business yourself?

8. **History** In the years surrounding the turn of the nineteenth to the twentieth century, John D. Rockefeller created the Standard Oil Company primarily by merging many smaller firms. Investigate how he accomplished this and what the impact was for the owners and customers of the merged firms. What costs and benefits may have resulted from these mergers for the economy as a whole?

movers & shakers

Paul Gbodi *Jani-King Franchise Owner*

Paul Gbodi was 24 years old when he came to the United States from Nigeria. Although he had attended a junior college in Nigeria, he said, "I wanted to come to the United States because of the educational opportunities it provides." After earning his bachelor's degree from Langston University in Langston, Oklahoma, Paul went on to earn his master's degree from the University of Central Oklahoma in Edmond, Oklahoma.

Paul originally intended to return to Nigeria after earning his college degrees. "But after spending some time in the United States, I realized the tremendous opportunities in business that it held for me," he said. So he, his wife, and daughter decided to remain in Oklahoma. After finishing college, Paul began working in the restaurant and food service industries. In 1990, he decided his best career option was to start his own business.

After months of research, Paul and a friend selected the $17.8 billion commercial cleaning market. They decided to purchase a franchise cleaning business instead of starting a company on their own. "Because we were foreigners, we knew it would be difficult to convince the owner of a company to give us the keys to their building so that we could clean it in the evening while they were away," Paul said. In 1990, they purchased a Jani-King commercial cleaning franchise. Within months of starting the business, Paul was making more money than he did in his previous full-time job.

Jani-King is the world's largest commercial cleaning franchiser with more than 9,500 franchise owners in 15 countries. Jani-King franchises typically cost between $8,000 and $50,000 in start-up fees. The fees depend on the number of established customers the purchaser receives and the services the purchaser wishes to provide. Like Paul, each franchise owner operates independently and has a full stake in the success of his or her company.

Today, Paul is the sole owner of the Jani-King franchise in Oklahoma City. His company has more than 200 clients. Paul's staff provides daily, weekly, monthly, or semi-annual cleaning, trash removal, window washing, floor care, and other specialty cleaning services. His office staff includes an accountant, a payroll clerk, and an office manager. The Jani-King regional office provides franchisers with ongoing marketing support and invoicing of clients. Paul pays Jani-King 10 percent of gross revenues each month for these services. He spends most of his time training his employees and doing paperwork at home.

Paul doesn't find much time for vacations, but he is thrilled with his work. "I love what I'm doing," he says enthusiastically. In 2003, selected from among all the Jani-King franchisees, Paul was named Jani-King Franchisee of the Year by the International Franchise Association. He credits his success to a positive attitude and the support and training provided to him by Jani-King. "The people at Jani-King really believed in me from the start. The support they provide me has definitely helped me live a better life, own a home, and make my family proud," he said. He is quick to point out that anyone can be successful "if you put your mind to it, stay positive, and work hard."

SOURCE READING
Re-read the quotations from Paul Gbodi. What characteristics does he possess that make him a successful entrepreneur?

ENTREPRENEURS IN ACTION
Divide into pairs. You and your partner are considering starting a residential maid service. Decide whether to start your business from scratch or purchase a franchise from a franchiser. List the pros and cons of both starting from scratch and purchasing a franchise.

to History

United States Steel

On December 12, 1900, Charles M. Schwab, president of the Carnegie Steel Company, spoke before a group of 80 industrial executives at the University Club of New York. He discussed the advantages of consolidation in such industries as steel. Whether Carnegie Steel owner Andrew Carnegie encouraged Schwab to make the speech—or if Carnegie even was in attendance—is not known. Within five months, however, the largest corporation in the world, United States Steel, was created.

The U.S. steel industry was growing quickly during the last two decades of the nineteenth century. In 1880, the United States produced only half the amount of crude pig iron as Britain. By 1900, it was making 50 percent more than Britain, as production rose from 4 to 14 million metric tons. Up to 1880, the steel industry was driven by the railroad industry, and 85 percent of production went to making rails. By 1900, rail production had increased almost 300 percent, but rails represented only 31 percent of the rolled steel output.

As demand grew, advantages in economies of scale became apparent. However, integrating the various stages of production and modernizing plants to achieve the economies were costly. Some in the industry viewed acquisition as a safer method of growth. Still, as long as prices remained high, success was insured for most steel producers. When competition turned more predatory, however, prices dropped, causing the smaller, weaker companies to struggle.

Consolidation of the industry already had begun by the late 1900s. Many of the companies that specialized in finished steel were combining horizontally as the market diversified. Sheet making, wire making, and tube making were just a few of the activities that were subject to mergers. For these companies, most of the semi-finished steel was supplied along regional lines by one of two steel-producing giants—Federal or Carnegie Steel.

Two developments threatened to upset this arrangement. First, some of the companies that made finished steel began trying to reduce costs by producing their own steel. Some new companies were formed just to supply steel to these finishing companies. The reaction of Federal Steel and Carnegie Steel was to go into the finished steel business as well. At the threat of cut-throat competition, smaller companies feared that lower profits would destroy them.

J.P. Morgan was in attendance during Schwab's University Club speech. Morgan had been involved in the formation of both Federal Steel and National Steel, and railroads were an important part of his business empire. Morgan recognized that he could secure the financial success of his companies by following Schwab's proposal. After the speech, Morgan pulled Schwab aside and spoke with him for half an hour. He followed up the conversation with a meeting a few weeks later. Morgan secured a list of the companies Schwab had proposed for consolidation in his speech. The list also included values for what each company was worth. Morgan then asked Schwab to find out the amount for which Carnegie would sell his steel company. Carnegie came up with a figure of $480 million. Morgan accepted Carnegie's price, and U.S. Steel was created on April 1, 1901.

THINK CRITICALLY

Economies of scale were critical to the success of U.S. Steel. Still, some believe that the firm eventually became too large and difficult to manage. Its plants were spread over a large area. Also, because it was profitable, it was hard to justify modernizing old plants. What kind of diagram would you use to illustrate economies of scale? Draw a suitable diagram and show the effect of economies of scale in the long run.

10 Chapter Assessment

Summary

10.1 Production, Consumption, and Time

a It takes time to produce goods and services. Investments in capital can increase labor productivity but also require time and an accumulation of savings to use while investments are being made. Financial intermediaries help financial capital flow from savers to borrowers.

b Consumers generally value current consumption more than future consumption. This can be seen in their willingness to pay interest to borrow funds that allow them to consume now. A *demand for loans curve* slopes down. As interest rates decline, the amount of loans demanded increases.

c Loans are supplied by people willing to give up current consumption to consume more later. Interest is their reward for giving up current consumption. The higher the interest rate, the more money will be made available for loans. This is why the *supply of loans curve* slopes up. As interest rates increase, the amount of loans supplied also increases.

10.2 Banks, Interest, and Corporate Finance

a Banks act as *financial intermediaries* when they accumulate funds from savers and lend these funds to borrowers. By depositing funds in banks, savers earn interest. The banks then lend these funds at higher interest rates to borrowers that have been evaluated for their creditworthiness. If one borrower defaults, other borrowers are still likely to keep up their repayments.

b Interest rates differ for many reasons. The most important reason is the risk associated with a loan. Higher risks require borrowers to pay higher rates of interest. Other factors that influence interest rates include the duration of the loan, its cost of administration, and the way in which interest is taxed.

c Corporations raise money in a variety of ways. They may sell stock to the public or corporate bonds. Funds received from the sale of stock do not have to be repaid. *Dividends* will be paid on stock only when the corporation's board of directors chooses to do so. *Bonds* are debts of the business that must be repaid with interest, regardless of whether the firm earns a profit. Transactions of corporate stocks and bonds are carried out on stock exchanges.

10.3 Business Growth

a Businesses that are profitable are better able to grow than those that are not profitable. Profits may be reinvested in a firm. Banks are more likely to make loans to firms that are profitable. Individual investors are more likely to purchase stocks or bonds issued by profitable firms.

b Many entrepreneurs go into business by purchasing a franchise. These businesses benefit from having an established and successful business plan. The franchisees typically receive training from the franchiser. Although franchises have a better chance of being successful, there are significant fees that must be paid to the franchiser.

c There have been four waves of mergers in U.S. history. Although most mergers have created stronger, more successful businesses, some have not. A number of giant mergers in the 1990s lost billions of dollars, and some of these mergers were dissolved.

d In recent years many corporations have expanded beyond the borders of any individual nation. These *multinationals* often are better able to control their costs and market their products in many countries. It has been suggested that multinationals may exploit workers by producing goods and services in nations that have the lowest wage rates. But the wages offered by mulitinationals are typically higher than prevailing wages in those low-wage countries. Critics also claim that multinationals also may inappropriately influence governments because of their great economic power.

Review Economic Terms

Choose the term that best fits the definition. On a separate sheet of paper, write the letter of the answer. Some terms may not be used.

_____ 1. An asset owned by the borrower that can be sold to pay a loan in the event the loan is not repaid

_____ 2. The interest rate banks charge their most trustworthy business borrowers

_____ 3. Banks and other institutions that serve as go-betweens, accepting funds from savers and lending them to borrowers

_____ 4. A large corporation that makes and sells products in many different nations

_____ 5. An arrangement with a bank through which a business can quickly borrow needed cash

_____ 6. Corporate stock and corporate bonds

_____ 7. The portion of after-tax corporate profit that is reinvested in the firm

_____ 8. The initial sale of corporate stock to the public

_____ 9. The ability to borrow now, based on a promise of repayment in the future

_____10. Annual interest as a percentage of the amount borrowed or saved

a. bond

b. collateral

c. conglomerate merger

d. credit

e. demand for loans curve

f. dividend

g. equilibrium interest rate

h. financial intermediaries

i. initial public offering (IPO)

j. interest rate

k. line of credit

l. market for loans

m. multinational corporation (MNC)

n. prime rate

o. retained earnings

p. securities

q. supply of loans curve

r. vertical merger

Review Economic Concepts

11. **True or False** Production depends on savings because it requires time during which consumer goods cannot be produced.

12. The fact that people generally prefer to consume now rather than in the future is shown by their willingness to

    a. pay tuition to attend college.

    b. pay interest for an automobile loan.

    c. pay for life insurance.

    d. deposit their savings in a bank account.

13. The __?__ brings together borrowers and savers to determine the market rate of interest.

14. **True or False** The more valuable the collateral backing a loan, the higher the interest rate charged on the loan.

15. When the quantity supply of money supplied for loans exceeds the quantity of money for loans, there will be a

    a. shortage of loans, and interest rates will soon fall.

    b. surplus of loans, and interest rates will soon grow.

    c. shortage of loans, and interest rates will soon grow.

    d. surplus of loans, and interest rates will soon fall.

16. A(n) __?__ is extended to businesses by banks to provide them with funds when their sales are low.

17. __?__ are profits that a corporation earns but does not pay to its stockholders in dividends.

18. Which of the following situations will cause a bank to charge a lower *interest rate*?

    a. A loan is to be paid off in 60 days instead of 3 years.

    b. A loan is used to purchase an automobile instead of a house.

    c. A loan is made to a person who just changed jobs rather than a person who has been employed at the same job for 10 years.

    d. A loan is made to a small business instead of one that is very large.

19. Which is not a form of merger used by U.S. firms in the past?

    a. vertical mergers

    b. conglomerate mergers

    c. horizontal mergers

    d. diagonal mergers

20. **True or False** A firm's profits have little to do with that firm's ability to grow.

21. A corporation that operates globally is called a(n) __?__.

22. Which of the following statements about *multinational corporations* is not true?

    a. MNCs usually develop new products in their native countries.

    b. MNCs usually manufacture products in their native countries because costs usually are lower there.

    c. MNCs introduce less-developed countries to new technologies.

    d. MNCs benefit consumers and workers around the world by supplying products and creating jobs.

Apply Economic Concepts

23. **Different Types of Mergers** Organize these businesses into three groups as they would form horizontal, vertical, and conglomerate mergers. You may not need to use all of the firms to complete this activity.

    Ajax Trucking Co

    Apex Super Markets

    Clean Soap Co.

    Dad's Ice Cream Co.

    Harold's Fruit Co

    Joe's Wholesale Co.

    Mom's Detergent Co.

    Sue's Sandwich Co.

    XYZ Soap Co.

24. **Lines of Credit** Justin and Carla own a ski resort. All of their income is earned in the months between November and April, but they have expenses throughout the year. During the summer, they must repair their equipment and clear their ski trails. The table to the right shows their income and expenses from the end of last year's ski season through April of this year. Explain why Justin and Carla need a line of credit from their bank.

Justin and Carla's Income and Expenses

Month	Income	Expenses
May	$0	$ 42,810
June	$0	$ 38,291
July	$0	$ 36,743
Aug.	$0	$ 34,805
Sept.	$0	$ 40,283
Oct.	$0	$ 52,939
Nov.	$ 10,832	$ 66,380
Dec.	$134,640	$103,592
Jan.	$288,902	$154,021
Feb.	$275,010	$152,831
March	$152,345	$100,438
April	$ 56,832	$ 83,921
Total	$918,561	$806,576

25. **Sharpen Your Life Skills: Make Inferences** Imagine that in the past few months, interest rates have been growing steadily. They now stand about two percentage points higher for most types of loans than they did just one year ago. However, the demand for loans seems to be strong. Leaders of the Fed have announced that they are worried about increasing rates of inflation. Given this situation, what is the Fed likely to do, and what do you expect will happen to interest rates in the near future? Explain your answers.

26. **Demand and Supply for Loans** On a separate sheet of paper complete the table, indicating what would happen in each situation by placing a (+) for increase, (−) for decrease, or (0) for stay the same, in each box to the right of the event. Also, explain the reasons for each of the signs you place in the table.

Event	Demand for Loans	Supply of Loans	Interest Rates
A new electric motor is invented that is expensive but uses only half as much electricity as older motors.			
There is a new baby boom, and millions of children are born.			
There is a downturn in the economy and many workers are laid off.			
Many foreigners decide they want to buy more U.S.-made products.			

 *e*-con @pps   econxtra.swlearning.com

27. Access **EconData Online** through econxtra.swlearning.com. Read the article entitled "Stock Prices: S&P 500." Write a paragraph that describes the S&P 500, and why this index is useful to investors.

Investing In Your Future

The Situation

Aleesha sat quietly in her room at home, lost in thought about her junior year at college. Since moving away to go to school, a great deal had changed in Aleesha's life, yet some things had remained constant. She broke up with her boyfriend—their relationship a victim of the priority Aleesha placed on her studies. She still felt the passion for animals and their care that had carried her to this point. This had been reinforced by working at the zoo during the summers.

She declared a major in zoology, one of the educational cornerstones for a career in zoo keeping. This year, she would begin to take the courses specific to her career plan, including animal management and animal behavior. Her first two years at school had been pretty rough. She forced herself to concentrate, but some of the required courses seemed to have little to do with her area of interest. Even so, she maintained an A- average and easily retained her scholarship. Now, just before the beginning of junior year, she faced another major choice.

The Decision

The decision facing Aleesha at the moment came out of her sophomore history class. Aleesha had written a research report on the tools used by ancient engineers, such as those used to build the pyramids. One of these tools, an Egyptian level, had sparked in her an idea for a new type of animal-restraint muzzle. During the summer, Aleesha had created a prototype of the device and had adjusted it for various species. The result was an innovative product that was far more animal friendly and cost-effective than current alternatives on the market. The head zookeeper allowed her to test the device throughout the zoo. Several of the animal keepers suggested that she patent the product, and then make and sell it commercially.

Unfortunately, patenting the idea would take money—at least half her budget for the upcoming school year. She then would have to make and sell the devices to earn money in order to stay in school spring semester. She knew little about business. However, that could be remedied by switching her minor to business and changing some fall-semester courses. Aleesha knew that if she did not act soon, someone else would claim the idea for the device.

Activities

Divide into teams or work individually, as directed by your teacher, to perform the following tasks.

Apply the steps in the following decision-making process to Aleesha's situation:

1. *Define the problem.* Define Aleesha's problem in a way that will allow a clear solution. Should Aleesha become an entrepreneur?

2. *Identify the choices.* List the various alternatives among which she must choose.

a. Research the patent-application process. Also research firms that offer help in securing patents.

b. Which business courses would be most advantageous for Aleesha to take to enhance her chances in marketing her idea?

c. What form of business organization would be best for Aleesha?

3. *Evaluate the pluses and minuses of each choice.* Carefully weigh the value Aleesha puts on each alternative and the opportunity cost(s) for each.

4. *Make a choice.* Which course of action should she choose? Be prepared to present and defend your choice in class.

5. *Provide "action" steps that are appropriate to the decision.* Make sure these are realistic and timely to ensure the necessary action(s) are taken to resolve the problem.

6. *Critique the decision.* The class will assist in the review and evaluation of your plan of action. In real life, you should review not only the decision and its result, but also the process by which you make it.

Research

Research for the information you need to effectively make the decision, such as the patent-application process, business courses Aleesha might take, and the forms of business organization she might choose.

Present

Arrive at a decision. Then prepare a presentation for the class on the six steps you took to achieve this decision.

Unit 4

The National Economy

11 **Economic Performance**

12 **Economic Growth**

13 **Economic Challenges**

Since 1776, when Adam Smith inquired into the *Wealth of Nations,* economists have been trying to figure out why some economies prosper while others don't. Because a market economy is not the product of conscious design, it does not reveal its secrets readily. There is no clear blueprint of the economy, so policy makers can't simply push here and pull there to create prosperity for everyone. Still, economists are learning more every day about how the U.S. economy works. You, too, can discover the challenges and opportunities facing the largest and most complex economy in world history.

11 Economic Performance

Consider

How is the economy's performance measured?

What's gross about the gross domestic product?

What's the impact on gross domestic product if you make yourself a sandwich for lunch?

How can you compare the value of production in one year with that in other years if prices change over time?

What's the business cycle?

What's the big idea with the national economy?

© Getty Images/PhotoDisc

POINT YOUR BROWSER

econxtra.swlearning.com

11.1 Gross Domestic Product

Objectives

> Describe what the gross domestic product measures.

> Learn two ways to calculate the gross domestic product, and explain why they are equivalent.

Overview

The Great Depression of the 1930s convinced economists and the government to get a better handle on what was happening with the economy. Economists began assembling huge quantities of data collected from a variety of sources across America. These data were organized and reported periodically by the federal government. The resulting system for measuring the nation's economy has been hailed as one of the great achievements of the twentieth century. Its primary developers won a Nobel Prize for their work.

Key Terms

economy

gross domestic product (GDP)

consumption

investment

aggregate expenditure

aggregate income

[In the News]

● Tracking a $12 Trillion Economy

How does the government keep track of the most complex economy in history? Ever since Article I of the U.S. Constitution required that a census be taken every 10 years, the federal government has been gathering data. The three main data-gathering agencies are the Census Bureau, the Bureau of Economic Analysis, and the Bureau of Labor Statistics. Since 1980, the market value of all final goods and services produced in the United States has doubled. Employment has increased by nearly 40 million workers. Foreign trade has tripled. Yet the federal budget for these agencies has declined. Only 0.2 percent of the federal budget goes toward keeping track of the economy. Federal budget cuts have eliminated some data-collection efforts and have slowed down others. For example, the monthly household sample that tracks unemployment was cut from 60,000 to 50,000. Some agencies must do more with the same staff. In 1980, the Bureau of Labor Statistics had 18 analysts to keep track of productivity in 95 different industries. The number of industries they now track has increased four times. However, the number of analysts has changed little.

Think About It

Why do you think it is important for the U.S. government to keep track of the size of the economy?

The National Economy

economy

The structure of economic activity in a locality, a region, a country, a group of countries, or the world

National economics, or macroeconomics, focuses on the overall performance of the *economy*. The term **economy** describes the structure of economic activity in a locality, a region, a country, a group of countries, or the world. You could talk about the Chicago economy, the Illinois economy, the Midwest economy, the U.S. economy, the North American economy, or the world economy.

Gross Domestic Product

An economy's size can be measured in different ways. The value of production, the number of people employed, or their total income can be measured. The most commonly used measure is the *gross product*. This is the market value of production in a geographical region during a given period, usually one year.

gross domestic product (GDP)

The market value of all final goods and services produced in the United States during a given period, usually a year

The **gross domestic product**, or **GDP**, measures the market value of all final goods and services produced in the United States during a given period, usually a year. GDP measures production during the year by individuals and businesses located in the United States. GDP includes production in the United States by foreign firms, such as a Japanese auto plant in Kentucky. It excludes foreign production by U.S.

firms, such as a General Motors plant in Mexico.

GDP measures the economy's total production of goods and services, from trail bikes to pedicures. GDP can be used to track the same economy over time. It also may be used to compare different economies at the same time.

National Income Accounts

National income accounts organize huge quantities of data collected from a variety of sources across the United States. These data are summarized and reported periodically by the federal government. National income accounts keep track of the value of *final goods and services*. These are goods and services sold to the final, or end, users. A toothbrush, a pair of contact lenses, and a bus ride are examples of final goods and services.

Gross domestic product includes the value of only final goods and services. Your purchase of chicken from a grocer is reflected in GDP. When KFC purchases chicken, however, this transaction is not recorded in GDP because KFC is not the final consumer. Only after KFC deep fries that chicken and sells it to customers is the sale recorded as part of GDP.

No Double Counting

Intermediate goods and services are those purchased for additional processing and resale, such as the chicken purchased by KFC. This additional processing may be minor, as when a grocer buys canned goods to stock the shelves. The intermediate goods may be altered dramatically. For instance, oil paint costing $20 and a canvas costing $25 may be transformed into a work of fine art that sells for $5,000.

Sales of intermediate goods and services are excluded from GDP to avoid the problem of *double counting*. This is counting an item's value more than once. For example, suppose the grocer buys a can of tuna for $0.60 and sells it for $1.00. If GDP counted both the intermediate transaction of $0.60 and the final transaction of $1.00, that can of

NETBookmark

The Bureau of Economic Analysis is charged with estimating GDP and its components. You can access selected National Income and Product Account tables through econxtra.swlearning.com. Summary Table S1 tells you by how much each component has grown. Summary Table S2 shows the contribution of each component to GDP growth. Can you explain the difference between these two types of statistics?

econxtra.swlearning.com

tuna would be counted twice in GDP. Its recorded value of $1.60 would exceed its final value of $1.00 by $0.60. Therefore, GDP counts only the final value of the product.

GDP also ignores most of the secondhand value of used goods, such as existing homes and used cars. These goods were counted in GDP when they were produced. However, the value of services provided by realtors and used-car dealers is counted in GDP. For example, suppose a new-car dealer gives you a $1,500 trade-in allowance for your used car. The dealer cleans and repairs the car, and then resells it for $2,500. The $1,000 increase in the car's value is included in GDP.

CHECKPOINT
What does the gross domestic product measure?

Calculating GDP

The national income accounts are based on the idea that *one person's spending is another person's income.* This is expressed in a double-entry bookkeeping system of accounting. Spending on final goods and services is recorded on one side of the ledger and income created by that spending is recorded on the other side. GDP can be measured either by total spending on U.S. production or by total income earned from that production.

GDP Based on the Expenditure Approach

The *expenditure approach to GDP* adds up the spending on all final goods and services produced in the economy during the year. The easiest way to understand the spending approach is to divide spending into its four components: consumption, investment, government purchases, and net exports.

Consumption consists of purchases of final goods and services by households during the year. Examples of *services* include dry cleaning, haircuts, and air travel. Consumption of goods includes *nondurable goods,* such as soap and soup, and *durable goods,* such as televisions and furniture. Durable goods are those expected to last at least three years. On average, consumption makes up about two-thirds of all spending in the economy. Figure 11.1 shows the composition of U.S. spending since 1960.

consumption

Household purchases of final goods and services

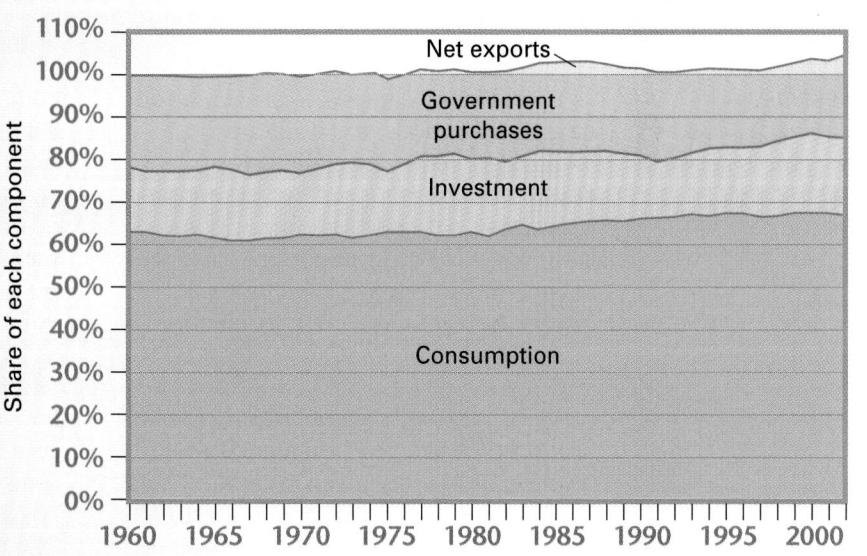

U.S. Spending Components as Percentages of GDP Since 1960

Figure **11.1**

Consumption's share of total U.S. spending increased slightly from 1960 to 2002. Most recently, it accounted for about 67 percent of the total.

Source: Computed from annual estimates from the U.S. Department of Commerce.

Which of the shoppers in these photos is shopping for durable goods, and which one is shopping for nondurable goods?

investment

The purchase of new plants, new equipment, new buildings, new residences, and net additions to inventories

Investment consists of spending on new capital goods and additions to inventories. More generally, investment consists of spending on current production that is not used for current consumption. The most important category of investment is new *physical capital*, such as new buildings and new machinery purchased by firms and used to produce goods and services. Spending by households on new residential construction also is considered to be investment.

Changes in firms' inventories are another category of investment. Inventories include stocks of goods in process, such as computer parts. They also include stocks of finished goods, such as new

computers awaiting sale. Investment changes more from year to year than any other spending component. On average it accounts for about 15 percent of U.S. GDP.

In the national income accounts, investment does not include purchases of *existing* buildings and machines. Nor does it include purchases of financial assets, such as stocks and bonds. Existing buildings and machines were counted in GDP in the year they were produced. Purchases of stocks and bonds sometimes provide firms with the funds to invest. However, stocks and bonds are not investments. They are simply indications of ownership.

Government purchases include spending by all levels of government for goods and services—from clearing snowy roads to clearing court dockets, from library books to the librarian's pay. Government purchases at all levels account for about 20 percent of U.S. GDP. Government purchases, and therefore GDP, exclude transfer payments such as those for Social Security, welfare, and unemployment. These transfer payments are outright grants from the government to the recipients and are not true purchases by the government or true earnings by the recipients. Transfer payments typically are used by recipients to purchase consumer goods. This portion of transfer payments is, therefore, counted in consumption totals.

The final component of the expenditure approach to GDP is net exports. This results from the interaction between U.S. residents and the rest of the world. Some spending for consumption, investment, and government purchases goes for imports. However, spending on imports does not count as part of U.S. GDP. To figure out the net effect of the rest of the world on GDP, the value of imports must be subtracted from the value of exports. *Net exports* equal the value of U.S. exports of goods and services minus the value of U.S. imports of goods and services.

The expenditure approach considers the nation's *aggregate expenditure.* Any time an economist uses the term *aggregate,* you can substitute the word *total* for it to determine the meaning. **Aggregate expenditure** equals the sum of consumption, *C,* investment, *I,* government purchases, *G,* and net exports, which is the value of exports, *X,* minus the value of imports, *M,* or $(X - M)$. Summing these spending components yields aggregate expenditure, or GDP:

$$C + I + G + (X - M) = GDP$$

The value of U.S. imports has exceeded the value of U.S. exports nearly every year since the 1960s. This means U.S. net exports $(X - M)$ have been negative. Negative net exports means that the sum of consumption, investment, and government purchases exceeds GDP. You can see negative net exports in Figure 11.1. It is that portion of consumption, investment, and government purchases that exceeds 100 percent of GDP.

GDP Based on the Income Approach

The expenditure approach sums, or aggregates, spending on production. The income approach sums, or aggregates, income arising from that production. The *income approach to GDP* adds up the aggregate income earned during the year by those who produce that output. Again, double-entry bookkeeping ensures that the value of aggregate output equals the aggregate

aggregate expenditure

Total spending on all final goods and services produced in the economy during the year

SPAN THE GLOBE

Japanese Economic Revival Plan

Japan once was a powerful economic force in the world. But as of 2003, the country had not yet recovered from more than a decade-long downturn in its GDP. Falling prices, lack of growth, and increasing unemployment continued. Japan's successful economy began to contract in the early part of the 1990s, when sky-high real-estate prices suddenly dropped. The drop in prices wiped out the value of much of the collateral that Japanese banks were holding against business loans. To make matters worse, Japan's export-driven companies were under increasing pressure to reduce prices—and therefore profits. They faced intense competition from other Asian nations with much lower labor costs. In October 2002, the Japanese government launched an economic revival plan. The plan involved a special loan program that rewarded companies that hired people who had been laid off. Its goal was to erase more than $336 billion of the banks' bad debts and create more jobs for Japanese workers. Though it seems like a big step and a lot of money, most observers think the Japanese government will need to spend much more money to effectively stimulate the economy.

Think Critically

How would creating more jobs for Japanese workers help to raise the GDP in Japan?

income paid for resources used to produce that output. **Aggregate income** equals the sum of all the income earned by resource suppliers in the economy. Thus

Aggregate expenditure
= GDP
= Aggregate income

A finished product usually is processed by several firms on its way to the consumer. A wooden desk, for example, starts as raw timber, which usually is cut by one firm. It is milled by another, made into a desk by a third, and retailed by a fourth. You avoid double counting either by focusing only on the market value of the desk when it is sold to the final user or by *calculating the value added at each stage of production.*

The *value added* by each firm equals that firm's selling price minus the amount paid for intermediate goods, This is the amount spent on inputs purchased from other firms. The value added at each stage represents income to individual resource suppliers at that stage. *The sum of the value added at all stages equals the market value of the final good. The sum of the value added for all final goods and services equals GDP based on the income approach.*

For example, suppose you buy a wooden desk for $200, which is the

final market value counted in GDP. Consider the production of that desk. Suppose the tree that gave its life for your studies was cut into a log that was sold to a mill for $20. That log was milled into lumber and sold for $50 to a manufacturer, who built your desk and sold it for $120 to a retailer. The retailer then sold it to you for $200. If all these transactions were added up, the total of $390 would exceed the $200 market value of the desk.

To avoid double counting, you include only the value added at each stage of production. In this example, the logging company adds $20, the miller $30, the manufacturer $70, and the retailer $80. The total value added is $200, which also is the selling price of the desk. All this is illustrated in Figure 11.2.

CHECKPOINT
What are two ways of calculating gross domestic product, and how are they equivalent?

Computation of Value Added for a New Desk   **Figure 11.2**

The value added at each stage of production is the sale value minus the cost of intermediate goods, or column (1) minus column (2). The sum of the values added at all stages equals the market value of the final good, shown at the bottom of column (3).

Stage of Production	(1) Sale Value	(2) Cost of Intermediate Goods	(3) Value Added
Logger	$ 20	——	$ 20
Miller	50	$ 20	30
Manufacturer	120	50	70
Retailer	200	120	80
		Market value of final good	**$200**

Key Concepts

1. Why should people care about the amount of production that takes place within the economy?

2. Why wouldn't you add $100 to GDP if you produced a table that you sold for $100?

3. Why are the values of spending and income always assumed to be the same?

4. In what way are investment by businesses and some spending by the government similar?

5. What would your teacher mean if she said, "The aggregate income of all students in this class was $52,315.28 last year?"

Graphing Exercise

6. Use the data in the table to construct two grouped bar graphs showing the percentage of spending for $C + I + G + (X - M)$ for the U.S. GDP in 1970 and 2000. The vertical axis should show the percent of GDP purchased. Each of the spending types should be represented by bars placed along the horizontal axis. Make separate bars for each of the different types of spending. Show the negative net exports in 2000 by extending that bar below the horizontal axis of the graph. What conclusions about changes in the economy can you draw from your graphs?

Different Types of Spending in 1970 and 2000
Values in Billions of Dollars

Spending	1970	% of GDP	2000	% of GDP
Consumption	$648.1	62.6%	$6,728.4	68.2%
Investment	150.2	14.5	767.5	18.0
Government	236.1	22.8	741.0	17.7
Net Exports	1.2	0.1	−364.0	−3.9
Total GDP	$1,035.6	100.0	$9,872.9	100.0

Think Critically

7. **Mathematics** Calculate the final price consumers would pay for a gallon of gasoline given the following costs. How does this example demonstrate the need for calculating added value when measuring GDP?

   • Crude oil is extracted from the ground at a cost of $20 per 40-gallon barrel.

   • Crude oil is transported to a refinery at a cost of 18 cents per gallon.

   • It takes 1.25 gallons of crude oil to produce 1 gallon of gasoline.

   • Crude oil is refined into gasoline at a cost of 7 cents per gallon of finished product.

   • Gasoline is transported to gas stations at a cost of 8 cents per gallon.

8. **Consumer Economics** A 5-pound bag of potatoes can be purchased for $2.49. At the same time, a 24-ounce bag of frozen french fries is priced at $2.99. Explain why the frozen potatoes are more expensive. What impact does this difference have on the measurement of GDP?

Limitations of GDP Estimation  11.2

Objectives

> Identify what types of production GDP calculations neglect.

> Determine why and how to adjust GDP for changes over time in the general price level.

Overview

Imagine the difficulty of developing an accounting system that must describe such a complex and dynamic economy. In the interest of clarity and simplicity, certain features are neglected. Features that are easier to measure and to explain may get too much attention. The problem is that the more comprehensive the national income accounts become, the more complicated they get. Trackers of the U.S. economy are always making tradeoffs between simplicity and comprehensiveness. Some production is not accounted for in GDP, however. GDP also must be adjusted for changes in the general price level over time.

Key Terms

depreciation

nominal GDP

real GDP

consumer price index (CPI)

[In the News]

● The Yard Sale Police Are Coming

Given the current state of the economy, the underground economy—also called the informal economy, the shadow economy, or the black market—is flourishing. You may associate the underground economy with the drug trade, money laundering, and other such activities. However, this uncharted sector of the U.S. GDP is booming and spreading into all walks of life. It's found in the market for recycled aluminum cans, day labor, pawnshops, and unreported tips at restaurants. It's at farmer's markets, under-the-table work sites, used book and clothing stores, and—yes—even yard sales. U.S. governmental agencies largely have ignored the underground economy—until now, that is. The IRS and state tax departments currently are developing programs to keep track, and get their share, of tax money from the underground activities. The focus of these new big-brother programs is the dollar, the exchange medium of choice in the black market. The new identification markers in almost all new currency will allow tracking of the currency. It also will allow the government to pinpoint large amounts of unexplained cash placed in people's bank accounts or used for purchases. So be careful: The Yard Sale Police are recruiting and getting ready for a yard sale near you.

Think About It

Do you participate in the underground economy? If so, do you buy or sell in it? If not, do you think you will in the future? What it is about this activity that keeps it from being included in the GDP measurement?

What GDP Misses

With some minor exceptions, GDP includes only those products that are sold in legal markets. It thereby neglects all household production and all illegal production. GDP accounting also has difficulty capturing changes in the quality and variety of products, and in the amount of leisure time available.

Household Production

Do-it-yourself household production, such as childcare, meal preparation, house cleaning, and home repair, is not captured in GDP. Consequently, an economy in which householders are largely self-sufficient will have a lower GDP than will an otherwise similar economy in which households specialize and sell products to one another.

During the 1950s, more than 80 percent of American mothers with small children stayed at home, caring for the family. All this care did not add one cent to GDP, however. Today more than half of all mothers with small children are in the workforce. Their market labor is counted in U.S. GDP. What's more, GDP also has increased because meals, childcare, and the like are now more apt to be purchased in markets than provided by households. In less-developed economies, more economic activity is do-it-yourself or provided by the extended family.

Because official GDP figures ignore most home production, these figures understate actual production in economies where families do more for themselves and buy less in the market.

Underground Economy

GDP also ignores production in the *underground economy,* which includes activity that goes unreported either because it's illegal or because those involved want to evade taxes on otherwise legal activity. The underground economy also is called the black market or "working off the books." A federal study suggests production in the underground economy is the equivalent of 7.5 percent of GDP. This amounted to about $750 billion in 2003.

Leisure, Quality, and Variety

GDP indicates the value of goods and services produced in the economy. This gives economists some idea of the economy's *standard of living,* or its level of economic prosperity. However, GDP fails to capture some features of the economy that also play a part in living standards. For example, more leisure time contributes to a higher standard of living, but GDP offers no information

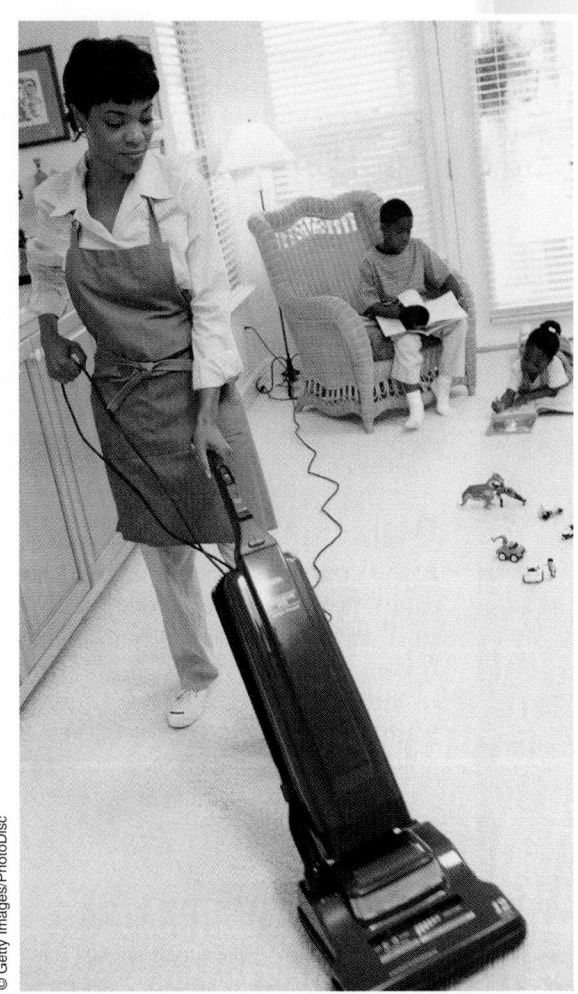

© Getty Images/PhotoDisc

Is the value of the activity of the woman in this photograph captured in GDP? Explain your answer.

depreciation
The value of the capital stock that is used up or becomes obsolete in producing GDP during the year

about the amount of leisure time available in an economy. If the amount of leisure remained relatively constant over time, then ignoring leisure would not change the picture.

However, the average U.S. workweek is much shorter now than it was a century ago. This means people work less to produce today's output. People also retire at an earlier age, and they live longer after retirement. Thus, over the years, there has been an increase in the amount of leisure time available. However, leisure is not reflected in GDP because leisure is not explicitly bought and sold in a market.

The quality and variety of products available also have improved over the years because of technological advances and market competition. Recording systems, computers, tires, running shoes, and thousands of other products have been improved. Also, new products are introduced all the time, such as high-definition television, the Internet, and wireless Internet connectors. Yet most of these improvements and innovations are not captured in GDP.

The gross domestic product fails to capture changes in the availability of leisure time. It also often fails to reflect changes in the quality of existing products and the availability of new ones. These factors make GDP a less-reliable measure of an economy's standard of living.

Depreciation

In the course of producing GDP, some capital wears out, such as the delivery truck that finally dies. Other capital becomes obsolete, such as an aging computer that can't run the latest software. A new truck that logs 100,000 miles its first year has been subject to wear and tear. It is now less valuable as a productive resource.

Depreciation measures the value of the capital stock that is used up or becomes obsolete in the production process. Gross domestic product is called "gross" because it does not take into account this depreciation. A picture of the *net* production that actually occurs during a year is found by subtracting this depreciation from GDP. *Net domestic product* equals gross domestic product minus depreciation, the value of the capital stock used up in the production process. By failing to account for depreciation, GDP gives a misleading total of what's actually produced.

Economists distinguish between two definitions of investment. *Gross investment* measures the value of all investment during a year. Gross investment is used in computing GDP. *Net investment* equals gross investment minus depreciation. The economy's production possibilities depend on what happens to net investment. If net investment is negative—that is, if depreciation exceeds gross investment—the capital stock declines, so its contribution to output will decline as well. If net investment is zero, the capital stock remains constant, as does its contribution to output. If net investment is positive, the capital stock grows, as does its contribution to output. As the names indicate, *gross* domestic product reflects gross investment and *net* domestic product reflects net investment.

GDP Does Not Reflect All Costs

Some production and consumption degrades the quality of the environment. Trucks and cars pump carbon monoxide into the atmosphere. Housing developments gobble up forests. Paper mills foul lungs and burn eyes. These negative externalities—costs that fall on those not directly involved in the market transactions—largely are ignored in GDP accounting, even though they diminish the quality of life and may limit future production. To the extent that growth in GDP also involves growth in such negative externalities, a rising GDP may not be as attractive as it would first appear.

Net national product captures the depreciation of buildings, machinery,

---

THE WALL STREET JOURNAL

Reading It Right What's the relevance of the following statement from *The Wall Street Journal:* "The economic package approved by the Italian Parliament includes measures to encourage firms operating in the underground economy to come out in the open."

vehicles, and other manufactured capital. Both GDP and net national product ignore the depletion of natural resources, such as standing timber, fish stocks, and soil fertility. The federal government is now in the process of developing so-called *green accounting*, or green GDP, to reflect the impact of production on air pollution, water pollution, lost trees, soil depletion, and the loss of other natural resources.

Despite the limitations and potential distortions associated with official GDP estimates, the trend of GDP over time provides a fairly accurate picture of the overall performance of the U.S. economy. Inflation, however, distorts comparisons of dollar amounts from one year to the next. That problem is discussed next.

CHECKPOINT
What types of production does the calculation of GDP neglect?

Adjusting GDP for Price Changes

The national income accounts are based on the market values of final goods and services produced in a particular year. Gross domestic product measures the value of output in *current dollars*—that is, in the dollar values at the time the output is produced. The system of national income accounting based on current dollars allows for comparisons among income or expenditure components in a particular year. For example, you could say that consumption last year was about five times greater than investment. Because the economy's general price level changes over time, however, current-dollar comparisons across years can be misleading.

Nominal GDP versus Real GDP

When GDP is based on current dollars, the national income accounts measure the *nominal value* of national output. Thus, the current-dollar GDP, or

NETBookmark

The Bureau of Labor Statistics (BLS) web site features an "Inflation Calculator." You can access this tool through econxtra.swlearning.com. The inflation calculator lets you adjust for inflation the price of a good in one year to its price in another year. Use this tool to find the current year's prices for the following goods: (1) Bicycle purchased in 1992 for $250. (2) Candy bar purchased in 1980 for $.50. (3) College tuition of $3,000 per year in 1974.

econxtra.swlearning.com

TEAM WORK

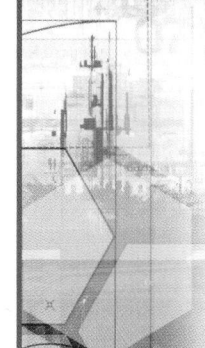

Choose a partner. Each partner should list five goods and the cost of each good today. Next to each item, write a year as early as 1913. Your partner, using the BLS inflation calculator, will determine the price of each good on your list in the year you have indicated.

nominal GDP, is based on the prices when the output is produced. Because of inflation, however, focusing on the nominal value of GDP over time distorts the true picture. For example, between 1979 and 1980, nominal GDP increased by about 9 percent. That sounds impressive, but the economy's general price level rose more than 9 percent. So the growth in nominal GDP resulted entirely from inflation. **Real GDP**, or GDP adjusted for inflation, in fact declined. Recall that *inflation* is an increase in the economy's average price level.

If nominal GDP increases in a given year, part of this increase may simply result from inflation—pure hot air. To make meaningful comparisons of GDP across years, you must take out the hot air, or *deflate* nominal GDP. To focus on *real* changes in production,

nominal GDP
GDP based on prices at the time of the transaction; current-dollar GDP

real GDP
The economy's aggregate output measured in dollars of constant purchasing power; GDP measured in terms of the goods and services produced

Computer Prices and GDP Estimation

Computer prices have fallen by an average of about 13 percent per year since 1982. Based on this rate of decline, a computer that cost, say $10,000 in 1982 cost about $5,000 in 1987 but only about $650 in 2001. According to these prices, that computer cost about the same in 1982 as a minivan. In 2001, you could buy about 35 computers for the cost of a minivan. So computers became much less expensive between 1982 and 2001. The sharp decline in computer prices spurred purchases of computers for offices and homes. Suppose the number of computers jumped from 1 million in 1982 to 5 million in 2001. If computers are valued at their 1987 price of $5,000, computer spending would have increased five times, from $5 billion in 1982 to $25 billion in 2001. If priced in current, or nominal, dollars of $10,000 in 1982 and $650 in 2001, spending on computers would have declined two-thirds from $10 billion in 1982 to only $3.3 billion in 2001.

Think Critically

How would you explain the sharp decline in computer prices from 1982 to 2001?

you must eliminate changes due solely to inflation.

Price Indexes

To compare the price level over time, you need a point of reference, a base year to which prices in other years can be compared. An *index number* compares the value of a variable in a particular year to its value in a base year, or reference year. Suppose bread is the only good produced in the economy. As a reference point, consider the price in some specific year. The year selected is called the base year. Prices in other years are expressed relative to the base-year price.

Suppose the base year is 2002, when a loaf of bread sold for $1.25. The price of bread increased to $1.30 in 2003 and to $1.40 in 2004. To construct a *price index*, each year's price is divided by the price in the base year and then multiplied by 100, as shown in Figure 11.3. For 2002, the base year, the base price of bread is divided by itself, $1.25/$1.25, which equals 1. So the price index in 2002 equals $1 \times 100 = 100$. *The price index in the base year, or base period, is always 100.*

Example of a Price Index (base year = 2002)

Figure 11.3

The price index equals the price in the current year divided by the price in the base year, all multiplied by 100.

Year	(1) Price of Bread in Current Year	(2) Price of Bread in Base Year	(3) Price Index (3) = (1)/(2) × 100
2002	$1.25	$1.25	100
2003	1.30	1.25	104
2004	1.40	1.25	112

The price index in 2003 is $1.30/$1.25, which equals 1.04, which multiplied by 100 equals 104. In 2004, the index is $1.40/$1.25, or 1.12, which multiplied by 100 equals 112. Thus, when compared to the base year, the price index is 4 percent higher in 2003 and is 12 percent higher in 2004.

The price index permits comparisons between any two years. For example, what if you were presented with the indexes for 2003 and 2004 and were asked what happened to the price level between the two years? By dividing the 2004 price index by the 2003 price index, 112/104, you find that the price level rose by 7.7 percent.

Consumer Price Index

The **consumer price index (CPI)**, measures changes over time in the cost of buying a "market basket" of goods and services purchased by a typical family. For simplicity, suppose that market basket for the year includes 365 pounds of bananas, 500 gallons of fuel oil, and 12 months of cable TV. Prices in the base year are listed in column (2) of Figure 11.4. Multiplying price by quantity yields the total cost of each product in the base year, as shown in column (3). The cost of the market basket in the base year is $1,184.85, shown as the total of column (3).

Prices in the current year are listed in column (4). Note that not all prices changed by the same percentage since the base year. The price of fuel oil increased by 50 percent, but the price of bananas fell. The cost of purchasing that same basket in the current year is $1,398.35, shown as the total of column (5).

To compute the consumer price index for the current year, you simply divide the total cost in the current year by the total cost of that same basket in the base year, $1,398.35/$1,184.85, and then multiply by 100. This yields a price index of 118. You could say that between the base year and the current year, the "cost of living" increased by 18 percent, although not all prices changed by the same percentage.

The federal government uses the years 1982 to 1984 as the base period for calculating the CPI for a market basket of 400 goods and services. The CPI is reported monthly, based on prices from thousands of sellers across the country.

GDP Price Index

Price indexes are weighted sums of various prices. Whereas the CPI focuses on just a sample of consumer purchases, a more comprehensive price index, the *GDP price index*, includes all goods and services produced. The GDP price index is found by dividing the

consumer price index (CPI)

Measure of inflation based on the cost of a fixed "market basket" of goods and services purchased by a typical family

---

Example Market Basket Used to Develop the Consumer Price Index

Figure 11.4

Good or Service	(1) Quantity in Market Basket	(2) Prices in Base Year	(3) Cost of Basket in Base Year (3) = (1) × (2)	(4) Prices in Current Year	(5) Cost of Basket in Current Year (5) = (1) × (4)
Bananas	365 pounds	$0.89/pound	$ 324.85	$ 0.79	$ 288.35
Fuel Oil	500 gallons	1.00/gallon	500.00	1.50	750.00
Cable TV	12 months	30.00/month	360.00	30.00	360.00
			$1,184.85		$1,398.35

The cost of a market basket in the current year, shown at the bottom of column (5), sums the quantities of each item in the basket, shown in column (1), times the price of each item in the current year, shown in column (4).

nominal GDP by the real GDP and then multiplying by 100:

GDP price index

$$= \frac{\text{Nominal GDP}}{\text{Real GDP}} \times 100$$

Nominal GDP is the dollar value of this year's GDP measured in current-year prices. Real GDP is the dollar value of this year's GDP measured in base-year prices. If you know both nominal GDP and real GDP, then finding the GDP price index is easy. The federal government most recently has used 1996 as the base year for computing real GDP. The base year moves forward every few years and could be a later year by the time you read this.

CHECKPOINT
Why and how is GDP adjusted for changes in the general price level?

11.2 Assessment

Key Concepts

1. Why wouldn't our nation's GDP grow if you mow your own lawn, but would grow if you were paid to mow your neighbor's lawn?

2. How do many young people participate in the underground economy?

3. Why wouldn't the purchase of a $20,000 truck by a business necessarily represent a $20,000 net investment in the economy?

Graphing Exercise

4. U.S. citizens watch television for more hours than people in any other nation. Although they value their time in front of the "tube," this value is not included in GDP. Construct a bar graph showing the hours the average U.S. citizen spends watching TV from the data in the table. Is there a way the value of this time should or could be included in national income accounting? Explain your point of view.

Average Hours Spent Watching Television Programming Per Year, 1996–2004

Year	Average Viewing Hours
1996	1,559
1998	1,551
2000	1,633
2002	1,655
2004	1,673

(Values for 2002 and 2004 are projected.)

Think Critically

5. **Government** In 1990, the federal government spent $1,253.2 billion when the CPI was 130.7. Ten years later, in 2000, the federal government spent $1,788.8 billion when the CPI was 172.2. Did the federal government's real spending increase in these years? If you had been a politician running for election in 2002, how would you have used this information? Explain your answer.

Objectives

> Distinguish between the two phases of the business cycle, and compare the average length of each.

> Differentiate among leading, coincident, and lagging economic indicators.

Overview

Economic activity, like cycles in nature, fluctuates in a fairly regular way. The U.S. economy and other industrial market economies historically have experienced alternating periods of expansion and contraction in the level of economic activity. These fluctuations vary in length and intensity, yet some features appear common to all. The ups and downs usually involve the entire nation and often the world. They affect nearly all dimensions of economic activity, not simply employment and production. Despite these ups and downs, the U.S. economy has grown dramatically over the long run.

Key Terms

business cycle

recession

expansion

leading economic indicators

[In the News]

● Taking the Pulse of the Economy

In mid-April 2003, after the war in Iraq, the U.S. economy was in a state of flux. Financial market observers and Washington policymakers were paying attention to economic indicators that provided a general picture of what the economy looked like right then. Some of the best of these indicators—termed coincident indicators—are the financial markets. Fluctuations in the prices of stocks and bonds offer investors a reasonable basis for predictions about inflation, earnings, and economic growth. Additionally, investors also can keep close tabs on other indicators—from weekly sales reports of major retailers to home mortgage applications. By the time most official government data are released, they're more than a month old. The coincident indicators can provide an up-to-the-moment snapshot of how the economy is performing. However, caution must be used in looking at these indicators. Coincident indicators can change quickly and register sharp spikes, false starts, or temporary dips. On April 15, 2003, the coincident data showed the economy was reacting positively to the quick end of the war in Iraq. Jobless claims were down by 38,000 and Wal-Mart sales were up 5 to 7 percent. However, complete economic recovery was a long time coming.

Think About It

What would be the problems associated with using only coincident indicators in making economic decisions?

U.S. Economic Fluctuations

business cycle

Fluctuations reflecting the rise and fall of economic activity relative to the long-term growth trend of the economy

The **business cycle** reflects the rise and fall of economic activity relative to the long-term growth trend of the economy. Perhaps the easiest way to understand the business cycle is to examine its components. During the 1920s and 1930s, Wesley C. Mitchell, director of the National Bureau of Economic Research (NBER), noted that the economy experiences two phases: periods of expansion and periods of contraction.

Recessions and Expansions

A contraction might be so severe as to be called a *depression*. This is a sharp reduction in the nation's total production lasting more than a year and accompanied by high unemployment. A milder contraction is called a **recession**, which is a decline in total production lasting at least two consecutive quarters, or at least six months. The U.S. economy experienced both recessions and depressions before World War II. Since then, there have been recessions but no depressions.

recession

A decline in total production lasting at least two consecutive quarters, or at least six months

Long-Term Growth

Despite these ups and downs, the U.S. economy has grown dramatically over the long run. The economy in 2003 was more than 11 times larger than it was in 1929, as measured by real gross domestic product, or real GDP. With real GDP, the effects of changes in the economy's price level have been stripped away. Therefore, the remaining changes reflect real changes in the value of goods and services produced.

Production tends to increase over the long run because of

1. increases in the amount and quality of resources, especially labor and capital

2. better technology

3. improvements in the *rules of the game* that facilitate production and exchange, such as property rights, patent laws, legal systems, and customs of the market.

Figure 11.5 shows a long-term growth trend in real GDP as an upward-sloping straight line. Economic fluctuations reflect movements around this growth trend. A recession begins after the previous expansion has reached its *peak*, or high point, and continues until the economy reaches a *trough*, or low point. The period between a peak and trough is a recession. The period between a

---

Business Cycles

Figure **11.5**

Business cycles reflect movements of economic activity around a trend line that shows long-term growth. A recession (shown in pink) begins after a previous expansion (shown in blue) has reached its peak and continues until the economy reaches a trough. An expansion begins when economic activity starts to increase and continues until the economy reaches a peak. A complete business cycle includes both the recession phase and the expansion phase.

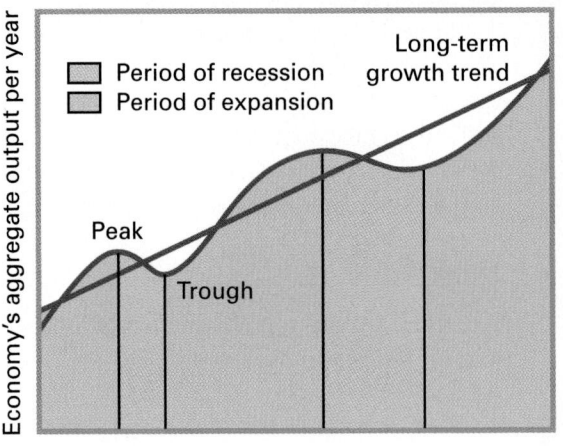

trough and subsequent peak is an **expansion**, or the phase of economic activity during which the economy's total output increases. Note that expansions last longer than recessions, but the length of the full cycle varies.

History of U.S. Business Cycles

Economists at the NBER have been able to track the U.S. economy back to 1854. Since then, the nation has experienced 31 business cycles. No two have been exactly alike. The longest expansion began in the spring of 1991 and broke the record during the first quarter of 2001. The longest contraction lasted five and a half years from 1873 to 1879.

Output changes since 1929 appear in Figure 11.6. The figure shows the annual percentage change in real GDP, with declines in red and increases in green. The big decline during the Great Depression of the early 1930s and the sharp jump during World War II stand in stark contrast. Growth since 1929 has averaged 3.4 percent a year.

Different Impact on States

The intensity of the business cycle varies from region to region across the United States. A recession hits hardest

The National Bureau of Economic Research maintains a Web page devoted to business cycle expansions and contractions. Take a look at this page and see if you can determine how the business cycle has been changing in recent decades. Has the overall length of cycles been changing? Have recessions been getting longer or shorter?

econxtra.swlearning.com

those regions that produce durable goods, such as appliances, furniture, and automobiles. This is because the demand for these goods falls more during hard times than does the demand for other goods and services.

Because of seasonal fluctuations and random events, the economy does not move smoothly through phases of business cycle. At the time of their occurrence, economists cannot always distinguish between temporary setbacks in economic activity and the beginning of a downturn. The drop in production in a particular quarter may result from a snowstorm or a poor harvest rather than

Ask the Xpert!

econxtra.swlearning.com

Gross Domestic Product increased between 1973 and 1974, but they say we had a recession. How could this be?

expansion

The phase of economic activity during which the economy's total output increases

---

Annual Percentage Change in U.S. Real GDP Since 1929   **Figure 11.6**

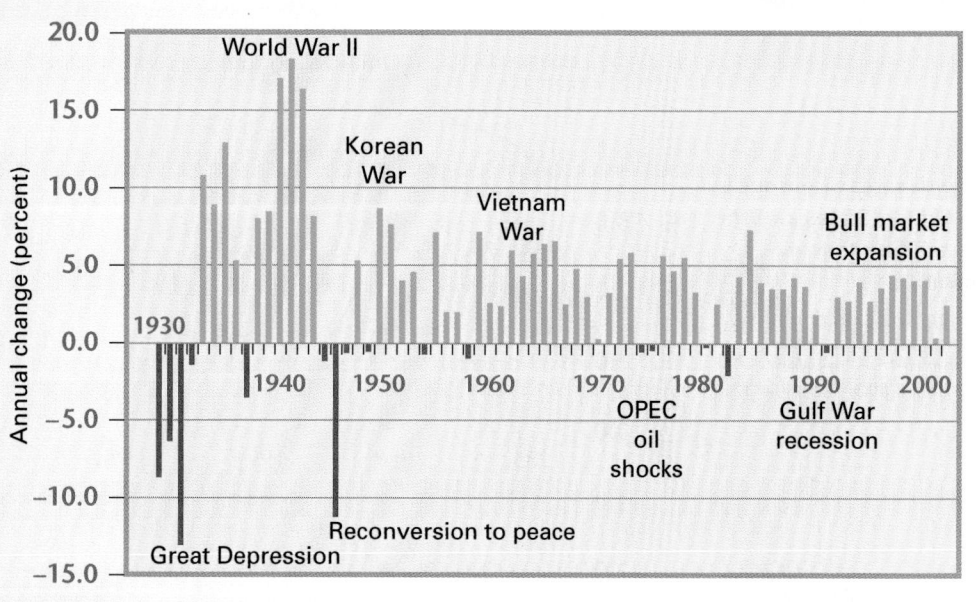

Since the end of World War II in 1945, the economy has gone through 10 business cycles. Expansions averaged just under five years. Recessions averaged just under one year. Note: In this chart, declines are shown in red and increases, in blue.

Source: Based on annual estimates from the U.S. Department of Commerce.

Is the job security of a construction worker who helps to build new homes likely to be affected by a recession? Why or why not?

mark the onset of a recession. Turning points—peaks and troughs—are thus identified by the NBER only after the fact. Because recession means that output declines for at least two consecutive quarters, a recession is not so designated until at least six months after it begins.

Business Cycles Around the Globe

Business cycles usually involve the entire nation. Indeed, market economies around the world often move together. Though economic fluctuations do not also happen at the same time across countries, a link often is apparent. Consider the recent experience of two leading economies—the United States and the United Kingdom. Figure 11.7 shows for both economies the year-to-year percentage change since 1985 in their real GDP. Again, *real* means that the effects of inflation have been erased. Remaining changes reflect *real* changes in the total amount of goods and services produced.

If you follow the annual changes in each economy, you will notice the similarities. For example, in 1991, U.S. real GDP declined, or had a negative growth

U.S. and U.K. Growth Rates

Figure **11.7**

Growth rates of output in the United States and the United Kingdom are similar.

Source: *OECD Economic Outlook* and *Economic Report of the President,* February 2003, Table B-112.

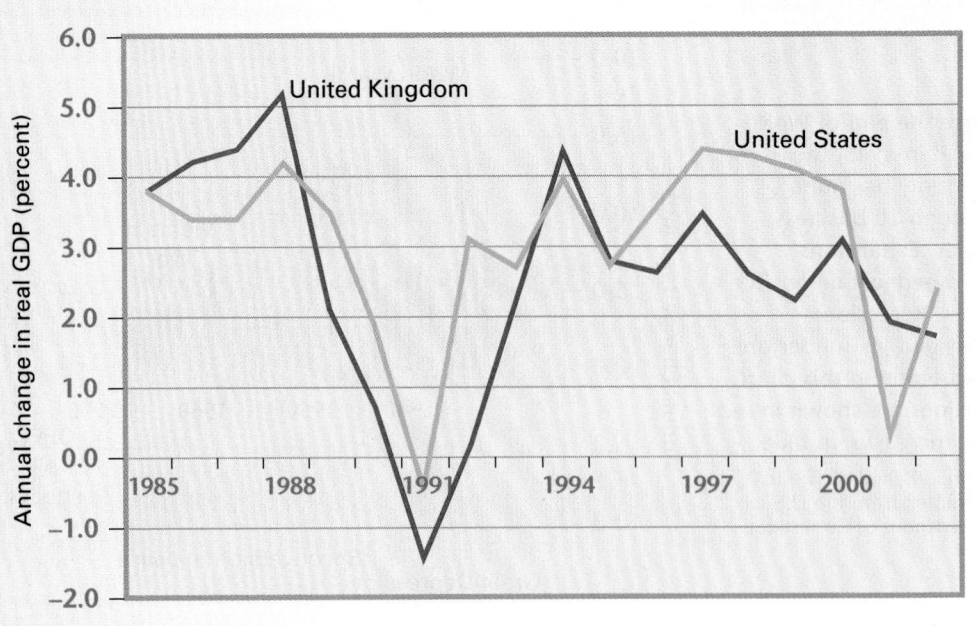

rate, reflecting a recession. The United Kingdom also experienced a recession that year. Likewise, in both economies, growth in 1994 jumped to at least 4 percent, and then slowed the following year.

One problem with the linkage across economies is that a slump in other major economies could worsen a recession in the United States, and vice versa. For example, the terrorist attacks on the United States in September 2001 affected economies and stock markets around the world.

Although year-to-year fluctuations in output are of interest, even more important to an economy's standard of living is its long-term growth trend. U.S. real GDP growth averaged 3.1 percent per year between 1985 and 2002, compared with 2.6 percent in the United Kingdom. This seemingly small difference compounded over the years to raise the level of real GDP much more in the United States. For example, if U.S. GDP had averaged only 2.6 percent growth since 1985, output by 2002 would have been $600 billion below that achieved with its 3.1 percent growth. The lower growth rate would have reduced U.S. production and income in 2002 by about $2,100 per person.

CHECKPOINT
What are the two phases of the business cycle, and what has been the average length of each?

Economic Indicators

During the Great Depression, economists identified measures that would keep better track of the economy. These economic indicators are classified according to their timing relative to the ups and downs of the business cycle. Those that predict future changes are called *leading indicators.* Those that measure the ups and downs as they occur are called *coincident indicators.* Those that measure the ups and downs after they have already occurred are called *lagging indicators.*

To understand economic indicators better, consider weather indicators as an example. A leading indicator tells you what the weather will be like tomorrow. A coincident indicator tells you what's it's like outside right now. The lagging indicator tells you what the weather was yesterday. Leading economic indicators get the most attention because people want to know where the economy is headed.

Leading Indicators

Certain events foretell a turning point in economy. Months before a recession begins, changes in leading economic indicators point to the coming storm. In the early stages of a recession, business slows, orders for machinery and computers slip, and the stock market, anticipating lower profits, turns down. Consumer confidence in the economy's future also begins to sag. Households cut back on their spending, especially for big-ticket items like new cars and new homes.

All these activities are called **leading economic indicators** because they usually predict, or *lead to,* a downturn. There are 10 leading indicators combined into the *index of leading indicators* and reported monthly. Upturns in leading indicators point to an economic recovery. The index of leading indicators is a closely followed measure of economic activity.

Leading indicators cannot predict precisely *when* a turning point will occur, or even *whether* one will occur. Sometimes the leading indicators sound a false alarm. Leading indicators also do not work when there is an external shock to the economy, such as a terrorist attack, drought, earthquake, or hurricane. For example, when Iraq invaded Kuwait, the price of crude oil increased from $25 to $40 per barrel. This caused an economic downturn throughout the world that could not have been predicted by the leading indicators.

leading economic indicators

Measures that usually predict, or *lead to,* recessions or expansions

Coincident Indicators

Some economic indicators measure what's going on in the economy right now. *Coincident economic indicators* are those measures that reflect peaks and troughs as they happen. There are four coincident indicators combined into the *index of coincident indicators,* including total employment, personal income, and industrial production.

Before new houses may be constructed, contractors must obtain building permits from local government. Find out the number of building permits issued in your community in the last two months. In light of this information, what will probably happen to the local economy in the next few months?

What type of economic indicator is provided in a chart that tracks the daily activity of a particular stock?

Lagging Indicators

Some economic indicators measure what has already happened. *Lagging economic indicators* follow, or trail, changes in overall economic activity. There are seven economic measures combined into *the index of lagging indicators,* including the interest rate, measures of loans outstanding, and the average duration of unemployment.

This introduction to the business cycle has been largely mechanical, focusing on the history and measurement of these fluctuations. Why economies fluctuate has not been addressed, in part because such a discussion requires a fuller understanding of the economy and in part because the causes are not always clear. The next section begins to build a framework by introducing a key model of the national economy.

CHECKPOINT
What are the differences among leading, coincident, and lagging economic indicators?

Key Concepts

1. Decide whether the U.S. economy is currently in an expansion or a recession. Identify and explain the types of information that allow you to make this decision.

2. Do you think a recession would harm your community more or less than the average of all communities in the United States? Explain your answer.

3. How would a major expansion of the economies in Europe affect the U.S. economy?

4. If the GDP increased from $1.1 trillion last year to $1.6 trillion this year, would you think the economy is in a recession or an expansion? Explain your answer.

Xtra!
Study Tools
econxtra.swlearning.com

Graphing Exercise

5. Use data in the table to construct a line graph that shows the rate of growth in the real GDP from 1990 through 2001. If the long-range growth rate averaged 3.4 percent per year, which years exceeded this growth rate and which had lower rates of growth? How does your graph demonstrate the business cycle?

Real GDP Growth Rates, 1990–2001

Year	Real GDP Growth	Year	Real GDP Growth
1990	1.8%	1996	3.6%
1991	−0.5%	1997	4.4%
1992	3.1%	1998	4.3%
1993	2.7%	1999	4.1%
1994	4.4%	2000	3.8%
1995	2.7%	2001	0.3%

Think Critically

6. **History** During the early years of the Great Depression of the 1930s, average prices fell in the United States. Explain what this would have done to the real value of the products that were produced in these years.

7. **Management** Explain why the managers of a home construction business would be more concerned with the business cycle than would the owners of a dairy.

movers & shakers

Norman Mayne *CEO, Dorothy Lane Markets*

Headquarters for one of the nation's largest grocery store chains is less than an hour away. Even so, Norman Mayne is proud to say that his three Dorothy Lane Markets are nothing like the chains. In fact, "we ignore what they do," he says.

Mayne is CEO of Dorothy Lane Markets in Dayton and Springboro, Ohio. His father started the business as a fruit stand in 1948. The fruit stand, located on Dorothy Lane, brought in $35 on its first day of business. This was the start of what would become one of the world's leading independent grocery stores. The stores attract visiting grocers from as far away as Europe, Japan, and Australia. The grocers are eager to learn as much as they can about how Dorothy Lane Markets operate.

"Most companies advertise three things," according to Mayne. These are "cheapest prices, best quality, and best service." But, as Mayne has learned, "it's impossible to do all three." In order to offer the cheapest prices, you have to compromise one of the other two, he explains. So after years of spending thousands of dollars each week advertising special prices, Mayne decided to focus his stores on quality and service. He ran his last ad in 1995. He now spends his promotional dollars rewarding his best, most loyal customers, all members of Club DLM.

Mayne gives members of Club DLM special prices. "It's not ethical *not* to give our best customers the best deal," he says. In addition, members receive a monthly newsletter. During Christmas, each store's 100 best customers typically receive a gift and a thank-you note. One year the company's 5,000 best customers received invitations to a popular oldies show that played for one night only in the Dayton area.

Overall, Club DLM allows Mayne and his staff to focus attention on their customers instead of on the competition. Here's how he responded to a recent price war on milk: "Grocers were paying $1.70 for a gallon of milk, yet during the price war they were selling it for 99 cents. We knew that one way to go broke was to lose 71 cents on an item that people buy 200 times a year. So, for Dorothy Lane's best customers we printed coupons that let them buy milk for 49 cents a gallon, limit five. People who just stopped into the store paid full price."

Half of Dorothy Lane's profits come in the fourth quarter of each calendar year. "The three biggest holidays—Thanksgiving, Christmas, and New Year's—all occur during this quarter and are built around great meals," says Mayne. Grocery stores are somewhat recession-proof because people continue to eat during a recession. However, Mayne does notice a difference in spending when customers' pocketbooks are tighter. "We might see our customers purchase lesser-priced cuts of meat, or a less-expensive brand," he says. But one thing seems certain. With Mayne at the helm, Dorothy Lane customers will continue to be rewarded for their business, and Dorothy Lane Markets will continue to be rewarded with loyal customers.

SOURCE READING
Norman Mayne states, "It's not ethical *not* to give our best customers the best deal." How does this thinking differ from that of many major retail chains? When the economy is in a recession, how might Mayne's business gain from this type of thinking?

ENTREPRENEURS IN ACTION
Pretend you are the owner of a car repair shop. A major car repair chain moves in across the street, offering better prices. Think of three things that you and your staff can do to retain customers and continue to grow your business.

Objectives

> Explain what is meant by aggregate output and the economy's price level.

> Describe the aggregate demand curve and the aggregate supply curve, and show how they determine the equilibrium level of price and aggregate output.

Overview

In the study of market economics, the focus is on a particular market, such as the market for pizza. However, the national economy is so complex that you need to simplify in order to focus on the big picture. The perspective broadens from the market for pizza, computers, or cell phones to the market for everything produced in the economy. Aggregate demand and supply curves help you understand how the price and output for the economy as a whole are determined. Like other theoretical models, these can be used to predict what will happen as a result of economic policies and events.

Key Terms

aggregate output

aggregate demand

price level

aggregate demand curve

aggregate supply curve

[In the News]

● Defense Spending and the Economy

In 2003, the war on terrorism and a war in Iraq caused government spending on defense and homeland security to increase dramatically. The spending helped a number of areas of the economy and several industries. Spending on new military equipment increased quite a bit in 2003, and the Pentagon planned to continue increasing its budgets. However, in a growing economy, billions in increased spending should have prompted industry to expand facilities and increase hiring. That didn't happen after the war in Iraq. A major reason sharp economic growth didn't take place was that most companies had excess capacity. Defense spending was preventing some layoffs and allowing some firms to maintain profitability. However, many industries still had a shortage in their private-sector orders. Firms had no need to add workers or open new factories to address increased demands. The increased spending by government to support the war in Iraq did not benefit the economy as much as it did following earlier wars. For example, increased defense spending to support the Korean War between late 1950 and the end of 1951 amounted to about 8 percent of the economy. In today's dollars, that amount would be about $800 billion. Total government spending for defense and homeland security was projected to be almost $600 billion in 2003. That's equal to about 6 percent of projected 2003 GDP.

Think About It

Why do you think the increased spending for defense in 2003 had a smaller impact on the economy than did the increased spending on defense for the Korean War?

◀ ▮ ▶

343

Aggregate Output and the Price Level

Picture a pizza. Now picture food more generally. Food includes not just pizza but thousands of edibles, from eggplant to omelets. Although food is more general than pizza, you probably have no difficulty picturing food. Now make the leap from food to all goods and services produced in the economy—food, housing, clothing, entertainment, education, transportation, medical care, and so on.

Aggregate Output

Aggregate output is the total amount of goods and services produced in the economy during a given period. The best measure of aggregate output is *real GDP.* Just as you can talk about the demand for pizza or the demand for food, you can talk about the demand for aggregate output. **Aggregate demand** is the relationship between the average price of aggregate output and the quantity of aggregate output demanded.

The Price Level

The average price of aggregate output is called the **price level**. You are more familiar than you may think with these aggregate measures. Headlines refer to changes in the growth of aggregate output—as in "Growth Slows in Second Quarter." News accounts also report on changes in the economy's price level—as in "Prices Up Slightly in June." You already have some idea how the economy's price level is computed. What you need to know now is that the price level in any year is an *index number,* or reference number. This compares average prices that year to average prices in some base, or reference, year. If you say that the price level is higher, you mean it's higher compared to where it was. The focus here is on the *price level* of all goods and services produced in the economy *relative to the price level in some base year.*

As discussed in the section about price indexes, the price level in the *base year* has a benchmark value of 100. Price levels in other years are expressed relative to the base-year price level. The price level, or price index, is used not only to compare price levels across time but also to make accurate comparisons of real aggregate output over time.

Real Gross Domestic Product

Economists use the GDP price index to eliminate any year-to-year changes in GDP due solely to changes in the general price level. After this adjustment is made, remaining changes are simply changes in real output, or changes in the amount of goods and services produced. After adjusting GDP for price changes, you end up with real GDP.

CHECKPOINT
What is aggregate output, and what is the economy's price level?

Aggregate Demand and Aggregate Supply Curves

In Chapters 4 and 5, you learned about the demand and supply of a particular product. Now the focus turns to the demand and supply of the total measure of output—aggregate output, or real GDP.

The Aggregate Demand Curve

Just as you can talk about the demand for pizza or the demand for movie tickets, you can talk about the demand for aggregate output in the economy. The **aggregate demand curve** shows the relationship between the price level in the economy and the real GDP

---

aggregate output

A composite measure of all final goods and services produced in an economy during a given period; real GDP

aggregate demand

The relationship between the economy's price level and the quantity of aggregate output demanded, with other things constant

price level

A composite measure reflecting the prices of all goods and services in the economy relative to prices in a base year

aggregate demand curve

A curve representing the relationship between the economy's price level and real GDP demanded per period, with other things constant

---

demanded, other things constant. Figure 11.8 shows a hypothetical aggregate demand curve, *AD*. The vertical axis measures an index of the economy's price level relative to a 1996 base-year price level of 100. The horizontal axis shows real GDP, which measures aggregate output in dollars of constant purchasing power (here, based on 1996 prices).

The aggregate demand curve in Figure 11.8 reflects an inverse relationship between the price level in the economy and real GDP demanded. Aggregate demand sums the demands of the four economic decision makers: households, firms, governments, and the rest of the world. As the price level increases, other things constant, households demand less housing and furniture, firms demand fewer trucks and tools, governments demand less computer software and military hardware, and the rest of the world demands less U.S. grain and U.S. aircraft.

Here's a quick explanation of the inverse relationship between price level and real GDP demanded. Real GDP demanded depends in part on household wealth. Some wealth is typ-ically held in bank accounts and in currency. An increase in the price level, other things constant, decreases the purchasing power of bank accounts and currency. Households, therefore, are poorer in real terms when the price level increases, so the quantity of real GDP demanded decreases. Conversely, a reduction in the price level increases the purchasing power of bank accounts and currency. Because households are richer as the price level decreases, the quantity of real GDP demanded increases.

Among the factors held constant along a given aggregate demand curve are the price levels in other countries as well as the exchange rates between the U.S. dollar and foreign currencies. When the U.S. price level increases, U.S. products become more expensive relative to foreign products. Consequently, households, firms, and governments both here and abroad decrease the quantity of U.S. real GDP demanded. On the other hand, a lower U.S. price level makes U.S. goods relatively cheap compared with foreign goods, so the quantity of U.S. real GDP demanded increases.

Aggregate Demand Curve

Figure 11.8

The quantity of output demanded is inversely related to the price level, other things constant. This inverse relationship is reflected by the aggregate demand curve AD.

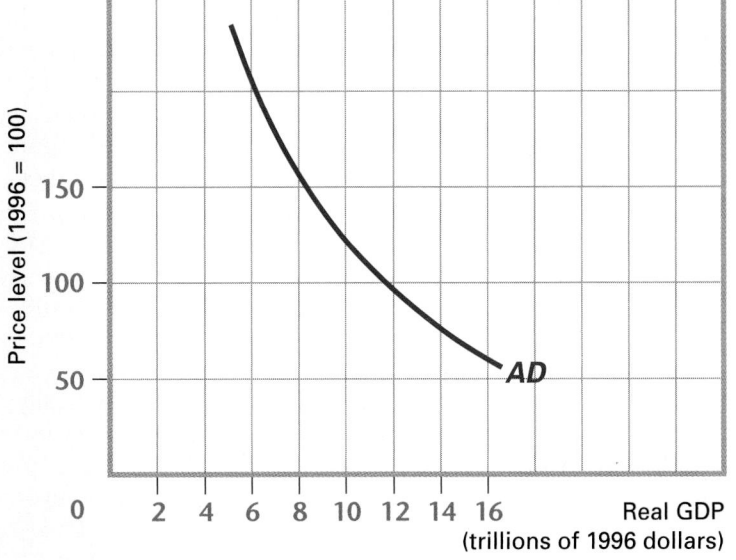

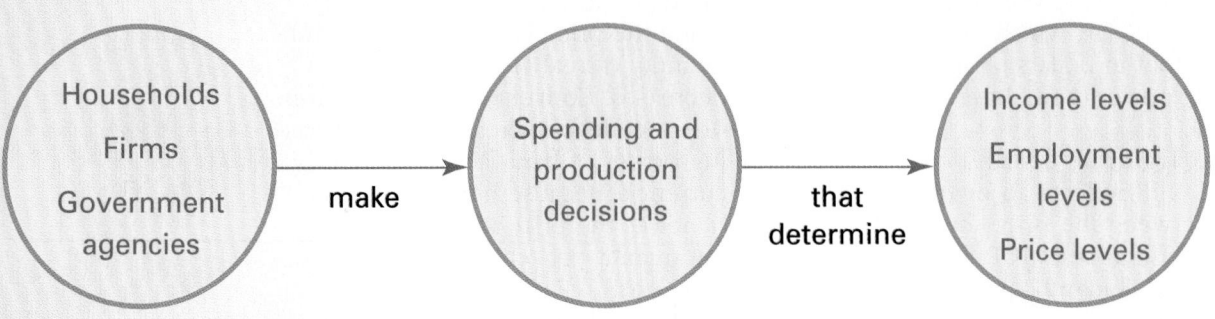

Households, firms, and government agencies make spending and production decisions that determine income levels, employment levels, and price levels.

aggregate supply curve

A curve representing the relationship between the economy's price level and real GDP supplied per period, other things constant

The Aggregate Supply Curve

The **aggregate supply curve** shows how much output U.S. producers are willing and able to supply at each price level, other things constant. How does the quantity supplied respond to changes in the price level? The upward-sloping aggregate supply curve *AS* in Figure 11.9 shows a positive relationship between the price level and the quantity of aggregate output that producers supply, other factors remaining constant.

Assumed constant along an aggregate supply curve are (1) resource prices, (2) the state of technology, and (3) the rules of the game that provide production incentives, such as patent and copyright laws. Wage rates are typically assumed to remain constant along the aggregate supply curve. With wages constant, firms find a higher price level more profitable, so they increase real GDP supplied. *Whenever the prices firms receive rise faster than the cost of production,*

firms find it profitable to expand output. Therefore, real GDP supplied varies directly with the economy's price level, other things constant

Equilibrium

The intersection of the aggregate demand curve and aggregate supply curve determines the equilibrium levels of price and real GDP in the economy. Figure 11.9 is a rough depiction of aggregate demand and supply in 2002. Equilibrium real GDP in 2002 was about $9.4 trillion, measured in dollars of 1996 purchasing power. The equilibrium price level in 2002 was 110.6, compared with a price level of 100 in the base year of 1996. At any other price level, quantity demanded would not match quantity supplied.

Although employment is not measured directly along the horizontal axis, firms usually must hire more workers to produce more output. Greater levels of real GDP are beneficial because (1) more goods and services are available

The total output of the economy and its price level are determined at the intersection of the aggregate demand and aggregate supply curves. The equilibrium reflects real GDP and the price level for 2002, using 1996 as the base year.

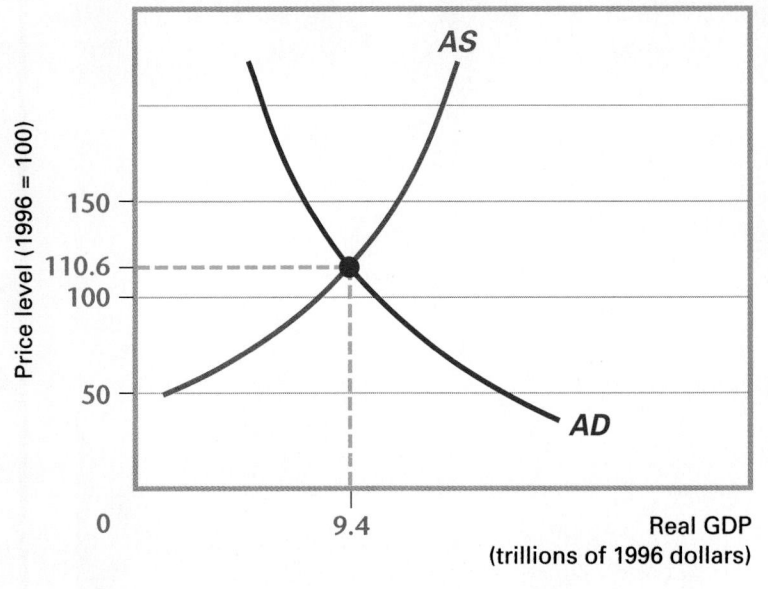

Seven Decades of Real GDP and Price Levels

Figure 11.10 traces the U.S. real GDP and price level since 1929. Aggregate demand and aggregate supply curves for 2002 are shown as an example, but all points in the series reflect such intersections. Years of growing GDP are indicated as blue points and years of declining GDP as red ones. Despite the Great Depression of the 1930s and 10 recessions since World War II, the long-term trend of economic growth is unmistakable.

Real GDP, measured along the horizontal axis in 1996 constant dollars, grew from $0.8 trillion in 1929 to $9.4 trillion in 2002—an eleven-fold increase and an average annual growth rate of 3.4 percent. The price level also rose, but not as much, rising from only 12.6 in 1929 to 110.6 in 2002—an eight-fold increase and an average inflation rate of 3.0 percent per year.

Because the U.S. population is growing all the time, the economy must create new jobs just to employ the additional people looking for work. For example, the U.S. population grew from 122 million in 1929 to 289 million in 2002, a rise of 137 percent. Fortunately, employment grew even faster, from 48 million in 1929 to 134 million in 2002, for a growth of 179 percent. During the last seven decades, employment grew more than enough to keep up with a growing population. The United States has created more jobs than any other economy in the world.

Not only did the number of workers more than double, but workers' average level of education increased as well.

CNN video
Consumer Tales
econxtra.swlearning.com

NETBookmark

Would you like to learn more about the economic history of the past century? J. Bradford De Long's brief article, "Slouching Toward Utopia," provides one economist's evaluation of key developments. Access this article through econxtra.swlearning.com. According to the article, what changes were history's driving force during the twentieth century?

econxtra.swlearning.com

Employment of other resources, especially capital goods, also rose sharply. What's more, the level of technology improved steadily, thanks to breakthroughs such as the computer chip. The availability of more and higher-quality human capital and physical capital increased the productivity of each worker. This contributed to the eleven-fold jump in real GDP since 1929.

Real GDP is important, but the best measure of the standard of living in an economy is *real GDP per capita*, which indicates how much an economy produces on average per resident. Because real GDP grew much faster than the population since 1929, real GDP *per capita* jumped five-fold from $6,740 in 1929 to about $32,800 in 2002. The United States is the largest economy in the world and has been a leader in real GDP per capita.

The Graphing Workshop

What factors led to the increase in the productivity of the individual worker?

 **CHECKPOINT**

What are the aggregate demand and aggregate supply curves, and how do they determine the economy's equilibrium price level and aggregate output?

U.S. Real GDP and Price Level Since 1929

Figure 11.10

Both real GDP and the price level increased since 1929. Blue points indicate years of growing real GDP, and red points are years of declining real GDP. Real GDP in 2002 was more than 11 times greater than it was in 1929. The price level was more than 8 times greater.

Source: Based on annual estimates from the U.S. Department of Commerce.

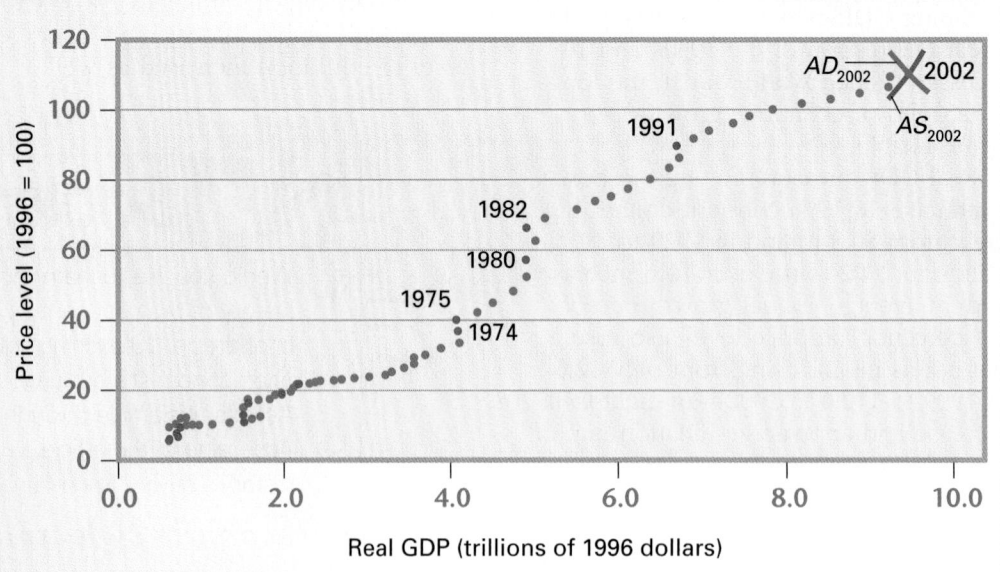

CHAPTER 11 Economic Performance

Ethics in Action

A New, Improved CPI There is no perfect way to measure changes in the price level. The Consumer Price Index (CPI) tends to overstate the true impact of inflation on the price level. The problem occurs in part because the CPI does not take into consideration that higher prices could result from improved quality rather than inflation. Another reason CPI tends to overstate inflation is that it does not recognize that the prices of items in the market basket may change at different rates. Researchers have concluded that the CPI overestimates inflation by about 1 percentage point per year. About 30 percent of all federal outlays are tied to changes in the CPI. The Internal Revenue Service uses the CPI to determine changes in tax brackets. Firms and unions determine changes in cost-of-living allowances based on the CPI. The government also bases Social Security benefits and welfare payments on changes in the CPI. A 1 percent downward correction in the CPI would save the federal budget $180 billion annually by the year 2008. The Bureau of Labor Statistics is now working on this problem. It has introduced an experimental version of the CPI that would reduce measured inflation.

Think Critically

Who would benefit from a more accurate measurement of CPI? Who would be hurt financially? Should government use the more accurate measurement? Why or why not?

Sharpen Your Life Skills

Evaluate Data

The data in the table below can be used to draw conclusions about the average standard of living enjoyed by people in Mexico between 1997 and 2000. In evaluating data, you first identify the subject. Next, identify the types of data given. Then determine the quantities in which the data are recorded. Lastly, compare the values of the data.

Apply Your Skill

1. What happened to the real GDP in Mexico during these years?

2. What impact would the growth in population have had on the standard of living in Mexico?

3. Why would lower rates of inflation tend to cause most people in Mexico to have better standards of living?

4. Why do nations that have lower birth rates tend to have higher standards of living?

Data About Mexico, 1997–2000

Year	1997	1998	1999	2000
Nominal GDP (billions of U.S. dollars)	$401	$421	$480	$574
Population (millions of people)	97.6	98.6	99.5	100.4
Change in Prices	——	15.9%	16.6%	9.5%

Key Concepts

1. Explain how your spending would be affected by a 10 percent average increase in prices. How would this change affect aggregate demand for goods and services throughout the economy?

2. How is it possible for aggregate output to fall at the same time that nominal GDP increases by 2 percent?

3. What effect would an increase in the cost of productive resources have on the aggregate supply curve and on the equilibrium prices of products?

4. What would you need to know to be able to determine whether the real GDP per capita increased from last year?

Graphing Exercise

5. Use the data in the table to construct a bar graph that shows the change in real GDP per capita in the years from 1990 through 2001. What was the average rate of growth in the value over these years?

Real GDP Per Capita, 1990–2001

Year	Real GDP Per Capita	Year	Real GDP Per Capita
1990	$26,834	1996	$28,993
1991	$26,354	1997	$29,915
1992	$26,804	1998	$30,834
1993	$27,160	1999	$31,727
1994	$27,914	2000	$32,663
1995	$28,321	2001	$32,646

Think Critically

6. **History** Study the data in the table. How do you think the lives of many U.S. citizens changed during the Great Depression of the 1930s?

Real GDP Per Capita, 1929–1938
Values in 1929 Prices

Year	Real GDP Per Capita	Year	Real GDP Per Capita
1929	$857	1934	$639
1930	$772	1935	$718
1931	$721	1936	$787
1932	$611	1937	$845
1933	$590	1938	$794

The Panic of 1907

During the 1800s, economic panics were a familiar feature of the American economy. Before 1907, the economy had suffered through four such events in the course of 34 years. In the summer of 1907, the American economy began another downturn. Each fall, the financial system suffered stress because money was needed to move crops from the Midwest to the markets in the East and Europe. Thousands of banks across the country, needing to maintain their reserves, withdrew cash from the country's 47 regional banks. These banks, in turn, withdrew cash from other banks in one of three cities that acted as central reserves—most notably, New York City. While not unexpected, the situation did cause short-term interest rates to rise. What was different in 1907 was that the money supply did not increase to meet the demand for money. Gold that usually would have flowed into the United States from Europe due to the higher interest rate did not do so. In 1907, the banking system that had been able to contain the earlier panics failed.

The panic accentuated an already declining stock market, which had lost 8.9 percent of its value since March 12. It would bottom out on November 15 with a decline of 39 percent as people turned their investments into cash.

Although the New York banking community publicly pledged to support the New York banks, depositors of the Knickerbocker Trust Company began a run. Another bank, not wanting to be stuck with worthless checks, refused to process checks from the Knickerbocker bank. On October 22, $8 million was paid out to depositors and the company closed it doors. New Yorkers lined up outside their banks, fearing for their deposits.

Financier J.P. Morgan decided to take action to restore confidence and end the panic. He called a committee of bankers, which first decided that the Knickerbocker's finances were in such bad shape that it could not be helped. It would be allowed to fail while other more sound banks were helped. The panic extended to banks around the country as they worried that New York banks would refuse them loans, and they began to pull out their reserves.

Morgan and his bankers could not contain the crisis and turned to the federal government. After making a direct plea to President Theodore Roosevelt, Morgan secured the aid of the U.S. government, which agreed to deposit $25 million in New York banks. Industrialist John D. Rockefeller also contributed $10 million in an effort to boost depositor confidence. Morgan also was able to get New York bankers to put another $25 million into ailing banks.

Over the next several weeks, the situation slowly got better. By mid-October, the panic had subsided, but the downturn in the business cycle lasted until June 1908. Banks around the country, afraid of being cut off by larger banks, continued to draw down their reserves and hoarded what cash they had. They stopped extending credit to their customers and suspended making cash payments. Thousands of firms that depended on short-term loans went bankrupt, and thousands of individuals lost their jobs. Much of the trade in the country ground to a halt.

THINK CRITICALLY
Draw a diagram illustrating the effect that a panic and the drawing down of reserves had on local, regional, and national (or central reserve) banks. Your diagram should show the cause and effect of a situation that could cause a banking panic such as that described above for (1) central reserve banks, (2) regional banks, and (3) local banks.

11 Chapter Assessment

Summary

11.1 Gross Domestic Product

a *Gross domestic product (GDP)* measures the market value of all final goods and services produced in a country in a year. GDP can be used to track an economy's performance over time or compare different economies with each other at a point in time.

b To measure GDP accurately, it is necessary to avoid double counting. This can be done only by totaling the value of final goods and services produced or by finding the sum of the value added at each step in producing a product.

c The expenditure approach to calculating GDP counts all spending carried out to purchase goods and services produced. The income approach totals the value of all income earned producing goods and services.

d These two methods reach the same total because one person's spending is automatically another person's income.

11.2 Limitations of GDP Estimation

a There are several difficulties that must be overcome to measure GDP. Chief among these is complex nature of production. A number of simplifications are made. GDP includes only products that are sold in legal markets. GDP is sometimes adjusted for *depreciation* to calculate *net domestic product.* Finally, GDP usually ignores the cost of pollution arising from production.

b GDP often is adjusted for price changes. When prices increase, it is possible for the *nominal GDP* to grow with no actual increase in the amounts of goods and services produced.

c The *Consumer Price Index (CPI)* measures the change in prices charged for a market basket of 400 goods and services sold by retailers across the nation. The GDP price index is found by dividing nominal GDP by *real GDP* and multiplying by 100.

11.3 Business Cycles

a Over time, the level of economic activity fluctuates in a fairly regular way. These fluctuations are commonly called the *business cycle.*

b Business cycles involve periods of *expansion* and periods of *recession.* Expansions are periods of time in which production grows. Recessions occur when real GDP declines for at least two successive quarters, or at least six months.

c Production tends to increase over time because of (1) increases in the amount and quality of resources, especially labor and capital, (2) improvement in technology, and (3) improvement in the *rules of the game.*

d There are factors within the economy that change with the business cycle. Factors that change before the overall economy are *leading indicators.* Those that change at the same time as the overall economy are *coincident indicators.* Those that change after the overall economy are *lagging indicators.*

11.4 Aggregate Demand and Aggregate Supply

a The total production of all goods and services within an economy is called the *aggregate output.* The total demand for all goods and services within an economy is called the *aggregate demand.* Price levels in an economic system are determined by the interaction of aggregate output and aggregate demand.

b The *aggregate demand curve* slopes downward, indicating that the quantity of aggregate output demanded increases as the price level falls. The *aggregate supply curve* slopes upward, indicating that the quantity of aggregate output supplied increases as the price level increases.

c Over the past seven decades, real GDP in the United States has increased by 1,100 percent. The best measure of a nation's standard of living is its real GDP per capita.

Review Economic Terms

Choose the term that best fits the definition. On a separate sheet of paper, write the letter of the answer. Some terms may not be used.

_____ 1. The market value of all final goods and services produced in the United States during a given period, usually a year

_____ 2. The structure of economic activity in a locality, a region, a country, a group of countries, or the world

_____ 3. Fluctuations reflecting the rise and fall of economic activity relative to the long-term growth trend of the economy

_____ 4. Measures that usually predict recessions or expansions in the economy

_____ 5. Household purchases of final goods and services except for new residences, which count as investment

_____ 6. Total spending on all final goods and services produced in the economy during the year

_____ 7. The purchase of new plants, new equipment, new buildings, new residences, and net additions to inventories

_____ 8. The value of capital stock that is used up or becomes obsolete in producing GDP

_____ 9. GDP based on prices at the time of the transaction; current-dollar GDP

_____10. The economy's aggregate output measured in dollars of constant purchasing power, GDP measured in terms of the goods and services produced

_____11. A composite measure reflecting the prices of all goods and services in the economy relative to prices in a base year

_____12. A measure of inflation based on the cost of a fixed market basket of goods and services purchased by a typical family

_____13. A decline in total production lasting at least two consecutive quarters, or at least six months

_____14. The phase of economic activity during which the economy's total output increases

a. **aggregate demand**

b. **aggregate demand curve**

c. **aggregate expenditure**

d. **aggregate income**

e. **aggregate output**

f. **aggregate supply curve**

g. **business cycle**

h. **consumer price index (CPI)**

i. **consumption**

j. **depreciation**

k. **economy**

l. **expansion**

m. **gross domestic product (GDP)**

n. **investment**

o. **leading economic indicators**

p. **nominal GDP**

q. **price level**

r. **real GDP**

s. **recession**

Review Economic Concepts

15. Which of the following would be included in GDP?

    a. the value of a used car your family purchased

    b. the amount you received in your pay check

    c. the weekly allowance your parents give you

    d. the $30 you received from your aunt for your birthday

16. The __?__ is a method of measuring GDP that adds up all spending on final goods and services produced in the economy.

17. **True or False** If you bake a cake from a cake mix and sell it for $8, you have added $8 to GDP.

18. __?__ GDP has not been adjusted for changes in price.

19. If last year's *consumer price index* was 185.0, and this year's is 192.4 how much inflation has there been in the past year?

  a. 7.4%

  b. 3.8%

  c. 5.0%

  d. 4.0%

20. **True or False** The value of capital *depreciation* is not considered when GDP is calculated.

21. __?__ usually predict what is likely to happen to the economy in the near future.

22. **True or False** A *business cycle* will affect all states, people, and businesses equally.

23. The *business cycle* consists of two phases that are called

  a. expansions and recessions.

  b. recessions and contractions.

  c. inflation and recessions.

  d. expansions and inflation.

24. *Aggregate demand* and *aggregate supply* interact to determine

  a. business profits.

  b. government tax receipts.

  c. investment.

  d. real GDP and the price level.

Apply Economic Concepts

25. **Measuring GDP** Identify which of the following activities would be included in the measurement of GDP. For those that would be included, tell whether they would be used in the income approach or expenditure approach.

Activity	Included in GDP?	Expenditure Approach	Income Approach
Buying a used bicycle	_____	_____	_____
Paying for a movie ticket	_____	_____	_____
Being paid to sell magazines	_____	_____	_____
Buying a new coat	_____	_____	_____
Mending your own shirt	_____	_____	_____
Earning interest on your savings	_____	_____	_____
Earning profit from a business	_____	_____	_____
Paying a toll to use a bridge	_____	_____	_____

26. **Calculating Real GDP** Suppose the gross domestic product of Germany was 3,420 billion euros in 2004 and 3,560 billion euros in 2005. Between the same years, the German CPI increased from 120.0 to 122.4. What was the real growth in Germany's real GDP in this time period?

27. **Evaluating Leading Indicators** Suppose the following events took place in the U.S. economy. Explain why each would be a leading indicator and what each would predict about future economic activity in the U.S. economy.

- The value of the stock market increases by 12 percent.
- The number of orders businesses have received but not filled falls by 8 percent.
- The number of hours employees work each week grows from 42.1 to 44.6.
- Business inventories of finished goods decline by 20 percent.

Real Spending in the U.S. Economy, 1996–2000
Values in Billions of 1996 Dollars

Year	Consumption	Investment	Government	Net Exports
1996	$5,237.5	$1,242.7	$1,422.9	−$ 89.0
1997	$5,423.9	$1,392.8	$1,455.4	−$113.3
1998	$5,683.7	$1,557.7	$1,483.3	−$221.1
1999	$5,968.4	$1,659.0	$1,531.8	−$316.9
2000	$6,257.8	$1,772.7	$1,572.6	−$399.1

28. **Skills Check: Evaluate Data** The data in the table indicate real spending in the economy in the years from 1996 through 2000. Use these data to calculate the real GDP for each of these years. How much growth was there in the real GDP from 1996 through 2000? What does the real GDP per capita in 2000 show about the state of the economy in that year?

29. **Mathematics** In 2001, real GDP was $10,208 billion. Suppose that the real GDP for the United States increased at the following rates in the five years following 2001.

Calculate the real value of GDP in 2001 dollars for each of these years. What would this mean for aggregate demand and supply in our economy?

Year	Rate of Increase in Real GDP	Real GDP in Billions
2002	2.4%	_____
2003	2.6%	_____
2004	3.3%	_____
2005	4.1%	_____
2006	2.5%	_____

 *econxtra.swlearning.com*

30. Access **EconData Online** through econxtra.swlearning.com. Read the article on Real Gross Domestic Product (GDP). Is it possible for nominal GDP to rise at the same time real GDP declines? Why or why not? For help with answering this question, access the data series for nominal GDP and real GDP. These links are provided on the second page of the article.

12 Economic Growth

Consider

Why do surgeons earn more than barbers, and accountants earn more than file clerks?

Why is the standard of living so much higher in some countries than in others?

How can a nation boost its standard of living?

Why is the economy's long-term growth rate more important than short-term fluctuations in economic activity?

What is labor productivity, and why has it grown faster in recent years?

POINT YOUR BROWSER

econxtra.swlearning.com

© Getty Images/PhotoDisc

Objectives

> Use the production possibilities frontier to analyze economic growth.

> Define labor productivity, and discuss what can increase it.

Overview

Throughout history, economic growth has been the primary way of easing poverty and raising living standards. Over the last century, there has been an incredible increase in the U.S. standard of living as measured by the goods and services available per capita. An economy's standard of living grows because of (1) increases in the amount and quality of resources, (2) better technology, and (3) improvements in the rules of the game—such as tax laws, property rights, patent laws, the legal system, and customs of the market—that enable production and exchange.

Key Terms

standard of living

productivity

labor productivity

human capital

physical capital

capital deepening

rules of the game

[In the News]

● The Chinese Are Coming on Strong

China's GDP grew approximately 8.3 percent in 2002. Its projected rate for GDP growth in 2004 was 8.5 percent. If China keeps up this rate of growth, it should have the third largest GDP in the world—behind only the United States and Japan and ahead of France, Great Britain and Germany—in three to four years. For 2002 in particular, Chinese GDP totaled $1.2 trillion. In comparison, France's GDP for that year totaled $1.4 trillion, Great Britain's $1.6, and Germany's $2.0. Significantly, however, the growth rates of these three competitors were much lower than China's 8.3 percent rate. France's economy grew at a 1.2 percent rate in 2002. Great Britain's grew at 1.9 percent, and Germany's, at less than 0.75 percent. Of course, it should be many years before the Chinese come close to Japan's $4.0 trillion economy or the United States' 2002 GDP of $10.4 trillion, which exceeded the total GDPs of all other nations in the top six. Nonetheless, the Chinese are in the race and accelerating.

Think About It

China's current population is about 1.3 billion people. To control its population growth rate, the government enforces a "one-child" policy that penalizes people for having more than one child and rewards them for having only one. What effects, if any, do you think this policy might have on China's future economic growth?

◄ | ►

The PPF and Economic Growth

The easiest way to introduce the idea of economic growth is to begin with the production possibilities frontier, or PPF. The *production possibilities frontier,* first introduced in Chapter 2, shows alternative combinations of goods that the economy can produce if available resources are used efficiently. Here are the assumptions used to develop the frontiers shown in Figure 12.1. During the period under consideration, usually a year, the quantity of resources in the economy and the level of technology are assumed to remain unchanged. Also assumed fixed during the period are the rules of the game that enable production and exchange. These "rules" will be discussed at the end of this section.

In Figure 12.1, production is sorted into two broad categories—consumer goods and capital goods. Capital goods are used to produce other goods. For example, the economy can make both pizzas and pizza ovens. Pizzas are consumer goods, and pizza ovens are capital goods.

When resources are employed efficiently, the production possibilities frontier *CI* in each panel of Figure 12.1 shows the possible combinations of consumer goods and capital goods that can be produced in a given year. Point *C* depicts the quantity of consumer goods produced if all the economy's resources are employed efficiently to produce them. Point *I* depicts the same for capital goods. Points inside the frontier are inefficient. Points outside the frontier are unattainable, given the resources, technology, and rules of the game. The production possibilities frontier is bowed out because resources are not perfectly adaptable to the production of both goods. Some resources are specialized and better suited for a particular good.

Economic Growth and the PPF

An outward shift of the production possibilities frontier reflects economic growth. This is shown in each panel of Figure 12.1. What can generate this growth? Any increase in the availability of resources, such as a growth in the labor supply or in the capital stock, shifts the frontier outward. Labor can increase because of an increase in either the quantity or the quality of labor. For example, growth in

---

Economic Growth Shown by Outward Shifts of the Production Possibilities Frontier | **Figure 12.1**

An economy that produces more capital goods will grow more, as shown by a shifting outward of the production possibilities frontier. More capital goods and fewer consumer goods are produced in panel (b) than in panel (a), so the PPF shifts outward more in panel (b).

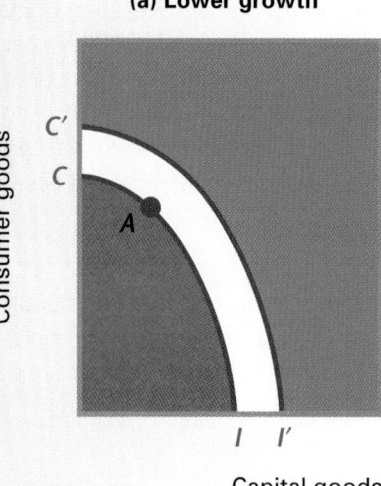
(a) Lower growth

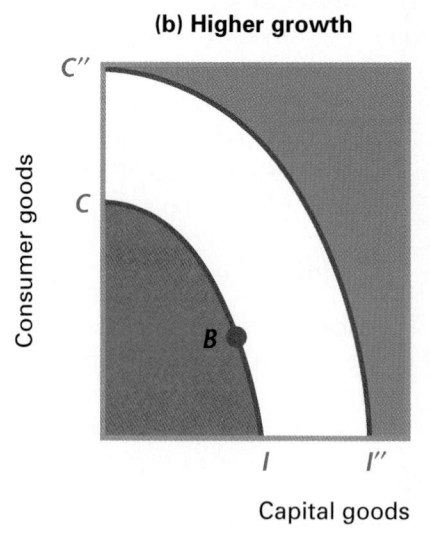
(b) Higher growth

the population can increase the number of workers. An increase in education levels can increase the quality of workers. The greater the quantity or quality of workers, the more the economy can grow, as shown by an outward shift of the PPF.

The capital stock expands if the economy produces more capital goods this year. Any improvement in technology also expands the frontier by making more efficient use of existing resources. Technological change often improves the quality of capital goods. It also can increase the productivity of any resource.

Finally, any improvements in the rules of the game—such as tax laws, property rights, patent laws, the legal system, and customs of the market—that encourage production and exchange will promote growth and expand the frontier. For example, the economy can grow as a result of a patent law revision that encourages more inventions or legal reforms that reduce transaction costs. In summary, *the economy grows because of a greater availability of resources, an improvement in the quality of resources, technological breakthroughs that make better use of resources, or improvements in the rules of the game that enhance production incentives.*

Capital and Growth

The amount of capital produced this year will affect the location of the PPF next year. For example, in panel (a) of Figure 12.1, the economy has chosen point *A* from possible points along *CI*. The capital produced this year shifts the PPF next year out to *C′I′*. However, if more capital is produced this year, as reflected by point *B* in panel (b), the economy will grow more next year. The PPF will shift farther outward next year, to *C″I″*.

An economy that produces more capital this year is said to *invest* more in capital. As you can see, to invest more in capital goods, people must give up some consumer goods. Thus, the opportunity cost of more capital goods this year is having fewer consumer goods available this year. More generally, to invest in capital, people in the economy must save more now—that is,

they must give up some current consumption. Investment cannot occur without saving. Economies that save more can invest and grow more.

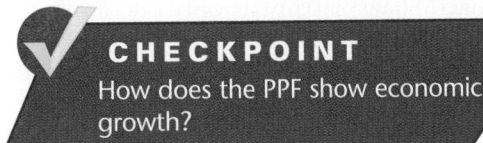

CHECKPOINT
How does the PPF show economic growth?

Productivity

Productivity measures how efficiently resources are employed. In simplest terms, the greater the productivity, the more goods and services can be produced from a given amount of resources. Economies that use resources more efficiently create a higher **standard of living**, meaning that more goods and services are produced per person.

Labor Productivity

Productivity compares total output to a specific measure of input. It usually reflects an average, expressing total output divided by the amount of a particular kind of resource employed, such as bushels of grain per acre of farm land. **Labor productivity** is the output per unit of labor. It measures total output divided by the hours of labor employed to produce that output.

Economists can focus on the productivity of any resource, such as labor, capital, or land. When agriculture made up the bulk of output in the economy, land productivity, such as bushels of grain per acre, shaped the standard of living. Where soil was rocky and barren, people were less well off than where soil was fertile and fruitful. Even today, in many countries around the world, land productivity determines the standard of living.

Industrialization and trade have freed many economies from dependence on land fertility. Today some of the world's most productive economies have relatively little land or have land of poor fertility. For example, Japan has a relatively

standard of living

An economy's level of economic prosperity; best measured by the value of goods and services produced per person

productivity

Compares output to a specific measure of input; usually reflects an average, such as bushels of grain per acre of farm land

labor productivity

Output per unit of labor; measured as total output divided by the hours of labor employed to produce that output

Glossary Terms

human capital

The accumulated knowledge, skill, and experience of the labor force

physical capital

The machines, buildings, roads, airports, communications networks, and other manufactured creations used to produce goods and services; also called capital goods

capital deepening

An increase in the quantity and quality of capital per worker; one source of rising labor productivity

rules of the game

The formal and informal institutions that provide production incentives and promote economic activity, such as laws, customs, and conventions

high living standard even though its population, which is about 40 percent that of the United States, lives on a land area that is only 4 percent of the U.S. land area. Put another way, compared to the United States, Japan has only one tenth the land area per capita.

Human and Physical Capital

Labor is the resource most commonly used to measure productivity. Why labor? First, labor accounts for a large share of the cost of production—about 70 percent on average. Second, labor is more easily measured than other inputs, whether it's in hours of work per week or number of full-time workers per year. Measures of employment and hours worked are more readily available and more reliable than measures of other resources.

The resource most responsible for increasing labor productivity is capital. The two broad categories of capital are human capital and physical capital. **Human capital** is the accumulated knowledge, skill, and experience of the labor force. As individual workers acquire more human capital, their productivity and incomes grow. That's why surgeons earn more than barbers, and accountants earn more than file clerks. You are reading this book right now to increase your human capital.

Physical capital, or *capital goods,* includes the machines, buildings, roads, airports, communications networks, and other manufactured cre-

ations used to produce goods and services. Think about the difference between digging a ditch with your bare hands and digging it with a shovel. Now compare that shovel to an excavating machine, such as a backhoe. More physical capital obviously makes a digger more productive.

As an economy accumulates more human and physical capital per worker, labor productivity increases and the standard of living grows. The most productive combination of all is human capital combined with physical capital. For example, one certified public accountant with a computer and specialized software can sort out a company's finances more quickly and more accurately than could a hundred high-school-educated file clerks with pencils and paper.

Capital Deepening

Two kinds of changes in capital can improve worker productivity:

1. An increase in the *quantity* of capital per worker, and

2. An improvement in the *quality* of capital per worker, as reflected by technological change.

More capital per worker and better capital per worker generally result in more output per worker.

An increase in the quantity and quality of capital per worker is called **capital deepening**. This is one source of rising labor productivity. *Capital deepening contributes to labor productivity and to economic growth.* Over time, more output per worker translates into more output per person, meaning a higher standard of living.

Changes in the *quantities* of labor and capital account for less than half of economic growth. Most growth comes from improvements in the *quality* of resources. As technological breakthroughs lead to new and better capital, total output increases. Thus, capital serves as the primary engine for economic growth.

Rules of the Game

Perhaps the most complex ingredients of productivity and growth are the **rules of the game**. These include the

Access the Bureau of Labor Statistics (BLS) web page on Quarterly Labor Productivity through econxtra. swlearning.com. Find the latest news release on productivity. Read the information about productivity growth in the manufacturing sectors of the U.S. economy. Then summarize the trends in productivity growth in one or two sentences.

econxtra.swlearning.com

© Getty Images/PhotoDisc

© Getty Images/PhotoDisc

Identify the human capital and physical capital in each of these images. Why do you think human capital is more productive in combination with physical capital?

Ethics in Action

Training Foreign Workers to Take Your Job

To reduce costs, a growing number of technology companies in the United States are replacing U.S. workers with less-expensive foreigners. In many cases, the U.S. workers are paid to train their own replacements before being laid off. The situation is spurred by the government's nonimmigrant visa program and the L-1 classification. The L-1 visa permits companies to transfer workers from overseas offices to the United States for up to three years. Moreover, the L-1 allows those companies to pay the foreign workers the lower wage they would be earning in their own country. An American computer programmer earns about $60 per hour in wages and benefits. Indian, Pakistani, or Chinese programmers working in their native countries receive about $10 an hour.

Think Critically

Do you think importing less-expensive foreign workers via the L-1 visa classification is an ethical business practice? Why or why not?

Investments that increase the quality and quantity of capital per worker contribute to rising labor productivity. This, in turn, *leads to* more output per worker, and *higher standards of living.*

THE WALL STREET JOURNAL

Reading It Right What's the relevance of the following statement from *The Wall Street Journal:* "Some economists say productivity growth will take an additional and longer-lasting hit in the terrorist attack's aftermath."

formal and informal institutions that provide production incentives and promote economic activity. Rules of the game include the laws, customs, and conventions that encourage people to undertake productive activity. A stable political environment and a system of well-defined property rights are important. Little investment will occur if potential investors think their capital might be taken over by government, stolen by thieves, destroyed by civil unrest, or blown up by terrorists.

Improvements in the rules of the game can affect the incentives that reward successful innovation and investment. Better incentives can boost economic growth and improve the standard of living. For example, a more stable political climate could promote investment in the economy. Conversely, destabilizing events such as wars and terrorist attacks can discourage investment and harm productivity and economic growth.

CHECKPOINT
What is labor productivity, and what can increase it?

What "rule" do you think this sign represents? How would it affect productivity in the economy?

Key Concepts

1. Why does the U.S. production possibilities frontier shift outward in May and June of each year? What does this have to do with the graduation of many students from high school or college?

2. Why is it more difficult for poorer nations to invest in capital goods than it is for wealthier nations?

3. Why wouldn't the act of giving new computers to the rural residents of a less-developed country add much to that nation's labor productivity?

4. How is capital deepening demonstrated by an increased number of students who purchase computers to help them in their studies?

5. How could a cut in payroll taxes make businesses more productive?

Xtra!
Study Tools
econxtra.swlearning.com

Graphing Exercise

6. Use the data in the table to construct a bar graph of investment in physical capital during the 1990s. Explain how changes in the level of investment in physical capital are likely to affect productivity in our economy.

Year	Investment in Physical Capital (in billions of real 1996 dollars)
1992	$ 630.6
1994	$ 744.6
1996	$ 899.4
1998	$1,135.9
2000	$1,350.7

Think Critically

7. **Management** You are the president of a small corporation. Your firm made good profits last year and could afford to pay increased dividends. You, however, think those funds should be used to purchase a new computer system to improve the efficiency of your firm's production. Write a letter to your firm's stockholders, explaining the benefits of your proposed use of the firm's profits.

8. **Research** Use newspapers or Internet sources to find information about college programs you might enroll in to improve your human capital. Explain how completing a college degree could increase your productivity.

Sharpen Your Life Skills

Categorize Information

Each of the following events contributed to the stock of either human capital or physical capital in the United States. Make two lists. The term *human capital* should head the first one and *physical capital* should head the second. Then place each event in the appropriate list. Some of these events may have contributed to stocks of both human and physical capital. Describe how each event contributed to increased productivity in the U.S. economy.

A.   In 2000, more than $264 billion was spent on research and development in the United States.

B.   In 2000, more than 2.5 million students graduated from high school.

C.   In 2000, the U.S. government provided more than $85 billion in aid for education.

D.   In 1999, 81 percent of all public-school students attended schools that had some access to the Internet. Fifty-three percent of all schools provided access to the Internet for instruction in at least one classroom.

E.   In 2000, U.S. government agencies provided grants of more than $17 billion to colleges and universities for research and development.

F.   In 2000, the federal Small Business Administration (SBA) provided more than $48 billion in loans to businesses.

G.   In 2000, U.S. businesses spent more than $758 billion to purchase new machinery

H.   In 1999, more than 88 million seats were taken by adults in continuing education courses.

Apply Your Skill

1.   In 1998, a law was passed that eliminated federal taxes on interest earned on U.S. savings bonds that was used to pay for the education of taxpayers or their children. Was this law intended to encourage investment in human or physical capital? Explain your answer.

2.   Soon after 2000, the state of New York passed a law that allowed residents to deduct as much as $2,000 from their state income tax liability if they purchased a new hybrid gasoline/electric-powered automobile. Was this law intended to encourage investment in human or physical capital? Explain your answer.

movers & shakers

Jerry Yang and David Filo *Founders, Yahoo!*

When Jerry Yang was 10 years old, his mother moved him and his brother from Taipei, Taiwan, to San Jose, California. Although his mother was an English teacher, Yang knew just one word of English when he moved to the United States. He quickly caught on to the language, however, and within three years he was a straight-A student. Yang's good grades earned him a spot in Stanford University's electrical engineering program. After earning bachelor's and master's degrees, Yang intended to look for a job. Because the labor market was in a slump at the time, however, he stayed at Stanford instead to work toward a Ph.D.

David Filo grew up in Moss Bluff, Louisiana, and attended nearby Tulane University. There he earned a bachelor's degree in computer engineering. Afterwards he attended Stanford University and earned a master's degree in electrical engineering. Filo, too, remained at Stanford to work towards a Ph.D.

Then the two got sidetracked.

"I was terribly bored," Filo recalls, as he discussed the outline of his unfinished graduate thesis. Yang was not anxious to complete his coursework, either. To fight the boredom, the two began surfing the still-developing World Wide Web. "Really, we'd do anything to keep from working on our theses," Yang remembers. In February 1994, as a hobby, Yang and Filo started a guide to keep track of their favorite online destinations on the Internet. Eventually their lists became too long, so they broke the lists into categories. When the categories became too full, the partners created subcategories.

Yang and Filo first called their web site "Jerry's Guide to the World Wide Web." Later, with the help of a dictionary, they settled on "Yahoo!" Although the guide was initially created for their own use, they later shared it with fellow students. "And then, a funny thing happened," Yang smiles. Within months, Yahoo! celebrated its first million-hit day.

"The first ingredient in our success was that we created Yahoo! as a hobby while students at Stanford—we never thought it would become a business," Yang explains. They created the site "because we loved it . . . not to make money." In March 1995, Yang and Filo incorporated the business and met with dozens of venture capitalists. Just one month later, Sequoia Capital agreed to an initial investment of almost $2 million.

Today, Yahoo! Inc. is a leading Internet communications, commerce, and media company that provides services to more than 237 million people each month worldwide. Total sales for 2002 reached just over $953 million with net income close to $43 million. In October 2003, the stock market valued the company at $25 billion. Not bad for a couple of college guys who started their business as a way to avoid completing their college coursework!

SOURCE READING

Using direct quotations from this feature, describe the human capital that Yang and Filo brought to the venture at its start. What type of physical capital do you think is used in running Yahoo today?

ENTREPRENEURS IN ACTION

In small groups, brainstorm a list of hobbies that might provide the potential for wealth. Are there specific areas of the country, or the world, that would provide a performance advantage for each business? Who might be interested in investing in the business? Why?

Objectives

> Explain why there is such a difference among countries in the standard of living.

> Evaluate the record of U.S. labor productivity growth, and explain why even small differences in growth rates are important.

Overview

The single most important determinant of a nation's standard of living over the long run is the productivity of its resources. A nation prospers by getting more from its resources. Even a relatively small growth in productivity, if continued for years, can have a huge effect on the average living standard—that is, on the average availability of goods and services per capita. Growing productivity is critical to a rising standard of living. It has kept the United States ahead of every other major economy in the world.

Key Terms

industrial market countries

developing countries

Group of Seven (G-7)

[In the News]

• Standard of Living and the Poverty Threshold

Living standards vary both within a country and among countries. However, no matter what the standard of living, poverty exists in all countries to some degree. In 1963, Mollie Orshansky of the U.S. Social Security Administration developed the idea of identifying a certain income level that she termed the "poverty threshold." If an individual or family received less than that amount in income each year, they would be considered as living in poverty. Orshansky started with the fact that food expenditures usually were 30 percent of total expenditures for food, clothing, and shelter. She then based her figures on how much it would cost to buy the necessary amount of food called for in the Department of Agriculture's "economy food plan." The percentage living in poverty in the United States has been at or near its all-time low for more than a decade—between 11 and 12 percent, or about 33 million people. Compare this figure to the approximately 23 percent living in poverty in Scotland, more than 55 percent in Zambia, and 60 percent of Palestinians living in the West Bank and Gaza. Over the years, the dollar amounts of the U.S. poverty-threshold income level have been increasing, due to inflation and other factors. For individuals it is now at $8,980, up from $1,539 in 1963. Similarly, the level for a family of four has risen from $3,169 in 1963 to $18,400 in 2003. The poverty threshold will continue to rise with the general level of prices in the economy.

Think About It

According to the latest estimates, more than half the world's population lives on less than the equivalent of $2 per day. Do you think the United States has a duty to help feed the poor of the world? Why or why not?

Standard of Living

There are vast differences in the standards of living among countries. For example, per capita output in the United States is more than 50 times that of the world's poorest countries. With only 5 percent of the world's population, the United States produces more than the nations making up the bottom 50 percent of the world's population put together. You might say that poor countries are poor because they experience low labor productivity.

Industrial and Developing Economies

The world's economies can be sorted into two broad groups. **Industrial market countries**, or *developed countries*, make up about 20 percent of the world's population. They include the advanced market economies of Western Europe, North America, Australia, New Zealand, and Japan. Industrial market countries were the first to experience long-term economic growth during the nineteenth century. Today they have the world's highest standard of living, based on their abundant human and physical capital.

The rest of the world—the remaining 80 percent of the population—consists of **developing countries**, which have a lower standard of living because they have relatively little human and physical capital. On average, more than half the workers in developing countries are in agriculture. Farming methods in developing countries are primitive. Labor productivity there is low, and most people barely subsist. In the United States, only about 2 percent of all workers are in agriculture. However, U.S. farmers are so productive that they grow enough to feed the nation and export to other countries.

Education and Economic Development

An important source of productivity is the quality of labor—the skill, experience, and education of workers. If knowledge is lacking, other resources may not be used efficiently. For example, a country may have fertile land, but farmers lack knowledge of irrigation and fertilization techniques.

What exactly is the contribution of education to the process of economic development? Education makes workers aware of the latest production techniques and more receptive to new ideas and methods. Countries with the most advanced educational systems also were the first to develop.

One distinguishing feature between industrial economies and developing economies is the literacy of the population. Literacy is the ability to read and write. Among countries that make up the poorest third of the world's population, most adults are illiterate. In contrast, fewer than 5 percent of adults in industrial market economies are illiterate.

industrial market countries

The advanced market economies of Western Europe, North America, Australia, New Zealand, and Japan; also called developed countries

developing countries

Countries with a lower standard of living because they have relatively little human and physical capital

© Getty Images/PhotoDisc

The farm workers in this photo are planting onions. Do you think this photo was taken in a developed country or in a developing country? Why?

Figure 12.2 shows the average years of schooling of the working-age population in the United States and six other leading industrial market economies. Together these seven economies are called the **Group of Seven (G-7)**. In 1970, the average education of the U.S. working population was 11.6 years. This was higher than any other nation in the world. Among other advanced economies, average education ranged from a low of 6.6 years in Italy to 11.3 years in Canada. By 1998, the U.S. edu-

cation average had grown to 12.7 years, but other countries had become even more educated. Americans ranked third behind Germany, at 13.6 years, and Canada, at 12.9 years.

CHECKPOINT
Why is there such a difference among countries in standard of living?

Group of Seven (G-7)

The seven leading industrial market economies, including the United States, United Kingdom, France, Germany, Italy, Japan, and Canada

Research the average years of schooling in your school district for more than one year. Then determine the gross state product per capita for your state for the same years. Is there a correlation?

U.S. Labor Productivity and Output Per Capita

Labor productivity is measured by real output per work hour. The higher the level of labor productivity, the more output per labor hour and the higher the standard of living in the economy. Thus, differences across economies in labor productivity determine differences in living standards. The key to a rising standard of living is the growth in labor productivity.

Average Years of Education of Working-Age Populations in 1970 and 1998

Figure 12.2

The United States has been surpassed by Germany and Canada in average years of education of its working-age population.

Source: Based on estimates developed by the Organization for Economic Cooperation and Development. The 1998 figure for Japan is based on 1990 data.

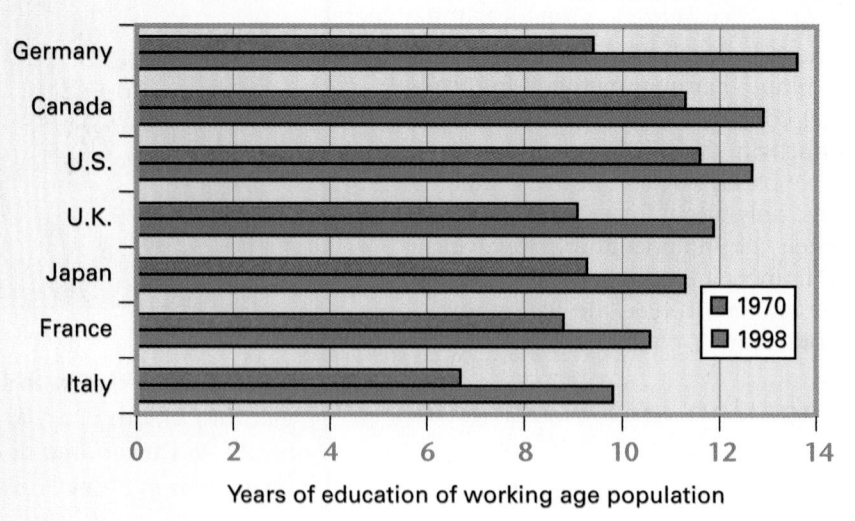

Years of education of working age population

Record Over the Long Run

Figure 12.3 offers a long-run perspective, showing U.S. productivity growth stretching back more than a century. Annual productivity growth is averaged by decade. Note the slowdown during the 1930s because of the Great Depression and the rebound during the 1940s because of World War II. Productivity growth slowed again during the 1970s and 1980s but recovered somewhat after 1990.

For the entire period since 1870, productivity growth averaged 2.1 percent per year. This may not seem like much, but growth has a powerful cumulative effect. Real output per work hour has grown a total of 1,400 percent since 1870. To put this in perspective, if a carpenter in 1870 could build one house in a year, today's carpenter could build 15 houses in a year.

Small differences in productivity growth can amount to huge differences in the economy's ability to produce and, therefore, in the standard of living. For example, if productivity growth had averaged only 1.1 percent per year instead of 2.1 percent, output per work hour since 1870 would have increased by only 325 percent, not 1,400 percent. On the other hand, if productivity growth had averaged 3.1 percent per year, output per work hour since 1870 would have jumped 5,500 percent! The wheels of progress seem to grind slowly, but the cumulative effect can be powerful.

Slowdown and Rebound in Productivity Growth

You can see in Figure 12.3 that productivity growth declined during the 1970s and 1980s and recovered somewhat since 1990. To focus on productivity

Long-Term Trend in U.S. Labor Productivity Growth: Annual Average by Decade   Figure **12.3**

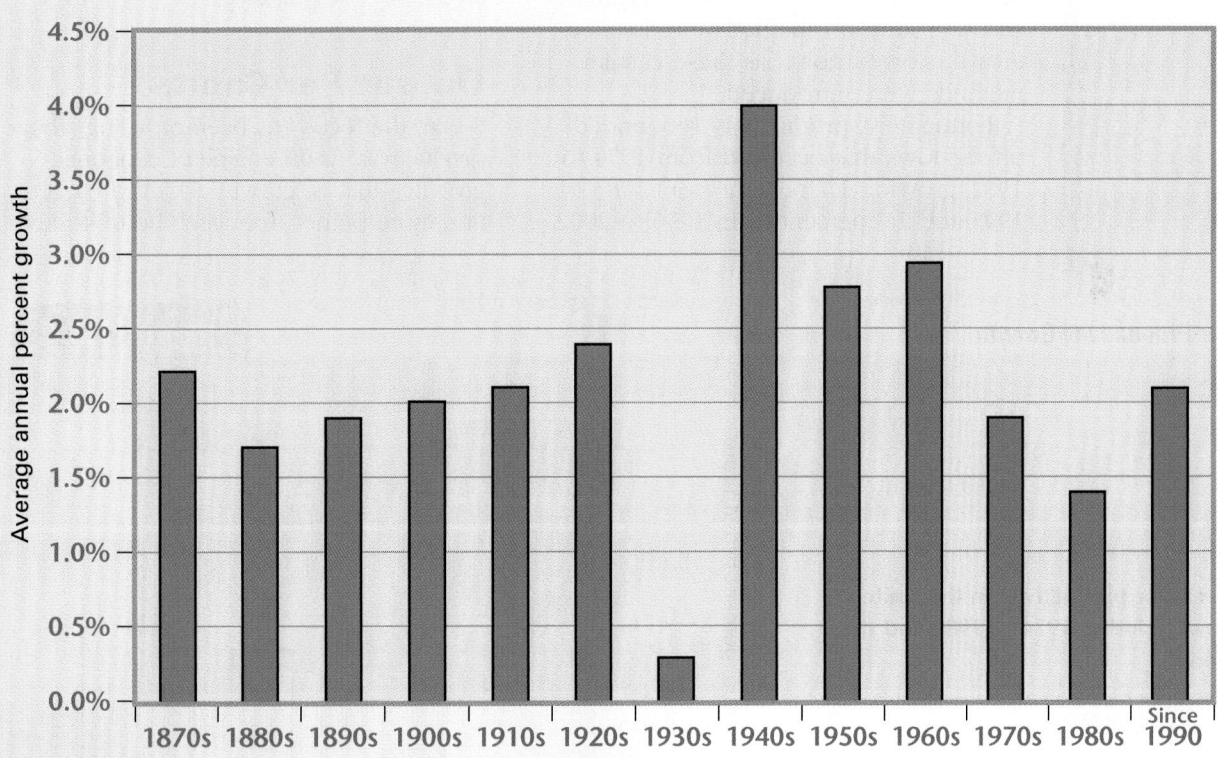

For the entire period since 1870, productivity growth averaged 2.1 percent per year.

Sources: Angus Maddison, *Phases of Capitalist Development* (New York: Oxford University Press, 1982) and U.S. Bureau of Labor Statistics.

trends since World War II, Figure 12.4 offers the average annual growth for four distinct periods. Labor productivity growth declined from an average of 2.9 percent per year between 1948 and 1973 to only 0.8 percent between 1974 and 1982. The rate of growth in labor productivity from 1974 to 1982 was less than a third the rate during the quarter century following World War II. Except for the Great Depression, the rate of growth in labor productivity during this period was less than the average for any decade during the previous century.

Why the slowdown? First, the price of oil quadrupled from 1973 to 1974 as a result of OPEC actions. Spikes in energy prices fueled inflation during the period. This contributed to three recessions, which slowed productivity growth. Second, in the early 1970s, several laws were passed to protect the environment and improve the quality and safety of the workplace. These measures ultimately led to cleaner air, purer water, and safer working conditions. However, they also required more costly production methods. Productivity growth slowed down as these costlier methods were introduced.

Fortunately, productivity rebounded off the lows that occurred from 1974 to 1982, growing 1.7 percent from 1983 to 1995 and 2.7 percent from 1996 to 2002.

Why the rebound? The most dramatic technological development in recent years has been the information revolution powered by computers and the Internet. New technology helps workers produce more. Computers also increase the flexibility of machines, which can be reprogrammed for different tasks. See the E-conomics feature on page 372 for a discussion about the effects of computers on productivity growth.

Higher labor productivity growth easily can make up for output lost during recessions. For example, if over the next 10 years the U.S. labor productivity grows an average of 2.7 percent per year (the average from 1996 to 2002) instead of 1.7 percent (the average from 1983 to 1995), that higher growth would add more than $1 trillion to real GDP in the tenth year. This would more than make up for the output lost during two typical recessions. *This cumulative power of productivity growth is why economists now worry less about short-term fluctuations in output related to the business cycle and more about long-term growth.*

Output Per Capita

So far, the focus has been on rising labor productivity as an engine of economic growth—that is, growth achieved by getting more output from each hour worked.

U.S. Labor Productivity Growth

Figure 12.4

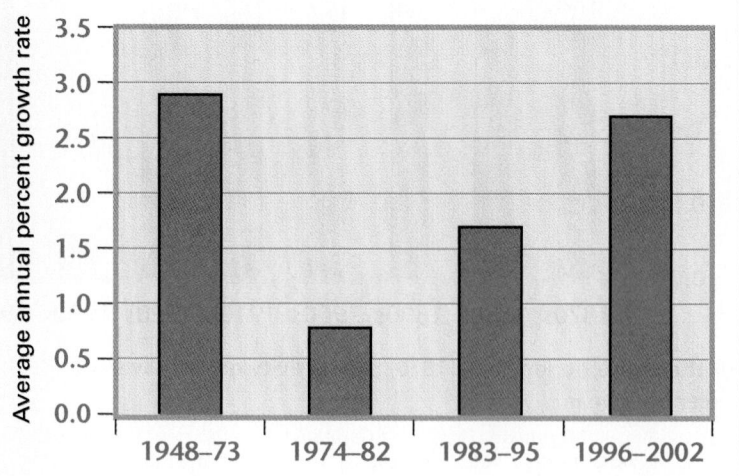

Growth in labor productivity in the United States slowed during 1974 to 1982 and then rebounded.

Source: Averages based on annual estimates from the U.S. Bureau of Labor Statistics.

Even if labor productivity remained unchanged, real GDP would grow if the quantity of labor increased. Total output can grow as a result of greater labor productivity, more labor, or both.

The best measure of an economy's standard of living is output per person, or per capita. *Output per capita,* or real GDP divided by the population, indicates how much an economy produces on average per resident. Labor productivity in the U.S. economy in 2002 was about $65,600 per worker per year. In the United States, one of every two people in the economy is a worker. Therefore, *output per capita* equals output per worker divided by two. In this example, output per capita would be $65,600/2, or $32,800.

Figure 12.5 presents real GDP per capita for the United States since 1959. Notice the general upward trend, interrupted by seven recessions, indicated by the pink shading. Real GDP per capita more than doubled (measured in 1996 dollars) from about $13,100 in 1959 to

about $32,800 in 2002 for an average annual growth rate of 2.2 percent. Since 1959, labor productivity grew an average of 2.1 percent. Output per capita grew faster than did labor productivity because the number of workers grew faster than did the population.

International Comparisons

How does U.S. output per capita compare with that of other major industrial economies? Figure 12.6 compares GDP per capita for the United States and the six other leading industrial nations. The United States produced more output per capita than any other major economy.

Ask the Xpert!
econxtra.swlearning.com

Have computers affected worker productivity?

CNN video
UK Butcher Shops
econxtra.swlearning.com

CHECKPOINT
What has been the record of U.S. labor productivity growth, and why are even small differences in average growth important?

U.S. Real GDP Per Capita Since 1959

Figure 12.5

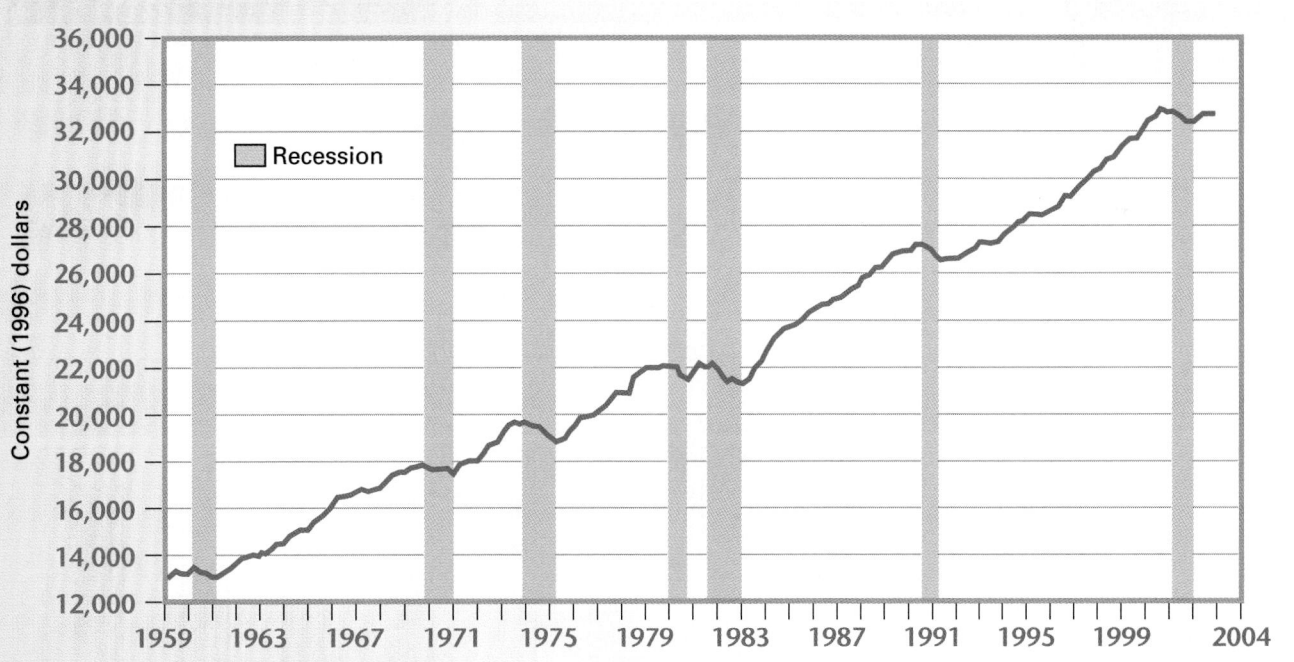

Despite the recessions since 1959, U.S. real GDP per capita has more than doubled. Periods of recession are indicated by the pink-shaded columns.

Source: U.S. Department of Commerce.

E-CONOMICS

Computers and Productivity Growth

The first microprocessor, the Intel 4004, could carry out about 400 computations per second when it hit the market in 1971. Today desktop computers can crunch 2 billion computations per second. This is 5 million times what the Intel 4004 could handle. Such advances in computing power have fueled a sharp increase in computer use. Since 1982, the growth rate of the computer sector has averaged 26 percent annually. PCs are moving beyond word processing and spreadsheet analysis to help people work together. For example, design engineers in California use the Internet to test new ideas with marketers in New York. This cuts development time for new products in half. Sales representatives on the road can use laptops or wireless devices to log orders and provide customer service. New-generation computer systems even monitor themselves and send messages to service centers detailing problems when they arise. For example, General Electric uses these systems and the Internet to keep tabs on factory equipment thousands of miles away. A recent study concludes that information technology (IT) was a leading force behind the improved productivity growth during the second half of the 1990s. Computers affect productivity through two channels: (1) efficiency gains in the production of computers and (2) greater computer use by industry.

Think Critically

Since their introduction to the workplace, what effects have computers had on the quality of human capital in the United States? How has this influenced productivity?

U.S. GDP Per Capita as Compared to Other Major Economies

Figure 12.6

The U.S. per capita income in 2000 stood 25 percent above that of second-ranked Canada and 48 percent above that of France, ranked last among these major economies.

Source: Based on OECD figures, which are adjusted across countries using the purchasing power of the local currency as of 2000.

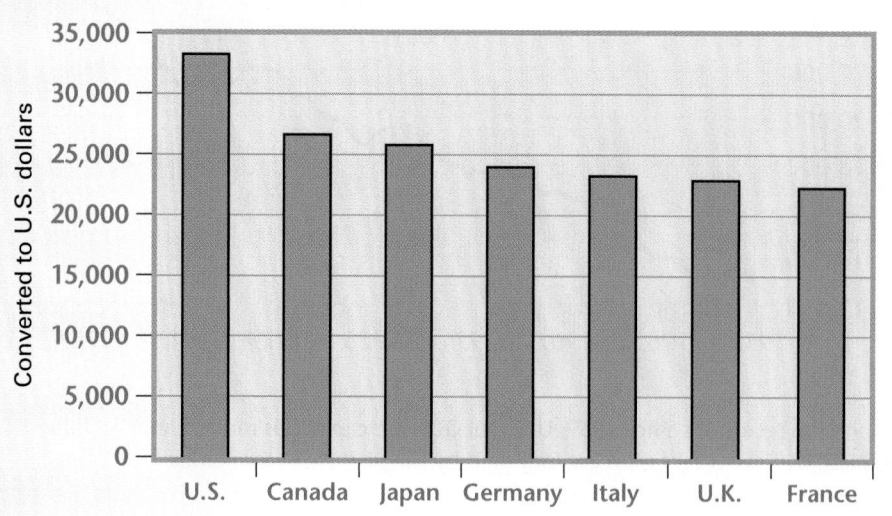

Key Concepts

1. Do you think your standard of living is better than that of your parents when they were your age? Explain your answer.

2. Why is providing education to all residents a difficult task for many developing countries?

3. What if by earning a high-school diploma you are able to produce 25 percent more each year than you could have produced without graduating from high school? How important would this extra production be to you, your family, and the economy in general if you work until you are 67 years old?

4. Identify a specific event or new technology that you think has increased labor productivity in the past five years. Explain how this increase has been accomplished.

5. Measures of output per capita do not consider production that takes place within households. In the past 50 years, a much larger share of U.S. citizens work outside the home. How may this have affected output per capita?

Graphing Exercise

6. As labor productivity grows, the value of output per hour worked increases. The data in the table show the increase in the real output per hour worked in the years from 1992 through 2001. The year 1992 represents 100 percent. Values for years after 1992 show the percentage growth from 1992. For example, the value 101.9 for 1994 shows that 1.9 percent more was produced per hour worked in 1994 than in 1992. Use these data to construct a line graph that shows the change in output per hour worked for these years. Explain what this information shows about the economy.

Real Output Per Hour Worked, 1992–2001

Year	Output	Year	Output	Year	Output
1992	100.0	1996	105.4	1999	113.4
1993	100.5	1997	107.8	2000	117.3
1994	101.9	1998	110.7	2001	119.5
1995	102.6				

Think Critically

7. **Science** Identify and describe a scientific advancement you have studied that has contributed to increases in labor productivity in this country or other countries in the world.

8. **Literature** Identify and describe advances in communications technology that have changed the way books are written and published in recent years. If Shakespeare had lived today, how might his work have been different?

Issues of Technological Change

12.3

Objectives

> Discuss the impact of research and development on the standard of living.

> Explain the relationship between technological change and employment levels.

> Describe industrial policy, and argue for and against its use.

Overview

A major contributor to productivity growth and a rising standard of living is an improvement in the quality of human and physical capital. Improvement of human capital results from better education and more job training. Improvement of physical capital springs from better technology. Some other issues of technological change include the role of research and development and the relationship between technological change and the employment level.

Key Terms

basic research

applied research

industrial policy

cluster

[In the News]

● Defense Spending: How Much Is Enough?

The U.S. defense budget for the fiscal year 2004 stood at almost $400 billion—up from $283 billion in 1999—with more funding requested by President George W. Bush for the war on terror and operations in Afghanistan and Iraq. The $400 billion represented approximately 4.1 percent of projected GDP for the period. Critics said that such an amount was unnecessary, as it took away needed funding from other programs. In addition, they argued that the United States was preparing to fight twenty-first century wars with needless spending on outmoded twentieth-century defense programs. Others maintained that we were not spending enough: that we could and should spend almost double the projected $400 billion without hardship. Such a level, they maintained, would allow us to "go it alone" in many future conflicts and not be subject to potential "vetoes" from allies. Compare U.S. 2004 defense spending to that of other countries for the same year:

- Russia, $65 billion, about 6 percent of its GDP
- Japan, $42.6 billion, about 1 percent of its GDP
- China, $47 billion, about 6 percent of its GDP
- United Kingdom, $38.4 billion, about 2.7 percent of its GDP

Also, contrast the 4 percent of 2004 GDP spent on defense with the percentages the United States spent during earlier wars and conflicts. In the Vietnam War, the country spent approximately 10 percent of GDP on defense; during Korea, 15 percent; during World War II, 43 percent; and during World War I, 14 percent.

Think About It

Is the United States spending enough on defense? Why or why not?

◀ ▮ ▶

Research and Development

Improvements in technology arise from scientific discovery, which is the product of research. Economists distinguish between basic research and applied research.

Basic and Applied Research

The search for knowledge without regard to how that knowledge will be used is called **basic research**. Basic research is a first step toward technological advancement. In terms of economic growth, however, scientific discoveries are meaningless until they are implemented, which requires applied research.

Applied research seeks to answer particular questions or to apply scientific discoveries to the development of specific products. Technological breakthroughs may or may not have commercial possibilities. Thus the payoff is less immediate with basic research than with applied research.

R&D Comparisons Across Countries

Technological change is the fruit of research and development (R&D). Investment in R&D reflects the economy's efforts to improve productivity through technological discoveries. One way to track R&D spending is to measure it relative to gross domestic product, or GDP. Figure 12.7 shows R&D spending as a share of GDP for the United States and the six other major economies for the 1980s and 1990s. Overall R&D spending in the United States averaged 2.7 percent of GDP in both the 1980s and the 1990s. During the 1990s, R&D as a share of GDP ranked the United States second among the major economies. It ranked slightly behind Japan, at 2.9 percent, but well ahead of last-place Italy, at only 1.1 percent.

Bar segments in the chart distinguish between R&D by businesses and R&D by governments and nonprofit institutions. Business R&D is more likely for applied research and innovations. R&D spending by governments

basic research

The search for knowledge without regard to how that knowledge will be used; a first step toward technological advancement

applied research

Research that seeks answers to particular questions or applies scientific discoveries to develop specific products

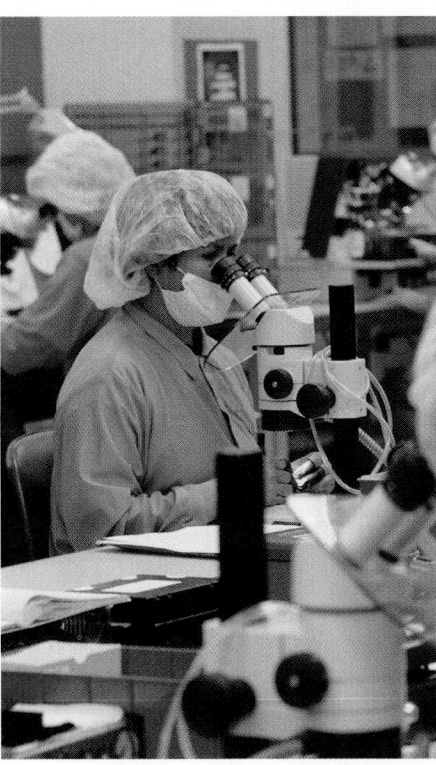

Which of these photos best illustrates basic research, and which best illustrates applied research? Justify your answers with evidence from the photos.

Growth: R&D Spending as a Percentage of GDP for Major Economies During the 1980s and 1990s

Figure 12.7

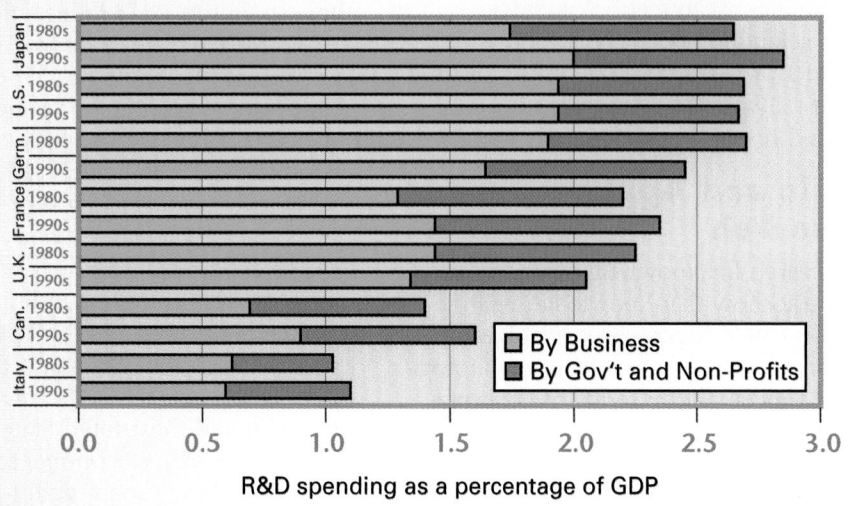

R&D spending as a percentage of GDP

The United States devotes relatively more resources to R&D than most other advanced economies.
Investment in R&D results in a higher standard of living for Americans.

Source: Based on figures from the Organization for Economic Cooperation and Development.

and nonprofits, such as universities, is more likely for basic research. This basic research may generate valuable ideas that ultimately have specific applications. For example, the Internet developed out of U.S. government research for a national defense communications system.

R&D by U.S. businesses averaged 1.9 percent of GDP in the 1990s, the same as in the 1980s. Three of the six other major countries experienced an increase in business R&D between the 1980s and 1990s, and three saw a decrease. Again, only Japan had higher business R&D than the United States had in the 1990s, at 2.0 percent of GDP. Italy had the lowest at 0.6 percent.

In short, the United States devotes relatively more resources to R&D than most other advanced economies. This results in a higher standard of living for Americans.

 CHECKPOINT
What is the impact of research and development on the standard of living?

Technological Change and Employment Levels

Technological change affects the economy in a variety of ways. Most of these effects are beneficial. However, technological change usually reduces the number of workers needed to produce a given amount of output. Consequently, some critics charge that new technology will throw people out of work and lead to lower employment levels.

Technological Change and Labor Productivity

Technological change may increase production and employment by making products more affordable. For example, the introduction of the assembly line made automobiles more affordable to the average household. This stimulated production and employment in the auto industry. The same happened with personal computers.

Technological change also may lead to workers losing their jobs—or being displaced—in some industries. Even in industries where some workers are displaced by machines, those who keep their jobs are more productive, so they earn more. As long as human wants are unlimited, displaced workers usually will find jobs producing other goods and services demanded in a growing economy. Sometimes finding another job requires a worker to be retrained for a new occupation.

Technological Change and Employment Levels Across Countries

There is no evidence that employment levels today are any lower than they were in 1870. Since then, however, worker productivity has increased more than 1,400 percent. The length of the average workweek has been cut nearly in half. Although technological change may displace some workers in the short run, long-run benefits include higher real incomes on average and more leisure—in short, a higher standard of living.

If technological change leads to lower levels of employment, then employment levels should be higher in economies where the latest technology has not yet been introduced, such as in developing countries. In fact, employment levels there usually are much lower. Those who do find work earn relatively little because they are not very productive.

Again, there is no question that technological change sometimes creates hardships in the short run, as workers scramble to adjust to a changing world. Some workers who lose their jobs due to advances in technology may not find jobs that pay as well as the ones they lost. These lost jobs are one price of progress. Over time, however, most of these workers find other jobs, often in new industries created by technological change. In a typical year, the U.S. economy creates many more jobs than it eliminates.

CHECKPOINT
How does technological change affect employment levels?

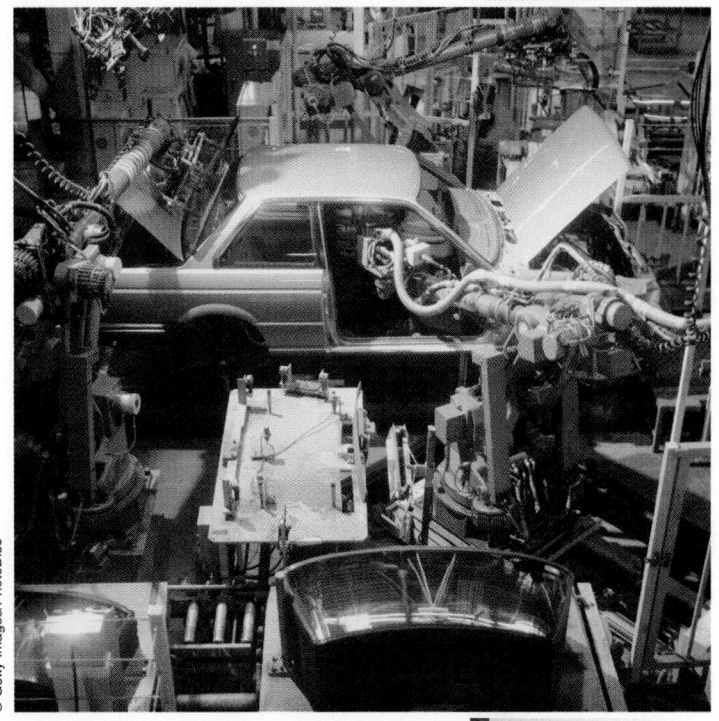
© Getty Images/PhotoDisc

Human workers on some assembly lines have been replaced by automated systems. In a growing economy, what happens to workers who become displaced by technological change?

Industrial Policy

Because technological change is so important to a rising standard of living, some argue that government should become more involved in shaping an economy's technological future. One concern is that technologies of the future will require huge sums to develop and implement. An individual firm cannot easily raise these sums and so will be put at risk. Another concern is that individual firms have less incentive to carry out basic research even though that research eventually has a high payoff for the economy as a whole. The fruits of basic research are not immediately embodied in something the firm can sell. Therefore, an individual firm may go bankrupt before applications are marketable.

industrial policy

The view that government—using taxes, subsidies, and regulations—should nurture the industries and technologies of the future, thereby giving domestic industries an advantage over foreign competition

Government Involvement

One possible solution to the problem of underinvestment is greater government involvement to promote investment in particular industries. **Industrial policy** is the idea that government—using taxes, subsidies, regulations, and coordination in the private sector—could help nurture the industries and technologies of the future. This would give U.S. industries an advantage over foreign competition. The objective of U.S. industrial policy is to ensure adequate investment in research and to secure a leading global role for U.S. industry. See the Span the Globe feature for an example of European industrial policy.

U.S. industrial policy over the years was aimed at creating the world's most advanced military production capacity. With the demise of the Soviet Union, however, defense technologies became less important.

Identifying Industry Clusters

Economists have long recognized that firms in some industries gain a performance advantage by forming a **cluster**. That is, they locate in a region already thick with firms in that same industry or in related industries. Examples of industry clusters include the movie business in Hollywood, Broadway theaters, Wall Street finances, Silicon Valley software, and Orlando theme parks.

Clusters aid communication and promote healthy competition among cluster members. The flow of information and cooperation between firms, as well as the competition among firms located together, stimulates regional innovation and promotes growth. By locating in a region that has similar businesses, a firm also can tap into an established customer base and into local markets for specialized labor and for other inputs.

Many state and local governments are trying to identify the industries that should be promoted in their area. Governments try to attract firms in favored technologies by adopting favorable tax policies. They also may help to pay for the construction of support facilities.

Pitfalls of Picking Technological Winners

Skeptics of industrial policy wonder whether the government should be trusted to identify emerging technologies and to pick the industry clusters that will lead the way. Critics of industrial policy say that markets allocate scarce resources better than governments do. For example, in the early 1980s, the U.S. government spent $1 billion to help military contractors

SPAN THE GLOBE

European Industrial Policy

Airbus, a four-nation aircraft maker, exemplifies European industrial policy in which companies from two or more countries combine efforts to compete more effectively in world markets. Airbus was established as a consortium of French, German, Spanish, and British companies in order to compete effectively with U.S. aircraft manufacturers. In its infancy, Airbus had to integrate the four different business cultures involved. It also had to agree on a common set of measurements and a common language. The company was first created in 1970 between Aerospatiale of France and Deutsche Aerospace of Germany. CASA of Spain and two British companies joined in 1971. The company has received an estimated $20 billion in government aid from the countries involved. It has now become Boeing's main rival. When Airbus seeks aircraft orders around the world, it can draw on government backing to promise special advantages. These include landing rights at key European airports and an easing of regulatory constraints. U.S. aircraft producers do not receive such government backing.

Think Critically

What advantages does Airbus enjoy that U.S. aircraft producers do not?

develop a high-speed computer circuit. However, Intel, a company that received no federal support, actually was the first to develop the circuit.

Japan has had the most aggressive policy for regulating and supporting favored industries. Its approach includes discouraging competition in the industry and encouraging joint research. Those Japanese industries

TEAM WORK

In small groups, brainstorm to identify any business clusters in your region. Then discuss the effects you think the clusters have on economic growth in the region.

subject to the most regulation and support, such as chemicals and aircraft manufacturing, simply became uncompetitive in the world market. Meanwhile, the Japanese industries that had received little government backing, such as automobiles, cameras, and video games, turned out to be dynamic, innovative world competitors.

There also is concern that the government aid and the competitive advantages would be awarded based on political connections rather than on the promise of the technologies. Most economists would prefer to let private firms bet their own money on the important technologies of the future.

cluster

Firms in the same industry or in related industries that group together in a region, such as Wall Street, Hollywood, or Silicon Valley

 CHECKPOINT
What is industrial policy, and what are the arguments for and against its use?

© Getty Images/PhotoDisc

The business of making movies is carried out primarily in Hollywood, California. What are the careers associated with the movie business? Why would people working in these fields benefit from living in or near Hollywood?

NETBookmark

The Bureau of Labor Statistics compiles international data on manufacturing productivity. Access this information through econxtra.swlearning.com. For the most recent period, which nations have enjoyed the most rapid growth in manufacturing productivity? Which nations have experienced the slowest growth?

econxtra.swlearning.com

Key Concepts

1. Which of the following research topics would have a more immediate impact on our nation's productivity: research into new types of genetically engineered plants or research about how genes control the development of fish embryos? Explain your choice.

2. A good deal of R&D in the United States and other countries is devoted to creating new types of consumer products such as shampoo, dish soap, or frozen pizza. Do you think this type of R&D adds significantly to our nation's productivity? Explain your answer.

3. There are many fewer manufacturing jobs in the U.S. economy today than there were in the past. Many people who once held manufacturing jobs have not been able to find new jobs that allow them to earn as much as they did in the past. Do you think government should provide such workers with special benefits? Why or why not?

4. Do you think that government-supported student aid for college students is similar to industrial policy in any way? Explain your answer.

Graphing Exercise

5. The use of computer technology in production in the United States has dramatically increased productivity. Use the data in the table to create a line graph that shows the growth of spending on new computer hardware in the United States during the 1990s. To what extent do you think this investment was responsible for the rapid growth in productivity in these years? Explain your answer.

Spending for New Computer Hardware in the United States, 1990 Through 1999
Values in Billions of Dollars

Year	Spending	Year	Spending
1990	$102.7	1997	$197.4
1995	$155.4	1998	$210.9
1996	$171.9	1999	$225.4

Think Critically

6. **Government** In 1981, Congress passed a law that allowed businesses to deduct 10 percent of the cost of investments they made from their federal income taxes. A firm that purchased a $1 million machine could subtract $100,000 from its federal taxes. This law expired in 1986. Some people think a similar law should be passed today. Would you support such a law? Why or why not?

7. **Science** The federal government has provided many billions of dollars to the National Science Foundation (NSF) to support scientific research and development. Although some of the discoveries made by researchers supported by NSF grants have been of great value to our economy, others have not. Do you think that using several billion dollars each year for the NSF research is a good use of your tax payments? Explain your answer.

Interchangeable Parts and the Assembly Line

First proposed for the gun industry, the idea of interchangeable parts depended on machinery and precise measurements to build parts that were exactly the same. This allowed lesser-skilled workers to use machines to construct identical parts that could be assembled quickly and easily. The result was that productivity increased and cost was reduced. The amount of work that skilled craftspeople did in half a day now could be completed in three-and-a-half minutes.

By the 1850s, meat packers in Cincinnati began to combine slaughtering and processing under one roof. Set up as "disassembly" lines, they were noted as models of efficiency. The hogs were killed with a sledgehammer. Their bodies were then hung from a hook and moved along a pulley through the slaughterhouse. Along the line they were bled, scalded, gutted, and cleaned. Finally the carcasses were dismembered in about 35 seconds by a team of butchers.

Ransom Olds was the first person to mass-produce automobiles. Before mass production, the cars remained stationary in the factory. The workers moved from chassis to chassis assembling parts. Other workers would bring the parts to the workers wherever they were needed. Olds manufactured the cars by bringing all the material, including both the chassis and the parts, to the workers, who remained in one place. Henry Ford used the same process. Frames were arranged in a line in the plant, and teams of assemblers moved down the line performing one assembly operation. Parts already delivered to each station were ready for installation when the assemblers arrived. Following a suggestion by scientific management expert Clarence Avery, Ford installed conveyer belts to deliver the parts.

In 1913, Ford adopted the moving assembly line to automobile manufacturing in his Highland Park plant. Assembly time dropped from 17 hours to six. Workers were more productive, and the cost of the automobile fell— making it affordable to most Americans. Ford was able to give his unskilled workers wages that previously had been available only to skilled workers. In 1914, Ford was selling cars at $440. By 1916 the price had dropped to $345. Following World War I, the Model T roadster was priced at $260.

© Hulton Archive

THINK CRITICALLY

Look at your own life and home and determine the things that make your life more productive, such as computers, telephones, dishwashers, etc. Ask your parents, grandparents, or both to estimate the time they spent on household tasks when they were young, and compare it to the time spent doing them today. What is the effect on everyday life? Write your findings down, and be prepared to compare them with what your classmates have found.

12 Chapter Assessment

Summary

 The PPF, Economic Growth, and Productivity

a Economic growth is the primary way to reduce poverty and raise living standards. When a greater share of a nation's resources is allocated to the production of capital goods, there will be increased rates of economic growth. When this is graphed on a production possibilities frontier, the frontier will shift out over time.

b *Productivity* measures how efficiently resources are employed to create goods and services. The more efficiently resources are used, the higher a nation's *standard of living* is likely to be. Measures of productivity include *labor productivity,* capital productivity, and land productivity. Labor productivity can be enhanced through investments in *human capital.*

c Investments in *physical capital* can take the form of *capital deepening,* which involves adding more or better physical capital to production. Investment in physical capital also may involve the creation and use of new types of capital. Capital embodies the fruits of technological breakthroughs and serves as the primary engine for economic growth.

12.2 *Living Standards and Labor Productivity Growth*

a The single most important determinant of a nation's standard of living is the productivity of its resources. There are great differences in the standards of living among nations. *Developing countries* have a lower standard of living than *industrial market countries* because they have less human and physical capital.

b The quality of a nation's labor is an important source of productivity. Countries with the most advanced educational systems also are those that were first to develop. Over the past 130 years, the productivity has grown at an average rate of just over 2 percent per year in the United States. Small differences in productivity growth can cause huge differences in an economy's ability to produce over time.

c The best measure of an economy's standard of living is its output per capita. There has been an upward trend in this measure of productivity in the United States that has been interrupted by recessions in our economy. The output per capita in the United States is much greater than that in most other nations, whether they are industrial market economies or developing economies.

12.3 *Issues of Technological Change*

a Improvements in technology arise from scientific discovery, which is the product of research that may either be basic or applied. *Basic research* investigates general fields of knowledge but has no direct application to production. *Applied research* seeks to answer particular questions that will assist in the production of specific products. As a greater share of a nation's resources are devoted to research and development, that nation should enjoy a greater increase in its productivity.

b Technological improvements that are brought about through research lead to increases in *labor productivity.* Workers who are trained to use new technologies are able to produce goods and services that have greater value. New technologies, however, can cause some workers who lack needed skills to become unemployed. This unemployment may occur within a nation or across national boundaries.

c Some nations have created and implemented *industrial policies* that are intended to shape their economies' futures. These nations use taxes, subsidies, and regulations to coordinate business activity in their private sectors to nurture industries and technologies of the future. This type of government policy has been used in a limited way in the United States. It has been much more common in Europe and Japan. Although industrial policies have assisted some types of production, they also have resulted in allocating resources to industries that could not use them efficiently.

Review Economic Terms

Choose the term that best fits the definition. On a separate sheet of paper, write the letter of the answer. Some terms may not be used.

_____ 1. The machines, buildings, roads, airports, communications networks, and other manufactured creations used to produce goods and services

_____ 2. An economy's level of economic prosperity

_____ 3. Firms in the same industry or in related industries that group together in a region

_____ 4. The advanced market economies that include Western Europe, North America, Australia, New Zealand, and Japan

_____ 5. Output per unit of labor

_____ 6. The accumulated knowledge, skill, and experience of the labor force

_____ 7. Countries with a lower standard of living because they have relatively little human and physical capital

_____ 8. The search for knowledge without regard to how that knowledge will be used

_____ 9. The ratio of output to a specific measure of input

_____10. Research that seeks answers to particular questions or applies scientific discoveries to develop specific products

_____11. The view that government—using taxes, subsidies and regulations—should nurture the industries and technologies of the future, thereby giving domestic industries an advantage over foreign competition

_____12. The formal and informal institutions—such as laws, customs, and conventions—that provide production incentives and promote economic activity

a. applied research

b. basic research

c. capital deepening

d. cluster

e. developing countries

f. Group of Seven (G-7)

g. human capital

h. industrial market countries

i. industrial policy

j. labor productivity

k. physical capital

l. productivity

m. rules of the game

n. standard of living

Review Economic Concepts

13. **True or False** _Capital deepening_ involves adding more or better physical capital to production.

14. __?__ measures how efficiently resources are employed to create goods and services.

15. **True or False** The more of a nation's resources that are allocated to the production of capital goods, the greater that nation's rate of economic growth will be.

16. __?__ takes place when there is an increase in the quantity or quality of capital per worker.

17. Which of the following will shift a nation's production possibilities frontier outward over time?

a. switching production away from capital goods

b. an increase in resources that are devoted to Social Security benefits

c. switching production away from consumer goods towards capital goods

d. an increase in resources that are devoted to employee salaries

18. Which of the following is an example of a change in the *rules of the game* that should increase a nation's productivity?

    a. Farmers are given a tax deduction when they buy new farm equipment.

    b. Lunches are provided free to students at an elementary school.

    c. Taxes on imported automobiles are increased.

    d. Welfare payments are increased for the nation's poor.

19. *Labor productivity* in most __?__ countries is very low, so most of their residents barely subsist.

20. The single most important determinant of a nation's *standard of living* is the

    a. productivity of its resources.

    b. size of its population.

    c. quality of its natural resources.

    d. nature of its government.

21. Some nations have created and implemented __?__ that are intended to nurture the industries and technologies of the future.

22. __?__ investigates general fields of knowledge but has no direct application to production.

23. Which of the following is regarded as the best measure of a nation's *standard of living*?

    a. total output

    b. output per capita

    c. spending on research and development

    d. spending on capital goods

24. __?__ seeks to answer particular questions or to use scientific discoveries to develop specific products.

25. **True or False** Technological advances will benefit all people equally.

26. Which of the following is not a common argument applied against the use of *industrial policy*?

    a. Industrial policy may result in investments that do not add to productivity.

    b. Industrial policy may give politicians too much control over the economy.

    c. Industrial policy may cause businesses to become uncompetitive in international trade.

    d. Industrial policy may prevent businesses from investing in new technologies.

27. **True or False** Productivity in the United States has increased at a constant rate of 2.1 percent per year over the past century.

28. Although technological improvements can lead to increased *labor productivity*, they also

    a. often reduce the quality of production.

    b. can cause some workers who lack needed skills to become unemployed.

    c. can weaken a nation's ability to compete in the global economy.

    d. may lower a nation's average standard of living.

Apply Economic Concepts

29. **Calculating Labor Productivity** The ABC Bowling Pin Company employs 20 workers who all work 40 hours per week, 50 weeks per year. Last year ABC produced 480,000 bowling pins that were sold for $2.50 each. What was the average hourly value of each ABC's worker's production?

30. **Graphing Land Productivity** The amount of corn that Sara is able to grow on her farm depends on many things, including the amount of fertilizer she adds to the soil. She has studied her production over many years and has found the data in the table. Use these data to construct a bar graph that relates the land productivity per acre of Sara's farm to the amount of fertilizer she applies. Why does production per acre decrease when she applies more than 5 tons of fertilizer per 100 acres?

Fertilizer Use and Corn Production Per Acre

Tons of Fertilizer Applied Per 100 Acres	Bushels of Corn Produced Per Acre
0	100
1	130
2	160
3	185
4	200
5	210
6	200

31. **Comparing Growth Rates in Different Nations** Suppose that two nations currently have exactly the same GDP this year. Country A allocates 10 percent of its resources to producing capital goods, while country B devotes only 6 percent of its resources to this type of production. As a result, country A's production grows at a rate of 2.5 percent per year while country B's rate of growth is only 1.8 percent per year. After five more years, how much larger will country A's GDP be than country B's? Make the amount of production in the first year equal to 100 in both countries.

32. **Sharpen Your Life Skills: Categorizing Information** Identify which of the following activities would add to human capital, which would add to physical capital, and which would add to neither type of capital.

- Ted buys a new bicycle so he can deliver more newspapers in his neighborhood.

- Shakir buys a new pizza oven for her restaurant.

- Tyekeesha buys a take-out pizza on her way home from work.

- Carmen buys a calculator to help her keep records for her pet shop.

- Martin reads a book that teaches him how to repair his lawn mower.

- Tanya completes a class in automotive repair at a community college.

 econxtra.swlearning.com

33. Access **EconData Online** through econxtra.swlearning.com. Read the article entitled "What Is Labor Productivity?". Then click on "Diagrams/Data" and examine the line graph entitled "Labor Productivity and the Consumer Price Index." Judging from the graph, describe the relationship between production and inflation. Explain why you think this type of relationship exists.

13 Economic Challenges

Consider

Would a high school senior who is not working be considered unemployed?

What type of unemployment might be healthy for the economy?

What's bad about inflation?

What's stagflation?

Why don't some families benefit from a strong economy?

How might government transfers change work incentives?

Food for Forecasters
econxtra.swlearning.com

POINT YOUR BROWSER

econxtra.swlearning.com

© Getty Images/PhotoDisc

Objectives

> Distinguish among four types of unemployment.

> Discuss the unemployment rate, and describe how it differs over time and across groups.

> Explain who is eligible for unemployment benefits in the United States.

Overview

"They scampered about looking for work.... They swarmed on the highways. The movement changed them. The highways, the camps along the road, the fear of hunger and the hunger itself, changed them. The children without dinner changed them, the endless moving changed them." There is no question, as John Steinbeck wrote in *The Grapes of Wrath*, that a long stretch of unemployment deeply affects the individual and the family. Unemployment also imposes costs on the economy. When there is high unemployment, the economy will not achieve its potential level of output. Not all unemployment harms the economy, however. Even in a healthy economy, some of the unemployment reflects the voluntary choices of workers and employers seeking their own self-interests.

Key Terms

full employment

underemployment

labor force

unemployment rate

labor force participation rate

unemployment benefits

[In the News]

● Will Work for Anything

Vicky K. was laid off from her job as a computer engineer. At the time, she earned $21.50 per hour with full benefits. To make ends meet after the layoff, she took a seasonal job at an amusement park for $7.00 per hour with no benefits. Joseph B. lost his job as a computer programmer and worked part-time as a gas meter reader while he looked for full-time work for more than two years. One morning, Joseph joined 700 other people who lined up to answer a want ad for 18 technical jobs in city government. According to some economists, the U.S. economy slowly began to recover from a recession in the fall of 2001. However, despite some small improvements in the stock market and other parts of the economy, jobs continued to disappear. Some 9 million people were out of work on Labor Day, 2003. Many were finding it difficult to find any jobs in their field, especially if they had worked in high-tech industries. Almost a quarter of all people without jobs in 2003 spent more than six months looking for employment before they were hired again. Those who had used up all of their unemployment benefits were forced to look for any work they could find. Many people were forced to change careers just a few years before they had once expected to retire.

Think About It

Has anyone close to you ever lost a job? What emotional impact did this job loss have on him or her?

Types of Unemployment

Think about all the ways people can become unemployed. They may quit or be fired from their job. They may be looking for a first job, or they may be re-entering the labor force after an absence. A look at the reasons behind unemployment in 2000 indicates that 42 percent of the unemployed lost their previous jobs, 13 percent quit their previous jobs, 9 percent were entering the labor market for the first time, and 36 percent were re-entering the market.

The help-wanted section of a big-city newspaper may list thousands of job openings, from accountants to yoga instructors. Why are people unemployed when so many jobs are available? To understand the answer to this question, take a look at the four types of unemployment: frictional, structural, seasonal, and cyclical.

Frictional Unemployment

Just as employers do not always hire the first applicant who comes through the door, job seekers do not always accept their first offer. Both employers and job seekers need time to explore the job market. Employers need time to learn about the talent available, and job seekers need time to learn about employment opportunities. The time required to bring together labor suppliers and labor demanders creates *frictional unemployment*. Frictional unemployment does not usually last long and results in a better match-up between workers and jobs. The entire economy becomes more efficient. A marketing major who graduated in June and is taking the summer to look for the perfect sales job is frictionally unemployed. A high school teacher who quits his job at the end of the school year to look for a job in another field is frictionally unemployed.

Structural Unemployment

In a dynamic economy, the demand for some labor skills declines while the demand for other labor skills increases.

For example, automatic teller machines have put many bank tellers out of work. At the same time, those with certain computer skills are in greater demand. *Structural unemployment* results when job seekers do not have the skills demanded. Structural unemployment poses more of a problem than frictional unemployment because the unemployed may need to retrain to develop the required skills.

Seasonal Unemployment

Unemployment caused by seasonal changes in labor demand during the year is called *seasonal unemployment*. During cold winter months, for example, demand for farm hands, lifeguards, and construction workers shrinks. Workers in these seasonal jobs know they will probably be unemployed in the off-season. Some may have even chosen a seasonal occupation to complement their lifestyles or academic schedules.

Cyclical Unemployment

As output declines during recessions, firms reduce their demand for inputs, including labor. *Cyclical unemployment* is the increase in unemployment caused by the recession phase of the business cycle. Cyclical unemployment increases during recessions and decreases during expansions.

Full Employment

In a dynamic, growing economy, changes in consumer demand and in technology continually affect the market for particular types of labor. Thus, even in a healthy, growing economy, there will be some frictional, structural, and seasonal unemployment. The economy is said to be at **full employment** if there is no cyclical unemployment.

When economists talk about "full employment," they do not mean zero unemployment but relatively low unemployment, say between 4 and 5 percent. Even when the economy is at full employment, there will be some frictional, structural, and seasonal unemployment.

Ask the Xpert!

econxtra.swlearning.com

What are the principal types of unemployment?

full employment
Occurs when there is no cyclical unemployment; relatively low unemployment

Problems with Official Unemployment Estimates

Official unemployment statistics have limitations. For example, some people may have become so discouraged by a long, unsuccessful job search that they have given up looking for work. These *discouraged workers* have, in effect, dropped out of the labor force, so they are not counted as unemployed. Because the official unemployment rate ignores discouraged workers, it may underestimate unemployment in the economy.

Official employment figures also ignore the problem of **underemployment**. This arises because people are counted as employed even if they can find only part-time jobs or are overqualified for their job. For example, if someone with a Ph.D. in English can find work only as a bookstore clerk, that individual would be considered underemployed.

Counting the underemployed as employed tends to understate the true amount of unemployment.

On the other hand, there are reasons why unemployment figures may over-state the true extent of employment. For example, to qualify for some government transfer programs, beneficiaries must look for work. If some of these

NETBookmark

The Bureau of Labor Statistics provides abundant data on labor market conditions, including unemployment rates, labor force estimates, and earnings data. Access the web site through econxtra.swlearning.com. What is the unemployment rate for the most recent month listed in the table?

econxtra.swlearning.com

under-employment

Workers are overqualified for their jobs or work fewer hours than they would prefer

What type of unemployment results for members of the ski patrol when changing weather patterns no longer permit skiing in an area?

© Getty Images/PhotoDisc

people do not in fact want to find a job, then counting them as unemployed overstates the true unemployment rate. Also, people working in the underground economy may not readily admit they have a job if their intent is to evade taxes or skirt the law. Many of those in the underground economy end up being counted as unemployed even though they are working.

 CHECKPOINT
What are the four types of unemployment?

The Cost and Measure of Unemployment

labor force

Those in the adult population who are either working or looking for work

unemployment rate

The number looking for work divided by the number in the labor force

The most obvious cost of unemployment is the loss of a steady paycheck for the unemployed individual. However, many who lose their jobs also suffer a loss of self-esteem. No matter how much people complain about their jobs, they rely on them not only for income but also for part of their personal identity. A long stretch of unemployment can have a lasting effect on both self-esteem and economic welfare.

Main Idea

Unemployment

What are *the costs of unemployment* for unemployed individuals? What are some other costs associated with unemployment?

Hires and Fires
econxtra.swlearning.com

© Getty Images/PhotoDisc

In addition to these personal costs, unemployment imposes a cost on the economy as a whole because fewer goods and services are produced. When the economy does not generate enough jobs to employ all who seek work, that unemployed labor is lost forever. *This lost output together with the economic and psychological damage to unemployed workers and their families represents the true cost of unemployment.*

Unemployment Rate

The most widely reported measure of the nation's economic health is the unemployment rate. To see what the unemployment rate measures, you need to understand its components. A measurement of unemployment begins with the U.S. *noninstitutional adult population,* which consists of all those 16 years of age and older, except people in the military, in prisons, or in mental hospitals. When the expression "adult population" is referred to in this section, it means the noninstitutional adult population.

The **labor force** consists of those in the adult population who are either working or looking for work. *Those with no job who are looking for work are counted as unemployed.* Thus, a high school student at least 16 years of age, Nicole Kidman, and Barry Bonds would all be counted as unemployed if they want a job but can't find one. The **unemployment rate** equals the number unemployed—that is, people without jobs who are looking for work—divided by the number in the labor force.

Unemployment rate

$$= \frac{\text{Number unemployed}}{\text{Number in the labor force}}$$

Only a fraction of those not working are considered unemployed. People may not be working for all kinds of reasons. They may be full-time students, retirees, homemakers, or disabled. Or they may simply not want to work.

Labor Force Participation Rate

Employment measures are illustrated in Figure 13.1. In this figure, circles represent the various groups, and the millions of people in each category and subcategory are shown in parentheses. The circle on the left depicts the entire U.S. labor force, including both those employed and those looking for work. The circle on the right represents members of the adult population who are not working. Together, these two circles include the adult population.

The overlapping area identifies *unemployed* workers—that is, people in the labor force who are not working but looking for work. Using the fomula given above, in this example 8.4 million people were unemployed in a labor force of 145.9 million. This resulted in a U.S. unemployment rate of 5.8 percent.

The productive capability of any economy depends in part on the proportion of adults in the labor force, measured as the *labor force participation rate*. In Figure 13.1, the U.S. adult population equals those in the labor force (145.9 million) plus those not in the labor force (74.2 million), for a total

Research to find the unemployment rates in your city and state. Compare these rates with the most current unemployment rate for the United States. If these rates differ, propose an explanation for why they differ.

of 220.1 million. The **labor force participation rate** therefore equals the number in the labor force divided by the adult population. For February 2003, that was 145.9 million divided by 220.1 million, which equals 66.3 percent. So, on average, two out of three adults were in the labor force then. The labor force participation rate increased from about 60 percent in 1970 to about 67 percent in 1990. Since then, it has remained relatively constant.

labor force participation rate

The number in the labor force divided by the adult population

---

Composition of Adult Population, February 2003 (in millions)

Figure 13.1

The labor force consists of employed and unemployed people. Those not working consist of individuals not in the labor force and those unemployed. The adult population sums the employed, the unemployed, and people not in the labor force.

Source: U.S. Bureau of Labor Statistics.

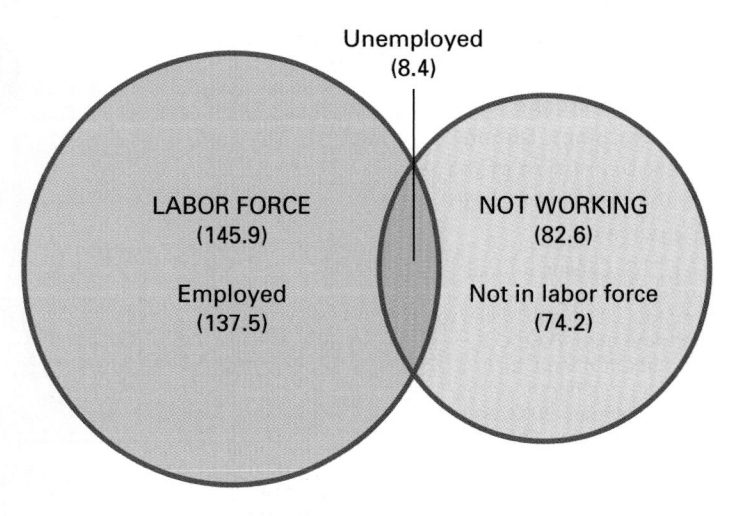

Unemployed
(8.4)

LABOR FORCE
(145.9)

Employed
(137.5)

NOT WORKING
(82.6)

Not in labor force
(74.2)

Changes in Unemployment Rate

Figure 13.2 shows the U.S. unemployment rate since 1900, with shading to indicate periods of recession and depression. As you can see, the rate increased during recessions and fell during expansions. Perhaps the most striking feature of the graph is the dramatic jump that occurred during the Great Depression of the 1930s, when the unemployment rate reached 25.2 percent.

Unemployment for Various Groups

The unemployment rate says nothing about who is unemployed or for how long. Even a low overall rate often hides wide differences in unemployment rates across age, race, gender, and geographic area. For example, when the U.S. unemployment rate was 5.8 percent, the rate was 17.1 percent among teenagers, 10.5 percent among blacks, and 7.7 percent among Hispanics. These reflect differences in job opportu-nities, work experience, education, skills, as well as discrimination.

Unemployment rates for different groups appear in Figure 13.3. As you can see, rates are higher among blacks than among whites. They also are higher among teenagers than among those aged 20 and older. During recessions, the rates climbed for all groups. Rates peaked during the recession of 1982 and then trended down. After the recession of the early 1990s, unemployment rates continued downward, with the rate among blacks falling in 2000 to the lowest on record. Rates then turned up again with the recession of 2001.

Why are unemployment rates among teenagers so much higher than among workers age 20 and older? Because young workers enter the job market with little training, they take unskilled jobs and are the first to be fired if the economy slows down. Young workers also move in and out of the job market more frequently during the year as they juggle school demands. Even those who have left school often shop around for jobs more than older workers do.

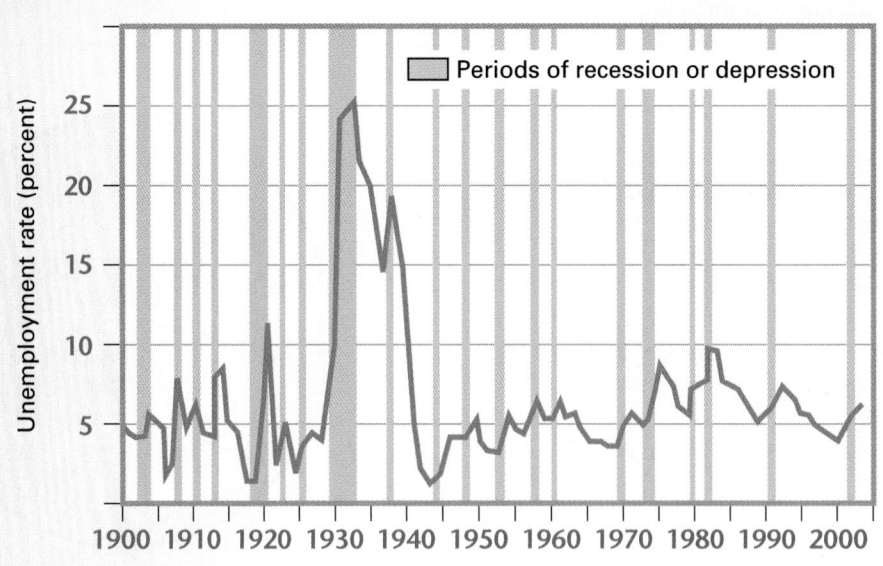

The U.S. Unemployment Rate Since 1900

Figure 13.2

Since 1900, the unemployment rate has fluctuated widely, rising during recessions and falling during expansions. During the Great Depression of the 1930s, the rate rose as high as 25.2 percent.

Sources: U.S. Census Bureau, *Historical Statistics of the United States: Colonial Times to 1970* (Washington, D.C.: U.S. Government Printing Office, 1975); *Economic Report of the President,* February 2003; and U.S. Bureau of Labor Statistics.

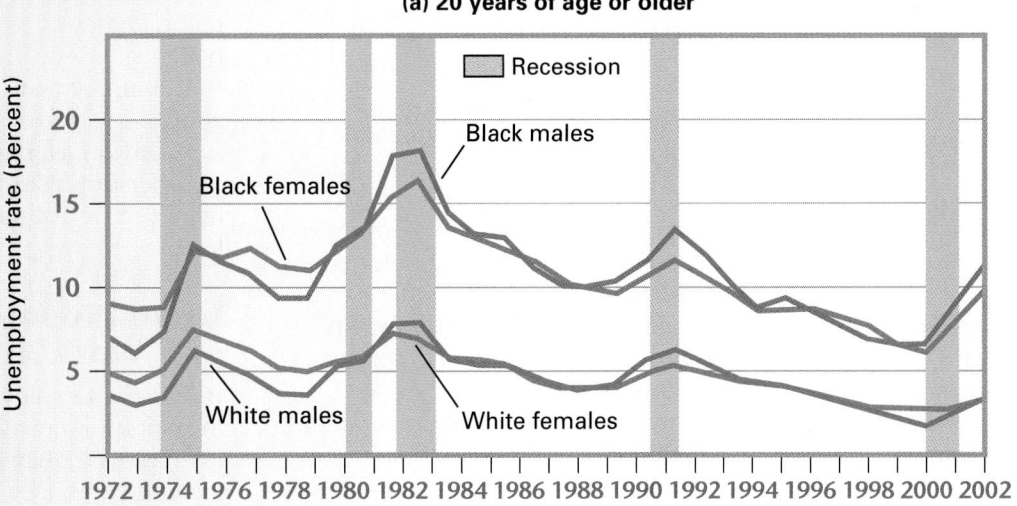

(a) 20 years of age or older

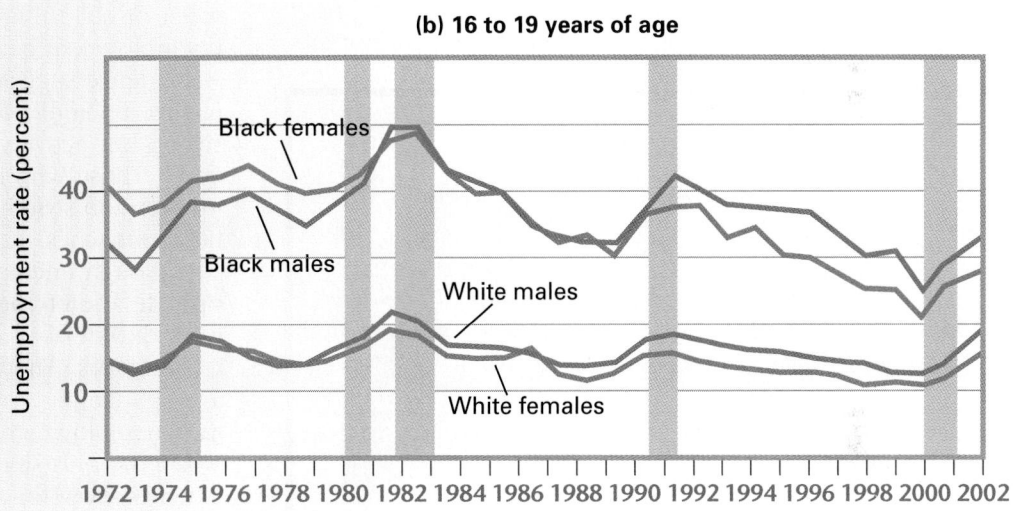

(b) 16 to 19 years of age

Unemployment affects different groups in different ways. The unemployment rate is higher for blacks than for whites and higher for teenagers than for older persons.

Sources: *Economic Report of the President,* February 2003; U.S. Bureau of Labor Statistics.

The U.S. unemployment rate also covers up much variation in rates across the country. For example, recent unemployment rates in Alaska, Oregon, and Washington were more than double those in Nebraska, North Dakota, and South Dakota.

 CHECKPOINT

What is the unemployment rate and how has it differed over time and across groups?

Unemployment Benefits

As noted earlier, unemployment often imposes both an economic and psychological hardship on the unemployed worker and the family. Today, a large proportion of households have two workers in the labor force, so if one becomes unemployed, another is likely to still have a job that may provide health insurance and other benefits. Having more than one family member

Lesson 13.1 ∘ *Unemployment*   **393**

in the labor force cushions the economic shock of unemployment.

Unemployment Compensation

Workers who lose their jobs today often receive unemployment benefits. In response to the massive unemployment of the Great Depression, Congress passed the Social Security Act of 1935. This act provided unemployment insurance financed by a tax on employers. Unemployed workers who meet certain qualifications can receive **unemployment benefits** for up to six months, provided they actively seek work.

During recessions, unemployment benefits often extend beyond six months in states with especially high unemployment. Insurance benefits go mainly to people who have lost jobs. Individuals just entering or re-entering the labor force are not covered, nor are those who quit their last job or those fired for just cause, such as excessive absenteeism or theft. Because of these restrictions, fewer than half of all unemployed workers receive unemployment benefits.

Unemployment benefits averaged about $240 per week in 2002. This replaced on average about 40 percent of a person's take-home pay, with a higher share for those whose jobs paid less.

Unemployment Benefits and Work Incentives

Because unemployment benefits reduce the opportunity cost of remaining unemployed, they also may reduce the incentive to find work. For example, what if you faced the choice of taking a job washing dishes that pays $200 per week or collecting $150 per week in unemployment benefits?

Evidence suggests that those who receive unemployment benefits tend to search less actively than those who don't. Those who receive benefits step up their job search as the end of benefits approaches.

Although unemployment benefits provide a safety net for the unemployed, they also may reduce the need to find work. They may increase the average length of unemployment and the unemployment rate as well.

On the plus side, unemployment benefits allow for a more careful job search, because the job seeker has some money and need not take the first job that comes along. As a result of a better search, there is a better match between job skills and job requirements, and this promotes economic efficiency. In addition, unemployment compensation payments allow the unemployed to continue to spend. This spending reduces the likelihood that other workers will be laid off.

unemployment benefits

Cash transfers to unemployed workers who actively seek work and who meet other qualifications

© Getty Images/PhotoDisc

What are the advantages of having more than one family member in the labor force?

CHECKPOINT

Who is eligible for unemployment benefits in the United States?

Key Concepts

1. How may people who keep their jobs be harmed by high levels of unemployment?

2. Are you currently a member of the labor force? Explain your answer.

3. Why do you think the government considers as unemployed only those adults who are without employment but are looking for work?

4. Do you know anyone who has chosen to change jobs? Why did this person make this choice? How long was he or she unemployed? Was this person satisfied with the job he or she eventually accepted? Do you think this person made a rational choice?

5. Unemployment compensation payments can make up for some of the income workers lose when they are laid off. However, such payments do not provide medical insurance coverage. Why might this be an important incentive for a person who is out of work to seek new employment as quickly as possible?

6. How can unemployment compensation payments help workers who are not unemployed?

Graphing Exercise

7. In general, young people suffer from higher rates of unemployment than older people. Use data from this table to construct a double line graph that compares the rates of unemployment for people who are 16–19 years of age with the average for all members of the labor force. Identify and explain three possible reasons for young people having higher unemployment rates.

Unemployment Rates, 1985–2002

Year	Unemployment Rate For People 16–19	Unemployment Rate For Entire Labor Force
1985	18.6%	7.2%
1990	15.5%	5.6%
1995	17.3%	5.6%
2000	13.1%	4.0%
2002	16.5%	5.8%

Think Critically

8. **History** The Great Depression of the 1930s was the deepest and most well-known economic downturn in recent U.S. history. There have been many other recessions since 1776. Years in which these recessions occurred include 1837, 1873, 1893, and 1907. Investigate one of these events. What happened to employment in the recession you chose to study?

9. **Sociology** Look through a sociology textbook or on the Internet to find information about how society is affected by high rates of unemployment. You should particularly investigate its impact on families. Are there more divorces when unemployment is high? Why might this be true?

movers & shakers

Jeff Taylor *CEO, Monster.com*

Being a leader is part of Jeff Taylor's make-up. While attending the University of Massachusetts, he set his sights on becoming pledge master of the Pi Kappa Alpha fraternity. Not only did he achieve that goal, Taylor eventually became fraternity vice-president and then president. At the same time, he also managed the university's tour guide service. As advertising manager and later business manager for the University of Massachusetts paper, *The Collegian,* Taylor helped make the paper profitable after a 30-year history of operating in the red. To earn living expenses during college, Taylor came up with the idea to assemble and sell "freshmen survival kits," a box of snacks intended to help freshmen survive exam week.

After graduating, Taylor earned an executive MBA from Harvard Business School. In 1989, he started his own advertising agency, Adion. The name, he explains, "stood for what we did, which was create ads, and for the particle of energy—ion—that represented the energy we put into creating ads." While running his ad agency, Taylor became intrigued by the then-new concept of computer bulletin boards. "So I started learning everything I could about them. At the same time, the World Wide Web was being invented." Taylor combined his interests in advertising and the new communications technologies, and what resulted was Monster.com.

Now the company's CEO, Taylor created Monster.com for companies looking for employees and individuals looking for jobs. At its inception, the site posted 200 job openings at 20 different companies.

Today, the Monster web site typically posts more than 400,000 job openings and is visited by more than 15 million job seekers each month. It is the largest careers web site in the world. In 2003, Monster.com had 8,500 employees and annual sales of more than $1 billion. The stock market valued the company at $3.2 billion as of October 2003.

Monster.com has special services that enable visitors to develop one or more online resumes that can be stored for free. Visitors also can apply online for jobs, all at no charge. For a membership fee, users can utilize software components that will continuously search for their self-described "ideal" job.

At 39 years of age, Taylor is not your typical CEO. He equipped the company's headquarters, located in Maynard, Massachusetts, with pool, ping-pong, and foosball tables. "We encourage our employees to be excellent foosball players as long as they have some other core competency, like doing their job well." He practices what he preaches. "I can hold my own during employee foosball tournaments."

Taylor's leadership abilities have made him an attractive employer. "I think a big part of being a leader is learning how to identify talent. The people you surround yourself with are going to directly influence your ability to build a successful organization, so you must be very careful and selective of the people you hire." He adds, "Being able to recognize good ideas from okay ideas is also a key aspect of leadership." Taylor is a fan of the saying that the shortest distance between two points is a good idea. A popular speaker, Taylor likes to tell his audience, "If you have good ideas, pursue them!" His other favorite expression—one that promotes his belief in hard work—is, "you can only coast one way, and that is downhill."

SOURCE READING
What type of unemployment do you think Monster.com affects? Explain your answer. How does Monster.com help to make the economy more efficient?

ENTREPRENEURS IN ACTION
Jeff Taylor's success is self-made. In small groups, discuss the qualities Jeff Taylor possesses that helped lead to his success.

Objectives

> Describe the types of inflation, and identify two sources of inflation.

> Identify the problems that unexpected inflation creates.

Overview

As a result of incredibly high inflation, Brazilian prices in 1994 were 3.6 million times higher than in 1988. To put this in perspective, with such inflation in the United States, the price of gasoline would have climbed from $1.25 a gallon in 1988 to $4.5 million a gallon in 1994. A pair of jeans that sold for $25 in 1988 would have cost $90 million in 1994. With such wild inflation, Brazilians had difficulty keeping track of prices. People couldn't lug around enough money to make even small purchases. Inflation, particularly high inflation, makes market exchange much more difficult.

Key Terms

inflation

demand-pull inflation

cost-push inflation

nominal interest rate

real interest rate

[In the News]

● Who's the Box Office Champion?

Almost every year, the total amount of movie box office receipts increases. The 1997 movie *Titanic* grossed more than $600 million in the United States—more than any movie ever. However, in 1997 the average ticket price for a movie was around $5.00. When adjusted for inflation, *Titanic* was only the seventh highest-grossing film of all time. The film that made the most money, when adjusted for inflation, was the 1939 epic *Gone with the Wind.* At the time it came out, the average price of a movie ticket was only 25 cents. When its revenues are adjusted for inflation, it earned the equivalent of $1.3 billion in 1997 dollars, more than twice as much as *Titanic*. This means that many more people actually saw *Gone with the Wind* when it came out than saw *Titanic.* This trend is reflected in movie attendance records as well. Even though films today gross much more than films of the 1930s, more people went to the movies back then. Today about 25 million Americans see a movie each week. In the 1930s, about 90 million people went to the movies every week. Because of this difference, it is very unlikely that even the most popular modern film will ever surpass *Gone with the Wind,* or even the second-runner up, *Snow White and the Seven Dwarves* (1937), which, in inflation-adjusted dollars, grossed more than $1 billion in the United States.

Think About It

Why is it necessary to adjust for inflation when comparing economic situations from different eras, such as movie box office receipts?

Inflation Basics

inflation

An increase in the economy's general price level

demand-pull inflation

Inflation resulting from a rightward shift of the aggregate demand curve

You were introduced to the concept of inflation earlier in this book. **Inflation** is an increase in the economy's general price level. Inflation reduces the value of money and is usually measured on an annual basis. The *annual inflation rate* is the percentage increase in the general price level from one year to the next.

Types of Inflation

Extremely high inflation, such as the experience in Brazil, is called *hyperinflation*. A reduction in the rate of inflation is called *disinflation*, as occurred in the United States during the 1980s. A decrease in the general price level is called *deflation*, as occurred in the United States during the Great Depression and most recently in Japan, Hong Kong, and Taiwan.

Two Sources of Inflation

Inflation is an increase in the economy's price level resulting from an increase in aggregate demand or a decrease in aggregate supply. Panel (a) of Figure 13.4 shows an increase in aggregate demand that raises the price level from P to P'. Inflation resulting from increases in aggregate demand is often called **demand-pull inflation**. In such cases, a rightward shift of the aggregate demand curve *pulls up* the price level.

NETBookmark

The Brazilian embassy in Washington, D.C., maintains a web site that you can access through econxtra.swlearning.com. Put your cursor on "The Economy" and then click on "Brazil Economic Briefing" to access the latest news and reports on the Brazil's economy. What's the current status of Brazil's inflation rate?

econxtra.swlearning.com

Inflation Caused by Shifts of the Aggregate Demand and Aggregate Supply Curves   **Figure 13.4**

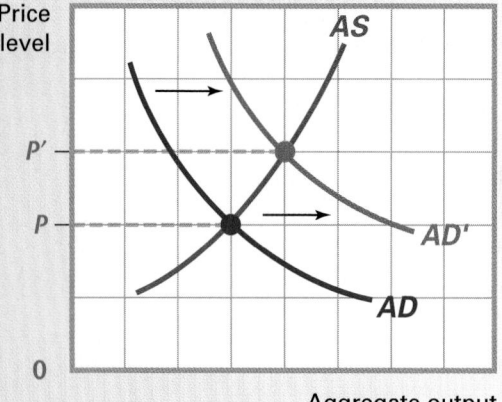

(a) Demand-pull inflation: inflation caused by an increase of aggregate demand

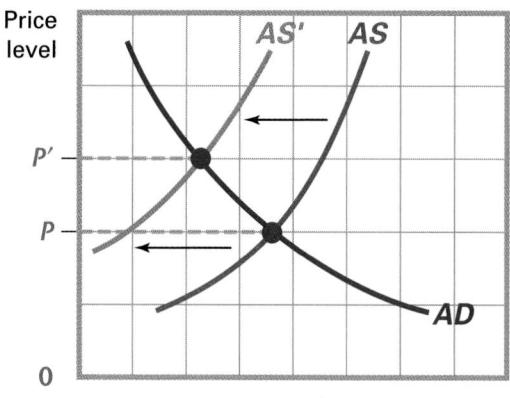

(b) Cost-push inflation: inflation caused by a decrease of aggregate supply

Panel (a) illustrates demand-pull inflation. An outward shift of the aggregate demand curve to *AD'* "pulls" the price level up from *P* to *P'*. Panel (b) shows cost-push inflation, in which a decrease of aggregate supply to *AS'* "pushes" the price level up from *P* to *P'*.

To generate continuous demand-pull inflation, the aggregate demand curve would have to keep shifting out along a given aggregate supply curve. Rising U.S. inflation rates during the late 1960s resulted from demand-pull inflation. At this time, federal spending for the Vietnam War and for expanded social programs boosted aggregate demand.

Alternatively, inflation can arise from reductions in aggregate supply. This is shown in panel (b) of Figure 13.4, where a leftward shift of the aggregate supply curve raises the price level. For example, crop failures and cuts in OPEC oil supplies reduced aggregate supply during 1974 and 1975, thereby raising the price level.

Inflation stemming from decreases in aggregate supply is called **cost-push inflation**, suggesting that increases in the cost of production *push up* the price level. If prices increase and real GDP decreases, this combination is called *stagflation,* which will be discussed later in this chapter. Again, to generate sustained and continuous cost-push inflation, the aggregate supply curve would have to keep shifting to the left along a given aggregate demand curve.

An Historical Look at Inflation and the Price Level

The consumer price index is the price measure you most often encounter, so it gets more attention here. As you have already learned, the *consumer price index (CPI)* measures the cost of a "market basket" of consumer goods and services over time. Figure 13.5 shows prices in the United States since 1913, using the consumer price index. The price *level* is measured by an index relative to the base period of 1982 to 1984. As you can see, the price level actually was lower in 1940 than in 1920. Since 1940, however, the price level has risen steadily, especially during the 1970s.

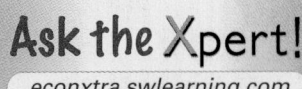

Ask the Xpert!
econxtra.swlearning.com

Which is worse: demand-pull inflation or cost-push inflation?

What the Fed Watches
econxtra.swlearning.com

cost-push inflation

Inflation resulting from a leftward shift of the aggregate supply curve

 CHECKPOINT
Name the types of inflation and two sources of inflation.

Consumer Price Index Since 1913

Figure 13.5

Despite fluctuations, the price level, as measured by the consumer price index, was lower in 1940 than in 1920. Since 1940, the price level has risen almost every year.

Source: U.S. Bureau of Labor Statistics.

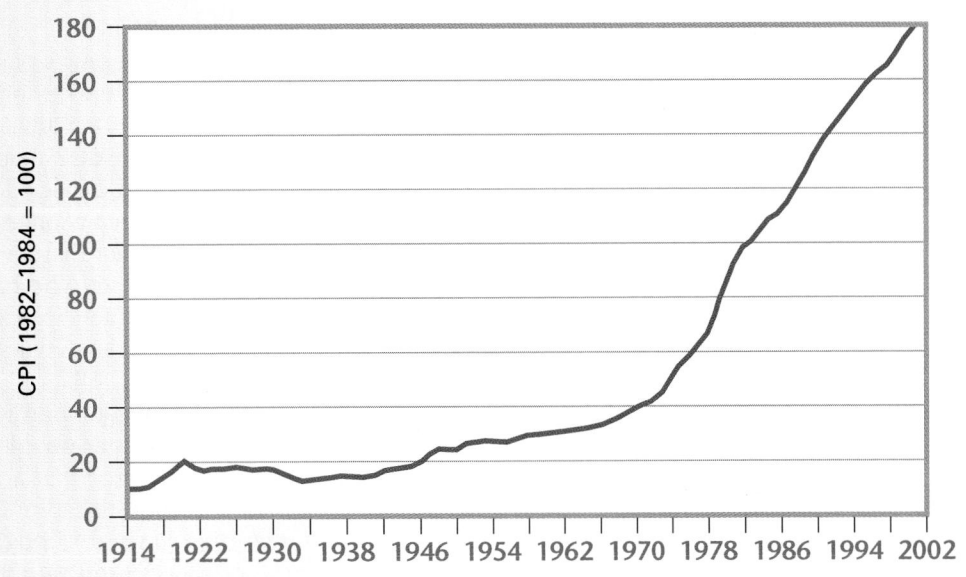

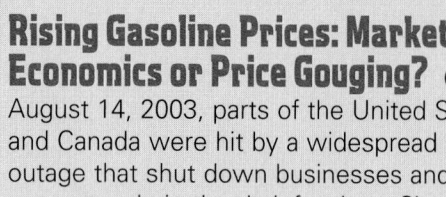

Ethics in Action

Rising Gasoline Prices: Market Economics or Price Gouging?

On August 14, 2003, parts of the United States and Canada were hit by a widespread power outage that shut down businesses and left some people in the dark for days. Shortly after that, gasoline prices nationwide jumped dramatically. From August 18 to 25, the average price of gasoline jumped 12 cents per gallon—the biggest one-week increase ever. By the end of that week, gasoline prices were at a record average high of $1.75 per gallon. The Energy Department immediately launched an investigation. It wanted to determine whether this increase was due to real market economics or to price gouging, an illegal practice of charging unreasonably high prices. This practice usually occurs by taking advantage of public anxiety during times of crisis. The price of gasoline often fluctuates greatly, depending on supply and demand. For example, gasoline prices generally go up during the summer, when more people are traveling and using more gas. However, there have been several occasions when gasoline prices have shot up dramatically after some kind of crisis that has had no real effect on gasoline supplies. These events have led some people to accuse gasoline suppliers of price gouging. Widespread reports of gouging appeared in the days following the September 11, 2001, terrorist attacks on the United States. In some cases, gasoline stations more than doubled their prices within hours of the attacks. Local authorities acted to stop these practices as quickly as possible and to fine those who engaged in price gouging.

Think Critically

From an economic perspective, how could the economy benefit from price increases immediately after a crisis? From an ethical perspective, should the government be concerned about price gouging? Why or why not?

Impact of Inflation

Changes in the price level are nothing new. Prior to World War II, periods of inflation and deflation balanced out over the long run. Therefore, people had good reason to think the dollar would retain its purchasing power over the long term. Since the end of World War II, however, the CPI has increased by an average of 3.9 percent per year. That may not sound like much, but it translates into a *nine-fold* increase in the consumer price index since 1946. Thus, it now takes $9 to purchase what $1 would buy in 1946. *Inflation reduces the value of the dollar and takes away confidence in the value of the dollar over the long term.*

Expected Versus Unexpected Inflation

What is the effect of inflation on the economy's performance? *Unexpected* inflation creates more problems for the economy than does *expected* inflation. To the extent that inflation is higher or lower than expected, it arbitrarily creates economic winners and losers. If inflation is higher than expected, the winners are the people who had agreed to pay a price that anticipates lower inflation. The losers are those who agreed to sell at that price.

If inflation is lower than expected, the situation is reversed: The winners are the people who contracted to sell at a price that anticipates higher inflation, and the losers are all those who contracted to buy at that price.

Suppose inflation next year is expected to be 3 percent, and you agree to work next year for a wage that is 4 percent higher than your wage this year. In this case, you expect your *real* wage—that is, your wage measured in dollars of constant purchasing power—to increase by 1 percent. If inflation turns out to be 3 percent, you and your employer will both be satisfied with your nominal wage increase of 4 percent.

If, however, inflation turns out to be 5 percent, your real wage will fall. You will be a loser and your employer will be a winner. If inflation turns out to be only 1 percent, your real wage will increase by 3 percent. In this case, you will be a winner and your employer, a loser.

The arbitrary gains and losses arising from unexpected inflation are one reason that inflation is so unpopular. To the extent that inflation is fully expected by market participants, it is of less concern than unexpected inflation. Unexpected inflation arbitrarily redistributes income and wealth from one group to another.

The Transaction Costs of Unexpected Inflation

During long periods of price stability, people correctly think that they can predict future prices and can, therefore, plan accordingly. If inflation changes unexpectedly, the future is cloudier and planning gets harder.

Firms that deal with the rest of the world face added complications. These firms must not only plan for U.S. inflation. They also must anticipate how the value of the dollar might change relative to foreign currencies. Inflation uncertainty and the resulting exchange-rate uncertainty increase the difficulty of making international business decisions.

As inflation becomes less predictable, firms must spend more time coping with the effects of inflation. This reduces productivity. The transaction costs of market exchange increase. *High and variable inflation interferes with the ability to make long-term plans. It also forces buyers and sellers to pay more attention to prices.* For example, high and variable inflation rates in the United States during the 1970s and early 1980s slowed economic growth during that period.

Inflation and Interest Rates

No discussion of inflation would be complete without some mention of the interest rate. *Interest* is the cost of borrowing and the reward for saving. As noted in Chapter 10, the *interest rate* is the interest per year as a percentage of the amount loaned.

The **nominal interest rate** measures interest in terms of current dollars. The nominal rate is the one that appears on the borrowing agreement and the rate discussed in the news media. In contrast, the **real interest rate** equals the nominal interest rate minus the inflation rate:

Real interest rate =
    Nominal interest rate − Inflation rate

With no inflation, the nominal interest rate and the real interest rate would be identical. But with inflation, the real interest rate is less than the nominal interest rate. For example, if the nominal interest rate is 5 percent and the inflation rate is 3 percent, then the real interest rate is 2 percent. Lenders and borrowers are concerned more about the real rate than the nominal rate. The real interest rate, however, is known only after the fact—that is, only after inflation actually occurs.

Because the future is uncertain, lenders and borrowers must form expectations about inflation. They base their willingness to lend and to borrow on these expectations. Lenders and borrowers base their decisions on the *expected* real interest rate, which equals the nominal rate of interest minus the expected inflation rate. Other things constant, the higher the expected inflation rate, the higher the nominal rate of interest that lenders require and that borrowers are willing to pay.

CHECKPOINT
What problems does unexpected inflation create for the economy?

nominal interest rate

The interest rate expressed in current dollars as a percentage of the amount loaned; the interest rate on the loan agreement

real interest rate

The interest rate expressed in dollars of constant purchasing power as a percentage of the amount loaned; the nominal interest rate minus the inflation rate

Key Concepts

1. How have recent changes in gasoline prices affected your family?

2. If you thought that prices would be 10 percent higher one year from now, how would your current demand for goods and services be affected?

3. Suppose that the government reduced personal income taxes by 10 percent. At the same time, it increased social insurance payments by 10 percent. Why would these changes tend to cause inflation? Would this inflation be demand-pull or cost-push inflation?

4. Why would a 10 percent increase in prices be bad for an economy if most people expected prices to go up by only 2 percent?

Graphing Exercise

5. Consider this graph of the aggregate demand and aggregate supply curves. What would happen to the location of each of these curves, the average price level, and the amount of production as a result of each of the following events? Would the change in the price level be the result of a demand-pull or cost-push in the economy?

   • Many more foreign consumers choose to buy products made in the United States.

   • There is a 20 percent increase in the cost of crude oil.

   • A new technology is invented that allows automobiles and trucks to be driven 100 miles per gallon of gasoline.

   • Federal income taxes are increased by 10 percent.

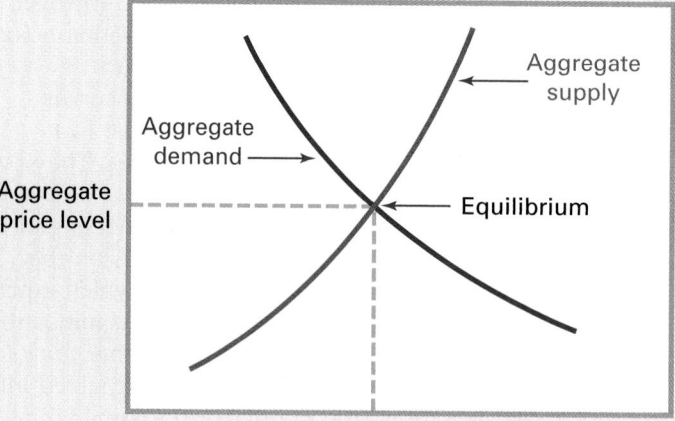

Amount of production (GDP)

Think Critically

6. **Management** Suppose there was a 3 percent rate of inflation last year. This year the rate of inflation is 5 percent. You are the manager of a large business. It is your job to set the prices your firm will charge next year. How much will you choose to increase prices? Why will you make this choice?

Objectives

> Use aggregate demand and aggregate supply to analyze the Great Depression.

> Use aggregate demand and aggregate supply to analyze demand-side economics.

> Use aggregate demand and aggregate supply to analyze stagflation.

> Use aggregate demand and aggregate supply to analyze supply-side economics.

Overview

The recent history of the U.S. economy can be divided into four economic eras: (1) before and during the Great Depression; (2) after the Great Depression to the early 1970s; (3) from the early 1970s to the early 1980s; and (4) since the early 1980s. The first era was marked by recessions and depressions, ending in the Great Depression of the 1930s. The second era was one of strong economic growth, with only moderate increases in the price level. The third era saw high unemployment combined with high inflation. The fourth era showed good growth on average with only moderate increases in the price level. Government leaders in all four eras had to deal with the challenge of economic instability.

Key Terms

laissez-faire

demand-side economics

stagflation

supply-side economics

[In the News]

● Global Crisis and Economic Uncertainty

As war with Iraq loomed in the spring of 2003, many people were nervous and uncertain about how the war might affect the U.S. economy. Such feelings are very common in the face of global crises. Some crises, such as the SARS epidemic that struck much of Asia and other parts of the world in 2003, can have a serious impact on global markets as well as the U.S. economy. Yet it is often difficult to tell how much a crisis is going to affect the economy. In uncertain times, is it better to play it safe and avoid large investments? Or should you take advantage of the uncertainty to build for the future? When a foreseeable crisis like a war is looming, most people plan for the worst by cutting spending and saving as much as they can. However, such action actually can make the economy worse off. Some economists suggest that when faced with economic uncertainty, it is better be optimistic about the future and to take bold risks.

Think About It

Suppose there is significant uncertainty regarding next year's economic conditions. What actions might be good for a typical individual to take that would be bad for the economy as a whole?

The Great Depression and Before

Before World War II, the U.S. economy alternated between periods of prosperity and periods of sharp economic decline. The longest contraction on record occurred between 1873 and 1879. During this time, 80 railroads went bankrupt and most of the nation's steel industry shut down. During the depression of the 1890s, the unemployment rate topped 18 percent. In October 1929, the stock market crashed. This began what was to become the deepest—though not the longest—economic contraction in the nation's history. This period is known as the Great Depression of the 1930s.

Decrease in Aggregate Demand

In terms of aggregate demand and aggregate supply, the Great Depression can be viewed as a leftward shift of the aggregate demand curve, as shown in Figure 13.6. AD_{1929} is the aggregate demand curve in 1929, before the onset of the depression. Real GDP in 1929 was $822 billion, measured in dollars of 1996 purchasing power. The price level was 12.6, relative to a 1996 base-year price level of 100.

By 1933, aggregate demand had shifted leftward, decreasing to AD_{1933}. Why did aggregate demand decline so much? Though the causes are still debated, the list of possibilities is long. It includes the stock market crash of 1929, grim business expectations, a drop in consumer spending, widespread bank failures, a sharp decline in the nation's money supply, and severe restrictions on world trade.

Because of the decline in aggregate demand, both the price level and real GDP dropped. Real GDP fell 27 percent, from $822 billion in 1929 to $603 billion in 1933, and the price level fell 26 percent, from 12.6 to 9.3. As real GDP declined, the unemployment rate soared, climbing from 3 percent in 1929 to 25.2 percent in 1933. This was the highest U.S. unemployment rate ever recorded.

Laissez-Faire

Before the Great Depression, macroeconomic policy was based primarily on the **laissez-faire** doctrine that said government should not intervene in a market economy beyond the minimum required to maintain peace and property rights. This doctrine dates back at

---

laissez-faire

The doctrine that the government should not intervene in a market economy beyond the minimum required to maintain peace and property rights

---

The Decrease of Aggregate Demand Between 1929 and 1933

Figure 13.6

The Great Depression of the 1930s can be represented by a leftward shift of the aggregate demand curve, from AD_{1929} to AD_{1933}. In the resulting depression, real GDP fell from $822 billion to $603 billion. The price level dropped from 12.6 to 9.3.

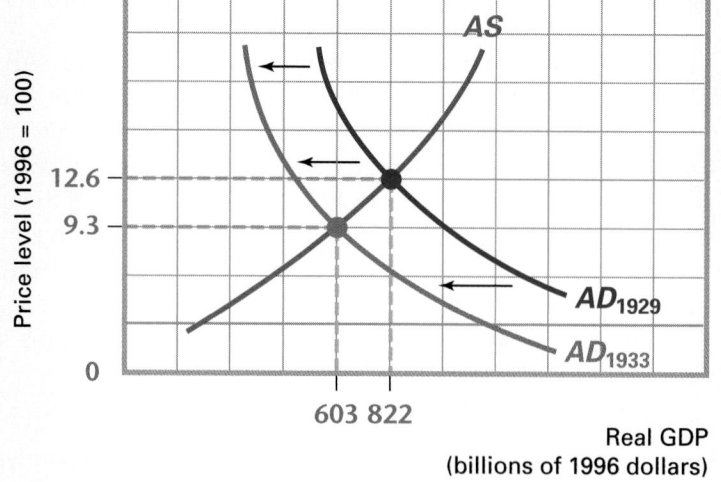

© Getty Images/Image Bank

Day-to-day life during the Great Depression was grim. The unemployment rate reached 25.2 percent in 1933. Many people could not afford to buy food and gathered in "breadlines" to receive free food from charities. How did the sharp drop in aggregate demand from 1929 to 1933 lead to such high unemployment?

least to Adam Smith. In his 1776 book *The Wealth of Nations,* Smith argued that if people were allowed to pursue their self-interest in free markets, resources would be guided as if by an "invisible hand" to produce the greatest, most efficient level of aggregate output.

Although the U.S. economy had suffered several sharp contractions since the beginning of the nineteenth century, most economists of the day viewed these as a natural phase of the economy—unfortunate, but ultimately good for the economy.

 CHECKPOINT
Use aggregate demand and aggregate supply to analyze the Great Depression.

From the Great Depression to the Early 1970s

The Great Depression was so severe that it stimulated new thinking about how the economy worked—or didn't

work. In 1936, John Maynard Keynes (1883–1946) published *The General Theory of Employment, Interest, and Money,* the most famous economics book of the twentieth century. In it, Keynes argued that aggregate demand was unstable, in part because investment decisions were often guided by the unpredictable "animal spirits" of business expectations.

If businesses grew pessimistic about the economy, they would cut investment spending. This, in turn, would reduce aggregate demand. This reduction in aggregate demand would cut output and employment. For example, investment dropped more than 80 percent between 1929 and 1933. Keynes saw no natural market forces operating to ensure that the economy would return to a higher level of output and employment.

Stimulating Aggregate Demand

Keynes proposed that the government shock the economy out of its depression by increasing aggregate demand. The government could achieve this stimulus directly by increasing its own spending, or indirectly by cutting taxes to stimulate consumption and investment. One problem was that either action could create a federal budget deficit. A *federal budget deficit* measures the amount by which total federal spending exceeds total federal revenues.

To understand what Keynes had in mind, imagine federal budget policies that would increase aggregate demand in Figure 13.6. This would shift the aggregate demand curve to the right, back to its original position. Such a shift would raise equilibrium real GDP, which would increase employment.

Demand-Side Economics

According to Keynes, *fiscal policy*—or changes in government spending and taxes—was needed to compensate for what he viewed as the instability of private spending, especially investment. If demand in the private sector declined, Keynes said the government should pick up the slack.

You can think of the Keynesian approach as **demand-side economics** because it focused on how changes in aggregate demand could promote full employment. Keynes argued that government stimulus could jolt the economy out of its depression and back to health. Once investment returned to normal, the government stimulus would no longer be necessary.

World War II and Aggregate Demand

World War II boosted demand for tanks, ships, aircraft, and the like. This increased output and employment. It also seemed to confirm the powerful impact that government spending could have on the economy. The increase in government spending, with no increase in tax rates, created federal budget deficits during the war.

Immediately after World War II, memories of the Great Depression were still fresh. Trying to avoid another depression, Congress approved the *Employment Act of 1946,* which imposed a clear responsibility on the federal government to foster "maximum employment, production, and purchasing power." The act also required the president to report annually on the state of the economy and to appoint a *Council of Economic Advisers.* This council is a three-member panel of economists, with a professional staff, to provide the president with economic advice.

The Golden Age of Keynesian Economics

The economy seemed to prosper during the 1950s, largely without the added stimulus of fiscal policy. The 1960s, however, proved to be the *golden age of Keynesian economics.* During this period, some economists thought they could "fine-tune" the economy to avoid recessions—just as a mechanic could fine-tune a race car to achieve top performance. During the early 1960s, nearly all advanced economies around the world enjoyed low unemployment and healthy growth with only modest inflation. In short, the world economy was booming, and the U.S. economy was on top of the world.

The economy was on such a roll that toward the end of the 1960s, some economists began to think the business cycle was history. In the early 1970s, however, the cycle returned with a fury. Worse yet, the problem of recession was compounded by rising inflation, which increased during the recessions of 1974–1975 and 1979–1980. Until then, inflation was limited primarily to periods of expansion. Confidence in demand-side policies was shaken.

> ✓ **CHECKPOINT**
> Use aggregate demand and aggregate supply to analyze demand-side economics.

The Great Stagflation: 1973–1980

During the late 1960s, federal spending increased on both the war in Vietnam and social programs at home. This combined stimulus increased aggregate demand enough that in 1968, the inflation rate jumped to 4.4 percent, after

---

demand-side economics

Macroeconomic policy that focuses on shifting the aggregate demand curve as a way of promoting full employment and price stability

averaging only 2.0 percent during the previous decade. Inflation climbed to 4.7 percent in 1969 and to 5.3 percent in 1970.

Reduction in Aggregate Supply

Inflation rates were so alarming that in 1971, President Richard Nixon tried to put a ceiling on price and wage increases. The ceiling was eliminated in 1973, about the time that crop failures around the world caused grain prices to climb. To compound these problems, OPEC cut its supply of oil, thus increasing oil prices. Decreases in the supplies of grain and oil reduced aggregate supply in the economy.

This reduction in aggregate supply is shown in Figure 13.7 by the leftward shift of the aggregate supply curve from AS_{1973} to AS_{1975}. This created the **stagflation** of the 1970s, meaning a *stag*nation, or a contraction, in the economy's aggregate output combined with in*flation*, or a rise, in the economy's price level. Real GDP declined by about $40 billion between 1973 and 1975. At the same time, the price level jumped nearly 20 percent.

The unemployment rate climbed from 4.9 percent in 1973 to 8.5 percent in 1975. Stagflation created higher unemployment and higher inflation.

Stagflation Repeats in 1980

Stagflation hit again at the end of 1980, fueled partly by another jump in OPEC oil prices. Between 1979 and 1980, real GDP declined and the price level increased by 9.2 percent. Because the problem of stagflation was primarily on the supply side, not on the demand side, Keynesian demand-management solutions seemed ineffective. Increasing aggregate demand might reduce unemployment, but it would worsen inflation.

CHECKPOINT
Use aggregate demand and aggregate supply to analyze stagflation.

stagflation
A decline, or *stagnation*, of a nation's output accompanied by a rise, or *inflation*, in the price level

Stagflation Between 1973 and 1975

Figure 13.7

The stagflation of the mid-1970s can be represented as a reduction of aggregate supply from AS_{1973} to AS_{1975}. Aggregate output fell from $4.12 trillion to $4.08 trillion (stagnation), and the price level rose from 33.6 to 40.0 (inflation).

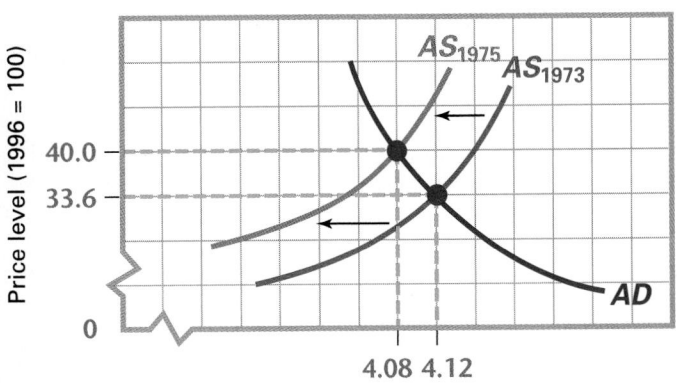

Since 1980

Increasing aggregate supply, or shifting the aggregate supply curve rightward, seemed an appropriate way to combat stagflation. Such a move would both lower the price level and increase output and employment. Attention thus turned from aggregate demand to aggregate supply.

Supply-Side Economics

A key idea behind **supply-side economics** was that cutting tax rates would stimulate aggregate supply. Lower tax rates would increase the incentive to supply labor. According to advocates of the supply-side approach, the resulting increase in aggregate supply would expand real GDP and reduce the price level. This, however, was easier said than done.

In 1981, President Ronald Reagan and Congress cut personal income tax rates by an average of 23 percent to be phased in over three years. They hoped the tax cuts would stimulate economic growth enough that the government's smaller share of a bigger pie would exceed what had been its larger share of a smaller pie.

Before the tax cut was fully implemented, recession hit in 1982. The unemployment rate shot up to 10 percent. After the recession, the economy began what at the time was the longest peacetime expansion on record. During the rest of the 1980s, output grew, unemployment declined, and inflation declined. However, the growth in federal spending exceeded the growth in federal tax revenues during this period. Therefore, federal budget deficits swelled.

Giant Federal Deficits

Federal budget deficits worsened with the onset of a Gulf War recession in 1990. That recession officially ended in early 1991. However, the deficit continued to grow and topped $290 billion in 1992. Annual deficits accumulated as a huge federal debt. *Government debt* measures the net accumulation of prior deficits. Measured relative to GDP, the federal debt nearly doubled from 33 percent in 1980 to 64 percent in 1992.

During the 1990s, policy makers began to worry more about huge federal deficits. To reduce them, President George H. W. Bush increased taxes in 1990. President Bill Clinton increased taxes on the rich in 1993. A newly elected Republican Congress reduced federal spending growth beginning in 1995. Higher tax rates and a slower growth in federal spending combined with an improving economy to reduce federal deficits. By 1998, the federal budget yielded a surplus.

By early 2001, the U.S. economic expansion became the longest on record. During this stretch, 22 million jobs were added, the unemployment rate dropped from 7.5 percent to 4.2 percent, and inflation remained low.

After achieving this record, the economy softened in 2001. Job losses increased after the terrorist attacks of September 2001. This added to the recession that began in March 2001. Federal deficits then began to grow again. The stock market declined three years in a row. The 2003 war in Iraq to topple Saddam Hussein added to the economic uncertainty of the times.

CHECKPOINT
Use aggregate demand and aggregate supply to analyze supply-side economics.

Getty Images/Photo Disc

Describe the trends in employment since 1980.

⊘ E-CONOMICS

Layers of the Onion Reveal How to Succeed with an Online Business

During the 1990s, dozens of new companies emerged in an attempt to cash in on the success of the Internet. When the high-tech boom went bust at the end of the decade, most of these firms folded. In the unstable new world of Internet commerce, many companies earned revenues, but few turned a profit. One popular Internet company survived and became more profitable than ever. TheOnion.com, a free online humor magazine, thrived due to a business strategy based on diversification. *The Onion* started out as a satirical humor magazine that poked fun at current news events. When the magazine went online in 1996, it quickly gained a popular following with its bizarre stories and attention-getting

headlines, such as "Clinton Deploys Vowels to Bosnia: Cities of Sjlbvdnzv, Grny to Be First Recipients." As it gained more than one million readers, it kept its spending under control and did not rely entirely on revenues from online advertisers. It continued to publish a print edition, branching out into regional editions mocking local personalities, It also published a series of popular books. Onion leaders expanded the brand into movie deals and a subscription service offering more humor for readers.

Think Critically

By 2003, TheOnion.com was earning annual profits of $7 million that were expected to grow by 25 percent over the next five years. What assumptions about aggregate demand were made in estimating this growth rate?

Key Concepts

1. Before 1929, most economists thought the federal government should always have a balanced budget (government tax revenues = government spending). When the Great Depression began in 1929, government tax revenues fell rapidly. The federal government responded by cutting spending. What was the impact of this policy on the economy?

2. People who support the economic theories of Keynes think that a stable economy will result from a steady increase of aggregate demand. Given this idea, what would Keynes have recommended the federal government do if consumption and investment declined because people and business owners started to worry about the future?

3. How could stagflation result from a large increase in the costs of production throughout the economy?

Graphing Exercise

4. Study this graph of aggregate demand and supply. The aggregate supply curve has shifted to the left from AS to AS´ because of an increase in the costs of production. This has increased the average price level and reduced the amount of production. Which of the policies listed below might reduce costs of production and cause the aggregate supply curve to return to its original location at AS? Why are these policies examples of supply-side economics?

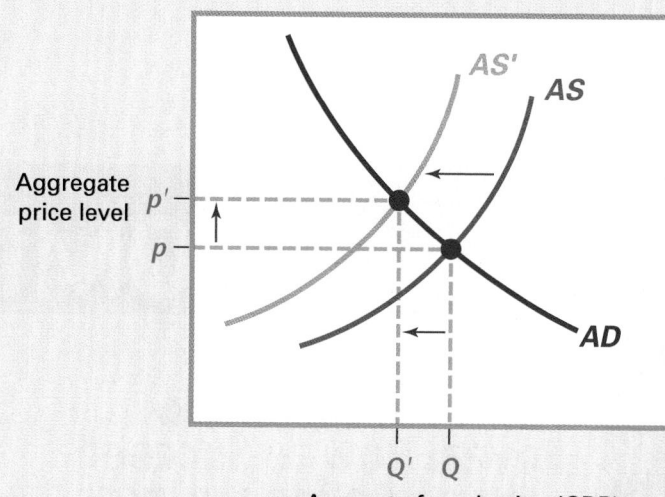

a. The government reduces taxes for businesses that buy new technology.

b. The government helps pay the wages of newly hired workers.

c. The government lowers taxes on imported raw materials.

d. The government reduces taxes on business profits.

e. The government gives grants to people who carry out applied research.

Think Critically

5. **History** The U.S. government borrowed most of the money it used to pay for its military efforts during World War II. The national debt increased by $23.5 billion in 1943, $64.3 billion in 1944, and $10.7 billion in 1945. In these years, the unemployment rate fell from its 1940 level of 14.6 percent, to 4.4 percent in 1942, 1.7 percent in 1943, and 1.0 percent in 1944. Why would these data have supported Keynes's theory that the way to combat a depression is to have more government spending?

to History

The
New Deal and the Deficit

During the early years of the Great Depression, many people—who believed that the economy would correct itself—suggested a laissez-fare approach to the business cycle. They viewed depressions as a helpful and necessary purge of the economy. Budget deficits were feared as inflationary and considered a bad example for the nation's citizens.

Still, from 1929 to 1933, prices dropped severely and the government deficit increased. Early attempts by President Herbert Hoover to balance the budget, such as sharply increasing tariffs on imports, made matters worse. In the face of increasing deficits, Hoover resisted more government intervention in the economy. He continued to advocate spending cuts and tax increases, telling Congress that "nothing is more necessary at this time than balancing the budget."

When Franklin D. Roosevelt swept into office in 1932, he initiated a host of programs known collectively as the New Deal. Although Roosevelt believed in a balanced budget, he was—unlike Hoover—willing to accept deficits in order to pump government money into the economy. The Reconstruction Finance Corporation, first begun under Hoover, was beefed up. New programs—such as the Public Works Administration, the Agricultural Adjustment Administration, National Recovery Administration, and later the Works Progress Administration—were designed to use federal money to stimulate the economy.

Under the New Deal, the economy began a slow recovery until 1937, when Roosevelt, believing that the nation's economy was strong enough to continue on its own, announced a reduction in federal spending and a plan to balance the budget by 1939. Instead, by the fall of 1937, the economy began to falter and the president called for a resumption of deficit spending in April 1938.

By this time, many in the government had become supporters of the ideas of John Maynard Keynes. Keynes himself, however, believed Roosevelt's latest attempts to build up the economy needed far more government spending than the $3 billion prescribed by the president. Before the results of the Second New Deal could be fully judged, World War II intervened and the country was brought back to full employment. The events of the 1930s, however, changed how many Americans viewed fiscal policy. As deficit spending became more accepted, they saw the government as having a crucial role in the nation's economy

© Hulton Archive

British economist and the founder of 'Keynesian economics', John Maynard Keynes (1883–1946).

THINK CRITICALLY

Evaluate and compare the wisdom of deficit spending by the government from an economic perspective, from a social perspective, and from a political perspective.

Objectives

> Describe the link between jobs, unmarried motherhood, and poverty.

> Identify some unplanned results of income-assistance programs.

Overview

In a market economy, your income depends primarily on how much you earn, which depends on the productivity of your resources. The problem with allocating income according to productivity is that some people have difficulty earning income. How should the government respond to the challenge of poverty? Families where the head of household has a job are much more likely to escape poverty than are families with no workers. Thus, the government's first line of defense in fighting poverty is to promote a healthy economy, thereby providing job opportunities for all who want to work.

Key Terms

cycle of poverty

welfare reform

[In the News]

● The Homeless Czar

In the spring of 2002, President George W. Bush named Philip Mangano to be the country's "homeless czar," or head of the government's Interagency Council on Homelessness. This position had been created many years earlier, but no one had filled the position since 1996. Why was this position left empty for so long, and why did President Bush feel the need to fill it in 2002? In 2000, the U.S. poverty rate fell to its lowest levels in two decades. The robust economy of the 1990s had helped ease poverty somewhat. As the economy began to decline in the early 2000s, however, many families only slightly above the brink were among the first to slip back into poverty. By 2001, the poverty rate was on the rise again. With this came a rise in homelessness as people lost their jobs and could not pay their rent or mortgages. Many of these new homeless were families like David and Gina C. and their four children. He was a rental car mechanic, and she worked in a nursing home. When the tourism industry began to decline in late 2001, David lost his job. Gina did not make enough money to support the family. Although David got a new job, that business soon failed, and he had difficulty finding new employment. The family was homeless for 10 months until it received new housing from a charity organization.

Think About It

Do you think the position of "homeless czar" is needed? What steps can people take to ensure that they will not become homeless in the event of job loss?

Poverty and the Economy

The best predictor of whether a family is poor is whether someone in that family has a job. Thus the most direct way the government can help reduce poverty is to nurture a healthy economy. The stronger the economy, the greater the job opportunities, and the more likely people will find jobs.

Poverty and Jobs

The poverty rate is much higher among families with no workers. Figure 13.8 shows the poverty rate based on the type of family and on the number of workers in the family. Overall, the poverty rate is about four times greater in families with no workers than in families with at least one worker. The poverty rate of families headed by a female with no workers is 15 times greater than the rate for married-couple families with at least one worker.

Poverty and Unemployment

Perhaps the best indicator of whether or not job opportunities are readily available is the unemployment rate. The lower the unemployment rate, the greater the likelihood that someone who wants to work has found a job. The more jobs, the lower the poverty rate.

Figure 13.9 shows poverty rates and unemployment rates in the United States each year since 1969. As you can see, the poverty rate tends to rise when the unemployment rate increases and fall when the unemployment rate declines. For example, between 1979 and 1982 the unemployment rate climbed from 5.8 percent to 9.7 percent. During that time period, the nation's poverty rate rose from 11.7 percent to 15.0 percent.

More recently, the unemployment rate fell from 7.5 percent in 1992 to 4.0 percent in 2000. During that time period, the poverty rate declined from 14.8 percent to 11.3 percent. Both unemployment and poverty increased in the recession year of 2001.

Unmarried Motherhood and Poverty

Even when the unemployment rate is low, the poverty rate remains stubbornly high. A strong economy with low unemployment is little aid to families with nobody in the labor force. Chapter 3 noted that young, single motherhood is a recipe for poverty. Often the young mother drops out of school, which reduces her future earning possibilities when and if she seeks work outside the home.

U.S. Poverty Rates by Family Type and Number of Workers

Figure **13.8**

Poverty rates in the United States are much higher in families with no workers.

Source: U.S. Census Bureau, *Current Population Survey*, 2002 Annual Demographic Supplement.

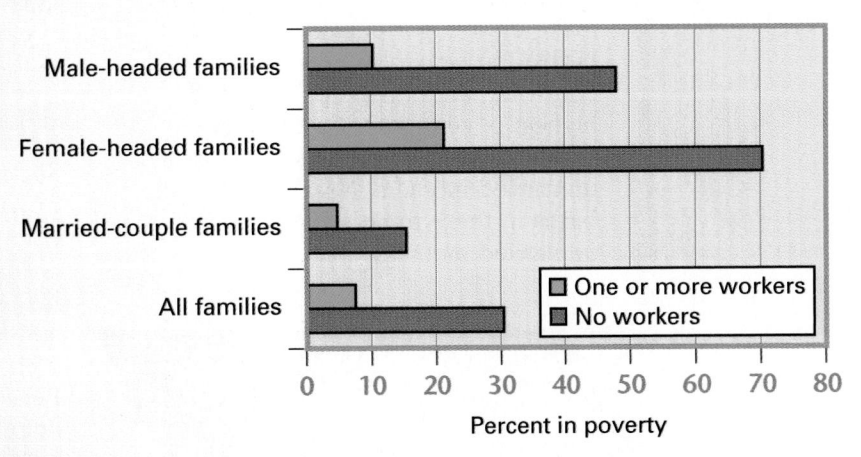

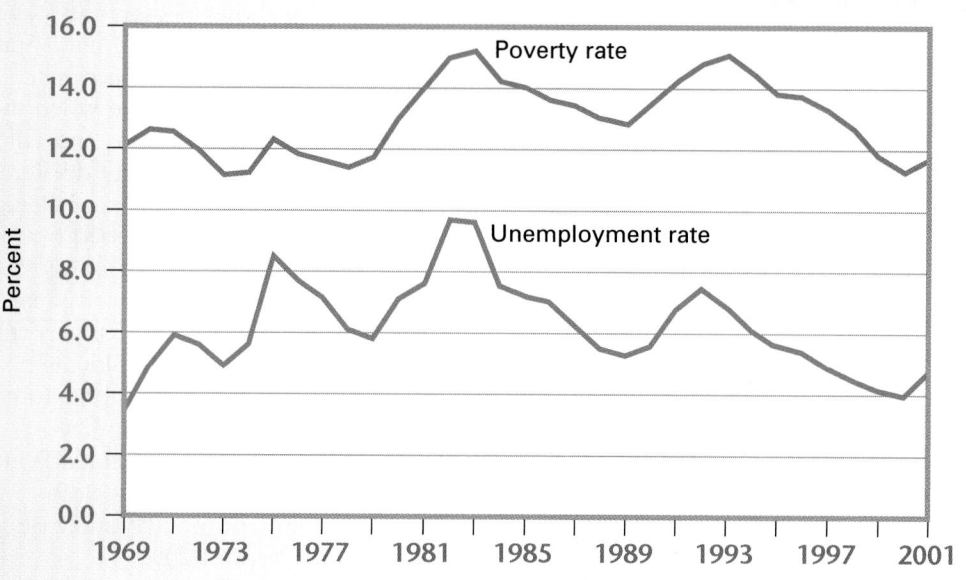

The top line shows the percentage of the U.S. population below the official poverty level. The bottom line shows the percentage of the U.S. labor force that is unemployed.

Sources: U.S. Census Bureau and U.S. Bureau of Labor Statistics.

Because of a lack of education and limited job skills, most young single mothers go on welfare. Before recently imposed lifetime limits on welfare, the average never-married mother had been on welfare for a decade.

Figure 13.10 shows the poverty rates for each of the 50 states. Those states with a deeper shade of pink have higher poverty rates. States with no shading have lower rates. As you can see, poverty rates are higher across the bottom half of the United States. Poverty rates tend to be higher in states where births to single mothers make up a larger percentage of all births. For example, New Mexico, Louisiana, and Mississippi had the highest poverty rates in 2001. They also had the highest rates of births to unmarried mothers. Nearly half of all births in these three states were to unmarried mothers.

✓ **CHECKPOINT**
What is the link between jobs, unmarried motherhood, and poverty?

Unplanned Results of Income Assistance

On the plus side, antipoverty programs increase the consumption possibilities of poor families. This is important because children are the largest group living in poverty. However, programs to assist the poor may have other effects that limit their ability to reduce poverty. Consider some unplanned results of these programs.

Why Work?

Society, through government, tries to provide families with an adequate standard of living, but society also wants to ensure that only the poor receive benefits. As you saw in Chapter 3, income assistance consists of a combination of cash and in-kind transfer programs. Because these programs are designed to help the poor and only the poor, welfare benefits decline as income from other sources increases. This has

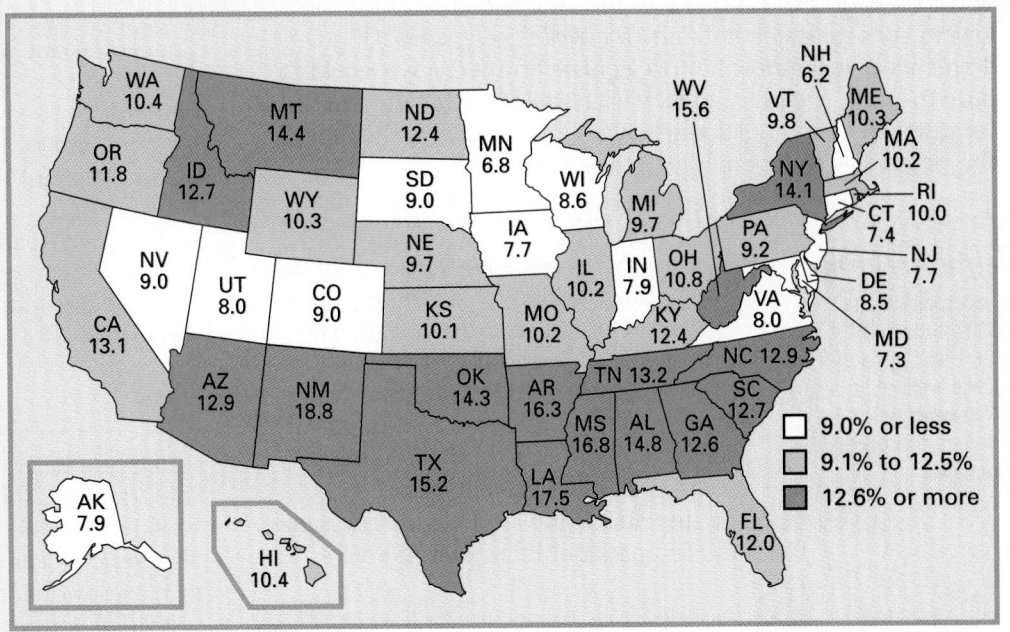

States with a deeper shade of pink have higher poverty rates. States with no shading have lower rates.

Source: U.S. Census Bureau. Rates are averages for 1999, 2000, and 2001.

WA 10.4 · OR 11.8 · ID 12.7 · MT 14.4 · WY 10.3 · ND 12.4 · SD 9.0 · MN 6.8 · WI 8.6 · MI 9.7 · NH 6.2 · VT 9.8 · ME 10.3 · MA 10.2 · NY 14.1 · RI 10.0 · CT 7.4 · NJ 7.7 · WV 15.6 · PA 9.2 · DE 8.5 · MD 7.3 · NV 9.0 · UT 8.0 · CO 9.0 · NE 9.7 · IA 7.7 · IL 10.2 · IN 7.9 · OH 10.8 · KY 12.4 · VA 8.0 · CA 13.1 · KS 10.1 · MO 10.2 · NC 12.9 · AZ 12.9 · NM 18.8 · OK 14.3 · AR 16.3 · TN 13.2 · SC 12.7 · MS 16.8 · AL 14.8 · GA 12.6 · TX 15.2 · LA 17.5 · FL 12.0 · AK 7.9 · HI 10.4

- 9.0% or less
- 9.1% to 12.5%
- 12.6% or more

---

resulted in a system in which transfer payments decline sharply as earned income increases.

An increase in earnings reduces benefits from cash assistance, Medicaid, food stamps, housing assistance, energy assistance, and other poverty programs. In some cases, total welfare benefits are cut by $1 or more as earned income increases by $1. Because welfare benefits decline with earnings, this reduces the incentive to find work.

Why work if doing so simply reduces your income and your standard of living? After all, holding even a part-time job involves additional expenses—for transportation and childcare, for instance—not to mention the loss of free time.

In many cases, the value of welfare benefits exceeds the disposable income resulting from full-time employment. Such a system can frustrate people trying to work their way off welfare. *The high tax rate on each additional dollar earned discourages employment and self-sufficiency.*

Long-Term Dependency

The longer people are out of work, the more their job skills weaken. As a result, when those who have been on welfare for years finally do look for work, their productivity and their pay are lower than when they were last employed. This lowers their expected wage, thus making work even less attractive. Some economists argue that in this way, welfare benefits can lead to long-term dependency on welfare. While welfare seems to be a rational choice in the short run, it has unfavorable long-term consequences for both the family and for society.

By tracking welfare recipients over time, economists have learned that most recipients received welfare for less than a year, but about one third had remained on welfare for at least eight years. Thus there was a core of long-term recipients.

Cycle of Poverty

A second and more serious concern is that children in welfare families may end up on welfare themselves when they grow up. This is referred to as the **cycle of poverty**. Why might this occur? Children in welfare households may learn the ropes about the welfare system and may come to view welfare

CNN video
Welfare Reform
econxtra.swlearning.com

cycle of poverty

Children in welfare families may end up on welfare themselves when they grow up

welfare reform

An overhaul of the welfare system in 1996 that imposed a lifetime welfare limit of five years per recipient and other conditions

as a normal way of life rather than as a temporary bridge over a rough patch.

Research indicates that daughters from welfare families are more likely than daughters in other families to participate in the welfare system themselves. It is difficult to say whether welfare "causes" the link between mother and daughter, because the same factors that contribute to a mother's

welfare status also can contribute to her daughter's welfare status.

Welfare Reforms

Concern about welfare dependency and a cycle of poverty prompted **welfare reform**, or an overhaul of the welfare system in 1996. The reform imposed a lifetime welfare limit of five years per recipient. As a condition of receiving welfare, the head of the household also must participate in education and training programs, search for work, or take some paid or unpaid position. The idea is to help people on welfare to learn about the job market. Those who find work are able to maintain some of their welfare benefits, such as free medical care, during a transition period from welfare to work. Those who find jobs also get childcare services. This increases the incentive to work.

Evidence from various states indicates that programs involving mandatory job searches, short-term unpaid work, and training increase employment. Those involved in such programs left welfare rolls sooner. Between 1995 and 2001, the number of welfare recipients fell by more than half.

NETBookmark

The U.S. Department of Health and Human Services' Administration for Children and Families (ACF) maintains a web site about welfare reform. Access this site through econxtra.swlearning.com.

Choose one of the links to find out about Temporary Assistance for Needy Families. Write down five facts you learned about this program.

econxtra.swlearning.com

✓ CHECKPOINT
What are some unplanned results of income-assistance programs?

What are the benefits of free or low-cost childcare programs for families trying to work their way out of the welfare system?

© Getty Images/PhotoDisc

SPAN THE GLOBE

Pro-Poor Tourism

For many people in the world's poorest countries, poverty is an ongoing fact of life. About 80 percent of the world's poorest people live in just 12 countries. In many of these countries, a variety of factors make it difficult to build an economic structure that can support the majority of citizens. Recently, though, some economists and developers have begun to promote the idea of building up pro-poor tourism in these countries. This idea involves promoting tourism so as to provide jobs and ongoing economic growth that will allow the majority of the people to rise out of poverty. Because many of these countries have no industry, their undeveloped environments are an attractive draw for tourists. Advocates of pro-poor tourism warn, however, that great care must be taken to ensure that these environments are not harmed by the growth of tourism. In the past, the growth of tourism in some areas has come at the expense of poor people. In Indonesia, for example, land that poor people once used for agriculture was bought up by developers for hotels and golf courses. These projects cut off land and water resources to the poor without providing them with jobs. Pro-poor tourism seeks to minimize these negative results. Development is focused on preserving the natural environment and culture while helping to build a system of public works that can be used by both tourists and local residents. In the Mekong River Basin of Asia, for example, pro-poor tourism loans have been used to help build roads, piers, and better walking paths. These projects improve mobility yet preserve the beauty of the countries in this region and help its residents earn money.

Think Critically

Do you think pro-poor tourism is an effective way to help the people in the world's poorest countries? Why or why not?

Getty Images/PhotoDisc

Key Concepts

1. Why is living in poverty in rural areas often different from living in poverty in an urban area?

2. What reasons can you identify to explain why the number of welfare recipients in the United States fell by more than half between 1995 and 2001?

3. Does the fact that fewer people receive social benefits necessarily mean that fewer people are living in poverty? Explain why or why not.

Graphing Exercise

4. Many people think the bulk of federal government transfers are used to support the poor. This is not the case. In 2000, the total of all federal government transfer payments to individuals was $1,013 billion. The table shows how these payments were distributed. Use the data in the table to construct a pie graph that shows how federal transfer payments were distributed. Is there any information in the graph that you find surprising? Explain why or why not.

Federal Transfers by Use, 2000 (in billions of dollars)

Type of Spending	Amount	Percent of Total
Retirement and Disability Insurance (Social Security)	$425.3	42.0%
Medical Payments (Medicare and Medicaid)	$423.2	41.8%
Income Maintenance (SSI and Welfare)	$106.4	10.5%
Unemployment Insurance Benefits	$ 20.7	2.0%
Veteran's Benefits	$ 24.9	2.4%
Other transfers to Individuals	$ 12.8	1.3%

Think Critically

5. **Psychology** Investigate the impact of poverty on people's self-image. Do people who live in poverty feel they are victims of circumstances that are beyond their control? Do they feel there is something that they have done that has caused them to be poor? How might these feelings change the way poor people live and relate to other people in society?

6. **Management** Suppose that you are the owner of a small business that produces precision parts for specialized machines. Your workers are very skilled. If one of your workers were to leave, it would take a long time to find and retrain a replacement. The economy has been in a recession for the past six months, and your firm's sales have fallen by 30 percent. You are having trouble selling enough product to pay your workers and keep them busy. You are thinking of laying off three of your ten workers. What reasons are there for you to do this or not do this? Explain each reason.

Sharpen Your Life Skills

Make Inferences

People who are unemployed typically experience a reduced standard of living. It is therefore reasonable to expect that poverty rates will increase during times of recession and fall during times of economic expansion.

Apply Your Skill

Study the data in the table and consider whether they support this expectation. Write a brief essay that discusses your findings.

Poverty and Unemployment Rates, 1992–2000

Year	Poverty Rate	Unemployment Rate	Year	Poverty Rate	Unemployment Rate
1992	14.8%	7.5%	1997	13.3%	4.9%
1993	15.1%	6.9%	1998	12.7%	4.5%
1994	14.5%	6.1%	1999	11.8%	4.2%
1995	13.8%	5.6%	2000	11.3%	4.0%
1996	13.7%	5.4%			

(13) Chapter Assessment

Summary

 13.1 *Unemployment*

a Unemployment occurs when people who are over 16 are seeking, but unable to find, employment. The *labor force* is made up of all people over 16 who are either employed or seeking work. The *labor force participation rate* is the number of people in the labor force divided by the non-institutionalized adult population.

> **Xtra! Quiz Prep**
> econxtra.swlearning.com

b Unemployment is more common among individuals who have less education, experience, or training. It also is more likely to affect young people, minorities, and women. In recent years, the differences in unemployment rates among various groups have declined somewhat.

c There is always some unemployment in the economy as workers move from job to job. Economists have identified four types of unemployment: *frictional, structural, seasonal,* and *cyclical.* Discouraged workers are not counted as unemployed because they are no longer seeking employment.

d Unemployment compensation is paid to workers who lose their jobs through no fault of their own. In general these benefits last for 26 weeks. The benefits may reduce the incentive unemployed workers feel to find new jobs.

13.2 *Inflation*

a *Inflation* is an increase in the economy's general price level. Inflation may be divided into two basic types: *demand-pull* and *cost-push.* Demand-pull inflation results from an increase of aggregate demand. Cost-push inflation is caused by an increase in the costs of production that causes the aggregate supply curve to shift to the left.

b Prior to World War II, inflation in the United States was temporary. Since World War II, there has been sustained inflation that has not been followed by periods of falling prices.

c When people do not expect inflation, they often are harmed when prices increase. That is because they made agreements based on a price level that is lower than what actually exists. Higher rates of inflation are associated with higher interest rates.

13.3 *Economic Instability*

a Before the Great Depression, most economists held a *laissez-faire* doctrine that said the government should not intervene in a market economy. The economic difficulties of the 1930s convinced many people that government intervention in the economy was necessary for it to work well. Keynes suggested that the government should adjust its own spending and taxing to assure that there is sufficient aggregate demand in the economy to keep production and employment stable.

b By the 1970s, it was clear that Keynes's theories could not solve all economic problems. In these years, a combination of high rates of unemployment and inflation called *stagflation* occurred. In the 1980s, some economists suggested that stagflation could be reduced or eliminated by implementing government policies that would reduce the costs of production. The tax cuts of 1981–1983 were intended to stimulate investment in the economy. The most apparent result of these tax cuts, however, was growth in the national debt.

13.4 *Poverty*

a A significant proportion of people in the United States lives in poverty. Poverty is associated with unemployment, single parenthood, and physical or mental disabilities. People with limited education or training also are likely to live in poverty.

b Income-assistance programs help people who live in poverty, but they also may cause some people not to seek employment. This has caused a long-term dependency on social programs that lead to what has been called a *cycle of poverty. Welfare reforms* passed in 1996 attempted to eliminate this cycle.

Review Economic Terms

Choose the term that best fits the definition. On a separate sheet of paper, write the letter of the answer. Some terms may not be used.

_____ 1. Workers who are overqualified for their jobs or who work fewer hours than they would prefer

_____ 2. An increase in the economy's general price level

_____ 3. Macroeconomic policy that focuses on shifting the aggregate demand curve as a way of promoting full employment and price stability

_____ 4. The number of people looking for work divided by the number in the labor force

_____ 5. Macroeconomic policy that focuses on a rightward shift of the aggregate supply curve through tax cuts or other changes that increase production incentives

_____ 6. Doctrine that the government should not intervene in a market economy beyond the minimum required to maintain peace and property rights

_____ 7. Inflation that results from a leftward shift of the aggregate supply curve

_____ 8. A decline of a nation's output accompanied by a rise in the price level

_____ 9. Inflation that results from a rightward shift of the aggregate demand curve

_____ 10. Children in welfare families may end up on welfare themselves when they grow up

_____ 11. The interest rate expressed in current dollars as a percentage of the amount loaned; the interest rate on a loan agreement

_____ 12. Occurs when there is no cyclical employment

a. **cost-push inflation**

b. **cycle of poverty**

c. **demand-pull inflation**

d. **demand-side economics**

e. **full employment**

f. **inflation**

g. **labor force**

h. **labor force participation rate**

i. **laissez-faire**

j. **nominal interest rate**

k. **real interest rate**

l. **stagflation**

m. **supply-side economics**

n. **underemployment**

o. **unemployment benefits**

p. **unemployment rate**

q. **welfare reform**

Review Economic Concepts

13. Imagine there are 150 million adults in a country. Of these, 45 million adults are not seeking work, and 105 million adults are either working or looking for work. In this case, the labor force participation rate is

    a. 40 percent.

    b. 70 percent.

    c. 30 percent.

    d. 60 percent.

14. **True or False** The _labor force_ is made up of all the people who would like a job but lack employment.

15. Job seekers who lack skills that are demanded by employers are __?__.

16. **True or False** Interest rates tend to increase when the inflation rate increases.

17. Which of the following events would cause *cost-push inflation*?

    a. The price of natural gas increases by 20 percent.

    b. The stock market's value grows by 20 percent.

    c. The federal government cuts income taxes by 20 percent.

    d. The amount of grain produced in the United States grows by 20 percent.

18. __?__ inflation is particularly harmful to people in businesses because they are not able to plan for it.

19. __?__ results in higher unemployment and higher inflation.

20. Before the Great Depression, most economists believed that the government should

    a. intervene in the economy when there was a problem.

    b. intervene in the economy only when the federal government had a large debt.

    c. try not to intervene in the economy at any time.

    d. intervene in the economy at all times to make sure there was full employment.

21. **True or False** Poverty is closely associated with unemployment.

22. Which group is not likely to suffer from higher rates of unemployment and poverty than the average for all people?

    a. single parents

    b. minorities

    c. people with limited education

    d. two-parent families

Apply Economic Concepts

Identify Types of Unemployment Identify each of the following as an example of

    A. Structural Unemployment

    B. Cyclical Unemployment

    C. Seasonal Unemployment

    D. Frictional Unemployment

    E. Discouraged Worker

23. Rosetta quit her job at the public library to look for a job with better pay.

24. Brandon was laid off from his construction job last December.

25. Peter was laid off from his job at Ford when Ford's sales declined.

26. Serena gave up looking for work after she got no job offers in six months of looking.

27. Walter was laid off from his bookkeeping job after his employer installed a new automated inventory control system.

Calculate the Unemployment Rate Use the data below to calculate

28. The labor force

29. The labor force participation rate

30. The number of people who are unemployed

31. The unemployment rate for this imaginary economy.

Total population: 10,000 people

Non-institutionalized adult population: 7,000 people

Adults who do not work and are not looking for work: 2,000 people

People who have employment: 4,750 people

32. **History** Investigate the inflation that took place in Germany after World War I. In 1914, $1 was equal in value to 4.2 marks. By the end of November 1923, $1 had about the same value as 1 trillion marks. What impact did this hyperinflation have on the German economy and German people?

33. Sharpen Your Life Skills: Make Inferences

In 1996, U.S. government public-assistance programs were reformed, and limits were placed on the length of time over which people could receive such assistance. How do you think this change has affected single mothers with young children? Do you think that more of these women would have looked for employment after 1996? What impact might this have on the environment in which their children live? Do the data in the table support your answers?

Labor Force Participation Rates for All Adults and for Single Mothers of Children through Six Years of Age, 1980–2000

Year	Labor Force Participation Rate for All Adults	Labor Force Participation Rate for Single Mothers with Children
1980	63.8%	44.1%
1985	64.8%	46.5%
1990	66.5%	48.7%
1995	66.6%	53.0%
2000	67.2%	70.5%

34. Graphing Inflation

Use data in the table to construct a line graph that shows the rate of inflation in the United States as measured by the Consumer Price Index (CPI). In 1989 and 1990, prices went up more quickly because the cost of energy increased when Iraq invaded Kuwait. Why were interest rates high in 1989 and 1990?

Rates of Inflation as Measured by the CPI, 1985–2001

Year	Inflation	Year	Inflation	Year	Inflation
1985	3.6%	1991	4.2%	1997	2.3%
1986	1.9%	1992	3.0%	1998	1.6%
1987	3.6%	1993	3.0%	1999	2.2%
1988	4.1%	1994	2.6%	2000	3.4%
1989	4.8%	1995	2.8%	2001	2.8%
1990	5.4%	1996	3.0%	2002	1.6%

 *econxtra.swlearning.com*

35. Access EconDebate Online

at econxtra.swlearning.com. Read the policy debate entitled "Do technological advances result in higher unemployment?" Analyze this issue from both points of view, and write a paragraph summarizing each side.

Investing In Your Future

The Situation

It was the end of a long day. Shortly, Aleesha would get up and drive to her home a few miles away in the suburbs. There her two children, Tomas, four, and Aleece, two, would come bubbling up to her with stories of what they had done today with their daddy. First, though, Aleesha needed some quiet time to sort things out. She knew how lucky she was. Just seven years ago, she was a struggling college student trying to finance her education and guide the small company she founded into profitability. The company was anchored by a patent Aleesha had received on her invention of a new type of animal-restraint muzzle.

While she was in college, she ran the business out of her parents' garage. After graduation, she devoted her full energies to the enterprise, and sales increased dramatically. Aleesha then bought a small building in the downtown area, and the company had been there ever since. She now had 24 employees, most of whom were single mothers. These women valued not only their chance to work but also the day-care center Aleesha provided as an employee benefit. Aleesha met her husband Tom during a trip to Kenya to observe gorillas. They married four months later and, with the arrival of Tomas, their first child, Tom elected to stay home and care for him.

The Decision

Now Aleesha faced some vital decisions about which direction to take the company. Demand for its basic products—based on the patent and tailored to each species of animal—continued to increase dramatically. As a consequence, however, the present building was too small, even with the three shifts currently running. Also, the company's machinery now was depreciated fully, and the breakdown rate was increasing, due to its heavy use. The company's small research and development group, comprised of two ex-zookeepers and a mechanical engineer, had several products ready for market. These included more "humane" animal-restraint devices than the cage and a better means for capturing animals. Regrettably, the country's economy as a whole was having problems. Governmental expenditures on zoos were very low. Some economic forecasters predicted that the economic cycle would reverse and a recovery would follow.

Activities

Divide into teams or work individually, as directed by your teacher, to perform the following tasks.

Apply the steps in the following decision-making process to Aleesha's current situation:

1. *Define the problem.* Define Aleesha's problem in a way that will allow a clear solution. Should Aleesha invest in new equipment and a new location?

2. *Identify her choices.* List the various alternatives among which Aleesha must choose.

a. If the company must move to a distant new location, how should Aleesha provide for her current employees?

b. How should a new factory and equipment be financed? What are the risks of using debt to do so? What about selling stock instead?

c. Should Aleesha bring out the new products? What would be good way to determine if the new products will sell?

3. *Evaluate the pluses and minuses of each choice.* Carefully weigh the value Aleesha puts on each alternative and the opportunity cost(s) for each. Consider what problems each choice might pose for her personal life.

4. *Make a choice.* Which course of action should she choose? Be prepared to present and defend your selection to the class.

5. *Provide "action" steps that are appropriate to the decision.* Make sure these are realistic and timely to ensure the necessary actions are taken to resolve the problem.

6. *Critique the decision.* The class will assist in the review and evaluation of your plan of action. In real life, you should review not only the decision and its result, but also the process by which you make it.

Research

Research for the information needed to effectively make the decision, such as financing the new factory with debt versus stock and techniques available to assess the marketability of new products.

Present

Arrive at a decision. Then prepare a presentation for the class on the six steps you took to achieve this decision.

Unit 5

Public Policy and the National Economy

Does the economy function pretty well on its own, or does it need government intervention to keep on track? According to one view, the economy can get off track quite easily, resulting in falling output and rising unemployment. To get the economy moving again, government must step in to boost employment and output. According to another view, the economy is fairly stable on its own. Even when things do go wrong, the economy can bounce back pretty quickly. If this second view is true, not only is government intervention unnecessary, it could do more harm than good.

14 Government Spending, Revenue, and Public Choice

Consider

How does the demand for public goods differ from the demand for private goods?

How are responsibilities divided among levels of government?

How big is the federal budget, and where does the money go?

Why do politicians need to deal with special interest groups?

Why do most people remain largely ignorant about what's happening in the public sector?

POINT YOUR BROWSER

econxtra.swlearning.com

© Getty Images/PhotoDisc

Objectives

> Calculate the optimal quantity of a public good.

> Distinguish between the two principles of taxation.

> Identify other government revenue sources besides taxes.

Overview

Markets are marvelous devices, but they are not perfect. They have limitations and shortcomings. For example, firms have little incentive to supply public goods because such goods, once produced, are available to all, regardless of who pays and who doesn't. Because a firm cannot limit the good just to those who pay for it, firms can't earn a profit selling public goods. Governments attempt to compensate for this market failure by supplying public goods and paying for them with taxes. People who don't pay their taxes could go to prison.

Key Terms

benefits-received tax principle

ability-to-pay tax principle

tax incidence

proportional taxation

progressive taxation

regressive taxation

marginal tax rate

[In the News]

● Will a Heavier Beer Tax Combat Underage Drinking?

A recent National Academy of Sciences report has proposed that the excise tax on alcohol, in particular beer, be raised to help curtail the $53 billion that underage drinking costs taxpayers each year. Alcohol-related traffic accidents involving minors cost almost $20 billion alone. The federal excise tax on beer, currently about 33 cents per six-pack, was last raised in 1991 from around 16 cents. This tax increase resulted in a reported drop of nearly 10 percent in beer sales, according to a spokesperson for beer wholesalers. However, the same spokesperson also commented, "To try to engineer a social problem out of existence [through taxation] is unfair to people who use a product responsibly."

Think About It

Do you think a tax increase on beer would be effective in reducing underage drinking? Why or why not?

429

Public Goods

You already learned about the market demand for a private good. For example, the market quantity of pizza demanded when the price is $10 is the quantity demanded by Alan plus the quantity demanded by Maria plus the quantity demanded by all other consumers in the pizza market. Because private goods are rival in consumption, the market quantity demanded of a private good is the sum of the quantities demanded by each consumer.

The Demand for Public Goods

A public good is different because it is nonrival in consumption. A public good is available to all consumers in an identical amount. For example, if the town sprays a neighborhood for mosquitoes for two hours a week, each resident benefits from the two hours of spraying. The spraying is a public good that spreads through the neighborhood.

The market demand for the spraying reflects the marginal benefit that Alan gets from each hour of spraying plus the marginal benefit that Maria gets from each hour plus the marginal benefit that all others in the community get from each hour.

For simplicity, suppose the neighborhood consists of only two households, one headed by Alan and the other by Maria. Alan spends a lot more time in the yard and therefore values a mosquito-free environment more than Maria does. Maria spends more time away from home. Alan's demand curve, D_a, is shown in the bottom panel of Figure 14.1. Maria's demand curve, D_m, appears in the middle panel. These demand curves reflect the marginal benefits that each person enjoys from each additional hour of spraying.

For example, when the town sprays two hours a week, Maria values the second hour at $5 and Alan values it at $10. To derive the sum of the marginal benefits for the neighborhood, simply add up the marginal benefit to get $15, as identified by point *e* in the top panel. By vertically summing up marginal

valuations at each rate of output, you derive the neighborhood demand curve, *D,* for mosquito spraying.

Note again that the demand for private goods is found by summing quantities *across* consumers at each price. Pizza and other private goods are rival in consumption. A pizza sold to Alan cannot also be sold to Maria. But public goods are nonrival, so any given quantity of mosquito spraying benefits both Alan and Maria. They may value that public good differently, but the same quantity is available to each.

Optimal Quantity of the Public Good

How much mosquito spraying should the town government provide? To determine the optimal level of a public good, compare the sum of the marginal benefits of the good with the marginal cost. Suppose the marginal cost of spraying for mosquitoes is a constant $15 an hour, as shown in the top panel of Figure 14.1.

The efficient level of the public good is found where the sum of the marginal benefits equals the marginal cost of providing the good. This occurs where the neighborhood demand curve intersects the marginal cost curve. These curves intersect at two hours per week. Thus, two hours is the efficient amount of spraying. That's where the marginal benefit enjoyed by the community just equals the marginal cost. If the town sprayed three or more hours per week, the marginal cost would exceed the marginal benefit.

CHECKPOINT
What is the optimal quantity of a public good?

Tax Principles

Two hours per week is the efficient, or optimal, level of the public good. How should the government pay for it? Taxes are the source of most government revenue. The way a tax is imposed often is justified on the basis of one of two general principles: the benefits received or the ability to pay.

The Graphing Workshop

| Market Demand for a Public Good | Figure 14.1 |

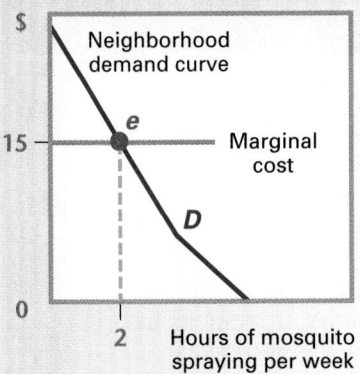

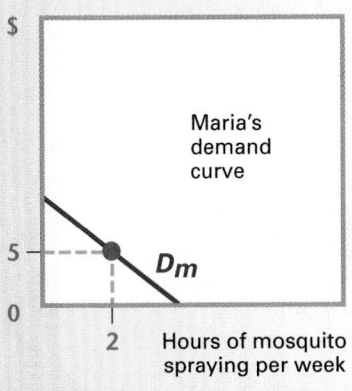

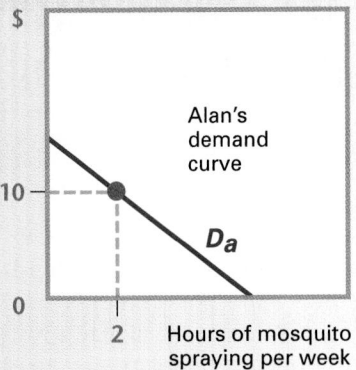

Because public goods, once produced, are available to all in identical amounts, the market demand for a public good sums up each person's demand at each quantity. In this example, the neighborhood demand for mosquito spraying sums up Alan's demand, D_a, and Maria's demand, D_m. The efficient level is found where the marginal cost of mosquito spraying equals the sum of the marginal benefits. This occurs where the marginal cost curve intersects the neighborhood demand curve, resulting in point e in the top panel. The optimal output is two hours of mosquito spraying per week.

Benefits-Received Taxation

The **benefits-received tax principle** relates taxes to the benefits taxpayers receive from a public good. In the mosquito-spray example, the government would impose a tax on each resident equal to his or her marginal benefit from the good. In this case Alan would pay $10 per hour of spraying, or $20 in all. Maria would pay $5 per hour of spraying, or $10 in all. This seems simple enough, but there are at least two problems with it.

First, once people realize that their taxes are based on how much the government thinks they value the good, they tend to understate their true valuation. Why admit how much you value the good if, as a result, you get hit with a higher tax bill? Therefore, taxpayers are reluctant to offer information about their true valuation of public goods. This creates the *free-rider* problem, which occurs because people try to benefit from the public good without paying for it or by paying less than they think it's worth.

Even if the government has accurate information about how much people value the good, the resulting tax may not seem fair if those who value the good more highly have lower incomes. In this example, Alan values mosquito control more than Maria does because he spends more time in the yard than she does. What if Alan is around more because he can't find a job? Maria is around less because she has a job. Should Alan's taxes be double those of Maria? Taxing people according to their marginal benefit may seem reasonable, but it may not be fair if the ability to pay differs sharply across taxpayers.

Ability-to-Pay Tax Principle

The second approach to taxes is based on the **ability-to-pay tax principle**. Those with a greater ability to pay are taxed more. In the mosquito-spray example, Maria would pay more taxes because she has the greater ability to pay. For example, Maria might pay twice

benefits-received tax principle

Those who receive more benefits from the government program funded by a tax should pay more of that tax

ability-to-pay tax principle

Those with a greater ability to pay, such as those with a higher income, should pay more of a tax

E-CONOMICS

Library Internet Access for Some but Not All?

You head for the nearest public library to do research on human anatomy for your science project. Sitting down at a computer Internet station, you type in a search request. Unfortunately, when you try to access a useful site, the download is blocked by the library's pornography filtering system. You talk to a librarian about getting the material but the librarian responds that, unlike adults, minors are not empowered by federal law to have the filters removed at their request. Your situation reflects a choice that was made by the library under the Children's Internet Protection Act. Under the Act, if the library wanted to receive federal money supporting Internet access for its patrons, it had to agree to install the filters and to enforce the rules surrounding their use. The Supreme Court upheld the Act over a challenge by libraries, their patrons, web-site publishers, and the like. These groups maintained that the software filters blocked a great deal of useful, non-offending information on topics such as health issues. Other recipients of federal subsidies—for example, publicly supported radio and TV stations and the National Endowment for the Arts—worry that, as a consequence of the Court's decision, the material they present may be censored by the government.

Think Critically

Is Internet access at the library a public good? Do you think Internet access at the library should be available to adults and minors alike with no restrictions? Why or why not?

---

as much as Alan. Income and property taxes usually rely on the ability-to-pay approach. The ability-to-pay tax principle focuses more on taxpayer's income than on the taxpayer's benefit from the public good. Maria might not think the tax is fair, because she is paying twice as much as Alan even though she values the good only half as much as he does. Fairness is not necessarily an issue when it comes to taxation.

Public goods are more complicated than private goods in terms of what goods should be produced, in what quantities, and who should pay. These decisions are sorted out through public choices, which are examined later in the chapter.

tax incidence

Indicates who actually bears the burden of a tax

proportional taxation

The tax as a percentage of income remains constant as income increases; also called a *flat tax*

> ✓ **CHECKPOINT**
> What are the two principles of taxation?

Other Revenue Issues

Taxes provide most revenue at all levels of government. The federal government relies primarily on the individual income tax. State governments rely on income and sales taxes. Local governments rely on the property tax. In addition to taxes, other revenue sources include (1) aid from higher levels of government; (2) user fees, such as highway tolls; (3) fines, such as speeding tickets; and in some states (4) monopoly profits from having the exclusive right to sell certain goods, such as lottery tickets and liquor. If revenues fall short of expenditures, governments cover the resulting deficit by borrowing from the public.

Tax Incidence

Tax incidence indicates who actually bears the burden of the tax. One way to evaluate tax incidence is by measuring the tax as a percentage of income. Under **proportional taxation**, taxpayers at all income levels pay the same percentage of their income toward that tax. A proportional income tax is called a *flat tax,* because the tax as a percentage of income remains constant, or flat, as income increases.

Under **progressive taxation**, the percentage of income paid in taxes increases as income increases. The federal income tax and most state income taxes are progressive, because tax rates increase as taxable income increases.

Finally, under **regressive taxation**, the percentage of income paid in taxes decreases as income increases, so the tax rate declines as income increases. For example, Social Security taxes in 2003 collected 6.2 percent of the first $87,000 of a workers' earnings. The tax rate imposed on income above that level dropped to zero. The average tax rate declines as income increases above $87,000.

Marginal Tax Rate

The **marginal tax rate** indicates the percentage of each additional dollar of a taxpayer's income that goes to taxes. High marginal rates reduce the after-tax income from working, saving, and investing. Therefore, high rates can reduce people's incentives to work, save, and invest. As of 2003, there were six marginal rates for those who pay federal income taxes, ranging from 10 percent to 35 percent, depending on income. Millions of low-income households pay no income taxes. Many with low earnings receive tax refunds that exceed the amount paid in.

Income tax rates are, therefore, progressive. Figure 14.2 shows the top marginal tax rate on federal personal income taxes since the tax was introduced in 1913. Note that most recently the highest rate was relatively low by historical standards. Still, the top 10 percent of tax filers, based on income, pay about two-thirds of all federal income taxes collected.

Pollution Taxes and Sin Taxes

At times, taxes and fines are imposed to discourage some activities. For example, government may impose a tax or a fine on pollution emissions. Fines for littering, disturbing the peace, and having a defective muffler are designed to reduce these externalities. To discourage activities deemed socially undesirable, governments also impose *sin taxes* on cigarettes, liquor, and legal gambling.

User Fees

Sometimes the government can easily exclude those who don't pay for a good and so can charge a user fee. For example, states charge entrance fees to state parks and tuition to state colleges.

progressive taxation

The tax as a percentage of income increases as income increases

regressive taxation

The tax as a percentage of income decreases as income increases

marginal tax rate

The percentage of each additional dollar of income that goes to pay the tax

Why would the local government of this beach town impose a $1,000 fine for littering?

Those unwilling to pay are not admitted. User fees are just like prices for private goods except that the fees often do not cover the cost.

Borrowing

Governments sometimes borrow from households and firms to fund public programs. Borrowing by the public sector can be justified for capital projects that increase the economy's productivity—investments such as highways, airports, and schools. The cost of these capital projects should be borne in part by future taxpayers, who also will benefit from these investments. Governments also borrow when revenues fall short of expenditures. Borrowing by the federal government will be examined in the next chapter.

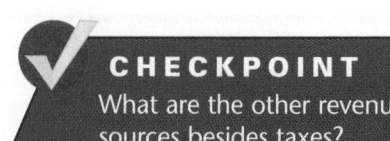

CHECKPOINT
What are the other revenue sources besides taxes?

THE WALL STREET JOURNAL

Reading It Right What's the relevance of the following statement from *The Wall Street Journal:* "Simply put, the IRS data demonstrate once again that the income tax system is steeply progressive . . . The top 10% of taxpayers [in 2001] continued to cough up well over half of all tax revenues—about 65%."

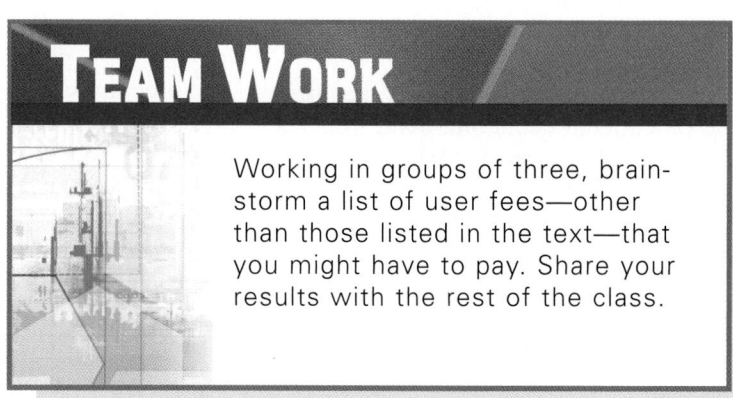

TEAM WORK

Working in groups of three, brainstorm a list of user fees—other than those listed in the text—that you might have to pay. Share your results with the rest of the class.

Top Marginal Tax Rate on Personal Income, 1913–2003   Figure 14.2

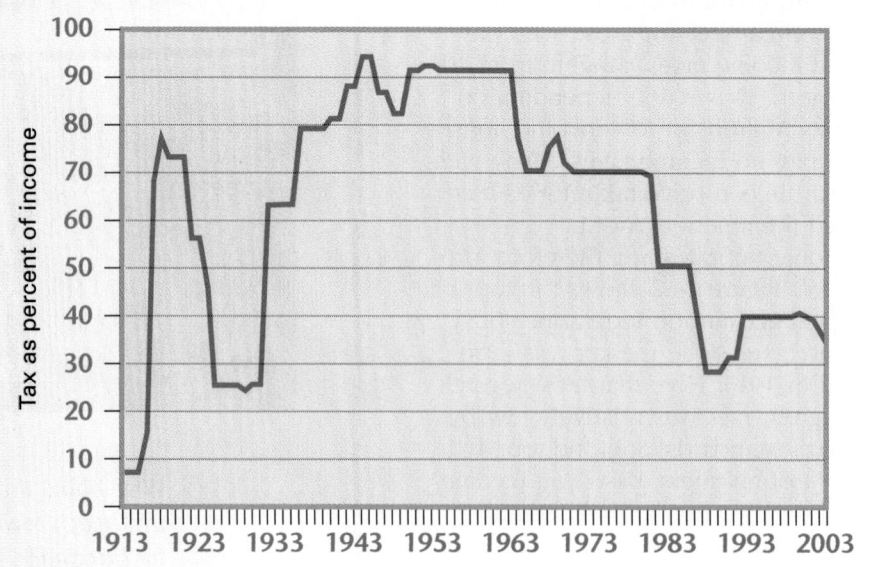

The top 10 percent of tax filers, based on income, pay about two-thirds of all federal income taxes collected.

Source: U.S. Internal Revenue Service.

14.1 Assessment

Key Concepts

1. Why isn't a campsite you rent in a national park a perfect example of a public good?

2. Suppose your town council has determined that it would need to spend $1 million to repave and widen the road that leads to your school. How should the members of the town council decide whether to undertake this project?

3. Why isn't it logical for the government to try to pay for a welfare program by imposing a *benefits-received principle* tax?

4. Why aren't property taxes, particularly for older people, always examples of *ability-to-pay principle* taxes?

5. Why is it difficult for people to agree on a tax structure that is fair for all?

6. How willing would you be to work 10 hours next week at a local store to earn $100? If $25 of your earnings were taken to pay taxes, what would happen to your willingness to work? What if $50 or $75 were taken? How does this example demonstrate the importance of the marginal tax rate to production in the economy?

Graphing Exercise

7. Many residents of Oakwood, a small town, have asked to have the town's swimming pool kept open for eight hours each day during the summer instead of only six hours. The cost of operating the pool is $80 per hour. Draw a graph that shows the efficient level of swimming-pool hours per day to be eight hours. The marginal cost should be shown by a horizontal line that hits the vertical axis at $80. The sum of the marginal benefit or demand curve should slope downward from left to right and intersect the marginal cost above eight hours of daily operation. Explain how your graph demonstrates that this is the optimal quantity of this public good.

Think Critically

8. **Math** Patty is a loan officer for a bank. She earns $60,000 per year and drives a new Jaguar. Tony is a night janitor who works for the same bank. He earns $20,000 per year and drives an old Ford. Both Patty and Tony buy 1,000 gallons of gasoline for their cars each year. The tax per gallon of gasoline is $.50. How much does each person pay in gasoline tax? What percent is this payment of each person's income? Is the tax on gasoline proportional, progressive, or regressive? Explain how you know.

Apply Math Skills

To make rational decisions, people need to quantify and evaluate the costs and benefits of alternative choices they might make. This can be seen in choosing among job offers you might receive when you finish your education. Taking a job that pays a high wage may not be your best financial choice if it is located in a city that has high taxes and costs of living. A lower wage could provide you a better standard of living in a different community. Study the two job offers described below. Then use your math skills to answer the questions that follow.

Job A in Florida

- You would work as an assistant manager in a retail clothing store.

- Your salary would begin at $23,000 per year.

- There is no state income tax in Florida.

- The sales tax in Florida is 7%.

- You can rent an apartment you like for $550 per month.

- You won't need to pay high heating costs, but your air conditioning could cost as much as $200 per month during the six months of summer.

Job B in New York State

- You would work as an assistant manager in a jewelry store.

- Your salary would begin at $28,000 per year.

- You would pay state income tax at an average rate of 5 percent.

- The sales tax in New York is 8.25%.

- You can rent an apartment you like for $675 per month.

- You would expect to pay an average of $75 per month to heat your apartment during the six months of winter and $40 per month to air condition it in summer.

Apply Your Skill

1. How much state income tax would you pay in each state?

2. If you spent $8,000 buying products that are subject to sales tax, how much would you pay in tax in each state?

3. How much would you pay per year to rent an apartment in each state?

4. How much would you pay per year to heat or cool your apartment in each state?

5. How much more per year would taxes and costs of living be in New York than in Florida?

6. Why do you think many people have moved from higher-tax states to lower-tax states in recent years?

Objectives

> Identify the top spending category in the federal budget and the top source of revenue.

> Identify the top spending category in state budgets and the top source of revenue.

> Identify the top spending category in local budgets and the top source of revenue.

> Compare the relative size of the U.S. government during the last decade with other major economies.

Overview

The United States has a federal system of government, meaning that responsibilities are shared across levels of government. State governments grant some powers to local governments and surrender some powers to the national, or federal, government. As the system has evolved, the federal government has assumed primary responsibility for national security and the stability of the economy. State governments fund public higher education, most prisons, and—with grants from the federal government—highways and welfare. Local governments are responsible mainly for local schools, though some funding for this comes from the state.

Key Terms

government budget

payroll taxes

[In the News]

● Which Way Does the Tax Cut Cut?

Recent reports on the effect of the $350 billion income tax cut of 2003 have given it mixed reviews. As a result of the tax cut, a typical middle-income family with two children had approximately $1,200 extra to spend. However, some analysts believed that families would spend this windfall in the same way they spent the 2001 tax cut funds—on foreign-made consumer goods. As a consequence, sales of domestic manufacturers would not increase, nor would these manufacturers spend money on machinery or hire new employees. The decreased taxes on stock dividends and other investments, however, had positive effects. They encouraged more people to buy stock, which sent stock prices higher. This came at a good time for baby boomers and others whose savings and retirement plans, dependent on stock prices, gained back much of the value lost in the market decline of the previous years. Finally, the loss of federal revenue from the tax cut contributed to massive actual and projected budget deficits. In fact, in a little more than three years, a federal budget surplus of more than $230 billion dollars in 2000 became a deficit of $374 billion for 2003.

Think About It

What are the benefits and downsides of income tax cuts?

Federal Budgets

A **government budget** is a plan for outlays and revenues for a specified period, usually a year. The word *budget* derives from the Old French word *bougette,* meaning "little bag." The federal budget is now more than $2,300,000,000,000—$2.3 trillion a year. If this "little bag" contained $100 bills, it would weigh more than 25,000 *tons*! These $100 bills could cover a 14-lane highway stretching from northern Maine to southern California.

Federal Spending

One way to track the impact of government spending over time is to compare that spending to the U.S. gross domestic product, or GDP. In 1929, the year the Great Depression began, government spending at all levels totaled about 10 percent of GDP. Local government spending accounted for about half that total. The federal government played a minor role in the economy. In fact, during the nation's first 150 years, federal spending, except during war years, never exceeded 3 percent relative to GDP.

The Great Depression, World War II, and a change in economic thinking have boosted government spending, particularly at the federal level, to 32 percent of GDP most recently. The federal portion totals 20 percent and state and local governments, 12 percent. Thus, since 1929, government spending has more than tripled as a share of GDP, and the federal portion has increased more than six times.

Figure 14.3 shows the share of federal spending by major category since 1960. The share of the budget going to national defense fell from 52 percent in 1960 to only 18 percent in 2004. Redistribution, which consists largely of Social Security, Medicare, and welfare, grew steadily as a share of the total, climbing from 21 percent in 1960 to 49 percent in 2004. In 1960, the federal government focused primarily on national defense. By 2004, spending had shifted to income redistribution.

Interest payments on the federal debt stood at 8 percent of the budget in 1960, grew during the middle years, and then returned to 8 percent by 2004 (thanks to record-low interest rates). Spending on all other programs, from federal prisons to the environment, went from 20 percent in 1960 to 26 percent in 2004.

Defense Spending as a Share of the Federal Budget

Figure 14.3

As a share of the federal budget, defense spending has declined and redistribution has increased since 1960.

Source: *Economic Report of the President,* February 2003, Table B-80. Figures for 2003 and 2004 are estimates.

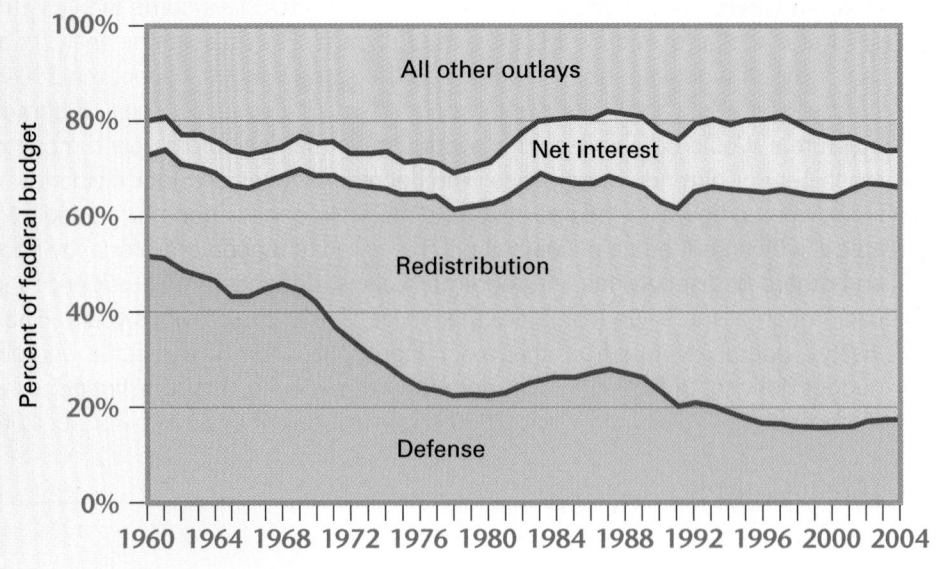

CHAPTER 14 Government Spending, Revenue, and Public Choice

Federal Revenue

During its first century, the federal government raised most of its revenue from taxes on imports, taxes on specific goods, and property taxes. All that changed with the Sixteenth Amendment to the U.S. Constitution. This empowered Congress to levy a tax on personal income. The personal income tax was introduced in 1913. The tax originally affected only the top 10 percent of households based on income. Rates were raised to help pay for World War II. Since then the personal income tax has remained the primary source of federal revenue.

Figure 14.4 shows the composition of federal revenue since 1960. The individual income tax fluctuated from 42 percent to 50 percent of the total during the period. In part because of income tax cuts in 2001 and 2003 and in part because the economy remained weak, income taxes made up 44 percent of total revenue in 2004, the same as in 1960.

The share from payroll taxes more than doubled from 15 percent in 1960 to 40 percent. **Payroll taxes** are deducted from paychecks to support Social Security, which is a retirement program, and Medicare, which funds medical care for the elderly. The abbreviation *FICA* on your paycheck stub refers to these payroll taxes. FICA stands for the Federal Insurance Contributions Act. Corporate income taxes and revenue from other taxes and user fees have declined as a share of the total from 40 percent in 1960 to 16 percent in 2004.

Note that Figure 14.4 shows the composition of revenue sources and ignores borrowed funds. Most years the federal government spends more than it takes in and makes up the difference by borrowing

Access the current fiscal year's federal budget document through econxtra.swlearning.com. Click on the link to the current year's budget. Choose one topic in the Table of Contents for the budget. Click on that link, read the document, and then write a paragraph explaining how the topic relates to the budget.

econxtra.swlearning.com

payroll taxes

Taxes deducted from paychecks to support Social Security and Medicare

Ask the Xpert!

econxtra.swlearning.com

Why do we keep the income tax if it is so unpopular?

Payroll Taxes as a Share of Federal Revenue

Figure 14.4

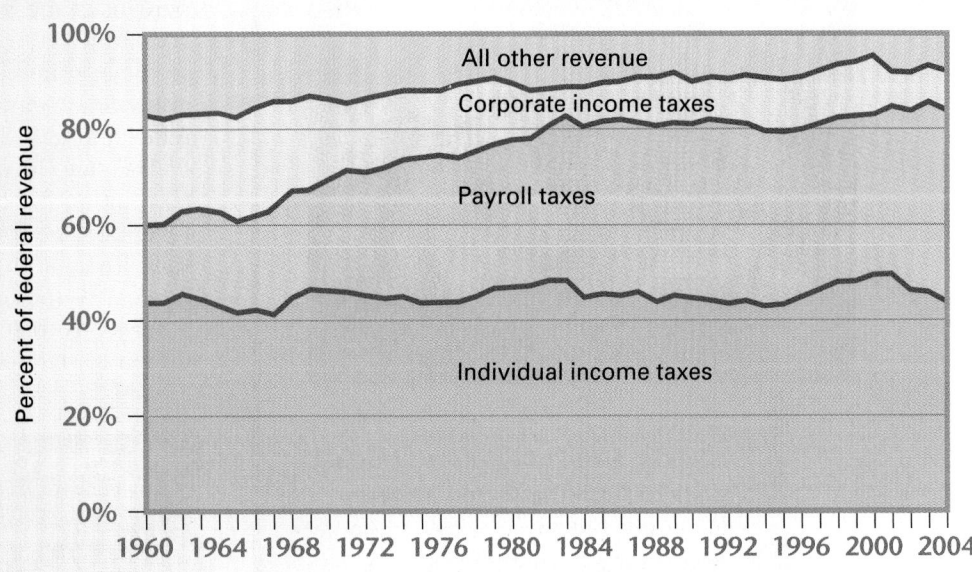

Payroll taxes have grown as a share of federal revenue since 1960.

Source: Based on fiscal year revenue figures from the *Economic Report of the President,* February 2003. Figures for 2003 and 2004 are projections.

from the public. This is discussed in the next chapter.

✓ CHECKPOINT
What is the top spending category in the federal budget and the top source of revenue?

State Budgets

You already know something about state government. You travel on state roads, visit state parks, and may be planning to attend a state college. State regulations dictate how old you must be to get a driver's license, how fast you may drive on most roads, and how many days a year school is in session. You pay state excise taxes on certain items, including gasoline and movie tickets. If you earn a paycheck, you may pay state income taxes. You also may pay state sales taxes on most purchases. From the department of motor vehicles to the department of education, state government affects your life in many ways.

State Spending

The pie chart on the left of Figure 14.5 shows the composition of state spending. The biggest outlay, 34 percent of the total, goes toward grants to local governments, mostly to help pay for schools. The next biggest share, 20 percent, consists of welfare payments, most of which go toward medical care for the poor, especially elderly in nursing homes. Higher education ranks third at 14 percent of the total. The remaining 32 percent pays for highways, state police, prisons, interest on state debt, administration, and other state activities.

State Revenue

The right pie chart in Figure 14.5 lays out the sources of state revenue. The largest source, 28 percent of the total, is aid from the federal government, which covers more than half of state welfare costs. The second biggest source, sales and excise taxes, makes up 25 percent of state revenue. Sales taxes apply to broad categories of goods. All but five states impose a general sales tax, with rates ranging from 3 percent to 7 percent of the purchase price. Does your state have a general sales tax? If so, what's the tax rate? Excise taxes apply to specific goods such as cigarettes and gasoline.

The state income tax ranks third, accounting for 19 percent of state revenue. The fourth greatest source of state revenue is user fees, making up 17 percent of the total. Examples include admissions to state campgrounds and tuition at state colleges.

© Getty Images/PhotoDisc

A small portion of a state's budget goes to fund the prison system. What are the top two spending categories for state government?

CHECKPOINT
What is the top spending category in state budgets and the top source of revenue?

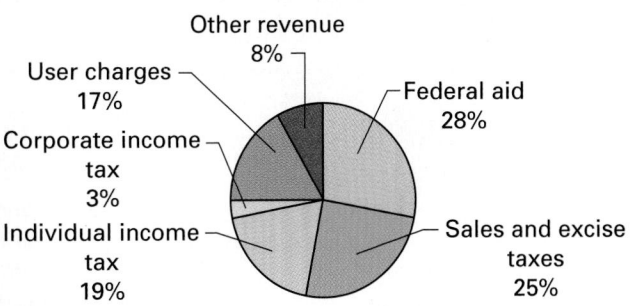

Composition of State Spending

Administration and interest 6%

Police and prisons 5%

Highways 6%

Higher education 14%

Other spending 15%

Aid to local government 34%

Welfare 20%

Composition of State Revenue

Other revenue 8%

User charges 17%

Corporate income tax 3%

Individual income tax 19%

Federal aid 28%

Sales and excise taxes 25%

The biggest portion of state spending goes toward grants to local governments. The largest source of state revenue is aid from the federal government.

Source: Based on general expenditure figures for fiscal year 2000 from the U.S. Census Bureau.

Local Budgets

Of all government levels, you may be most familiar with the local one. You may be attending a public school. You may get to school in a government-funded bus on roads maintained by local government and patrolled by local police. Local schools decide school hours, what you may wear to school, and when you eat lunch. You may stroll on city sidewalks to visit city parks or the local library. Your family pays property taxes either directly as property owners or as part of the rent. Your family also may pay user fees for water, garbage collection, and other local services.

Local Spending

Before the Great Depression, local government accounted for half of all government spending. However, the growing importance of the federal government has decreased the local share to one-sixth of the total. The left pie chart in Figure 14.6 shows the composition of local spending. No other spending category comes close to education, which accounts for 47 percent of the total. Police and fire protection combine for 11 percent of local spending.

Environment and housing issues also combine for 11 percent.

Local Revenue

As the right-hand pie chart in Figure 14.6 shows, state and federal aid make up 40 percent of local revenue, by far the largest source. Most of this aid goes toward local schools. Local governments raise from their own sources only $6 out of every $10 they spend. The property tax accounts for 27 percent of

Investigate Your Local Economy

Research to find out the size of your local government's budget and how much of this budget is spent on local schools. What are the other items in the budget, and how much is spent on each item? Present your findings in a pie chart.

Composition of Local Spending

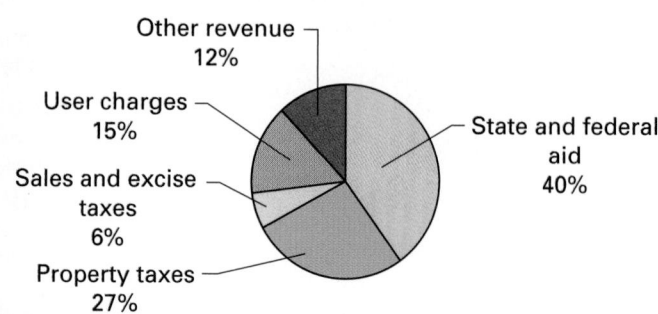

Administration and interest
8%

Other spending
8%

Environment and housing
11%

Education
47%

Highways
7%

Health and hospitals
8%

Police and fire
11%

Composition of Local Revenue

Other revenue
12%

User charges
15%

State and federal aid
40%

Sales and excise taxes
6%

Property taxes
27%

The largest category of local spending is education. State and federal aid make up the largest percent of local revenue.

Source: Based on general expenditure figures for fiscal year 2000 from the U.S. Census Bureau.

the total. User fees rank third at 15 percent. Examples include fees for water usage and school lunches.

CHECKPOINT
What is the top spending category in the local budget and the top source of revenue?

Relative Size and Growth of Government

So far, the focus has been on each level of government, but a fuller picture includes all three levels. How has the size of government in America changed

Nearly half of local spending goes to schools. What spending categories might be included in a local school district's budget?

© Getty Images/PhotoDisc

in the last decade, and how does that size compare with what's been going on in other major economies around the world?

An International Comparison

Figure 14.7 shows government outlays at all levels relative to GDP in 10 industrial economies for 1993 and 2003. Government outlays in the United States in 2003 were 32 percent relative to GDP, the smallest share in the group. This is down slightly from 34 percent in 1993, a year when only Japan among the 10 industrial economies had a smaller government share.

Between 1993 and 2003, government outlays relative to GDP decreased in 9 of the 10 industrial economies. The average dropped from 44 percent to 40 percent. Why the drop? The breakup of the Soviet Union in the early 1990s reduced defense outlays in major economies. The poor performance of most socialist economies around the world shifted attitudes more toward private markets, thus lessening the role of government. Growing prosperity of market economies during most of the period made it less important for governments to spend funds to stimulate their economies or provide social services to their people.

The world economy began to sour beginning in 2001. The terrorist attacks on America temporarily stalled the trend toward a shrinking government. Government stepped up spending to fight terrorism and help revive the economy.

 CHECKPOINT
How did the relative size of government change between 1993 and 2003 compared with other major economies?

Government Outlays as Percentage of GDP

Figure 14.7

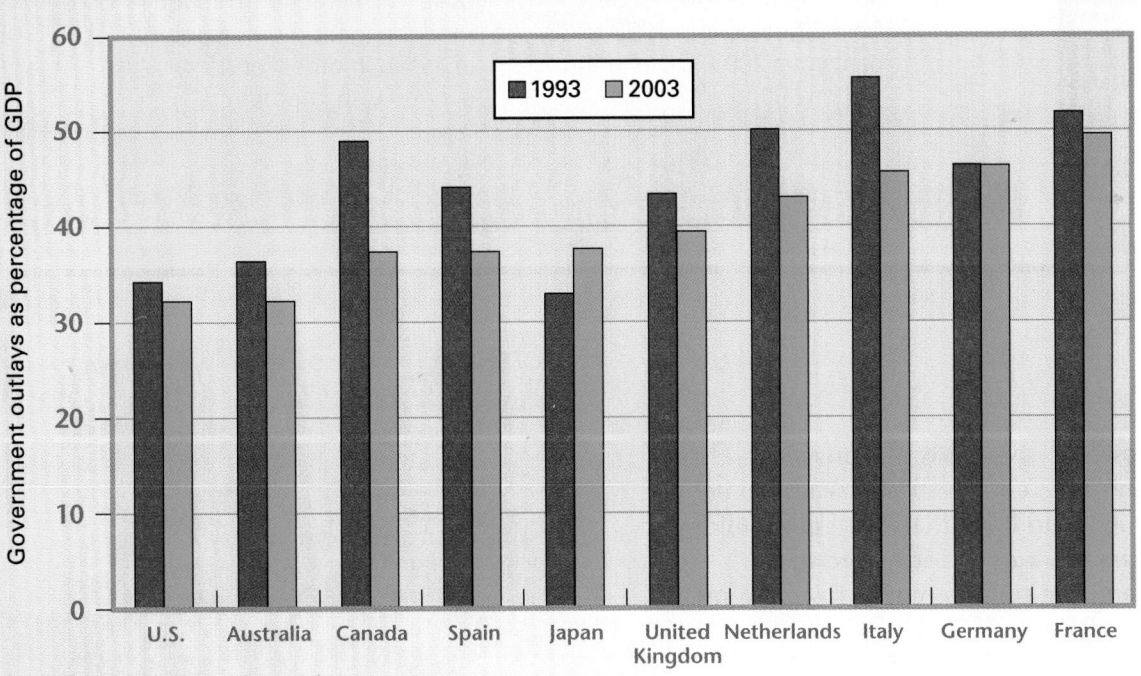

Government outlays as percentage of GDP declined between 1993 and 2003 in major industrial economies except Japan.

Source: Based on outlays at all government levels as reported in *OECD Economic Outlook*, June 2003. Figures for 2003 are projections.

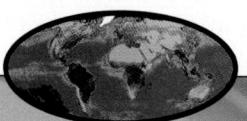

SPAN THE GLOBE

Why Japan Is Different

The exception to the trend toward a smaller GDP share for government outlays is Japan, where the economy has been suffering for more than a decade. The troubles began with a collapse in real estate values and stock prices in 1990. The crash of these two sources of wealth crushed consumer confidence. With consumers unwilling to spend as much, the government tried to stimulate aggregate demand by increasing its spending for government projects. Government outlays relative to GDP in Japan rose from 33 percent in 1993 to 38 percent in 2003. Despite the stepped-up role for govern-ment, the unemployment rate in Japan more than doubled from 2.5 percent in 1993 to 5.4 percent in 2003. Japan remains one of the most troubled economies in the world.

Think Critically

According to a *Wall Street Journal* editorial, "Japan is stuck in an awkward stage of development between two worlds....The government can no longer solve Japan's problems, but effective market mechanisms have yet to take over." What does this statement suggest must happen in Japan in order for its economy to improve?

Will the Sun Rise Again?
econxtra.swlearning.com

Japan's growth in the 1980s was driven by government-directed industrial policies. Some politicians in Japan think that these economic policies, mired in bureaucracy, need to be reformed and the country moved toward a more entrepreneurial system. One area where reform is needed is the Japan Highway Corporation, which spends trillions of yen on wasteful projects.

© Getty Images/PhotoDisc

Key Concepts

1. Why were most Americans willing to accept a larger role for the government in the economy during the Great Depression and World War II?

2. Why does the share of federal tax revenue that comes from personal income taxes change from year to year even when the tax rates remain unchanged?

3. What has made it possible for state spending to grow more rapidly than state tax collection in many recent years?

4. Why have some state courts ruled that funding public schools from local property tax receipts results in unequal educational opportunities for school children?

5. Why do governments in countries that experience rapid economic growth often spend smaller portions of GDP?

Graphing Exercise

6. Since its creation in 1967, the Medicare program that provides medical coverage for our nation's elderly population has accounted for a growing proportion of our GDP in most years. Use data in the table to construct a double line graph that shows the rates of growth of federal Medicare payments and GDP from 1995 through 1999. What does your graph show about the relative rates of growth in these amounts in these years? Given the large number of people born in the baby boom from 1946 through 1964, what will happen to the relationship between these amounts in future years?

Growth in Federal Medicare Payments and GDP, 1995–1999

Year	Growth in Medicare Payments	Growth in GDP
1995	9.5%	4.9%
1996	7.1%	5.6%
1997	5.1%	6.7%
1998	1.4%	5.7%
1999	3.7%	5.8%

Think Critically

7. **Government** An important part of state government spending is governed by federal laws that require these governments to provide Medicaid programs for people who are unable to pay for their own medical care. Investigate Medicaid spending in your state. Have these payments grown more rapidly than other types of government spending? What reasons can you think of that could explain the growth in your state's Medicaid payments?

The Evolution of the Income Tax

One trigger for the American Revolution was a tax revolt. It was through trade that England lightly taxed its American colonies. When England attempted to impose an internal tax through the Stamp Act, the American colonists reacted against the government's attempt to impose taxes on them. They saw it as a violation of the British Bill of Rights, which historically had held that taxes could not be imposed without the approval of Parliament. Because the colonies had no direct representation in Parliament, they rejected the government's right to tax them directly.

Following the Revolution, the first American constitution, the Articles of Confederation, did not give the central government the power to levy taxes. Therefore, taxation was one of the problems addressed at the Constitutional Convention held in Philadelphia. Through the U.S. Constitution, the new government was given the power to "lay and collect Taxes, Duties, imports, and Excises."

During the nation's early days, the federal government relied primarily on tariffs (taxes on imports) and land sales to fund its operations. An early attempt to increase revenue by levying excise taxes on items such as carriages, sugar, salt, and distilled spirits met with armed resistance in Western Pennsylvania. The "Whisky Rebellion" was quickly put down. However, with the election of Thomas Jefferson in 1800, most of the excise taxes were repealed.

The government returned to relying on tariffs for revenue until the demands of the Civil War led to a need for new sources of revenue. The nation's first income tax was imposed during the conflict, as well as taxes on many commodities. Following the war, the high tariffs imposed during the war remained.

However, the income tax was first cut and then allowed to expire by 1872.

In the 1890s, the idea of an income tax resurfaced, and a new income tax was passed in 1894. The following year, the Supreme Court declared it unconstitutional. A decade later, following the Panic of 1907, a federal income tax once again emerged as an issue. President William Howard Taft, not wanting to directly challenge a Supreme Court decision, suggested a constitutional amendment permitting an income tax. He also suggested a tax on corporate profits. The corporate profits tax passed a Supreme Court challenge, and Congress and the states passed the Sixteenth Amendment, which was adopted in 1913. Later that year, President Woodrow Wilson signed the personal income tax into law.

The tax burden from the income tax fell on the wealthy. In its first year, only 357,598 tax forms were filed. In 1910, the tariff on imported goods supplied 90 percent of the government's revenues. Today that figure is about one percent. Where previously the debate over tariffs pitted regions of the country against each other, today the argument is between economic classes.

THINK CRITICALLY

A century ago the United States underwent a fundamental change in how it funds the government—from relying on tariffs to relying on personal and corporate income taxes. Could the country undergo such a change today? What alternate forms of taxation could it employ?

Objectives

> Discuss how representative democracy may favor special interests at the expense of the public interest.

> Distinguish between bureaus and firms, and explain why bureaus might be less responsive to customers than firms are.

Overview

This book, for the most part, has assumed that governments make optimal adjustments to the shortcomings of the private sector. In other words, when confronted with market failure, governments adopt just the right program to address the problem. However, there are limits to government's effectiveness, just as there are limits to the market's effectiveness. For example, elected officials may side more with special interests than with the public interest. Government bureaus get less consumer feedback and face less competition than private firms do.

Key Terms

maximizing political support

rational ignorance

bureaus

[In the News]

● Special Interests vs. the Interests of Seniors

Congress has set aside $400 billion dollars to be spent between now and 2010 on prescription drug benefits for seniors. However, tens of billions of dollars of that money are being redirected, thanks to the lobbying efforts of healthcare providers such as HMOs, ambulance companies, hospitals in rural areas, kidney dialysis providers, psychologists, and others. Each of these special interests has lobbied successfully for a spending provision for their cause to be added to the main bill. Taken together, these provisions reduce the benefits seniors were intended to receive. One of the authors of the Senate bill said that these "add-ons" for healthcare providers are being paid for with cuts in other parts of the Medicare program. Seniors' organizations point out that these resulting cuts bring on costs for their members to cover the "add-on" expenditures. These costs include a provision that seniors pay 20 percent of the cost for important diagnostic tests performed at hospital or doctors' office laboratories. Currently there is no charge to beneficiaries for these tests, and many lower-income patients could not afford to pay even such a small percentage.

Think About It

What types of activities do you think the lobbying groups engage in to see that their special interests are addressed? In this specific case, who wins and who loses?

Representative Democracy

In market choice, each person votes for what should be produced with dollars. The rule is: one dollar, one vote. People with more to spend get more votes. In public choice, each person has a single vote to decide what should be produced. The rule is: one person, one vote, regardless of income. People vote directly on public choices at New England town meetings and on the occasional referendum, but direct democracy is unusual. When you consider the thousands of public choices required to run a government, it would be impractical for voters to make all those choices. Instead, voters elect representatives, who—at least in theory—make public choices that reflect constituent views. Delegating choices to representatives involves complications, however.

Maximizing Political Support

Economists assume that households try to maximize their utility and firms try to maximize profit, but what about governments—or, more specifically, what about elected representatives? What do they try to maximize? One problem is that the U.S. system of federal, state, and local governments consists of not one government but more than 87,000 separate governments in all. These range from a local school district to the federal government.

What's more, even a particular government does not act as a single, consistent decision maker. For example, the federal government relies on a system of checks and balances to limit the executive, legislative, and judicial branches.

Even within the federal executive branch, there are so many agencies and bureaus that at times they seem to work at cross-purposes. For example, for decades the U.S. Surgeon General has required health warnings on cigarette packages. During that same time,

however, the U.S. Department of Agriculture has been subsidizing tobacco farmers.

Economists assume that elected representatives try to maximize their political support, including votes and campaign contributions. In this theory, **maximizing political support** guides the decisions of elected officials who, in turn, direct government employees.

Role of Special Interest

Elected representatives often appear to cater to special interests rather than the public interest. Consider only one of the thousands of decisions made by elected representatives: funding an obscure federal program that subsidizes U.S. wool production. Under the wool-subsidy program, the federal government guarantees sheep farmers a certain price for each pound of wool they produce. This subsidy costs taxpayers more than $75 million per year. During deliberations to renew the program, the only person to testify before Congress was a representative of the National Wool Growers Association, who claimed that the subsidy was vital to the nation's economic welfare. Why didn't a single taxpayer challenge the subsidy?

As a consumer, you do not specialize in woolen goods. You buy thousands of different goods and services, from software to underwear. You have no special interest in wool legislation. Wool producers do have a special interest, because that's how they earn a living. As a result of this mismatch of interest, legislation often favors producers rather than consumers. Well-organized producer groups, as squeaky wheels in the legislative machinery, get the most grease in the form of favorable legislation.

Special interest groups expend abundant resources to secure these advantages. For example, political action committees, known more popularly as PACs, contribute millions to congressional campaigns. More than 4,000 PACs try to shape federal legislation. Top contributors recently included tobacco companies and the American Trial Lawyers

Association. Tobacco interests want to influence cigarette legislation, and lawyers fear reforms that would limit liability suits.

Rational Ignorance

How do elected officials get away with serving special interests? Why don't voters elect someone else? Sometimes voters do. However, some people don't bother to vote and even those who do vote consume so many different goods and services that they have neither the time nor the incentive to keep up with public choices that affect any particular product. For example, the $75 million subsidy for wool growers amounts to only about 30 cents per U.S. citizen. Would you make the effort to protest passage of this law to save 30 cents?

Therefore, unless voters have a special interest in the legislation, they adopt a stance of **rational ignorance**. This means the costs and benefits of the thousands of proposals considered by elected officials remain largely unknown to voters. The cost to the typical voter of acquiring and acting on such information usually is greater than any possible benefit.

In contrast, consumers have much more incentive to gather and act on information about market choices. For example, a consumer in the market for a new car has an incentive to examine the performance records of different models, test-drive a few, and check prices at dealerships and on the Internet. That person has complete control over the choice of a new car. *Because information and the time required to acquire and digest it are scarce, consumers focus more on private choices than on public choices. The payoff in making wise private choices usually is more direct, more immediate, and more substantial.*

CHECKPOINT
Why does representative democracy favor special interests?

rational ignorance
A stance adopted by voters when they find that the cost of understanding and voting on a particular issue exceeds the benefit expected from doing so

Ethics in Action

Minors Banned from Making Political Contributions
A lawsuit argued before the U.S. Supreme Court affects both political campaign reform and the rights of minors. The Bipartisan Campaign Reform Act, known popularly as the McCain-Feingold bill, includes a provision that bans political campaign contributions by minors. Evidently, such donations made in the name of the actual donor's children were a means used to avoid donation limits imposed on individuals. These limits previously were set at $2,000 but have now been boosted to $4,000. The result was a prohibition (or ban) on such donations in the new campaign finance law that closed the loophole. However, it also eliminated the potential for legitimate contributions by minors. A lawsuit was brought against the bill by a group of minors along with other plaintiffs—including the National Rifle Association *and* the American Civil Liberties Union—versus the Federal Election Commission. The Court heard the case in September of 2003 on appeal from a 1,600-page decision of a three-judge federal appeals court that threw out numerous sections of the law as unconstitutional.

Think Critically
What ethical balance is being struck by the law? Do you support the prohibition? Why or why not?

Bureaus Versus Firms

Elected representatives approve legislation, but the task of implementing that legislation typically is delegated to **bureaus**. These are government departments and agencies whose activities are financed through legislative bodies. Examples include the FBI, FDA, FCC, EPA, the Pentagon, your state's department of motor vehicles, and your public school system.

Voluntary Exchange Versus Coercion

Market exchange relies on the voluntary behavior of buyers and sellers making private choices. Don't like tofu? No problem—don't buy any. Nobody can force you to buy something you don't want. In political markets the situation is different. Any voting rule except for unanimous consent will involve some government influence. Even if you object to certain government programs, you must still pay the taxes that ultimately fund those programs. Public choices are enforced by the police power of the state. If you fail to pay your taxes, you could go to jail.

Product Prices

For-profit firms sell products for prices that at least cover the cost of production. Bureaus usually offer products for either a zero price or some price below cost. For example, if you plan to attend a public college or university in your

state, your tuition will probably cover only about half the cost of providing your education.

Because the revenue side of the government budget usually is separate from the expenditure side, there is no necessary link between the cost of a public program and the benefit. Contrast this with the private sector, in which the marginal benefit of a good is at least as great as its marginal cost. Otherwise, people wouldn't buy it.

Customer Feedback

Markets offer firms a steady stream of consumer feedback. If prices are too high or too low, surpluses or shortages become obvious. Not only is consumer feedback abundant in markets, but firms have a profit incentive to act on that feedback. The firm's owners stand to gain from any improvement in customer satisfaction or any reduction in the cost of production.

Because public goods and services are not sold in markets, government bureaus receive less consumer feedback. There usually are no prices for public goods and no obvious shortages or surpluses. For example, how would you know whether there was a shortage or a surplus of police protection in your community?

Voter Incentives

Voters can move from a jurisdiction if they think the government there is inefficient. This mechanism, whereby people "vote with their feet," promotes some efficiency at the state and local levels. Voters who are not satisfied with the federal government, however, cannot easily vote with their feet.

In the private sector, competition makes firms more responsive to customers. If a firm does not know consumer preferences, it will either have to shape up or go out of business. Bureaus that do not know about public preferences do not necessarily go out of business. A bureau that is inefficient may continue to be funded and waste resources indefinitely. Thus, bureaus face less pressure to satisfy consumer demand or to minimize costs. A variety

bureaus

Government agencies charged with implementing legislation and financed through legislative bodies

of studies compares costs for products that are provided by both public bureaus and private firms, such as garbage collection. Of those studies that show a difference, most find private firms are more efficient. A competitive private firm that is inefficient will earn no profit and go out of business.

Private Versus Public Production

Just because some goods and services are *financed* by the government does not mean they must be *produced* by the government. Elected officials may contract directly with private firms to produce public output. This could introduce more competition and more efficiency. For example, a city council may contract with a firm to handle garbage collection for the city. Profit-making firms now provide everything from fire protection to prisons to schools in certain jurisdictions.

Elected officials also may use some combination of bureaus and firms to produce the desired output. For example, the Pentagon, a giant bureau, hires and trains military personnel. Yet the Pentagon contracts with private firms to develop and produce weapons systems. State governments typically hire private contractors to build roads but employ state workers to maintain them.

The mix of firms and bureaus varies over time and across jurisdictions. However, the trend is toward greater production by the private sector. These goods and services are still financed by government, usually with taxes.

When governments produce public goods and services, they are using *the internal organization of the government*—the bureaucracy—to supply the product. When governments contract with private firms to produce public goods and services, they are using *the market* to supply the product. Legislators may prefer dealing with bureaus rather than with firms for two reasons. First, in situations where it is difficult to specify in a contract just what is being produced, as with education or social work, bureaus may be more responsive to the legislature's concerns. Second, bureaus provide legislators with more opportunities to reward political supporters with government jobs.

CHECKPOINT
Why might bureaus be less responsive to customers than firms are?

 **Main Idea**

Cost/Benefit Analysis for Government Programs

Government policies are carried out through bureaus. The costs of carrying out policies sometimes exceed the benefits derived from them. This may occur due to the following factors: incentives facing voters, government officials, and government employees; actions by special interest groups; or other social goals. **The EPA is a government bureau that, among other activities, oversees programs that control the cleanup of hazardous wastes. How could the costs versus the benefits of the hazardous waste cleanup programs be evaluated?**

© Getty Images/PhotoDisc

Key Concepts

1. Imagine that your class has decided to earn money to take a class trip in their senior year. The big question is deciding where the class should go. Some students want to visit Washington, D.C., some would prefer New York City, others would choose Disney World or other well-known destinations. Describe how this decision might be made and why this decision-making process is similar to the way in which choices are made by government.

2. Suppose a school's sports director decided to spend $15,000 to purchase new equipment for the football team. Although this decision left only $5,000 to pay for equipment for all of the school's other teams, most of the students at the school didn't complain. Explain how this situation demonstrates the idea of *rational ignorance.*

3. Why does the saying "the squeaky wheel gets the grease" often describe how government decisions are made?

4. What would happen to a private firm that employed clerks who were rude or unresponsive to customer requests? Why may bureaucracies employ such workers and still continue to exist over many years?

5. Why might parents demand fewer services from public schools if they were required to pay for these services directly from their own funds?

Graphing Exercise

6. Use data in the table to construct a bar graph that shows the per-student spending in selected states for public schools. What might explain the difference in the levels of funding among states? Do you think that there is a direct relationship between the amount spent and the quality of education provided? Explain your answer.

Per-Student Public School Spending in Selected States, 2000

State	Per-Student Spending	State	Per-Student Spending
Connecticut	$10,711	Texas	$ 6,588
Rhode Island	$ 8,773	Nevada	$ 6,283
Indiana	$ 7,254	Mississippi	$ 4,905
Ohio	$ 7,152	North Dakota	$ 4,621

Source: *Statistical Abstract of the United States, 2001,* p. 154.

Think Critically

7. **Government** Identify and describe a current public policy issue that is important to you. Explain how you could work to influence legislation that would affect government policy toward this issue. Why might you be more successful acting as a member of a group rather than as an individual voter?

movers & shakers

Kathleen Sebelius *Governor of Kansas*

You might say that politics is in Kathleen Sebelius's blood. When she was young, her father John J. Gilligan served as a councilman in Cincinnati, Ohio; a U.S. Representative; and Governor of Ohio. Kathleen decided to pursue a political science degree from Trinity College in Washington, D.C. Later she earned a master's degree in public administration from the University of Kansas. Along the way she met and married Gary Sebelius, the son of a former congressman from Kansas.

Sebelius won a seat in the Kansas House of Representatives, where she served from 1987 to 1994. She then was elected Insurance Commissioner for Kansas and earned a reputation as a tough, innovative, and tight-fisted leader. She was named one of America's Top Ten Public Officials in 2001 by *Governing Magazine.* In 2003, Kathleen Sebelius began her first term as Governor of Kansas.

In her campaign for the governorship, Sebelius promoted her ability to rid the government of wasteful spending, indicating that "I know firsthand you find waste in state government." She added, "As Insurance Commissioner, I reduced the department's budget by 19 percent while vastly improving department services." During her tenure she fired two state attorneys, who she believed "were double-billing the state and charging exorbitant fees." She lowered the fees paid to other state attorneys and, in all, saved the state more than $4 million.

Throughout her campaign, she called for a strict accounting of where Kansas was spending its money, something not done for more than 20 years. She promised voters she would begin "an in-depth look at government operations and initiate an extensive review of state government, looking for waste and inefficiency."

As Sebelius took over as Governor, the Kansas sales tax was designed to tax only tangible goods such as groceries, cars, and clothing. Service providers, such as accountants, beauticians and veterinarians, were not taxed. Asked if she thought such a tax structure was fair, she replied, "I will fight to make sure that no single sector of our economy or group of our citizens bears a disproportionate share of our tax burden."

Throughout her campaign for governor, Sebelius declared her commitment to education. "Education is the key to our children's future and Kansas' economic prosperity," she told voters. She promised she would "fight to see that Kansas schools will have the funds they need." This promise helped her win the hearts of many Kansans who were unhappy with statements made by her opponent, state Treasurer Tim Shallenburger. He maintained that the schools in Kansas "can make it with 1 or 2 or 3 percent" less funding." Although a Democrat in a state where only 28 percent of voters are registered Democrats, Sebelius easily beat Shallenburger, a Republican.

SOURCE READING

Kathleen Sebelius promised "to fight to make sure that no single sector of our economy or group of our citizens bears a disproportionate share of our tax burden." Does this statement support the benefits-received principle of taxation or the ability-to-pay principle? Explain your answer.

ENTREPRENEURS IN ACTION

In small groups, discuss the pros and cons of running for political office and serving the public as an elected official. How might the need to maximize political support conflict with the elected official's ability to follow through with his or her political goals?

14 Chapter Assessment

Summary

14.1 Public Goods and Taxation

a Public goods are different from private goods in that they are nonrival in consumption. The market demand for public goods is equal to the sum of the marginal benefit for all members of a community. The efficient level of a public good is found where the sum of the marginal benefits is equal to its marginal cost.

b There are two generally recognized principles of taxation: the *benefits-received principle* and *the ability-to-pay principle.* According to the benefits-received principle, taxpayers should pay in proportion to the benefit they receive from the service the tax supports. According to the ability-to-pay principle, people should be taxed at higher rates as their ability to pay in terms of income or wealth grows.

c *Tax incidence* indicates who actually bears the burden of a tax. Under a *proportional tax,* all people would pay the same percent of their incomes in tax. When there are *progressive taxes,* people pay a greater share of their incomes in tax as their incomes grow. This is true of personal income taxes. When there are *regressive taxes,* people pay a smaller share of their income in tax as their incomes grow. This is true of most excise taxes such as the tax on tobacco products or gasoline.

d The *marginal tax rate* is the percentage of each additional dollar of a taxpayer's income that is paid in taxes. High marginal tax rates reduce a person's after-tax income and can discourage people from working to earn additional income. The government gathers additional revenue by imposing sin taxes to discourage certain types of behavior, user fees, and by borrowing funds.

14.2 Federal, State, and Local Budgets

a Through the first 150 years of U.S. history, federal spending amounted to about 3 percent of GDP except during times of war. In the past 70 years, however, this share has grown to roughly 20 percent of GDP, or more than $2.3 trillion in 2004. The largest share of federal spending goes to income redistribution (49 percent). The largest source of federal revenue is the personal income tax (44 percent).

b The largest share of state spending is devoted to aid to local government (34 percent). The largest source of state revenue is aid received from the federal government (28 percent).

c Local governments spend the largest share of their incomes for education (47 percent). The greatest source of local government revenue is received as aid payments form the state and federal governments (40 percent).

d On average, at 32 percent, the United States takes a smaller share of GDP than governments in any other major industrial nation. The average share of GDP taken by governments in most industrial nations fell between 1993 and 2003.

14.3 Economics of Public Choice

a When government leaders make decisions, they do not necessarily try to bring about economic efficiency. They may instead work to optimize their political support and chances of being reelected. Special interest groups often work to influence governments to make choices beneficial to their interests. Many voters are not concerned or even aware of these efforts to influence legislation. They adopt a stance of *rational ignorance* because the cost of learning about legislation exceeds any benefits they might receive from working to influence the legislation.

b Many laws are implemented or enforced by government *bureaus* that are not always responsive to interests of the population as a whole. Bureaus administer government programs that often have little link between costs and the value of benefits provided by the programs. Inefficient use of government funds and resources may result from this situation.

c Some governmental units have attempted to supply services more efficiently by contracting with private firms to provide them.

Review Economic Terms

Choose the term that best fits the definition. On a separate sheet of paper, write the letter of the answer. Some terms may not be used.

_____ 1. A tax as a percentage of income increases as income increases

_____ 2. Government agencies charged with implementing legislation and financed through legislative bodies

_____ 3. A plan for government outlays and revenues for a specified period, usually a year

_____ 4. Those who receive more benefits from a government program funded by a tax should pay more of that tax

_____ 5. A tax as a percentage of income decreases as income increases

_____ 6. Those with a greater ability to pay should pay more of a tax

_____ 7. The percentage of each additional dollar of income that goes to pay a tax

_____ 8. A tax as a percentage of income remains constant as income increases

_____ 9. Taxes deducted from paychecks to support Social Security and Medicare

_____ 10. A stance adopted by voters when they find that the cost of understanding and voting on a particular issue exceeds the benefit expected from doing so

a. **ability-to-pay tax principle**

b. **benefits-received tax principle**

c. **bureaus**

d. **government budget**

e. **marginal tax rate**

f. **maximizing political support**

g. **payroll taxes**

h. **progressive taxation**

i. **proportional taxation**

j. **rational ignorance**

k. **regressive taxation**

l. **tax incidence**

Review Economic Concepts

11. Public goods are __?__ in consumption.

12. **True or False** The efficient level of production of a public good is found where the marginal benefit of additional units of that good is zero.

13. Which of the following is an example of the *benefits-received tax principle*?

    a. the excise tax on cigarettes

    b. a tariff on imported automobiles

    c. a sales tax on purchases of new clothing

    d. the toll that is paid to cross a bridge

14. **True or False** Taxes that fall more heavily on people who earn larger incomes represent the *ability-to-pay principle of taxation.*

15. An *ability-to-pay tax* also is likely to be

    a. regressive.

    b. progressive.

    c. proportional.

    d. reactionary.

16. If a tax structure is *progressive* and we know that Tom pays $1,000 on his $10,000 income, then Alicia, who earns $30,000, must pay

    a. more than $3,000 in tax.

    b. exactly $3,000 in tax.

    c. less than $3,000 in tax.

    d. more than $4,000 in tax.

17. The part of the next dollar you earn that is taken in tax is your __?__.

18. **True or False** High *marginal tax rates* encourage people to work and earn additional income.

19. The largest share of federal spending is allocated to

    a. national defense.

    b. income redistribution.

    c. interest on the national debt.

    d. government employee salaries.

20. **True or False** The largest source of federal government revenue is borrowing.

21. The biggest type of outlay for state governments is __?__.

22. Which of the following is not a source of revenue for state or local governments?

    a. tariffs on imported goods

    b. aid from the federal government

    c. income taxes

    d. sales taxes

23. **True or False** The largest part of local government spending is used for schools.

24. Government spending in the United States accounts for roughly _____ percent of the nation's GDP.

    a. 21

    b. 27

    c. 32

    d. 36

25. **True or False** Some political leaders appear to be more interested in whether they are reelected than in how efficiently the economy works.

26. Voters sometimes choose not to learn about how their taxes are spent because

    a. they are not able to influence government decisions.

    b. there is little information available to them about how their tax money is spent.

    c. they are not affected by how the government spends tax money.

    d. they think the cost of learning about how tax money is spent is greater than the benefits of working to influence legislation.

27. One theory states that unless voters have a special interest in a piece of legislation, they are likely to adopt a stance of __?__.

28. Which of the following is not an example of a government *bureau*?

    a. your community's public school system

    b. the state highway department

    c. a firm that has been hired to collect garbage in your community

    d. the federal court system

29. **True or False** *Bureaus* usually offer products for either a zero price or some price below cost.

Apply Economic Concepts

30. **Identify the Optimal Quantity of a Public Good** Imagine that many residents of a riverside community wish to have a break wall built around their town to protect their homes when the river floods. The cost of construction is $100,000 per 100 yards. The break wall will have no value unless it is 1,800 yards long to surround the entire community. The people of the community have voted to spend up to $1,000,000 for the break wall. How much of this amount should they spend? How does this situation demonstrate a problem of achieving an efficient level of public goods?

31. **Decide Which Tax Is Best** Suppose that the Environmental Protection Agency (EPA) has

determined that the sewer system in your town is inadequate and must be replaced. Your community will need to borrow $20,000,000 to build a new system. This loan must be repaid from tax revenues over the next 20 years. There is a debate over the type of tax that should be imposed to collect the needed money. One idea is to charge people an extra $1 for each thousand gallons of water they use. The other is to impose a city income tax and charge people 5 percent of their annual federal income tax payment. What principle of taxation is each of these proposals based on, and which would you support? Explain your answer.

32. **Evaluate the Marginal Tax Rate** Members of Congress often have debated the importance of the marginal income tax rate to the economy. Suppose that your marginal federal income tax rate is 30 percent. You pay Social Security and Medicare taxes at a rate of 7.65 percent, and your state income tax will take 6 percent of any additional income you earn. Your boss has asked you to go on a sales trip to Chicago next weekend. She has offered to pay you an extra $1,000 if you agree to go. Would you accept this offer? If you did, how much of the $1,000 will you keep?

33. **Petition Your Congressional Representative** The national debt is growing rapidly, and you are concerned that you will grow up to owe debts that have been taken on by older generations. Write a letter to your congressional representative expressing your concern and listing steps you think the government should take to reduce the size of the deficit. Explain why the representative may pay only limited attention to what you have to say.

34. **Assess a Proportional Income Tax** Some politicians believe that high marginal tax rates discourage people from working. They have suggested that it would be better to charge all taxpayers the same percent of their income so that the lower marginal tax rates for many people would encourage them to work and earn more. It has been estimated that the same amount of tax revenue could be collected if all taxpayers paid roughly 23 percent of what they earn in tax. This would mean that a person who earns $10,000 per year would pay $2,300 in tax while a person who earns $100,000 would pay $23,000. Decide whether you believe this is a good or a bad idea. Then write several paragraphs that identify and explain reasons for your point of view. Be careful to discuss the impact of such a tax structure on the economy as well as your opinion of its fairness.

35. **Calculate Historical Tax Liabilities** In the past, maximum federal income tax rates have been much higher than they are today. In 1944, for example, those who had taxable incomes of $1,000,000 or more paid a marginal tax rate of 90 percent. If a person's taxable income increased from $1 million to $1.1 million in that year, how much of the additional income would he or she have been able to keep? What might have justified such a high tax rate at that time? What impact do you think such a high tax rate would have on the U.S. economy today?

36. **Construct a Bar Graph to Show Marginal Income Tax Rates** The federal marginal income tax rates for single individuals in 2003 are shown in the table. Construct a bar graph to show these rates. What has happened to these rates since 2003? Why have changes been made in these rates or why have they remained unchanged?

Federal Income Tax Rates For Single Filers

Taxable Income In 2003	Marginal Tax Rate
$0 – $14,000	10%
$7,001 – $28,400	15%
$28,401 – $68,800	25%
$68,801 – $143,500	28%
$143,501 – $311,950	33%
$311,951 or more	35%

e-con @pps   econxtra.swlearning.com

37. **Access the Policy** Debate entitled "How should we reform the current tax system?" in the **EconDebate Online** at econxtra.swlearning.com. Read the Issues and Background. Write a paragraph summarizing both sides of this debate. Then choose one of the links listed under "Different Perspectives in the Debate." Write another paragraph that explains which side of the debate the writer of the article is on and summarizes the writer's basic argument.

15 Fiscal Policy, Deficits, and Debt

Consider

What is your normal capacity for academic work, and when do you usually exceed that effort?

If the economy is already operating at full employment, how can it produce more?

Can fiscal policy reduce swings in the business cycle?

Why has the federal budget been in deficit most years?

How is a strong economy like a crowded restaurant?

What did President George W. Bush mean when he proposed a tax cut to "get the economy moving again"?

© Reuters NewMedia Inc./CORBIS

POINT YOUR BROWSER

econxtra.swlearning.com

Objectives

> Identify the economy's potential output level.

> Distinguish between fiscal policy before and after the Great Depression.

Overview

Government spending for national defense, education, the environment, and other programs aims to achieve specific objectives, such as national security, a more educated work force, cleaner air, and the like. Fiscal policy has a broader focus. Fiscal policy considers the overall impact of the government's budget on the economy, especially on employment, output, and prices. Fiscal policy tries to promote full employment and price stability by targeting changes in aggregate demand.

Key Terms

potential output

natural rate of unemployment

classical economists

annually balanced budget

multiplier effect

[In the News]

• The Challenge of Protecting Social Security

One of the greatest fiscal policy challenges political leaders have faced in recent years is what to do about the future of Social Security. This program was created in the 1930s to help make sure that older Americans received an income after retirement. Payroll taxes from current workers pay for the program. For many years, whenever tax revenues exceeded the cost of the program, Congress raised benefits, expanded eligibility, or spent the surplus on something else. By the 1980s, however, lawmakers began to realize that the retirement of baby boomers—persons born between 1946 and 1964—would place a heavy burden on the system. In 1983, Congress passed reforms to save money for the future baby-boomer retirement era. These reforms included raising payroll taxes, expanding the tax base by the rate of inflation, gradually increasing the retirement age from 65 to 67, increasing penalties for early retirement, and offering incentives to delay retirement. Congress also called for any surpluses to be saved in trust funds. Despite these reforms, experts expect Social Security to be bankrupt by 2039, when payroll taxes will cover only about 73 percent of payments to retirees. Saving the system is a difficult challenge. Both of the ideas of cutting benefits to retirees or raising payroll taxes are unpopular. President George W. Bush proposed allowing younger workers to direct part of their Social Security payroll taxes to private investments, such as the stock market. While such investments usually provide larger returns over the long run, the stock market crash raised concerns about the plan. Also, Bush's plan would have taken away funds needed to pay current retirees. Recognizing the need to help the system, in 2002 President Bush proposed spending an extra $600 billion over 10 years to help support Social Security.

Think About It

Do you think it's important for government to continue to fund the Social Security system? Why or why not?

Fiscal Policy and Potential Output

Fiscal policy uses government taxing and spending to move the economy toward full employment with price stability. It focuses mainly on shifts of the aggregate demand curve. If unemployment is high, fiscal policy aims to increase aggregate demand as a way of boosting output and employment. If aggregate demand is already so strong that it threatens to trigger higher inflation, fiscal policy tries to relieve that pressure by reducing aggregate demand.

Potential Output

Fiscal policy tries to move the economy to its potential output. **Potential output** is the economy's maximum sustainable output in the long run, given the supply of resources, the state of technology, and the rules of the game that nurture production and exchange. Potential output also is referred to as the full-employment output. When the economy produces its potential output,

it is operating on its production possibilities frontier.

Suppose potential output equals a real GDP of $12 trillion. Potential output in Figure 15.1 is the vertical line where real GDP is $12 trillion. If potential output is achieved, the economy reaches full employment with no inflationary pressure. At full employment, the economy is doing as well as possible in the long run. In theory, fiscal policy can be used to ensure the economy achieves its potential, with full employment and price stability.

The unemployment rate that occurs when the economy is producing its potential GDP is called the **natural rate of unemployment**. At this rate, there is no cyclical unemployment. Generally accepted estimates of the natural rate of unemployment are in the range of 4 percent to 5 percent of the labor force.

Output Below Potential

If the aggregate demand curve and aggregate supply curve intersect in the pink-shaded area of Figure 15.1, then output falls short of the economy's potential. The economy is not producing

natural rate of unemployment

The unemployment rate when the economy is producing its potential level of output

potential output

The economy's maximum sustainable output in the long run

Main Idea

Fiscal Policy and Potential Output

Figure 15.1

Potential output is the economy's maximum sustainable output in the long run. The pink-shaded area indicates real GDP below the economy's potential. The blue-shaded area indicates real GDP exceeding the economy's potential. *When the economy, through federal fiscal policy, reaches potential output, there is full employment and price stability.*

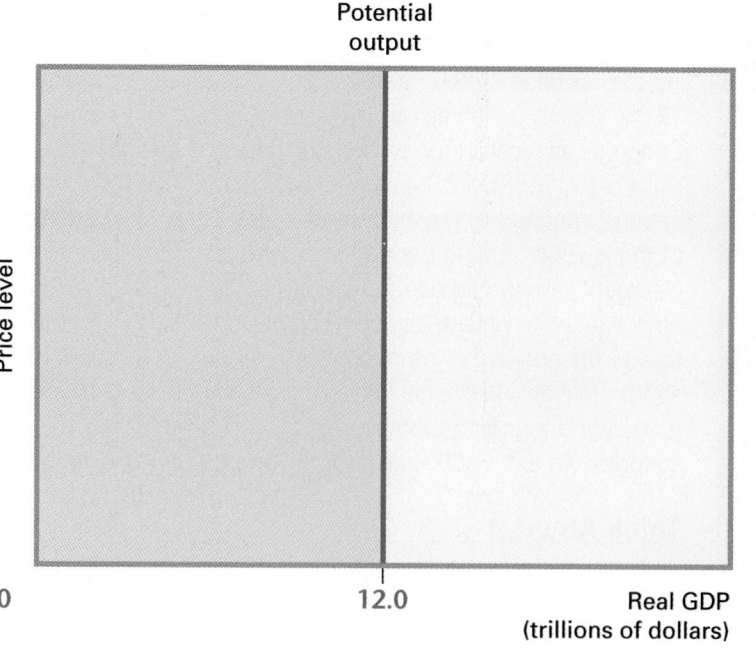

as much as it can. Unemployment exceeds its natural rate. The amount by which short-run output falls below the economy's potential output is called a *contractionary gap*. If output is below the economy's potential, policy makers often decide to reduce taxes or increase government spending. The idea is to stimulate aggregate demand as a way of increasing output to its potential. Figure 15.2 illustrates this situation.

Output Exceeding Potential

If the aggregate demand curve and aggregate supply curve intersect in the blue-shaded area of Figure 15.1, then output exceeds the economy's potential. Unemployment is below its natural rate. The amount by which actual output in the short run exceeds the economy's potential output is called the *expansionary gap*.

This seems like a good outcome. However, production beyond the economy's potential creates inflationary pressure in the economy. Production exceeding the economy's potential is not sustainable in the long run. The result is higher inflation and a return to the economy's potential output. To head off this higher inflation, policy makers sometimes increase taxes or reduce government spending to reduce aggregate demand.

How Can Output Exceed the Economy's Potential?

You probably have no problem understanding that output may fall below its potential. But how can the economy produce more than its potential? Remember, potential output means not zero unemployment, but the natural rate of unemployment. Even in an economy producing its potential

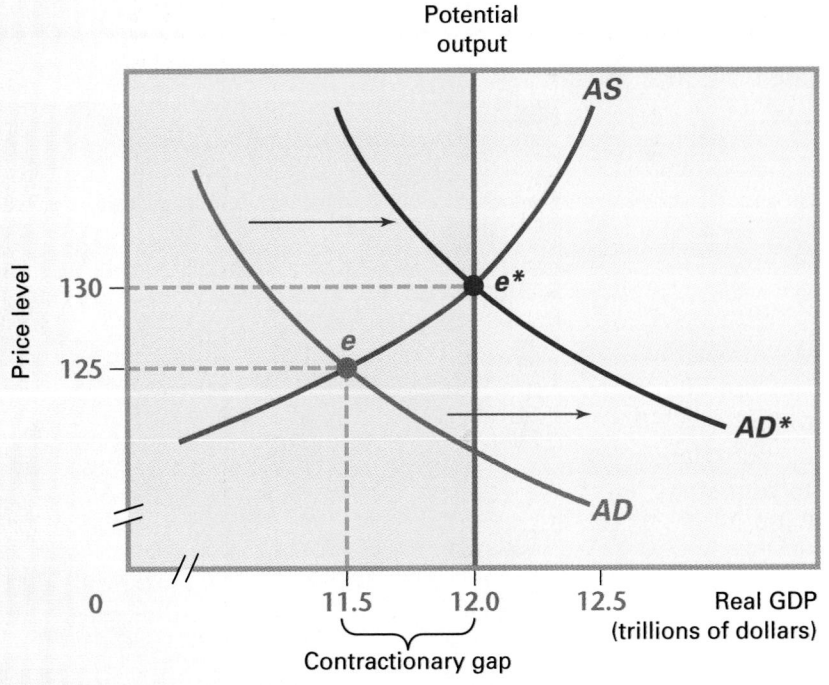

The Graphing Workshop
econxtra.swlearning.com

Discretionary Fiscal Policy to Close a Contractionary Gap

Figure 15.2

The aggregate demand curve *AD* and the aggregate supply curve *AS* intersect at point *e*. Output of $11.5 trillion falls short of the economy's potential of $12.0 trillion. The result is a contractionary gap of $0.5 trillion. This gap could be closed by discretionary fiscal policy that increases aggregate demand by just the right amount. An increase in government spending, a decrease in taxes, or some combination of the two could shift aggregate demand to *AD**, moving the economy to its potential level of output at *e**.

NETBookmark

The University of Washington's Fiscal Policy Center provides an extensive list of links about U.S. fiscal policy. Access that site through econxtra.swlearning.com and use the links to determine what tax and spending proposals have been made in Congress during the past six months. Choose one of those proposals and use aggregate demand and aggregate supply to explain its likely impact.

econxtra.swlearning.com

output, there is still some unemployed labor and some unused production capacity.

If you think of potential output as the economy's *normal production capacity*, you get a better idea of how the economy can temporarily exceed that capacity. Consider your own study habits. During most of the school year, you display your normal capacity for academic work. As the end of a grading period draws near, however, you may step it up a notch to finish long-standing assignments. You may study more than usual and make an extra push trying to pull things together. During these brief stretches, you study beyond your normal capacity, beyond the schedule you follow on a regular or sustained basis.

Producers, too, can exceed their normal capacity in the short run to push output beyond the economy's potential. For example, during World War II, businesses pulled out all the stops to win the war. The unemployment rate fell below 2 percent. However, in the long run, the economy does not exceed its potential, just as you don't boost your study effort permanently. Output in the long run gravitates back to the economy's potential. Production beyond the economy's potential usually leads only to inflation in the long run. For example, despite price controls put in place during World War II, inflation was still relatively high.

CHECKPOINT
What is the economy's potential output?

How does the concept of potential output relate to your study habits?

© Getty Images/PhotoDisc

The Rise of Fiscal Policy

Before the Great Depression, most policy makers believed that an economy producing less than its potential in the short run would move to its potential in the long run without intervention from the federal government. They thought the government should just balance its budget and forget about trying to stabilize the economy in the short run. Besides, before the Great Depression, the federal government itself played a minor role in the economy. At the onset of the Great Depression, for example, federal outlays were less than 3 percent of GDP, compared to about 20 percent today.

View of Classical Economists

Before the 1930s, fiscal policy was seldom used to influence the overall performance of the economy. Prior to the Great Depression, public policy was shaped by the views of **classical economists**. They advocated *laissez-faire,* the belief that free markets without government intervention were the best way to achieve the economy's potential output.

Classical economists did not deny the existence of depressions and high unemployment. They argued, however, that the sources of such crises lay outside the market system, in the effects of wars, tax increases, poor growing seasons, and the like. Such external events could shock the economy, reducing output and employment in the short run. Classical economists believed, however, that natural market forces, such as declining prices, wages, and interest rates, would end any recession in a relatively short time by encouraging people and businesses to spend more.

Simply put, classical economists argued that if the economy's average price level was too high to sell all that was produced, prices would fall until the quantity supplied equaled the quantity demanded. If wages were too high to employ all who wanted to work, wages would fall until the quantity of labor supplied equaled the quantity demanded. If interest rates were too high to invest all that had been saved, they would fall until the amount invested equaled the amount saved.

The classical approach claimed that natural market forces, through flexible

SPAN THE GLOBE

Laissez-Faire Policies in France

The French term laissez-faire literally means "allow to do." The exact origins of the term are unknown. It was first associated with a group of French economists called the Physiocrats. This group was popular in the late 1700s and is generally considered the founders of a scientific school of economic thought. Physiocrats believed that economies worked best if grounded in agriculture and allowed to run freely based on natural laws, not regulation by the government. Physiocrats strongly opposed the growing European policies of mercantilism, in which governments heavily regulated trade and manufacturing more for their own good than that of individual property owners. Physiocrats also believed that land and the products grown from it were the basis of wealth. Mercantilists believed that hard currency and precious metals were the basis of wealth. In the end, the mercantilists' theories of wealth became more widely accepted than those of the Physiocrats. Nevertheless, the Physiocrats' laissez-faire ideas were embraced by many people. When the French Revolution was launched in 1789, the new government instituted a number of reforms aimed at easing regulations on trade. The French government today is far from laissez-faire. Modern France has a mixed economy, which includes heavy regulation over the economy but not complete control of private property.

Think Critically

Why do you think the French government moved away from applying the ideas of the Physiocrats to its economy? With which philosophy regarding wealth—the mercantilist or the Physiocrat—do you most agree? Justify your answer.

prices, wages, and interest rates, would move the economy toward its potential GDP in the long run. Classical economists saw no need for changes in spending or taxing to "correct" the economy.

Instead, fiscal policy prior to the Great Depression aimed to maintain an **annually balanced budget**, except during wartime. Tax revenues tend to rise during expansions and fall during recessions. Therefore, an annually balanced budget means that spending increased during expansions and declined during recessions. However, such a pattern magnified fluctuations in the business cycle. This overheated the economy during expansions and increased unemployment during recessions.

The Great Depression and Keynes

Classical economists acknowledged that market economies could produce less than potential in the short run. The prolonged depression of the 1930s strained belief in the economy's ability to correct itself. The Great Depression was marked by unemployment reaching 25 percent and much unused plant capacity. With vast unemployed resources, output and income fell far short of the economy's potential for many years.

The market adjustments predicted by classical theory and the years of unemployment experienced during the Great Depression represented a clash between theory and fact. In 1936, John Maynard Keynes of Cambridge University, England, published *The General Theory of Employment, Interest, and Money*. This book challenged the classical view and touched off what would later come to be called the Keynesian revolution. *Keynesian theory and policy were developed to address the problem of unemployment during the Great Depression.*

Keynes's main quarrel with the classical economists was that prices and wages did not appear flexible enough even in the long run to ensure the full employment of resources. According to Keynes, prices and wages were relatively inflexible—they were "sticky." So

if unemployment was high, natural market forces would not return the economy to full employment in a timely fashion. Keynes also believed business expectations might at times become so grim that even very low interest rates would not encourage firms to invest.

The Multiplier Effect

Keynes also argued that any change in taxing or government spending had a magnified effect on aggregate demand. For example, suppose the government spends $100 million on a new presidential plane, Air Force One. Workers and suppliers at Boeing, the manufacturer of the 747, see their incomes rise by $100 million. These people will spend at least part of that higher income on products such as food, clothing, housing, cars, appliances, and the like. As a result, the people who make all those products will have more income. They will spend some of that higher income on yet more stuff.

Each round of income and spending increases aggregate demand a little more. This is called the **multiplier effect** of fiscal policy, which says that any change in fiscal policy affects aggregate demand by more than the original change in spending or taxing.

The multiplier effect also could result from a change in business investment and even a change in consumption. However, Keynes focused on changes in government spending and taxing.

The Rise of Fiscal Policy

Three developments in the years following the Great Depression supported the use of fiscal policy in the United States. The first was the influence of Keynes's *General Theory*. Keynes thought the economy could get stuck at a level of output that was well below its potential, well below the full-employment level. He argued that increasing government spending or cutting taxes could have a multiplier effect on aggregate demand. According to Keynes, fiscal policy should be used in times of high unemployment to increase aggregate demand enough to boost output and employment.

annually balanced budget

Matching annual spending with annual revenue, except during war years; approach to the federal budget prior to the Great Depression

multiplier effect

Any change in fiscal policy affects aggregate demand by more than the original change in spending or taxing

CNN video
A Matter of Priorities
econxtra.swlearning.com

The second development giving credibility to fiscal policy was the powerful impact World War II had on output and employment. The demands of war greatly increased production and cut unemployment sharply, ending the depression.

The third development, largely a consequence of the first two, was the passage of the Employment Act of 1946, which gave the federal government the responsibility for promoting full employment and price stability.

Again, prior to the Great Depression, the dominant fiscal policy was pursuit of a balanced budget. Indeed, in 1932, when the economy was in the depths of the Depression, federal taxes were increased to head off a budget deficit. This made things worse. In the wake of Keynes's *General Theory* and World War II, however, policy makers grew more receptive to the idea that fiscal policy could improve economic performance. The objective of fiscal policy was no longer to balance the budget but to promote full employment with price stability, even if this resulted in budget deficits.

 CHECKPOINT
How did the Great Depression change fiscal policy?

 **TEAM WORK**

Working with a partner, perform a role play. Acting as a classical economist, one partner will explain that economic approach to the partner. Acting as a Keynesian economist, the other partner will explain that approach. Make a list of the issues about which these two schools of thought disagree.

© Time Life Pictures

What role did fiscal policy play in ending the Great Depression?

Key Concepts

1. How close do you think the U.S. economy is currently to its potential output? Explain your answer.

2. Why can the economy have a 4 to 5 percent rate of unemployment when it is at its natural rate of unemployment?

3. In 2001, the U.S. economy was in recession. Why would classical economists have believed that this downturn in the economy would not last very long?

4. If the federal government borrows and spends an additional $5 billion, why are aggregate demand, production and income likely to grow by more than $5 billion?

Graphing Exercise

5. Draw a bar graph to show five rounds of the multiplier effect on spending when the federal government implements fiscal policy by borrowing and spending an additional $10 million. Remember that all money that is spent becomes someone else's income. Assume that each person who receives additional income saves 10 percent and spends 90 percent of these funds, as shown in the table below. How does your graph demonstrate the power of government spending?

Five Rounds of the Multiplier Effect

Round	Additional Spending	Additional Income	Amount Saved
1	$10,000,000	$10,000,000	$1,000,000
2	$ 9,000,000	$ 9,000,000	$ 900,000
3	$ 8,100,000	$ 8,100,000	$ 810,000
4	$ 7,290,000	$ 7,290,000	$ 729,000
5	$ 6,561,000	$ 6,561,000	$ 656,100

Think Critically

6. **History** When Keynes first asserted that the government could stabilize the economy by adjusting its spending and taxing, his ideas were met with skepticism from many economists and politicians. Events during World War II, however, caused most people to change their minds and come to believe that his ideas were correct. Investigate government borrowing and spending that took place during World War II and explain how they supported Keynes's ideas.

Sharpen Your Life Skills

Evaluate and Construct Pie Graphs

In its 2002–2003 budget, the state of New York anticipated revenues and expenditures that are shown in these pie graphs. Study the graphs and then answer the four questions in Apply Your Skill.

Apply Your Skill

1. Which of New York state's sources of tax revenue would you expect to have fallen the most below expectations because of the economic downturn in 2003?

2. Which type of government spending would have been easiest to cut when New York leaders found that their tax revenues fell below expectations in 2003?

3. Why were cuts in aid to local governments an important issue in preparing the budget for 2003–2004 in New York state?

4. Find the budgeted revenue and spending in your state's current budget. Use these data to construct similar pie graphs for your state. What might explain differences between sources of revenue and types of spending between your state and New York state?

New York State Sources of Revenue, 2002–2003 Budget

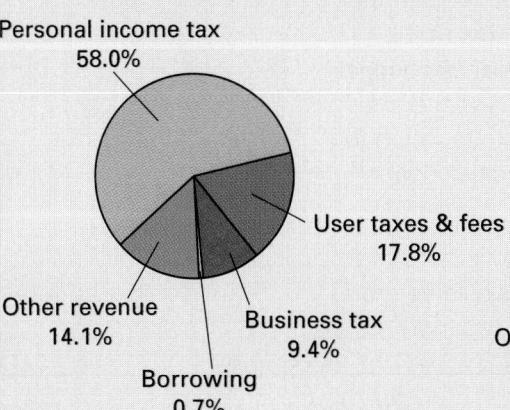

Personal income tax 58.0%
User taxes & fees 17.8%
Other revenue 14.1%
Business tax 9.4%
Borrowing 0.7%

New York State Expenditures, 2002–2003 Budget

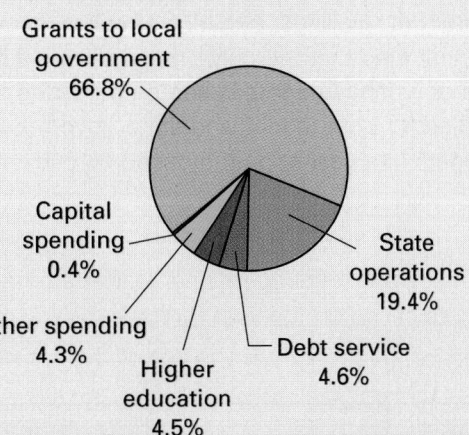

Grants to local government 66.8%
Capital spending 0.4%
Other spending 4.3%
Higher education 4.5%
Debt service 4.6%
State operations 19.4%

Objectives

> Identify the two tools of fiscal policy.

> Evaluate discretionary fiscal policy in light of the time lags involved.

Overview

From the Great Depression through the 1960s, fiscal policy appeared to be the miracle drug to cure what ailed the economy. Policy makers would adopt the necessary spending and tax policies to move the economy to its potential. The 1970s brought a new set of problems—problems that seemed beyond the reach of fiscal policy. Policy makers face the challenge of lags between the time they select and implement a policy and when it actually has an effect on the economy.

Key Terms

discretionary fiscal policy

automatic stabilizers

recognition lag

decision-making lag

implementation lag

effectiveness lag

[In the News]

● Requiring a Balanced Budget

By the early 1980s, the U.S. national debt had reached more than $2 trillion. To force the government to curb spending and balance the budget, Congress in 1985 passed the Gramm-Rudman-Hollings Act. This act required automatic cuts if government spending exceeded income. In its first year, the law cut the deficit by $70 billion. However, the Supreme Court struck down the automatic spending cuts as unconstitutional. Congress responded by passing several new versions of the law, the most significant being the Budget Enforcement Act of 1990. This new law tried to control the budget by limiting discretionary spending. It also required that any attempt to increase spending or reduce revenues had to be offset by other actions to provide money for those changes. By the end of the 1990s, it looked as if this legislation was working, as the federal government experienced budget surpluses for the first time in years. This was during an era of widespread economic growth, however. Many lawmakers feared that an economic downturn would lead to more deficits, despite the laws in place. In 2001, Senator Fritz Hollings, one of the original sponsors of the Gramm-Rudman-Hollings Act, argued that the only way to secure a balanced budget was to abandon the practice of writing budgets based on projected ten-year economic forecasts. Hollings called for both federal and state governments to return to the tradition of planning budgets one year at a time based on current situations.

Think About It

Do you agree with Hollings that planning budgets one year at a time would be more effective than planning budgets based on ten-year forecasts? Why or why not?

Fiscal Policy Tools

The tools of fiscal policy sort into two broad categories: discretionary fiscal policy and automatic stabilizers.

Discretionary Fiscal Policy

This chapter so far has focused mostly on discretionary fiscal policy. **Discretionary fiscal policy** requires congressional action to change government spending or taxing. These actions are designed to promote macroeconomic goals such as full employment and price stability. President Bush used discretionary fiscal policy in proposed plans for tax cuts in 2001 and 2003.

Automatic Stabilizers

Once adopted, a discretionary fiscal policy measure usually becomes an ongoing part of the federal budget. Most taxing and spending programs, once implemented, become **automatic stabilizers**. They automatically change with the ups and downs of the economy to stabilize *disposable income,* the income available after taxes. By smoothing fluctuations in disposable income, automatic stabilizers also smooth fluctuations in consumption and in aggregate demand.

One automatic stabilizer is unemployment insurance. During a recession, unemployment benefits automatically flow to the unemployed. This increases disposable income and props up consumption and aggregate demand. Likewise, welfare spending automatically increases as more people become eligible during hard times.

As another example of an automatic stabilizer, the federal income tax takes a bigger bite out of income as income increases. During an economic expansion, income taxes claim a growing percentage of income. This slows the growth in disposable income, which slows the growth in consumption. Therefore, the progressive income tax relieves some of the inflationary pres-sure that might otherwise arise when output increases during an economic expansion.

On the other hand, when the economy goes into a recession, real GDP declines, but taxes decline faster. Therefore disposable income does not fall as much as real GDP does. This props up consumption and aggregate demand during recessions. The progressive income tax protects against declines in disposable income, in consumption, and in aggregate demand.

Automatic stabilizers smooth fluctuations in disposable income over the business cycle. They boost aggregate demand during periods of recession and dampen aggregate demand during periods of expansion.

Automatic stabilizers do not eliminate economic fluctuations, but they do reduce their magnitude. The stronger and more effective the automatic stabilizers, the less need there is for discretionary fiscal policy. Because of automatic stabilizers introduced during the Great Depression, *the economy is more stable today than it was during the Great Depression and before.* Without much fanfare, automatic stabilizers have been quietly doing their work, keeping the economy on a more even keel.

Ask the Xpert!

econxtra.swlearning.com

In theory, how does a tax cut work to stimulate the economy?

discretionary fiscal policy

Congressional changes in spending or taxing to promote macroeconomic goals

automatic stabilizers

Government spending and taxing programs that year after year automatically reduce fluctuations in disposable income, and thus in consumption, over the business cycle

CHECKPOINT

What are the two tools of fiscal policy?

NETBookmark

In the United States, fiscal policy is determined jointly by the president and Congress. The Congressional Budget Office provides analysis to Congress. The Office of Management and Budget does the same for the executive branch. Access the web sites for these offices to get a sense of the kinds of analysis being done and how they might be used in determining fiscal policy. Write a one-page paper describing your findings.

econxtra.swlearning.com

Problems with Discretionary Fiscal Policy

Discretionary fiscal policy is a type of demand-management policy. The idea is to increase or decrease aggregate demand to smooth economic fluctuations and move the economy toward its potential output. This seemed to work between the Great Depression and the 1960s. The 1970s, however, turned out to be different.

Stagflation

The problem during the 1970s was stagflation. A decrease in aggregate supply created the double trouble of higher inflation and higher unemployment. The aggregate supply curve shifted left because of crop failures around the world, sharply higher oil prices, and other adverse supply shocks. Demand-management policies are not suited to solving the problem of stagflation. This is because in the short run, it is impossible to fight unemployment and inflation at the same time with fiscal policy. An increase in aggregate demand would worsen inflation, whereas a decrease in aggregate demand resulting from reduced government spending or higher taxes would worsen unemployment.

Calculating the Natural Rate of Unemployment

The unemployment rate that occurs when the economy is producing its potential output is called *the natural rate of unemployment*. Before adopting discretionary fiscal policies, public officials must correctly estimate this natural rate. That's no easy task, and they may get it wrong.

For example, suppose the economy is producing its potential output of $12.0 trillion, as shown in Figure 15.3, where the natural rate of unemployment is 5 percent. Also suppose that public officials mistakenly think the natural rate of unemployment is 4 percent. They then attempt to increase output and reduce unemployment through discretionary fiscal policy. This attempt would only lead to inflation in the long run.

When Discretionary Fiscal Policy Underestimates the Natural Rate of Unemployment   **Figure 15.3**

If public officials underestimate the natural rate of unemployment, they may attempt to stimulate aggregate demand even if the economy is producing its potential output, as at point *a*. In the short run, this expansionary policy yields a short-run equilibrium at point *b*. At this point the price level and output are higher and unemployment is lower. The policy appears to be working. Thus, attempts to increase production beyond potential GDP lead only to inflation in the long run.

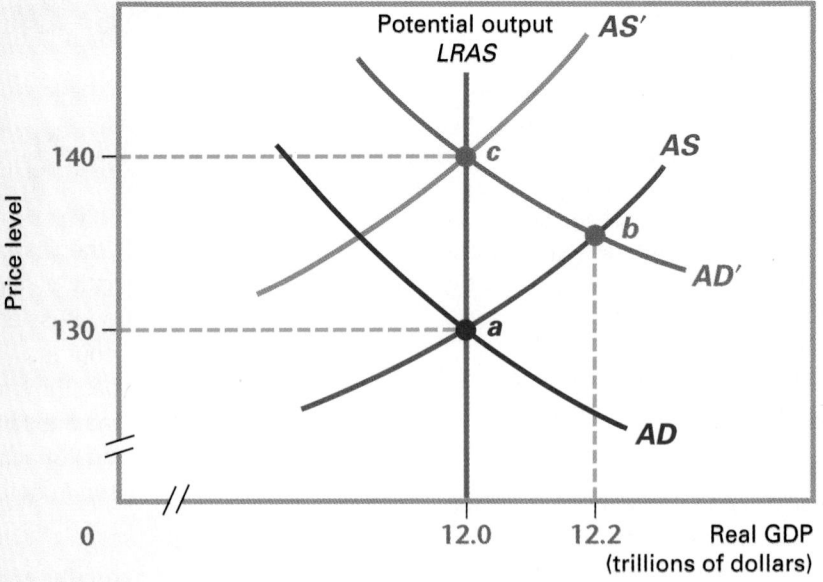

The Problem of Lags

So far, the discussion has ignored the time required to implement discretionary fiscal policy. The assumption has been that the desired policy is selected and implemented instantaneously. The presentation also has assumed that, once implemented, the policy works fast. Actually, there may be long, sometimes unpredictable, lags at several stages in the process. These lags reduce the effectiveness of discretionary fiscal policies.

Recognition Lag

First, there is a **recognition lag**, which is the time it takes to identify a problem and determine how serious it is. Because a recession is not identified until more than six months after it begins and the average recession lasts only about 11 months, a typical recession will be more than half over before it is officially recognized as such.

Decision-Making Lag

Even after it becomes clear that the economy is in trouble, Congress and the president must develop and agree on an appropriate course of action. Because policy makers usually take time deciding what to do, there is a **decision-making lag**. Changes in fiscal policy usually take months to approve, but they could take more than a year.

Implementation Lag

Once a decision has been made, the new policy must be introduced. This often involves an **implementation lag**. For example, in early 2001, President Bush proposed a tax cut to stimulate the economy. Although Congress passed the measure relatively quickly, tax rebate checks were not mailed until six months after Bush introduced the legislation.

Effectiveness Lag

Once a policy has been implemented, there is an **effectiveness lag** before the full impact of the policy registers on the economy. Fiscal policy, once implemented, takes between 9 and 18 months to register its full effect.

© Getty Images/PhotoDisc

Once government decision makers implement a policy, there is a lag before the full impact of the policy registers on the economy. What is this lag called, and how long does it usually last?

These lags make it difficult to carry out discretionary fiscal policy. Discretionary fiscal policy to address a recession could take hold only after the economy has recovered on its own. Thus, discretionary fiscal policy aimed at increasing output and employment may end up just fueling inflation. These lags are reasons why policy makers need to be careful with dscretionary fiscal policy.

recognition lag

The time needed to identify a macroeconomic problem

decision-making lag

The time needed to decide what to do once the problem has been identified

implementation lag

The time needed to execute a change in policy

effectiveness lag

The time needed for changes in policy to affect the economy

THE WALL STREET JOURNAL

Reading It Right What's the relevance of the following statement from *The Wall Street Journal*: "Inevitably, there is a big, long lag between the time spending is ordered by Congress and the time spending actually shows up in the economy."

Fiscal Policy and Aggregate Supply

So far the discussion of fiscal policy has been limited to effects on aggregate demand. Fiscal policy also can affect aggregate supply, although often that effect is unintentional. For example, suppose the government increases unemployment benefits by imposing higher taxes on the employed. This redistributes income from workers to the unemployed. These offsetting effects may leave aggregate demand unchanged.

What about the possible effects of these changes on aggregate supply? Those who receive higher unemployment benefits have less incentive to find work, so they may search at a more leisurely pace. On the other hand, the higher marginal tax rate makes work less attractive. In short, the supply of labor could decrease as a result of offsetting changes in taxes and transfers. A decrease in the supply of labor would decrease aggregate supply, reducing output and employment.

Both automatic stabilizers, such as unemployment insurance and the progressive income tax, and discretionary fiscal policies, such as changes in tax rates, may affect individual incentives to work, spend, save, and invest, although these effects are usually unintended. Policy makers should keep these secondary effects in mind when they evaluate fiscal policies.

CHECKPOINT
What are the various lags involved with discretionary fiscal policy?

E-CONOMICS

Using Technology to Make Economic Forecasts

Predicting economic developments can be as tricky as predicting the weather. It is based on a number of factors and calculations involving current and past economic data. Computer technology has aided economists greatly in their ability to recognize and predict economic trends. One economic forecasting tool using computers is input-output analysis. This method looks at the interdependence of all the various productive sectors in an economy by analyzing each product as both a commodity to be consumed and as an input in the production of other goods. The method is used to predict the total amount of various goods that are affected by a given amount of spending. As an example, economists might be trying to project the future development of the shipping industry. They must figure out the distribution of the total production of ships, broken down into the quantity of ships used in different parts of the economy. The purpose of such a chart is to foresee how a change in one part of the economy would affect other parts of the economy. For example, if the amount of food the United States exported to other countries increased by a certain amount, then the number of ships needed to transport that food would increase as well. Economic forecasters use methods like this to predict "economic ripples" that can have far-reaching effects. However, input-output analysis requires an enormous amount of data from countries throughout the world. Computer programs can help economists quickly compile this data and predict outcomes.

Think Critically

How do you think making economic forecasts before computer technology differed from economic forecasting today?

Key Concepts

1. Why is the unemployment compensation program an example of an automatic stabilizer for the economy?

2. Inflation often results when the economy is growing rapidly. Why is it politically difficult for Congress to use discretionary fiscal policy by passing tax increases that could slow economic growth and reduce inflation?

3. If the government decided to extend unemployment compensation payments for an extra 13 weeks beyond the 26 that normally are paid, what would happen to the incentive unemployed people have to find work? How might this affect the economy?

4. Why do many economists believe that the decision-making lag is the longest of the lags that reduce the effectiveness of discretionary fiscal policy?

5. Suppose that the federal government borrowed and spent an additional $10 billion to stimulate the economy. Because of this extra government borrowing, interest rates increased by 1 percent on average. How might this increase affect the willingness of people and businesses to borrow and spend? What could this do to the effectiveness of the government's attempt to stimulate the economy?

Graphing Exercise

6. The so-called *misery index* is found by summing the unemployment rate and the inflation rate by year. Construct a line graph of the misery index based on data in the table. How does the misery index appear to be related to the economic conditions of the country? What would you expect to happen to the misery index if the economy began to grow rapidly?

Think Critically

7. **History** In 1980 and 1981, there was a deep recession in the U.S. economy. Unemployment exceeded 10 percent. To try to help the economy recover, Congress passed a law in 1982 that increased federal excise taxes on gasoline. The funds collected were intended to create additional jobs when they were spent to repair roads and highways throughout the nation. The tax increase went into effect on April 1, 1983. The first contracts were awarded to construction companies in the fall of that year. Actual construction began early in 1984, when the economy was already well on its way to recovery. Explain how this situation demonstrates a problem with using discretionary fiscal policy.

Inflation, Unemployment, and Misery Index, 1993–2003

Year	Unemployment	Inflation	Misery index
1993	6.9%	2.7%	9.6%
1994	6.1	2.7	8.6
1995	5.6	2.5	8.1
1996	5.4	3.3	8.7
1997	4.9	1.7	6.6
1998	4.5	1.6	6.1
1999	4.2	2.7	6.9
2000	4.0	3.4	7.4
2001	4.7	1.6	6.3
2002	5.8	2.4	8.2
2003*	6.1	3.6	9.7

*Projections based on first four months of 2003.

movers & shakers

Philip Knight *Chairman, President, CEO, and Co-Founder, NIKE, Inc.*

Philip Hampson Knight grew up in Portland, Oregon. He attended the University of Oregon, majoring in accounting. Knight was a member of the school's track team—at the time, one of the best college teams in the country. His coach, Bill Bowerman, was always experimenting with running shoes in order to make his team faster. Not happy with the shoes available at that time, Bowerman began making his own shoes. "Since I wasn't the best guy on the team, I was the logical one to test the shoes," Knight explains.

After graduation and a year in the army, Knight enrolled in Stanford University's Graduate School of Business. It was there, as an assignment for one of his business classes, that Knight came up with the idea for Blue Ribbon Sports, later named NIKE. Once up and running, Blue Ribbon Sports operated by selling shoes from a van at high-school track meets and other athletic events. Within a few years, a retail site was secured, and the company was renamed NIKE. A local designer was paid $35 to come up with a logo, and the NIKE "swoosh" was born. The new shoe, with its new logo, debuted at the 1972 U.S. Olympic trials in Eugene, Oregon. The launch was a success. That year, $3.2 million worth of NIKE shoes were sold. Profits doubled each of the next 10 years. In 1980, NIKE passed Adidas to become the industry leader.

Astronomical growth in the 1980s and 1990s was a result of Knight's idea to sign 21-year-old Michael Jordan to endorse a basketball shoe. It wasn't long before Air Jordans were must-have shoes among American youths. Later, athletes including Tiger Woods, Bo Jackson, Gabrielle Reese, and Andre Agassi kept NIKE sneakers in the minds of aspiring athletes, and the company's success continued. When speaking of his company's advertising campaigns, Knight stated, "We didn't invent it [advertising], but we ratcheted it up several notches." The company typically budgets $200 million each year for advertising and celebrity endorsements.

In fiscal year 2003, NIKE—still the world's number-one shoemaker—had sales of $10.7 billion, with net income of just over $1 billion. The company employs 23,300 and manufactures and sells shoes for baseball, cheerleading, golf, volleyball and other sports. The company also sells Cole Haan dress and casual shoes, manufactures a line of athletic apparel and equipment, and operates numerous retail outlets. NIKE products are sold throughout the United States and in 200 other countries. The company's "swoosh" is recognizable today even without the name.

Although shy and aloof, Knight is known as one of the smartest brand builders ever. He inspires employees with the "NIKE Spirit" and motivates them to help take the company to the next level time after time. In addition to his trademark sunglasses—he is rarely seen without them—and wrinkled, casual wardrobe, one of Knight's trademark sayings is: "The trouble in America is not that we are making too many mistakes, but that we are making too few." His belief in making mistakes clearly has served him well.

SOURCE READING
Knight is fond of saying: "The trouble in America is not that we are making too many mistakes, but that we are making too few." Explain what you think he means by this. How did his belief in making mistakes serve him—and NIKE—well?

ENTREPRENEURS IN ACTION
Imagine you are an entrepreneur building your own company. What are some of the choices you likely will face in the process of helping your company grow? Explain what you would consider to be two good decisions regarding company growth and two bad decisions regarding company growth.

Objectives

> Discuss why federal deficits have been common since the Great Depression.

> Distinguish between crowding out and crowding in.

> Discuss changes in the relative size of federal debt since World War II.

> Explain who bears the burden of the federal debt.

Overview

When governments spend more than they take in, budget deficits result. These deficits can have their own effect on the economy, beyond the stimulus provided by changes in spending and taxing. These deficits add up to the federal debt, which also can have its own effect on the economy. Policy makers usually focus on the immediate impact of a policy and ignore the long-term effects.

Key Terms

crowding out

crowding in

[In the News]

● The National Debt Clock

The old saying "time is money" usually refers to someone wasting money by wasting time. The phrase also could be applied to the U.S. National Debt Clock, which literally ticks out how much the U.S. national debt is increasing every second, down to the penny. The clock is located in New York City and was the brainchild of real estate developer Seymour Durst. In 1989, Durst funded the building of the National Debt Clock in Times Square to draw public attention to how much the debt was growing. At the time the clock started, the national debt was increasing by $13,000 per second. By the mid-1990s, the national debt was rising so fast that it crashed the computer used to run the clock. By the end of 1999, however, as budget surpluses were able to help pay down some of the national debt, the clock started to reverse itself. This caused some confusion for observers and led the clock's owners to shut it down on September 7, 2000. At the time it shut down, the clock read, "Our national debt: $5,676,989,904,887. Your family share: $73,733." Less than two years later, however, the debt was rising again, and the National Debt Clock restarted on July 11, 2002, showing a debt of $6,126,597,702,503, or about $66,800 per family.

Think About It

Do you think the display of a National Debt Clock is a good idea? Why or why not?

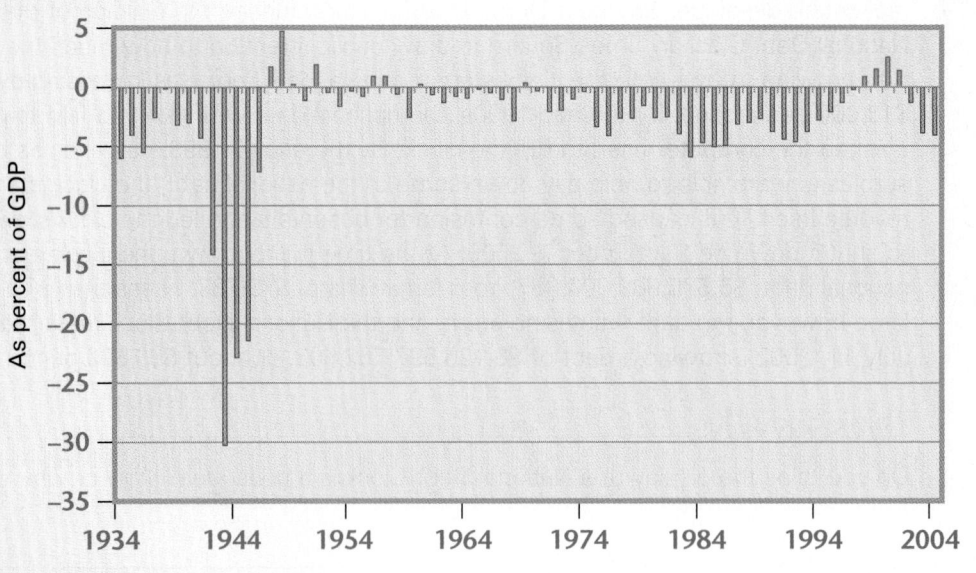

NETBookmark

The Office of Management and Budget prepares *A Citizen's Guide to the Federal Budget* each year. This publication contains numerous easy-to-read charts and graphs indicating sources of revenue and the types of spending. Access these guides and other budget documents for the current year and previous years through econxtra.swlearning.com. Choose one of the links in the Table of Contents, and write a one-paragraph summary of web page you access.

econxtra.swlearning.com

Budget Deficits

When government spending exceeds government revenue, the result is a *budget deficit*. The federal budget deficit measures the amount by which total federal spending exceeds total federal revenues. The federal government finances a deficit by selling U.S. government securities, such as bonds. People and businesses buy them because the bonds earn interest.

Federal Deficits Over the Years

Between 1789, when the U.S. Constitution was officially adopted, and 1930, the first full year of the Great Depression, the federal budget was in deficit 33 percent of the time. Federal deficits during that stretch occurred primarily during war years. Because wars involved much personal hardship, public officials were understandably reluctant to increase taxes much to finance war-related spending. After a war, government spending dropped more than government revenue. Thus, deficits arising during a war were largely self-correcting once the war ended.

Since the Great Depression, the federal budget has been in deficit 85 percent of the time. Figure 15.4 shows federal deficits and surpluses as a percentage of GDP during the last 70 years. Unmistakable are the huge deficits during World War II.

The federal budget experienced a surplus from 1998 to 2001. However, before that it had been in deficit every year but one since 1960 and in all but eight years since 1930. The average annual deficit grew from less than 1 percent of GDP in the 1960s to an

---

Federal Deficits and Surpluses as Percent of GDP

Figure 15.4

Between 1934 and 2004, the federal budget has been in deficit 85 percent of the time.

Source: Fiscal-year figures from *Economic Report of the President,* February 2003. Figures for 2003 and 2004 are projections based on the President's 2004 budget proposal and estimates from the Congressional Budget Office.

average of about 4 percent during the 1980s, during the first half of the 1990s, and in 2003 and 2004.

Why Is the Budget Usually in a Deficit?

Why has the federal budget been in deficit for all but 12 years since 1930? One obvious reason is that, unlike legislatures in 49 states, Congress is not required to balance the budget. Why does Congress approve budgets with deficits most years?

One widely accepted model of the public sector discussed in the previous chapter argues that elected officials try to maximize their political support. Voters like public spending programs but hate paying taxes. Therefore, spending programs win voters' support and taxes lose it. Public officials try to maximize their political support by spending more than they tax. This results in chronic deficits. Why were deficits more common after the Great Depression? The answer can be traced back to Keynes and his followers, who thought deficits were a justifiable result of fiscal policy. They were less worried about the long-run consequences. As Keynes once said, "In the long run we are all dead."

The Surplus of 1998–2001

What about the budget surpluses from 1998 to 2001? Where did they come from? Concern about rising deficits during the 1980s led to two tax hikes in the early 1990s. The Republican Congress elected in 1994 imposed more discipline on federal spending. Meanwhile, the economy experienced a healthy recovery resulting from technological innovation, market globalization, and the strongest stock market in history.

As a result of tax increases and a strengthening economy, revenues gushed into Washington, growing an average of 8.3 percent per year between 1993 and 1998. Meanwhile, federal spending was held in check, growing by an average of only 3.2 percent per year. By 1998, that one-two punch

knocked out the federal deficit, a deficit that only six years earlier had reached $290 billion, a record to that point. The federal surplus grew from $69 billion in 1998 to $236 billion in 2000, the highest ever.

The economy entered a recession in March 2001. In the spring of 2001, the newly elected President George W. Bush pushed through an across-the-board cut in income tax rates to, in his words, "get the economy moving again." On September 11, 2001, 19 men in four hijacked airplanes ended thousands of lives and squelched chances of a quick rebound from the recession. The attacks grounded commercial flights across the country for weeks, and knocked down the travel industry for months. Stock markets and insurance markets also suffered.

Since peaking in early 2001, job totals fell 2.5 million by May 2003. The stock market went into a three-year funk. As the economy softened, automatic stabilizers reduced federal revenues and increased federal spending. All this fueled the federal deficit, which reached $374 billion by 2003. The federal surpluses seemed at that point like ancient history.

CHECKPOINT
Why have federal deficits been so common since the Great Depression?

Deficits and Interest Rates

What effect do federal deficits have on interest rates? Recall that interest rates affect investment, a critical component of economic growth. In fact, year-to-year fluctuations in investment are the primary source of shifts in aggregate demand and in GDP. Figure 15.5 compares the percent change in real investment and the percent change in real GDP since 1960. As you can see, investment fluctuates much more than GDP.

The Graphing Workshop

Crowding Out

How do federal deficits affect investment? Here's a way of looking at the question. Were you ever unwilling to go to a particular restaurant because it was too crowded? You simply did not want to put up with the hassle and long wait. You were "crowded out." Some version of this also can result from federal deficits.

The higher the deficit, the more that must be borrowed. This increased demand for borrowed funds drives up the market rate of interest. Higher interest rates discourage, or *crowd out,* some private investment. **Crowding out** occurs when higher government deficits drive up interest rates and thereby reduce private investment. Decreased investment spending reduces the effectiveness of federal deficits that are intended to stimulate aggregate demand.

Crowding In

Did you ever pass up an unfamiliar restaurant because the place had few customers? If you had seen just a few more customers, you might have stopped in—you might have been willing to "crowd in." Similarly, businesses may hesitate to invest in a seemingly lifeless economy.

crowding in

Government spending stimulates private investment in an otherwise stagnant economy

crowding out

Private investment falls when higher government deficits drive up interest rates

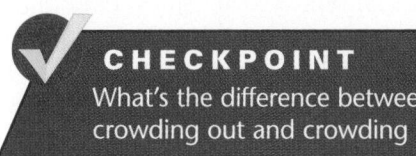

Ask the Xpert!

econxtra.swlearning.com

What is fiscal policy, and what is it supposed to accomplish?

If government stimulates a weak economy, the business outlook may improve. As expectations grow more favorable, firms become more willing to invest. This ability of government deficits to stimulate private investment is sometimes called **crowding in**.

CHECKPOINT

What's the difference between crowding out and crowding in?

Federal Debt

Federal deficits add up. It took 39 presidents, six wars, the Great Depression, and more than 200 years for the federal debt to reach $1 trillion, as it did in 1981. It took only three presidents and another 15 years for that debt to triple in real terms, as it did by 1996. The federal deficit measures the amount by which annual spending exceeds annual revenue. The *federal debt* measures the accumulation of past deficits, the total amount owed by the federal government. Federal debt adds up all federal deficits and subtracts federal surpluses.

Investment Fluctuations

Figure 15.5

Investment fluctuates much more from year to year than does GDP.

Source: U.S. Department of Commerce. Investment and GDP are in real terms—that is, adjusted for changes in the price level.

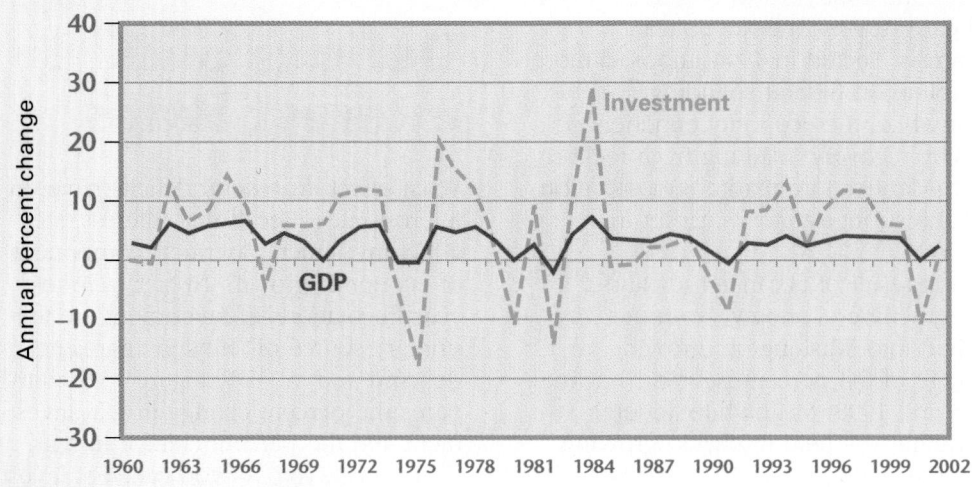

Gross Debt Versus Debt Held by the Public

In talking about the federal debt, economists often distinguish between gross debt and debt held by the public. The gross debt includes U.S. Treasury securities purchased by various federal agencies. Since this is debt the federal government owes to itself, economists often ignore it and focus instead on debt held by the public. Debt held by the public includes debt held by households, firms, non-profit institutions, and foreign entities. As of 2003, gross federal debt totaled $6.8 trillion, and debt held by the public totaled $4.0 trillion. Public debt amounted to about $14,000 per capita.

Debt Relative to GDP

One way to measure debt over time is relative to the economy's production and income, or GDP. In a sense, GDP shows the economy's ability to carry debt, just as household income shows that family's ability to carry a mortgage.

Figure 15.6 shows federal debt held by the public relative to GDP. The cost of World War II increased the debt to more than 100 percent relative to GDP in 1946. *Despite recent setbacks, the federal debt held by the public relative to GDP dropped nearly two-thirds between 1946 and 2004.*

Note that usual measures of the federal debt do not capture all future liabilities. The Social Security programs and other retirement programs promise benefits that must be paid from taxes or further borrowing.

CHECKPOINT
What has happened to federal debt levels relative to GDP since World War II?

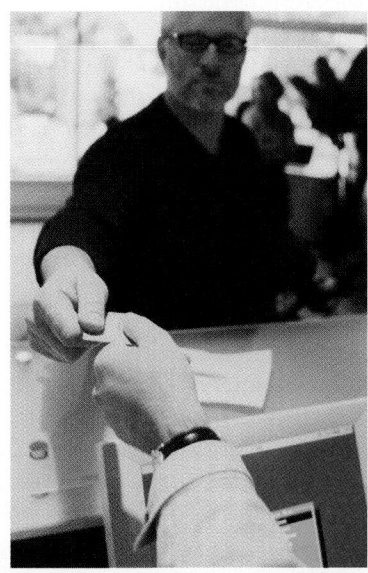

Credit card debt accounts for much of the debt held by the public. What types of expenditures does the $14,000 in debt per capita represent?

Federal Debt Held by the Public as Percent of GDP, 1940 to 2004

Figure 15.6

The federal debt held by the public relative to GDP dropped nearly two-thirds between 1946 and 2004.

Source: Fiscal year figures from *Economic Report of the President,* February 2003, Table 79. Figures for 2003 and 2004 are projections.

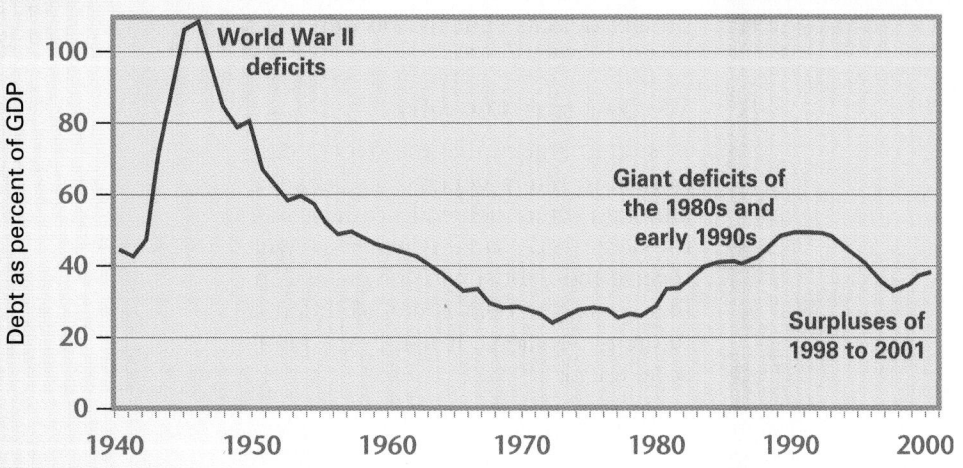

Economic Impact of the Debt

What is the impact of a large federal debt on the economy?

Debt and Interest Rates

The federal government seldom pays off any debt. When bonds mature, the federal government simply sells more to pay off maturing bondholders. Nearly half the debt is refinanced every year. With nearly $200 billion in bonds coming due each month, debt service payments are quite sensitive to changes in interest rates. Based on a $4.0 trillion debt held by the public in 2003, a one-percentage point increase in the interest rate raises annual interest costs by about $40 billion.

Interest payments on the federal debt were about 8 percent of the federal budget in 1978. Thanks to record-low interest rates, interest payments in 2003 were also about 8 percent of the federal budget. When interest rates rise from their low levels, so will the cost of servicing the debt.

Who Bears the Burden of the Debt?

Deficit spending is a way of billing future taxpayers for current spending. The federal debt raises questions about the right of one generation to pass on to the next generation the burden of its borrowing. To what extent do budget deficits shift the burden to future generations?

We Owe It to Ourselves

It is often argued that the debt is not a burden to future generations because, although future generations must service the debt, those same generations will receive the debt service payments. In that sense, the debt is not a burden on future generations. It's all in the family, so to speak.

Foreign Ownership of Debt

But the "we-owe-it-to-ourselves" argument does not apply to that portion of the federal debt purchased by foreigners. Foreigners who buy U.S. government bonds forgo present consumption. *As foreigners buy more government bonds, this increases the burden of the debt on future generations because future debt service payments no longer remain in the country.* Foreigners owned about 20 percent of all federal debt in 2003, compared to 14 percent in 1991.

CHECKPOINT
Who bears the burden of the federal debt?

Investigate Your Local Economy

Interview three or four adults about the federal budget deficit. Ask if they know the size of the federal deficit. Ask if they think having a budget deficit is a good idea or a bad idea for the economy, and why. Then compare the answers you receive with the answers your classmates receive. Did you uncover any trends? If so, what are they?

Ethics in Action

Preventing Deficits from Harming Future Generations

One common concern about deficit spending is that it will place an unfair burden on future generations. One economist argued that people can prevent this from happening by saving more and spending less now. Harvard economist Robert Barro argued that when governments increase deficits, they generally keep taxes low. Eventually, however, taxes on future generations will have to be raised to make up for this deficit. If no one cared about future generations, then adults today would support deficit spending because they would be dead before the tax bills would come due. Barro argued that people concerned about the well-being of their children and grandchildren will offset the future harm of deficits by spending less and saving more today. This saved money will be passed along to their children and grandchildren, who can use it to pay the higher taxes that will come due when they are adults. Many economists disagree that Barro's idea really works, however. Many point out that during the 1980s, when deficits were very high, people's tendency to save money was very low. Barro's supporters argue that this may have been because people in the 1980s were optimistic about the future growth of the economy and believed that the deficits would be offset by lower government spending, not by future higher taxes. Barro's critics also argue that the growing number of people with no children may be less concerned about the welfare of future generations. Also, his theory assumes a great deal of public knowledge and understanding about the national debt and its effects on the future. One survey found that few adults had any idea about the size of the federal deficit. This would make it very difficult for them to plan ahead and spend with the idea of protecting future generations in mind.

Think Critically

Do you agree with Barro's supporters or his critics? Explain your reasons.

© Getty Images/PhotoDisc

Do you think the federal government is acting responsibly in passing debt on to future generations? Why or why not?

Key Concepts

1. In 1930, the national debt was just over $16.8 billion. Why doesn't this fact provide much information about the size or importance of this debt? What other information would you need in order to evaluate the debt's importance?

2. Why didn't the across-the-board income tax cut of 2001 immediately cause people to spend more and get the economy moving?

3. The Social Security system has invested many billions of dollars by purchasing bonds from the U.S. treasury. Some economists believe this is simply a matter of taking money from one of the government's pockets and putting it in another. Others do not agree. When the Social Security system cashes in its bonds to pay benefits to retired workers in the future, where will the funds come from? Are these bonds really less of a financial responsibility of the government than other bonds held by the public?

4. If interest rates increased by 3 percent across the board, what would happen to interest payments on the debt over a period of several years?

Graphing Exercise

5. During the 1980s and 1990s, tax payments received by the Social Security system far exceeded the amount paid to beneficiaries. Money that the system accumulated was invested in government bonds and held in the Social Security Trust Fund to be used to make future payments. Use the data in the table to construct a line graph that shows the growth in this trust fund. Why will this trend toward larger balances in the Social Security Trust Fund be reversed in the future?

Social Security Trust Fund Balance, 1980–2000
(in billions of dollars)

Year	Balance
1980	$ 22.8
1985	35.8
1990	214.2
1995	458.5
2000	931.8

Think Critically

6. **Math** The federal debt was approximately $6.8 trillion dollars in 2003. If this debt grew at a rate of 3 percent per year in each of the following 10 years, how much would the debt total be in 2013? Should such an increase in the debt be a concern for U.S. citizens? Why or why not?

Alexander Hamilton
and the Question of the National Debt

Economic issues played a major role in causing the American Revolution, and the United States emerged from the struggle in poor financial shape. It had fought the war on borrowed money. It stopped paying interest on its bonds. It was behind in paying the army. It also had issued more than $200 million in near worthless money, or "continentals." When representatives from the various states met in Philadelphia during the summer of 1787 to correct these problems, the result was a new constitution. The new U.S. Constitution gave the government powers to tax, borrow, and spend.

President George Washington appointed Alexander Hamilton as the first secretary of the treasury in 1789. Hamilton was not the first choice. Robert Morris, the "financier of the Revolution," turned Washington down and recommended Hamilton. Hamilton realized he needed to establish the country's credit by resolving the problems of the nation's debt. The United States and its credit were held in low esteem, and no one was willing to lend money. Hamilton realized that establishing the nation's credit would set the conditions for its future prosperity and economic success. It also would provide an incentive for individuals and nations to invest in the United States. For Hamilton, the prospect of a federal debt was desirable, as he felt it would bind the moneyed class to the new government. Hamilton had written to Morris, "A national debt, if not excessive, will be to us a national blessing."

Three types of debt arose from the Revolution: (1) federal debt owed to foreigners, (2) federal debt owed to Americans, and (3) state debts. There was no question about paying the foreign debt at face value. Domestic debt had depreciated to about 25 cents on the dollar, but Hamilton proposed to pay it at face value as

well. Because many speculators who had purchased the depreciated certificates would stand to profit, some in Congress resisted this solution. They felt it would enrich speculators rather than those who originally had purchased the debt. Despite the opposition, Hamilton's solution prevailed. He proposed to repay the debt by issuing new bonds for the full amount of the old debts. The new debt would be repaid over time from tariff revenues.

Hamilton also proposed that the federal government assume state debts. Much of the debt had been incurred during the Revolution for the benefit of all the states. In addition, wealthy residents held many state bonds. If their investments could be shifted from the states to the federal government, he believed their long-term interests in the nation's success would be ensured. Southern states defeated these proposals four times, putting Hamilton's entire financial plan in danger. It was only when he gained Thomas Jefferson's support by agreeing to locate the capital to the south—in the area of Washington, D.C.—that Hamilton was able to gain enough votes to pass his plan.

Hamilton was successful, and the nation's credit was insured. By 1794, the United States had a high credit rating and its bonds were highly sought.

THINK CRITICALLY

The perfect solution at one time in history may not be the proper solution in another. Hamilton saw that the national debt could be a positive factor in the nation's economy. How does that differ from attitudes today?

Chapter Assessment

Summary

 The Evolution of Fiscal Policy

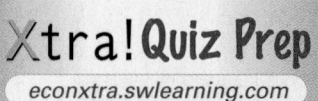

a Fiscal policy is intended to move the economy toward full employment at its potential output with price stability. It does this primarily by working to shift aggregate demand. The *potential output* is the level of production that that is sustainable in the long run. Some unemployment will occur at the potential output. This level of unemployment is called the *natural rate of unemployment.*

b When output is below its potential, government may use fiscal policy to stimulate production by increasing its spending or cutting taxes. If output exceeds its potential, government may use fiscal policy to reduce production by cutting its spending or increasing taxes.

c Before the Great Depression of the 1930s, *classical economists* believed that natural market forces would cause the economy to automatically recover from recessions without government intervention. During the Great Depression, it became apparent the classical economic theory had some problems.

d Keynes developed a theory in the 1930s that argued prices, wages, and interest rates were "sticky" and would not quickly fall in a recession to bring about economic growth. Keynes argued that it is the responsibility of the government to get the economy moving again by adjusting government spending and taxes.

 Fiscal Policy Reconsidered

a Fiscal policy may either be automatic or *discretionary*. Automatic fiscal policy takes place without passage of new legislation. An example of automatic fiscal policy is the progressive federal income tax. When the economy is in recession, people pay a smaller share of their reduced incomes in tax while in an expansion their greater incomes force them into higher tax brackets.

b There are a number of limitations on the effectiveness of fiscal policy. Because fiscal policy is designed to adjust aggregate demand, it is not effective in fighting stagflation, when there is both unemployment and inflation. Time lags that slow the carrying out and impact of fiscal policy reduce its effectiveness.

c Changes in aggregate demand that result from fiscal policy decisions may have unforeseen results on aggregate supply. When unemployed workers are provided with additional weeks of unemployment compensation, for example, the result may be that they choose not to look for work. This would reduce production and aggregate supply from what it might have been if they had looked for work aggressively and succeeded in finding it.

 Federal Deficits and Federal Debt

a Before the Great Depression, the federal government normally spent only as much money as it collected in taxes, except in time of war. Since the 1930s the government has spent more than it received from taxes in most years. These annual deficits have accumulated over time to create a federal debt that totaled $6.8 trillion by 2003.

b In most years in the 1980s and 1990s, the federal deficit averaged about 4 percent of GDP. This trend was reversed between 1998 and 2001, when tax hikes of the early 1990s and reduced spending increases temporarily eliminated the annual deficits. A recession in 2001 triggered automatic stabilizers that increased the federal deficit. Bush's tax cuts to revive the economy also worsened the deficit after 2001.

c Deficit spending often has been linked to higher interest rates. When the federal government borrows additional money to fund a deficit, interest rates often have increased. These higher interest rates can discourage borrowing and spending by business and consumers.

d Some economists argue that the importance of the federal debt should be evaluated in terms of our nation's ability to carry it.

Review Economic Terms

Choose the term that best fits the definition. On separate paper, write the letter of the answer.

_____ 1. Private investment falls when higher government deficits drive up interest rates

_____ 2. The unemployment rate when the economy is producing its potential level of output

_____ 3. Congressional changes in spending or taxing to promote macroeconomic goals

_____ 4. The economy's maximum sustainable output in the long run

_____ 5. The time needed for changes in government policy to affect the economy

_____ 6. A group of laissez-faire economists, who believed that economic downturns were short-run problems that corrected themselves in the long run through natural market forces

_____ 7. The time needed to execute a change in government policy

_____ 8. Matching annual spending with annual revenue, except during war years

_____ 9. The time needed for the government to decide what to do once an economic problem has been identified

_____10. Any change in fiscal policy affects aggregate demand by more than the original change in spending or taxing

_____11. Government spending and taxing programs that, year after year, automatically reduce fluctuations in disposable income and thus in consumption over the business cycle

_____12. The time needed to identify a macroeconomic problem

_____13. Government spending stimulates private investment in an otherwise lifeless economy

a. **annually balanced budget**

b. **automatic stabilizers**

c. **classical economists**

d. **crowding in**

e. **crowding out**

f. **decision-making lag**

g. **discretionary fiscal policy**

h. **effectiveness lag**

i. **implementation lag**

j. **multiplier effect**

k. **natural rate of unemployment**

l. **potential output**

m. **recognition lag**

Review Economic Concepts

14. An economy's *potential output* is reached

   a. when there is no unemployment.

   b. at the natural rate of unemployment.

   c. when there is only cyclical unemployment.

   d. at the frictional rate of unemployment.

15. **True or False** Output can only exceed the potential rate in the short run.

16. When output is less than the potential rate, there is a(n) __?__ gap in the economy.

17. The *natural rate of unemployment* in the United States is estimated to fall between

   a. 2 and 3 percent.

   b. 3 and 4 percent.

   c. 4 and 5 percent.

   d. 5 and 6 percent.

18. *Classical economists* believed that the federal government should always have a(n) __?__ budget.

19. **True or False** *Classical economists* believed that in a recession prices, wages, and interest rates would fall, and this would bring the recession to an end.

20. Keynes developed a theory that was intended to address which problem during the Great Depression?

    a. unemployment

    b. inflation

    c. government deficits

    d. high interest rates

21. Keynes believed that the __?__ would cause an increase in government spending or reduction in taxes to have a larger impact on aggregate demand.

22. Which of the following is an automatic stabilizer for the economy?

    a. Congress decides to increase welfare benefits during a recession.

    b. An increase in income tax rates is passed by Congress during a period of inflation.

    c. More welfare compensation is paid because more people are unemployed in a recession.

    d. Congress decides to require people to work until they are 68 years old to collect their full Social Security benefit.

23. **True or False** According to Keynes, prices and wages are quite inflexible—they are "sticky."

24. Which of the following is an example of *discretionary fiscal policy*?

    a. Income tax payments grow during an economic expansion.

    b. Congress spends an extra $2 billion to provide jobs for unemployed workers.

    c. Fewer workers receive unemployment compensation payments in an expansion.

    d. More people apply for and receive welfare benefits in a recession.

25. **True or False** Keynes believed that it was necessary for the government to balance its budget in every year.

26. __?__ takes place when there are both high rates of inflation and high unemployment.

27. **True or False** Because of lags, it is difficult for the government to implement *discretionary fiscal policy* effectively.

28. Which of the following situations would indicate that the economy is below its *potential output*?

    a. Many workers have been laid off because of a decline in sales.

    b. A large number of construction workers are unemployed each February.

    c. In June, many graduating students spend several months looking for a job.

    d. There are many people who need to be trained to qualify for job openings.

29. The time that it takes the government to realize that there is a problem in the economy is called the __?__

30. The federal government accumulated most of its debt during the 20 years following

    a. 1920.

    b. 1940.

    c. 1960.

    d. 1980.

31. **True or False** Between 1946 and 2002, the federal debt held by the public as a percentage of GDP declined by about 10 percent.

32. **True or False** *Crowding out* refers to people and businesses choosing to borrow and spend less money because of higher interest rates that result from greater federal borrowing.

33. Gross debt refers to debt the federal government owes to itself, whereas debt held by the public refers to debt held by

    a. households and firms.

    b. non-profit institutions.

    c. foreign entities.

    d. all of the above.

Apply Economic Concepts

34. Evaluate Government Policy In the late 1970s, President Jimmy Carter and Congress expanded spending under the Comprehensive Employment and Training Act (CETA) to provide temporary employment to as many as 500,000 unemployed workers. Most of this money was made available to state and local governments that were supposed to hire and train workers so that they would eventually be able to find permanent employment working for private industry. Explain why this was an example of discretionary fiscal policy. How successful do you imagine this program was? Investigate the program at your library or online to find out whether your expectations were correct.

35. "Sticky" Wages Imagine that you are 20 years older and married with two children. You have purchased a car, a house, and furniture on credit. Most of your income goes to pay bills. You work for a business where you are a member of a union. Your contract states that you will be paid $13.50 per hour. Yesterday your employer announced that its sales have declined 30 percent and that if workers don't agree to a 15 percent pay cut, the business will lay off 10 percent of its employees and may fail in the next year. Would you agree to the pay cut? Explain your answer. Why are wages "sticky"?

36. Calculate the Impact of the Multiplier Effect In 1993, President Bill Clinton asked Congress to approve an additional $15 billion in spending to repair and upgrade the nation's highways. In addition to improving the nation's roads, President Clinton argued that this spending would increase output and employment in the economy. Assume that each person who received any of this extra spending as income would have spent 80 percent of it. Describe how the multiplier effect would have increased the total increase in spending to far more than the original $15 billion President Clinton wanted to spend. What does this show about the importance of changes in government spending?

37. Explain the Benefits of Unemployment Compensation When there is a downturn in the economy, unemployment grows and more workers receive unemployment compensation. How do these payments benefit workers who have not lost their jobs?

38. Evaluate a Proposed Constitutional Amendment Members of Congress have from time to time argued in favor of a constitutional amendment that would require the federal government to maintain a balanced budget except in times of war. Discuss whether you think this would be a good idea. Be sure to explain the reasons for your point of view.

39. Sharpen Your Life Skills: Graphs of Interest on the National Debt Interest on the national debt is an important part of the federal budget. The amount of this cost depends on the size of the federal debt and the interest rate the government pays on the debt. Use the data in the table to construct three pie graphs showing the part of the federal budget that was devoted to paying interest in 1950, 1980, and 2000. Why did this proportion of the budget first decline and then grow?

Payments on the National Debt as a Percent of the Federal Budget 1950, 1980, and 2000

Year	Interest Payment as a Percent of the Federal Budget
1950	14.51%
1980	8.89%
2000	12.47%

econxtra.swlearning.com

40. Access EconNews Online at econxtra. swlearning.com. Find the article under Fiscal Policy entitled "Promises, Promises." Read the article, and then write a sentence describing what the article says is the problem with Social Security. What did President Bush propose as a solution to this problem?

Money and Banking

Consider

Why are you willing to exchange a piece of paper bearing Alexander Hamilton's portrait and the number 10 in each corner for a pepperoni pizza?

Why is paper money more efficient than gold coins?

Why was a Montana bank willing to cash a check written on a clean but frayed pair of underpants?

How do banks create money?

When were thousands of different currencies circulating in the U.S. economy?

Why is there so much fascination with money, anyway?

POINT YOUR BROWSER

econxtra.swlearning.com

© Getty Images/PhotoDisc

Objectives

> Trace the evolution from barter to money.

> Describe the three functions of money.

> Identify the properties of ideal commodity money.

Overview

The word *money* comes from the name of the goddess in whose temple Rome's money was coined. Money has come to symbolize all personal and business finance. You can read *Money* magazine and the "Money" section of *USA Today*. You can watch TV shows such as *Moneyline* and visit hundreds of web sites about money, such as the web site of the federal agency that prints money (www.moneyfactory.com). With money, you can express your preferences—after all, money talks. When it talks, it says a lot, as in "Put your money where your mouth is" and "Show me the money."

Key Terms

medium of exchange

commodity money

[In the News]

● The Price of Admission to the Barter

Can you imagine Kevin Spacey, Meg Ryan, and Quentin Tarantino walking around with signs reading "Will work for food"? Well, many famous actors, actresses, and directors did just that during the Great Depression at the Barter Theatre in Abingdon, Virginia. Created in 1933 under the Depression-era "Will Work for Food" program, the Barter was founded by a troupe of unemployed actors who headed south from New York to offer live theater in exchange for produce. With an original admission price equivalent to 35 cents in barter, the first ticket was purchased with a pig. Community members, including a local barber, provided services as well in return for tickets. Tradition has it that the first season ended with a net profit of $4.35 and a total weight gain among the players of some 300 pounds. Today, cash generally has replaced produce as the medium of exchange at the Barter. Nonetheless, in a recent season, non-perishable food items were accepted as payment of admission for several performances and donated to a local food bank.

Think About It

Why was barter originally used at the Barter Theatre? Why do you think cash eventually replaced barter as the main admission medium?

The Evolution of Money

In the beginning, there was no money. The earliest families were self-sufficient. Each produced all it consumed and consumed all it produced, so there was no need for exchange. Without exchange, there was no need for money. When specialization first emerged, as some families farmed the land and others went hunting, farmers and hunters began to trade. Thus, the specialization of labor resulted in exchange. The kinds of goods people traded were limited enough that they easily could exchange their products directly for other products. This is a system called *barter,* which you read about in Chapter 2.

Problems with Barter

As long as specialization was limited to just a few goods, mutually beneficial trades were relatively easy to discover. As the economy developed, however, greater specialization increased the kinds of goods produced. As the variety of goods increased, so did the difficulty of finding mutually beneficial trades. For example, a heart surgeon in a barter economy would have to find people willing to accept a heart operation in exchange for what the surgeon wanted. Barterers also had to agree on an exchange rate. Negotiating such exchanges every time the surgeon

needed to buy something would prove difficult and time consuming. *Greater specialization increased the transaction costs of barter.*

A huge difference in the values of the units to be exchanged also made barter difficult. For example, suppose a hunter wanted to buy a home that exchanged for 2,000 hides. A hunter would be hard-pressed to find a home seller in need of that many hides.

The Birth of Money

The high transaction costs of barter gave birth to money. Nobody actually recorded the emergence of money, so we can only speculate about how it developed. Through barter experience, traders may have found that certain goods always had ready buyers. If a trader could not find a good that he or she desired, some good with a ready market could be accepted instead.

Thus, traders began to accept certain goods not for personal use but because the goods were readily accepted by others and so could be held for exchange later. For example, corn might become accepted because traders knew that corn was always in demand. As one good became generally accepted in return for all other goods, that good began to function as money. *Money is anything that is widely accepted in exchange for goods and services.*

CHECKPOINT
How did money evolve from barter?

Three Functions of Money

Money fulfills three important functions: it is a *medium of exchange,* a *unit of account,* and a *store of value.*

Medium of Exchange

If a society, by luck or by design, can find one good that everyone will accept in exchange for whatever is sold,

TEAM WORK

Working with a partner, role-play a barter situation. One partner will have a portable radio to barter. The other student will barter another item or items for the radio. After completing your role-play barter, compare your results with those of other students. Were the items bartered for the radios of comparable value?

traders can save time, disappointment, and sheer aggravation. Suppose corn plays this role—a role that clearly goes beyond its role as food. Corn becomes a medium of exchange because it is accepted in exchange by all buyers and sellers, whether or not they want corn to eat. A **medium of exchange** is anything that is generally accepted in payment for goods and services sold. The person who accepts corn in exchange for some product believes corn can be used later to purchase whatever is desired.

In this example, corn is both a *commodity* and *money*, so corn is called **commodity money**. The earliest money was commodity money. Gold and silver have served as money for at least 4,000 years. Cattle were used as money, first by the Greeks, and then by the Romans. In fact, the word *pecuniary* (meaning "of or relating to money") derives from the Latin word for cattle, *pecus*. Salt also served as money. Roman soldiers received part of their pay in salt. The salt portion was called the *salarium*, the origin of the word *salary*.

Commodity money used at various times included wampum (polished shells strung together) and tobacco in colonial America, tea pressed into small cakes in Russia, and palm dates in North Africa.

Unit of Account

As one commodity, such as corn, became widely accepted, it also served as a *unit of account,* a standard on which to base prices. The price of shoes or pots or hides could be measured in bushels of corn. Thus, corn became a common denominator, a yardstick, for measuring the value of all goods and services. Rather than having to determine the exchange rate between each good and every other good, as was the case in a barter economy, buyers and sellers could price everything using a common measure, such as corn.

Store of Value

Because people do not want to buy something every time they sell something, the purchasing power acquired

What are the functions of money?

medium of exchange

Anything generally accepted by all parties in payment for goods or services

commodity money

Anything that serves both as money and as a commodity, such as gold

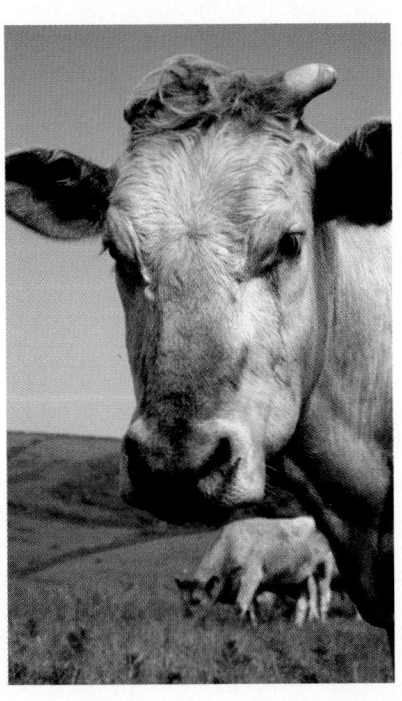

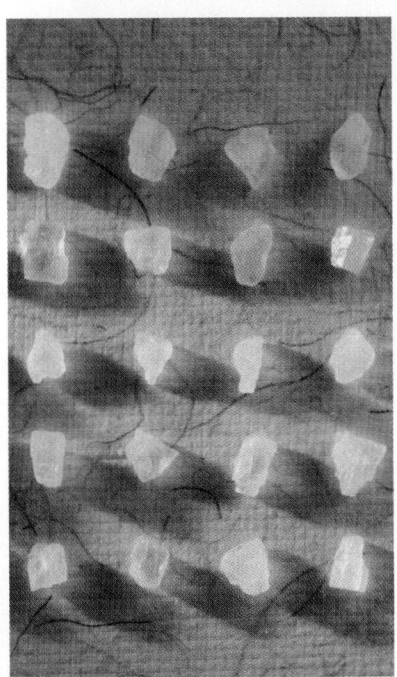

© Getty Images/PhotoDisc

Why were cattle, salt, and corn all useful as commodity money?

through a sale must somehow be preserved. Money serves as a *store of value* when it retains purchasing power over time. The better it preserves its purchasing power, the better money serves as a store of value.

To understand the store-of-value function of money, consider the distinction between a stock and a flow. A *stock* is an amount measured at a particular point in time, such as the amount of food in your refrigerator this morning, or the amount of money you have with you right now. In contrast, a *flow* is an amount received or expended within a period of time, such as the calories you consume per day, or the income you earn per week.

Income has little meaning unless the period is specified. For example, you would not know whether to be impressed that a friend earns $300 unless you know whether this is earnings per week, per day, or per hour. Don't confuse money with income. *Money* is a stock measure, and *income* is a flow measure.

CHECKPOINT
What are three functions of money?

Commodity Money

The introduction of commodity money reduced the transaction costs of exchange compared with barter. Commodity money does involve some transaction costs, however.

Limitations of Commodity Money

The ideal money is durable, portable, divisible, of uniform quality, has a low opportunity cost, does not fluctuate wildly in value, and is in limited supply. The ideals are brought to life in Figure 16.1. As you will see, most commodity money falls short of these ideals.

Durable

If the commodity money is perishable, as is corn, it must be properly stored or its quality deteriorates. Even then, it won't last long. The ideal money is *durable*.

Portable

If the commodity money is bulky, exchanges for major purchases can become unwieldy. For example, if a new home cost 5,000 bushels of corn, many cartloads of corn would be needed to purchase that home. The ideal money is *portable*.

Divisible

Some commodity money is not easily divisible into smaller units. For example, when cattle served as money, any price involving a fraction of a cow posed an exchange problem. The ideal money is *divisible*.

Uniform Quality

If commodity money like corn is valued equally in exchange, regardless of quality, people will keep the best corn and trade away the rest. Over time, the quality remaining in circulation deteriorates and becomes less acceptable. The ideal money is of *uniform quality*.

Low Opportunity Cost

Commodity money usually ties up valuable resources, so it has a relatively high opportunity cost compared with, say, paper money. For example, corn that is used for money cannot at the same time be used as food. The ideal money has a *low opportunity cost*.

Supply or Demand Must Not Fluctuate Erratically

The supply and demand of commodity money determine the prices of all other goods. A record harvest would increase the supply of corn. An increase in the popularity of corn as food would increase the demand for corn. Each would alter the price level measured in corn. Erratic fluctuations in the supply or demand for corn limit its usefulness as money, particularly as a unit of account and as a store of value.

The ideal money is durable, portable, divisible, of uniform quality, has a low opportunity cost, does not fluctuate wildly in value, and is in limited supply.

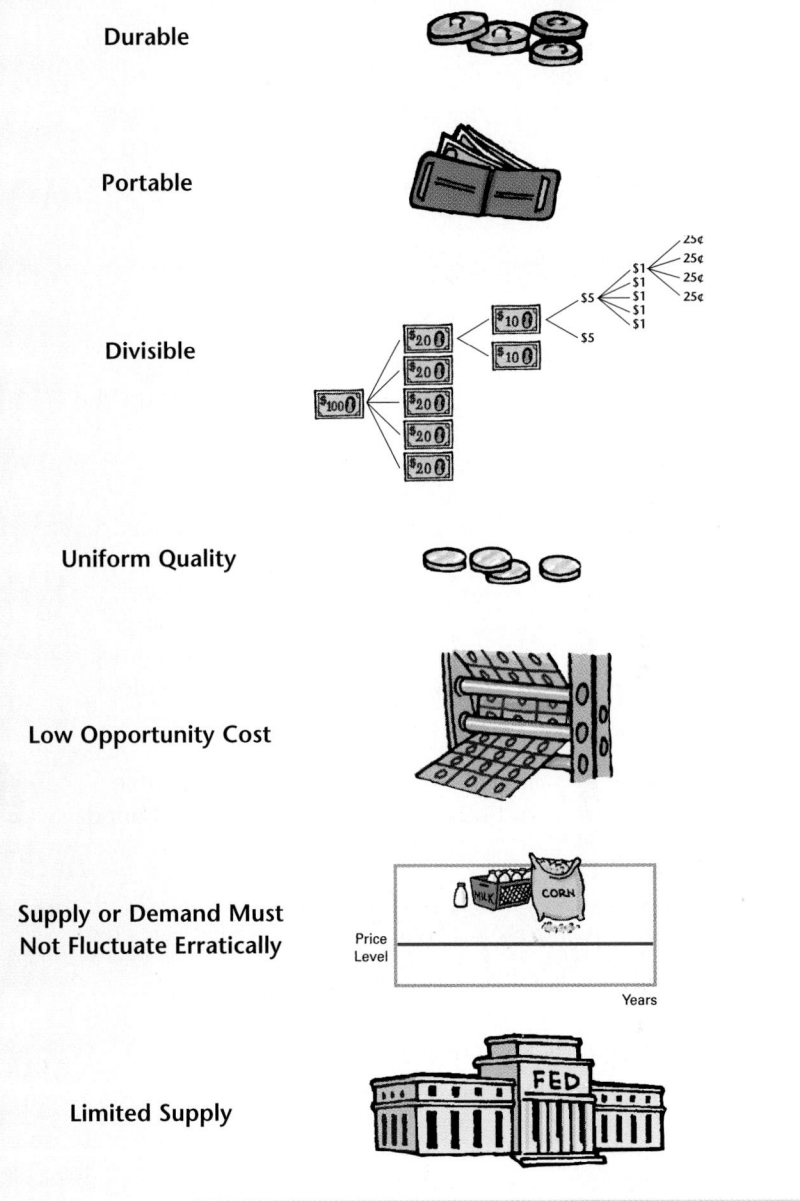

Durable

Portable

Divisible

Uniform Quality

Low Opportunity Cost

Supply or Demand Must Not Fluctuate Erratically

Limited Supply

The supply or demand for the ideal money *should not fluctuate wildly*.

Limited Supply

Because the value of money depends on its limited supply, anything that can be gathered or produced easily would not serve well as commodity money. For example, tree leaves or common rocks would not serve well as commodity money. The ideal money should be in *limited supply*.

Coins

Measuring a unit of commodity money often was quite natural, as in a bushel of corn or a head of cattle. When rock salt served as money, it was cut into bricks. Because salt was usually of consistent quality, a trader could simply count the bricks to determine the amount of money. However, when silver and gold were used as money, both their quantity and quality were open to question. When these precious metals were combined with cheaper metals, their quality lessened. Thus, the quantity and the quality of the metal had to be determined with each exchange.

This quality-control problem was solved by coining silver and gold. *Coinage determined both the amount and quality of the metal.* The earliest known coins appeared in the seventh century B.C. in Asia Minor to assist sea trade. The use of coins allowed payment by count rather than by weight. Coins were attractive because they were durable and easy to carry. They also contained

precious metals, so they were intrinsically valuable. The table on which money was counted during this era came to be called the *counter,* a term still used today.

Originally, the power to coin was vested in the feudal lord, or *seignior.* If the exchange value of the coin exceeded the cost of making it, minting coins became a source of revenue to the seignior. Revenue earned from coinage is called *seigniorage* (pronounced "seen´-your-edge").

Token money is money whose exchange value exceeds the cost of production. Coins and paper money now in circulation in the United States are token money. For example, a quarter (a 25-cent coin) costs the U.S. Mint only about 4 cents to make. Coin production alone nets the federal government more than $500 million per year in seigniorage. Paper money is a far greater source of seigniorage, as you will learn later.

CHECKPOINT
What seven properties would the ideal commodity money exhibit?

Ethics in Action

Identity Theft—Revisited People who steal the identities of others basically have one motive—that is, to steal money. This crime can be carried out in a variety of ways. One common means is someone pulling the mail from your unlocked mailbox and sending in for a credit card in your name to be sent to a "new" address. You are eventually sued for nonpayment of the bills that result. Your credit standing may suffer, perhaps permanently. According to the FTC, more than 10 million instances of such identify theft occurred during a recent year. Much of the increase in these numbers is due to the use of the Internet and fraudulent phone solicitations. What's to be done? One avenue of approach for the victims is to contact the Identity Theft Resource Center

(ITRC), a nationally recognized business operated by the Foley family of San Diego, California. The Foleys feel a moral duty to assist those who call or read the warnings posted on their web site. They have organized former victims into a volunteer support and legislative lobbying network. The Foleys also serve as a resource for legislation intended to curtail this "fastest-growing crime in the United States."

Think Critically

According to the ITRC web site, "the burden of proving innocence rests on the shoulders of the victim." Why do you think this is so? What can you do to keep your identity from being stolen? How can you help others from being victimized?

Key Concepts

1. Why could it be difficult for you to exchange your collection of 500 CDs for a good-quality used car in a world with no money?

2. Why have wheat and corn been used as commodity money in the past while strawberries and lettuce have not?

3. On the Pacific island of Yap, commodity money took the form of donut-shaped pieces of stone that could weigh one ton or more. In what ways did these stones fall short of being ideal forms of money?

4. At times in history the value of the gold or silver in coins has been greater than the face value of the coins themselves. What did this give people an incentive to do? How would this have affected the economy?

5. What would happen if there were more than one type of commodity money in use—one that people trusted to hold its value and one that they did not? If you had some of both types of money, which would you spend and which would you save? How would this affect the economy?

Graphing Exercise

6. Fred has an electric saw he would like to trade for a tire for his boat trailer. Mary has a tire for a boat trailer that she would be willing to trade for an electric lawn mower. Rachel has an electric lawn mower she would like to trade for a portable TV. Tony has a portable TV he would be willing to trade for an electric saw. Draw a chart that shows the trades that must take place for each of these people to obtain the product he or she wants. Explain why barter is not an efficient way to carry out complicated transactions.

Think Critically

7. **History** When gold and silver coins were the primary type of money in circulation, merchants often weighed the coins before accepting them. Why do you think they did this? What problem of using gold or silver coins as money does this situation demonstrate?

8. **English** You probably have either read or seen a televison production of *A Christmas Carol,* a short novel written by Charles Dickens, published in 1843. In his book, Dickens told the story of Ebenezer Scrooge, a miser who accumulated wealth more for the sake of having money than to be able to use it to buy goods or services. Scrooge was regarded by all who knew him as a sour old man who hated everything about Christmas. His lack of charity kept even the poorest of the poor from asking him for help. However, after being visited by the ghosts of Christmas Past, Christmas Present, and Christmas Yet to Come, Scrooge came to view his wealth in a different way. Write an essay in which you identify and explain Scrooge's original point of view about the three functions of money (medium of exchange, unit of account, and store of value). How did the the three Christmas ghosts change his perspective on money? If you have never read this publication, it can be found in almost every library or online, and it is only 124 pages long.

Objectives

> Describe how the earliest banks made loans.

> Based on whom they lend to, identify two types of depository institutions.

> Explain when and why the Federal Reserve System was created.

Overview

The word *bank* comes from the Italian word for bench, *banca*. Italian moneychangers originally conducted their business on benches. Banking spread from Italy to England, where London goldsmiths offered people "safekeeping" for their gold, or money. When people needed to make purchases, they would visit the goldsmith to withdraw some money. Deposits by some people tended to offset withdrawals by others, so the amount of money in the goldsmith's vault remained relatively constant over time. Goldsmiths found they could earn interest by lending some of these idle deposits. Today's banks still earn a profit by lending some of the money deposited with them.

Key Terms

check

fractional reserve banking system

representative money

fiat money

commercial banks

Federal Reserve System (the Fed)

reserves

discount rate

Federal Open Market Committee (FOMC)

open-market operations

[In the News]

● Will Gold Return as a World Currency?

After three quarters of a century without it, the Muslim world and its bankers are considering creating a currency of their own to rival the dollar and the euro. The currency would be in the form of the gold *dinar*, a coin that had been used for almost 1,500 years but then dropped from circulation in 1924. National paper currencies would still be allowed. However, the central banks of the various Muslim countries on the gold standard would settle the differences in their trade accounts by shifting gold from the debtor to the creditor country's account in a bank. Currently such settling of accounts is done in either dollars or euros. The return to gold is being advocated by many countries that believe the United States has an unfair advantage when the dollar is used for such purposes. The change also may protect against problems like the 1997 currency crisis that swept Asia, seemingly as a result of currency speculation. The potential for such speculation would be reduced greatly by tying paper currencies to something with real value—like gold. Paper currency has value only if its users believe it will continue to be accepted for trade in goods and services.

Think About It

What practical problems might occur if all paper currencies were replaced with precious metals like gold and silver?

The Earliest Banks

Keeping money, such as gold coins, on deposit with a goldsmith was safer than carrying it around or leaving it at home, where it could be easily stolen. Still, visiting the goldsmith every time one needed money was a nuisance. For example, a farmer might visit the goldsmith to withdraw enough gold to buy a horse. The farmer would then pay the horse trader, who would promptly deposit the receipts with the goldsmith. Thus, money made a round trip from goldsmith to farmer to horse trader, back to goldsmith.

Bank Checks

Depositors eventually grew tired of visiting the goldsmith every time they needed cash. They began writing notes instructing the goldsmith to pay someone, such as the horse trader, a given amount from the depositor's account. This payment amounted to moving gold from one stack (the farmer's) to another (the horse trader's). These written instructions to the goldsmith were the first bank checks. A **check** is a written order for the bank to pay money from amounts deposited.

Checks have since become official-looking instruction forms. However, they need not be, as evidenced by the actions of a Montana man who paid his speeding fine by writing a payment instruction on a clean but frayed pair of underpants. The Western Federal Savings and Loan of Missoula cashed the check.

Bank Loans

By combining the ideas of cash loans and checks, the goldsmith soon discovered how to make loans by check. Rather than lend idle cash, the goldsmith could simply create a checking account for the borrower. *The goldsmith could extend a loan by creating an account against which the borrower could write checks. In this way goldsmiths, or banks, were able to create a medium of exchange—to*

"create money." This money, based only on an entry in the bank's ledger, was accepted because of the public's confidence that the bank would honor these checks.

The total claims against the bank consisted of claims by people who had deposited their gold plus claims by people for whom the bank had created deposits. So both groups were depositors. Because the claims by those with deposits at the bank exceeded the value of gold on reserve, this was the beginning of a **fractional reserve banking system**. In this system, the goldsmith's reserves amounted to just a fraction of the claims by depositors.

The *reserve ratio* measures bank reserves as a share of deposits. For example, if the goldsmith had gold reserves valued at $40,000 but deposits totaling $100,000, the reserve ratio would be 40 percent.

Bank Notes

Another way early banks could create money was by issuing bank notes. *Bank notes* were pieces of paper promising the bearer a specific amount of gold or silver when the notes were redeemed at the issuing bank. In London, goldsmiths introduced bank notes about the same time they introduced checks. *Checks could be redeemed for gold only if endorsed by the payee. Bank notes, however, could be redeemed for gold by anyone who presented them to the issuing bank.*

A bank note was "as good as gold," because the bearer could redeem it for gold. In fact, this paper money was more convenient than gold because it was more portable. Bank notes that exchanged for a specific commodity, such as gold, were called **representative money**. The paper money *represented* gold in the bank's vault. Initially, these promises to pay were issued by banks. Over time, governments took a larger role in printing and circulating bank notes.

Fiat Money

Once representative money became widely accepted, governments began issuing **fiat money** (pronounced "fee´at"). Fiat money is not redeemable

---

fractional reserve banking system

Only a portion of bank deposits is backed by reserves

check

A written order instructing the bank to pay someone from an amount deposited

representative money

Bank notes that exchange for a specific commodity, such as gold

fiat money

Money not redeemable for anything of intrinsic value; declared money by government decree

for anything of intrinsic value, such as silver or gold. Fiat money is money because the government says it is. People came to accept fiat money because they believed that others would accept it as well. You can think of fiat money as mere paper money. The currency issued by the U.S government and nearly all other governments throughout world today is fiat money.

A well-regulated system of fiat money is more efficient than commodity money or even representative money. Fiat money requires only some paper and a printing press. (Both $1 notes and $100 notes cost about 5 cents each to print). Commodity money and representative money, however, tie up more valuable resources, such as gold.

CHECKPOINT
How did the earliest banks make loans?

commercial banks

Depository institutions that make loans primarily to businesses

Depository Institutions

Banks evolved from London goldsmiths into a wide variety of institutions that respond to the economy's demand for financial services. *Depository institutions* accept deposits from the public and make loans from these deposits. These institutions, modern-day versions of the London goldsmith, are classified broadly into commercial banks and thrift institutions.

Commercial Banks

Commercial banks are the oldest, largest, and most diversified of depository institutions. They are called **commercial banks** because historically they lent primarily to *commercial* ventures, or businesses, rather than to households. There are about 8,000 commercial banks in the United States, holding more than two-thirds of all

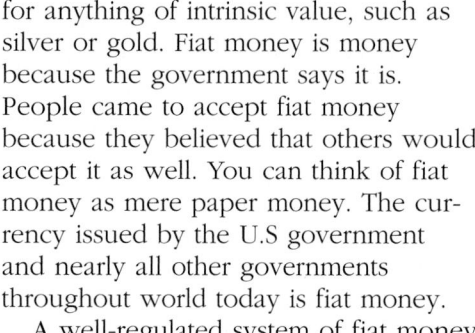

Main Idea

Role of Economic Institutions

Banks evolved from London goldsmiths into a wide variety of institutions that help individuals and groups accomplish their financial goals. What are the two broad classifications of depository institutions?

© Getty Images/PhotoDisc

Internet Banking: Full Service or Self-Help?

Consumers would be well advised to comparison shop before choosing an Internet bank. A recent study indicated that Internet banking service providers know that their users often do not have a chance to compare services and ease of use before setting up their accounts. As a result, some banks offer only the bare necessities, such as account history statements and fund transfers between accounts. However, the top sites in the survey were found to offer much more. For example, those on the cutting edge provide the customer not only with bill-payment services but also with a system of account alerts to warn the depositor of upcoming financial deadlines, loan deals, and potential overdrafts. Other features typically offered at no additional charge include online statements, automatically filled-out loan applications, and document image archives so you can download a copy of that disputed check. In short, consumers can receive a lot of enhancements that both aid and protect them—if they do their homework.

Think Critically

Can you think of some other services that banks might offer online? Would the services mentioned above make a difference to you in choosing an online bank? Why or why not?

---

bank deposits. Until 1980, commercial banks were the only depository institutions that offered demand deposits, or checking accounts. *Demand deposits* are so named because a depositor with such an account can write a check *demanding* those deposits.

Thrifts

Thrift institutions, or *thrifts,* include savings and loan associations, mutual savings banks, and credit unions. Historically, savings and loan associations and mutual savings banks specialized in making home mortgage loans. Credit unions, which tend to be small, account for most thrifts. They extend loans only to their "members" to finance homes or other major consumer purchases, such as new cars.

Dual Banking System

Before 1863, commercial banks in the United States were chartered, or authorized, by the states in which they operated, so they were called *state banks.* These banks, like the English gold-smiths, issued bank notes. Thousands of different notes circulated at the same time, and nearly all were redeemable for gold.

The National Banking Act of 1863 and its later amendments created a new system of federally chartered banks

Investigate Your Local Economy

Research a depository institution in your area to learn something about its history. When was it established, and by whom? In which category of depository institution does it fit now? Write a one-page report explaining your findings.

called *national banks.* Only national banks were authorized to issue notes and were regulated by the Office of the Comptroller of the Currency, part of the U.S. Treasury. The state banks survived by substituting checks for notes. To this day, the United States has a *dual banking system* consisting of both state banks and national banks.

CHECKPOINT
Based on whom they lend to, what are the two types of depository institutions?

The Federal Reserve System

During the nineteenth century, the economy experienced a number of panic "runs" on banks by depositors seeking to withdraw their funds. A panic was usually set off by the failure of some prominent bank. As depositors became alarmed, they tried to withdraw their money. But they couldn't because each bank held only a fraction of its deposits as reserves, using the rest to earn interest, as in making loans.

Birth of the Federal Reserve System

The failure of a large New York City bank set off the Panic of 1907. During this banking calamity, thousands of depositors lost their savings and many businesses failed. The situation so aroused public wrath that Congress began developing what would become the **Federal Reserve System**, or **the Fed** for short. The Fed was established in 1913 as the central bank and monetary authority of the United States.

By that time nearly all industrialized countries had established central banks, such as the Bundesbank in Germany, the Bank of Japan, and the Bank of England. The American public's suspicion of monopolies initially led to the establishment of 12 separate banks in 12 Federal Reserve districts around the country. The banks were named after the cities in which they were located—the Federal Reserve Banks of Boston, New York, Chicago, San Francisco, and so on, as shown in Figure 16.2. Later legislation passed during the Great Depression left the 12 Reserve Banks in place but centralized the power of the Federal Reserve System with a Board of Governors in Washington.

All national banks became members of the Federal Reserve System and were thus subject to new regulations. For state banks, membership was voluntary. Most state banks did not join the Federal Reserve System because they did not want to face tighter regulations.

Powers of the Federal Reserve System

The founding legislation directed the Federal Reserve Board of Governors "to exercise general supervision" over the Federal Reserve System to ensure sufficient money and credit in the banking system. The power to issue bank notes was taken away from national banks and turned over to the Federal Reserve Banks. (Take a look at paper currency and you will read "FEDERAL RESERVE NOTE" across the top.) These notes actually are printed by the U.S. Bureau of Printing and Engraving, which is part of the U.S. Treasury. The Treasury prints the notes, but the Fed has responsibility for putting them into circulation.

Federal Reserve Banks do not deal with the public directly. Each may be thought of as a bankers' bank. Reserve Banks hold deposits for member banks, just as commercial banks and thrifts hold deposits for the public. The name "Reserve Bank" comes from the responsibility to hold member-bank *reserves* on deposit.

Reserves consist of cash that banks have on hand in their vaults or on deposit with Reserve Banks. By holding reserves of member banks, a Reserve Bank can clear a check written by a depositor at one bank, such as Citibank, and deposited in another bank, such as your bank. This check-clearance process

Federal Reserve System (Fed)

Established in 1913 as the central bank and monetary authority of the United States

reserves

Cash that banks have on hand in their vaults or on deposit with the Federal Reserve

is, on a larger scale, much like the gold-smith's moving gold from the farmer's pile to the horse trader's pile.

Reserve Banks also extend loans to member banks. The interest rate charged for these loans is called the **discount rate**. By making loans to banks, the Fed can increase reserves in the banking system.

Directing Monetary Policy

The Federal Reserve's Board of Governors is responsible for setting and carrying out the nation's monetary policy. *Monetary policy,* as you will recall, is the regulation of the economy's money supply and interest rates to promote macroeconomic objectives such as full employment, price stability, and economic growth.

The Board of Governors consists of seven members appointed by the president and confirmed by the Senate. Each governor serves one 14-year nonrenewable term, with one member appointed every two years. One is also appointed to chair the Board of Governors for a four-year renewable term. Board members tend to be economists. In 2003, six of the seven Governors, including Chairman Alan Greenspan, held Ph.D.s in economics.

NETBookmark

For an online introduction to the Federal Reserve System, access the New York Federal Reserve Bank web site through econxtra.swlearning.com. This site provides a very readable overview of the Fed's structure and operations. Read the article under "About the Fed." Then make a list of activities that sets the New York Federal Reserve Bank apart from the other district banks in the system.

econxtra.swlearning.com

Board membership is relatively stable because a new U.S. president can be sure of appointing or reappointing only two members in a presidential term. *The Board structure is designed to insulate monetary authorities from pressure by elected officials.*

Federal Open Market Committee

Originally, the power of the Federal Reserve System was vested in each of the 12 Reserve Banks. Later reforms established the **Federal Open Market Committee (FOMC)** to consolidate decisions regarding the most important

discount rate
Interest rate the Fed charges banks that borrow reserves

Federal Open Market Committee (FOMC)
Twelve-member group that makes decisions about open-market operations

The Twelve Federal Reserve Districts

Figure 16.2

The twelve Federal Reserve districts are named after the cities in which they are located. Which district are you in?

Source: Federal Reserve Board.

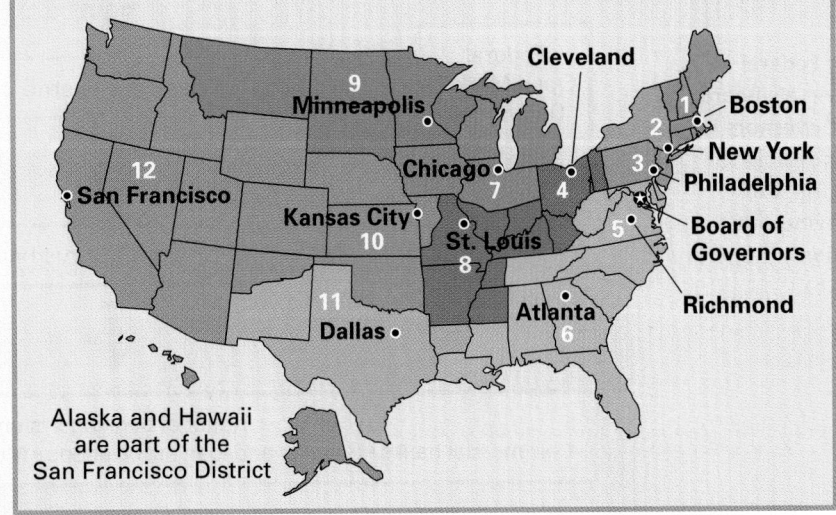

Alaska and Hawaii are part of the San Francisco District

open-market operations

Buying or selling U.S. government securities as a way of regulating the money supply

© Getty Images/PhotoDisc

The FOMC is required to meet at least four times each year in Washington, D.C. What tool of monetary policy is this group responsible for implementing?

tool of monetary policy—open-market operations. **Open-market operations** consist of buying or selling U.S. government securities to influence the money supply and interest rates in the economy.

The FOMC consists of the seven Board Governors plus 5 of the 12 presidents of the Reserve Banks. The chair of the Board of Governors heads the FOMC. The organizational structure of the Federal Reserve System as it now stands is presented in Figure 16.3. The FOMC and, less significantly, the Federal Advisory Committee advise the Board of Governors. The Federal Advisory Committee consists of one commercial banker from each of the 12 Reserve Bank districts.

 CHECKPOINT
When and why was the Federal Reserve System created?

Organization Chart for the Federal Reserve System

Figure 16.3

The Federal Reserve's Board of Governors is responsible for setting and carrying out the nation's monetary policy.

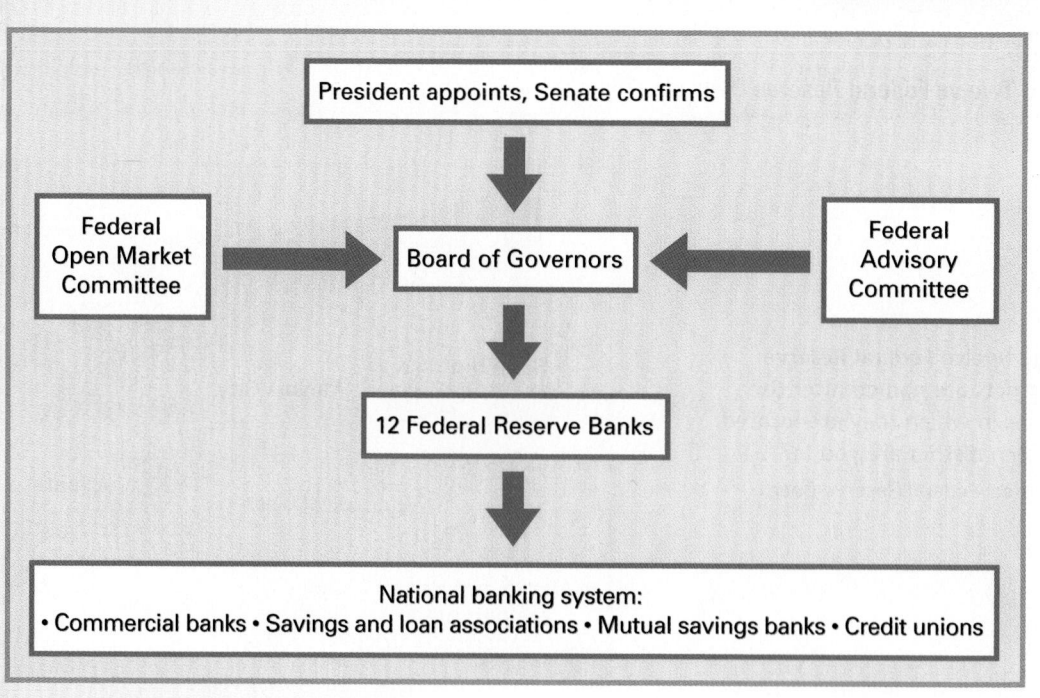

President appoints, Senate confirms

Federal Open Market Committee → Board of Governors ← Federal Advisory Committee

12 Federal Reserve Banks

National banking system:
• Commercial banks • Savings and loan associations • Mutual savings banks • Credit unions

Key Concepts

Xtra!
Study Tools
econxtra.swlearning.com

1. How would you feel about taking $10,000 in cash to an automobile dealership to purchase a used car? Why might you prefer to complete this type of transaction with a bank check instead?

2. Why are banks able to keep only 10 percent of checking deposits on reserve and still be reasonably sure that they will be able to pay all checks presented for payment?

3. Why are you willing to accept Federal Reserve Notes (fiat money) in payment for your labor? Remember, these notes are backed by nothing other than the government's statement that they are money.

4. Why is it important to the economy that people who save and deposit money in banks can be sure that they will be able to withdraw their savings at anytime in the future without suffering a loss?

5. How may banks obtain extra cash on short notice if the need arises?

Graphing Exercise

6. Although there were more than 8,000 commercial banks in the United States at the beginning of the twenty-first century, most of these banks were relatively small. Most of the business in the banking industry was dominated by a few large banks. Use data in the table to construct a double bar graph that shows the number of commercial banks of different sizes and the amount of assets held by each-size group in 2001. Do you think the smaller banks could compete successfully with the larger banks? Why might some of these banks merge in the future?

Commercial Banks by Asset Size, 2001

Asset Size of Banks	Number of Banks in Group	Total Assets for Group in Billions of Dollars
Less than $5.0 million	30	$ 0.1
$5.0 – $9.9 million	98	$ 0.8
$10.0 – $24.9 million	746	$ 13.6
$25.0 – $49.9 million	1,548	$ 58.2
$50.0 – $99.9 million	2,062	$ 148.8
$100.0 – $499.9 million	2,861	$ 592.0
$500.0 – $999.9 million	335	$ 227.6
$1.0 – $2.9 billion	219	$ 362.8
$3.0 billion and more	181	$5,165.4

Source: *Statistical Abstract of the United States*, 2002, p. 722.

Think Critically

7. **Government** Investigate the Banking Act of 1935 to find out how the creation of the Board of Governors changed the nature of the Federal Reserve System. Why do you think the government was willing to concentrate so much economic power in the hands of only seven people?

Early Banking
in the United States

When Alexander Hamilton approved the charter of the First Bank of the United States, there were only three commercial banks in the country. The Bank was 20 percent owned by the government. It immediately functioned as a central bank with a stabilizing influence on the nation's economy, especially in controlling the over-issuance of private bank notes. Still, many distrusted such a large institution. In 1811, its charter failed to be renewed by only one vote. The lapse was short lived, as the War of 1812 demonstrated to many in government the need for a strong central bank. In 1816, the Second Bank of the United States, chartered under the same basic rules, was formed.

The Second Bank of the United States also was unpopular in some parts of the country. For many, the bank seemed to serve the wealthy Eastern establishment at the expense of the Southern and Western parts of the country. When Andrew Jackson became president in 1829, he brought with him a dislike of banks in general and the Second Bank of the United States in particular. Rather than wait for the Bank's charter to expire in 1836, supporters of the bank pushed for renewal in 1832. It passed Congress, but Jackson vetoed the bill. Wanting to "kill the monster" (the bank), he ordered the government to begin to deposit its funds into various state-chartered banks, or "pet banks." The Second Bank of the United States, devoid of government deposits, limped along until 1849, when it finally went out of business.

Without the restraint imposed by a central bank, banks began to issue too much currency, and so the value of each piece of currency fell. By 1836, Jackson had become alarmed that government debts were being paid in currency of declining value. He ordered the Specie Circular, which stated that government debts could be paid only in hard currency—or in gold or silver coins. The result was a contraction of the money supply and the "Panic of 1837."

Nationally, Jackson's actions marked the beginning of what is called the "free banking era." Hundreds of state-chartered banks sprang up around the country. Many of these banks were established in such out-of-the-way places that they were called "wildcat banks." Each loosely controlled bank issued its own currency, thus flooding the nation with more than 9,000 denominations and types. People had no way of telling if a particular currency was sound or not. They resorted to "note detectors," which rated the currency according to the soundness of the bank that issued it. This caused many merchants to refuse to accept currency coming from outside their state or region.

The banking and currency problems were left unaddressed until the Civil War forced the passage of the National Banking Act. It wasn't until 1913, with the passage of the Glass-Stegall Act, that the country formed a new central bank, The Federal Reserve.

THINK CRITICALLY

Even today, historians debate Jackson's actions. Based on your understanding of banks and banking, examine Jackson's opposition to the Second Bank of the United States and his support for "hard money." Were his concerns valid and his veto justified? Are the same concerns about central banking and currency relevant today? Why or why not?

Objectives

> Describe the narrow definition of money.

> Explain why distinctions among definitions of money have become less meaningful over time.

Overview

When you think of money, what comes to mind is currency—notes and coins. Notes and coins, however, are only part of the money supply. If you deposit this currency in a checking account or a bank extends you a loan by creating a checking account deposit, the amount in that checking account also is money. Currency and checking accounts are money because each serves as a medium of exchange, a unit of account, and a store of value. Some other bank accounts also perform the store-of-value function and sometimes can be readily converted into cash. These bank accounts are viewed as money, based on a broader definition.

Key Terms

M1

checkable deposits

M2

[In the News]

● Traveler's Checks Go Electronic

As of October 2003, American Express, the largest and most well known issuer of traveler's checks, began issuing traveler's cards. The result of extensive focus-group research, the cards combine the safety of traveler's checks with the convenience of plastic. Unlike debit or credit cards, the new cards are not tied to an individual's bank or credit card account. Instead they are similar to a phone card; but in place of user minutes, the travel card is loaded with a particular amount of cash. It can then be reloaded from American Express locations around the world. Thus, currency you receive in a transaction overseas can be placed in a safe travel-card account and be accessible for later transactions without the risk of personally carrying the cash. In addition, and unlike regular credit or debit cards, the cards will be replaced in 24 hours if lost or stolen.

Think About It

With traveler's cards available, would you still want to carry traveler's checks on a trip overseas? Why or why not?

Narrow Definition of Money: M1

M1

The narrowest definition of the money supply; consists of currency (including coins) held by the nonbanking public, checkable deposits, and traveler's checks

Money aggregates are various measures of the money supply. The narrowest definition, called **M1**, consists of currency (including coins) held by the nonbanking public, checkable deposits, and traveler's checks. The money supply at any given time is a stock measure, just as is the amount of cash you have with you right now.

NETBookmark

Visit the U.S. Treasury Department web site for information about currency through econxtra.swlearning.com. Click on one of the "Latest Press Releases" links. Write a paragraph about the currency-related news reported in the press release.

econxtra.swlearning.com

SPAN THE GLOBE

Show Me the Dollar

Most Americans do not realize that more than half the dollars in circulation are held overseas. According to recent Federal Reserve figures, the amount of U.S. currency available for use around the world, including in the United States itself, was approximately $1,288 billion. Of that amount, about $620 billion was in general circulation in private hands outside banks and other financial institutions. Between $340 billion and $370 billion of the $620 billion was in use overseas. The number of dollars held outside the United States is approximately 15 to 20 times the number of Japanese yen held outside Japan and about 5 times the number of euros held outside Europe. The rate of counterfeiting, approximately one in every 10,000 bills, was approximately the same whether held in the United States or outside the country.

Think Critically

Why do you think the dollar is such a popular currency around the world? Do you think this helps the United States? Why or why not?

Currency in Circulation

Dollar bills and coins in circulation are part of the money supply as narrowly defined. Money in bank vaults or on deposit at the Fed is not being used as a medium of exchange and so is not counted in the money supply. Currency makes up about half of M1.

The paper currency circulating in the United States consists of Federal Reserve notes. These notes are issued by, and are liabilities of, the Federal Reserve System. Because Federal Reserve notes are redeemable for nothing other than more Federal Reserve notes, they are fiat money. The other component of currency is coins. Like paper money, U.S. coins are token money because their intrinsic value is less than their exchange value.

U.S. Currency Abroad

More than half of all Federal Reserve notes, particularly $100 notes, are in foreign hands. Wealthy people around the world, particularly in relatively unstable countries, often hoard U.S. currency as insurance against hard times. Some countries, such as Panama, Ecuador, and El Salvador, even use U.S. dollars as their own currency.

It's actually a good deal for Americans to have U.S. currency held abroad. Think about it this way: A $100 note that costs only about 5 cents to print can be "sold" to foreigners for $100 worth of their goods and services. It's as if these foreigners were granting the United States essentially free goods or services as long as that currency remains abroad, usually for years.

Counterfeiting

Improvements in copy machines, computers, and printers allow even amateurs to make passable counterfeits of U.S. currency. Of the fake notes found in the United States in 2002, about 40 percent were produced with computers, copiers, and printers.

U.S. currency is being redesigned to make it harder to copy. You may have noticed the new $20 note, issued in late 2003. The major difference is the subtle introduction of color, a feature hard to reproduce. A new $50 note is being issued in 2004, and a new $100 note, in 2005.

The Fed and the Treasury have announced plans to redesign the currency every 7 to 10 years. Their idea is to stay one step ahead of counterfeiters.

Checkable Deposits

Currency, or cash, makes up a little more than half of M1, the money supply narrowly defined. Suppose you have some cash with you right now—notes and coins. If you deposit this cash in a checking account, you can then write checks directing your bank to pay someone from your account. **Checkable deposits**, or deposits against which

THE WALL STREET JOURNAL

Reading It Right What's the relevance of the following statement from *The Wall Street Journal*: "The Bank of Mexico will begin issuing new high-denomination bills next week that include improved security features to dissuade counterfeiters. New counterfeit techniques allow for the mass production of false bills."

checks can be written, are part of the narrow definition of money.

Checkable deposits also can be tapped with an ATM card or debit card. Banks hold a variety of checkable deposits. About half of checkable deposits are *demand deposits.* These are held mostly at commercial banks and earn no interest. In recent years, banks have developed other types of accounts, such as negotiable order of withdrawal, or NOW, accounts, which carry check-writing privileges but also earn interest. Checkable deposits make up nearly half of M1.

Traveler's Checks

If you ever planned a vacation, you may have visited the bank to buy traveler's checks. You signed the checks at the bank, and then signed them again

checkable deposits
Deposits in financial institutions against which checks can be written and ATM or debit cards can be applied

Using an ATM is a convenient way to access your checking account. Can you think of any disadvantages of using ATMs?

when you spent them. This allowed a merchant to compare your two signatures as the rightful owner of these checks.

If your cash is stolen, you are out of luck. However, if your traveler's checks are stolen, you can get them replaced. Therefore, traveler's checks are safer than cash. Traveler's checks are a tiny part of the money supply, accounting for only about 1 percent of M1.

CHECKPOINT
What is the narrow definition of money?

Broader Definitions of Money

M1 serves as a medium of exchange, a unit of account, and a store of value. Some can be converted readily into M1. Because these other accounts are so close to M1, they are considered to be money, using a broader definition. Here are those bank accounts.

Savings Deposits

Savings deposits earn interest but have no specific maturity date. This means that you can withdraw them any time without a penalty. Banks often allow depositors to shift funds from savings accounts to checking accounts by using a phone, an ATM, or online banking. Because savings can be converted so easily into checkable deposits and cash, distinctions between narrow and broad definitions of money have become blurred. Savings deposits total more than twice the size of M1.

Time Deposits

Time deposits earn a fixed rate of interest if held for a specified period. The holding period ranges from several months to several years. Holders of time deposits are issued certificates of deposit, or CDs

for short. Early withdrawals are penalized by forfeiture of several months' interest. Neither savings deposits nor time deposits serve directly as media of exchange, so they are not included in M1, the narrowest definition of money.

Time deposits are sorted into two categories: Those of less than $100,000, called small-denomination time deposits, account for about half of all time deposits. Those in excess of $100,000 are called large-denomination time deposits and make up the other half.

Money Market Mutual Fund Accounts

Money market mutual fund accounts are another component of the money supply more broadly defined. Funds deposited in these accounts are used to purchase a collection of short-term interest-earning assets by the financial institution that administers the fund. Depositors are then able to write checks against the value of their deposited funds. Because of restrictions on the minimum balance, on the number of checks that can be written per month, or on the minimum amount of each check, these popular accounts are not viewed as money when narrowly defined.

M2 and M3

Recall that M1 consists of cash held by the nonbanking public, checkable deposits, and traveler's checks. **M2** includes M1 as well as savings deposits, small-denomination time deposits, and money market mutual fund accounts. *M3* includes M2 plus large-denomination time deposits. M3 is less liquid than M2, which is less liquid than M1.

The size and the relative importance of each of the three definitions of money are presented in Figure 16.4. As you can see, compared to M1, M2 is nearly five times larger, and M3 is nearly seven times larger. Distinctions between M1 and M2 become less meaningful as banks make it easier for depositors to transfer funds from one account to another.

M2

A broader definition of the money supply, consisting of M1 plus savings deposits, small-denomination time deposits, and money market mutual fund accounts

Debit Cards but Not Credit Cards

Why does the definition of money include funds accessible by debit (or ATM) cards but not include credit cards, such as VISA and MasterCard? After all, credit cards account for about 20 percent of all consumer spending in the United States. Most sellers accept credit cards as readily as they accept cash or checks. Online purchases and mail orders usually require credit cards.

A credit card itself is not money. Using a credit card, however, is a convenient way of obtaining a short-term loan from the card issuer. If you buy an airline ticket with a credit card, the card issuer lends you the money to pay for the ticket. You don't use money until you pay your credit card bill. The credit card has not eliminated your use of money. It has merely delayed it. On the other hand, when you use a debit card at a grocery store, a drugstore, or any of hun-

dreds of other retailers, you draw down your checking account—part of M1.

If a credit card itself is not money, what is it?

Alternative Measure of the Money Supply, April 2003

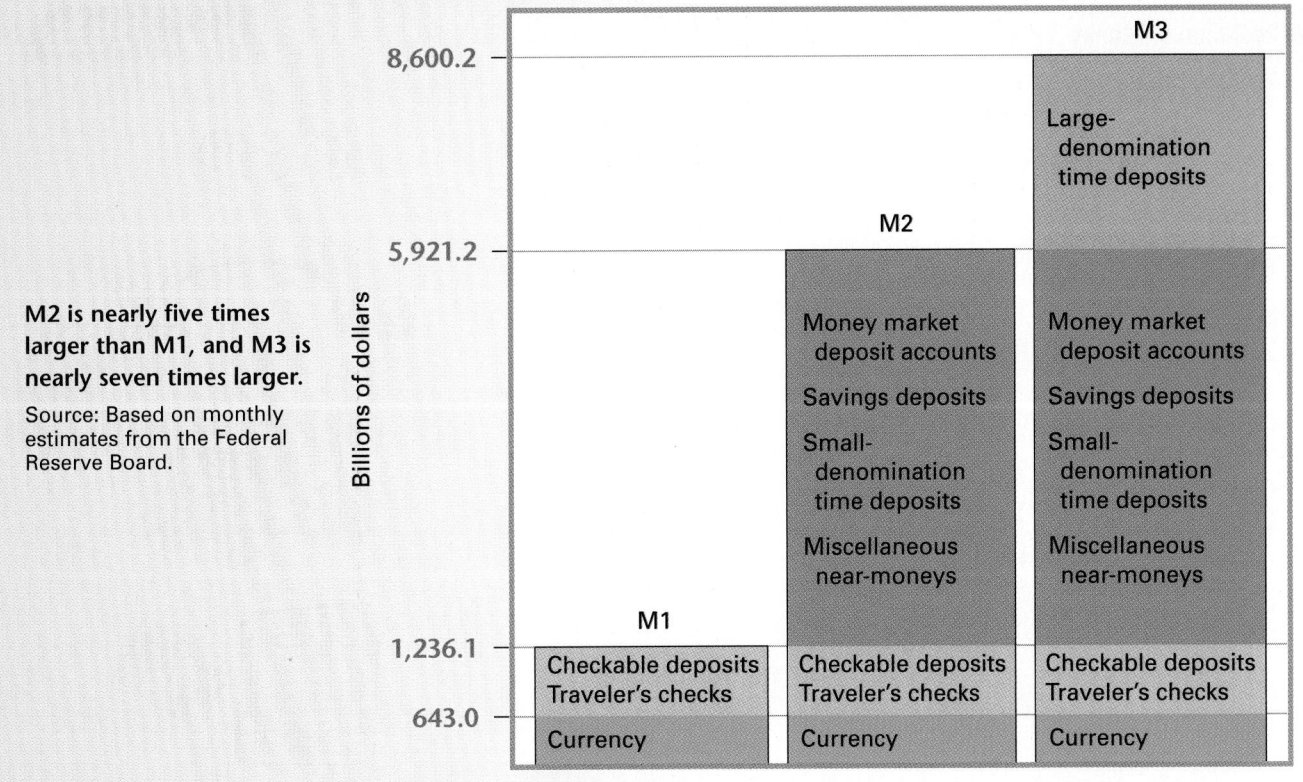

Figure 16.4

M2 is nearly five times larger than M1, and M3 is nearly seven times larger.

Source: Based on monthly estimates from the Federal Reserve Board.

Electronic Money

Money has grown increasingly more abstract over time, moving from commodity money to paper money that represented a claim on some commodity such as gold, to paper money with no intrinsic value, to an electronic entry at a bank that can be tapped with a debit card. Much of modern money consists of electronic entries in bank computers. So, money has evolved from a physical commodity to an electronic entry. This evolution is depicted in Figure 16.5. Money today not so much changes hands as it changes computer accounts.

CHECKPOINT
Why have distinctions among the broad aggregates of money become less meaningful over time?

The Evolution of Money

Figure 16.5

Money has evolved from a physical commodity to an electronic entry.

Commodity Money

Representative Money

Fiat Money

Electronic Money

Assessment

Key Concepts

1. Why can't the Fed be sure of exactly how much currency is in circulation at any specific time? Why does it have a much better idea of the amount deposited in checkable accounts?

2. If you had $100, would you be more likely to spend it if you held it in cash, had it deposited in a checking account, or had a traveler's check in that amount? Are these forms of money all equally easy to spend?

3. How would the effect of buying a $50 shirt with a credit card be different from buying the same shirt with a debit card from your bank?

4. Before electronic fund transfers became common, it could take days or weeks for checks to be presented to banks for payment. During this time, banks could use funds deposited in checking accounts even though they had already been spent by the depositor. This time was called *float time.* What do you imagine has happened to float time in recent years? Do you think this has had an important impact on the economy? Why or why not?

Graphing Exercise

5. Use data in the table to construct two bar graphs to show the components of M-1 and M-2 in May 2003. Calculate the percent each component represented of the total for these two measures of the money supply. Do any of these percentages surprise you? Why or why not?

Components of M-1 and M-2 in May 2003
Values in Billions of Dollars

M-1			M-2		
Currency	$645.7	51.3%	M-1	$1,258.3	21.0%
Traveler's Checks	7.5	0.6%	Savings Deposits	2,981.0	49.7%
Checkable Deposits	605.1	48.1%	Small Time Deposits	864.3	14.4%
Total	$1,258.3		Money Market Funds	896.3	14.9%
			Total	$5,999.9	

Source: Federal Reserve web site, July 21, 2003.

Think Critically

6. **Mathematics** Calculate the changes in M-1 and M-2 that would result from each of the following. Explain how you found your answers. Why don't the values of M-1 and M-2 always change when the value of their components change?

   a. The Fed buys a $10,000 bond from a person who then deposits the funds in her checking account.

   b. A depositor has $500 transferred from his checking account to his savings account.

   c. A depositor withdraws $1,000 from her savings account in cash.

   d. A depositor transfers $2,000 from her savings account to a time deposit.

movers&shakers

Tony Brown
Director, Community Development Financial Institutions (CDFI), U.S. Department of the Treasury

Tony Brown began his career in banking in 1982 after earning a Bachelor of Arts degree in International Affairs and Business and a Master of Business Administration degree in Finance from Xavier University in Cincinnati. In 1985, he joined Bank of America in Florida, serving as Senior Vice President of Community Development from 1990 to 2001. His work included community development lending and other financial services, resulting in more than $2 billion in annual loan production.

In August 2001, Brown was nominated by President George W. Bush as Director of the Community Development Financial Institutions (CDFI) Fund within the U.S. Department of Treasury. The purpose of the Fund, and Brown's overall role, is to expand the availability of credit, investment capital, and financial services in distressed communities. Since the Fund's creation in 1994, more than $534 million has been awarded to community development organizations and financial institutions.

Vicki and Maurice Marchman are shining examples of the impact CDFI Funds can have on a community. The Marchmans operate a small childcare business in an economically distressed neighborhood of Louisville, Kentucky. They wanted to expand their business, but they lacked the necessary collateral to qualify for a traditional bank loan. The couple found the necessary funding,

$112,000, through a loan from the Louisville Community Development Bank, a CDFI bank. Within the next few years, the business underwent several expansions, again receiving CDFI loans when traditional banks didn't find them eligible. Today the Marchman Learning Centers serve 300 children and provide jobs to 35 people. One of the centers is located in the Marchman Plaza, also home to a Social Security office, a county clerk's office, a laundromat, and a discount store. Once an eyesore, the Marchman Plaza now is a series of clean, well-maintained buildings, surrounded by attractive landscaping—all made possible through CDFI funds.

Success stories like this fuel Tony Brown's passion for serving as director of the CDFI Fund. His desire is to help Americans like the Marchmans, in economically distressed communities, realize a dream by providing better access to credit, capital, and financial services. The overall goal for Brown and his staff is to measurably improve the economic conditions of the residents of low-income communities by spurring economic growth and jobs through community development finance. To reach that goal, Brown requested a $51 million appropriation for the CDFI Fund from President Bush's fiscal year 2004 budget.

"We also have responsibility for administering the $15 billion new-markets tax credit program. These tax credits are provided to investors who invest in companies that in turn invest in businesses in low-income areas," Brown explains.

SOURCE READING
Analyze Brown's quote, above, about the new-markets tax credit program. Who benefits from the tax credit program he describes?

ENTREPRENEURS IN ACTION
In small groups, research the CDFI to find out if a small business owner could become eligible to receive one of these loans. Access the CDFI web site through econxtra.swlearning.com for information to use in completing this assignment.

Sharpen Your Life Skills

Decision-Making Skills

Banks use part of the money they receive from deposits in checking, savings, money market funds, and certificates of deposit (CDs) to make loans to their customers. The percent of interest they are willing to pay depositors depends on the type of account in which deposits are made. In general, the longer a bank expects to have a deposit, the greater the interest rate it pays. The reason for this relationship is the interest income banks are able to earn from loans they make. With a few exceptions, banks earn higher rates of interest from long-term loans than from short-term loans. This is why they are willing to pay more for long-term deposits. By carefully evaluating their situations, savers can make optimal decisions when they deposit their funds in banks.

The table below lists average interest rates paid for different types of deposits on July 22, 2003. Study this table, and use the information it contains to answer the questions that follow.

Apply Your Skill

In which type of account would you choose to deposit your funds in each of the following situations? Explain each of your choices.

1. You have $250 in cash that you must spend to pay your rent next Friday.

2. You have $1,000 in cash that you intend to spend sometime in the next few months when a new racing bicycle you have ordered arrives at a bike shop. You do not know precisely when it will arrive.

3. You have decided to start to save by setting aside $20 from each of your weekly paychecks.

4. You were given $2,000 by your uncle, who told you to set it aside for your college tuition after you graduate from high school in two years.

5. You inherit $10,000 and decide to set it aside to help you make a down payment on a house after you graduate from college and get settled in a career.

Interest Paid on Deposits, July 22, 2003

Type of Deposit	Interest Rate Paid
Small Checking Accounts	0.0%
Savings Accounts	1.2%
Money Market Deposits ($500 minimum deposit)	2.1%
1-Year CD ($500 minimum deposit)	2.2%
2-Year CD ($1,000 minimum deposit)	2.5%
5-Year CD ($1,000 minimum deposit)	3.8%

16 Chapter Assessment

Summary

16.1 Origins of Money

a The earliest families were self-sufficient and did not need money. When people began to specialize, transactions were carried out through barter at first. Problems with using barter centered on the difficulty of finding mutually beneficial trades of products with equal values. Making these exchanges involved large transaction costs that gave birth to money. People began to accept goods that they did not expect to use for themselves but rather to trade later for other products they wished to own. The goods that were used as money became known as *commodity money*.

Xtra! Quiz Prep
econxtra.swlearning.com

b Money must fulfill three functions. (1) It must be accepted as a *medium of exchange*. (2) It must serve as a unit of account. (3) It must provide a store of value over time. An ideal form of money would be durable, portable, divisible, of uniform quality, have a low opportunity cost of use, have a supply and demand that does not fluctuate wildly, and exist in limited quantity.

c Coins often replaced other types of commodity money in early commerce. They offered the advantages of being more portable, durable, and divisible than most types of commodity money. To assure that the precious metals they contained were pure, coins were stamped with an official seal by the issuing institution. Most coins were token money, which means that the value stamped on them was greater than the value of the gold or silver they contained.

16.2 Origins of Banking and the Federal Reserve System

a The earliest businesses that served as banks were goldsmiths who stored gold for their customers. Depositors often wrote checks to have gold transferred from one account to another. Goldsmiths learned that they could loan part of these funds to earn income and pay depositors a small return for their deposits. They came to operate under the *fractional reserve banking system*.

b Paper money was first issued in the form of notes printed by banks. Soon, governments also issued paper money that often was backed by nothing other than the government's statement that it was money. This *fiat money* is accepted because people trust the government and expect others to accept the money as well.

c Depository institutions are classified broadly into *commercial banks,* which hold more than two-thirds of bank deposits, and thrift institutions, which include mutual savings banks and credit unions. Banks may be chartered by either state or the federal government in the United States.

d The *Federal Reserve System, or Fed,* was established in 1913 to stop runs on banks. The Fed is responsible for supervising banking in the United States and for making and implementing monetary policy. The Fed may lend money to banks at the *discount rate*.

16.3 Money, Near Money and Credit Cards

a The Fed measures the money supply in the U.S. economy through several categories called money aggregates. *M1* includes currency in circulation, checkable deposits, and traveler's checks. The measurement of M1 is complicated by U.S. currency that has been sent abroad, and by counterfeiting.

b *M2* is a broader definition of the money supply. It includes M1 plus savings and time deposits, as well as funds placed in money market mutual fund accounts. Another, even broader measure of money is M3, which includes M2 and other less-liquid deposits.

c Electronic fund transfers carried out through debit cards have made it easier for people to spend their money. When people use credit cards to purchase goods or services, they are effectively taking out short-term loans.

Review Economic Terms

Choose the term that best fits the definition. On a separate sheet of paper, write the letter of the answer. Some terms may not be used.

_____ 1. Money not redeemable for anything of intrinsic value; declared money by government decree

_____ 2. Anything generally accepted by all parties in payment for goods or services

_____ 3. Buying or selling U.S. government securities as a way of regulating the money supply

_____ 4. Depository institutions that make loans primarily to businesses

_____ 5. A written order instructing a bank to pay someone from the amount deposited

_____ 6. Bank notes that exchange for a specific commodity, such as gold

_____ 7. Interest rate the Fed charges to banks that borrow reserves

_____ 8. Cash that banks have on hand in their vaults or on deposit with the Federal Reserve System

_____ 9. Deposits in financial institutions against which checks can be written

_____10. Anything that serves both as money and as a commodity, such as gold

a. **check**

b. **checkable deposits**

c. **commercial banks**

d. **commodity money**

e. **discount rate**

f. **Federal Open Market Committee (FOMC)**

g. **Federal Reserve System**

h. **fiat money**

i. **fractional reserve banking system**

j. **M1**

k. **M2**

l. **medium of exchange**

m. **open-market operations**

n. **representative money**

o. **reserves**

Review Economic Concepts

11. Without __?__ there is no need for money.

12. **True or False** The high transaction cost of money gave birth to barter.

13. Which of the following is not a function of money?

   a. medium of exchange

   b. unit of account

   c. standard of deposit

   d. store of value

14. Gold, silver, wheat, and tobacco have all served as __?__ at some time in the past.

15. **True or False** *Fiat money* is accepted when people trust the issuing agency.

16. Which of the following is probably the greatest limitation on the usefulness of diamonds as *commodity money*?

   a. They are not durable.

   b. They are not portable.

   c. They do not have value.

   d. They are not easily divisable.

17. Paper documents issued by banks that promised the bearer a specific amount of gold or silver were called __?__.

18. Goats or sheep make poor money because they

   a. are not portable.

   b. are not divisible.

   c. have no intrinsic value.

   d. exist in almost unlimited quantities.

19. **True or False** Money is a stock while income is a flow.

20. *Federal Reserve* notes are examples of

    a. fiat money.

    b. representative money.

    c. commodity money.

    d. full-bodied money.

21. **True or False** Banks in the United States may be chartered only by state governments.

22. In the past, savings and loans and mutual savings banks specialized in

    a. issuing credit cards.

    b. extending credit to businesses.

    c. maintaining checking accounts.

    d. making home mortgage loans.

23. When the Fed lends money to banks, it charges them the __?__.

24. Which of the following statements about the Federal Reserve's Board of Governors is not true?

    a. Its members are responsible for setting monetary policy.

    b. Its members are elected by commercial bank presidents.

    c. Its members also serve on the Federal Open Market Committee.

    d. Its members serve 14-year terms.

25. **True or False** The *FOMC* was established to coordinate the Fed's *open-market operations*.

26. *M1* includes each of the following except

    a. checkable deposits.

    b. currency.

    c. small savings account deposits.

    d. traveler's checks.

27. A part of a collection of short-term interest-earning assets that individuals are able to purchase is called a __?__.

28. **True or False** The use of a debit card will immediately impact the money supply while the use of a credit card will not.

29. __?__ carried out through debit cards make it easier for people to spend their money.

Apply Economic Concepts

30. **Decide When to Use Cash** Which of the following transactions would you complete with cash and for which would you write a check? Explain each of your choices. What generalizations can you make about when people choose to use cash to make their payments?

    • Pay your $850 rent.

    • Buy two $8 movie tickets for your friend and yourself.

    • Make a $199 monthly payment for your car loan.

    • Purchase your lunch for $5.99 at a fast-food restaurant.

    • Repay your uncle the $300 he loaned you last year.

31. **Assess What Makes a Piece of Paper Money** Some resort communities issue guests special pieces of paper that may be used to purchase goods or services within the resort. Guests may spend 50 credits to rent a small sailboat, 75 credits to purchase a meal, or 100 credits to play a round of golf or take a tennis lesson. In what ways are these pieces of paper similar to money and in what ways are they different from money?

32. **Calculate the Money Supply** The following table lists amounts of money held in a variety of forms in May 2002. Use these values to calculate the amount in M1 and M2 at that time.

Money Held in May 2002
Values in Billions of Dollars

Currency	$605.0
Checkable Deposits	570.5
Savings Deposits	$2,499.2
Small Time Deposits	927.7
Money Market Mutual Funds	896.3
Traveler's Checks	7.8

33. **Describe What Happens When the Fed Lends Money** Banks that are short on cash may ask to borrow funds from the Federal Reserve System. This sometimes happens when banks located in rural areas need money to make loans to farmers in the spring when they are preparing to plant crops. These loans are repaid the following fall, after farmers have harvested and sold their crops. Write an essay that describes what would happen in the economy if a bank borrowed $10 million from the Fed and used this money to make loans to farmers.

34. **Identify Depository Institutions** Make a list of all the depository institutions that have offices in your community. Identify them as commercial banks, savings and loans, mutual savings banks, credit unions, or other. How much difference is there in the services that they offer typical consumers?

35. **Diagram the Check-Clearing Process** When you deposit your paycheck in your bank, it must have the check cleared to obtain the funds it credits to your account. Here are the steps that take place.

    • You deposit your check for $250 in Bank ABC. The check was drawn on Bank XYZ, which is located in a different community in your state.

    • Your bank credits your account for $250 and sends the check to the nearest Federal Reserve Bank.

    • The Federal Reserve Bank credits Bank

ABC's account for $250 and deducts this amount from Bank XYZ's account.

    • The Federal Reserve Bank sends the cancelled check to Bank XYZ, which will draw down your employer's checkable deposits by the amount of the check, keep a record of the check and possibly send the cancelled check to your employer.

Draw and label a diagram to show this process.

36. **Sharpen Your Life Skills** Imagine that you have decided to save $5,000 over the next two years to make the down payment on a used car. You work 20 hours each week after school and take home $127.35 after taxes. You believe you could save $30 each week during the 42 weeks of the school year. In the summer, you plan to work 40 hours each week and take home about $250. During this time you could save more. Use this information to create a savings plan to reach your goal. Which of the following types of savings accounts would you open? How much could you save during each school year? How much would you need to save during each of two summers to reach your goal? Explain your plan in several paragraphs.

    Possible Ways to Save

    • a checking account that pays no interest

    • a savings account that pays 1 percent interest

    • a one-year certificate of deposit that pays 1.75 percent interest and has a minimum deposit of $500

 *econxtra.swlearning.com*

37. Access **EconNews Online** at econxtra. swlearning.com. Find the article entitled "Making It Tough on Counterfeiters." Read the article, and then answer this question: Why do you think the government is changing the $20 and $100 bills, but not the $1, $5, and $10 bills?

17 Money Creation, the Federal Reserve System, and Monetary Policy

Consider

How does the Fed create money?

Why don't you demand all the money you can get your hands on?

What's the price of holding money?

How does the supply of money in the economy affect your chances of finding a job, your ability to finance a new car, and the interest rate you pay on credit cards?

What's the impact of changes in the money supply on the economy in the short run and in the long run?

© Getty Images/PhotoDisc

POINT YOUR BROWSER

econxtra.swlearning.com

Objectives

> Discuss what's involved in getting a new banking operation up and running.

> Describe how the banking system can expand the money supply by a multiple of excess reserves.

Overview

Coins and paper money notes account for only a part of money supply in the U.S. economy. The narrow definition of money also includes checking accounts, which consist mostly of electronic entries in bank computers. The Federal Reserve System creates money not so much by circulating more Federal Reserve notes, but by having banks do what they do best—accept deposits and lend out some of them to borrowers. Bank reserves provide the raw material banks use to make loans, and these loans are how the banks add to the money supply.

Key Terms

net worth

asset

liability

balance sheet

required reserve ratio

required reserves

excess reserves

money multiplier

[In the News]

• Stealing the People's Money

Almost from the moment the first banks went into business, there have been bank robbers. Popular fiction and films often have portrayed bank robbers as daring outlaws who are able to gain large sums of money in a single heist. Several famous American outlaws, such as Jesse James, John Dillinger, and Bonnie and Clyde, became well known for their attempts to steal from banks. Some Americans sympathized with these thieves because they saw banks as tools of the rich, whose lending practices often hurt the poorest people. Although usually better guarded than local banks, central banks also can be robbed. These banks often hold billions of dollars in reserve currency and gold. The people of Iraq learned this in the aftermath of the 2003 U.S. war in Iraq. Fleeing dictator Saddam Hussein was discovered to have taken more than $1 billion in U.S. dollars from Iraq's central bank. In addition to raising fears that this money might be used to fund terrorist operations, it further weakened an already unstable Iraqi economy that needed to rebuild after the war.

Think About It

Do you think the security and strength of a country's banking system is important to a country's political stability? Why or why not?

Operating a Bank

asset

Any physical property or financial claim that is owned

liability

An amount owed

balance sheet

A financial statement showing assets, liabilities, and net worth at a given time; assets must equal liabilities plus net worth, so the statement is in balance

net worth

Assets minus liabilities; also called owners' equity

required reserve ratio

A Fed regulation that dictates the minimum percentage of deposits each bank must keep in reserve

Suppose some business leaders in your hometown want to establish a bank. The following section discusses what they would need to do and consider to get their new banking operation up and running. These things would apply to the operation of any depository institution, such as a commercial bank, a savings and loan, a mutual savings bank, or a credit union.

Getting a Charter

The bank founders first need to obtain a *charter,* or the right to operate. They would apply to the state banking authority to start up a state bank or to the U.S. Comptroller of the Currency to start up a national bank. In considering the application, the chartering agency would review the quality of management, the need for another bank in the community, the initial investment, and the likelihood of success.

The founders plan to invest $1,000,000 in the bank, and they indicate this on their charter application. Once their charter is granted, they incorporate, issuing themselves shares of stock, or certificates of ownership. Thus, they exchange $1,000,000 for shares of stock in a bank they name Home Bank. These shares are called the *owners' equity,* and represent the **net worth** of the bank.

The owners invest this $1,000,000 buying, furnishing, and building the bank. These become the bank's assets. An **asset** is any physical property or financial claim owned by the bank. The bank is now ready for business.

Bank Balance Sheet

Opening day is a lucky one for Home Bank because the first customer opens a checking account and deposits $100,000 in cash. The cash becomes the bank's asset. In accepting this deposit, the bank promises to repay the depositor that amount. That bank's promise becomes the bank's **liability**, which is an amount the bank owes.

As a result of this deposit, the bank's assets increase by $100,000 in cash and its liabilities increase by $100,000 in checkable deposits. At this point the money supply has not changed. The depositor simply converted $100,000 in cash to $100,000 in checkable deposits, which become part of the money supply. The bank's vault now holds the cash, which is no longer considered part of the money supply.

Look at the bank's **balance sheet**, presented in Figure 17.1. As the name implies, a balance sheet shows an equality, or a balance, between the two sides of the bank's account. The left side lists the bank's assets. At this stage, assets include the $1,000,000 in building and furnishings owned by Home Bank and the $100,000 in vault cash.

The right side shows two claims on the banks assets: claims by the owners, or net worth, amounting to $1,000,000, and claims by nonowners, or liabilities, which at this point consist of checkable deposits of $100,000. The two sides of the ledger must always be equal, or be in *balance,* which is why it's called a *balance sheet.* Assets must equal liabilities plus net worth.

Assets = Liabilities + Net Worth

Reserve Accounts

The Fed requires Home Bank to set aside, or to hold in reserve, a percentage of checkable deposits. The **required reserve ratio** dictates the minimum proportion of deposits the

The two sides of a balance sheet—assets and liabilities plus net worth—are always equal, or "in balance."

Assets		Liabilities and Net Worth	
Cash	$ 100,000	Checkable Deposits	$ 100,000
Building and Furniture	1,000,000	Net Worth	1,000,000
Total	$1,100,000	Total	$1,100,000

bank must keep in reserve. The dollar amount that must be held in reserve is called **required reserves**—checkable deposits multiplied by the required reserve ratio.

All banks and thrifts are subject to the Fed's reserve requirement. Reserves are either held as cash in the bank's vault or put on deposit at the Fed. In neither case are those reserves in circulation, so they are not counted as part of the money supply. Neither earns Home Bank any interest. If the reserve requirement on checkable deposits is 10 percent, as it has been in recent years, Home Bank must hold $10,000 as required reserves. That equals 10 percent times $100,000.

Home Bank's reserves now consist of $10,000 in required reserves and $90,000 in **excess reserves**, which are reserves that exceed required reserves.

So far Home Bank has not earned a dime. Excess reserves, however, can be used to acquire interest-earning assets. By law, a bank's interest-bearing assets are limited primarily to loans and to government securities. Suppose Home Bank uses the $90,000 excess reserves to make loans and buy government securities.

CHECKPOINT
What needs to be done to get a new banking operation up and running?

Money Multiplier

Home Bank has used all its excess reserves to make loans and buy U.S. government securities, assets that will

earn interest. The bank now has no excess reserves. What if, in addition to Home Bank having no excess reserves, there are no excess reserves in the entire banking system? In this setting, how can the Fed increase the money supply?

The Fed Makes a Move

To get the ball rolling, suppose the Fed buys a $10,000 U.S. government bond from Home Bank. This is called an open-market operation, and it's the primary way the Fed can alter the money supply. To pay for the bond, the Fed increases Home Bank's reserve account by $10,000. Where does the Fed get these reserves? It makes them up—creates them out of thin air, out of electronic ether!

In the process, Home Bank has exchanged one asset, a U.S. bond, for another asset, reserves held at the Fed. A U.S. bond is not money, nor are reserves, so the money supply has not yet changed. But Home Bank now has $10,000 in excess reserves, and excess reserves are the fuel for money creation.

Round One

What will Home Bank do with those excess reserves? Suppose Megan comes in and applies for a $10,000 car loan. Home Bank approves her loan and increases her checking account by $10,000. Home Bank has converted her promise to repay, her IOU, into a

required reserves

The dollar amount that must be held in reserve; checkable deposits multiplied by the required reserve ratio

excess reserves

Bank reserves in excess of required reserves

$10,000 checkable deposit. *Because her newly created checkable deposit is money, this loan increases the money supply by $10,000.*

She writes a $10,000 check for the car, and the dealer promptly deposits it in the company's checking account at Fidelity Bank. Fidelity Bank increases the car dealer's account by $10,000, and sends Megan's check to the Fed. The Fed transfers $10,000 in reserves from Home Bank's account to Fidelity Bank's account. The Fed then sends the check to Home Bank, which reduces Megan's checkable deposits by $10,000. The Fed has thus "cleared" her check by settling the claim that Fidelity Bank had on Home Bank.

At this point, the $10,000 in checkable deposits has simply shifted from Megan's account at Home Bank to the car dealer's account at Fidelity Bank. The increase in the money supply in this first round remains at $10,000.

Round Two and Beyond

Because the reserve requirement is 10 percent, Fidelity Bank sets aside $1,000 of the new deposit as reserves and lends the remaining $9,000 for a computer purchase by increasing the borrower's checking account. Thus, the money supply has increased by an additional $9,000, and the cumulative increase is $19,000 to this point.

An individual bank can lend no more than its excess reserves. When the borrower spends the amount loaned, reserves at one bank usually fall. However, total reserves in the banking system do not fall because the money that is spent is most often deposited in a bank by the person who received it. The recipient bank can use most of the new deposit to extend more loans, creating more checkable deposits. The potential expansion of checkable deposits in the banking system equals some multiple of the initial increase in reserves.

This cycle of borrowing, spending, and depositing continues round after round. As a result of the Fed buying this $10,000 bond, the money supply can eventually increase by a multiple of the excess reserves created by the Fed.

Because this money-creation process began with the Fed's open-market operation, the Fed can rightfully claim, "The buck starts here." This slogan appears on a large plaque in the Federal Reserve chairman's office.

Reserve Requirements and Money Expansion

The banking system as a whole eliminates excess reserves by expanding the money supply. With a 10 percent reserve requirement, the Fed's initial injection of $10,000 in fresh reserves could support up to $100,000 in new checkable deposits.

The **money multiplier** is the maximum multiple by which the money supply increases as a result of an increase in the banking system's excess reserves. The money multiplier equals 1 divided by the required reserve ratio. If r stands for the required reserve ratio, then the money multiplier is $1/r$. In this example, the required reserve ratio is 10 percent, or 0.1, so the money multiplier is $1/0.1$, which equals 10. The formula for the multiple expansion of checkable deposits can be written as:

Change in checkable deposits
  = Change in excess reserves $\times$ $1/r$

The higher the reserve requirement, the greater the fraction of deposits that must be held as reserves, so the smaller the money multiplier. A reserve requirement of 20 percent instead of 10 percent would require each bank to set aside twice as much in required reserves. The money multiplier in this case would be $1/0.2$, which equals 5. The maximum possible increase in checkable deposits resulting from an initial $10,000 increase in fresh reserves would be $10,000 $\times$ 5, or $50,000.

Excess reserves fuel the expansion of checkable deposits. A higher reserve requirement drains this fuel from the banking system, thereby reducing the amount of new money that can be created. The fractional reserve requirement is the key to the multiple expansion of checkable deposits. If each $1 deposit had to be backed by $1 in required reserves, the money multiplier would be cut to 1.

money multiplier

The multiple by which the money supply increases as a result of an increase in excess reserves in the banking system

Contraction of the money supply works in the same way, but in reverse. It begins with the Fed *selling* a $10,000 U.S. bond to Home Bank. Therefore, the Fed increases the money supply by buying bonds and decreases it by selling bonds.

Limitations on the Multiplier

For a given required reserve ratio, the multiplier is greatest if

1. banks do not allow excess reserves to sit idle

2. borrowed funds do not sit idle in checking accounts but are spent

3. the public does not choose to hold some of the newly created money as cash.

If excess reserves remain idle or if borrowed funds sit around in checking accounts, they are less able to fuel an expansion of the money supply. If people stash away some of the newly created money as cash rather than spend it or leave it in checking accounts, then that portion of borrowed funds held as cash cannot provide additional reserves in the banking system.

For the money multiplier to operate, a particular bank need not use excess reserves just to make loans. It could just as well use them to pay all its employees a Christmas bonus. As long as that spending ends up as checkable deposits in the banking system, the money multiplier can operate.

CHECKPOINT
How can the banking system expand the money supply by a multiple of excess reserves?

E-CONOMICS

Banking from the Big Rig

An unexpected development with the rise of online banking technology has been the growth of "specialty banks" created to serve particular types of customers. Most of these banks target members of a specific workforce who would be likely to use online banking. For example, in 2000 NationalInterbank formed a partnership with PNV Inc., a web site company aimed at truckers, to operate an online bank for truckers. Because truckers spend so much of their time on the road, traditional banking is not convenient for them. Truckers "are on the road, not at home, and probably not near a (bank) branch," notes online banking expert Richard Bell. "And most of these guys are sitting on a quarter of a million dollars worth of truck, so they either have money or owe money." With the creation of this specialty bank, a trucker can now do his or her banking from the seat of a big rig. In some ways, this trend in specialty banks is a throwback to credit unions, which originally were created to serve only members of particular groups, usually particular professions. Ironically, in recent years changes in banking laws have allowed many credit unions to expand their client base beyond the groups they originally were designed to serve. Some credit unions claimed that they had to broaden their client base in order to stay in business. The online specialty banks mark a reversal of this trend.

Think Critically

Do you think targeting a particular type of customer group would be effective? Why or why not? Would this strategy make more sense for online banking than it does for traditional depository institutions? Explain your answer.

Key Concepts

1. Why are people who organize a bank required to invest their own funds as owner's equity in the new business? How does this help to protect the bank's depositors?

2. Why is a loan made to help a consumer purchase a house an asset to the bank, while any funds the homeowner deposits in the same bank a liability?

3. Bank ABC holds $100 million in deposits upon which it must maintain a required reserve of 10 percent. The bank currently has $12 million on reserve. How much excess reserves does the bank hold? Why would it want to invest or loan these reserves as quickly as possible?

4. Why doesn't the money multiplier work as effectively if people decide to hold additional funds they receive in cash?

Graphing Exercise

5. Construct a bar graph to show four rounds of the money-creation process that would result from a new deposit of $2,000 in a checking account when the required reserve is 10 percent.

Expansion of a New $2,000 Deposit

	New Deposit	Required Reserve	New Loan
Round 1	$2,000.00	$200.00	$1,800.00
Round 2	$1,800.00	$180.00	$1,620.00
Round 3	$1,620.00	$162.00	$1,458.00
Round 4	$1,458.00	$145.80	$1,312.20

Think Critically

6. **Math** Recalculate the table in exercise 5 above, assuming that the Fed increased the required reserve ratio from 10 to 12 percent. Why is the required reserve an important factor in determining the amount of money that banks are able to lend? What would happen to consumers' ability to borrow funds from banks if the required reserve was increased?

Objectives

> Explain the shape of the money demand curve.

> Explain how changes in the money supply affect interest rates and real GDP in the short run.

> Discuss the federal funds rate and why the Fed uses this rate to set monetary policy goals.

Overview

So far the focus has been on how the banking system creates money. A more fundamental question is how the money supply affects the economy as a whole. When the Fed expands the money supply, this drives down interest rates in the short run. Because the cost of borrowing falls, firms borrow more to buy capital goods and households borrow more to buy cars, homes, and other "big ticket" items. Thus, an increase in the supply of money increases aggregate demand, output, and employment in the short run.

Key Terms

money demand

money supply

federal funds market

federal funds rate

[In the News]

• Cutting the Federal Funds Rate

In December 2001, the Federal Reserve announced that it was cutting the federal funds rate—the interest rate that banks charge to each other for overnight loans—to 1.75 percent. This was the lowest federal funds rate since 1958, and it marked the eleventh time that the Fed had lowered this rate in 2001. The idea is that lowering the rate reduces the cost of covering any reserve shortfalls, making banks more willing to lend money. For nearly four decades, the Fed has focused its monetary policy on this interest rate. Banks use this rate to help set their prime lending rates for other items. For example, the lowering of the federal funds rate in 2001 helped keep mortgage rates low, boosting the housing market. The Fed lowered its rates so much in 2001 because of rising unemployment and consumer uncertainty caused by the war on terrorism. In 2002, the economy had mixed results, with continuing unemployment but gains in automobile and housing loans thanks to lower interest rates. As a result, the Fed left its federal funds rate alone for more than a year.

Think About It

Why do you think lower interest rates boost consumers' willingness to make major purchases?

Money Demand

Recall the distinction between a *stock* and a *flow*. A stock measures something at a point in time, such as the amount of money you have with you right now. A flow measures something over an interval of time, such as your income per week. It may seem odd to even talk about the demand for money. You might think people would demand all the money they could get their hands on. Remember, however, that *money,* the stock, is not the same as *income,* the flow. People express their demand for money by holding some of their wealth as money rather than holding other assets. People express their demand for income by selling their labor and other resources to earn income.

A Medium of Exchange

Why do people demand money? Why do people maintain checking accounts and have cash in their pockets, purses, wallets, desk drawers, lockers, and coffee cans? The reason is obvious. *People demand money to carry out market transactions.* Money is a convenient medium of exchange.

Your demand for money is based on your expected spending. If you plan to buy lunch tomorrow, you will carry enough money to pay for it. You may also have extra money on hand in case of an emergency or in case you come across something else you want to buy. You may have a little extra cash with you right now for who knows what. Even you don't know.

A Store of Value

The demand for money is related to money's role as a medium of exchange. However, money also is a store of value. People save for a new home, for college, for retirement. People can store their purchasing power as money or as other financial assets, such as corporate and government bonds. When people purchase bonds and other financial assets, they are lending their money and earning interest for doing so. The interest rate indicates the cost of borrowing and the reward for lending.

The Cost of Holding Money

The demand for any asset is based on the flow of services it provides. The big advantage of money is its general acceptance in market exchange. In contrast, other financial assets, such as corporate bonds, government bonds, and some bank accounts, must first be liqui-

Main Idea

Role of Money

As a medium of exchange, *money makes it easier to trade, borrow, save, invest, and compare the value of goods and services.* Which of these activities do you regularly do?

dated, or exchanged for money, before they can fund market transactions.

Money, however, has one major drawback when compared with other financial assets. Money in the form of currency, demand deposits, and travelers checks earns no interest. Checkable deposits that do earn interest earn less than other financial assets.

Holding wealth in the form of money means passing up some interest that could be earned by holding some other financial asset. For example, suppose a business could earn 4 percent more interest by holding some financial asset other than money. Holding $1 million in money would have an opportunity cost of $40,000 per year. *The interest given up is the opportunity cost of holding money.*

Money Demand and Interest Rates

Money demand is the relationship between how much money people want to hold and the interest rate. The interest earnings that are given up are the cost of holding money. When the interest rate is low, other things constant, the cost of holding money is low. People hold more of their wealth as money. When the interest rate is high, the cost of holding money is high. People hold less money and more

Research interest rates offered on savings accounts at local banks or online banks. Would these rates motivate people to deposit their money in these accounts? Record the interest rates you find, and write a paragraph to explain your answer to the question.

assets that pay higher interest. Thus, *other things constant, the quantity of money demanded varies inversely with the market interest rate.*

The money demand curve, D_m, in Figure 17.2 shows the quantity of money people in the economy demand at alternative interest rates, other things constant. *The quantity of money demanded is inversely related to the price of holding money, which is the interest rate.* Movements along the curve reflect the effects of changes

money demand
The relationship between how much money people want to hold and the interest rate

---

The Graphing Workshop

econxtra.swlearning.com

Demand for Money

Figure 17.2

The money demand curve, D_m, slopes downward. As the interest rate falls, so does the opportunity cost of holding money. The quantity of money demanded increases.

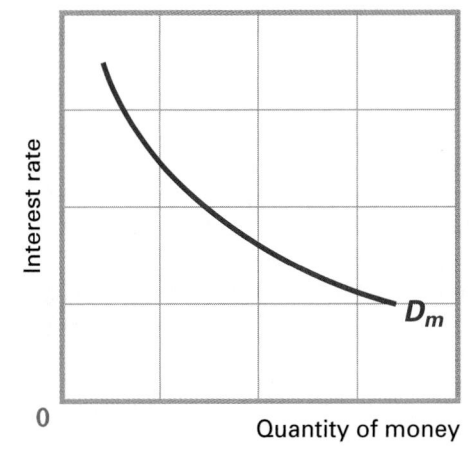

in the interest rate on the quantity of money demanded, other things constant.

✔ **CHECKPOINT**
What explains the shape of the money demand curve?

Money Supply and the Market Interest Rate

CNN video
About Landings
econxtra.swlearning.com

The money demand curve has the usual downward sloping shape of other demand curves. The only difference is that the price is measured not by dollars but by an interest rate. What about money supply?

Money Supply

Money supply is the stock of money available in the economy at a particular time. Money supply is determined primarily by the Fed through its control over currency and excess reserves in the banking system. The *money supply*

money supply
The stock of money available in the economy at a particular time

curve does not have the usual upward sloping shape of other supply curves. The supply of money, S_m, is depicted as a vertical line in Figure 17.3. A vertical supply curve indicates that the quantity of money in the economy is fixed by the Fed at any given time and is therefore independent of the interest rate. The assumption is that the Fed determines the money supply.

Market Interest Rate

The intersection in Figure 17.3 of the money demand curve, D_m, with the money supply curve, S_m, determines the market interest rate, i. That rate equates the quantity of money demanded in the economy with the quantity of money supplied by the Fed. At interest rates above the equilibrium level, the opportunity cost of holding money is higher, so the quantity people demand is less than the quantity supplied. At interest rates below the equilibrium level, the opportunity cost of holding money is lower, so the quantity of money people demand exceeds the quantity supplied.

An Increase in the Money Supply

If the Fed increases the money supply, by, for example, purchasing U.S. bonds, the money supply curve shifts to the

The Graphing Workshop
econxtra.swlearning.com

Effect of an Increase in the Money Supply

Figure 17.3

Because the supply of money is determined by the Federal Reserve, money supply can be represented by a vertical line. The intersection of the supply of money, S_m, and the demand for money D_m, determines the equilibrium interest rate, i. Following an increase in the money supply to S'_m, the quantity of money supplied exceeds the quantity demanded at the original interest rate, i. People who are holding more money than they would like attempt to exchange money for bonds or other financial assets. In doing so, they drive the interest rate down to i', where quantity demanded equals the new quantity supplied.

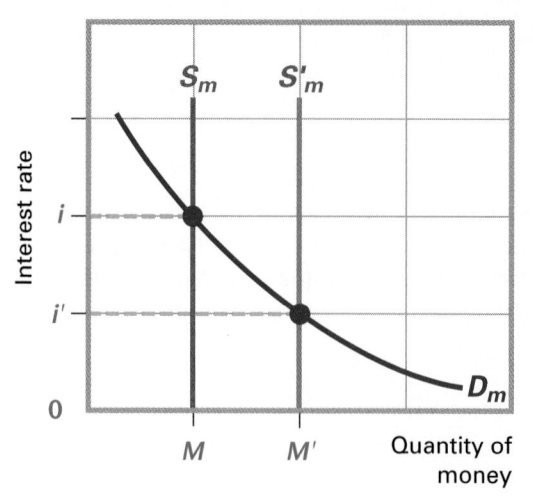

right, as shown by the movement from S_m to S_m' in Figure 17.3. The interest rate must fall to encourage people to hold the increased supply of money. The interest rate falls until the quantity of money demanded just equals the quantity supplied. With the decline in the interest rate to i' in Figure 17.3, the opportunity cost of holding money falls enough that the public is willing to hold the now-larger supply of money. *For a given money demand curve, an increase in money supply pushes down the market interest rate, and a decrease in the supply of money pushes up the market interest rate.*

Now that you have some idea how money demand and supply determine the market interest rate, you are ready to see how money fits into the economy in the short run. Specifically, how do changes in the supply of money affect aggregate demand and real GDP?

Effect of Lower Interest Rates

Suppose the Federal Reserve believes that the economy is operating below its potential and decides to stimulate

output and employment by increasing the money supply. The Fed can expand the money supply by

1. purchasing U.S. government securities

2. reducing the *discount rate* (the rate at which banks can borrow from the Fed), or

3. lowering the required reserve ratio to create excess reserves.

An increase in the money supply reduces the market interest rate. A lower interest rate encourages consumers to save less and borrow more. A lower rate also encourages businesses to invest more in capital goods. Thus, a lower interest rate stimulates consumption and investment. This greater aggregate demand will increase real GDP in the short run, as shown by the movement from Y to Y' in Figure 17.4. Note that the price level also increases.

Thus, monetary policy in the short run influences the market interest rate, which in turn stimulates aggregate demand and increases real GDP. *In the short run, changes in the money supply affect*

Ask the Xpert!

econxtra.swlearning.com

Why should we care how fast the money supply grows?

© Getty Images/PhotoDisc

What effect would lower interest rates have on each of the three topics explained in the brochure—time deposits (checking accounts), individual retirement accounts, and investments?

A lower interest rate encourages households to spend more and save less. It also encourages businesses to invest more. More consumption and investment increases aggregate demand. Therefore, a lower interest rate shifts the aggregate demand curve to the right, thereby increasing employment and output in the short run. In the short run, this increases real GDP and the price level.

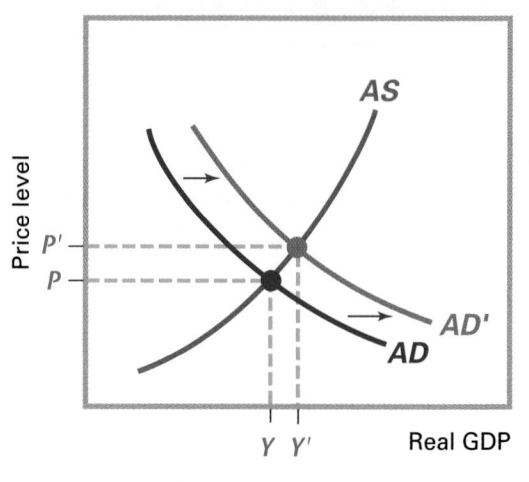

the economy through changes in the interest rate.

Increasing Interest Rates

Now consider the effect of an increase in the interest rate. Suppose Fed officials decide to reduce the money supply to cool down an overheated economy. The Fed can reduce the money supply by

1. selling U.S. government securities

2. increasing the discount rate, or

3. raising the required reserve ratio.

A decrease in the money supply would increase the equilibrium interest rate. At the higher interest rate, businesses find it more costly to finance plants and equipment. Households find it more costly to finance new homes and other major purchases. Thus a higher interest rate reduces aggregate demand, and this reduction in aggregate demand will reduce real GDP in the short run.

federal funds market
A market for overnight lending and borrowing of reserves held by the Fed for banks

 CHECKPOINT
How do changes in the money supply affect interest rates and real GDP in the short run?

The Federal Funds Rate

At 2:15 P.M. on June 25, 2003, immediately following a meeting, the Federal Open Market Committee (FOMC) announced that it would lower its target for the federal funds rate by one quarter of a percentage point to 1 percent, the lowest rate since 1958. What is the federal funds rate, and how did the Fed's action affect the economy?

Federal Funds Market

Because reserves earn no interest, banks usually try to keep excess reserves to a minimum. Banks continuously "sweep" their accounts to find excess reserves that can be put to some interest-bearing use. They do not let excess reserves remain idle even overnight. The **federal funds market** provides for overnight lending and borrowing among banks of excess reserves on account at the Fed.

For example, suppose that at the end of the business day, Home Bank has excess reserves of $10,000 on account with the Fed and wants to lend that amount to another bank that finished the day requiring reserves of $10,000. These two banks make a deal in the federal funds market—that is, the market for borrowing and lending reserves at the Fed. The interest rate paid on such loans is called the **federal funds rate** or the *interbank loan rate*. This is the interest rate targeted by the Fed's monetary policy.

Aggressive Rate Cuts

Between early 2001 and June 2003, the Fed cut the federal funds rate 5.5 percentage points in 13 steps. This was the most aggressive effort to stimulate the economy ever. In cutting the target rate on that June afternoon, the FOMC said the series of cuts was "providing important ongoing support to economic activity." Yet the economy "has yet to exhibit sustained growth."

To lower the federal funds rate, the FOMC made open-market purchases of government securities, increasing reserves in the banking system until the rate fell to the target level.

Why Target This Rate?

For nearly four decades, the Fed has influenced the money supply by focusing mostly on changes in the federal funds rate. There are many interest rates in the economy—for credit cards, new car sales, mortgages, home equity loans, personal loans, and so on. Why does the Fed choose to focus on the federal funds rate? First, by changing bank reserves through open-market operations, the Fed has a direct lever on this rate. The Fed's ability to influence this rate is stronger than it is for any other market rate. Second, the federal funds rate serves as a benchmark in the economy for determining many other interest rates. For example, after the Fed announces a change in its target federal funds rate, major banks around the country often change by the same amount their prime interest rate—the interest rate they charge their best corporate customers.

federal funds rate

The interest rate charged in the federal funds market; the Fed's target interest rate

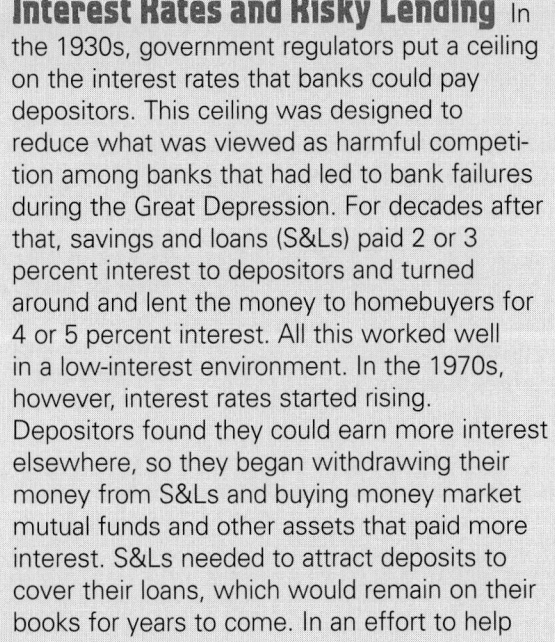

Ethics in Action

Interest Rates and Risky Lending In the 1930s, government regulators put a ceiling on the interest rates that banks could pay depositors. This ceiling was designed to reduce what was viewed as harmful competition among banks that had led to bank failures during the Great Depression. For decades after that, savings and loans (S&Ls) paid 2 or 3 percent interest to depositors and turned around and lent the money to homebuyers for 4 or 5 percent interest. All this worked well in a low-interest environment. In the 1970s, however, interest rates started rising. Depositors found they could earn more interest elsewhere, so they began withdrawing their money from S&Ls and buying money market mutual funds and other assets that paid more interest. S&Ls needed to attract deposits to cover their loans, which would remain on their books for years to come. In an effort to help the situation, Congress eliminated the ceiling on interest rates that S&Ls could pay depositors. However, getting more deposits didn't do the S&Ls much good because they had to pay more for deposits than they were making on the loans those deposits supported. They were on a collision course, and many of them failed. S&Ls began looking to make loans that would pay more interest. Many were too eager to lend money to customers who turned out to be poor credit risks. There was questionable behavior on both sides—S&L operators who were willing to go for broke in making loans and borrowers who misrepresented the potential success of their projects. Ultimately the taxpayers paid for much of the mess left in the wake of these questionable practices.

Think Critically

What was the ethical problem in this scenario?

Access the web page for the Federal Open Market Committee through econxtra.swlearning.com. Under the heading "Meetings and Proceedings of the FOMC," you will find a calendar of meetings. Choose one of the years, and click on "Statement" for all of the meetings in that year. Write a paragraph summarizing the decisions the FOMC made regarding the federal funds rate for that year.

econxtra.swlearning.com

TEAM WORK

Work in groups of three to four students to research the federal funds rate on the Federal Open Market Committee web page, as directed in the Net Bookmark activity. Each group member should choose a different year to research. Compare and discuss your findings as a group, referring to the line graph in Figure 17.5.

Recent History of Federal Funds Rate

Figure 17.5 shows the federal funds rate since early 1996. Consider what was going on in the economy during the period. Between early 1996 and late 1998, the economy grew nicely with low inflation, so the FOMC kept the federal funds rate relatively stable in a range of 5.25 percent to 5.5 percent. In late 1998, fears of a global financial crisis prompted the FOMC to drop its target rate to 4.75 percent.

By the summer of 1999, those fears had subsided, and the FOMC became concerned that robust economic growth would trigger higher inflation. In a series of six steps, the FOMC raised the federal funds rate from 4.75 percent to 6.5 percent. In early 2001, concerns about declining consumer confidence, weaker capital spending, falling manufacturing output, and a sinking stock market prompted the FOMC to reverse course. That began the series of rate cuts into 2003.

CHECKPOINT
What is the federal funds rate, and why does the Fed use it to set monetary policy?

Recent Ups and Downs in the Federal Funds Rate

Figure 17.5

To understand the fluctuations of the federal funds rate, consider what was going on in the economy during the periods shown here.

Source: Based on monthly averages from the Federal Reserve Bank.

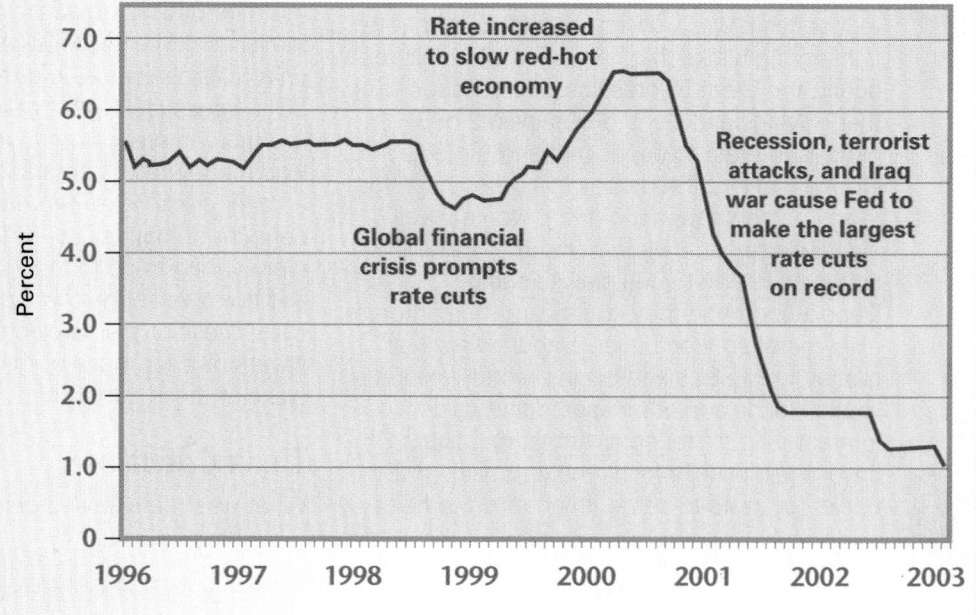

Key Concepts

1. The demand for money normally grows when there is economic growth. What effect does this growth in the demand for money have on interest rates? Explain your answer.

2. If something happened to cause savers to lose faith in the safety of banks, what might happen to the economy? Explain your answer.

3. People tend to spend, deposit, or invest their cash quickly when interest rates are high. This increases the speed at which financial transactions take place. What then would happen if interest rates are low? How would this affect the economy?

4. If the Fed purchased $2 billion in government bonds, what would happen to the money supply and interest rates in the economy? Why might the Fed implement such a policy?

5. Why might the Fed set a target rate for the federal funds rate that is 1 percent higher than its current rate? What steps would the Fed be likely to take to accomplish its goal?

Graphing Exercise

6. Use data in the table to construct a double line graph to show changes in the federal funds rate and the prime interest rate over the years from 1993 through 2003. Does there appear to be a relationship between these interest rates? Would you expect to find similar relationships between the federal funds rate and other interest rates? Why or why not?

Think Critically

7. **Government** Investigate the policies of the Reagan administration that were intended to stimulate the economy in 1981 and 1982. Compare these policies with the monetary policy implemented at the same time under the Federal Reserve's Chairman Paul Volcker. How does this show that government policies are not always coordinated?

Average Annual Federal Funds Rate and Prime Interest Rate, 1993–2003

Year	Federal Funds Rate	Prime Interest Rate
1993	3.02%	6.00%
1994	4.21	7.15
1995	5.83	8.83
1996	5.30	8.27
1997	5.46	8.44
1998	5.35	8.35
1999	4.97	8.00
2000	6.24	9.23
2001	3.88	6.91
2002	1.67	4.67
2003	1.26 *	4.25 *

* 2003 interest rates based on first six months of that year.

Source: *Economic Indicators,* June 2003.

Xtra!
Study Tools
econxtra.swlearning.com

Sharpen Your Life Skills

Make Predictions

In general, people are pretty smart. They tend to know what's happening in the world by keeping up with the news. Government decisions often come as no surprise to them, including decisions of the Federal Reserve System. In fact, many people think they know what the Fed is going to do long before it does it. If this is true, can the Fed make decisions that surprise people and cause them to change their plans? Or, put more simply, would an interest-rate increase have any impact on your plans if you had been sure for weeks it would take place? Making predictions about the future of the economy is important to ordinary consumers and business managers alike.

What do you think the Fed would do in each of the situations described below? How would your expectations affect your own choices? Explain the reasons for your choice.

Apply Your Skill

1. You have a $100,000 mortgage on a house that has a flexible interest rate of 6.0 percent that could change at any time. The economy has been growing rapidly for the past six months, and the rate of inflation has been going up steadily. You can refinance your mortgage at a fixed rate of 6.5 percent if you do it now. Would you refinance your mortgage now?

2. You plan to sell your home at some time in the next year or two. Right now, mortgages can be obtained at an interest rate of 6.0 percent. The economy has been growing rapidly for the past six months, and the rate of inflation has been going up steadily. Would your choose to put your home on the market right now, or would you wait awhile?

3. You have found a home you wish to buy. You need to take out a $100,000 mortgage to make this purchase. Your bank offers to lend you the money at either a 7 percent fixed rate or at a flexible rate that currently is 6.5 percent. On one hand, you like the idea of having a fixed rate that you know won't change in the future. On the other, you would like to pay the lower rate now. The economy has been in decline for six months, and the unemployment rate has reached 7 percent. Which mortgage would you choose?

movers & shakers

Howard Schultz *Chairman, Chief Global Strategist,*
Starbucks Corporation

Howard Schultz's family lived in a Brooklyn, New York, housing project. Thanks to a football scholarship, Howard was able to attend Northern Michigan University. After graduating he worked a variety of jobs until becoming the manager of U.S. operations for Hammarplast, a Swedish maker of stylish kitchen equipment.

While at Hammarplast, Schultz noticed that a company in Seattle, Washington, seemed to be purchasing an unusual number of specialty coffee makers. So in 1981 he traveled there to see what the company, called Starbucks, was doing with them. He fell in love with the rich aroma of the Starbucks store and with the extraordinary care the owners of the store put into selecting and roasting coffee beans. "I walked away...saying, 'What a great company, what a great city. I'd love to be a part of that.'"

Schultz convinced the Starbucks owners to hire him, and he became director of marketing and operations. During a trip to Italy, Schultz noticed the popularity of Italian coffee bars. There were, in fact, 200,000 such coffee bars in Italy at that time. Unlike his bosses, Schultz couldn't shake his enthusiasm for opening coffee bars in the United States, so he opened one of his own, called "Il Giornale." A year later, with the backing of local investors, he bought Starbucks for $3.8 million. By year's end, 17 Starbucks coffee bars were established. Within five years, 165 Starbucks were open, in such cities as San Francisco, San Diego and Denver.

By 1995, the company began opening Starbucks in Barnes & Noble and in Canada's Chapters bookstores. It finalized deals to have Starbucks served to all United Airlines customers and to guests of some of the finest U.S. hotels. It also opened a second roasting plant. By the end of 1995, Starbucks operated 676 coffee bars. The next five years saw growth into foreign markets, the introduction of Starbucks ice cream, and Starbucks coffee being sold in grocery stores.

"Our first priority is to take care of our people (employees), because they are the ones responsible for communicating our passion to our customers. If we do that, we accomplish our second priority, taking care of our customers," Schultz believes. He is true to his word, offering stock options to all employees and comprehensive health insurance for any employee working 20 or more hours a week.

Starbucks began to sell its common stock in 1992 under the trading symbol SBUX. The trend has been upward ever since. "Our stock market listing provided the liquidity that has allowed many people at Starbucks, including me, to cash in stock options and buy things we need or have long wished for. It has likewise served as a great incentive to attract talented people, who join us not only because of the excitement of building a fast-growing company but also because of the value we are creating."

Today there are more than 6,200 Starbucks throughout the world. Revenues for fiscal year 2003 were $4.1 billion, which represented a 24 percent increase from fiscal year 2002 and marked 12 consecutive years of growth.

SOURCE READING
Is it more beneficial for Starbucks employees to receive stock options instead of cash bonuses? Why or why not? Find the passage in Lesson 17.2 of this textbook that supports your answer.

ENTREPRENEURS IN ACTION
What traits does Howard Schultz possess that have helped him be successful in business? If you were starting your own business, which of these traits would you want to have, and why?

Objectives

> Understand why changes in the money supply affect only prices in the long run, not real GDP.

> Examine the historical link between money supply growth and inflation.

> Determine why political independence of central banks results in lower inflation.

Overview

In the short run, money influences aggregate demand and real GDP through its effect on interest rates. In the long run, the impact of money on aggregate demand is more direct. If the Fed increases the money supply, people will try to spend more. However, because the economy's potential output remains fixed from one year to the next, this greater spending simply increases the price level—there is more money chasing the same output. Thus, in the long run, increases in the money supply result only in inflation.

Key Term

euro

[In the News]

● The Problems of Too Much or Too Little Money

What happens when there is too much money in circulation? In the 1990s, extremely high inflation in Russia following the breakup of the Soviet Union increased Russian demand for so-called hard currencies, including the U.S. dollar. As a result, Russians traded their rubles and hoarded their dollars. In 1995, a Russian central banker claimed that the value of Russians' dollar holdings exceeded the value of their ruble holdings. What about the opposite problem when there is not enough money to go around? This happened a few years ago to Panama, a country that relies on the U.S. dollar as its currency. In 1988, in response to charges that Panama's leader was involved in drug dealing, U.S. officials froze Panamanian assets in the United States. This touched off a panic in Panama as bank customers tried to withdraw their deposits. Banks were forced to close for nine weeks. Dollars were hoarded, and people resorted to barter. Because barter is less efficient than a smoothly functioning monetary system, Panama's GDP fell by 30 percent in 1988. Both of these examples show that when a country has too much or too little of its currency available, people will come to rely on another mechanism for exchange. This alternative is seldom as efficient as a smoothly functioning monetary system, however. It has been said that no machine increases the economy's productivity as much as properly functioning money.

Think About It

Why did Panama's GDP decrease as a result of people hoarding their money?

Long-Run Effect of Money Supply Changes

Monetary authorities try to keep the economy on an even keel by smoothing fluctuations in the economy over the business cycle. These are based mostly on short-run adjustments in the federal funds rate. What happens in the long run?

Production in the Long Run

In the short run, the aggregate supply curve slopes upward. Thus, an increase in aggregate demand increases both real GDP and the price level, as was shown in Figure 17.4. In the long run, the economy produces its potential level of output, which is the economy's maximum sustainable output. Potential output is determined by the supply of resources in the economy, the state of technology, and the rules of the game that nurture production and exchange. Potential output is the economy's normal capability on a regular or sustained basis. The economy can't produce any more than potential output in the long run.

An increase in the money supply doesn't change potential output. An increase in the money supply means only that there is more money chasing the same potential output.

Changes in Aggregate Demand

The economy cannot produce more than its potential output in the long run. You could think of the economy's long-run supply curve as a vertical line drawn at the economy's potential level of output, as shown in Figure 17.6. That figure also shows the long-run effect of an increase in the money supply. An increase in the money supply causes a rightward shift of the aggregate demand curve from *AD* to *AD'*. Because output in the long run is fixed at the economy's potential output, the rightward shift of the aggregate demand curve leads only to a higher price level. Output remains unchanged at its potential level. The economy's potential output level is not affected by changes in the money supply. In the long run,

---

An Increase in the Money Supply in the Long Run

Figure 17.6

An increase in the supply of money in the long run results in a higher price level, or inflation. Because the long-run aggregate supply curve is fixed, increases in the money supply affect only the price level, not real output.

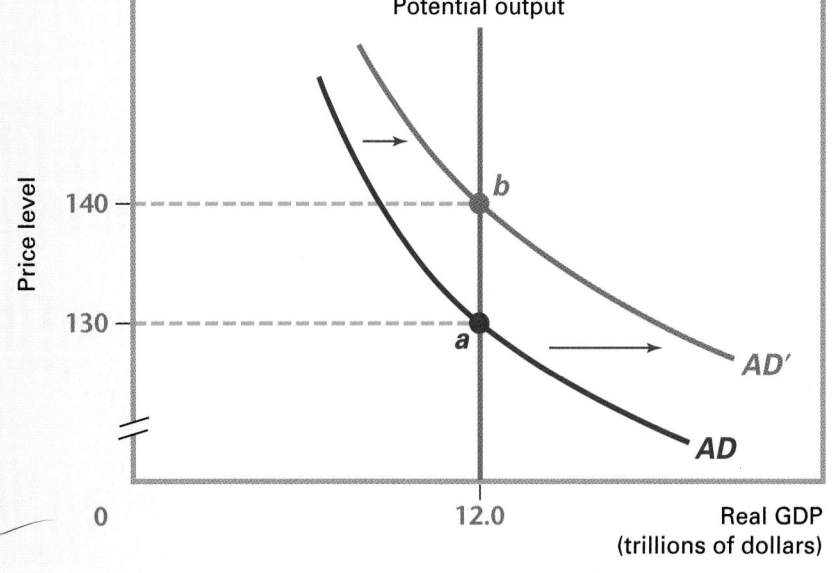

---

increases in the money supply result only in higher prices, or inflation.

CHECKPOINT
Why do changes in the money supply affect only the price level in the long run, not real GDP?

Long-Run Evidence

In the United States and around the world, what has been the long-run relationship between increases in the money supply and inflation?

Money Supply Growth and Inflation in U.S. History

Since the Federal Reserve System was established in 1913, the United States has suffered three bouts of high infla-

tion. These periods occurred from 1913 to 1920, 1939 to 1948, and 1967 to 1980. Each was preceded and accompanied by a corresponding growth in the money supply. Each U.S. episode of high inflation was related to a rapid growth in the money supply.

Money Supply Growth and Inflation Around the World

What has been the link around the world between changes in the money supply and inflation in the long run? Again, monetary theory points to a relationship in the long run between the percentage change in the money supply and the percentage change in the price level. Figure 17.7 illustrates this using the average annual growth rate in M2 over a 10-year period and the average annual inflation rate during that period for 85 countries around the world. As you can see, the points fall rather neatly along the line, showing a positive relation between money growth, measured

---

Inflation and Money Growth Worldwide

Figure 17.7

Inflation is higher in countries where the money supply grows faster.

Source: The World Bank, *World Development Report 1992* (New York: Oxford University Press, 1992), Table 13. Figures are annual averages for 85 countries between 1980 and 1990.

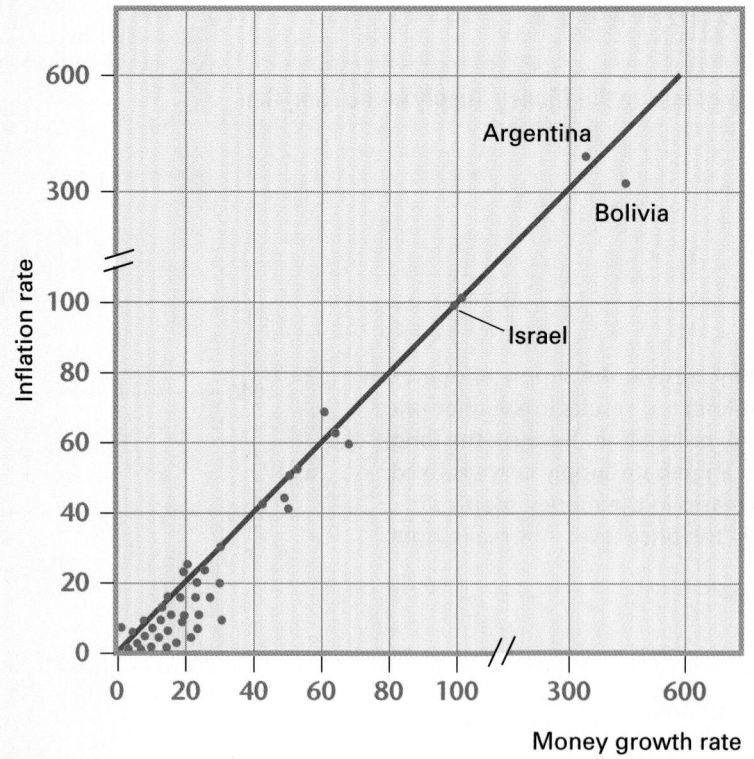

CHAPTER 17 Money Creation, Federal Reserve, Monetary Policy

along the horizontal axis, and inflation, measured along the vertical axis.

Extremely high inflation, or *hyperinflation,* became a problem for some countries in the twentieth century. In every case, hyperinflation has been accompanied by extremely rapid growth in the supply of paper money. For example, Argentina—which had the highest average annual inflation rate over the 10-year period in the sample, at 395 percent—also had the highest average annual rate of growth in the money supply, at 369 percent.

Argentina, Bolivia, and Israel all managed to tame inflation. Households in all three countries, perhaps mindful of their experience with hyperinflation, still hoard a lot of U.S. currency.

The most famous hyperinflation during the last century was in Germany between August 1922 and November 1923, when inflation averaged 322 percent *per month.* Inflation was halted when the German government created an independent central bank that issued a limited supply of new currency convertible on demand into gold.

CHECKPOINT
What has been the link between money growth and inflation in the United States and around the world?

Other Issues in Monetary Policy

Three issues remain with regard to monetary policy:

1. the relationship between inflation and the central bank's independence from political pressure,

2. the problem of deflation, and

3. the lags involved with monetary policy.

Fed Independence

Some economists argue that the Fed would do better in the long run if it were committed to the single goal of price stability. To focus on price stability, a central bank would have to remain insulated from political pressure. Elected officials usually urge the Fed to

SPAN THE GLOBE

Hyperinflation and Political Instability

Incidents of hyperinflation have often been accompanied by political upheaval. Almost every country that has experienced hyperinflation has had subsequent political instability as desperate citizens looked for ways to protect themselves. In Germany, the hyperinflation following World War I led many people to lose faith in the democratic government. Both the Communist Party and the rising Nazi Party thought they could use this uncertainty to gain control of the country. The democratic government was able to remain in power by undertaking currency reform, but the memories of hyperinflation played a role in the eventual rise of the Nazis in the 1930s. More recently, hyperinflation in Bolivia resulted in no less than ten different governments ruling the country between 1978 and 1982. These included several military governments as the result of numerous overthrow attempts. Not until after a democratically elected government issued reforms to stop the inflation did political stability begin to emerge in Bolivia. The same kind of situation happened in Argentina. Hyperinflation in that country sparked a massive economic crisis, which ended in the country having four different presidents during one two-week period in 2001. After weeks of public rioting and looting, it looked as if democracy might be dead in Argentina. However, a caretaker president then instituted a series of reforms that helped ease the economic crisis. The violence stopped, and people were willing to give the government another chance. Argentineans finally went to the polls in the spring of 2003 to elect a new president.

Think Critically

Why do you think a country tends to experience political instability when hyperinflation occurs in its economy?

stimulate the economy whenever it's performing below its potential. All this short-run stimulation, however, can lead to inflation in the long run.

When the Fed was established in 1913, several features insulated it from politics, such as the 14-year terms with staggered appointments for members of its Board of Governors. Also, the Fed does not rely on a Congressional appropriation. The Fed has its own source of income.

Here's how the Fed earns a profit. The Fed, like any other bank, has a balance sheet. More than three-fourths of the Fed's assets are U.S. government securities. The Fed bought them through open-market operations. They are IOUs from the federal government, and they earn interest for the Fed.

More than three-fourths of the Fed's liabilities are Federal Reserve notes in circulation. These notes—U.S. currency—are IOUs from the Fed and are therefore liabilities of the Fed. However, the Fed pays no interest on Federal Reserve notes.

The Fed's primary assets—U.S. government securities—earn interest for the Fed. Its primary liabilities—Federal Reserve notes—require no interest payments by the Fed.

The Fed also earns income from various services it provides member banks. After covering its operating costs,

euro

The new European common currency

the Fed turns over any remaining income to the U.S. Treasury. In some years the Fed turns over more than $20 billion. You might think of this as profit resulting from the Fed's ability to issue notes and create bank reserves.

Central Bank Independence and Inflation

Does a central bank's independence from political pressure affect its performance? In one study, the central banks of 17 advanced industrial countries were ranked from least independent to most independent. It turned out that inflation during the 15-year span studied was lowest in countries with the most independent central banks and highest in countries with the least independent central banks. The U.S. central bank is considered relatively independent, and inflation here averaged about halfway between the most independent and least independent groups of banks.

Independence Trend

The trend around the world is toward greater central bank independence from political pressure. For example, Australia and New Zealand, two countries that had problems with inflation, have amended laws governing their central banks to make price stability the primary goal. Chile, Colombia, and Argentina—developing countries that have experienced hyperinflation—have legislated more central bank independence.

The framework that established the new European currency, the **euro**, identified price stability as the main objective of the new European Central Bank. That bank announced a policy to keep inflation under 2.0 percent. In fact, the bank came under criticism recently for appearing reluctant to cut its target interest rate even though a recession loomed and the unemployment rate exceeded 8 percent.

Could Deflation Pose a Problem?

Hyperinflation can bring an economy to its knees. But deflation, a decline in the average price level, is no picnic either.

NETBookmark

Argentina limited its central bank's ability to issue new currency by creating a currency board. The currency board required that each new peso be backed by one U.S. dollar held in reserve by the bank. Access the article "Are Currency Boards a Cure for All Monetary Problems?" through econxtra.swlearning.com. This article, from the IMF publication *Finance and Development,* explores the use of independent currency boards to control the supply of money in advanced industrial countries. What does the article note as the advantages and disadvantages of having a currency board in a country?

econxtra.swlearning.com

Falling prices during the Great Depression caused consumers to delay major purchases, waiting for prices to drop even more. This reduced aggregate demand, output, and employment. Investment also tanked because lower prices erased profits. Further, borrowers found it more difficult to pay off their debts as their incomes fell.

In recent years, Japan has suffered from deflation averaging about 1 percent a year. Germany, now the world's third largest economy (behind the United States and Japan) also is facing deflation. Fed Chairman Alan Greenspan has voiced concern about the possibility of deflation here. He said the Fed would fight deflation as fiercely as it fights high inflation. Most economists, including Greenspan, don't think the nation will experience deflation. Regardless, you should know that deflation can create as much havoc in an economy as high inflation.

Lags and Monetary Policy

One final consideration: How do the lags involved with monetary policy compare with those involved with fiscal policy? Recall that one problem with fiscal policy involves lags at several stages of the process. Does monetary policy face the same problems?

The *recognition lag,* the time required to identify a problem with the economy, is probably about the same for both policies. Monetary and fiscal decision makers are each supported by a competent team of economists tracking the economy.

With regard to the *decision-making lag,* monetary policy has the advantage, since the FOMC can make a decision during one meeting. Once a decision is made, monetary policy also has the advantage because the FOMC can begin executing open-market operations within minutes. Fiscal policy may take months to implement, so the *implementation lag* is shorter for monetary policy.

Finally, with regard to the *effectiveness lag,* it may be a toss-up. Market interest

THE WALL STREET JOURNAL

Reading It Right What's the relevance of the following statement from *The Wall Street Journal:* "[The Philadelphia Fed President] has warned about the danger of cutting interest rates too much this year because, given the 6- to 12-month lags with which monetary policy affects the economy, it could lead to the economy growing unsustainably quickly next year, fueling inflation pressure."

rates can move quickly in response to a change in Fed policy, but there is no way to know how long it will take businesses and consumers to react to changed interest rates. The full effect of changes in the money supply may take a year or more, as long as it may take fiscal policy to show its full effects.

✓ CHECKPOINT
What is the relationship between inflation and the political independence of central banks?

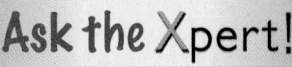

Ask the Xpert!
econxtra.swlearning.com

Why do so many people listen to Alan Greenspan?

© John Neubauer/Photo Edit Inc.

What advantage does monetary policy have over fiscal policy regarding decision-making lags? What role does the FOMC play in this?

Key Concepts

1. If the Fed worked to keep the unemployment rate at 3 percent by increasing the money supply year after year, what would happen to prices? Would the Fed be successful in reaching its goal in the long run? Why, or why not?

2. Why would deflation be harmful to the economy?

3. Why might it take many months or possibly more than a year for people and businesses to respond to a changes in the money supply? What does this tell you about the usefulness of monetary policy?

Graphing Exercise

4. Use data in the table to create a double line graph of interest rates and changes in real (adjusted for inflation) GDP from 1994 through 2002. Does there seem to be a relationship between these values? Which do you think is the cause and which is the effect? Explain your answer.

Interest Rate on 3-Year Government Bonds and Change in Real GDP, 1994–2002

Year	Interest Rate on 3-Year Government Securities	Percentage Growth in Real GDP
1994	6.27%	4.04%
1995	6.25	2.67
1996	5.99	3.57
1997	6.10	4.44
1998	5.14	4.32
1999	5.49	4.11
2000	6.22	3.75
2001	4.09	0.25
2002	3.10	2.43

Source: *Economic Indicators*, June 2003, pp. 2, 30.

Think Critically

5. **Management** Business owners cannot be sure what policy the Fed will follow. When they guess wrong, it can have a devastating effect. In 1978, for example, the owners of a small steel mill in upstate New York borrowed $50 million to purchase new equipment. They agreed to pay a flexible rate of interest set at prime plus 1 percent. (When prime was 8 percent, they were required to pay 9 percent.) When the loan was first taken out, they were paying 9 percent interest, or $4.5 million per year. Three years later, actions of the Federal Reserve System had caused the prime interest rate to grow to 20 percent, forcing the firm to pay 21 percent on its loan. This amounted to $10.5 million in interest per year. The firm was unable to make these payments and failed in 1983. If you owned a firm and were considering borrowing funds, how concerned would you be over what the Fed's future monetary policy might be? Would you avoid borrowing if you could? How might this uncertainty affect the economy?

to History

Deflation
in the Nineteenth Century

Following the Civil War, the United States' prices, especially for agricultural products, began to suffer from deflation. In the decade following 1866, wheat prices dropped from $2.06 a bushel to $1.00. Fifteen years later, farmers were receiving 60 cents a bushel for wheat. Over the same period, corn prices dropped from 66 cents a bushel to 30 cents. Some decline in prices was due to the introduction of new techniques and equipment, which helped farmers become more productive, thus increasing supply faster than demand. Farmers, however, wanted inflation. Many had run up debts to buy or expand farms, to buy equipment, or to support themselves after a bad year. While the cost to pay back their loans remained the same, lower prices meant they had to produce more to earn enough money to make the payments.

Farmers saw one solution to their problem in the government's issuance of Greenbacks. This was paper money issued during the Civil War, which had no backing in gold or silver. After the War, the government had been withdrawing Greenbacks, thereby leaving less money in circulation. The effect was that fewer dollars were chasing more goods, thus bringing lower prices. For farmers, the answer seemed to be the government's issuing as many Greenbacks as it took to raise prices. This idea was so strong that a political party—the Greenback Party—was formed around it. Business interests, however, opposed this solution, and most politicians pursued a policy of "sound money."

In 1873, the government passed the Coinage Act. The Act said that the government would no longer buy silver to turn into coins. The cost of silver was more than the government was willing to pay. Farmers were outraged because they believed more silver purchases would increase the money supply, resulting in inflation and higher farm prices. Farmers and

now silver miners, referring to the act as the "Crime of '73," demanded that the government resume the buying and coining of silver. The government responded by passing the Bland Allison Act (1878) and the Sherman Silver Purchase Act (1890). These acts authorized a limited amount of silver to be purchased and turned into coins. Neither created the inflation desired by the farmers and silver miners, however.

In the election of 1896, which pitted William Jennings Bryan for the Democratic and Populist parties against Republican William McKinley, a major issue was the gold standard. Bryan traveled the country, arguing against the government policy and demanding an increased money supply. Despite his defeat, Bryan's "cross of gold" speech stands as one of the most famous in American history. However, by the turn of the century the farmers got their wish, and prices stopped declining. This had nothing to do with their efforts to change government policy, but with the additional deposits of gold that were discovered in Alaska and other parts of the world, which doubled the world's supply of gold.

THINK CRITICALLY
Write a paragraph to explain the effect deflation had on farmers' income and their ability to meet their fixed costs (mortgages, etc.). Assume that a farmer's income and fixed costs are both $1,000 and that there is 10 percent deflation each year. What would the deflation do with the farmer's ability to meet his debts? Next, assume income and fixed costs of $1,000 and a 10 percent *inflation* rate. What would this do to the farmer's ability to meet his debts? In what way is the homebuyer of today similar to the farmer of the late 1800s?

Chapter Assessment

Summary

17.1 How Banks Work

a To establish a bank, a group of people must obtain a charter from either the federal or state government. They must agree to invest an amount of money in the new bank. The bank will report its financial status on a *balance sheet,* which lists its *assets* on one side and its *liabilities* and the amount of the owners' equity on the other. The amounts on both sides must be equal. Under the fractional reserve system, banks are required to maintain a portion of deposits on reserve.

Xtra! Quiz Prep
econxtra.swlearning.com

b New funds deposited in a bank can be multiplied into much larger increases in total deposits over time. When the Fed buys a bond from a bank, the money paid is new to the economy. The bank will have increased reserves that it will loan or spend in some other way. When the money is spent, it is received as income by someone else, who will deposit it back into a bank. The bank then, after holding back its required reserve, will make additional loans or invest these funds in some other way. This cycle of deposits, reserves, loans, spending, and more deposits is repeated many times, causing the amount of money in the economy to grow by much more than the amount of the original bond purchase.

c The *money multiplier* is limited by the *required reserve ratio.* When banks are required to keep more deposits on reserve, they are able to make fewer loans and the process will be slowed.

17.2 Monetary Policy in the Short Run

a People demand money so they can complete financial transactions and to hold as a store of value. The amount they wish to hold at any time depends on many factors, including the interest rate. When interest rates are high, people are willing to hold less money.

b The *Money supply* is determined by the amount of money that the Federal Reserve System has placed in the economy. It can be viewed as a vertical line graph. The intersection of a demand for money with the supply of money determines the market interest rate in the economy. An increase in the money supply will lead to a lower interest rate while a decrease in the money supply will cause a higher market interest rate. Lower interest rates stimulate the economy while higher rates slow its growth.

c The Fed sets targets for the *federal funds rate,* which is the rate banks charge each other for borrowing bank reserves. The Fed targets this rate because it has tighter control over it than other interest rates. When the Fed changes its target for the federal funds rate, most other interest rates change, too.

17.3 Monetary Policy in the Long Run

a Production in the long run cannot be sustained above the economy's potential. Efforts to expand aggregate demand and production beyond its potential can succeed in the short run, but will cause prices to rise and production to fall back to its potential in the long run.

b All economically developed nations have a monetary authority similar to the Fed. In some nations, this authority is quite independent of the political process. In others, it is controlled by political figures in the government. In these latter nations, rates of inflation have tended to be higher than in other nations where the monetary authorities are more independent.

c Deflation makes it more difficult for those in debt to repay their loans and discourages businesses from investing in new facilities or hiring as many workers. Some people think there is a danger of deflation in the United States and in other developed nations.

d There are lags in the effectiveness of monetary policy. It takes time for the Fed to recognize that there is a problem, decide what action to take, implement the policy, and for the economy to react to the changed policy.

Review Economic Terms

Choose the term that best fits the definition. On a separate sheet of paper, write the letter of the correct answer. Some terms may not be used.

_____ 1. Bank reserves in excess of required reserves

_____ 2. The stock of money available in the economy at a particular time

_____ 3. Any physical property or financial claim that is owned

_____ 4. The dollar amount that must be held in reserve

_____ 5. The interest rate charged in the federal funds market

_____ 6. The relationship between how much money people want to hold and the interest rate

_____ 7. A Fed regulation that dictates the minimum percentage of deposits each bank must keep in reserve

_____ 8. A financial statement showing assets, liabilities, and net worth at a given time

_____ 9. An amount owed

_____10. The multiple by which the money supply increases as a result of an increase in excess reserves in the banking system

a. **asset**

b. **balance sheet**

c. **euro**

d. **excess reserves**

e. **federal funds market**

f. **federal funds rate**

g. **liability**

h. **money demand**

i. **money multiplier**

j. **money supply**

k. **net worth**

l. **required reserve ratio**

m. **required reserves**

Review Economic Concepts

11. **True or False** Anyone who has enough money has the legal right to start a banking business.

12. A bank's _balance sheet_ lists its _assets_ on one side and its _liabilities_ and the amount of the owner's __?__on the other.

13. The _required reserve ratio_ is the
    a. amount of money a bank's owners must invest in the bank.
    b. share of its deposits that a bank may lend.
    c. amount of its deposits that a bank must hold on reserve.
    d. share of its deposits that a bank must hold on reserve.

14. **True or False** If the Fed bought a $100,000 government bond from a bank, the money supply would immediately grow by more than $100,000.

15. If the Fed lowered the _required reserve ratio_ from 10 percent to 8 percent, the money __?__ would increase from 10 to 12.5.

16. If people choose to hold a smaller share of income they receive in cash and deposit more of their earnings in checking accounts, the money expansion will be
    a. greater than it was in the past.
    b. the same as it was in the past.
    c. smaller than it was in the past.
    d. carried out more slowly than it was in the past.

17. **True or False** The demand for money is a measure of a stock. It is the amount of money people wish to hold at a particular time.

18. Which of the following events would reduce the impact of the _money multiplier_?
    a. The Fed purchases additional government bonds.
    b. People choose to hold more of their money in cash.
    c. The Fed lowers the required reserve ratio.
    d. The federal government borrows and spends more money.

19. If the Fed increases the *money supply,* the demand curve for money will

    a. remain unchanged.

    b. immediately shift to the right.

    c. immediately shift to the left.

    d. eventually shift to the left.

20. **True or False** The opportunity cost of holding cash is the interest that could have been earned but is forgone.

21. Lower interest rates stimulate the economy, while higher rates slow its __?__.

22. The Fed could increase interest rates by

    a. buying additional government bonds.

    b. lowering the required reserve ratio.

    c. lowering the discount rate.

    d. selling some of its government bonds.

23. The Fed sets interest rate targets for the __?__.

24. **True or False** Inflation is likely to occur if the Fed increases the *money supply* when the economy is already at its potential level of output.

25. By increasing the *money supply,* the Fed can

    a. increase output to its potential in the short run.

    b. increase output beyond its potential in the long run.

    c. decrease output to its potential in the short run.

    d. decrease output below its potential in the long run.

26. Countries that have experienced high rates of inflation also have usually had

    a. totalitarian forms of government.

    b. independent monetary authorities.

    c. rapid growth in their money supplies.

    d. large government budget surpluses.

27. __?__ may result from a decline in aggregate demand that forces the price level to fall.

Apply Economic Concepts

28. **Calculate the Impact of a Change in the Reserve Ratio** Suppose that the Fed decided to increase the reserve ratio from 10 to 12.5 percent. In theory, how would this change the value of the money multiplier? What would this do to the amount of each checking deposit that banks could lend? How would this decision affect interest rates and the economy? Explain your answer.

29. **Decide How Much Cash to Hold** Imagine that it is 10 years in the future. You are married and have two young children. Every month you pay $800 for your rent, $300 for your car loan, and at least $1,900 in other costs of living. You are trying to save $300 from every paycheck to make a down payment on a house in a few years. You earn a salary that provides you with a take-home pay of $2,000 every two weeks. Your savings account currently pays 2 percent interest. How much of your bi-weekly pay would you take in cash, deposit in your checking account, and put in your saving account? How would your decision change if the interest rate on your saving account increased to 10 percent?

30. **Choose When to Borrow** Imagine that you have a job that pays you a good wage. You have decided to borrow $20,000 to buy a new car. Right now the interest rate on a new-car loan is 9 percent. You have read in the newspaper that the Fed is likely to lower interest rates soon because many workers are being laid off and unemployment is on the rise. You believe that if you wait a few months, you might be able to borrow the money you need at only 7 percent interest. Would you buy the car now or wait for lower interest rates? What else should concern you? Explain your answers.

31. Decide Whether to Accept an After-School Job You spend many hours every week doing school work and helping around your home. You like to go out with your friends on the weekend. You really don't have much spare time. The economy is booming, and interest rates are low. On your way home from school, you notice a sign in the window of a store that promises a $10 per-hour wage for anyone who accepts a job as a sales clerk. When you ask about the job, the store owner says she will hire you only if you agree to work 16 hours each week. You accept the job, but you're not happy with the number of hours you must work. After you receive your first paycheck, you go shopping and find that because of taxes and inflation your money doesn't go very far. You decide you really don't want the job so you hand in your resignation and go back to asking your parents for money. Explain how this story is related to economic problems that take place when the Fed tries to move production in the economy to exceed its potential.

32. Sharpen Your Life Skills: Make Predictions On October 28, 2003, the Fed announced that it had left the target federal funds rate at 1.0 percent and that there was no expectation that this rate would be increased at any time in the near future. This was the lowest rate that had been targeted by the Fed in more than 40 years. The Fed chose to keep interest rates low at that time because the economy was suffering from a relatively high unemployment rate of more than 6 percent and a low rate of economic growth of about 2.5 percent. Inflation was of little concern because it was running at only about 2.0 percent. What if two years later the economy had recovered with unemployment down to 4.0 percent, production growing at a rate of more than 6 percent per year, and inflation up to a rate of 5.2 percent? Predict what the Fed would do to its target for the federal funds rate under these circumstances. Explain what the likely results would be for the economy.

33. Construct a Graph of Demand and Supply for Money The hypothetical data in the table represents the demand and supply for money in the U.S. economy. Construct a graph from these data. What is the equilibrium interest rate in this example? What are two events that might cause the equilibrium interest rate to increase? What are two events that might cause the equilibrium interest rate to fall?

Demand and Supply for Money (in billions of dollars)

Amount Demanded	Amount Supplied	Interest Rate
$ 500	$1,000	12.0%
750	1,000	10.0%
1,000	1,000	8.0%
1,250	1,000	6.0%
1,500	1,000	4.0%

e-con @pps — econxtra.swlearning.com

34. Access EconNews Online at econxtra. swlearning.com. Find the article entitled "Will the Fed Raise Rates?" Read the article, and then answer this question: What was the relationship between the lack of inflation in the economy in late 2003 and the large numbers of unemployed and underemployed workers?

Investing In Your Future

Project 5   SHIFTING PERSPECTIVES

🌀 The Situation

As she walked past security at the airport, Aleesha looked back at her family. Aleesha regretted taking this business trip more than anyone. She and Tom recently had been talking about the children's future schooling and needed to make a decision. However, discussions were to begin Monday in Washington with representatives of the Department of Defense about a possible deal to sell animal-restraint devices for use by the military. Later in the week, she was to meet with the law firm of Winston and Bailey on another matter.

So much had changed over the last two years. The sales figures for the new products were increasing monthly and should soon show a profit. The most dramatic success, the company's Capturecare device, had been purchased by several leading animal-control departments throughout the United States. In addition, the company also was test-marketing several spin-off consumer products for use by hunters. The new factory, located near the zoo, had started operations several months ago, and it was running smoothly. Unfortunately, the introduction of the new products and the new factory's financing had been based on predictions for an economic upturn. When the predictions proved incorrect, the future of the entire company was placed in jeopardy.

🌀 The Decision

Once in the air, Aleesha pulled out her laptop, opened a file, and began listing the pros and cons of the children's schooling. Tom wanted to send the children to the local public grade school. Aleesha preferred a nearby private school that would assure the children more individual attention. Thanks to the earlier profits of the business, she and Tom now owned their own home and had plenty in savings to pay the private school tuition for many years. Aleesha worked on the lists for some time. Then she took a moment to reflect on how different her life had become.

Finally, her thoughts turned to the upcoming meetings. The first, with representatives of the Armed Services, resulted from months of preparation. Aleesha had been awarded a government contract to supply animal capture, restraint, and other devices to the Army and the Marines. At first Aleesha was elated, as the contract payout would solve most of the company's current financial problems. However, she soon realized that one of the contract provisions could commit her company to develop devices used to capture animals used as weapons by opposing military forces and terrorist organizations. Her animal-capture devices would be used by U.S. forces to capture animals used to carry explosives, and the animals then would be put to death. The thought horrified her, and she knew she would be reluctant to agree to the contract.

The meetings later in the week also concerned her. Over the last two years, because of her factory's location, the company had been given tax breaks. Now, due to the economic downturn, the tax-relief program was about to be eliminated. As there was no national group representing her type of business, Aleesha hired the lobbying firm of Winston and Bailey to try to keep the program alive.

Activities

Divide into teams or work individually, as directed by your teacher, to perform the following tasks.

Apply the steps in the following decision-making process to Aleesha's current situation:

1. *Define the problem.* Aleesha faces multiple decisions this time. Define each problem in a way that will allow a clear solution. The issues involve:

a. her children's schooling

b. the Department of Defense contract

c. the law firm of Winston and Bailey

2. *Identify her choices.*

3. *Evaluate the pluses and minuses of each choice.*

4. *Make a choice.*

5. *Provide "action" steps that are appropriate to the decision.*

6. *Critique the decision.*

Research

Research for the information needed to make the decision, such as the pros and cons of public versus private school, the use of animals in modern warfare, and the world of Washington lobbyists.

Present

Arrive at a decision. Then prepare a presentation for the class on the six steps you took to achieve this decision.

Unit 6

The International Economy

Comparative advantage, specialization, and exchange help people get the most from their scarce resources. Despite the clear benefits from free international trade, trade restrictions date back centuries. Pressure from producers on governments to impose trade barriers continues to this day. Still, the United States plays a major role in the world economy, not only as the largest importer but also as the largest exporter. While the U.S. dollar remains the currency of choice in world trade, all nations face the challenge of achieving greater stability in their global finances.

18 International Trade

Consider

If the United States is such a rich and productive nation, why are so many goods and services imported?

Why isn't the United States self-sufficient?

If free trade is such a good idea, why do some producers try to restrict foreign trade?

What's up with the euro?

Is a growing U.S. trade deficit a growing worry?

POINT YOUR BROWSER

econxtra.swlearning.com

© Getty Images/PhotoDisc

Objectives

> Identify sources of comparative advantage.

> Discuss the gains from international trade even without comparative advantage.

> Describe U.S. exports and imports.

Overview

This morning you put on your Levi jeans made in Mexico, pulled on your Benetton sweater from Italy, and laced up your Timberland boots from Thailand. After a breakfast that included bananas from Honduras, you headed for school in a Swedish Volvo fueled by Venezuelan oil. The world is a giant shopping mall, and Americans are big spenders. Foreigners buy American products, too—products such as grain, personal computers, aircraft, movies, trips to Disney World, and thousands of other goods and services.

[In the News]

● Mexico Bleeds Workers and Jobs

When the North American Free Trade Agreement (NAFTA) took effect January 1, 1994, it was praised as a way to improve economic conditions in the United States, Canada, and Mexico. Mexico immediately benefited from the shifting of manufacturing jobs from the United States into Mexican factories. However, today Mexico is caught in a situation that is bleeding it of its work and workers. The recent downturn in the U.S. economy led U.S. companies to redirect to China the manufacturing jobs it had been sending to Mexico. In China, labor costs are roughly one-third of the $13 a day paid on average in Mexico. In other words, Mexico no longer enjoyed the comparative advantage of providing the lowest-cost labor force for these jobs. Many Mexicans then decided to move north to the United States, where they would receive higher wages than they could in Mexico. Consequently, a river of undocumented workers totaling well over five million people began to flow into the United States, where transplanted Mexicans can make as much in a day as they can in a week in Mexico.

Think About It

What might motivate these undocumented workers to return to Mexico? Is having these workers in the U. S. a good or bad thing? Explain your answer.

Comparative Advantage

Recall the discussion in Chapter 2 about how you and your neighbor could increase output by specializing. The law of comparative advantage says that the individual with the lowest opportunity cost of producing a particular good should specialize in that good. Just as individuals benefit from specialization and exchange, so do businesses, states, and nations.

To reap the gains that arise from specialization, countries engage in international trade. *To maximize the benefits of trade, each country specializes in the goods that it produces at the lowest opportunity cost.* As a result, all countries can become better off than if each tried to go it alone. World output increases when countries specialize.

How does a country decide what to produce? In other words, how does it determine its comparative advantages? Trade based on comparative advantage is usually prompted by differences in the quantity and quality of resources across countries. These resources include labor and capital, soil and seasons, and mineral deposits.

Labor and Capital

Two key resources are labor and capital. Countries differ not only in their availability of labor and capital but also in the qualities of these resources. Countries with a well-educated and well-trained labor force will specialize in producing goods that require such talent. Similarly, countries with state-of-the-art manufacturing technologies will specialize in producing goods that require high-tech capital.

Some countries, such as the United States and Japan, have an educated labor force and abundant high-tech capital. Both resources result in greater productivity per worker. This makes each nation quite competitive globally in producing goods that require skilled labor and technologically advanced capital.

Soil and Seasons

Some countries are blessed with fertile land and favorable growing seasons. The United States, for example, has been called the "bread basket of the world." The country's rich farmland is ideal for growing corn, wheat, and other grains. Honduras has the ideal climate for growing bananas. Coffee grows best in the climate and elevation of Colombia, Brazil, and Jamaica. Thus, the United States exports grain and imports coffee and bananas.

Seasonal differences across countries also create gains from trade. For example, during America's winter months, Chileans sell Americans fruit and Canadians travel to Florida for sun and fun. During the summer months, Americans export fruit to Chile and Americans travel to Canada for fishing and camping.

Mineral Deposits

Mineral resources often are concentrated in particular parts of the world, such as oil in Saudi Arabia, bauxite in Jamaica, and diamonds in South Africa. The United States has abundant coal deposits but not enough oil to satisfy domestic demand. Thus, the United States exports coal and imports oil.

In summary, *countries export what they can produce at a lower opportunity cost and import products that other countries can produce at a lower opportunity cost. As a result of this trade, all countries can produce and consume more.*

CHECKPOINT
What resources lead to a country's comparative advantage?

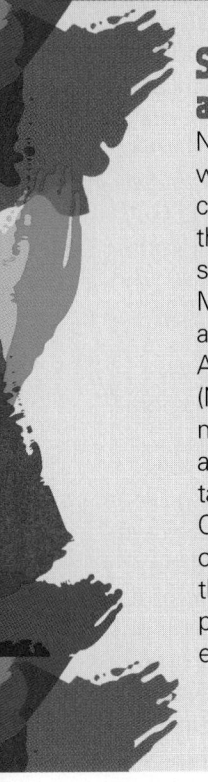

Should Lax Environmental Laws Be a Comparative Advantage?

When the North American Free Trade Agreement (NAFTA) was negotiated 10 years ago, environmental concerns were addressed by what was called the "green guardian." This phrase referred to a side accord among the signers of NAFTA—Mexico, the United States, and Canada. This accord officially was named the North American Agreement on Environmental Cooperation (NAAEC). It set up a Commission for Environmental Cooperation (CEC) to help coordinate and implement policy solutions to environmental problems. Unfortunately, the creation of the CEC seems to have been the high point of its operations, with things going downhill from there. Critics claim the NAAEC actually aided polluters by allowing the referral of recognized environmental problems to a commission (the CEC) that lacked the powers to take effective corrective action. In a recent self-analysis report, the CEC itself concluded that the free trade allowed by NAFTA had the partial effect of allowing companies to move severely polluting factories to jurisdictions with less-strict anti-pollution laws. In particular, industries such as pulp and paper, mining, iron and steel production, and chemicals all found relatively safe havens in Mexico under the free-trade umbrella. A provision similar to the "green guardian" is being considered for inclusion in the Free Trade Area of the Americas (FTAA) agreement that will create a similar free-trade zone stretching throughout North and South America.

Think Critically

Do you think moving plants that cause pollution to Mexico is ethical? Why or why not?

Other Benefits of Trade

If each country had an identical stock of resources and each country combined those resources with equal efficiency, then there would be no comparative advantage. Yet international trade could still benefit both sides. Here are two reasons why.

Economies of Scale

If a producer experiences *economies of scale*—that is, if the average cost of output declines as a firm expands its scale of production—countries can gain from specialization and trade. Such specialization allows firms in each nation to produce enough to enjoy economies of scale.

As you will see later in the chapter, the primary reason for establishing one single market in Europe was to offer producers there a large, open market of more than 330 million consumers. European producers can increase production, have economies of scale, and sell for less. In the process, these producers also will become more competitive trading outside of Europe.

Differences in Tastes

Even without comparative advantage, countries can gain from trade as long as tastes and preferences differ across countries. Consumption patterns do differ across countries, and some of these differences likely stem from differences in tastes. For example, the Danes eat twice as much pork as do Americans. Americans eat twice as much chicken as do Hungarians.

Soft drinks are four times more popular in the United States than in Western Europe. The English like tea. Americans like coffee. Algeria has an ideal climate for growing grapes, but its large Muslim population abstains from alcohol. Thus, Algeria exports wine.

Comparative advantage stimulates trade, but countries still may benefit from international trade even if all countries have identical resources and even if all countries produce with identical efficiency.

CHECKPOINT
How might countries benefit from trade even if there is no comparative advantage?

U.S. Exports and Imports

Countries trade with one another—or, more precisely, people and firms in one country trade with those in another—because each side expects to gain from the exchange. People expect to increase their consumption possibilities.

U.S. Exports

Just as some states are more involved in interstate trade than others, some nations are more involved in international trade than others. For example, exports account for about one-quarter of the gross domestic product (GDP) in Canada and the United Kingdom; about one-third of the GDP in Germany, Sweden, and Switzerland; and about half of the GDP in the Netherlands. Despite the perception that Japan has a giant export sector, exports there make up only about one-seventh of GDP.

In the United States, exports of goods and services amounted to about one-tenth of GDP in 2002. Although relatively small compared to most other countries, exports play a growing role in the U.S. economy.

The left-hand panel of Figure 18.1 shows the composition of U.S. exports by major category. Capital goods account for nearly half of all exports. Capital goods include high-tech products, such as computers and jet aircraft. Next most important is industrial supplies and materials, at 23 percent of the total. Together, capital goods and industrial supplies and material make up 67 percent, or two-thirds, of U.S. exports. It seems that most U.S. exports help foreign manufacturers make things. Consumer goods account for only 12 percent of exports. This category includes entertainment products, such as movies and recorded music.

Specialization and Trade

When nations specialize in what they can produce at the lowest cost and then trade with others, both production and consumption increase. The largest category of U.S. exports is capital goods, such as machinery used in the textile industry. The largest U.S. import category is consumer goods, which inclues men's suits from Italy. How do U.S. exports of textile machinery to Italy boost production and consumption of the men's suits that country produces?

© Getty Images/PhotoDisc

© Getty Images/PhotoDisc

U.S. Imports

America is a rich country and Americans spend more on imports than foreigners spend on U.S. exports. *U.S. imports of goods and services were one-seventh the size of U.S. GDP in 2002.* The right-hand panel of Figure 18.1 shows the composition of U.S. imports. Whereas consumer goods accounted for only 12 percent of U.S. exports, they are the largest category of imports at 27 percent of the total. Imported consumer goods include consumer electronics from Taiwan, shoes from Brazil, and kitchen gadgets from China.

The next most important category of imports is capital goods, at 25 percent, such as printing presses from Germany. A close third, at 23 percent, is industrial supplies and materials, such as crude oil from the Middle East and raw metals, including lead, zinc, and copper, from around the world. Note that automotive vehicles are only 11 percent of exports but are 17 percent of imports.

To give you some feel for America's trading partners, here are the top 10 destinations for U.S. goods in order of importance: Canada, Mexico, Japan,

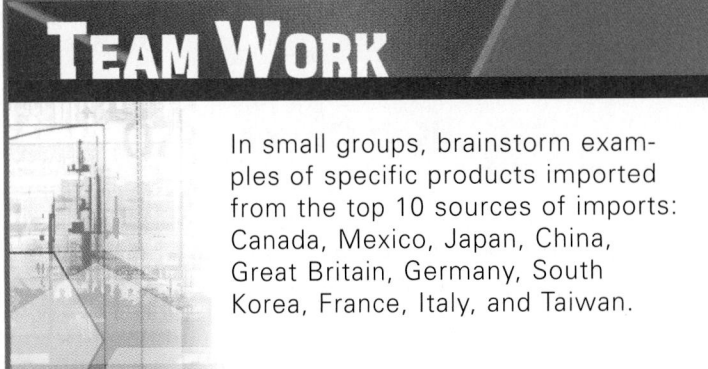

TEAM WORK

In small groups, brainstorm examples of specific products imported from the top 10 sources of imports: Canada, Mexico, Japan, China, Great Britain, Germany, South Korea, France, Italy, and Taiwan.

Great Britain, Germany, South Korea, France, the Netherlands, China, and Taiwan. The top 10 sources of U.S. imports consist of this same group in the same order, except Italy replaces the Netherlands and China jumps from ninth to fourth.

CHECKPOINT

What are the most important categories of U.S. exports and imports?

Composition of U.S. Exports and Imports in 2002   **Figure 18.1**

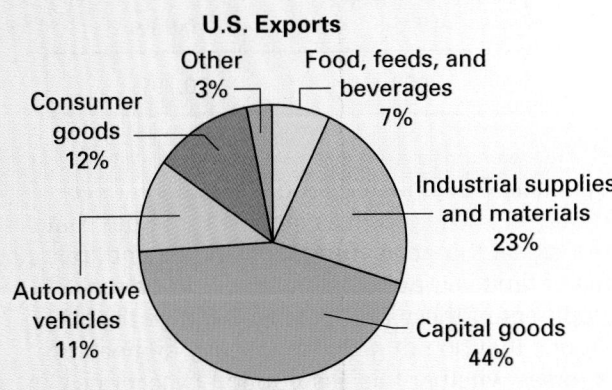

U.S. Exports

- Other 3%
- Food, feeds, and beverages 7%
- Consumer goods 12%
- Industrial supplies and materials 23%
- Automotive vehicles 11%
- Capital goods 44%

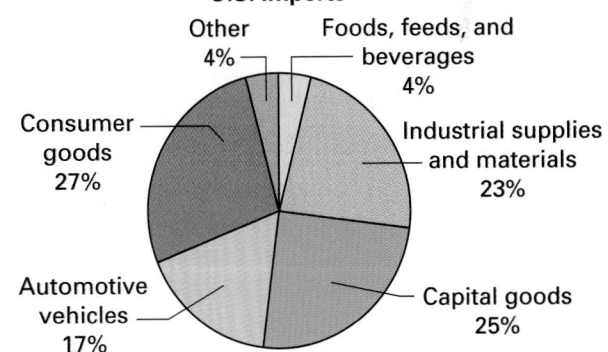

U.S. Imports

- Other 4%
- Foods, feeds, and beverages 4%
- Consumer goods 27%
- Industrial supplies and materials 23%
- Automotive vehicles 17%
- Capital goods 25%

Capital goods account for nearly half of U.S. exports, while consumer goods are the largest category of imports.

Source: Developed from export and import estimates in "U.S. International Transactions," *Survey of Current Business,* U.S. Department of Commerce, April 2003, Table E.

Key Concepts

1. Why does the United States have a comparative advantage over New Zealand in the production or lamb during April and May, while New Zealand enjoys a similar comparative advantage over the United States during the months of October and November?

2. Why wouldn't the purchase of the most advanced technology necessarily provide a nation with a comparative advantage relative to other nations?

3. In the Far East, some people think that soup made from boiled bats is a special delicacy. How does this give nations in which people who do not share this taste a comparative advantage?

4. Why do wealthy nations import a larger proportion of consumer goods than nations that are not as wealthy?

5. Why doesn't it make sense for the United States to try to export coffee or bananas?

Graphing Exercise

6. Although exports have accounted for roughly 10 percent of U.S. production in recent years, there have been periods of time when these sales have been smaller. Construct a line graph that shows the value of U.S. exports as a percent of U.S. GDP in recent years using data in the table. What happened in 1985 to cause U.S. exports to decline as a percent of GDP? How did this affect the U.S. economy?

U.S. Exports of Goods and Services as a Percent of U.S. GDP, 1980–2000

Year	Percentage
1980	9.76%
1985	6.92%
1990	9.32%
1995	10.93%
2000	10.79%

Think Critically

7. **Biology** In recent years, many genetically engineered foods have been developed and marketed in the United States. These products include tomatoes that are firm and easy to ship, corn and wheat that resist fungus diseases, and fruit that can be stored for long periods of time without spoiling. It would be reasonable to assume that the development of these products would give the U.S. a comparative advantage over nations that do not grow genetically engineered foods. Investigate these products to see whether this assumption is accurate. What do you find? Why does a comparative advantage benefit a nation only when there is a willingness by potential customers to purchase the product?

Objectives

> Identify trade restrictions and evaluate their impact.

> Explain why nations seek free-trade agreements.

Overview

International trade expands the consumption possibilities of trading nations. Despite the benefits of such trade, nearly all countries at one time or another have erected trade barriers across national borders. Trade restrictions usually benefit domestic producers but harm domestic consumers. The losses to domestic consumers typically exceed the gains to domestic producers. If free trade is such a good deal, why do most countries impose trade restrictions? Producer groups are well organized and are able to encourage governments to restrict imports. Consumers are disorganized and seldom even make the connection between trade restrictions and higher prices. The good news is that trade restrictions are diminishing around the world.

Key Terms

world price

tariff

quota

General Agreement on Tariffs and Trade (GATT)

Uruguay Round

World Trade Organization (WTO)

[In the News]

● Tariffs on Steel Trigger Conflict Among American Industries

In 2002, the U.S. government imposed tariffs on steel imports in order to save the domestic steel industry from what might have been a deadly slump. Since then, a lobbying war has been waged over the tariffs' effect and continuation. In a little more than a year, the tariff added more than $600 million to the cost of imported steel and allowed domestic steel producers to profit from higher prices. Touting this success, representatives of the steel companies that benefited told of plant upgrades and consolidations that will, they say, better prepare the industry for competition. Countering this viewpoint, two dozen members of the Automotive Coalition met with U.S. government officials to detail the damage done to manufacturers of automotive parts and components. Plant closings, layoffs and permanent job losses, transfers of business to overseas suppliers, and other extremely negative effects were attributed to the tariffs. Consequently, on its behalf and the behalf of other users of steel products who were losing business and jobs, the Coalition begged the government to end the tariff.

Think About It

When should a government impose a tariff? Is it reasonable to expect a tariff to have a totally positive or negative impact? Why or why not?

Ask the Xpert!

econxtra.swlearning.com

What are some arguments for restricting trade with other nations?

world price

The price at which a good is traded internationally; determined by the world supply and world demand for the good

The Graphing Workshop

tariff

A tax on imports

quota

A legal limit on the quantity of a particular product that can be imported

The Graphing Workshop

Trade Restrictions

For internationally traded goods, such as wheat, oil, or steel, a price is established on the world market. The **world price** is determined by world supply and world demand for the product. With free trade, U.S. consumers can buy any amount desired at the world price.

Tariffs

U.S. producers would like to be able to sell their product in the United States for more than the world price. To achieve this, they often try to persuade legislators to restrict competition from abroad. One way the government can put foreign producers at a disadvantage is to impose a tariff on imports. Simply put, a **tariff** is a tax on imports. The tariff reduces the quantity of imports supplied. With fewer imports, the supply of goods in the U.S. market declines, so the price of the goods goes up. As a result, U.S. producers get to sell their products for more on the U.S. market. A tariff on U.S. imports benefits U.S. producers. However, a tariff harms U.S consumers, who must pay that higher price. The revenue from tariffs goes to the government.

Quotas

Another way domestic producers try to limit foreign competition is by getting the government to impose import quotas. A **quota** is a legal limit on the amount of a particular commodity that can be imported. Quotas usually target imports from particular countries. For example, a quota may limit automobiles from Japan or shoes from Brazil. *By limiting imports, a quota reduces the supply in the U.S. market, which raises the U.S. price above the world price.* Again, this helps U.S. producers but harms U.S. consumers. Foreign producers who get to sell their goods for the higher U.S. price also benefit.

Producer support for quotas, coupled with a lack of opposition from consumers (who remain mostly unaware of all this), has resulted in quotas that have lasted for decades. For example, apparel quotas have been in effect for more than 30 years and sugar quotas for more than 50 years.

Tariffs and Quotas Compared

Consider the similarities and differences between a tariff and a quota. Both restrict supply, thereby increasing the price, which hurts U.S. consumers and helps U.S. producers. The primary difference is that the revenue from a tariff goes to the U.S. government, whereas the revenue from the quota goes to whoever has the right under the quota to sell foreign goods in the U.S. market. Usually the beneficiary of a quota is a foreign exporter.

Perhaps the worst part about tariffs and quotas is that foreign governments typically respond with tariffs and quotas of their own. This shrinks the U.S. export market, reducing specialization and exchange around the world.

Other Trade Restrictions

Besides tariffs and quotas, a variety of other measures restricts free trade. To promote exports, a country may provide subsidies to exporters or low-interest loans to foreign buyers. Some countries impose *domestic content requirements* specifying that at least a certain portion of a final good must be produced domestically.

Other requirements concerning health, safety, or technical standards often discriminate against foreign goods. For example, European countries prohibit beef from hormone-fed cattle, a measure aimed at U.S. beef. Food purity laws in Germany bar many non-German beers.

Until the European Community adopted uniform standards, differing technical requirements forced manufacturers to offer as many as seven different models of the same TV set for that market. Sometimes exporters will voluntarily limit exports, as when Japanese automakers agreed to cut auto exports to the United States. *The point is that tariffs and quotas are only two of many tools that restrict imports and reduce the benefits of comparative advantage.*

Problems with Trade Restrictions

Trade restrictions raise a number of problems. The biggest problem is that other countries often respond with tariffs and quotas of their own, thus shrinking the gains from trade. This can trigger still greater trade restrictions, and lead to an outright trade war.

Second, protecting one stage of production from international competition often requires protecting other stages of production. For example, protecting the U.S. textile industry from foreign competition raises the cost of cloth to U.S. garment makers. This reduces the competitiveness of U.S. garments compared to foreign ones. As a result, the domestic garment industry might need protection as well.

Third, the cost of protection also includes spending for lobbying fees, propaganda, and legal actions to secure and maintain this favorable treatment. All these outlays are, for the most part, a social waste for they reduce competition but produce nothing besides trade restrictions.

A fourth problem with trade restrictions is the high transaction costs of enforcing quotas, tariffs, and other restrictions. The U.S. Customs Service operates 24 hours a day, 365 days a year, inspecting the luggage of the 500 million people who enter the country each year via air, sea, and more than 300 border crossings. On highway I-35 in Laredo, Texas, for example, more than 6,000 18-wheeler trucks roll in from Mexico every day. Policing and enforcement costs add up.

Finally, research indicates that trade barriers slow the introduction of new goods and better technologies. So, rather than simply raising domestic prices and reducing the gains from specialization, trade restrictions also slow economic progress.

✓ CHECKPOINT

What are the two main trade restrictions and how do they affect U.S. prices?

Free Trade by Multilateral Agreement

International trade arises from voluntary exchange among buyers and sellers pursuing their self-interest. Since 1950, world output has risen seven-fold, but world trade has increased seventeen-fold. World trade offers many advantages to the trading countries. These include increased consumption possibilities, access to markets around the world, lower costs through economies of scale, improved quality from competitive pressure, and lower prices. Because of these advantages, the trend around the world is toward freer trade.

General Agreement on Tariffs and Trade (GATT)

Trade restrictions introduced during the Great Depression contributed to that economic disaster. To avoid a return to such dark times, after World War II the United States invited its trading partners to negotiate lower tariffs and quotas. The result was the **General Agreement on Tariffs and Trade (GATT)**, an international trade agreement adopted in 1947 by the United States and 22 other countries. Each signer of GATT agreed to reduce tariffs through multinational negotiations; reduce quotas; and treat all member nations equally with respect to trade.

Since then, a series of trade negotiations among many countries, called *trade rounds,* has continued to lower trade barriers. Trade rounds offer a package approach to trade negotiations rather than an issue-by-issue approach. A particular industry might not object to freer trade when it sees that other industries also agree to freer trade.

The most recent round of negotiations was completed in Uruguay in 1994. More than 140 countries have signed this agreement, called the **Uruguay Round**. This was the most

The Art of the Trade War
econxtra.swlearning.com

General Agreement on Tariffs and Trade (GATT)

An international tariff-reduction treaty adopted in 1947 that resulted in a series of negotiated "rounds" aimed at freer trade

Uruguay Round

The most recent and most comprehensive of the eight postwar multilateral trade negotiations under GATT; created the World Trade Organization

World Trade Organization (WTO)

The legal and institutional foundation of the multilateral trading system that succeeded GATT in 1995

comprehensive of the eight postwar multilateral trade rounds. The Uruguay Round phased in tariff reductions on 85 percent of world trade and will eventually eliminate quotas.

Figure 18.2 shows tariff revenue as a percentage of the value of merchandise imports since 1821. You can see that tariffs have been up and down. Note that during the Great Depression of the 1930s, tariffs spiked. These high tariffs were contributing factors to the global economic troubles of that period. Thanks to trade agreements, average tariffs are lower now than at any time in history. When the Uruguay Round is fully implemented, the average tariff will fall from 6 percent to 4 percent.

World Trade Organization

The Uruguay Round also created the World Trade Organization (WTO) as the successor to GATT. The **World Trade Organization (WTO)** now provides the legal and institutional foundation for world trade. Whereas GATT was a multilateral agreement with no staff or permanent location, the WTO is a permanent institution in Geneva, Switzerland, staffed mostly by economists. Whereas GATT involved only merchandise trade, the WTO deals with services and trade-related aspects of intellectual property, such as books, movies, and computer programs.

Common Markets

Some countries have looked to the success of the U.S. economy, which is

NETBookmark

The World Trade Organization's web site describes its role and functions and explains the value of reducing trade barriers. Browse the web site through econxtra.swlearning.com and choose a topic that interests you. Prepare a two-minute oral presentation explaining the topic you chose to your classmates.

econxtra.swlearning.com

U.S. Tariff Revenue as a Percentage of Merchandise Imports

Figure 18.2

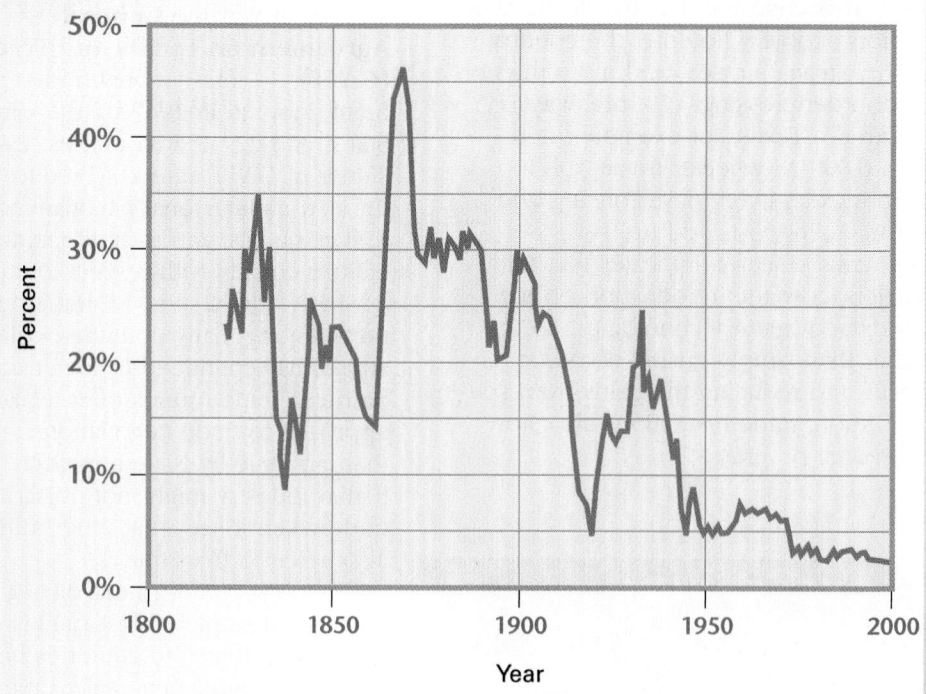

Over the years, tariffs have been up and down, spiking during the Great Depression.

Source: 1821–1970: U.S. Dept. of Commerce, Bureau of Census, *Historical Statistics of the United States,* Part 2, 1976, and *Economic Report of the President,* February 2003, Table B-81.

essentially a free-trade zone across 50 states, and have tried to develop free-trade zones of their own. The largest and best known is the European Union, which began in 1958 with six countries and has expanded to 15. The idea was to create a barrier-free European market in which goods, services, people, and capital flow freely to their highest-valued use. Twelve members of the European Union have adopted a common currency, the *euro*, which replaced national currencies in 2002.

The United States, Canada, and Mexico also have developed a free-trade pact called the North American Free Trade Agreement (NAFTA). Around the world, the trend is toward free-trade agreements.

CHECKPOINT

Why have nations signed free-trade agreements?

SPAN THE GLOBE

Proposal to Create World's Largest Free-Trade Area Under Attack

The North American Free Trade Agreement (NAFTA) was signed and put into effect by Mexico, Canada, and the United States in 1994 in order to lower tariffs and create economic prosperity in those three nations. In November 2003, the leaders of the 34 democracies of the Western Hemisphere met in Miami, Florida, to work out the details of a new trade agreement called the Free Trade Area of the Americas (FTAA). The FTAA would create the world's largest free-trade area—a tariff-free trade zone stretching from Canada to the tip of South America. The FTAA is touted as the logical successor to NAFTA, and it has many supporters. However, some governments and anti-globalization groups from the various countries involved oppose the creation of this free-trade area. Brazil, for example, is reluctant to enter the agreement due to issues involving import quotas, tariffs, and agricultural subsidies. Groups representing U.S. workers also oppose the free-trade area. Labor organizations blame NAFTA for hundreds of thousands of lost manufacturing jobs. These groups are concerned that an FTAA agreement will only increase this job loss. Manufacturers, on the other hand, argue that to survive they must be able to reduce costs.

Think Critically

What advantage is there in having a free-trade area such as FTAA? What are the disadvantages?

Key Concepts

1. Why do many fruit farmers in the United States think tariffs should be placed on fruit imported from South America and China? Whom would such tariffs benefit, and whom would they harm?

2. If a quota was placed on the number of automobiles that could be imported into the United States, how would U.S. consumers be affected?

3. Many nations require imported car models to be crash-tested before they can be marketed to consumers. They refuse to accept the results of crash tests performed in other countries. This process is expensive for firms involved in trade. How is such a requirement a barrier to trade? How are consumers in these nations affected by such laws?

4. Why have some less-developed nations argued that they have been discriminated against by first GATT and then the WTO rules that discourage tariffs and quotas?

5. What problems and benefits that might result from the creation of a free-trade organization can be seen within the U.S. economy?

Graphing Exercise

6. Nations are most likely to impose either tariffs or quotas on trade for products for which they do not have a comparative advantage. Study the data in the table, and use it to construct a double bar graph that shows the value of U.S. imports and exports for these classifications of goods in 2000. In which types of production would there have been the greatest pressure from U.S. businesses and labor organizations for the imposition of either tariffs or quotas? Explain your answer.

U.S. Exports and Imports of Selected Commodity Groups, 2000 (Values in billions of dollars)

Commodity Group	Exports	Imports
1. Soybeans	$ 5,284	$ 31
2. Fruits and Vegetables	$ 7,477	$ 9,286
3. Airplanes	$24,777	$ 12,412
4. Footwear	$ 663	$ 14,842
5. Scientific Instruments	$30,984	$ 22,007

Source: *Statistical Abstract of the United States,* 2002, p. 800.

Think Critically

7. **Government** The creation of a free-trade organization requires a formal international treaty. Approval of such treaties often involves political issues that go beyond economic considerations. The treaty that created the European Union, for example, was debated by governments in Europe for many years. Some nations, such as Norway and Switzerland, chose not to join the organization. What possible reasons could these nations have had for their choice? Why might they change their decision in the future?

movers & shakers

Yoshimi Inaba *Toyota Motor Sales*

When it comes to selling vehicles in the United States, Toyota is not eager to be the number one supplier. As president and chief executive officer of Toyota Motor Sales, U.S.A., Yoshimi Inaba didn't like the possibility that Toyota sales in the United States might exceed those of Ford, DaimlerChrysler, or General Motors. "I don't want to see any of them go into difficulty," Inaba said about the "Big Three" U.S. automakers. "If that happens, public sentiment will change," he explained.

Nearly all the vehicles Toyota sells in the United States come from the Japanese automaker's 11 manufacturing and parts facilities located in the United States. Together these facilities provide employment to more than 30,000 Americans.

In 2001, for the first time, more Toyotas were sold in the United States than in Japan, thus inching Toyota closer to overtaking the number-three U.S. carmaker, DaimlerChrysler. In spite of his company's success, Inaba wasn't celebrating. He worried that should DaimlerChrysler or another of the Big Three automakers face serious financial losses, many Americans would be forced out of a job, and Toyota could suffer as a result. Here's why:

The rise of foreign automakers has been a huge blow to the United Automobile Workers (UAW). The union has never succeeded in organizing a plant owned by a foreign manufacturer, including Toyota. Decreasing membership in a powerful labor union, combined with the loss of jobs should a U.S. automaker fail, could easily raise sentiment among Americans to buy only American-made vehicles. So, in spite of the 30,000 U.S. citizens that Toyota employs, and the money those employees churn back into the U.S. economy, the fact that Toyota is Japanese-owned could be enough to cause a backlash.

In spite of his concerns, Inaba continues to infuse Toyota with his innovative ideas.

Working for Toyota since graduating from Kyoto University with a degree in economics, Inaba has spent many years outside his homeland. After earning a master's degree from Northwestern University's Kellogg School of Business, he worked for three years at Toyota's German sales company. Later he returned to Japan but concentrated his efforts on the company's European division. In 1993, he moved to Toyota's U.S. sales company and within three years was named senior vice president.

Later, as president and chief executive officer of Toyota Motor Sales U.S.A. Inc., Inaba worked to develop direct web-based connections to Toyota's U.S. auto dealers and to Toyota's supply chain. He also was involved in developing technology in the navigation system of Toyota vehicles that will pay tolls and make payments at gas stations, parking lots, and restaurants.

In July 2003, Inaba returned to Toyota in Japan. He now serves as senior managing director and chief officer for the Americas, Oceania, Middle East and Southwest Asia Operations Group.

SOURCE READING
Why did Inaba say, "I don't want to see any [U.S. auto manufacturers] go into difficulty. If that happens, public sentiment will change." Why should he be concerned about this?

ENTREPRENEURS IN ACTION
In small groups, discuss the pros and cons of Toyota's success in the United States. Which groups benefit from its success? Which groups might suffer from this success?

Sharpen Your Life Skills

Critical Thinking

Some people think it is a wise and patriotic choice to pay higher prices to buy goods and services manufactured in the United States rather than to purchase similar products that have been imported from foreign countries. They point out that dollars spent on imported products deprive U.S. workers of employment and U.S. firms of profits.

Other people argue that consumers should look only for the best price and highest quality in the products they buy, regardless of where they were produced. They argue that paying more to buy American-made goods and services allows inefficient firms to stay in business and use scarce resources in ways that do not take advantage of our nation's comparative advantage.

Which of these two points of view seems most logical to you? Is it always possible to make choices that clearly support one side or the other? Use your critical thinking skills to evaluate each of the following situations and decide what you would do in each case. Explain your choice, and describe how it is consistent with the point of view you think is most logical.

Apply Your Skill

1. In 2003, more than 90 percent of athletic shoes (tennis, running, basketball, etc.) sold in the United States were imported from other countries. The relatively few athletic shoes produced in this country most often were designed for special uses and were more expensive than similar imported footwear. Suppose you needed a new pair of athletic shoes for a school team you joined. You could buy an imported pair for $80 or a similar pair made in the United States for $120. Which pair of shoes would you purchase?

2. In 2003, advancements in communications technology made it possible for U.S. manufacturers to provide "help lines" and technical support to their customers from people located in almost any nation of the world. When U.S. consumers called the toll-free number to ask for assistance in operating their new appliance, they were likely to end up talking with a person located in India or Pakistan. These workers were paid much less than workers in the United States. Would you try to avoid purchasing products from firms that outsourced their consumer support services to other nations? Why or why not?

3. In 2003, more than 60 percent of the petroleum consumed in the United States was imported from other nations. Some consumers chose to conserve gasoline by purchasing hybrid automobiles imported from Japan that were powered by both electric motors and gasoline engines. These vehicles could go 50 miles or more on each gallon of gasoline. Would you buy this type of vehicle if you were ready to purchase an automobile? Why or why not?

Objectives

> Describe the components of a nation's current account.

> Describe the components of a nation's financial account.

Overview

Money doesn't grow on trees. In the course of a week, a month, or a year, the amount you spend, save, and give away must equal the amount you earn, borrow, or are given. You, like everyone else in the world, face a budget constraint. Your outflow of money must not exceed your inflow. Just as you must make sure ends meet, so too must families, businesses, governments, and even countries. For example, the flow of receipts into the United States from the rest of the world must equal the outflow of payments to the rest of the world. There's no getting around it.

Key Terms

balance of payments

current account

merchandise trade balance

trade surplus

trade deficit

financial account

[In the News]

● Illegal Foreign Workers Make Dollars and Jobs Disappear

One significant source of inaccuracy in the balance of payments is the amount of money earned and transferred home by the millions of illegal workers in the United States. These workers may send this money home to family members by various means during the workers' stays in the United States. Or, they might keep it in an international account as a nest egg they will use once they return home. In either case, the dollars they earn but don't spend in the United States total in the hundreds of millions of dollars. The jobs lost to U.S. workers because of their presence here totals in the tens of thousands. Many of these illegal workers learn of work opportunities in the United States from web sites such as AmericaGo.biz, which advertises work in American stores such as Target, K-Mart, Home Depot, T.J. Maxx, and Wal-Mart. Once in this country, the workers are contacted and hired by firms who contract such services as housekeeping and domestic help to American firms.

Think About It

What effects do these workers and international transfers of dollars have on the U.S. economy?

Current Account

The U.S. **balance of payments** is the record of all economic transactions between U.S. residents and residents of the rest of the world. Because it reflects all the transactions that occur during a particular period, usually a year, the balance of payments is a *flow* measure. Balance-of-payments accounts are maintained according to the principles of *double-entry bookkeeping*, in which entries on one side of the ledger are called *credits*, and entries on the other side are called *debits*. Because total credits must equal total debits, there must be a *balance* of payments when all the separate accounts are added together.

The balance of payments is divided into two broad accounts: the current account and the financial account. The **current account** keeps track of trade in goods and services, the flow of interest and profits across international borders, and the flow of foreign aid and cash gifts. The most important of these is the trade in goods, also called *merchandise trade.*

The Merchandise Trade Balance

The **merchandise trade balance** equals the value of merchandise exports minus the value of merchandise imports. Merchandise trade reflects trade in goods, or tangible products, such as Irish sweaters and U.S. computers. The merchandise trade balance usually is referred to in the media as simply the *trade balance.*

The value of U.S. merchandise exports is listed as a credit in the U.S. balance-of-payments account because U.S. residents must *be paid* for the exported goods. The value of U.S. merchandise imports is listed as a debit in the balance-of-payments account because U.S. residents must *pay* foreigners for imported goods.

If the value of merchandise exports exceeds the value of merchandise imports, there is a *surplus* in the merchandise trade balance, or a **trade surplus**. If the value of merchandise imports exceeds the value of merchandise exports, there is a *deficit* in the merchandise trade balance, or a **trade deficit**. The merchandise trade balance, which is reported monthly, influences the stock market, currency exchange rates, and other financial markets.

The trade balance depends on a variety of factors, including the relative strength and competitiveness of the U.S. economy compared with other economies and the value of the dollar compared with other currencies. The U.S. merchandise trade balance since 1960 is depicted in Figure 18.3, where exports (the blue line) and imports (the red line) are expressed as a percentage of GDP. In the 1960s, exports exceeded imports, so there were trade surpluses, shaded in blue. Since 1976, imports have exceeded exports every year, resulting in trade deficits, shaded in pink. Trade deficits as a percentage of GDP have increased steadily in recent years, growing from 1.3 percent in 1991 to an all time high of 4.7 percent in 2002, when the U.S. trade deficit reached a record $484.3 billion.

The United States imports more from each of the world's major economies than it exports to them. Figure 18.4 shows the U.S. trade deficit with major economies or regions of the world in 2002. The $103 billion trade deficit with China was the largest. China bought $22 billion in U.S. goods, but Americans bought $125 billion in Chinese goods, including $82 billion in nonfood consumer goods. Chances are, most of the utensils in your kitchen were made in China.

NETBookmark

Access the Bureau of Economic Analysis data reports on U.S. international accounts through econxtra.swlearning.com. Click on the "Latest news release," and then write a paragraph summarizing the information in the release.

econxtra.swlearning.com

Figure 18.3

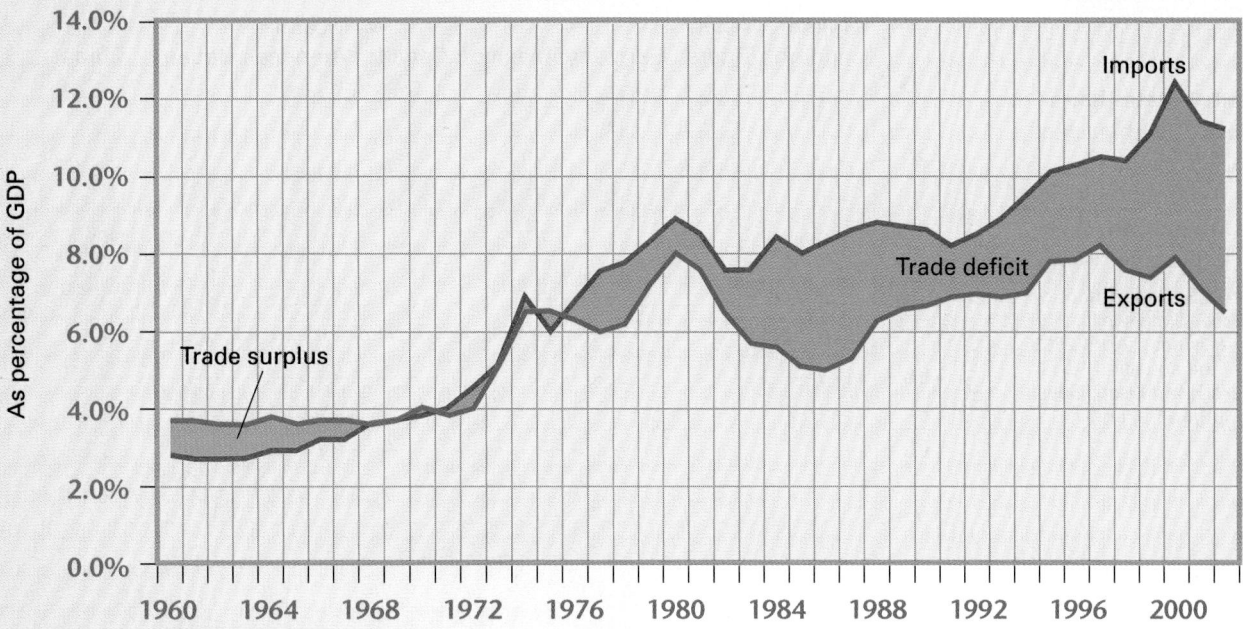

U.S. imports of goods have exceeded U.S. exports of goods since 1976, and the trade deficit has widened.

Source: Developed from merchandise trade data in the *Economic Report of the President,* February 2003, and the U.S. Bureau of Economic Analysis. Imports and exports are shown relative to GDP.

The Balance on Goods and Services

The merchandise trade balance focuses on the flow of goods, but some services also are traded internationally. *Services* are intangible products, such as transportation, insurance, banking, consulting, and tourism. Services also include the income earned from foreign investments less the income earned by foreigners from their investment in the U.S. economy.

The value of U.S. service exports, such as when an Italian visits Chicago, is a credit in the U.S. balance-of-payments account because U.S. residents receive payments for these services. The value of U.S. service imports, such as when a computer specialist in India enters data for a Connecticut insurance company, is a debit in the balance-of-payments account because U.S. residents must pay for the imported services. Because the United States exports more services than it imports, the balance on services has been in surplus for the last three decades.

The *balance on goods and services* is the value of exports of goods and services minus the value of imports of goods and services. Because the service account

Investigate Your Local Economy

Research to find an example of a good or service produced in your local economy that is exported. If possible, find out the annual dollar value of the exported good or service. Share your results in class.

The Troubles with Trade
econxtra.swlearning.com

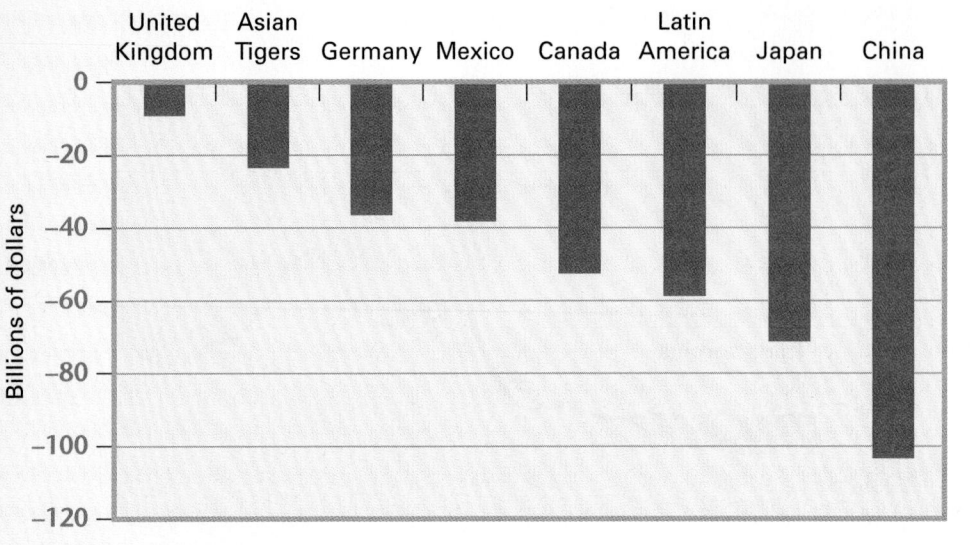

The United States has a trade deficit with each of the world's major economies because it imports more from them than it exports to them.

Source: U.S. Department of Commerce, *Survey of Current Business,* April 2003, Table K. The so-called Asian Tigers are Hong Kong, South Korea, Singapore, and Taiwan.

has been in surplus, the balance on goods and services has not been as negative as the merchandise trade balance.

Unilateral Transfers

Unilateral transfers consist of government transfers to foreign residents, foreign aid, personal gifts to friends and relatives abroad, personal and institutional charitable donations, and other

When Europeans visit U.S. beaches, is the money they spend considered a debit or a credit in the U.S. balance-of-payments account? Explain your answer.

© Getty Images/PhotoDisc

transfers. Money sent abroad by a U.S. resident to friends or relatives would be included in U.S. unilateral transfers and would be a debit in the balance-of-payments account. For example, immigrants to the United States often send money to families back home.

Net unilateral transfers equal the unilateral transfers received from abroad by U.S. residents minus unilateral transfers sent to foreign residents by U.S. residents. Included are U.S. government grants to foreign governments. U.S. net unilateral transfers have been negative each year since World War II, except for 1991, when the U.S. government received sizable transfers from foreign governments to help pay their share of the Persian Gulf War. In 2002, the U.S. net unilateral transfer was a negative $56 billion. To give you some feel for that amount, the net transfer abroad averaged about $500 for each U.S. household. These transfers represent an important source of spending power for many poor countries.

When net unilateral transfers are combined with the balance on goods and services, the result is the *current account balance,* a figure reported quarterly by the federal government. *The current account includes all international transactions in currently produced goods and services, flows of interest and profit, plus unilateral*

E-CONOMICS

U.S. Foreign Aid for Internet Use in Uzbekistan?

Foreign aid, the unilateral transfer payments by the United States to other countries that are intended to raise living standards and spur economic development, has gone through many changes over the years. The progression began with the post-World War II Marshall Plan, generally credited with helping to rebuild a Europe devastated by conflict. It then moved through the Alliance for Progress, aimed at increasing the standard of living in Latin America in the 1960s. Foreign aid during the 1980s was aimed at supporting governments in Latin America threatened by revolutionary movements. The George W. Bush administration planned to increase the size of foreign aid by half again, to help countries that are "ruling justly, investing in their people, and establishing economic freedom." Through it all, however, the actual good done by the programs has been difficult to see, due to the sheer size of the amounts paid out in these

programs and the political motives behind them. This may be changing, however. The Bush administration placed great emphasis on accountability for the use of the funds. The aid agencies, as proof of their undertakings, have begun publishing stories about their programs. A case in point is the foreign aid targeted at developing e-commerce in Uzbekistan. A central Asian country founded in 1991, Uzbekistan has some 22.5 million people and a literacy rate of 99 percent. To help boost the country's economic activity and the well-being of its people, seminars and training sessions about the Internet and how to use it as a marketing device recently have been held throughout the country. These seminars, sponsored by USAID, have been responsible for several millions of dollars of business being transacted.

Think Critically

How does the Uzbek program enhance economic freedom? Can you think of better uses for the money?

---

transfers. It can be negative, reflecting a current account deficit; positive, reflecting a current account surplus; or zero.

CHECKPOINT
What is included in a nation's current account?

Financial Account

The United States has been running a current account deficit for years. How can it pay for all the imports and all the

transfers? The United States gets the money from selling financial assets, such as stocks and bonds, and from selling real assets such as land, housing, factories, and other property. When the current account comes up short, asset sales make up the difference.

The **financial account** tracks the flow of financial capital by recording international transactions involving financial and real assets. For example, if U.S. residents buy foreign assets, money flows from the United States to pay for these assets. Money flows into the United States when foreigners buy U.S. assets, such as U.S. stocks and bonds, an office building in New York City, or a ski chalet in Colorado. The financial account deals with buying and selling assets across international borders.

financial account
That portion of the balance of payments that records international transactions involving financial assets, such as stocks and bonds, and real assets, such as factories and office buildings

Record of the Financial Account

Between 1917 and 1982, the United States ran a deficit in the financial account, meaning that U.S. residents purchased more foreign assets than foreigners purchased assets in the United States. Since 1983, however, the financial account has been in surplus nearly every year. This means foreigners have been buying more U.S. assets than Americans have been buying foreign assets. Foreign purchases of assets in the United States contribute to America's productive capacity and promote employment. However, the return on these investments flows to foreigners, not to Americans.

Statistical Discrepancy

Again, the U.S. balance of payments records all transactions between U.S. residents and foreign residents during a specified period. It is easier to describe the balance of payments than to compile it. Despite efforts to capture all international transactions, some are nearly impossible to trace. For example, the government can't easily monitor cross-border shopping or illegal drug trafficking. But as the name *balance of payments* suggests, the entire balance-of-payments account must by definition be in balance—debits must equal credits.

To ensure that the two sides balance, the *statistical discrepancy* was created. An excess of credits in all other accounts is offset by an equivalent debit in the statistical discrepancy, or an excess of debits in all other accounts is offset by an equivalent credit in the statistical discrepancy.

You might think of the statistical discrepancy as the official "fudge factor." The statistical discrepancy provides analysts with both a measure of the error in the balance-of-payments data and a means of satisfying the double-entry bookkeeping requirement that total debits equal total credits. In 2002, the current account and the financial account combined for a deficit of $29.2 billion. To offset that deficit, the statistical discrepancy added $29.2 billion back into the balance. Thus, the balance of payments for all accounts, including the statistical discrepancy, sums to zero.

CHECKPOINT
What is included in a nation's financial account?

The government has difficulty tracking cross-border transactions, such as when an American visiting Italy purchases gold jewelry. How does the government try to measure such purchases?

© Getty Images/PhotoDisc

Key Concepts

1. A large part of the U.S. national debt is owned by people who live in other nations. How is the U.S. current account affected by interest payments made by the federal government on its debt?

2. Would the merchandise trade balance be affected by millions of people in foreign nations choosing to pay to see a recent Hollywood action movie? Why or why not? If not, what measure of trade would this affect?

3. Why must the total value of all nations' trade surpluses and deficits be balanced?

4. If you received a gift of 100 euros from a relative who lives in Germany, how would this gift affect the U.S. balance of payments?

5. Suppose the value of stocks in the United States increased, causing many foreigners to sell their U.S. stock to earn a profit. They then have their funds sent to them in their own nations. What would this do to the U.S. financial account?

Graphing Exercise

6. When foreigners purchase or build businesses in the United States, their payments for these investments flow into this country. Construct a line graph from the data in the table that shows the growth in foreign investment in U.S. businesses from 1995 through 2000. What does your graph tell you about this investment? How would this investment affect the U.S. economy?

Value of U.S. Businesses Acquired or Established by Foreign Investors, 1995–2000 (Values in millions of dollars)

1995	$57,195	1998	$215,256
1996	$79,929	1999	$274,956
1997	$69,708	2000	$320,858

Source: *Statistical Abstract of the United States,* 2002, p. 787.

Think Critically

7. **Accounting** Keeping track of a nation's balance of payments is a major accounting problem that is never totally accurate. Determine whether each of the following would be a credit or a debit for a nation's balance of payments and how each would affect the nation's economy. Why is it difficult for government officials to keep track of some of these flows of value?

 • There is a $500 million increase in the nation's exports of computers.

 • People send $30 million more to their relatives in other countries.

 • Foreigners invest an additional $450 million in that nation's businesses.

 • There is an $800 million increase in the nation's imports of automobiles.

 • Residents of the nation spend $40 million more on travel in other nations.

 • Businesses in that nation pay $25 million more in dividends to foreigners.

Objectives

> Analyze the market for foreign exchange.

> Identify the participants in the market for foreign exchange.

> Distinguish between flexible and fixed exchange rates.

Overview

Now that you have some idea about international trade and the balance of payments, you can take a closer look at the forces that determine the rate of exchange between the U.S. dollar and other currencies. When Americans buy foreign goods or travel abroad, these transactions involve two currencies—the U.S. dollar and the foreign currency. What is the dollar cost of a British pound, a Mexican peso, a Japanese yen, or a European euro? As you will see, the exchange rates between the dollar and other currencies usually are determined just like other prices—by the forces of supply and demand.

Key Terms

foreign exchange

exchange rate

flexible exchange rates

[In the News]

● China Not Cited for Foreign Exchange Manipulation

In late 2003, the Chinese currency exchange rate was 8.3 yuan to the dollar, where it had been pegged for nine years. At the time, the Chinese were enjoying a more than $100 billion dollar trade surplus with the United States, with this figure rising by more than 20 percent annually. Some members of Congress called for imposing steep tariffs on Chinese goods. They also accused the Chinese government of manipulating its foreign exchange rate to improve its trading position. However, in testimony before the Senate Banking Committee, the U.S. Secretary of the Treasury announced that the Chinese government was not guilty of doing this. In their defense, the Chinese said that the pegging at 8.3 was a result of the last trade imbalance outcry by the United States almost 10 years before. The Chinese also pointed out that if the yuan was allowed to float, it might even drop in value against the dollar because the Chinese overall trade balance is far smaller than its surplus with the United States. This is because the Chinese have to import the raw materials and the unassembled parts for the goods they manufacture for sale in the United States. A cheaper yuan would cause an even greater trade imbalance with the United States in China's favor. Other analysts pointed out that the trade imbalance may be just a natural occurrence of a marketplace where China, with its overwhelming supply of labor, has a wide comparative advantage in producing toys, shoes, textiles, and other labor-intensive goods. More than 70 percent of the trade imbalance falls within this range of products. Therefore, these analysts believe the market should be left alone to make its own ultimate correction.

Think About It

Who would benefit from the imposition of a tariff on Chinese goods?

The Market for Foreign Exchange

Foreign exchange is foreign money people need to carry out international transactions. Typically, foreign exchange is made up of bank deposits in the foreign currency. When foreign travel is involved, foreign exchange may consist of foreign paper money. The **exchange rate** is the dollar price of purchasing a unit of another currency. The exchange rate, or price of another currency, is determined by the interaction of all those who buy and sell foreign exchange. The exchange rate between two currencies is set through the interaction of demand and supply for these currencies.

The Euro

The foreign exchange market involves all the arrangements used to carry out international transactions. This market is not so much a physical place as it is a network of telephones and computers connecting large financial institutions worldwide. The foreign exchange market is like an all-night diner—it never closes. A trading center is always open somewhere in the world.

Consider the market for a particular foreign currency, the euro. For decades the nations of Western Europe have tried to increase their economic cooperation and trade. These countries believed they would be more productive and more competitive with the United States if they acted more like the 50 United States and less like separate economies, each with its own trade regulations, trade barriers, and currency. Imagine the hassle involved if each of the 50 states had its own currency, which you had to exchange every time you wanted to buy something in another state.

In January 2002, *euro* notes and coins entered circulation in the 12 European countries that adopted the new common currency. The euro is now the common currency in the *euro area,* as the dozen countries are now called. The price, or exchange rate, of the euro is the dollar price of one euro. Because the exchange rate

foreign exchange

Foreign money needed to carry out international transactions

exchange rate

The price of one country's currency measured in terms of another country's currency

CNN video
The Ups and Downs of the Euro
econxtra.swlearning.com

© Getty Images/PhotoDisc

Why do you think adoption of the euro as a common currency in Europe has increased trade among the 12 countries in the euro area?

is a price, it is determined using supply and demand. *The equilibrium price of foreign exchange is the one that equates quantity demanded with quantity supplied.*

Demand for Euros

U.S. residents need euros to pay for goods and services from the euro area, to buy assets from there, to make loans to the euro area, or simply to send cash gifts to friends or relatives there. Whenever U.S. residents need euros, they must buy them in the foreign exchange market, which could be as near as the local bank, paying for them with dollars.

Figure 18.5 depicts a market for foreign exchange—in this case, euros. The horizontal axis shows the quantity of foreign exchange, measured here in millions of euros. The vertical axis indicates the dollar price of one euro. The demand curve *D* for foreign exchange shows the relationship between the dollar price of the euro and the quantity of euros demanded, other things assumed constant. Some of the factors assumed constant along the demand curve are the incomes and preferences of U.S. consumers, the expected inflation rates in the United States and the euro area, and interest rates in the United States and the euro area.

People have many reasons for demanding foreign exchange; but in the aggregate, the lower the dollar price of foreign exchange, the greater the quantity demanded. The cheaper it is to buy euros, the lower the dollar price of euro area products, so the greater the quantity of euros demanded by U.S. residents. For example, a cheap-enough euro might persuade you to tour Rome, climb the Austrian Alps, or wander the museums of Paris.

Supply of Foreign Exchange

The supply of foreign exchange is generated by the desire of foreign residents to acquire dollars—that is, to exchange euros for dollars. Residents of the euro area want dollars to buy U.S. goods and services, to buy U.S. assets, to make loans in dollars, or to make cash gifts in dollars to their U.S. friends and relatives. Europeans supply euros in the foreign exchange market to acquire the dollars they need.

An increase in the dollar-per-euro exchange rate, other things constant, makes U.S. products cheaper for

The Foreign Exchange Market

Figure 18.5

The fewer dollars needed to purchase one unit of foreign exchange, the lower the price of foreign goods and the greater the quantity of foreign goods demanded. The greater the demand for foreign goods, the greater the amount of foreign exchange demanded. The demand curve for foreign exchange slopes downward. An increase in the exchange rate makes U.S. products cheaper for foreigners. The increased demand for U.S. goods implies an increase in the quantity of foreign exchange supplied. The supply curve of foreign exchange slopes upward.

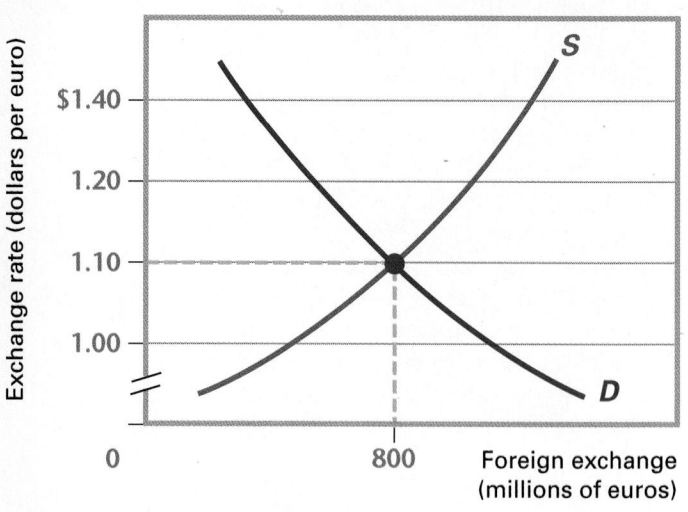

foreigners, because foreign residents need fewer euros to get the same number of dollars. More euros will be supplied on the foreign exchange market to buy dollars. Figure 18.5 shows the upward-sloping supply curve for foreign exchange (again, euros in this example).

The supply curve is drawn assuming other things remain constant. These include the euro area's incomes and preferences, inflation expectations in the euro area and the United States, and interest rates in the euro area and the United States.

Determining the Exchange Rate

Figure 18.5 brings together the supply and demand for foreign exchange to determine the exchange rate. At a rate of $1.10 per euro, the quantity of euros demanded equals the quantity supplied—in this example, 800 million euros.

What if this equilibrium exchange rate is upset by a change in one of the underlying forces that affect supply or demand? For example, suppose an increase in U.S. income causes Americans to increase their demand for all normal goods, including those from the euro area. An increase in U.S. income will shift the U.S. demand curve for euros to the right, as Americans seek euros to buy more German automobiles and European vacations.

This increased demand for euros is shown in Figure 18.6 by a rightward shift of the demand curve for euros. The supply curve does not change, because an increase in U.S. income should not affect the euro area's willingness to supply euros. The rightward shift of the demand curve from D to D' leads to an increase in the exchange rate from $1.10 per euro to $1.12 per euro. Thus, the euro increases in value, while the dollar falls in value. The higher exchange value of the euro prompts some people in the euro area to purchase more American products, which are now cheaper in terms of the euro.

An increase in the dollar price of a euro indicates a weakening of the

dollar, or *currency depreciation*. A decrease in the dollar price of a euro indicates a strengthening of the dollar, or a *currency appreciation*.

CHECKPOINT
What determines the rate of exchange between the dollar and the euro?

Who Buys Foreign Exchange?

Foreign exchange is purchased mainly by those who buy foreign goods or invest abroad, such as importers and exporters, investors in foreign assets, central banks, and tourists. Other groups also regularly participate in foreign exchange markets as well, including speculators, arbitrageurs, and people seeking a safe haven.

Speculators

Speculators buy or sell foreign exchange in hopes of profiting later by trading the currency at a more favorable exchange rate. By taking risks, speculators aim to profit from market fluctuations—that is, they try to buy low and sell high.

Arbitrageurs

Exchange rates between specific currencies are nearly identical at any given time in markets around the world. For example, the dollar price of a euro is nearly the same in New York, Frankfurt, Tokyo, London, Zurich, Hong Kong, Istanbul, and other financial centers. *Arbitrageurs* are money dealers who take advantage of tiny differences in exchange rates between markets. Their actions help to equalize exchange rates across markets. For example, if one euro trades for $1.10 in New York but for $1.11 in Paris, an arbitrageur could buy, say, $10,000,000 worth of euros in New York and at the same time sell them in Paris for $10,090,909, thereby earning $90,909 minus the transaction costs of the trades.

Abitrageurs take less risk than speculators because they *simultaneously* buy currency in one market and sell it in another. In this example, the arbitrageur increases the demand for euros in New York and increases the supply of euros in Paris. These actions increase the dollar price of euros in New York and decrease it in Paris.

Those Seeking a Safe Haven

Finally, people in countries suffering from economic and political turmoil may buy more stable currencies as a hedge against the depreciation and instability of their own currency. For example, the dollar has long been accepted as an international medium of exchange. It is also the currency of choice in world markets for oil and illegal drugs.

The euro may eventually challenge that dollar as the key world currency, in part because the largest euro denomination, the 500 euro note, is worth about five times a 100 dollar note, the top U.S. note. So it would be five times easier to smuggle currency or conduct cash transactions using euros rather than dollars.

CHECKPOINT
Who participates in the market for foreign exchange?

The **Graphing Workshop**

Effect on the Foreign Exchange Market of an Increase in Demand for Euros   **Figure 18.6**

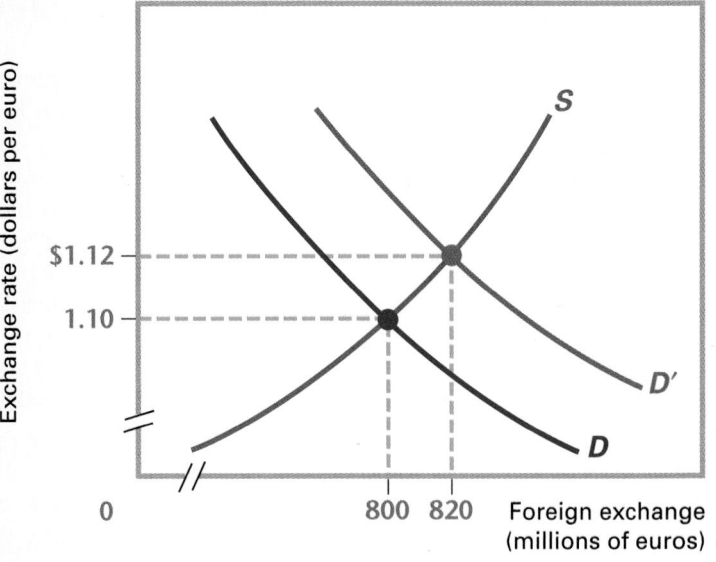

The intersection of supply curve *S* and demand curve *D* determines the exchange rate. At an exchange rate of $1.10 per euro, the quantity of euros demanded equals the quantity supplied. An increase in the demand for euros from *D* to *D'* leads to an increase in the exchange rate from $1.10 to $1.12 per euro.

Exchange Rate Systems

So far the discussion has been about **flexible exchange rates**, with the rate determined by supply and demand. A flexible, or *floating*, exchange rate adjusts continually to the many forces that affect the foreign exchange market. When the exchange rate is flexible, government officials usually have little direct role in foreign exchange markets.

However, if government officials try to set, or fix, the exchange rate, active and ongoing central bank intervention is often necessary to establish and maintain this **fixed exchange rate**. For example, prior to World War II, the value of each major currency was fixed in relation to gold. This was called the *gold standard*. Because currencies were fixed in relation to gold, they also were fixed in relation to each other.

From the end of World War II until 1971, other nations could redeem dollars for gold at a fixed exchange rate. The dollar during that period was tied to gold. The U.S. Treasury was by law required to sell foreigners gold at $35 per ounce. The values of other currencies were fixed in relation to the dollar, which was fixed in relation to gold.

In 1971, the United States developed a serious trade deficit and stopped selling gold to foreigners with dollars. No longer tied to gold, the value of the dollar began to float. Exchange rates among major world currencies became flexible, and they remain so today. Some smaller economies choose to fix the value of their currency in terms of dollars.

> ✓ **CHECKPOINT**
> Compare a system of flexible exchange rates to one of fixed exchange rates.

flexible exchange rate

Exchange rate determined by the forces of supply and demand without government intervention

fixed exchange rate

Exchange rate fixed within a narrow range of values and maintained by central banks' ongoing purchases and sales of currencies

THE WALL STREET JOURNAL

Reading It Right What's the relevance of the following statement from *The Wall Street Journal:* "U.S. Treasury Secretary John Snow repeated his view that exchange rates are best determined by market forces. He also repeated his desire to see China free the yuan from its close peg to the dollar 'as soon as possible' in order that the world see China isn't 'rigging' its exchange rate."

Main Idea

Gain from Trade

Exchange rate systems allow trade among nations to take place. *How do individuals gain from trade among nations?*

© Getty Images/PhotoDisc

Key Concepts

1. What effect would each of the following events have on the exchange rate for the U.S. dollar relative to other currencies? Explain each of your answers.

   • A new sports car is produced in Japan that many U.S. consumers choose to purchase.

   • U.S. banks offer higher interest rates for deposits. This causes many people in other nations to deposit funds in U.S. banks.

   • Many U.S. businesses choose to invest in businesses in other nations.

2. Why didn't the conversion by many European nations to the euro at the start of 2002 eliminate all trade problems between these nations?

3. How may the conversion by many European nations to the euro have helped U.S. firms that trade with these nations?

4. How are arbitrageurs able to change the exchange rates for different currencies?

5. Why did the fixed exchange rate system often result in imbalances in trade among nations?

Graphing Exercise

6. In August 2003, exchange rates for the U.S. dollar in other currencies varied widely. Suppose you were considering taking a package vacation in one of the nations listed below. Divide each price by the appropriate exchange rate to calculate the number of U.S. dollars you would have to pay for each trip. Construct a bar graph to show the relative cost of each trip. What other factors would you consider when choosing among these trips?

   Exchange Rate for U.S. Dollar in Selected Currencies, 2003

   $1 = 1.385 Canadian dollars $1 = 119.25 Japanese yen

   $1 = 0.888 euros $1 = 10.730 Mexican pesos

   • A one-week trip to Canada costs 1,662 Canadian dollars.

   • A one-week trip to Japan costs 238,500 Japanese yen.

   • A one-week trip to Germany costs 1,420.80 euros.

   • A one-week trip to Mexico costs 15,022 Mexican pesos.

Think Critically

7. **Math** Toward the end of 2000, the exchange rate for the euro fell to 0.90 euros to the U.S. dollar. By the summer of 2003, the euro had appreciated to 1.125 euros per dollar. What percentage increase was this in the value of the euro? How did this appreciation affect the ability of U.S. firms to sell their products to European Union member nations?

CONNECT to History

Tariffs
and Trade, Part I

Alexander Hamilton's vision of the United States included manufacturing. To protect the nation's young industries, he proposed a protective tariff. Because most Americans were doing well at agriculture, there was little incentive in the United States to engage in manufacturing. Therefore, Congress, which had passed a modest tariff in 1789 for revenue purposes, did not support Hamilton's proposal. Still, the tariff became the federal government's chief source of revenue until 1913.

The Napoleonic Wars provided the spark for American manufacturing and a move toward protective tariffs. This pattern, repeated during each war in the country's early history, would trigger protectionism. Tariff rates were increased for revenue purposes during the War of 1812, and they were not reduced when the war ended.

Throughout the nineteenth century, the tariff was the most important economic policy and became a huge political issue. The South supported low tariffs, and the North favored higher, more protective rates. Tariff rates inched up until the crisis caused by the 1828 "Tariff of Abominations" led to some rollback of duties. The South, believing the tariff favored the more industrial North, claimed the theory of "nullification," by which it could invalidate federal laws within its borders. President Jackson threatened to collect the tariff duties by force. Henry Clay defused the situation by negotiating a reduction of rates. The South did not renounce the theory of nullification, and the rift between it and the North was open.

When the split between the two sections of the nation erupted into the Civil War, the United States' tariff policy changed. Strapped for money, the government raised tariff rates by passing the 1861 Morrill Tariff, and tariffs were kept high until 1913. Following the Civil War, the South's political power diminished. As the United States began a period of rapid industrialization and became more self-sufficient, the importance of international trade declined. The nation's industrialists, supported by the Republican Party, were able to maintain high tariffs. Advocates of low tariffs feared that protective tariffs would cause manufacturing to grow, giving that sector more political power.

When tariff rates finally were reduced in 1913, they were replaced by an income tax so as to maintain (and shift the burden of) revenues. Still, the reductions of 1913 had less effect than predicted, primarily because of World War I. The return of higher tariffs reached a peak with the Smoot-Hawley Tariff. This tariff, enacted in 1930 during the beginning of the Great Depression, further decreased world trade.

THINK CRITICALLY

Imagine you are a member of Congress immediately after the Civil War. Take a position for or against keeping tariffs high. Then write a paragraph justifying your point of view.

18 Chapter Assessment

Summary

 Benefits of Trade

a Countries trade to improve the average standard of living of their people. Each country benefits from comparative advantage by specializing in the production of goods and services it is able to produce with the lowest opportunity cost.

b Trade can benefit nations even when they do not enjoy a comparative advantage. When nations trade, they produce larger quantities of goods and services and are able to take advantage of economies of scale.

econxtra.swlearning.com

c The United States exports many products, including capital goods, industrial supplies, services, and some consumer goods. The most important U.S. imports are consumer goods, capital goods, industrial supplies, and automobiles.

 Trade Restrictions and Free-Trade Agreements

a The flow of trade in the global economy is restricted by barriers that take the form of *tariffs, quotas,* and other measures. Tariffs are taxes placed on imported goods. Quotas are legal limits on amounts of goods that may be imported.

b All barriers to trade reduce supplies of goods and services and increase prices consumers pay for them. When one nation sets trade restrictions, other nations are likely to respond with their own restrictions. Resources are wasted when firms and groups pressure governments to impose trade restrictions.

c The *General Agreement on Tariffs and Trade (GATT)* encouraged the reduction of tariffs and quotas. Its members agreed to treat all other member nations equally. The *Uruguay Round* of trade agreements, which took place between 1986 and 1994, set the goals of

reducing tariffs by 85 percent and eliminating all quotas. The agreement also established the *World Trade Organization (WTO),* which provides the foundation for the world's multilateral trading system. Common markets or free-trade zones have been established worldwide to allow a free flow of goods, services, people, and capital among the member nations.

Balance of Payments

a The *balance of payments* is the record of all economic transactions between U.S. residents and residents of the rest of the world. Two broad accounts are included in each nation's balance of payments: the *current account* and the *financial account.* Trade of goods is measured by the *merchandise trade balance.*

b Individuals may make unilateral transfers of funds to people in other countries. This flow of money is a debit in the balance-of-payments account. Net unilateral transfers combined with the balance of goods and services results in the current account balance.

c The financial account tracks the flow of capital resulting from international transactions. It is impossible to keep track of every international transaction, so any discrepancy between credits and debits in the current account and the financial account is "balanced" by including an offsetting statistical discrepancy.

Foreign Exchange Rates

a *Foreign exchange* is the money used to carry out international transactions. The *exchange rate* is the amount of a foreign currency that can be purchased with one U.S. dollar.

b Twelve European nations have agreed to use a single currency, the euro.

c Foreign exchange is most often purchased to buy foreign goods or invest abroad.

d Before 1971, many nations fixed exchange rates for their currencies in terms of gold. This system was replaced in 1971 with a floating exchange rate system.

Review Economic Terms

Choose the term that best fits the definition. On a separate sheet of paper, write the letter of the answer. Some terms may not be used.

_____ 1. The amount by which the value of merchandise exports exceeds the value of merchandise imports during a given period

_____ 2. A tax on imports

_____ 3. A record of all economic transactions between residents of one country and residents of the rest of the world during a given period

_____ 4. Foreign money needed to carry out international transactions

_____ 5. The portion of the balance of payments that records exports and imports of goods and services, net investment income, and net transfers

_____ 6. An exchange rate determined by the forces of supply and demand without government intervention

_____ 7. The amount by which the value of merchandise imports exceeds the value of merchandise exports during a given period of time

_____ 8. A legal limit on the quantity of a particular product that can be imported

_____ 9. An exchange rate fixed within a narrow range of values and maintained by central banks' ongoing purchases and sales of currencies

_____ 10. The portion of the balance of payments that records international transactions involving financial assets

a. **balance of payments**

b. **current account**

c. **exchange rate**

d. **financial account**

e. **fixed exchange rate**

f. **flexible exchange rate**

g. **foreign exchange**

h. **General Agreement on Tariffs and Trade (GATT)**

i. **merchandise trade balance**

j. **quota**

k. **tariff**

l. **trade deficit**

m. **trade surplus**

n. **Uruguay Round**

o. **world price**

p. **World Trade Organization (WTO)**

Review Economic Concepts

11. **True or False** The law of comparative advantage states that the individual or firm with the lowest opportunity cost of producing a particular good should specialize in that good.

12. A nation may enjoy a comparative advantage as a result of possessing each of the following except

   a. superior labor.

   b. superior resources

   c. superior capital.

   d. superior consumers.

13. Countries can gain from specialization and trade if that trade results in __?__ for producers in that country. That is, the producers' average

costs of output decline as they expand their scale of production to meet the increased demand.

14. **True or False** Without comparative advantage, there is no reason for a nation to trade.

15. The category of exports from the United States that has the greatest value is

   a. capital goods.

   b. consumer goods.

   c. industrial supplies.

   d. agricultural products.

16. The __?__ for a good or service is determined by world supply and world demand for the product.

17. The category of imports to the United States that has the greatest value is

    a. capital goods.

    b. consumer goods.

    c. industrial supplies.

    d. agricultural products.

18. A *tariff* that is placed on an imported good will __?__ of the taxed product.

    a. harm consumers and producers

    b. harm consumers and benefit producers

    c. benefit consumers and producers

    d. benefit consumers and harm producers

19. **True or False** A *tariff* on imported goods will have no affect on the price of products made in that country.

20. A(n) __?__ is a legal limit on the amount of a product that may be imported into a nation.

21. Trade restrictions cause

    a. the value of international trade to grow.

    b. the price of products consumers purchase to decline.

    c. the selection of products from which consumers may choose to grow.

    d. the number of people employed in export industries to decline.

22. The __?__ provides the legal and institutional foundation for the world's multilateral trading system.

23. **True or False** When one nation sets trade restrictions, other nations are unlikely to respond with their own restrictions.

24. Trade of goods is measured by the *merchandise trade balance* that is equal to

    a. the value of a nation's exports plus the value of its imports.

    b. the value of a nation's imports less the value of its exports.

    c. the value of a nation's exports less the value of its imports.

    d. the value of a nation's exports.

25. **True or False** The *current account* keeps track of trade in goods and services, the flow of interest and profits across international borders, and the flow of foreign aid and cash gifts.

26. Which of the following would appear as a credit in a nation's *balance of payments*?

    a. Businesses in that country purchase resources from other nations.

    b. Banks in that country lend money to people in other nations.

    c. Farmers in that country sell grain to firms in other countries.

    d. Residents of that country send cash to their relatives in other countries.

27. When the unilateral transfers are combined with the balance of goods and services, the result is the __?__.

28. **True or False** The *exchange rate* for the U.S. dollar relative to other currencies is set and controlled by the U.S. government.

29. Before 1971, many nations fixed *exchange rates* for their currencies

    a. according to the value of crude oil.

    b. according to the value of a group of European currencies.

    c. according to the value of the Japanese yen.

    d. according to the value of gold.

30. A __?__ *exchange rate* system was created in 1971 under which exchange rates for major currencies are determined by demand and supply.

Apply Economic Concepts

31. **Determine the Price of an Imported Good** You have decided to buy a new camera while you are traveling in Germany. Its price is 275 euros. If the exchange rate for euros is 0.91 per one U.S. dollar, how many dollars will the camera cost? What other costs should you consider?

32. **Determine Comparative Advantage** In the following table, countries A and B are able to produce similar chairs from the resources

shown. Determine which nation has a comparative advantage in this type of production.

What should the other nation do to maximize the value of its production?

Type of Resource	Amount of Resource Required		Cost of Resource	
	A	B	A	B
Labor	2 hours	6 hours	$10 per hour	$6 per hour
Raw materials	20 lbs	20 lbs	$1.00 per lb	$.80 per lb
Power	150 kwh	80 kwh	$.03 per kwh	$.04 per kwh
Tools	1 robot system	20 hand tools	$3 per chair	$1 per chair

33. **Impose a Barrier to Trade?** Assume you are the prime minister of a poor nation that is located in another part of the world. Your government has been working to encourage economic growth by investing in new technology and training in modern skills for its workers. Although some progress has been made, there is a long way to go before your nation's businesses can compete successfully with those in other countries. Decide what type of barrier to trade (tariff or quota) you would impose in the following situations. You also may choose to impose no barrier at all. Explain each of your choices.

 a. Your nation has invested in firms that produce kitchen appliances. These firms' costs are about 25 percent higher than the cost of buying imported appliances from producers in other nations. The firms are selling few of their products and are in danger of failing. What barrier would you place on the importation of appliances?

 b. Your nation has no known oil reserves. It imports all the oil it uses from other nations. More money is spent paying for oil than is spent for any other imported product. A large part of the imported oil is used by consumers who like to take long weekend drives in the country. You would like to see more of your nation's money spent importing tools and machinery. What barriers would you place on the importation of oil?

 c. Your nation has fertile land that could be used to grow fruits it might export. Unfortunately, it lacks the ability to produce fertilizer, which the production of these crops requires. What barriers would you place on the importation of fertilizer?

34. **Sharpen Your Life Skills: Critical Thinking** Because of fears of terrorism and a general decline in economic activity in 2003, many airlines and hotels suffered from a reduced demand for their services. U.S. consumers were able to take discounted vacations either in the United States or in foreign nations. One New York City travel agency offered consumers a one-week vacation in London for $699 or a one-week vacation in California for the same price. If you had been looking for a vacation destination, which of these alternatives would you have chosen? What role would a desire to support the U.S. economy have played in your decision-making process?

 econxtra.swlearning.com

35. Access **EconDebate Online** at econxtra.swlearning.com. Read the policy debate entitled "Does the U.S. economy benefit from foreign trade?" Choose one side of this issue (for or against foreign trade) and write a paragraph arguing for that point of view.

19 Economic Development

Consider

Why are some countries poor while others are rich?

What determines the wealth of nations?

How much does foreign aid help poorer countries?

How does terrorism affect economic development?

What's the "brain drain," and how does it affect poorer countries?

Why are birth rates higher in poorer countries?

Are poorer countries catching up with the rest of the world?

POINT YOUR BROWSER

econxtra.swlearning.com

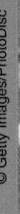

© Getty Images/PhotoDisc

Objectives

> Distinguish between developing countries and industrial market countries.

> Explain why labor productivity is so low in developing countries.

Overview

People around the world face the day under very different circumstances. Many Americans rise from a comfortable bed in their own home, select the day's clothing from a wardrobe, choose from a variety of breakfast foods, and ride to school or to work in one of the family's automobiles. In contrast, most of the world's 6.5 billion people have little housing, clothing, or food. They own no automobile, and many have no real job. Their health is poor, as is their education. Many cannot read or write. Rich nations are very different from poor ones.

Key Terms

developing countries

industrial market countries

fertility rate

[In the News]

• Longevity Differences Among Nations

On September 17, 2003, the world's oldest woman celebrated her 116th birthday. Kamato Hongo was born and raised on a small island in Japan. Her island also was home to the oldest confirmed person ever known to have lived—a woman who died at the age of 120. Less than two weeks after Hongo's 116th birthday party, the world's oldest man at that time died at the age of 114. Yukichi Chuganji also was from Japan. Coincidence? Not really. Japan, an industrial market economy, has a higher percentage of people over the age of 100 than any country in the world. It also has the highest average life expectancy (ALE)—85 years for women and 78 years for men. During the 1900s, Japan saw its ALE rate more than double. Why do the Japanese live so long? It's partly because their culture promotes a healthy lifestyle with a fish-based, low-fat diet. Even more important, the country has been able to nearly wipe out most infectious diseases. Eliminating tuberculosis and gastroenteritis accounted for nearly 40 percent of the ALE increase. The Japanese experience shows the positive effects of good medical care and a healthy lifestyle. Many developing countries do not have either, and so also have a low ALE. The African country of Sierra Leone has a low life expectancy of about 43 years for both men and women. Infectious diseases account for much of this difference. In Sierra Leone, AIDS, malaria, tuberculosis, even pneumonia and diarrhea are major causes of death. The country also has suffered through a civil war in which 50,000 people were killed. Not surprisingly, the countries that have the lowest ALEs also are among the poorest in the world.

Think About It

Based on the information in this article, what do you think is the relationship between average life expectancy and a country's economy?

econxtra.swlearning.com

Ask the Xpert!

Why are some nations rich but others are poor?

industrial market countries

Economically advanced market countries of Western Europe, North America, Australia, New Zealand, and Japan

developing countries

Nations with low GDP per capita, high rates of illiteracy, high unemployment, and high fertility rates

Worlds Apart

Countries can be classified in a variety of ways, based on their level of economic development. The yardstick used most often is to compare living standards across nations. The most common measure of living standards is a nation's *GDP per capita*. Recall that GDP per capita measures how much an economy produces on average per resident. Based on that measure, countries can be sorted into two broad categories:

1. developing countries, which have lower levels of GDP per capita income, and

2. industrial market countries, which have higher levels of GDP per capita.

Developing and Industrial Market Countries

Developing countries not only have lower GDP per capita. They also usually have higher rates of illiteracy, higher unemployment rates, extensive under-employment, and rapid population growth. On average, more than half the labor force in developing countries works in agriculture. Because farming methods are relatively primitive there, farm productivity is low, and most people barely subsist.

About 5 billion of the world's 6.5 billion people live in developing countries. China and India, the two population giants, are developing countries that together account for half the developing world's population.

Industrial market countries not only have higher GDP per capita. They also have lower illiteracy rates, lower unemployment, and slower population growth. Industrial market countries consist of the economically advanced nations of Western Europe, North America, Australia, New Zealand, and Japan. They were the first countries to experience long-term economic growth during the nineteenth century. About 1.5 billion of the world's 6.5 billion population live in industrial market countries.

Figure 19.1 shows 10 representative countries based on GDP per capita. GDP has been adjusted to reflect the actual buying power of currency in each respective economy. The United States, Canada, Japan, and the United Kingdom are industrial market economies. The rest are developing economies.

The United States had a GDP per capita in 2001 that was about five times that of Brazil, a developing country. But GDP per capita in Brazil, in turn, was about 15 times that of Sierra Leone, one of the poorest countries on Earth. Thus, developing countries are not uniformly poor. Residents of Brazil likely feel poor relative to industrial market countries such as the United States, but they are well off compared to the poorest developing countries. Per capita GDP in the United States was 70 times greater than in Sierra Leone. Thus, there is a wide range of productive performance around the world.

© Getty Images/PhotoDisc

How does this photograph suggest that the woman lives in a developing country?

Figure **19.1**

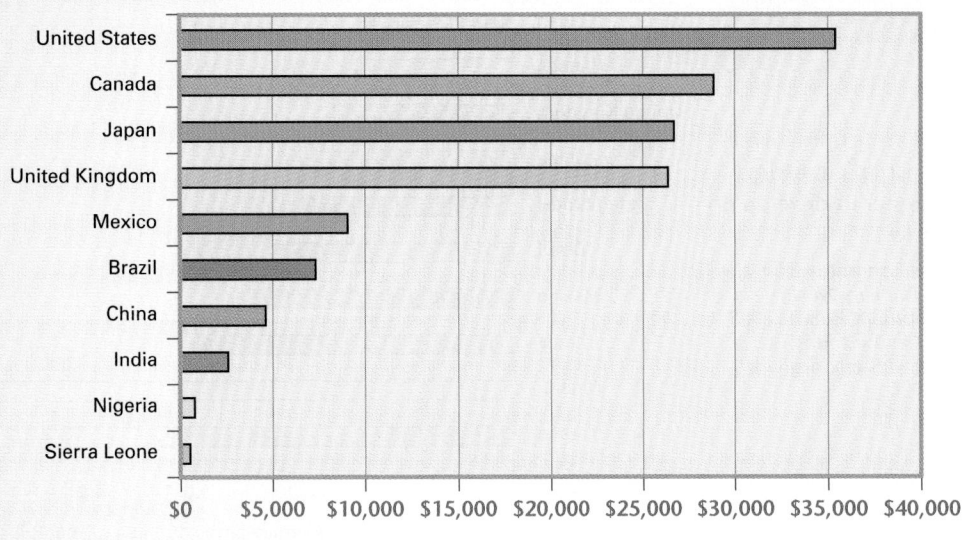

There is a wide range of productive performance around the world.

Source: The Central Intelligence Agency's *World Factbook 2002* and OECD estimates. Figures reflect the purchasing power of currencies in each country.

Life Expectancy

Differences in stages of development among countries are reflected in a number of ways besides GDP per capita. For example, many people in developing countries suffer from poor health as a result of malnutrition and disease. HIV/AIDS is devastating some developing countries, particularly those in Africa and the Caribbean. About 5,000 Haitian children are born with the HIV/AIDS virus each year.

The average life expectancy around the world ranges from about 43 years in the poor African country of Sierra Leone to 81 years in the industrial market economy of Japan. The world average is 67 years. Countries with the shortest life expectancies also have the highest infant mortality. *Infant mortality* refers to the death of a baby before its first birthday. For example, the infant mortality rate in Sierra Leone is about 35 times higher than the rate in Japan. Among industrialized nations in the world, the United States ranks 23rd in infant mortality.

Malnutrition is a primary or contributing factor in most deaths among young children in poor countries. Diseases that are easily controlled in industrial economies—malaria, whooping cough, polio, dysentery, typhoid, and cholera—can become epidemics in poor countries, where clean drinking water often is hard to find.

High Birth Rates

Developing countries also are identified by their high birth rates. This year, about 65 million of the 75 million people added to the world's population will be born in developing countries. In fact, the **fertility rate**, which is the average number of births during a woman's lifetime, is an easy way of distinguishing between developing and industrial countries. Few developing countries have a fertility rate of less than 2.2 births per woman, but no industrial country has a fertility rate above that level.

Figure 19.2 presents the average fertility rate for the 10 countries introduced in Figure 19.1. As you can see, fertility rates are lower in industrial countries and higher in developing countries. Sub-Saharan African countries are the poorest in the world and have the fastest-growing populations.

Fertility rates are higher in developing countries for a variety of reasons.

fertility rate

The average number of births during each woman's lifetime

Figure 19.2

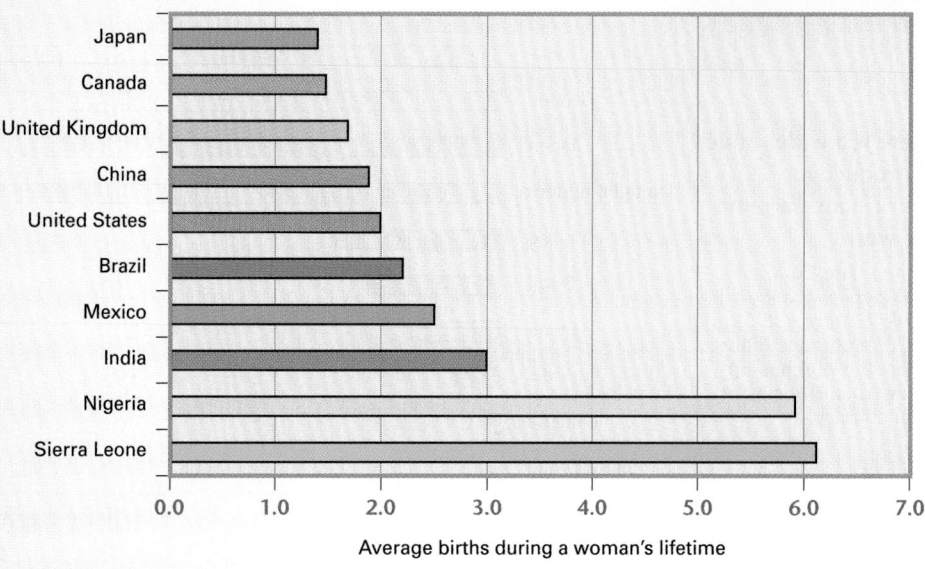

Fertility rates are lower in industrial countries and higher in developing countries.

Source: Estimates from the World Bank in *World Development Report 2003*, which can be found at econ.worldbank.org/wdr/wdr2003/.

Average births during a woman's lifetime

Among these is that parents there view children as a source of farm labor. Also, most developing countries have no pension or social security systems so parents want children to support them in old age. The higher infant mortality rates in poorer countries also lead to higher birth rates, as parents strive to achieve sufficiently large families.

Attitudes about family size are changing, however, even in the poorest countries. According to the United Nations, the birth rate during a typical woman's lifetime in a developing country has fallen from six in 1965 to less than three children today. As women become better educated, they earn more. Women who are pregnant or who have young children are less able to work. Thus, because their opportunity cost of child bearing has increased, women have chosen to have fewer children.

NETBookmark

The CIA World Factbook web site is a great source for information about the populations and economic situations of countries throughout the world. Access this site through econxtra.swlearning.com. Select a country that interests you. Find the following facts about that country's people: infant mortality rate, life expectancy at birth, and total fertility rate. Then examine the information about the country's economy. Read the "Economy—Overview" paragraph and the statistics given about the country's economy. Compare the facts you found about the country's people with the information about the economy. Write a paragraph that explains the relationship between the two sets of information.

econxtra.swlearning.com

CHECKPOINT

What are some clear differences between developing economies and industrial market economies?

Productivity and Economic Development

You have examined some symptoms of poverty in developing countries. However, you have yet to explore why poor countries are poor. Simply put, poor countries are poor because they do not produce many goods and services.

Low Labor Productivity

Labor productivity, measured as output per worker, is low in developing countries. Why? Labor productivity depends on the quality of the labor and on the amount of capital, natural resources, and other resources that combine with labor to create production. For example, a farmer who has abundant land and uses modern techniques and equipment, healthy seeds, and proper irrigation can grow more than a hundred farmers trying to scratch out a living on smaller plots using primitive tools.

One way a country raises its productivity is by investing more in human and physical capital. National savings usually finance this investment. Income per capita often is too low in developing countries to allow for much national saving or investment. In poor countries with unstable governments, the wealthy who can afford to save and invest in their nation's economy often send their savings abroad to invest in more stable economies.

What about foreign investments in developing countries? Governments of developing countries heavily regulate private international borrowing and lending. These countries are therefore less attractive for foreign investors. For example, some developing countries, such as China, have required foreign investors to find a local partner who must be granted controlling interest in the business.

Thus, in developing countries there is less financial capital available for investment in either human or physical capital. With less physical and human capital, workers produce less, so labor productivity is lower.

Less Education

Education enables workers to use modern production techniques and technology. Education also makes people more receptive to new ideas and methods. Countries with the most advanced educational systems also were the first to develop economically. For example, the United States has been a world leader in free public education and in economic development.

In the poorest countries, most adults can't read or write. For example, 70 percent of adults in Sierra Leone are illiterate. When knowledge is lacking, other resources are not used as efficiently. For

The literacy rate in the United States is 97 percent. This means that 97 percent of the U.S. population over the age of 15 can read and write. Why do you think that countries with the most advanced educational systems also have the most highly developed economies?

example, a country may be endowed with fertile land, but farmers may not understand irrigation and fertilization techniques. Farmers also may not know how to rotate crops to avoid soil depletion. Rates of illiteracy are much lower in industrial economies, where fewer than 5 percent of adults can't read or write.

Child labor in developing countries reduces educational opportunities. In Pakistan, for example, there are enough classrooms and teachers for only one-third of the country's school-age children. More than 10 million Pakistani children work full-time, usually in agriculture.

Inefficient Use of Labor

Another feature of developing countries is that they use labor less efficiently than do industrial nations. Unemployment and underemployment reflect inefficient uses of labor. Recall that underemployment occurs when skilled workers are employed in low-skill jobs or when people are working less than they would like—such as working only part time when a full-time job is preferred. Only a small proportion of the work force in developing countries have what you would call a regular job with normal hours and a steady paycheck. Most work as day laborers in the informal economy or scratch out a living in agriculture.

Few Entrepreneurs

In order to develop, an economy must have entrepreneurs who are able to bring together resources and take the risk of profit or loss. Many developing

E-CONOMICS

Technology Outsourcing to Developing Countries

American businesses have taken advantage of unemployment and underemployment in developing countries by outsourcing work to these countries. For many years, such outsourcing mainly involved moving factory work to developing countries, where the company could hire workers for a much lower pay rate than in the United States. The ability to outsource has only increased with the advent of the Internet. "With advancements in communications and the Internet," says Chris Kizzier, an offshore outsourcing consultant, "the world has shrunk to the size of a pea, and the fact that you might be 9,000 miles away is irrelevant." In recent years, many companies have saved as much as 60 percent in labor costs by moving information technology (IT) work to developing countries. India has been one of the primary beneficiaries of such outsourcing. An American company that outsources only a portion of its work can save huge amounts of money. For example, in 1999 an IT team that had 25 percent of its workers in the United States and 75 percent in India could average a combined hourly labor rate of $37 per worker. If 100 percent of the team was in the United States, the hourly labor costs would have averaged about $75 to $100 per worker. Companies as diverse as Amazon.com, DirectTV, and Delta Airlines have outsourced many of their customer service and telemarketing operations to India. The downside to this trend is that it moves jobs out of the United States. It also can leave those jobs vulnerable to political crises in the developing countries. The threat of war between India and Pakistan, for example, has concerned some American business leaders. Some experts also worry that outsourcing and the electronic communications it requires may make information less secure.

Think Critically

What are the advantages and disadvantages of U.S. firms outsourcing jobs to developing countries to (a) the firms themselves, (b) the U.S. economy in general, and (c) the economy to which the jobs are outsourced?

countries, particularly those in Africa, were once under colonial rule, where a foreign country governed. Under this system, the local population had few opportunities to develop leadership or entrepreneurial skills.

Reliance on Agriculture

In some developing countries, the average farm is as small as two acres, so the average farmer does not produce much. Even where more land is available, a lack of physical capital limits the amount of land that can be farmed. More than half the labor force in developing countries works in agriculture. However, because farm productivity is low, less than a third of GDP in those countries stems from agriculture.

In contrast, modern equipment helps a U.S. farmer to work hundreds of acres. Though only 2 percent of the U.S. labor force, American farmers grow enough to feed the nation and lead the world in agricultural exports.

Vicious Cycle of Low Income and Low Productivity

Low productivity obviously results in low income, but low income, in turn, affects worker productivity. Low income means less saving, and less saving means less investment in human and physical capital. These difficult beginnings are made even worse by poor diet and insufficient health care. Therefore, as children grow into adults, they are not well suited for regular employment. Thus, *low income and low productivity may reinforce each other in a vicious cycle of poverty.*

CHECKPOINT
Why is labor productivity low in developing countries?

© Getty Images/PhotoDisc

On rice plantations in Indonesia, much of the labor is performed by people rather than by modern farming equipment. How does this affect the productivity of Indonesian agriculture?

econxtra.swlearning.com

Key Concepts

1. Do you think it was easier for the United States to become an industrialized market economy in the nineteenth century than it is for developing countries today? Why or why not?

2. Why don't reductions in infant mortality rates necessarily cause an improvement in the standard of living in developing countries?

3. Why is labor productivity likely to be relatively low in nations that have rapid population growth?

4. Many developing countries rely on parents to teach their children how to produce goods and services. How does this contribute to their limited ability to increase production?

5. Why are 2 percent of U.S. residents able to produce more food than our nation needs while other nations cannot grow enough food for themselves with nearly 90 percent of their population working in agriculture?

Graphing Exercise

6. There are many indicators of a nation's economic wealth and development. One of these is the number of personal computers per 1,000 residents. In 2000, residents of the United States owned more computers than people in any other nation. In the same year, this rate was 3 computers per 1,000 people in Ghana. Use data in the table to construct a bar graph that shows the computer ownership rates in the identified nations. Why is computer ownership a good indicator of a nation's economic wealth and development?

Personal Computer Ownership Per 1,000 Residents in 2000

Country	PC Ownership	Country	PC Ownership
Switzerland	502	Norway	491
Australia	465	Belgium	344
Malaysia	105	Mexico	51
Turkey	38	Indonesia	10

Source: *Statistical Abstract of the United States*, 2002, p. 852.

Think Critically

7. **Management** Assume that you own a small business in a developing country that produces aluminum cooking pots. Through hard work and thrift, you have been able to save enough money to purchase a machine that can be used to produce cooking pots twice as fast as your business has in the past. In order to use this machine, you would need to hire someone to train your workers. This training would cost almost as much as the machine itself. Under these conditions, would it make sense for you to purchase the machine? What alternatives do you have if you really want your business to become more efficient and grow?

Sharpen Your Life Skills

Analyze Visuals

You can quickly compare economic conditions in different nations by constructing graphs that demonstrate different attributes of their population.

Apply Your Skill

Study the bar graph below and evaluate the information it provides about the economic conditions in each nation.

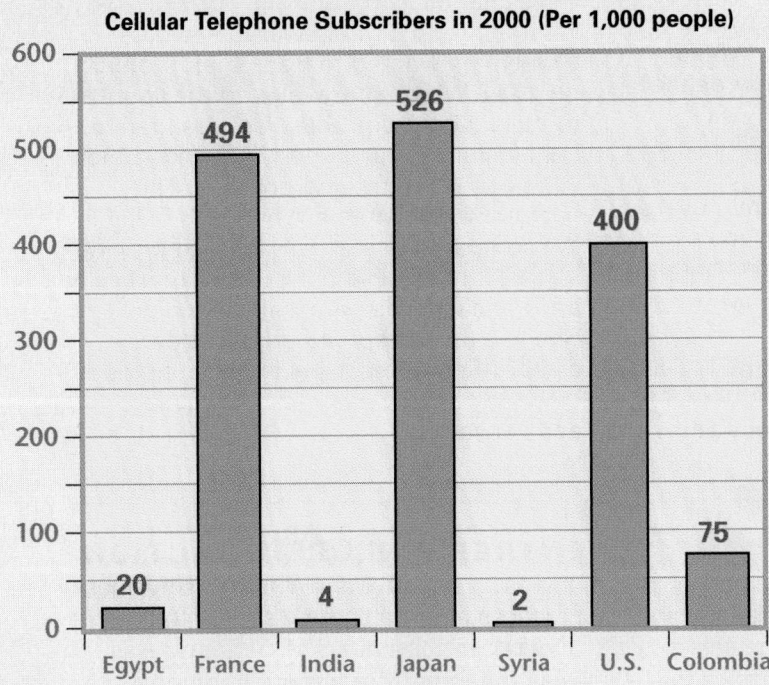

Cellular Telephone Subscribers in 2000 (Per 1,000 people)

Nation	Subscribers
Egypt	20
France	494
India	4
Japan	526
Syria	2
U.S.	400
Colombia	75

Source: *Statistical Abstract of the United States*, 2002, p. 852.

movers & shakers

Meg Whitman *CEO, eBay Inc.*

Meg Whitman had not planned to become a business executive. Growing up in Long Island, New York, she longed for a career in the medical field and entered college with medicine on her mind. However, a summer job selling advertising sparked an interest in business, and she returned to college after summer break, declaring herself an economics major. Two years after earning her economics degree from Princeton University, she graduated from Harvard Business School with an MBA. The next 20 years included stints at some of the most prestigious companies in the world: Procter & Gamble, Walt Disney Company, Stride Rite Corporation, Florists Transworld Delivery (FTD), and Hasbro Inc.

In 1998, while overseeing global marketing for Mr. Potato Head and Playskool brands at Hasbro, Whitman received an offer that would change her life. Would she be interested in running a tiny online auction company? She eventually said "yes" and has been CEO of eBay Inc. ever since. When she began her new position, eBay was a haven for Beanie Baby buyers and collectors. Today, eBay is on track to host more than $20 billion in gross annual sales of everything from cars to laptops to farm equipment.

Whitman considers eBay "a small economy," meaning it's a place where 62 million registered members meet each day to do business. These members, not eBay, control pricing for the items for sale on the web site. "If prices go up in a category, then sellers automatically bring more product to the marketplace. If prices are headed down, then sellers automatically reduce the amount of product they have because they're only willing to sell products at a certain price."

Although she's CEO, in some respects Whitman feels totally powerless over her company. "It's not something we can manage," she explains. "Our users are on to the next idea, the next hot thing, faster than we could ever be as a company. It's the millions of entrepreneurs who maximize their own business on eBay, which in turn maximizes the economy."

Whitman's passion for her customers drives the company's success. Some make their living on eBay. She refers to eBay customers as her partners and is eager for their feedback, which comes in the form of 100 to 500 e-mails a day. This feedback drives her decision making. For example, when a group of craftswomen in Guatemala wanted to trade their products on eBay, Whitman traveled to the country to meet with them. She also arranged to help install the technology needed in their village to make trading possible. This gesture demonstrates Whitman's belief in the company's stated mission "to provide a global trading platform where practically anyone can trade practically anything." She has further spread this mission by establishing global sites in 21 countries including Korea, Argentina, Singapore, and Taiwan.

SOURCE READING
Meg Whitman indicates eBay's stated mission is "to provide a global trading platform where practically anyone can trade practically anything." How does this mission serve developing countries? How does Whitman's passion for the customer help carry out this mission?

ENTREPRENEURS IN ACTION
In what ways are Meg Whitman's business practices and philosophy similar to those of other entrepreneurs? In what ways is eBay different from a more traditional firm that produces and sells goods and services?

Objectives

> Identify two foreign-trade strategies and assess their impact on economic development.

> Assess the impact of foreign aid on economic development.

Overview

Higher labor productivity and a higher standard of living go hand in hand. To boost labor productivity, developing countries must trade with developed countries to acquire the best capital and the latest technology. This deepening of capital will increase labor productivity on the farm, in the factory, in the office, and in the home. To import capital and technology, developing countries first must acquire the foreign exchange needed to pay for them. Exports usually generate more than half of the annual flow of foreign exchange in developing countries. Foreign aid and private investment make up the rest.

Key Terms

import substitution

export promotion

brain drain

foreign aid

bilateral aid

multilateral aid

U.S. Agency for International Development (USAID)

[In the News]

● Protests Against the WTO

In recent years, most major meetings of World Trade Organization (WTO) leaders have been met with angry protests. One of the most violent clashes occurred at the 1999 WTO meeting in Seattle, Washington. More than 50,000 protestors disrupted the city, more than 500 were arrested, and about $3 million in property was damaged. The violent protestors mainly targeted multinational corporations, smashing windows at Starbucks, McDonald's, Nike Town, and Old Navy, and burning khakis in front of the Gap. The Seattle protests marked the largest demonstration against free trade ever held in the United States. It brought together protestors with a variety of worries. Many expressed concerns that industrialized nations were exploiting workers and the environment in developing countries. Yet, the United States and European WTO members have pushed the hardest to protect workers around the world. In contrast, the leaders of many developing countries, including Mexico, Egypt, India, and Pakistan, have objected even to discussing labor rights. These poorer nations are most concerned that the tradable items they produce are not getting onto the markets of richer countries quickly enough. Many developing countries view attempts to impose labor and environmental standards as efforts to keep them poor. International groups like the WTO provide a forum for discussing labor and environmental issues around the world. The reality is that working conditions, especially in poor countries, are improving, thanks to trade opportunities along with pressure for labor rights from the WTO and other international groups.

Think About It

Why do you think the leaders of developing countries are reluctant to discuss the rights of workers?

Foreign Trade and Migration

What is the role of international trade in economic development? The least-developed economies rely on farming and on natural resources, such as wild game, timber, and mining. Economic development usually involves a shift from agricultural products and raw materials to manufacturing more complex products. If a country is fortunate, this transformation occurs gradually through natural market forces. Sometimes government pushes along the shift. How quickly an economy develops a manufacturing base depends on its trade relations with the rest of the world.

Import Substitution

Many developing countries, including Argentina and India, have pursued a trade policy called **import substitution**, whereby the country manufactured products that until then had been imported. Often the packaging and even the name of the product were quite similar to the import, such as "Crust" toothpaste instead of "Crest" toothpaste. To insulate domestic producers from foreign competition, the government usually imposed tariffs, import quotas, or other trade restrictions.

Import substitution became a popular development strategy for several reasons.

1. Demand already existed for these products, so the "what to produce" question was easily answered.

2. By reducing imports, the approach addressed a common problem among developing countries—the shortage of foreign exchange.

3. Import substitution was popular with those who supplied labor, capital, and other resources to the protected domestic industries.

Like all protection measures, however, import substitution wiped out the gains from specialization and comparative advantage among countries. Often the developing country replaced low-cost foreign goods with high-cost domestic goods. Domestic producers, insulated from foreign competition, usually failed to become efficient. They often produced goods of inferior quality, compared to the imports they replaced.

Even the balance-of-payments picture did not improve, because other countries typically retaliated with their own trade restrictions. Import substitution protected some domestic industries but hurt consumers with higher prices and lower quality.

Export Promotion

Critics of the import-substitution approach claim that export promotion is a surer path to economic development. **Export promotion** is a development strategy that focuses on producing for the export market. This approach begins with relatively simple products, such as textiles. As a developing country builds its educational and technological base, producers can then export more complex products.

Economists favor export promotion over import substitution because the emphasis is on comparative advantage and trade expansion, rather than trade

import substitution

A development strategy that emphasizes domestic manufacturing of products that are currently imported

export promotion

A development strategy that concentrates on producing for the export market

TEAM WORK

In groups of six or eight students, debate the pros and cons of the import substitution trade strategy versus the export promotion strategy. Divide the group into two smaller groups. One group will represent import substitution and the other, export promotion. Spend about 10 minutes in your small groups, studying the textbook in preparation for the debate. Start the debate by presenting your group's strategy to the other group. Then debate the effectiveness of the strategies.

restriction. Export promotion also forces producers to become more efficient in order to compete in world markets. Research shows that global competition increases domestic efficiency. What's more, export promotion requires less government intervention in the market than does import substitution.

Export promotion has been the more successful development strategy. For example, the newly industrialized "Asian Tigers" (Taiwan, South Korea, Hong Kong, and Singapore) have grown much more quickly than import-substituting countries such as Argentina, India, and Peru.

Most Latin American nations, which for decades favored import substitution, are now pursuing free-trade agreements with the United States. Even India is in the process of dismantling trade barriers, especially for high-technology capital goods such as computer chips. Trade barriers in India still are in place for many consumer goods. When it comes to imports, one slogan of Indian trade officials is "Microchips, yes! Potato chips, no!"

International Migration

International migration also affects developing economies. Because unemployment and underemployment are high in developing countries, job opportunities are better in industrial economies. This is a big reason why people in poorer countries try to move to richer countries. Some Mexicans, for example, risk their lives trying to get to the United States.

A major source of foreign exchange in some developing countries is the money sent home by migrants who find jobs in industrial countries. For example, Salvadorans working in the United States account for a significant chunk of spending power in El Salvador. In fact, the Salvadoran economy now uses the U.S. dollar as legal tender alongside its own currency. Thus, migration provides a valuable safety valve for poor countries.

There is a downside to migration, however. Sometimes the best and the brightest professionals, such as doctors, nurses, and engineers, migrate from developing to industrial countries. Because human capital is such a key resource, this **brain drain** hurts the developing economy in the long run.

✓ **CHECKPOINT**
What are two foreign trade strategies, and what is the impact of each on economic development?

brain drain
A developing country's loss of educated migrants to industrial market countries

© Getty Images/PhotoDisc

Nearly 30 million of the 105 million people of Mexico live in Mexico City. Since 1980, the population of that city has just about doubled. Many of these people have come to Mexico City from rural areas in Mexico. What, if anything, do you think this has to do with the migration of Mexicans to the United States?

multilateral aid

Development aid from an organization, such as the World Bank, that gets funds from a group of countries

foreign aid

An international grant or a loan made on especially favorable terms to promote economic development

U.S. Agency for International Development (USAID)

The federal agency that coordinates foreign aid to the developing world

bilateral aid

Development aid from one country to another

Foreign Aid

Because poor countries do not generate enough savings to fund an adequate level of investment, these countries often rely on foreign sources of financial capital. What is the role of foreign aid in economic development?

What Is Foreign Aid?

Foreign aid is any international transfer made on especially favorable terms, for the purposes of promoting economic development. Foreign aid includes grants, which need not be repaid. It also includes loans extended on more favorable terms than the recipient could receive otherwise. These loans have lower interest rates, longer repayment periods, and sometimes are wiped off the books entirely. Foreign aid can take the form of money, capital goods, technical assistance, food, and others.

Some foreign aid is granted by one country, such as the United States, to another country, such as the Philippines. Country-to-country aid is called **bilateral aid**. Other foreign aid goes through inter-

national bodies, such as the World Bank. Assistance provided by organizations that get funds from a number of countries is called **multilateral aid**. For example, the *World Bank* provides grants and loans to benefit development. This includes aid for health and education programs or for basic infrastructure projects like dams, roads, and communications networks. The *International Monetary Fund* extends loans to countries that have trouble with their balance of payments.

During the last four decades, the United States has provided more than $400 billion to aid developing countries. Most U.S. aid has been coordinated by the **U.S. Agency for International Development (USAID)**, which is part of the U.S. State Department. Its mission is

1. to further America's foreign policy interests in expanding democracy and free markets, and

2. to improve living standards in the developing world.

USAID concentrates primarily on health, education, and agriculture. It provides both technical assistance and loans.

Foreign aid is a controversial, though relatively small, part of the federal budget. In the last decade, official U.S. aid has been less than 0.2 percent of U.S. GDP, compared to an average of 0.3 percent of GDP in aid given by other advanced industrial nations.

Does Foreign Aid Promote Economic Development?

In general, foreign aid provides additional purchasing power to the country that receives it. It's not clear whether foreign aid *adds* to national saving, thus increasing investment, or simply *substitutes* for national saving, thereby increasing consumption rather than investment.

What is clear is that foreign aid often benefits not so much the poor as government officials, who decide how to allocate the funds. More than 90 percent of the funds distributed by USAID has been dispersed by local governments. There is reason to believe that much

THE WALL STREET JOURNAL

● **Reading It Right** What's the relevance of the following statement from *The Wall Street Journal*: "The prospect of Brazil emerging from economic recession offers a bright spot for the IMF in a troubled region that largely resents the fund's traditional prescription of budget austerity and free markets."

NETBookmark

Access the International Monetary Fund's web site through econxtra.swlearning.com. Click on Country Info, and then click on the same country you researched for Net Bookmark in Lesson 19.1. Read several articles about the IMF's involvement in that country. Then write a paragraph describing that involvement.

econxtra.swlearning.com

of this aid has been diverted from its intended purpose by government officials in recipient nations.

Much bilateral funding is tied to purchases of goods and services from the donor nation, and such programs can sometimes be counterproductive. For example, in the 1950s, the United States began the Food for Peace program, which required recipient nations to purchase food from the United States. Although this helped sell U.S. farm products abroad, it did little to help these nations develop their own agricultures. It also did not help them to become less dependent on imported food. Worse yet, the availability of low-priced food drove down farm prices in the developing countries, hurting farmers there.

Foreign aid may have raised the standard of living in some developing countries. However, it has not necessarily increased their ability to become self-supporting at that higher standard of living. Many countries that receive aid are doing less of what they had done well. Their agricultural sectors have suffered. For example, per capita food production in Africa has fallen since 1960. Much of this decline is the result of civil wars, the HIV/AIDs epidemic, and the end of colonization.

Because of disappointment with the results of government aid, the trend is now toward channeling funds through private nonprofit agencies such as CARE. More than half of all foreign aid now goes through private channels. The privatization of foreign aid matches a larger trend toward privatization of state enterprises around the world. This important development is discussed later in this chapter.

CHECKPOINT
What has been the impact of foreign aid on economic development?

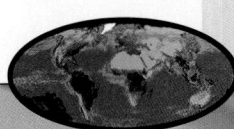

SPAN THE GLOBE

Enforcing Trade Restrictions

Many countries impose trade restrictions in the form of quotas or tariffs on goods that come into their country. These restrictions usually serve to prevent foreign countries from flooding their markets with cheap goods that compete with domestic producers of the same goods. Sometimes this can lead to a trade war, in which one country responds to another's trade restrictions by imposing restrictions of its own. In 2000, Korea and China engaged in a trade war after Korea imposed a tariff on Chinese garlic. The Chinese responded by banning the importation of Korean-made mobile telephones and petrochemicals. A year later, Japan and China entered into a similar conflict when Japan imposed quotas on three Chinese farm products—string onions, shiitake mushrooms, and the grass used to make a popular Japanese mat. Two months later, China cut Japanese car imports by half. In addition to the dangers of trade wars, enforcing trade restrictions can be very time consuming and expensive. Many countries try to find creative ways to get around those restrictions. For instance, if Country A allows a more generous quota to some countries than to others, exporters in countries under tight controls sometimes will ship their goods through Country A. For example, because Nepal is not subject to a U.S. clothing quota but India is, India ships clothing to the United States through Nepal. To get around U.S. quotas on sugar imports, Brazil exports molasses to Canada, from where it is then brought into the United States without a quota.

Think Critically

Why is it difficult for countries to enforce the quotas or tariffs they impose on imports from certain countries?

Key Concepts

1. In the 1980s, many U.S. automobile manufacturers introduced smaller, more fuel-efficient cars to compete with the flood of small Japanese cars that many consumers were buying. Was this an example of import substitution? Explain your answer.

2. How may developing countries be both harmed and helped when their people migrate to industrial market economies to obtain employment?

3. If the United States sent every person in a developing country enough food to eat for free, what would happen to farmers in that country? Why can foreign aid be a mixed blessing?

4. Why do some leaders in developing countries argue that the most effective aid they could receive would be a guarantee from industrial market economies that they will purchase imports from these countries at prices that allow their producers to earn a profit?

Graphing Exercise

5. The United States provides foreign aid though grants and loans to many developing countries. The amount given, however, is not constant or equally distributed among nations or regions. Construct a multiple bar graph using data in the table to show how U.S. foreign assistance was provided between 1994 and 2000. What reasons can you think of that might explain changes in how this aid was awarded?

U.S. Foreign Assistance Provided Through Grants and Loans, 1994–2000 (Values in Millions of Dollars)

Region	1994	1996	1998	2000
Africa	$2,031	$1,957	$1,366	$1,033
Near East & South Asia	$7,042	$7,666	$5,045	$7,669
Eastern Europe	$2,910	$1,957	$1,790	$1,818
Western Hemisphere	$1,005	$ 511	$1,033	$1,167

Source: *Statistical Abstract of the United States*, 2002, pp. 788–790.

Think Critically

6. **History** After World War II, the United States provided nearly $12 billion worth of assistance through the Marshall Plan to help the nations of Western Europe rebuild from the war. This effort was a great success. Between 1948 and the end of 1952, the nations of Western Europe increased their collective GDPs by well over 100 percent. What advantages did these nations have in rebuilding that are not shared by developing countries today?

19.3 Rules of the Game, Transition Economies, and Convergence

Objectives

> Assess the impact of a nation's physical infrastructure and rules of the game on its economic development.

> Discuss why many centrally planned economies are trying, with difficulty, to introduce market forces.

> Explain convergence theory, and discuss why the reality has not yet matched the theory's prediction.

Overview

Economic systems are classified based on the ownership of resources, the way resources are allocated to produce goods and services, and the incentives used to motivate people. Laws regarding resource ownership and the role of government in resource allocation determine the "rules of the game"—the incentives and constraints that guide the behavior of individual decision makers. Resources in centrally planned economies are owned mostly by the government and are allocated by central planners. Resources in market economies are owned mostly by individuals and are allocated through market coordination. Regardless of the economic system, economic development depends on establishing a trusted, reliable, and fair framework for productive activity.

Key Terms

physical infrastructure

soft budget constraint

privatization

convergence theory

[In the News]

● Africa Reaches Out to the Internet

In June 2000, African business leaders met in Sun City, South Africa, for their annual African Computing and Telecom Summit (ACT). In 1994, only one country in sub-Saharan Africa had Internet access. Now virtually all African countries are connected. During the annual ACT conferences, African leaders discuss such challenges as how to expand networking capabilities throughout Africa, protect technology, and encourage new business enterprises. Many African leaders believe the future of their economies depends on the ability to educate students in technology. In the late 1990s, the country of Ghana launched a major effort to expand technology training in schools. In some areas, they even bus students from rural schools to computer centers in central areas. In 1998, Ghana had only about 100,000 telephone lines for 18 million people. The government privatized the telecommunications industry in order to encourage the creation of more lines. To encourage Internet use, the government set up free Internet centers at post offices and other public places.

Think About It

Why do you think African leaders believe technology training will lead to economic development in their countries?

◀ ▮ ▶

Infrastructure and Rules of the Game

Key ingredients for economic development that have not yet been discussed are the physical infrastructure and rules of the game that support the economic system. Whether the system involves central planning or competitive markets, all economies rely on a stable and supportive institutional framework.

Physical Infrastructure

physical infrastructure

Transportation, communication, energy, water, and sanitation systems provided by or regulated by government

Production and exchange rely on the economy's **physical infrastructure**, which are transportation, communication, energy, water, and sanitation systems provided by or regulated by government. Roads, bridges, airports, harbors, and other transportation facilities are vital to production. Reliable mail and phone service along with a steady supply of electricity and water also are essential for advanced production techniques. Imagine how difficult it would be to run even a personal computer if the supply of electricity and phone service was continually interrupted, as is often the case in developing countries.

Investigate Your Local Economy

Think about the physical infrastructure in your area. List the infrastructure categories mentioned in this section of the book on the left side of a sheet of paper. On the right side, place a plus sign (+) next to the categories that seem to be working efficiently and a minus sign (−) next those that seem to need some attention. For the categories you think need attention, research to find out if the local, state, or federal government has any plans underway for improvement. If they do, write a paragraph describing these plans. If not, write a letter to a political leader describing the problem and asking for their office's help in solving it.

Fixed and Mobile Telephone Lines Per 1,000 Population by Country in 2001

Figure 19.3

Many developing countries have serious deficiencies in their physical infrastructures.

Source: Estimates reported by the World Bank in *World Development Report 2003*, which can be found at econ.worldbank.org/wdr/wdr2003/.

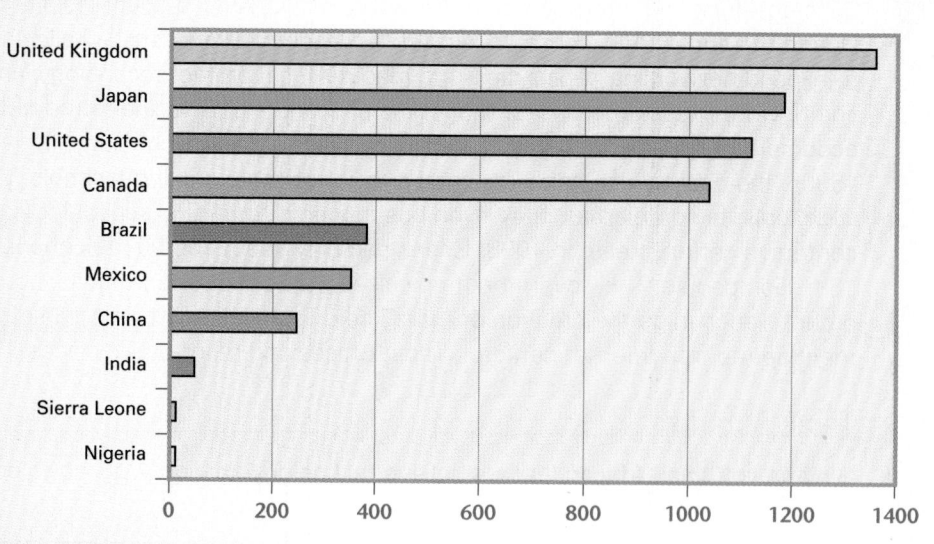

Many developing countries have serious deficiencies in their physical infrastructures. As just one measure of that infrastructure, Figure 19.3 shows the number of fixed and mobile telephone lines per 1,000 population in 2001 for the 10 countries examined earlier. Note how much greater is the number in the top four countries—which are industrial market economies—compared with the bottom six countries, which are developing economies. The United Kingdom, the top rated in this category, had 1,358 phone lines per 1,000 population. Compared this to only 10 phones lines per 1,000 in Sierra Leone and only 9 per 1,000 in bottom-rated Nigeria.

Worse still for the infrastructure, some of the poorest countries in Africa have been ravaged by internal political strife. For example, civil war raged in Sierra Leone for more than a decade. In Sudan, civil war has been going on for two decades. Wars destroy bridges, roads, electrical systems, water works, and other vital infrastructure. Without these things, efficient production will not take place.

Rules of the Game

Reliable and trusted rules of the game also are important for economic development. Recall that the rules of the game are the formal and informal institutions that promote production incentives and economic activity. They include the laws, customs, conventions, and other social and political elements that encourage people to undertake productive activity.

On the *formal* end of the spectrum, rules of the game include a country's codified rules and laws, along with the system for establishing and enforcing those rules and laws. On the *informal* end of the spectrum, rules of the game include the customs and informal mechanisms that help coordinate production.

Rules of the game are vital for economic development. When operating properly, they allow people to work, spend, and save to build a better future for themselves and their families. When they are weak, corrupt, or operate

© Getty Images/PhotoDisc

In the past four years, Egypt has been spending much of its budget on national infrastructure projects. What types of physical infrastructure do you think might be needed in this Egyptian farmers' village?

unfairly, people lack confidence in the economic system. Weak or corrupt rules of the game also encourage people to "take" rather than "make." This means they may find it easier to steal what others have, rather than to produce something of value themselves. When taking becomes more attractive than making, production declines and incomes fall.

Better incentives can boost productivity and improve the standard of living. For example, a more stable political climate promotes investment in the economy. Conversely, destabilizing events such as wars and terrorist attacks discourage investment, harm productivity, and reduce the standard of living.

CHECKPOINT
What is the impact of a nation's physical infrastructure and rules of the game on its economic development?

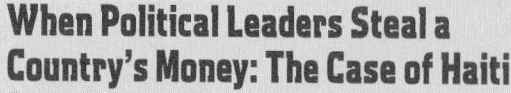

Ethics in Action

When Political Leaders Steal a Country's Money: The Case of Haiti

Developing countries face many difficulties in transitioning into a strong economy. Their ability to succeed depends largely on the strength and stability of their political leadership. In some countries, political leadership has been corrupt to the point that leaders have weakened the economy by stealing from the national treasury. One of the worst cases of such corruption was the experience of Haiti. Haiti had never been a rich country, but it had enjoyed some economic growth in the 1940s and 1950s, thanks to rising prices for the goods it exported. Then, in the 1950s, François Duvalier established a dictatorship. He imposed heavy taxes on the population to fund a powerful army and his own lavish lifestyle. Under his rule, government officials openly stole money from the public treasury for their own use. The harsh regime drove the most talented and skilled people out of the country, leaving only the very poor to suffer under heavy taxes and a draining economy. Haiti soon became the poorest country in the Western Hemisphere, and it fell far behind the rest of the world in economic growth. After Jean-Claude Duvalier took over from his father in 1971, some countries, including the United States, began to give aid money to Haiti. Much of this money was stolen as well. Fed up with government corruption and facing desperate poverty, the Haitian people staged a successful revolt to oust Duvalier in the mid-1980s. Slowly Haiti has started to build a more stable political structure. However, it remains one of the world's poorest countries as a result of years of political greed and economic neglect.

Think Critically

What "rules of the game" in Haiti under the Duvaliers prevented the country from achieving economic growth?

Economies in Transition

From the breakup of the Soviet Union to China's move toward freer markets, markets are replacing central plans in countries around the world The attempt to replace central planning with markets is one of the greatest economic experiments in history.

Prices and Profit in Centrally Planned Economies

Most prices in centrally planned economies are established not by market forces but by central planners. Once set, prices tend to be inflexible. As a result, consumers have less say in what's produced. Consumer goods often are priced below the market-clearing level, so shortages are common. For example, just prior to the collapse of the Soviet Union in 1991, the price of bread had not changed since 1954. That price amounted to only 7 percent of bread's production cost. Some rents had not changed in 60 years. Thus, prices had little relation to supply and demand, and shortages were common.

Evidence of shortages of consumer goods included long waiting lines at retail stores. Shoppers in the former Soviet Union sometimes would wait in line all night and into the next day. Consumers often relied on "connections" through acquaintances to obtain many goods and services. Scarce goods were frequently diverted to the black market, where prices were much higher.

Prices did not allocate products very well in centrally planned economies. To make matters worse, state enterprises faced little pressure to cover costs. With central planning, any "profit" earned by a state enterprise was appropriated by the state. Any "loss" was covered by a state subsidy. Thus, covering costs was not important for a state enterprise. Such enterprises face what has been called a **soft budget constraint**. Managers could ignore market forces, could allocate resources inefficiently, and could make poor investment decisions—yet still survive.

Privatization

One necessary step in the move from central planning to a market economy is **privatization**, which is the process of turning government enterprises into private enterprises. It is the opposite of *nationalization*, which is turning private enterprises into government enterprises.

The problem is that most centrally planned economies that are trying to privatize have no history of market interaction. They also have no established record of codified law or rules of conduct for market participants. For example, Russian privatization began in 1992 with the sale of municipally owned shops. Most property in countries of the former Soviet Union was owned by the state. Thus, it often remained unclear who had the authority to sell the property and who should receive the proceeds from the sale. This uncertainty resulted in cases in which different buyers purchased the same property from different officials. Yet there was no clear legal process for resolving title disputes to establish property rights. Russia did not have a reliable legal system.

Worse still, self-serving managers stripped some enterprises of their assets. The process of privatization does not work well when the general population perceives it to be unfair.

Thus, establishing a market system is easier said that done. Economists involved in structuring the transition from central planning to market systems are learning as they go. Many centrally planned economies have little experience with laws and customs that are trusted, reliable, and fair.

CHECKPOINT
Why are centrally planned economies trying to introduce market forces, and what has been slowing down the process?

Are the World's Economies Converging?

Given enough time, will poor countries eventually catch up with rich ones? The **convergence theory** argues that developing countries can grow faster than advanced ones and should eventually close the gap.

Reasons for Convergence

Countries that are far behind economically can grow faster by copying existing technology. It is easier to copy new technology once it is developed than to develop that technology in the first place. Advanced economies, which are already using the latest technology, can boost productivity only with a steady stream of technological breakthroughs.

Advanced countries, such as the United States, find their growth limited by the rate of creation of new knowledge and improved technology. Follower countries can grow more quickly by, for instance, adding computers where they previously had none. For example, the United States makes up just 5 percent of the world's population. But in 1995, Americans owned most of the world's personal computers. By 2001, most PC purchases were outside the United States.

Not Much Convergence

What is the evidence for convergence? Some poor countries have begun to catch up with richer ones. For example, the newly industrialized Asian economies of Hong Kong, Singapore, South Korea, and Taiwan have invested heavily in technology and in education. These Asian Tigers have moved from the ranks of developing countries to the ranks of industrial market economies.

The Asian Tigers are more the exception than the rule. Among the nations that make up the poorest third of the world's population, consumption per capita has grown by an average of only about 1.0 percent per year during the last two decades, compared with a 2.5

Singapore, one of the so-called Asian Tigers, is a highly developed and successful free market economy. *Due to investments in factories, machinery, new technology, and in the health, education, and training of people, the population of Singapore enjoys a high standard of living.* **The country boasts one of the highest per capita GDPs in the world. Singapore is an island country. How has this helped Singapore to successfully develop its economy?**

percent average growth in the rest of the world. Therefore, while the standard of living in the poorest third of the world has improved, that living standard has fallen further behind the rest of the world.

Higher Birth Rates and Less Human Capital

One reason per-capita consumption has grown so slowly in the poorest economies is that birth rates there are double those in richer countries. Therefore, poor economies must produce still more just to keep up with a growing population. Another reason why convergence has not taken hold, particularly for the poorest third of the world, is the vast difference in the amount of human capital across countries. Whereas

technology is indeed portable from industrial economies to developing economies, the knowledge, skill, and training usually required to take advantage of that technology are not portable.

Some poor countries, such as most of those in Africa, simply do not have the human capital needed to identify and absorb new technology. Consider personal computers. Figure 19.4 shows the number of personal computers per 1,000 people in 2001 for the 10 nations examined earlier. Notice how many more PCs the top four countries, which are industrial market economies, have than the bottom six, which are developing economies. The United States had 625 PCs per 1,000 people. Sierra Leone had only one PC per 1,000 people.

As already noted, poor economies tend to have low education levels and high illiteracy rates. Those persons who do become well educated often migrate to richer economies. This is part of the brain drain, discussed earlier.

Most developing countries lack the stable institutions needed to nurture economic development. Many developing countries have serious problems with their infrastructures. For example, they may lack a reliable source of electricity needed to power new technologies. Some of the poorest nations have been ravaged by civil war for years.

Reasons for Optimism

Despite all that, working conditions in most poor countries are improving, thanks to greater trade opportunities and pressure from international bodies such as the World Trade Organization. For example, Cambodia is extremely poor, but the highest wages in the country are earned by the 1 percent of the population working in the export sector. This tiny group makes products for companies such as Nike and Gap. Though pay is low by U.S. standards, workers in the export sector earn more

than twice what judges and doctors average in Cambodia. Child labor is still a problem in poor countries, but most children work on family farms. Because of world pressure on manufacturers, fewer and fewer children are working in factories.

The reduction in trade barriers resulting from the Uruguay Round, the latest round of trade negotiations, is projected to boost world income by more than $500 billion in 2005, the target date for full implementation. This amounts to an increase of about $400 for each household on Earth. That payoff may not impress those who object to greater globalization through freer trade, but for households in some poor countries, it can be a lifesaver.

CHECKPOINT
What does the convergence theory predict, and why hasn't the reality yet matched that prediction?

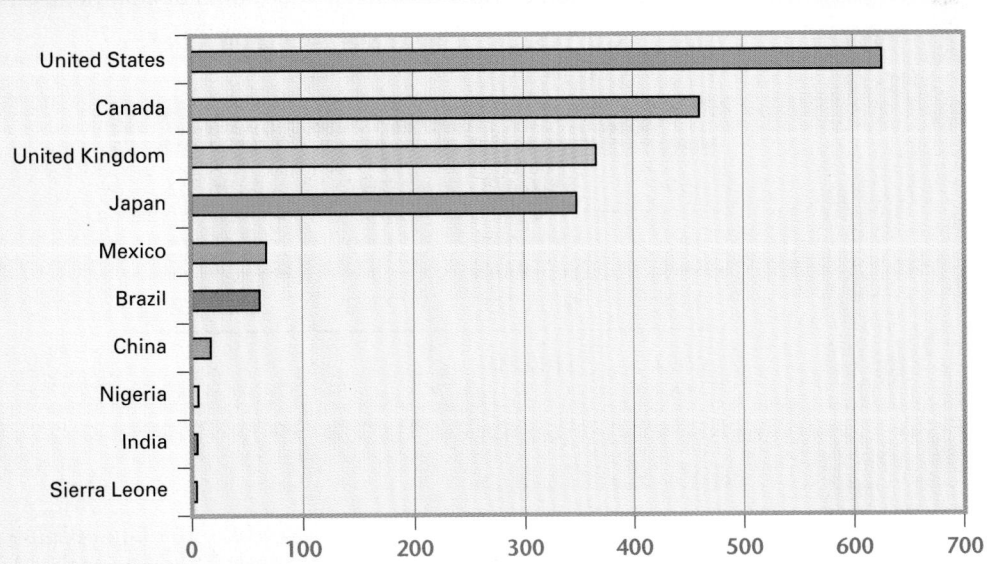

Personal Computers Per 1,000 Population by Country in 2001　　**Figure 19.4**

Some poor countries simply do not have the human capital needed to identify and absorb new technology.

Source: Estimates from the *World Bank in World Development Report 2003*, which can be found at econ.worldbank.org/wdr/wdr2003/.

Key Concepts

1. Choose a business in your community that employs many workers. How would this business be affected if suddenly there were no local roads and bridges, electric power, telephone service, water supplies, and waste removal services? Why is a country that lacks basic physical infrastructure unlikely to have a comparative advantage in manufacturing?

2. Many developing countries have created laws to regulate the production of goods and services. Regardless of this fact, many businesses in these nations largely ignore these laws and carry out production as they choose. What do these nations need in addition to their laws? Explain your answer.

3. Why do people who live in nations that once had government ownership and control of businesses often find it difficult to operate in a competitive market economic system?

4. Will giving individuals the right to own and operate businesses without government interference guarantee a nation's smooth transition from a centrally planned to a free market economy? Why or why not? What other conditions need to be created for this to take place?

5. Some people think that investments made in developing countries by businesses from industrial market economies help these nations improve in terms of their production and standards of living. Others think that this investment will not lead to a material improvement in the lives of these people. Which of these points of view do you think is nearest to the truth? Explain your answer.

Graphing Exercise

6. U.S. businesses invest billions of dollars every year in developing countries. Construct a line graph showing the total accumulated value of U.S. investments in Latin America in the years from 1994 through 2000. Why do businesses make these investments? How do such investments benefit people in Latin America?

Value of Total U.S. Direct Investments in Latin America, 1994–2000 (Values in Millions of Dollars)

Year	Investment	Year	Investment
1994	$116,478	1998	$196,755
1995	$131,377	1999	$220,705
1996	$155,925	2000	$239,388
1997	$180,818		

Source: *Statistical Abstract of the United States,* 2002, p. 788.

Think Critically

7. **Sociology** You have learned that poverty in the United States is frequently found in households led by single parents. These households often include many young children. In what ways are the problems of these households in the United States similar to those faced by people who live in developing countries? In what ways are their problems different?

to History

Tariffs
and Trade, Part II

The Reciprocal Trade Agreement Act of 1934 and its 12 extensions through 1962 ushered in an era of tariff reduction worldwide. The Act authorized the U.S. president to negotiate tariffs and give nations "most favored nation status."

In 1947, following World War II, 23 nations negotiated the General Agreement on Tariffs and Trade (GATT). The goal of this agreement was to encourage nations to lower tariffs and other trade barriers. For the United States, lowering tariffs also had a foreign-policy component in helping to rebuild Europe and develop poor nations. While the general principle is for a country to treat all members equally, some exceptions were allowed for developing countries to protect necessary industries. These reductions were tied to a "no injury" clause, which limited the impact of tariff reductions if they were determined to have a negative effect on domestic industries. It also allowed for free-trade areas to be created, such as the European Community and the North American Free Trade Agreement (NAFTA). The first five agreements, or "rounds," were characterized primarily by countries negotiating an agreement on a product for tariff reductions. They would then apply the agreement to all members on a "most favored nation" basis.

During the 1964 Kennedy Round, the United States proposed across-the-board reductions to the 62 member nations. The negotiations, which lasted three years, focused primarily on deciding what items to include. Success was obvious as average tariff rates, which were at 47 percent in 1947, dropped to 9 percent in 1972, and reached 4 percent in 2003. Following the Kennedy Round, discussions began to focus more on non-tariff barriers, such as dumping, subsidized exports, and other exclusionary practices. Most industrialized nations agreed to the provisions that were resisted by developing countries.

By the Uruguay Round (1986–1994), membership in GATT had grown to 123 countries. This round led to the creation of the World Trade Organization (WTO). The WTO now has nearly 150 members, accounting for more than 97 percent of the world's trade. Fifty additional nations are now negotiating membership in the organization.

The WTO operates principally under the rules formed by GATT. Documentation of those rules runs to 50,000 pages and incorporates 30 agreements, called schedules. WTO decisions are not put to a vote. In fact, voting rarely is used under GATT. Decisions typically are made by consensus, and then agreements are ratified by member parliaments.

The system allows countries to bring disputes to the WTO if they believe that their rights or agreements are being infringed. The organization encourages disagreements to be settled by consultation. In the eight years from 1995 to 2003, the WTO had about 300 cases before it. This was about the same number dealt with by GATT from 1947 to 1994.

With 75 percent of its membership consisting of developing countries, the WTO faces huge challenges. The latest round of negotiations (the Doha round, 2001) is scheduled to end in 2005. In the current round of negotiations, developing countries, which typically depend on agriculture for a large portion of their exports, are asking for the elimination of export subsidies. The agricultural sectors in industrialized nations, however, rely on these subsidies to stay afloat. Therefore, ending export subsidies on agricultural goods is difficult for industrialized countries.

THINK CRITICALLY
Given a world economy, do you think a country can both promote free trade and protect its domestic industries at the same time? What would be the advantages to a country of doing both?

Chapter Assessment

Summary

econxtra.swlearning.com

19.1 Developing Economies and Industrial Market Economies

a Countries may be classified in a variety of ways based on their levels of economic development. *Developing countries* have lower levels of GDP per capita income and higher rates of illiteracy, unemployment, underemployment, and rapid population growth than *industrial market countries*. They also have relatively short average life expectancies and high birth rates.

b Developing countries suffer from low labor productivity. Their workers often lack skills and basic education. Income per capita is low and does not allow individuals to save to make investments in physical capital.

c Developing countries have few entrepreneurs who are able to bring together resources and take the risks necessary to develop new and more efficient means of production.

19.2 Foreign Trade, Foreign Aid and Economic Development

a Developing countries have used many techniques to try to speed their economic growth. One method is *import substitution*. This policy places barriers on specific types of imported products that are targeted to be replaced with domestic production. Domestic producers then are able to sell products in a proven market without foreign competition. Another method used to speed growth is *export promotion*. Under this policy, a government provides assistance to businesses targeted for export expansion.

b Many people who live in developing countries move to *industrial market economies* each year. This allows them to earn greater incomes, some of which they send home to their friends and relatives. When skilled workers migrate, however, they are no longer able to contribute to production in their native lands. This movement of skilled workers has been called the *brain drain*.

c Countries with industrial markets have attempted to assist developing countries through various programs that encourage investment in human and physical capital. *Foreign aid* has been extended through *bilateral* agreements between individual countries and *multilateral* organizations. Over the past 40 years, the United States has extended more than $400 billion in assistance to developing countries. Most of this aid was coordinated by the *U.S. Agency for International Development (USAID)*. Foreign aid provides additional purchasing power in developing countries. There is, however, a question about its effectiveness.

19.3 Rules of the Game, Transition Economies, and Convergence

a For a country to produce goods and services efficiently and to experience economic growth, its economy must provide businesses with both a *physical infrastructure* and a stable environment in which to operate. Many developing countries lack sufficient roads, bridges, airports, harbors, and other transportation facilities. They do not have reliable mail, phone service, or steady supplies of electricity, water, and other necessary services.

b Political stability is a necessary component for production and growth in many developing countries. Entrepreneurs will not work to expand production if they are not convinced they will benefit from that production.

c Inefficiencies in centrally planned economic systems led most to move to market-based economies. However, *privatization*, transferring ownership of businesses to private individuals, does not mean that these people have the entrepreneurial skills needed to run them efficiently.

d Some economists and politicians believe that the world's economies are gradually converging into one global system. A reduction in trade barriers, increased international investments, and a spread of technology and education may allow many people to escape poverty in the future.

Review Economic Terms

Choose the term that best fits the definition. On separate paper, write the letter of the answer. Some terms may not be used.

_____ 1. The process of turning public enterprises into private enterprises

_____ 2. Development aid from one country to another

_____ 3. Nations with low GDP per capita, high rates of illiteracy, high unemployment, and high fertility rates

_____ 4. Transportation, communication, energy, water, and sanitation systems provided by or regulated by government

_____ 5. Development aid from an organization, such as the World Bank, that gets funds from a group of countries

_____ 6. A developing country's loss of educated migrants to industrial market countries

_____ 7. The average number of births during each woman's lifetime

_____ 8. Economically advanced market countries of Western Europe, North America, Australia, New Zealand, and Japan

_____ 9. A development strategy that concentrates on producing for the export market

_____10. A development strategy that emphasizes domestic manufacturing of products that are currently imported

a. **bilateral aid**

b. **brain drain**

c. **convergence theory**

d. **developing countries**

e. **export promotion**

f. **fertility rate**

g. **foreign aid**

h. **import substitution**

i. **industrial market countries**

j. **multilateral aid**

k. **physical infrastructure**

l. **privatization**

m. **soft budget constraint**

n. **U.S. Agency for International Development (USAID)**

Review Economic Concepts

11. **True or False** _Developing countries_ typically have low GDP per capita, high rates of illiteracy, high unemployment rates, and rapid population growth.

12. _Developing countries_ are likely to have each of the following except
    a. a limited physical infrastructure.
    b. few educational opportunities for students.
    c. easy access to high-quality medical care.
    d. a low savings rate.

13. A country's __?__ is the average number of children born during each woman's lifetime.

14. **True or False** Countries with low life expectancies also have high infant mortality rates.

15. People in _developing countries_
    a. are all equally poor.
    b. vary in their degree of poverty.
    c. are able to support their families because their prices are much lower.
    d. are provided with free medical care by their governments.

16. Countries that use tariffs or quotas to encourage the production of products that were formerly imported are following a policy of __?__.

17. **True or False** Like all protection measures, *export promotion* reduces the gains from specialization and comparative advantage.

18. Farms in *developing countries* are often inefficient for each of the following reasons except

    a. they are too small to be efficient.

    b. they lack tools and fertilizer that could make them more efficient.

    c. the farmers do not work hard enough to be efficient.

    d. the farmers do not understand modern farming techniques.

19. When skilled workers leave developing countries to find employment in industrial market countries, there is a(n) __?__.

20. Foreign assistance extended by one nation to another nation is called

    a. bilateral aid.

    b. unilateral aid.

    c. multilateral aid.

    d. quadrilateral aid.

21. Most U.S. assistance provided to developing countries in the past 40 years has been coordinated by the __?__.

22. Which of the following is an example of *physical infrastructure*?

    a. savings used to purchase machinery

    b. land upon which crops are grown

    c. roads upon which products are moved

    d. good weather that helps crops to grow

23. **True or False** For rules to be effective in regulating production, they must be written into laws.

24. __?__ in centrally planned economies allows inefficient producers to continue to operate over long periods of time, even when their costs were greater than the income they received from products they sold.

25. In the past decade, there has been

    a. a steady convergence of the world's economies.

    b. little evidence that the world's economies are converging.

    c. a narrowing of gaps in productivity among all the world's countries.

    d. no growth in productivity by any of the world's developing countries.

Apply Economic Concepts

26. **Evaluate the Cost of Education** In many of the world's poorest countries, nearly 50 percent of the population is under 15 years of age. If these people are to help improve the productivity of their economies, they must be trained in modern methods of production. In 2000, just over 4 million of the 8.8 million people of Chad were under 15. Explain why it would be difficult for many of these children to be educated and become productive members of a growing economy.

27. **Determine the Best Type of Aid** Imagine that you have been given control of the USAID program. You have the power to decide how to use the funds provided to this organization by the U.S. government. Unfortunately, there is a limit to what you can spend, and there are many nations that need assistance. You have allocated $20,000,000 to a developing country. These funds may be spent to do any of the following. How would you spend this money to do the most good? Explain your choice.

    • Spend the money to provide better education for 20,000 students.

    • Spend the money to provide better health care for 200,000 people.

    • Spend the money to purchase better farm equipment for 10,000 farmers.

    • Spend the money to build a highway that leads to the country's only port.

    • Spend the money to provide 1,000,000 people with better nutrition.

28. **Encourage Foreign Investment** Imagine you have been put in charge of a developing country's Office of Economic Growth. Your job includes setting policies intended to encourage foreign businesses to invest in your

country and provide jobs to your people. Which of the following policies would you support? Which would you oppose? Explain your answers.

- Allow foreign firms to pay any wage rate that your people are willing to accept. Have no required minimum wage, overtime pay, or days off.

- Assure foreign firms that their investment will not be nationalized by the government.

- Provide foreign firms with reduced tax rates

- Allow foreign firms to ignore pollution control laws

- Pass laws that make it illegal for workers to go on strike against foreign firms

29. **Sharpen Your Life Skills: Analyze Visuals** Study the graph below and evaluate the information it provides about newspaper sales. How does it show which countries are still developing and which are established industrial market economies?

Daily Newspaper Circulation Per 1,000 Residents

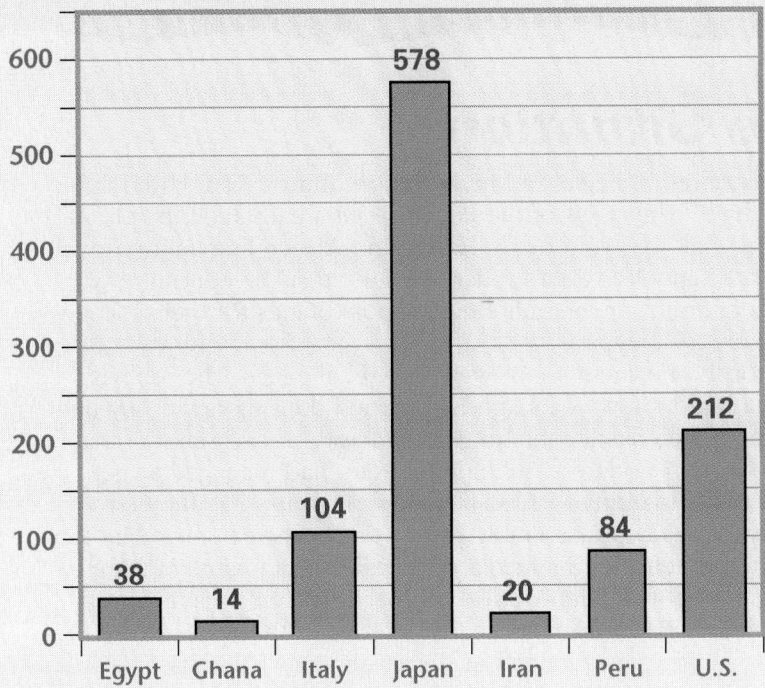

Source: *Statistical Abstract of the United States,* 2002, p. 852

econxtra.swlearning.com

30. Access **EconNews Online** at econxtra. swlearning.com. Read the article entitled "Grading the IMF and World Bank." Also reread the Ethics in Action feature on page 606 of this chapter. What political and economic circumstances in Haiti might explain why critics of the World Bank point to this country "as an example of the failure of the World Bank"? Do you think this criticism is wholly justified? Why or why not?

Investing In Your Future

Project 6 〉 FINDING NEW FRONTIERS

◉ The Situation

Aleesha stared at herself in the bathroom mirror. That couldn't be a gray hair! The stress of the last few years had taken its toll. At least the children were okay. Tomas and Aleece had adjusted well to private school. Even Tom had to agree that the education was first class, and it opened all kinds of possibilities for their college education and beyond.

As for the business, there were new challenges. The lobbyists Aleesha hired a few years ago had earned their money. They had kept the tax credits for the inner-city factory in each tax bill that rolled through Congress. In addition, they had managed to get other credits to apply to Aleesha's new program that allowed employees to do pre-assembly piecework in their homes. The lobbying firm even used its media contacts to bring national television attention to the innovative approach. A similar campaign by Winston and Bailey brought media interest to the wartime use of animals as weapons carriers. As a consequence, Aleesha was able to get the worrisome term on such potential use of her products dropped from her Defense Department contract and had signed the result. The contract kept both factories at near full production.

◉ The Decision

The government contract would not last forever, however. To keep up the current level of production, new markets would have to be found and developed. In addition, new problems in the United States consumer market recently had arisen. Funding for zoos and similar institutions around the country continued to dry up, due to decreasing tax revenues as a result of the economic downturn. Further, just last Monday Aleesha's vice-president for sales had discovered nearly identical rip-offs of two of the company's most important consumer products. The rip-offs, made in China, were of decent quality. They were now being sold by two discount chains around the country at half the price. Something had to be done about the situation.

Another problem surfaced, involving international trade. Japan, one of the most lucrative potential markets for Aleesha's pet consumer products, would allow only a small number of the products to be imported. Also on the international front, many nations in Africa represented wide-open markets for the company's products, in particular the Capturecare line. However, customers in these countries were unable to buy the products, due to the strength of the dollar against their currencies and the resulting higher prices than the competition was offering on its outmoded (and far less animal-friendly) devices. Aleesha wondered how she could change these situations to benefit her company.

6/24

1/5

5/14

Activities

Divide into teams or work individually, as directed by your teacher, to perform the following tasks.

Apply the steps in the following decision-making process to Aleesha's current situation:

1. *Define the problem.* Again, Aleesha faces multiple decisions. Define each problem in a way that will allow a clear solution.

2. *Identify her choices.* List the various alternatives among which Aleesha must choose for each problem.

3. *Evaluate the pluses and minuses of each choice.* Carefully weigh the value Aleesha puts on each alternative and the opportunity cost(s) for each.

4. *Make a choice.* Which course of action should she choose? Be prepared to present and defend your selection to the class.

5. *Provide "action" steps that are appropriate to the decision.* Make sure these are realistic and timely to ensure the necessary actions are taken to resolve the problem.

6. *Critique the decision.* The class will assist in the review and evaluation of your plan of action.

Research

Research for the information needed, such as the funding of zoos through taxation, rip-off products from nations such as China, and the trade situation with Japan and countries in Africa.

Present

Arrive at a decision. Then prepare a presentation for the class on the six steps you took to achieve this decision.

Economic Data

Economic Indicators

Consumer Price Index Since 1913

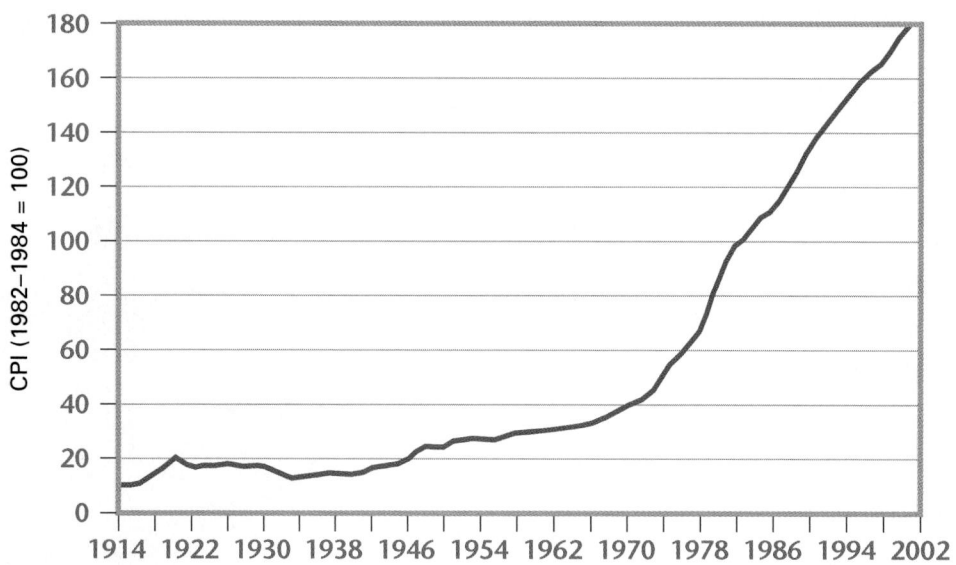

Despite fluctuations, the price level, as measured by the consumer price index, was lower in 1940 than in 1920. Since 1940, the price level has risen almost every year.

Source: U.S. Bureau of Labor Statistics.

U.S. Real GDP and Price Level Since 1929

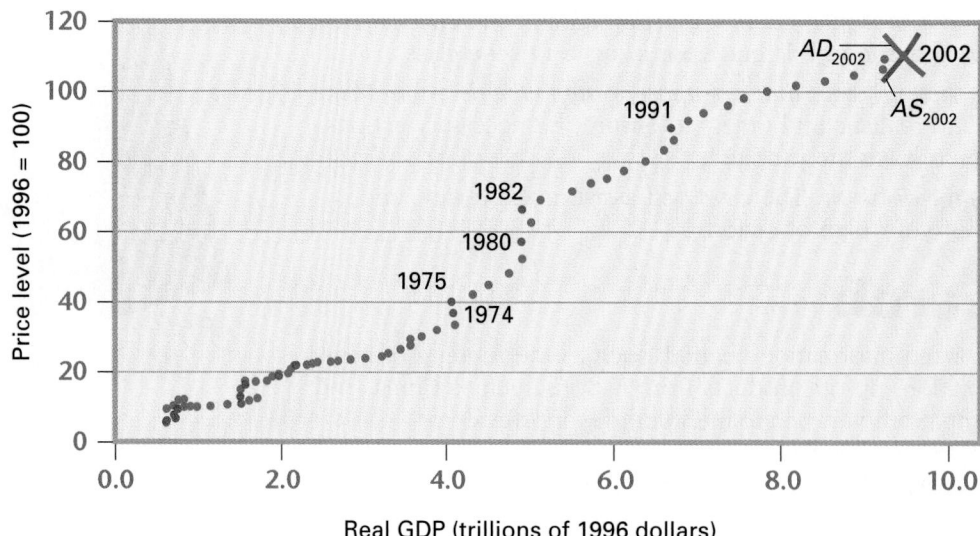

Both real GDP and the price level increased since 1929. Blue points indicate years of growing real GDP, and red points are years of declining real GDP. Real GDP in 2002 was more than 11 times greater than it was in 1929. The price level was more than 8 times greater.

Source: Based on annual estimates from the U.S. Department of Commerce.

U.S. Spending Components as Percentages of GDP Since 1960

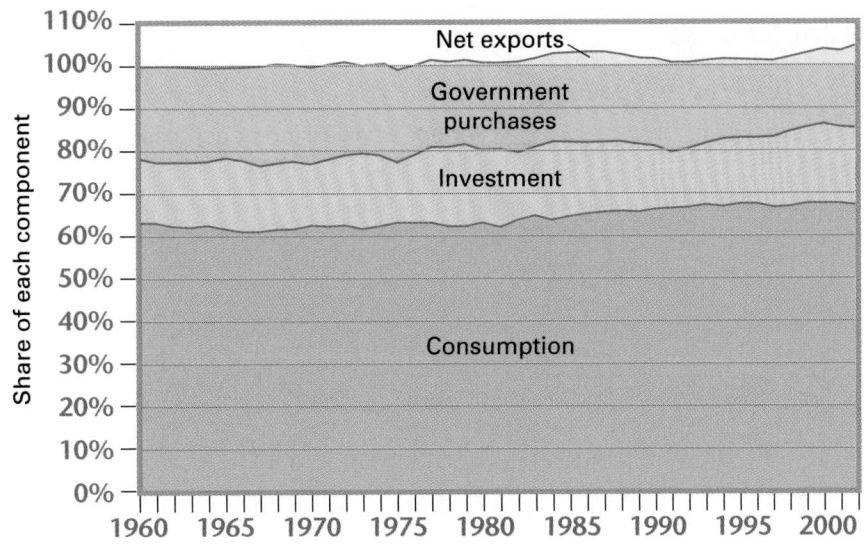

Consumption's share of total U.S. spending increased slightly from 1960 to 2002. Most recently, it accounted for about 67 percent of the total.

Source: Computed from annual estimates from the U.S. Department of Commerce.

Annual Percentage Change in U.S. Real GDP Since 1929

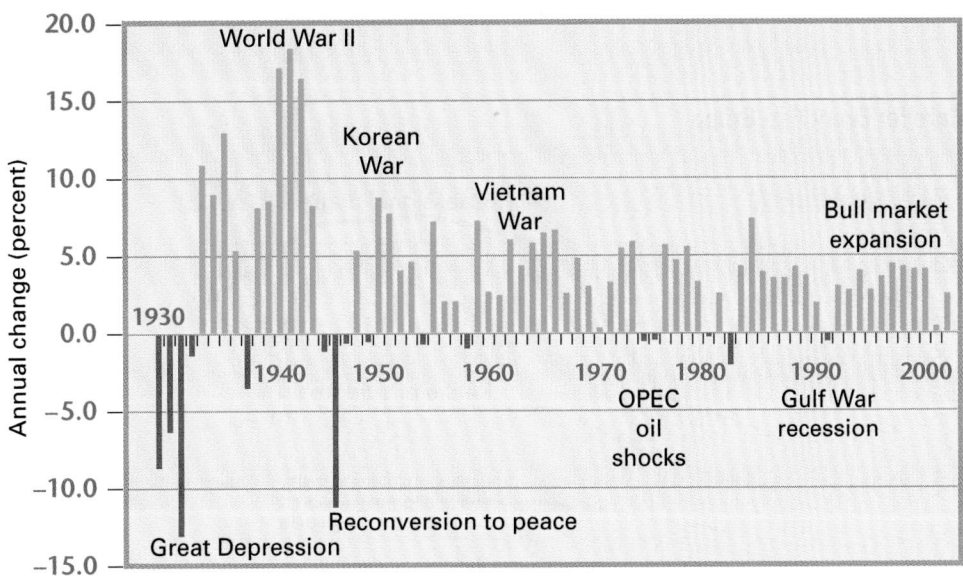

Since the end of World War II in 1945, the economy has gone through 10 business cycles. Expansions averaged just under five years. Recessions averaged just under one year. Note: In this chart, declines are shown in red and increases, in blue.

Source: Based on annual estimates from the U.S. Department of Commerce.

The U.S. Unemployment Rate Since 1900

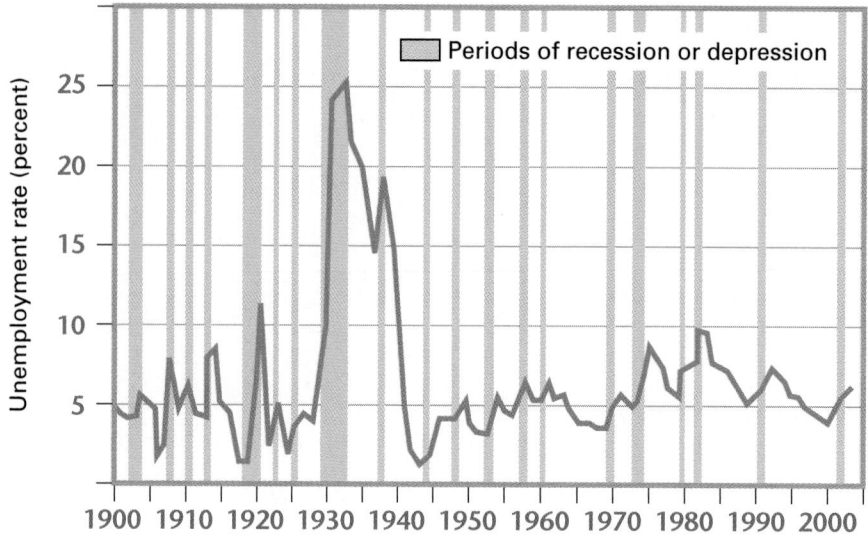

Since 1900, the unemployment rate has fluctuated widely, rising during recessions and falling during expansions. During the Great Depression of the 1930s, the rate rose as high as 25.2 percent.

Sources: U.S. Census Bureau, *Historical Statistics of the United States: Colonial Times to 1970* (Washington, D.C.: U.S. Government Printing Office, 1975); *Economic Report of the President*, February 2003; and U.S. Bureau of Labor Statistics.

Education Pays More for Every Age Group

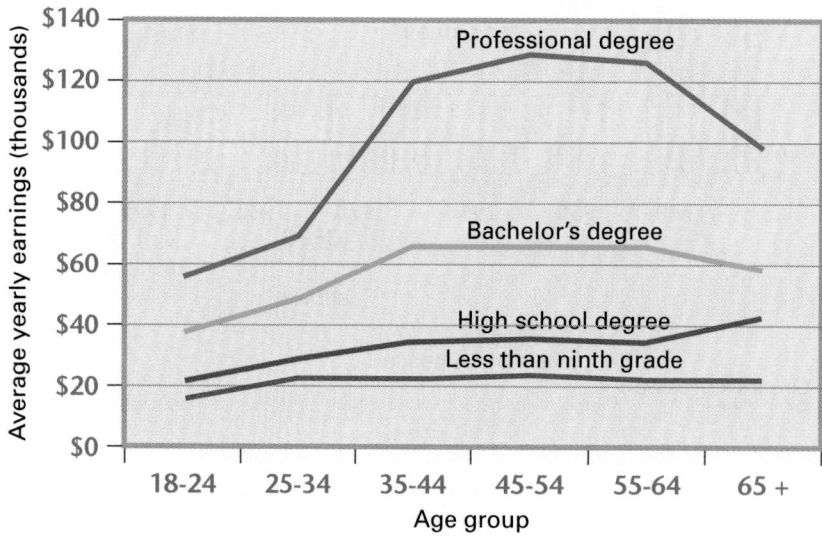

At every age, those with more education earned more. Earnings increased as workers gained more job experience and became more productive.

Source: U.S. Bureau of Labor Statistics. Figures are average earnings for all full-time, year-round workers in 2001.

U.S. Union Membership for Men and Women by Age

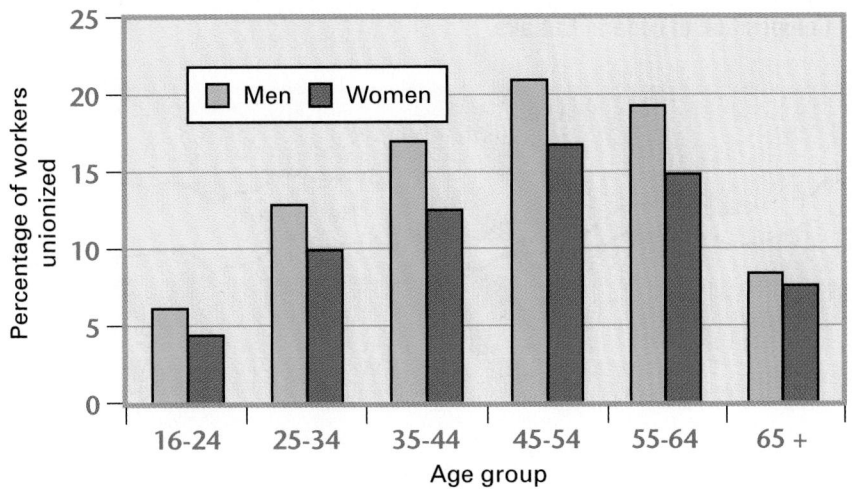

Men in the United States have higher rates of union membership than women, due to the nature of the work each group typically performs.

Source: U.S. Bureau of Labor Statistics. Percentages are for 2001.

Long-Term Trend in U.S. Labor Productivity Growth: Annual Average by Decade

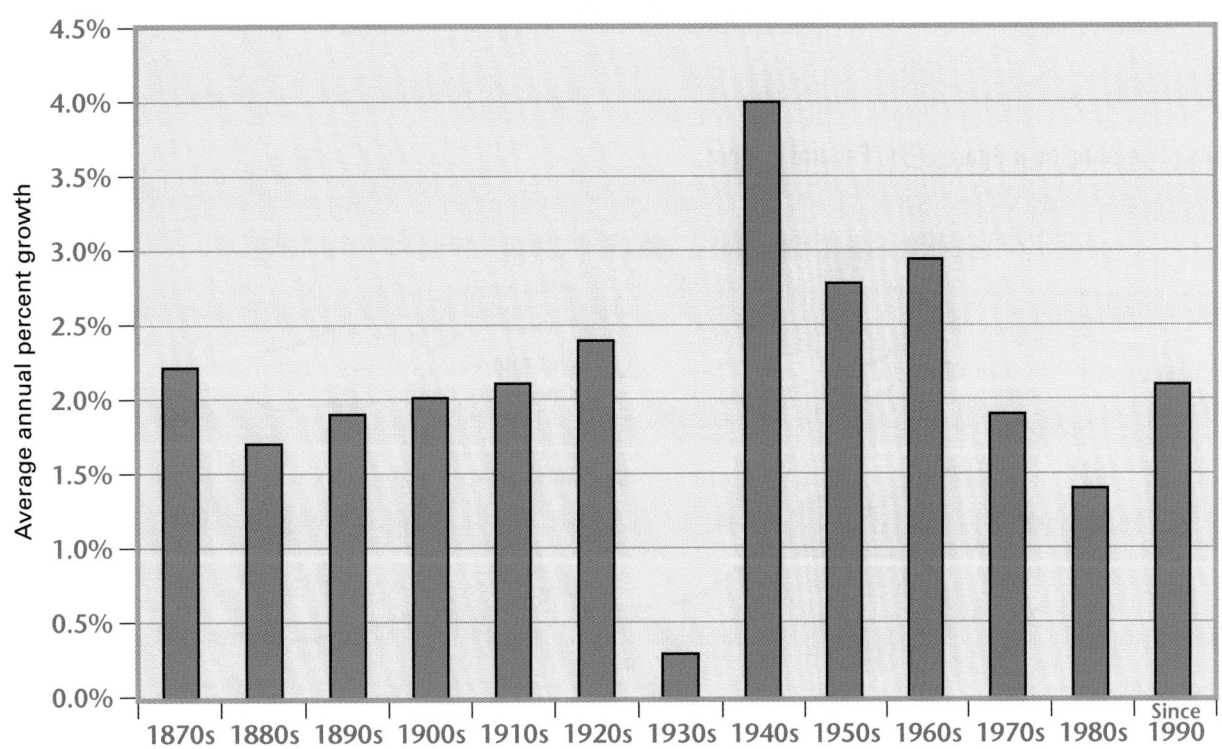

For the entire period since 1870, productivity growth averaged 2.1 percent per year.

Sources: Angus Maddison, *Phases of Capitalist Development* (New York: Oxford University Press, 1982) and U.S. Bureau of Labor Statistics.

Income Redistribution—Composition of Federal Outlays

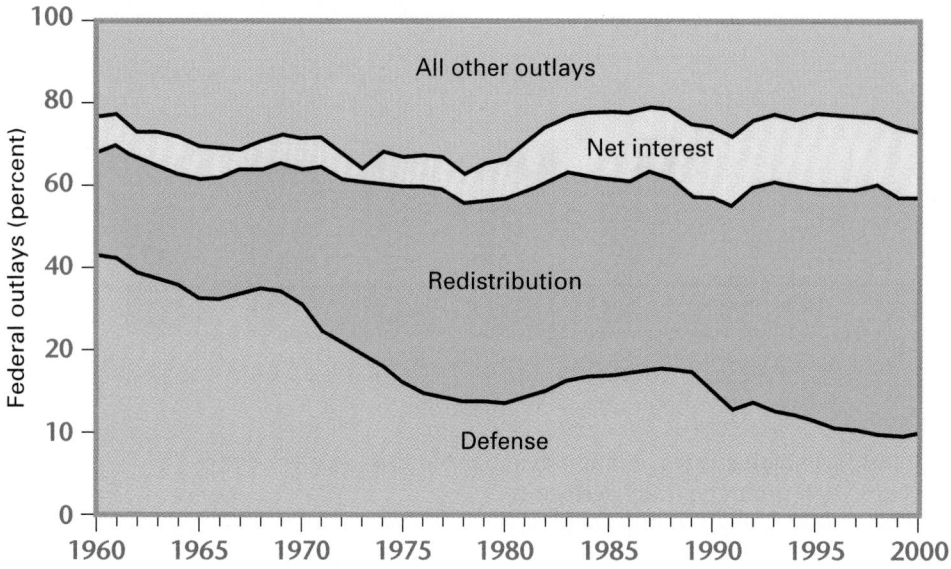

Since 1960, spending on income redistribution has increased and spending on defense has decreased as a share of federal outlays.

Source: Computed based on figures from the *Economic Report of the President,* January 2001, Table B-80. Access the most current report through econxtra.swlearning.com.

Defense Spending as a Share of the Federal Budget

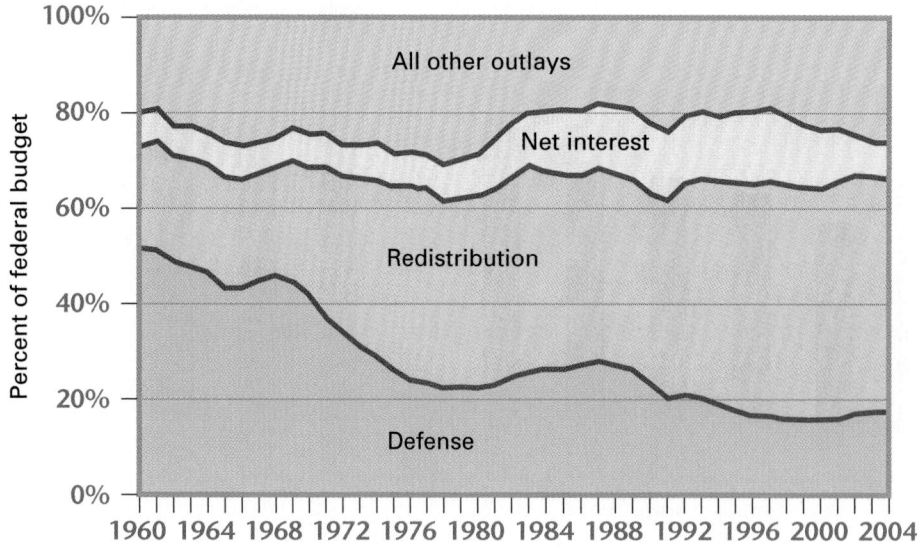

As a share of the federal budget, defense spending has declined and redistribution has increased since 1960.

Source: *Economic Report of the President,* February 2003, Table B-80. Figures for 2003 and 2004 are estimates.

Payroll Taxes as a Share of Federal Revenue

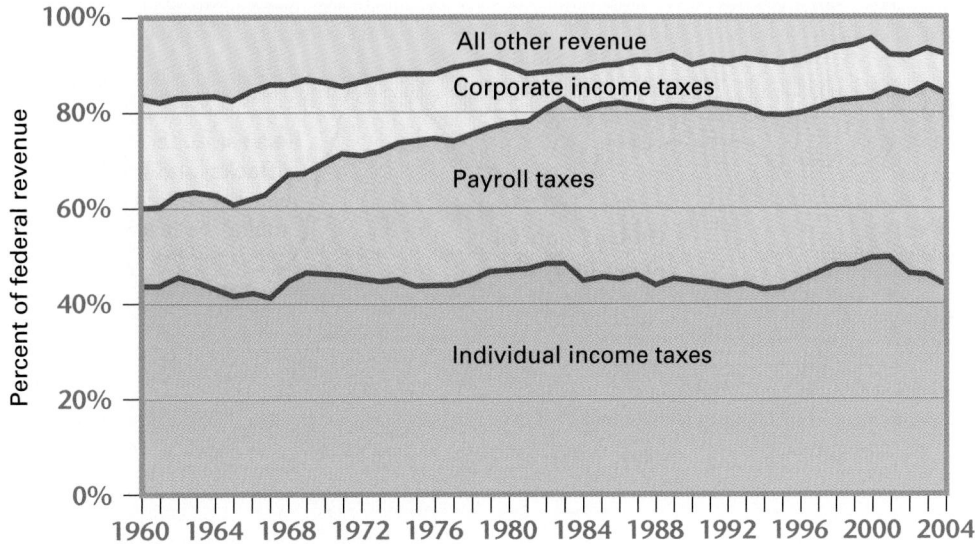

Payroll taxes have grown as a share of federal revenue since 1960.

Source: Based on fiscal year revenue figures from the *Economic Report of the President,* February 2003. Figures for 2003 and 2004 are projections.

Federal Debt Held by the Public as Percent of GDP, 1940 to 2004

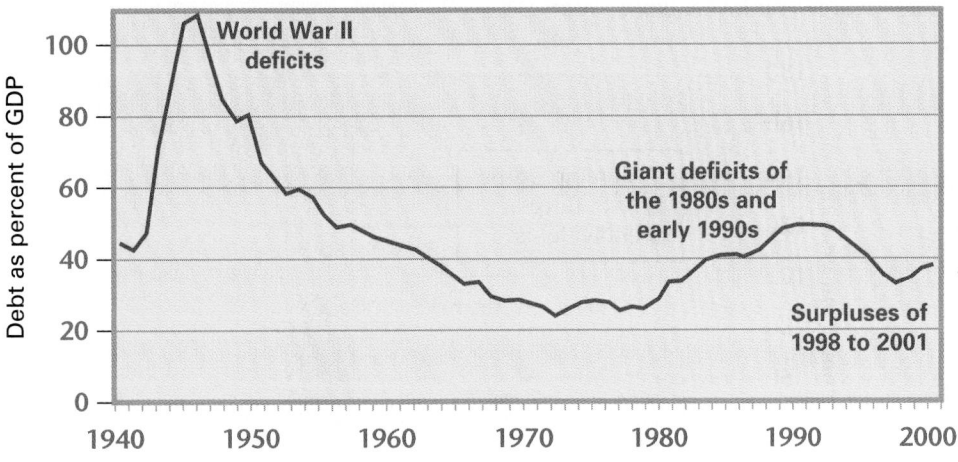

The federal debt held by the public relative to GDP dropped nearly two-thirds between 1946 and 2004.

Source: Fiscal year figures from *Economic Report of the President,* February 2003, Table 79. Figures for 2003 and 2004 are projections.

Recent Ups and Downs in the Federal Funds Rate

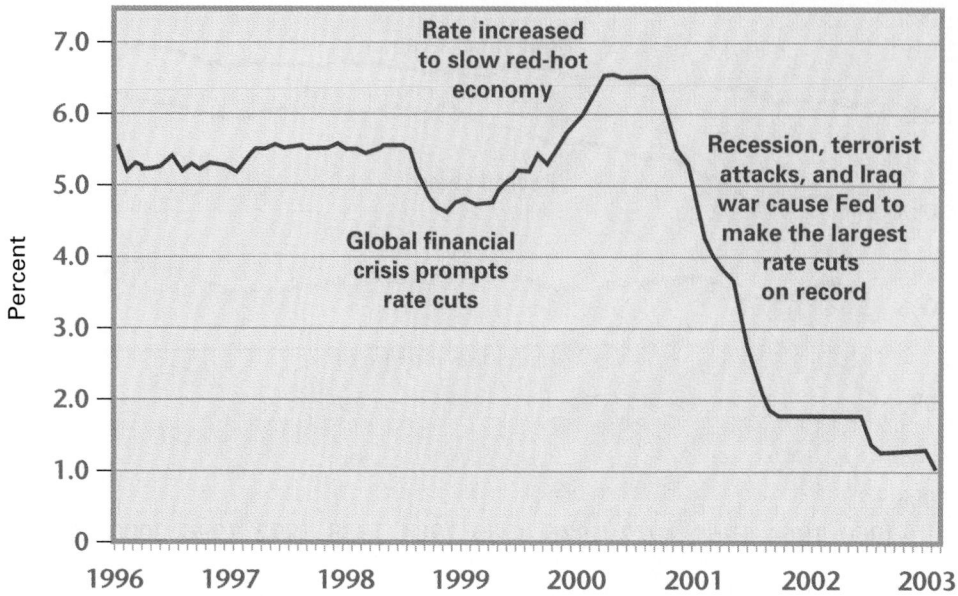

To understand the fluctuations of the federal funds rate, consider what was going on in the economy during the periods shown here.

Source: Based on monthly averages from the Federal Reserve Bank.

Source of U.S. Patents Awarded for Inventions by Year

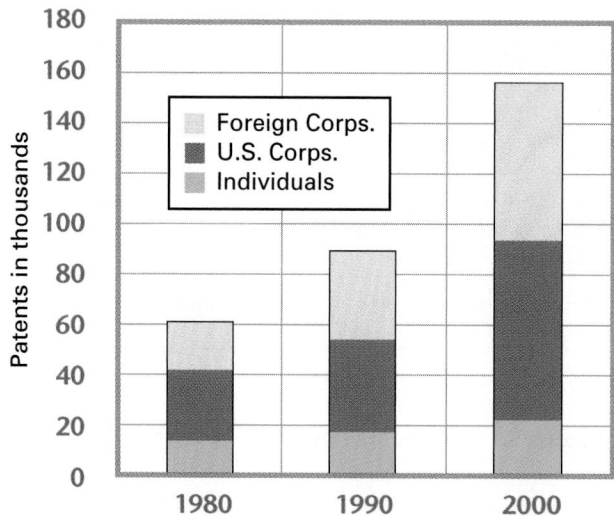

The number of patents grew from 61,800 in 1980 to 157,500 in 2000. In 1980, 22 percent of all patents were awarded to individuals. By 2000, only 14 percent went to individuals.

Source: U.S. Bureau of the Census, *Statistical Abstract of the United States,* 2001.

Composition of State Spending and State Revenue

Composition of State Spending

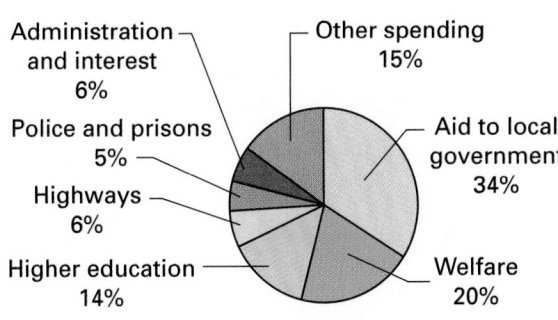

Administration and interest 6%
Police and prisons 5%
Highways 6%
Higher education 14%
Other spending 15%
Aid to local government 34%
Welfare 20%

Composition of State Revenue

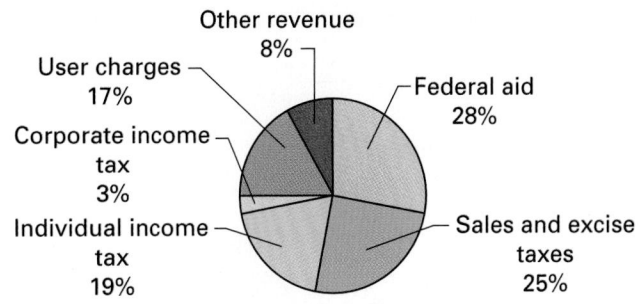

Other revenue 8%
User charges 17%
Corporate income tax 3%
Individual income tax 19%
Federal aid 28%
Sales and excise taxes 25%

The biggest portion of state spending goes toward grants to local governments. The largest source of state revenue is aid from the federal government.

Source: Based on general expenditure figures for fiscal year 2000 from the U.S. Census Bureau.

Composition of Local Spending and Local Revenue

Composition of Local Spending

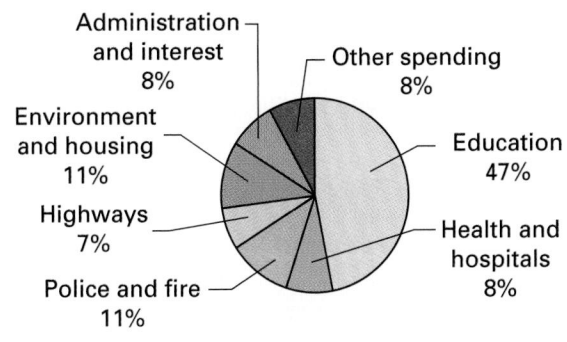

Administration and interest 8%
Environment and housing 11%
Highways 7%
Police and fire 11%
Other spending 8%
Education 47%
Health and hospitals 8%

Composition of Local Revenue

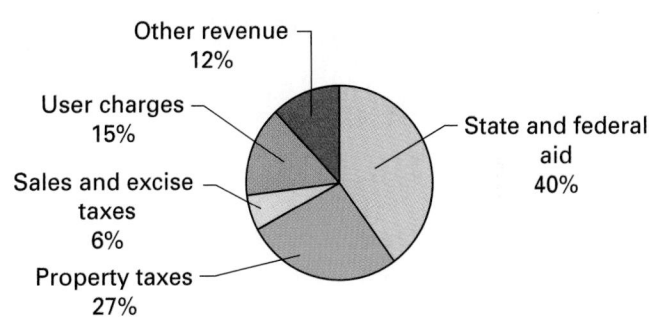

Other revenue 12%
User charges 15%
Sales and excise taxes 6%
Property taxes 27%
State and federal aid 40%

The largest category of local spending is education. State and federal aid make up the largest percent of local revenue.

Source: Based on general expenditure figures for fiscal year 2000 from the U.S. Census Bureau.

Distribution of Sole Proprietorships Based on Annual Sales and by Industry

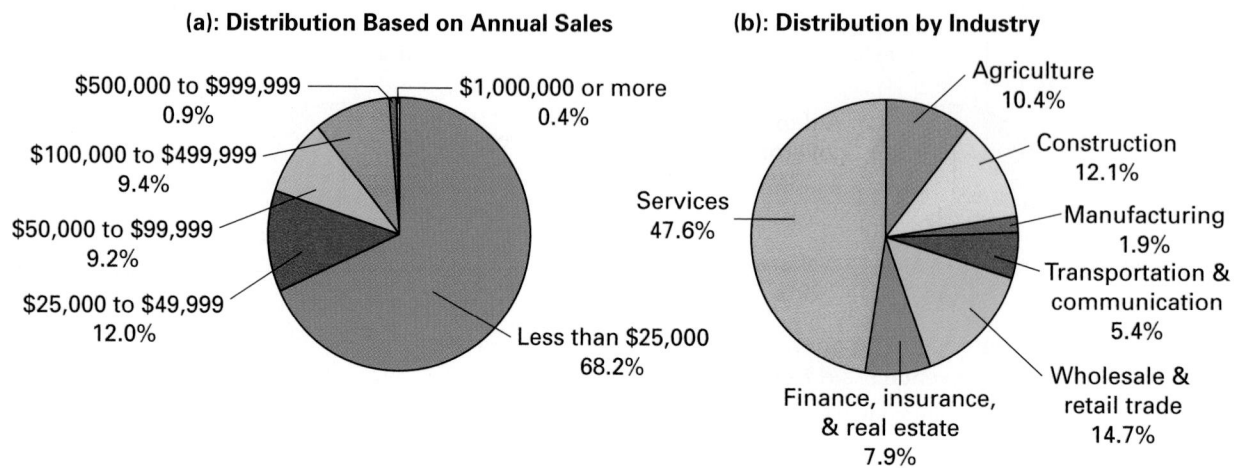

(a): Distribution Based on Annual Sales

$500,000 to $999,999 0.9%
$100,000 to $499,999 9.4%
$50,000 to $99,999 9.2%
$25,000 to $49,999 12.0%
$1,000,000 or more 0.4%
Services 47.6%
Less than $25,000 68.2%

(b): Distribution by Industry

Agriculture 10.4%
Construction 12.1%
Manufacturing 1.9%
Transportation & communication 5.4%
Wholesale & retail trade 14.7%
Finance, insurance, & real estate 7.9%

More than half of all sole proprietors earn $25,000 or less a year. Most sole proprietorships are service businesses.

Source: U.S. Bureau of the Census, *Statistical Abstract of the United States,* 2002.

Distribution of Partnerships Based on Annual Sales and Industry

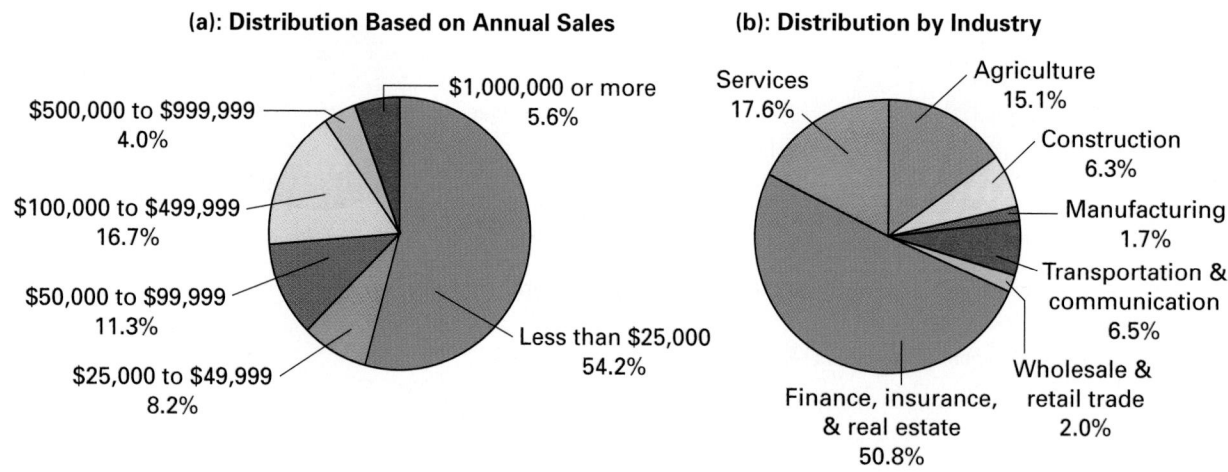

(a): Distribution Based on Annual Sales

$500,000 to $999,999 4.0%
$100,000 to $499,999 16.7%
$50,000 to $99,999 11.3%
$25,000 to $49,999 8.2%
$1,000,000 or more 5.6%
Less than $25,000 54.2%

(b): Distribution by Industry

Services 17.6%
Agriculture 15.1%
Construction 6.3%
Manufacturing 1.7%
Transportation & communication 6.5%
Wholesale & retail trade 2.0%
Finance, insurance, & real estate 50.8%

Most partnerships had annual sales of less than $25,000. About half of all partnerships are in finance, insurance, or real estate.

Source: U.S. Bureau of the Census, *Statistical Abstract of the United States,* 2002.

Distribution of Corporations by Annual Sales and by Industry

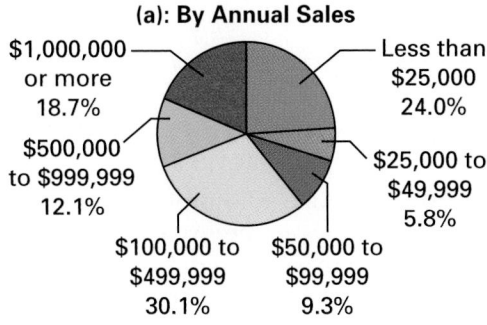

(a): By Annual Sales

- $1,000,000 or more 18.7%
- $500,000 to $999,999 12.1%
- $100,000 to $499,999 30.1%
- $50,000 to $99,999 9.3%
- $25,000 to $49,999 5.8%
- Less than $25,000 24.0%

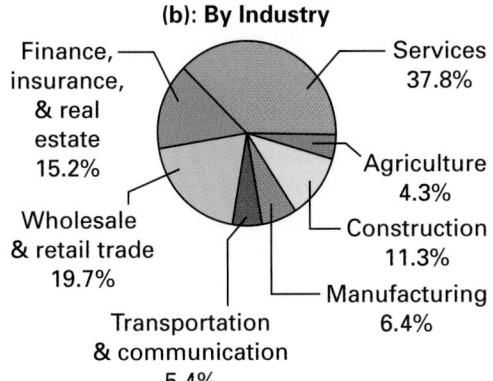

(b): By Industry

- Finance, insurance, & real estate 15.2%
- Services 37.8%
- Agriculture 4.3%
- Construction 11.3%
- Manufacturing 6.4%
- Transportation & communication 5.4%
- Wholesale & retail trade 19.7%

Nearly one in five corporations had annual sales of $1 million or more. About four in ten corporations are in services, such as health care.

Source: U.S. Bureau of the Census, *Statistical Abstract of the United States,* 2002.

Comparing Corporations with Sole Proprietorships and Partnerships

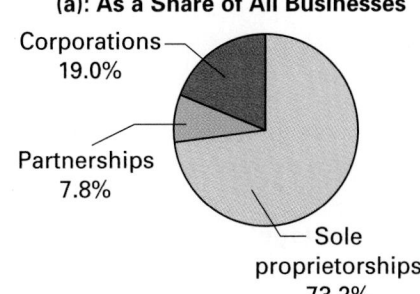

(a): As a Share of All Businesses

- Corporations 19.0%
- Partnerships 7.8%
- Sole proprietorships 73.2%

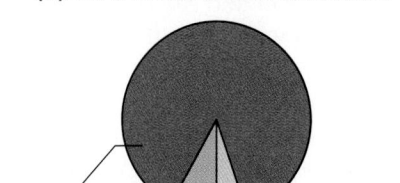

(b): As a Share of Business Sales

- Corporations 86.5%
- Partnerships 8.2%
- Sole proprietorships 5.3%

Sole proprietorships account for nearly three quarters of all U.S. businesses, but corporations account for most business sales.

Source: U.S. Bureau of the Census, *Statistical Abstract of the United States,* 2002.

Value of Business Structures and Equipment in the United States

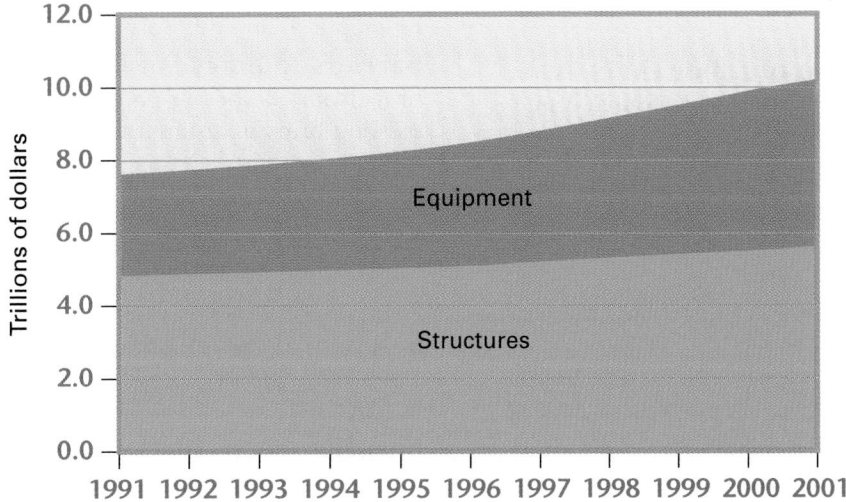

The combined value of business equipment and business structures increased nearly $3 trillion from 1991 to 2001.

Source: Developed from estimates in the U.S. Department of Commerce, *Survey of Current Business,* September 2002, Table 15. Structures include factories, buildings, and other permanent business fixtures. Figures are adjusted to eliminate the effects of inflation.

Glossary

A

ability-to-pay tax principle Those with a greater ability to pay, such as those with a higher income, should pay more of the tax (p. 431)

absolute advantage To be able to make something using fewer resources than other producers require (p. 51)

aggregate demand The relationship between the economy's price level and the quantity of aggregate output demanded, with other things constant (p. 344)

aggregate demand curve A curve representing the relationship between the economy's price level and real GDP demanded per period, with other things constant (p. 344)

aggregate expenditure Total spending on all final goods and services produced in the economy during the year (p. 325)

aggregate income The sum of all the income earned by resource suppliers in the economy during a given year (p. 326)

aggregate output A composite measure of all final goods and services produced in an economy during a given period; real GDP (p. 344)

aggregate supply curve A curve representing the relationship between the economy's price level and real GDP supplied per period, with other things constant (p. 346)

allocative efficiency Achieved when the firm produces the output most preferred by consumers (p. 179)

American Federation of Labor (AFL) An organization of national craft unions founded in 1886; not a union itself but a collection of independent unions (p. 274)

annual inflation rate The percentage increase in the economy's general price level from one year to the next (p. 398)

annually balanced budget Matching annual spending with annual revenue, except during war years; approach to the federal budget prior to the Great Depression (p. 464)

antitrust activity Government efforts aimed at preventing monopoly and promoting competition in markets where competition is desirable (p. 209)

antitrust laws Laws that prohibit anticompetitive behavior and promote competition in markets where competition is desirable (p. 71)

applied research Research that seeks answers to particular questions or applies scientific discoveries to develop specific products (p. 375)

arbitrageur Someone who profits from temporary geographic differences in the exchange rate by simultaneously purchasing a currency in one market and selling it in another market (p. 578)

articles of partnership A legal agreement spelling out each partner's rights and responsibilities (p. 243)

asset Any physical property or financial claim that is owned (p. 520)

automatic stabilizers Government spending and taxing programs that year after year automatically reduce fluctuations in disposable income, and thus in consumption, over the business cycle (p. 469)

average cost Total cost divided by output (p. 154)

B

balance of payments A record of all economic transactions between residents of one country and residents of the rest of the world during a given period (p. 568)

balance sheet A financial statement showing assets, liabilities, and net worth at a given point in time; since assets must equal liabilities plus net worth, the statement is in balance (p. 520)

bank note A piece of paper promising gold or silver to whoever presented it to the issuing bank for redemption; an early form of money (p. 497)

barriers to entry Anything that prevents new firms from competing on an equal footing with existing firms in an industry (p. 194)

barter A system of exchange in which products are traded directly for other products (p. 52)

basic research The search for knowledge without regard to how that knowledge will be used; a first step toward technological advancement (p. 375)

behavioral assumption The simplifying assumption about what motivates people, such as rational self interest (p. 11)

benefits-received tax principle Those who receive more benefits from the government program funded by the tax should pay more of that tax (p. 431)

bilateral aid Development aid from one country to another (p. 600)

binding arbitration When labor negotiations have broken down and the public interest is involved, a neutral third party is brought in to impose a settlement that both sides must accept (p. 274)

bond A contract promising to repay borrowed money on a designated date and pay interest along the way (p. 299)

brain drain A developing country's loss of educated migrants to industrial market countries (p. 599)

bureaus Government agencies charged with implementing legislation and financed by appropriations from legislative bodies (p. 450)

business cycle Fluctuations reflecting the rise and fall of economic activity relative to the long-term growth trend of the economy (pp. 72, 336)

C

capital deepening An increase in the quantity and quality of capital per worker; one source of rising labor productivity (p. 360)

capital goods all human creations used to produce goods and services; for example, factories, trucks, and machines (p. 8)

cartel A group of firms that agree to coordinate and pricing decisions to maximize group profits by behaving as a monopolist (p. 204)

charter The legal authorization to organize a business as a corporation (p. 243)

check A written order instructing the bank to pay someone from the amount deposited (p. 497)

checkable deposits Deposits in financial institutions against which checks can be written and ATM, or debit, cards can be applied; part of the narrow definition of money (p. 507)

circular-flow model A figure that describes the flow of resources, products, income, and revenue among economic decision makers (p. 15)

classical economists A group of laissez-faire economists, who believed that economic downturns were short-run problems that corrected themselves in the long run through natural market forces (p. 463)

cluster Firms in the same industry or in related industries that group together in a region, such as Wall Street, Hollywood, or Silicon Valley (p. 379)

coincident economic indicators Measures that reflect recessions or expansions as they occur (p. 339)

collateral An asset owned by the borrower that can be sold to pay off the loan in the event the loan is not repaid (p. 297)

collective bargaining The process by which representatives of the union and the employer negotiate wages, employee benefits, and working conditions (p. 274)

collusion An price-fixing agreement among firms to reduce competition and increase profit (p. 204)

commercial banks Depository institutions that make loans primarily to businesses (p. 498)

commodity money Anything that serves both as money and as a commodity, such as gold (p. 491)

commodity A product that is identical across sellers, such a bushel of wheat (p. 192)

common-pool problem People use an open-access resource until the benefit of additional use drops to zero, so open access resources are overused (p. 76)

competitive firm's supply curve The rising portion of a firm's marginal cost curve at or above the price that will allow the firm to cover variable cost (p. 153)

complements Goods, such as milk and cookies, that relate in such a way that a decrease in the price of one shifts the demand for the other rightward (p. 120)

conglomerate merger One firm combines with another firm in a different industry, such as a merger between a plastics maker and an electronics firm (p. 305)

Congress of Industrial Organizations (CIO) A national organization of unions in mass-production industries formed in 1935 (p. 274)

constant returns to scale Over a range of production in the long run, long-run average cost neither increases nor decreases with changes in the firm size (p. 154)

consumer cooperative A retail business owned and operated by some of all of its customers in order to reduce costs (p. 246)

consumer price index, or **CPI** Measure of inflation based on the cost of a fixed "market basket" of goods and services purchased by a typical family (p. 333)

consumer surplus The difference between the maximum amount that consumers are willing to pay for a given quantity of a good and what they actually pay (p. 181)

consumption Household purchases of final goods and services except for new residences, which count as investment (p. 323)

convergence theory A theory predicting that the standard of living in economies around the world will grow more similar over time, with poorer countries gradually closing the gap with richer ones (p. 607)

cooperative An organization consisting of people who pool their resources to buy and sell more efficiently than they could independently (p. 245)

copyright Assigns property rights to original expressions of an author, artist, composer, or computer programmer (p. 63)

corporation A legal entity with an existence that is distinct from the real people who organize, own, and run it (p. 245)

cost-push inflation Inflation resulting from a leftward shift of the aggregate supply curve (p. 399)

cottage industry system Entrepreneurs hired rural households to turn raw materials into finished goods (p. 64)

craft union A union whose membership is limited to workers with a particular skill, or craft—such as carpenters or plumbers (p. 274)

credit The ability to borrow now based on the promise of repayment in the future (p. 295)

crowding in Government spending stimulates private investment in an otherwise dead economy (p. 478)

crowding out Private investment falls when higher government deficits drive up interest rates (p. 478)

currency appreciation A decrease in the dollar price of a unit of foreign exchange in a flexible exchange rate system (p. 577)

currency depreciation An increase in the dollar price of a unit of foreign exchange in a flexible exchange rate system (p. 577)

current account That portion of the balance of payment that records exports and imports of goods and services, net investment income, and net transfers (p. 568)

current dollars Dollar values at the time the output is produced (p. 331)

cycle of poverty Children in welfare families may end up on welfare themselves when they grow up (p. 415)

cyclical unemployment Occurs because of the jobs lost during the recession phase of the business cycle (p. 388)

D

decision-making lag The time needed to decide what to do once the problem has been identified (p. 471)

decrease in demand Consumers are less willing and able to buy the product at every price (p. 171)

decrease in supply Producers are less willing and able to supply the product at every price (p. 173)

default To not pay back a loan (p. 297)

deflation A *decrease* in the general price level (p. 398)

demand A relation showing the quantities of a good that consumers are willing and able to buy at various prices per period, other things constant (p. 102)

demand curve A curve or line showing the quantities of a particular good demanded at various prices during a given time period, other things constant (p. 105)

demand deposits Originally, the only type of checking accounts (p. 499, 507)

demand for loans curve A downward sloping curve showing the negative relationship between the interest rate and the quantity of loans demanded, other things constant (p. 290)

demand-pull inflation Inflation resulting from a rightward shift of the aggregate demand curve (p. 398)

demand schedule Columns of numbers showing the quantities of a particular good demanded at various possible prices during a given period, other things constant (p. 105)

demand-side economics Macroeconomic policy that focuses on shifting the aggregate demand curve as a way of promoting full employment and price stability (p. 406)

depository institutions Financial institutions that accept deposits from the public and lend out a portion of those deposits (p. 498)

depreciation The value of the capital stock that is used up or becomes obsolete to produce GDP during the year (p. 330)

depression A sharp reduction in the nation's total production lasting more than a year and accompanied by high unemployment (p. 336)

deregulation A reduction in government control over prices and firm entry in previously regulated markets, such as airlines and trucking (p. 212)

derived demand The demand for a resource is derived from the demand for the product that resource produces (p. 256)

developing countries Countries with a lower standard of living because they have relatively little human and physical capital; also called Third-World countries (p. 367); nations with low GDP per capita, high rates of illiteracy, high unemployment, and high fertility rates (p. 588)

differentiated oligopoly Oligopoly market where firms sell products that differ across producers, such as Ford versus Toyota (p. 203)

discount rate Interest rate the Fed charges banks that borrow reserves (p. 501)

discouraged workers Someone who, unable to find a job, drops out of the labor force (p. 389)

discretionary fiscal policy Congressional changes in spending or taxing to promote macroeconomic goals (p. 469)

diseconomies of scale In some industries, forces that eventually increase a firm's average cost as the scale of operation increases in the long run (p. 154)

disequilibrium A mismatch between quantity demanded and quantity supplied as the market seeks equilibrium; usually temporary, except where government intervenes and sets the price (p. 180)

disinflation A reduction in the rate of inflation (p. 398)

dividend That portion of after-tax corporate profit paid out to shareholders (p. 299)

division of labor Sorting the production process into separate tasks to be carried out by separate workers (p. 53)

domestic content requirements Regulations specifying that a certain portion of a final good must be produced domestically (p. 560)

double counting The mistake of including the value of intermediate goods plus the value of final goods in computing gross domestic product; counting an item's value more than once (p. 322)

dual banking system The U.S. banking system, which consists of both state banks and national banks (p. 500)

durable goods Goods expected to last at least three years, such as televisions and furniture (p. 323)

E

earned-income tax credit A federal program that supplements wages of the working poor (p. 87)

economic growth An expansion in the economy's production possibilities or ability to produce (p. 45)

economic system The set of mechanisms and institutions that resolve the *what, how,* and *for whom* questions for an economy (p. 34)

economic theory, economic model A simplification of economic reality used to make predictions about the real world (p. 11)

economics The study of how people use their scarce resources to satisfy their unlimited wants (p. 6)

economies of scale Forces that reduce a firm's average cost as the firm's size, or scale, increases in the long run (p. 154)

economy The structure of economic activity in a locality, a region, a country, a group of countries, or the world (p. 322)

effectiveness lag The time needed for changes in policy to affect the economy (p. 471)

efficiency Producing the maximum possible output from available resources (pp. 42, 46)

elastic demand A change in the price has a relatively large effect on quantity demanded; the percentage change in quantity demanded exceeds the percentage change in price; the resulting elasticity is greater than 1.0 (p. 109)

elastic supply A change in the price has a relatively large effect on quantity supplied; the percentage change in quantity supplied exceeds the percentage change in price; the resulting elasticity is greater than 1.0 (p. 136)

elasticity of demand Measures how responsive quantity demanded is to a price change; the percentage change in quantity demanded divided by the percentage change in price (p. 110)

elasticity of supply A measure of the responsiveness of quantity supplied to a price change; the percentage change in quantity supplied divided by the percentage change in price (p. 135)

entrepreneur A profit-seeker who develops a new product or process and assumes the risk of profit or loss (p. 7)

equilibrium The quantity consumers are willing and able to buy equals the quantity producers are willing and able to sell (p. 164)

equilibrium interest rate The only interest rate at which the quantity of loans demanded equals the quantity of loans supplied (p. 292)

equilibrium point The point of intersection between the demand curve and the supply curve (p. 165)

equilibrium price The price that equates quantity demanded with quantity supplied; the market-clearing price (p. 165)

equilibrium quantity The quantity demanded and the quantity supplied when the market is in equilibrium (p. 165)

equilibrium wage The wage at which there is neither an excess quantity of labor demanded nor an excess quantity of labor supplied (p. 258)

euro The common currency put into circulation in 2002 by 12 European countries (pp. 540, 563)

excess capacity The amount by which a firm's actual production falls short of the firm's capacity; increasing output would reduce per unit cost (p. 203)

excess reserves Bank reserves in excess of required reserves (p. 521)

exchange rate The price of one country's currency measured in terms of another country's currency (p. 575)

exclusive Those who fail to pay for a good can be easily excluded from its consumption (p. 77)

exhaustible resource A natural resource that does not renew itself and so is available in a finite amount, such as oil or copper ore (p. 7)

expansion The phase of economic activity during which the economy's total output increases (p. 337)

expenditure approach to GDP A method of calculating GDP by adding up the spending on all final goods and services produced during the year (p. 323)

export promotion A development strategy that concentrates on producing for the export market (p. 598)

F

featherbedding Union efforts to force employers to hire more workers than demanded for the task (p. 276)

federal budget deficit The amount by which total federal outlays exceed total federal revenues (p. 408)

federal funds market A market for overnight lending and borrowing of reserves held by the Fed for banks (p. 531)

federal funds rate The interest rate charged in the federal funds market; the Fed's target interest rate (p. 531)

Federal Open Market Committee (FOMC) Twelve-member group that makes decisions about open-market operations (p. 501)

Federal Reserve System, or **Fed** Established in 1913 as the central bank and monetary authority of the United States (p. 500)

fertility rate The average number of births during each woman's lifetime (p. 589)

fiat money Money not redeemable for anything of intrinsic value; declared money by government decree (p. 497)

final goods and services Goods and services sold to the final, or end, users (p. 322)

financial account That portion of the balance of payments that records international transactions involving financial assets, such as stocks and bonds, and real assets, such as factories and office buildings (p. 571)

financial capital Money needed to start or expand a business (p. 229)

financial intermediaries Banks and other institutions that serve as go-betweens, accepting funds from savers and lending them to borrowers (p. 295)

firm A business unit or enterprise formed by a profit-seeking entrepreneur who combines resources to produce goods and services (p. 63)

fiscal policy The federal government's use of taxing and public spending to influence the national economy (p. 72)

fixed cost Any production cost that is independent of the firms output (p. 150)

fixed exchange rate Exchange rate fixed within a narrow range of values and maintained by central banks' ongoing purchases and sales of currencies (p. 579)

fixed resource Any resource that cannot be varied in the short run (p. 148)

flexible exchange rate Exchange rate determined by the forces of supply and demand without government intervention (p. 579)

foreign aid An international grant or a loan made on especially favorable terms to promote economic development (p. 600)

foreign exchange Foreign money needed to carry out international transactions (p. 575)

fractional reserve banking system Only a portion of bank deposits is backed by reserves (p. 497)

free-riders Those who consume a public good without paying for it (p. 76)

frictional unemployment Occurs because of the time required to match qualified job seekers with available openings (p. 388)

full employment Occurs when there is no cyclical unemployment; relatively low unemployment (p. 388)

G

GDP price index A comprehensive measure of inflation based on all goods and services included in GDP (p. 336)

General Agreement on Tariffs and Trade (GATT) An international tariff-reduction treaty adopted in 1947 that resulted in a series of negotiated "rounds" aimed at freer trade (p. 561)

general partnership Partners share both in the responsibility for running the business and in any liability from its operation (p. 237)

golden age of Keynesian economics The 1960s, when some economists thought they could "fine-tune" the economy to avoid recessions (p. 406)

good An item you can see feel and touch that requires scarce resources and satisfies human wants (p. 8)

government budget A plan for government outlays and revenues for a specified period, usually a year (p. 438)

government purchases Spending by all levels of government for goods and services; does not include transfer payments (p. 324)

green accounting Reflects the impact of production on air pollution, water pollution, lost trees, soil depletion, and the loss of other natural resources (p. 331)

gross domestic product (GDP) The market value of all final goods and services produced in the United States during a given period, usually a year (p. 322)

gross investment The value of all investment during a year; used to compute GDP (p. 330)

Group of Seven (G-7) The seven leading industrial market economies, including the United States, United Kingdom, France, Germany, Italy, Japan, and Canada (p. 368)

H

horizontal merger One firm combines with another that produces the same product, such as Exxon and Mobil (p. 209)

hostile takeovers One firm buys control of another firm against the wishes of the purchased firm's management; a common merger strategy during the 1980s (p. 300)

household The most important economic decision maker, consisting of all those who live under one roof (p. 62)

human capital The accumulated knowledge, skill, and experience of the labor force (p. 360)

human resources The broad category of human efforts, both physical and mental, used to produce goods and services (p. 7)

hyperinflation Extremely high inflation (p. 398)

I

implementation lag The time needed to execute a change in policy (p. 471)

import substitution A development strategy that emphasizes domestic manufacturing of products that are currently imported (p. 598)

income approach to GDP A method of calculating GDP by adding up all payments to owners of resources used to produce output during the year (p. 323)

income effect of a price change A fall in the price of a good increases consumers' real income, making consumers more able to purchase the good; for normal goods, the quantity demanded increases (p. 103)

income-assistance programs Government programs that provide money and in-kind assistance to poor people (p. 86)

increase in demand Consumers are more willing and able to buy the product at every price (p. 170)

increase in supply Producers are more willing and able to supply the product at every price (p. 172)

increasing returns The marginal product of a variable resource increases as each additional unit of the resource is employed, other resources assumed constant (p. 148)

index number Compares the value of some variable in a particular year to its value in a base year, or reference year (p. 333)

individual demand The demand of an individual consumer (p. 107)

industrial market countries Economically advanced market countries of Western Europe, North America, Australia, New Zealand, and Japan (p. 588)

industrial market countries The advanced market economies of Western Europe, North America, Australia, New Zealand, and Japan; also called developed countries (p. 367)

industrial policy The view that government—using taxes, subsidies, and regulations—should nurture the industries and technologies of the future, thereby giving domestic industries an advantage over foreign competition (p. 378)

Industrial Revolution Development of large-scale production under one roof during the eighteenth century (p. 64)

industrial union A union whose membership includes all workers in an industry, such as all autoworkers and all steelworkers (p. 274)

industry All firms that supply output to a particular market, such as the market for autos, shoes, or wheat (p. 191)

inelastic demand A change in price has relatively little effect on quantity demanded; the percentage change in quantity demanded is less than the percentage change in price; the resulting elasticity is less than 1.0 (p. 111)

inelastic supply A change in price has relatively little effect on quantity supplied; the percentage change in quantity supplied is less than the percentage change in price; the resulting elasticity is less than 1.0 (p. 136)

inferior good A good for which demand decreases, or shifts leftward, as consumer incomes rise (p. 119)

inflation An increase in the economy's general price level (p. 398)

initial public offering (IPO) The initial sale of corporate stock to the public (p. 299)

innovation The process of turning an invention into a marketable product (p. 229)

institutional investors Banks, insurance companies, mutual funds, and other businesses that buy, sell, and own securities (p. 300)

interest rate Annual interest as a percentage of the amount borrowed or saved (p. 289)

intermediate goods and services Goods and services purchased for additional processing and resale (p. 322)

inventories Stocks of goods in process, such as computer parts, and stocks of finished goods, such as new computers awaiting sale (p. 324)

investment The purchase of new plants, new equipment, new buildings, new residences, and net additions to inventories (p. 324)

L

labor force Those in the adult population who are either working or looking for work (p. 390)

labor force participation rate The number in the labor force divided by the adult population (p. 391)

labor productivity Output per unit of labor; measured as total output divided by the hours of labor employed to produce that output (p. 359)

labor union A group of workers who join together to seek higher pay and better working conditions by negotiating a labor contract with their employers (p. 273)

labor The physical and mental effort used to produce goods and services (p. 7)

lagging economic indicators Measures that follow, or trail, recessions or expansions (p. 340)

laissez-faire The doctrine that the government should not intervene in a market economy beyond the minimum required to maintain peace and property rights (p. 404)

law of comparative advantage The worker, firm, region, or country with the lowest opportunity cost of producing an output should specialize in that output (p. 51)

law of demand The quantity of a good demanded per period relates inversely to its price, other things constant (p. 102)

law of diminishing marginal utility The more of a good a person consumes per period, the smaller the increase in total utility from consuming one more unit, other things constant (p. 103)

law of diminishing returns As more of a variable resource is added to a given amount of fixed resources, marginal product eventually declines and could become negative (p. 148)

law of increasing opportunity cost Each additional increment of one good requires the economy to give up successively larger increments of the other good (p. 44)

law of supply The quantity of a good supplied in a given time period is usually directly related to its price, other things constant (p. 132)

leading economic indicators Measures that usually predict, or *lead to,* recessions or expansions (p. 339)

liability The legal obligation to pay any debts the business encounters (p. 235); An amount owed (p. 520)

limited liability company (LLC) Business with limited liability for some owners, single taxation of business income, and no ownership restrictions (p. 245)

limited liability partnership (LLP) Like a limited liability company but more easily converted from an existing partnership (p. 245)

limited partnership At least one general partner runs the business and bears unlimited personal liability; other partners provide financial capital but have limited liability (p. 245)

line of credit An arrangement with a bank through which a business can quickly borrow needed cash (p. 296)

liquidity The ability of any asset to be exchanged for cash (p. 300)

long run A period during which all resources can be varied (p. 148)

long-run average cost the lowest average cost of production at each rate of output when the firm's size is allowed to vary (p. 154)

long-run average cost curve A curve that indicates the lowest average cost of production at each rate of output when the firm's size is allowed to vary (p. 154)

M

M1 The narrowest definition of the money supply; consists of currency (including coins) held by the nonbanking public, checkable deposits, and traveler's checks (p. 506)

M2 A broader definition of the money supply consisting of M1 plus savings deposits, small-denomination time deposits, and money market mutual fund accounts (p. 508)

marginal Incremental, additional, or extra; refers to a change in an economic variable, a change in the status quo (p. 13)

marginal cost The change in total cost resulting from a one-unit change in output; the change in total cost divided by the change in output (p. 152)

marginal product The change in total product resulting from a one-unit change in a particular resource, all other resources constant (p. 148)

marginal revenue The change in total revenue from selling another unit of the good (p. 152)

marginal tax rate The percentage of each additional dollar of income that goes to pay the tax (p. 433)

marginal utility The change in total utility resulting a one-unit change in consumption of a good (p. 103)

market The means by which people buy and sell something (p. 15); an arrangement that allows buyers and sellers to exchange things for a market price (p. 163)

market-clearing price The price that equates quantity demanded with quantity supplied; the equilibrium price (p. 165)

market demand The sum of the individual demands of all consumers in the market (p. 107)

market economics Study of economic behavior in particular markets, such as the market for computers or for unskilled labor (p. 14)

market economy Describes the U.S. economic system, where markets plays a relatively large role (p. 38)

market for loans The market that brings together borrowers (the demanders of loans) and savers (the suppliers of loans) to determine the market interest rate (p. 291)

market power The ability of a firm to raise its price without losing all its customers to rivals (p. 193)

market structure Important features of a market such as the number of buyers and sellers, product uniformity across sellers, ease of entering the market, and forms of competition (p. 192)

maturity date The date when the money borrowed by issuing a bond must be repaid (p. 299)

maximizing political support Objective that guides the behavior of elected officials; comparable to profit maximization by firms and utility maximization by households (p. 448)

means-tested program To qualify for welfare benefits, a household's income and assets must fall below a certain amount (p. 87)

median income The middle income when a group of incomes is ranked from lowest to highest (p. 83)

mediator An impartial observer brought in when labor negotiations break down to suggest how to resolve differences (p. 274)

Medicaid A program that funds medical care for those with incomes below a certain level who are elderly, blind, disabled, or are living in families with dependent children (p. 87)

medium of exchange Anything generally accepted by all parties in payment for goods or services (p. 491)

merchandise trade balance The value of a country's exported goods minus the value of its imported goods during a given period (p. 568)

merger The combination of two or more firms to form a single firm (p. 209)

minimum acceptable price The lowest price that will allow the firm's total revenue to cover variable cost; the minimum price the firm needs to produce in the short run rather than shut down (p. 153)

minimum efficient scale The smallest size that allows the firm to take full advantage of economies of scale; the smallest output that minimizes long run average cost (p. 154)

minimum wage law Establishes a minimum price that an employer can pay a worker for an hour of labor (p. 270)

mixed economy Economic systems that mix central planning with competitive markets (p. 37)

monetary policy The central bank's attempts to control the money supply to influence the national economy (p. 72)

money Anything that everyone is willing to accept in exchange for goods and services (p. 53)

money demand The relationship between how much money people want to hold and the interest rate (p. 527)

money income The number of dollars received per period, such as $100 per week (p. 103)

money market mutual fund A collection of short-term interest-earning assets (p. 508)

money multiplier The multiple by which the money supply increases as a result of an increase in excess reserves in the banking system (p. 522)

money price The dollar price of the good (p. 122)

money supply The stock of money available in the economy at a particular time (p. 528)

monopolistic competition A market structure with no entry barriers and many firms selling products differentiated enough that each firm's demand curve slopes downward (p. 202)

monopoly A sole supplier of a product with no close substitutes (p. 193)

movement along a given demand curve Change in quantity demanded resulting from a change in the price of the good, other things constant (p. 122)

movement along a given supply curve Change in quantity supplied resulting from a change in the price of the good, other things constant (p. 143)

multilateral aid Development aid from an organization, such as the World Bank, that gets funds from a group of countries (p. 600)

multinational corporation (MNC) A large corporation that makes and sells its products around the world (p. 307)

multiplier effect Any change in fiscal policy affects aggregate demand by more than the original change in spending or taxing (p. 464)

mutual fund A financial institution that issues its own stock and with the proceeds buys a portfolio of securities (p. 300)

N

national banks Banks chartered, or authorized by the federal government (p. 500)

national economics Study of the economic behavior of the economy as a whole, especially the national economy (p. 14)

national income accounts System that organizes huge quantities of data collected from a variety of sources across America (p. 322)

natural monopoly One firm that can serve the entire market at a lower per-unit cost than can two or more firms (p. 71)

natural rate of unemployment The unemployment rate when the economy is producing its potential level of output (p. 460)

natural resources So-called "gifts of nature" used to produce goods and services; includes renewable and exhaustible resources (p. 7)

negative externalities By-products of production or consumption that impose costs on third parties, neither buyers nor sellers (p. 78)

net domestic product Gross domestic product minus depreciation (p. 324)

net exports The value of a country's exports minus the value of its imports (p. 325)

net investment Gross investment minus depreciation; used to compute net domestic product

net unilateral transfers Grants and gifts of cash received from abroad by U.S. residents minus grants and gifts of cash sent to foreign residents by U.S. residents (p. 570)

net worth Assets minus liabilities; also called owners' equity (p. 520)

nominal GDP GDP based on prices prevailing at the time of the transaction; current-dollar GDP (p. 331)

nominal interest rate The interest rate expressed in current dollars as a percentage of the amount loaned; the interest rate on the loan agreement (p. 401)

nondurable goods Goods expected to last less than three years, such as soap and soup (p. 323)

nonhorizontal merger One firm combines with another that does not produces the same product, such as Ford and U.S. Steel (p. 209)

noninstitutional adult population All those 16 years of age and older, expect people in the military, prisons, or mental hospitals; used to determine the unemployment rate (p. 390)

normal good A good for which demand increases or shifts rightward, as consumer incomes rise (p. 119)

normative economic statement An opinion, which cannot be shown to be true or false by reference to the facts (p. 13)

not-for-profit organizations Groups that do not pursue profit as a goal; they engage in charitable, educational, humanitarian, cultural, professional, or other activities often with a social purpose (p. 246)

O

oligopoly A market structure with a small number of firms whose behavior is interdependent (p. 203)

open-access good A good that is rival in consumption but exclusion is costly (p. 76)

open-market operations Buying or selling U.S. government securities as a way of regulating the money supply (p. 502)

opportunity cost The value of the best alternative passed up for the chosen item or activity (p. 20)

other-things-constant assumption The simplifying assumption that nothing else of importance changes except the variables in question (p. 11)

overhead Another word for fixed cost (p. 150)

P

partnership Two or more people agree to contribute resources to the business in return for a share of the profit (p. 236)

patent The exclusive right an inventor receives to sell that invention for up to 20 years (p. 70)

payroll taxes Taxes deducted from paychecks to support Social Security and Medicare (p. 439)

perfect competition A market structure with many fully informed buyers and sellers of an identical product with no barriers to entry (p. 192)

physical capital The machines, buildings, roads, airports, communications networks, and other manufactured creations used to produce goods and services; also called capital goods (pp 324, 360)

physical infrastructure Transportation, communication, energy, water, and sanitation systems provided by or regulated by government (p. 604)

positive economic statement An assertion about economic reality that can be supported or rejected by reference to the facts (p. 13)

positive externalities By-products of consumption or production that benefit third parties, neither buyers nor sellers (p. 79)

potential output The economy's maximum sustainable output in the long run (p. 460)

price What you pay when you buy something, and what you receive when you sell it (p. 164)

price ceiling A maximum legal price above which a product cannot be sold; to have an impact, a price floor must be set below the equilibrium price (p. 180)

price floor A minimum legal price below which a product cannot be sold; to have an impact, a price floor must be set above the equilibrium price (p. 180)

price level A composite measure reflecting the prices of all goods and services in the economy relative to prices in a base year (p. 344)

prime rate The interest rate banks charge for loans to their most trustworthy business borrowers (p. 297)

private good A good with two features: (1) the amount consumed by one person is unavailable for others and (2) nonpayers can easily be excluded (p. 76)

private property rights Legal claim that guarantees an owner the right to use a resource or to charge others for its use (p. 69)

privatization The process in transition economies of converting state-owned enterprises into private enterprises (p. 40, 607)

producer cooperative Producers join forces to reduce their costs by purchasing supplies and equipment as a group and selling their output as a group (p. 246)

product market A set of arrangements by which goods and services are bought and sold (p. 15)

production possibilities frontier (PPF) Shows the possible combinations of the two types of goods that can be produced when available resources are employed fully and efficiently (p. 42)

productive efficiency Achieved when a firm produces at the lowest possible cost per unit (p. 179)

productive resources The inputs, or factors of production, used to produce the goods and services that people want (p. 6)

productivity The value of output produced by each additional unit of a resource (p. 257); the ratio of output to a specific measure of input; usually reflects an average, such as bushels of grain per acre of farm land (p. 359)

profit Equals the revenue from sales minus the cost of production (p. 5)

progressive taxation The tax as a percentage of income increases as income increases (p. 433)

proportional taxation The tax as a percentage of income remains constant as income increases; also called a flat tax (p. 433)

public good A good that, once produced, is available for all to consume, but the producer cannot easily exclude nonpayers (p. 76)

public utility A government-owned or government-regulated monopoly (p. 63)

publicly traded corporation Owned by many shareholders; shares can be bought or sold (p. 243)

pure centrally planned economy An economic system in which all resources are government-owned and production is coordinated by the central plans of government (p. 37)

pure market economy An economic system with no government involvement so private firms account for all production (p. 35)

Q

quantity demanded The amount demanded at a particular price (p. 106)

quantity supplied The amount supplied at a particular price (p. 134)

quasi-public good A good that, once produced, is available to all, but nonpayers are easily excluded (p. 76)

quota A legal limit on the quantity of a particular product that can be imported (p. 560)

R

ration To allocate goods, not by markets, but based on a certain amount per household (p. 37)

rational Making the best choices one can based on the information available (p. 11)

rational ignorance A stance adopted by voters when they find that the cost of understanding and voting on a particular issue exceeds the benefit expected from doing so (p. 449)

real GDP The economy's aggregate output measured in dollars of constant purchasing power; GDP measured in terms of the goods and services produced (p. 331)

real GDP per capita Real GDP divided by the population; the best measure of an economy's standard of living (p. 348)

real income Income measured in terms of the goods and services it will buy (p. 103)

real interest rate The interest rate expressed in dollars of constant purchasing power as a percentage of the amount loaned; the nominal interest rate minus the inflation rate (p. 401)

recession A decline in total production lasting at least two consecutive quarters, or at least six months (p. 336)

recognition lag The time needed to identify a macroeconomic problem (p. 471)

regressive taxation The tax as a percentage of income decreases as income increases (p. 433)

renewable resource A natural resource that can be drawn on indefinitely if used conservatively, such as the atmosphere or water supply (p. 7)

representative money Bank notes that exchange for a specific commodity, such as gold (p. 497)

required reserve ratio A Fed regulation that dictates the minimum percentage of deposits each bank must keep in reserve (p. 520)

required reserves The dollar amount that must be held in reserve; checkable deposits multiplied by the required reserve ratio (p. 521)

reserve ratio Bank reserves as a share of bank deposits (p. 497)

reserves Cash that banks have on hand in their vaults or on deposit with the Federal Reserve (p. 500)

resource complements One resource works with the other in production; a decrease in the price of one increases the demand for the other (p. 260)

resource market A set of arrangements by which productive resources are bought and sold (p. 15)

resource substitutes One resource can replace another in production; an increase in the price of one resource increases the demand for the other (p. 260)

rest of the world Economic decision makers formed by households, firms, and governments in the more than 200 sovereign nations throughout the world (p. 65)

retained earnings That portion of after-tax corporate profit reinvested in the firm (p. 299)

right-to-work law State law that says a worker at a union company does not have to join the union or pay union dues to hold a job there (p. 274)

rival in consumption The amount consumed by one person is unavailable for others to consume; a feature of private goods (p. 76)

rules of the game The formal and informal institutions that provide production incentives and promote economic activity, such as laws, customs, and conventions (p. 360)

S

savings deposits Deposits that earn interest but have no specific maturity date (p. 507)

scarce The amount people want exceeds the amount available at a zero price (p. 9)

scarcity A condition facing all societies because there are not enough productive resources to satisfy people's unlimited wants (p. 6)

S corporation Limited liability combined with the single taxation of business income; must have no more than 75 stockholders with no foreign stockholders (p. 245)

seasonal unemployment Occurs because of seasonal changes in labor demand during the year (p. 388)

secondary markets Securities markets where stocks and bonds already sold by the corporation can be exchanged (p. 300)

secondhand securities Stocks and bonds that have already been sold by the corporation (p. 300)

securities Corporate stock and corporate bonds (p. 299)

security exchanges Markets where stocks and bonds can be traded, or bought and sold (p. 299)

seigniorage The difference between the exchange value of money and the cost of supplying it; the "profit" from issuing money (p. 494)

service Something not physical that requires scarce resources and satisfies human wants (p. 8)

shares of stock Proof of corporate ownership; owners are entitled to profits and to vote on directors of the corporation (p. 243)

shift of a demand curve Increase or decrease in demand resulting from a change in one of the determinants of demand other than the price of the good (p. 122)

shift of a supply curve Increase or decrease in supply resulting from a change in one of the determinants of supply other than the price of the good (p. 144)

short run A period during which at least one of a firm's resources is fixed (p. 148)

shortage At a given price, the amount by which quantity demanded exceeds quantity supplied; a shortage usually forces the price up (p. 164)

sin tax A tax on products that are deemed socially undesirable, such as cigarettes, liquor, and legal gambling (p. 432)

social insurance Cash transfers for retirees, the unemployed, and others with a work history and a record of contributions to the program (p. 86)

soft budget constraint In centrally planned economies, the budget condition faced by state enterprises that are subsidized when they lose money (p. 607)

sole proprietorship The simplest form of business organization; a firm is owned and run by one person (p. 234)

specialization Occurs when individual workers focus on single tasks, enabling each one to be more efficient and productive (p. 51)

speculator Someone who buys or sells foreign exchange in hopes of profiting from fluctuations in the exchange rate over time (p. 577)

stagflation A decline, or *stag*nation, of a nation's output accompanied by in*flation* in the price level (p. 407)

standard of living An economy's level of economic prosperity; best measured by the value of goods and services produced per capita (p. 359)

state banks Banks chartered, or authorized, by the states in which they operated (p. 499)

store of value Anything that retains its purchasing power over time (p. 492)

strike A labor union's attempt to withhold labor from the firm (p. 274)

structural unemployment Occurs because job seekers do not have the skills demanded (p. 388)

substitutes Goods, such as pizza and tacos, that relate in such a way that an increase in the price of one shifts the demand for the other rightward (p. 120)

substitution effect of a price change When the price of a good falls, consumers substitute that good for other goods, which are now relatively more expensive (p. 103)

sunk cost A cost you have already incurred and cannot recover, regardless of what you do now (p. 22)

Supplemental Security Income (SSI) Provides cash to the elderly poor and the disabled (p. 87)

supply A relation showing the quantities of a good producers are willing and able to sell at various prices during a given period, other things constant (p. 132)

supply curve A curve or line showing the quantities or a particular good supplied at various prices during a given time period, other things constant (p. 132)

supply of loans curve An upward sloping curve showing the positive relationship between the interest rate and the quantity of loans supplied, other things constant (p. 291)

supply schedule Columns of numbers showing the quantities of a particular good supplied at various possible prices during a given period, other things constant (p. 132)

supply-side economics Macroeconomic policy that focuses on a rightward shift of the aggregate supply curve through tax cuts or other changes that increase production incentives (p. 408)

surplus At a given price, the amount by which quantity supplied exceeds quantity demanded; a surplus usually forces the price down (p. 164)

T

Taft-Hartley Act Federal legislation approved in 1947 authorizing states to approve right-to-work laws (p. 274)

tariff A tax on imports (p. 560)

tastes Consumer preferences; likes and dislikes in consumption; assumed to be constant along a given demand curve (p. 122)

tax incidence Those who bear the burden of the tax (p. 432)

technology Knowledge about how best to combine resources to make goods and services (p. 42)

Temporary Assistance for Needy Families (TANF) Provides cash to poor families with dependent children (p. 87)

thrift institutions, or **thrifts** Depository institutions that make long-term loans primarily to households; savings and loan institutions, mutual savings banks, and credit unions (p. 499)

time deposits Deposits that earn a fixed rate of interest if held for a specified period (p. 508)

time price The time required for a good or service to provide its benefits (p. 122)

token money Money whose exchange value exceeds its intrinsic value (p. 497)

total cost Fixed cost plus variable cost; the cost of all resources used by the firm (p. 150)

total product A firm's total output (p. 148)

total revenue Price multiplied by the quantity demanded at that price (p. 111)

trade deficit The amount by which the value of merchandise imports exceeds the value of merchandise exports during a given period (p. 568)

trade surplus The amount by which the value of merchandise exports exceeds the value of merchandise imports during a given period (p. 568)

trademark Establishes property rights to unique commercial marks and symbols, such as McDonald's golden arches (p. 70)

traditional economy Economic system shaped largely by custom or religion (p. 40)

transaction cost The cost of time and information needed to carry out market exchange (pp. 63, 167)

transition economy Economic system in the process of shifting from central planning to competitive markets (p. 39)

U

U.S. Agency for International Development (USAID) The federal agency that coordinates foreign aid to the developing world (p. 600)

underemployment Workers are overqualified for their jobs or work fewer hours than they would prefer (p. 389)

underground economy Market exchange that goes unreported either because it is illegal or because those involved want to evade taxes; also called the black market (p. 329)

undifferentiated oligopoly Oligopoly market where firms sell an identical product, such as a barrel of oil (p. 203)

unemployment benefits Cash transfers to unemployed workers who actively seek work and who meet other qualifications (p. 394)

unemployment rate The number looking for work divided by the number in the labor force (p. 390)

Uniform Partnership Act (UPA) In most states, governs partnerships lacking their own agreement (p. 245)

unit of account A common unit for measuring the value of every good or service (p. 491)

unit-elastic demand The percentage change in quantity demanded equals the percentage change in price; the resulting elasticity equals 1.0 (p. 110)

unit-elastic supply The percentage change in quantity supplied equals the percentage change in price; the resulting elasticity equals 1.0 (p. 136)

Uruguay Round The most recent and most comprehensive of the eight postwar multilateral trade negotiations under GATT; created the World Trade Organization (p. 562)

utility The satisfaction from consumption; sense of well-being (p. 63)

V

value added At each stage of production, the value of a product minus the cost of intermediate goods used to produce it (p. 326)

variable cost Any production cost that changes as output changes (p. 150)

variable resource Any resource that can be varied in the short run to change output (p. 148)

vertical merger One firm combines with another from which it buys inputs or to which it sells output, such as a merger between a steel producer and an automaker (p. 305)

W

wages Payment to resource owners for their labor (p. 7)

welfare reform An overhaul of the welfare system in 1996 that imposed a lifetime welfare limit of five years per recipient and other conditions (p. 416)

world price The price at which a good is traded internationally; determined by the world supply and world demand for the good (p. 560)

World Trade Organization (**WTO**) The legal and institutional foundation of the multilateral trading system that succeeded GATT in 1995 (p. 562)

A

ability-to-pay tax principle *principio de la habilidad de pagar el impuesto* Aquellos con más habilidad de pagar, tal como aquellos que tienen más ingresos, deben pagar más del impuesto (p. 434)

absolute advantage *ventaja absoluta* El poder hacer algo usando menos recursos que lo que requieren otros productores (p. 51)

aggregate demand *demanda total* La relación entre el nivel del precio de la economía y la cantidad de producción total exigida, otras cosas constantes (p. 344)

aggregate demand curve *curva de demanda total* Una curva que representa la relación entre el nivel del precio de la economía y el verdadero PIB exigido por periodo, otras cosas constantes (p. 344)

aggregate expenditure *gastos totales* Gasto total en todo bien y servicio terminado y producido en la economía durante el año (p. 325)

aggregate income *ingresos totales* La suma de todo el ingreso ganado por proveedores de recursos en la economía durante un año asignado (p. 326)

aggregate output *producción total* Una combinación de medidas de todos los bienes y servicios producidos en una economía durante un periodo asignado; PIB verdadero (p. 344)

aggregate supply curve *curva de oferta total* Una curva que representa la relación entre el nivel del precio de la economía y el verdadero PIB ofrecido por periodo, otras cosas constantes (p. 346)

allocative efficiency *eficiencia de asignar* Se logra cuando una empresa produce el producto más preferido por los consumidores (p. 179)

annually balanced budget *presupuesto anual ajustado* Igualando gastos anuales con ingresos anuales, excepto durante años de guerra; aproximación al presupuesto federal antes de la Gran Depresión (p. 466)

antitrust activity *actividad de antimonopolio* Esfuerzos del gobierno dirigidos a prevenir monopolios y promover competencia en mercados donde competencia se desea (p. 209)

antitrust laws *leyes de antimonopolio* Leyes que prohiben comportamiento anticompetitivo y promueve competencia en mercados donde se desea la competencia (p. 71)

applied research *investigación aplicada* Investigación que busca respuestas a preguntas en particular o aplica descubrimientos científicos para desarrollar productos específicos (p. 375)

asset *activo* Cualquier propiedad física o reclamo financiero que sea propio (p. 520)

automatic stabilizers *estabilizadores automáticos* Programas de gastos e impuestos por el gobierno que año tras año automáticamente reducen fluctuaciones en poder adquisitivo, y por lo tanto en consumo, durante el ciclo de negocios (p. 471)

B

balance of payments *ajuste de pagos* Una constancia de todas las transacciones económicas entre residentes de un país y residentes del resto del mundo durante un tiempo asignado (p. 568)

balance sheet *balance* Un estado de cuentas que muestra los activos, los pasivos y el valor neto en una fecha asignada; como los activos tienen que igualar a los pasivos más el valor neto, el estado de cuentas está ajustado (p. 520)

barriers to entry *obstáculos al entrar* Cualquier cosa que previene nuevas empresas de competir en forma igual con empresas que existen en una industria (p. 194)

barter *intercambiar* Un sistema de comercio en el cual productos se intercambian directamente por otros productos (p. 52)

basic research *investigación básica* La búsqueda por conocimiento sin prestar atención a como se usará ese conocimiento; un primer paso hacia avances tecnológicos (p. 375)

benefits-received tax principle *beneficios recibidos principio de impuesto* Aquellos que reciben más beneficios del program de gobierno financiado por el impuesto debe pagar más de ese impuesto (p. 434)

bilateral aid *ayuda bilateral* Ayuda de desarrollo de un país a otro (p. 600)

binding arbitration *arbitraje fijo* Cuando negociaciones de trabajo se han quebrado y el interés del público está involucrado, un tercer partidiario neutro se trae para imponer un acuerdo que los dos lados deben aceptar (p. 274)

bond *bono* Un contrato prometiendo pagar dinero prestado en una fecha designada y pagar interés en el proceso (p. 299)

brain drain *drenaje cerebral* La perdida de migrantes educados de un país en desarrollo a paises con mercados industriales (p. 598)

bureaus *departamentos* Agencias del gobierno encargadas de implementar legislación y que son financiadas por apropiaciones de cuerpos legislativos (p. 452)

business cycle *ciclo de negocio* Cambios que reflejan aumentos y reducciónes de actividad económica en relación con la tendencia de crecimiento de largo plazo de la economía (p. 336)

C

capital deepening *profundizando en capital* Un aumento en la cantidad y la calidad del capital por trabajador; una fuente para aumentar productividad en el trabajo (p. 360)

capital goods *bienes de capital* Toda creación humana usada para producir bienes y servicios; por ejemplo, fábricas, camiones y máquinas (p. 8)

cartel *cartel* Un grupo de empresas que acuerda coordinar decisiones de precio para maximar beneficios del grupo al comportarse como un monopolista (p. 204)

check *cheque* Una orden escrita instruyendo al banco de pagarle a alguien del monto depositado (p. 497)

checkable deposits *depositos verificables* Depositos en instituciones financieras contra los cuales se puede escribir cheques y/o tarjetas de cajero automático o de débito se pueden aplicar (p. 507)

classical economists *economistas clásicos* Un grupo de laissez-faire economistas, que creían que fases de bajas en la economía eran problemas a corto plazo que se corregían por ellos mismos a largo plazo por fuerzas naturales del mercado (p. 465)

cluster *conjunto* Empresas en la misma industria o en industrias relacionadas que se agrupan en una región, tal como Wall Street (La Bolsa), Hollywood o Silicon Valley (p. 379)

collateral *garantía* Una propiedad del prestatario que se puede vender para pagar el prestamo en caso de que el prestamo no se pague (p. 297)

collective bargaining *negociación colectiva* El proceso por el cual representantes del sindicato y

del empresario negocean salarios, beneficios de empleados y condiciones de trabajo (p. 274)

commercial banks *bancos comerciales* Instituciones de deposito que hacen prestamos primariamente a negocios (p. 498)

commodity *bien de consumo* Un producto que es idéntico entre vendedores, tal como una medida de áridos de trigo (p. 192)

commodity money *dinero de producto* Cualquier cosa que sirve tanto como dinero que como producto, tal como el oro (p. 491)

competitive firm's supply curve *curva de oferta de una empresa competitiva* La porción de la curva de costo marginal de una empresa que aumenta al precio o más del precio que permitirá que la empresa cubra el costo variable (p. 153)

conglomerate merger *fusión de conglomeración* Una empresa combina con otra empresa en una industria diferente, tal como la fusión entre un productor de plásticos y una empresa de electrónicos (p. 305)

consumer price index (CPI) *índice del precio del consumidor* Medida de inflación basada en el costo de un canasto fijo de bienes y servicios que se compran por una típica familia (p. 333)

consumer surplus *excedente de consumidor* La diferencia entre la máxima cantidad que consumidores quieren pagar por una cantidad determinada de un bien y lo que en realidad pagan (p. 181)

consumption *consumo* Compras por un hogar de un bien o servicio terminado excepto por nuevas residencias, las cuales cuentan como inversiones (p. 323)

convergence theory *teoría de convergencia* Una teoría que predice que el nivel de vida en economías por todo el mundo crecera más similar sobre el tiempo, con los paises más pobres gradualmente cerrando el espacio con los paises más ricos (p. 607)

cooperative *cooperativa* Una organización que consiste de personas que unen sus recursos para comprar y vender más eficientemente que lo que pudieran hacer en forma independiente (p. 245)

corporation *corporación* Una entidad legal con una existencia que es distinta de las verdaderas personas que la organizan, la poséen y la dirigen (p. 245)

cost-push inflation *inflación de costo y empuje* Inflación que resulta de un cambio hacia la izquierda de la curva de oferta total (p. 399)

credit *crédito* La habilidad de prestar ahora basada en la promesa de pagar en el futuro (p. 295)

crowding in *alojamiento* Gastos del gobierno estimulan inversión privada en una economía muerta (p. 480)

crowding out *desplazamiento* Inversión privada cae cuando déficits más altos del gobierno hacen subir los intereses (p. 480)

current account *cuenta actual* La porción del estado de pagos que da constancia a exportaciones e importaciones de bienes y servicios, ingresos netos de inversión, y transferencias netas (p. 568)

cycle of poverty *ciclo de pobreza* Niños en familias de bienestar pueden terminar en bienestar ellos mismos cuando crezcan (p. 415)

cyclical unemployment *desempleo cíclico* Ocurre por los empleos perdidos durante la fase de recesión del ciclo de negocio (p. 388)

D

decision-making lag *lapso para hacer una decisión* El tiempo necesitado para decidir que hacer cuando el problema se ha identificado (p. 473)

decrease in demand *reducción en demanda* Los consumidores mucho menos quieren y pueden comprar el producto a cualquier precio (p. 171)

decrease in supply *reducción en oferta* Los productores mucho menos quieren y pueden ofrecer el producto a cualquier precio (p. 173)

demand *demanda* Una relación que muestra las cantidades de un bien que los consumidores quieren y pueden comprar a diferentes precios por periodo, otras cosas constantes (p. 102)

demand curve *curva de demanda* Una curva o linea que muestra las cantidades de un bien en particular en demanda a varios precios durante un periodo específico, otras cosas constantes (p. 105)

demand for loans curve *curva de demanda por prestamos* Una curva con inclinación hacia abajo mostrando una relación negativa entre el índice de interés y la cantidad de prestamos exigidos, otras cosas constantes (p. 290)

demand-pull inflation *inflación de demanda y hala* Inflación que resulta por cambios hacia la derecha de la curva de demanda total (p. 398)

demand-side economics *economía de lado de demanda* Póliza de macroeconomía que enfoca en cambiar la curva de demanda total como forma de promover empleo total y estabilidad de precio (p. 406)

depreciation *depreciación* El valor de la acción capital que se usa o se vuelve obsoleto al producir PIB durante el año (p. 330)

deregulation *deregulación* Una reducción en el control del gobierno sobre los precios y entradas de empresas en mercados previamente regulados, tal como las aerolineas y el transporte por carretera (p. 212)

derived demand *demanda derivada* La demanda por un recurso se deriva de la demanda por el producto que ese recurso produce (p. 256)

developing countries *paises en desarrollo* Paises con un nivel de vida más bajo porque tienen relativamente poco capital humano y físico; también se llaman paises del Tercer Mundo (p. 367, 588)

discount rate *taza de descuento* Taza de interés que el gobierno federal le cobra a los bancos que prestan reservas (p. 501)

discouraged workers *trabajadores desilucionados* Alguien que no ha podido encontrar trabajo, se sale de la fuerza de trabajo (p. 389)

discretionary fiscal policy *póliza fiscal discrecional* Cambios a gastos o impuestos por el Congreso para promover metas macroeconómicas (p. 471)

disequilibrium *desequilibrio* Algo desigual entre la cantidad exigida y la cantidad ofrecida al paso que el mercado busca equilibrio; usualmente temporal, excepto donde el gobierno interviene y fija el precio (p. 180)

dividend *dividendo* La porción que se paga a los accionistas, del beneficio de una corporación después de impuestos (p. 299)

division of labor *división de trabajo* Clasificación del proceso de producción en diferentes tareas que se llevan a cabo por diferentes trabajadores (p. 53)

E

economic growth *crecimiento económico* Una expansión en las posibilidades de producción en la economía o en la habilidad de producir (p. 45)

economic system *sistema económico* Un conjunto de mecanismos e instituciones que resuelven las preguntas del qué, cómo y para quién para una economía (p. 34)

economic theory, economic model *teoría de economía, modelo de economía* Una simplificación de la realidad de la economía usada para hacer predicciones sobre el mundo verdadero (p. 11)

economics *economía* El estudio de como la gente usa sus recursos escasos para satisfacer sus deseos ilimitados (p. 6)

economies of scale *economías de escala* Fuerzas que reducen el costo promedio al paso que el tamaño, o escala de la empresa aumenta a largo plazo (p. 154)

economy *economía* La estructura de actividad económica en una localidad, región, país, un grupo de paises, o el mundo (p. 322)

effectiveness lag *lapso en eficacia* El tiempo necesitado para cambios en póliza para afectar la economía (p. 473)

efficiency *eficiencia* Producir el máximo producto posible de los recursos disponibles (pp. 42, 46)

elasticity of demand *elasticidad de demanda* Mide como la cantidad receptiva exigida es al cambio del precio; el cambio de porcentaje en cantidad exigida dividida por el cambio de porcentaje en precio (p. 110)

elasticity of supply *elasticidad de oferta* Una medida de receptividad de la cantidad ofrecida a un cambio de precio; el cambio de porcentaje en la cantidad dividido por el cambio de porcentaje en el precio (p. 135)

entrepreneur *empresario* Un buscador de beneficio que desarrolla un nuevo producto o proceso y asume el riesgo de beneficio o perdida (p. 7)

equilibrium *equilibrio* La cantidad que los consumidores quieren y pueden comprar es igual a la cantidad que productores quieren y pueden vender (p. 164)

equilibrium interest rate *índice de interés en equilibrio* El único índice de interés al cual la cantidad de prestamos exigidos es igual a la cantidad de prestamos ofrecidos (p. 292)

equilibrium wage *salario de equilibrio* El salario al cual no hay ni un exceso en la cantidad de trabajo en demanda ni un exceso en la cantidad de trabajo en oferta (p. 258)

euro *euro* La nueva moneda común europea (p. 540)

excess reserves *reservas en exceso* Reservas del banco en exceso de las reservas requeridas (p. 521)

exchange rate *taza de cambio* El precio de la moneda de un país medido en términos de la moneda de otro país (p. 575)

expansion *expansión* La fase de actividad económica durante la cual la producción total de la economía aumenta (p. 337)

expenditure approach to GDP *método de gastos al PIB* Un método de calcular el PIB al sumar los gastos en todos los bienes y servicios terminados producidos durante un año (p. 323)

export promotion *promoción de exportaciones* Una estrategia de desarrollo que se concentra en producir para el mercado de exportación (p. 598)

F

featherbedding *prebendaje (contratar mano de obra que no es necesaria)* Esfuerzos de un sindicato de forzar a un empresario para emplear a más trabajadores que los que se necesitan para la tarea (p. 274)

federal funds market *mercado de fondos federales* Un mercado para hacer prestamos y prestar de un día para el otro de las reservas que mantiene el gobierno federal para los bancos (p. 531)

federal funds rate *taza de fondos federales* La taza de interés que se cobra en el mercado de fondos federales; el objetivo de la taza de interés que tiene el gobierno federal

Federal Open Market Committee (FOMC) *Comité Federal de Mercado Abierto* Un grupo de doce miembros que hacen decisiones sobre operaciones de mercado abierto (p. 501)

Federal Reserve System (the Fed) *Sistema Federal de Reserva* Establecido en 1913 como el banco central y autoridad monetaria de los Estados Unidos (p. 500)

fertility rate *nivel de fertilidad* El promedio en número de nacimientos durante la vida de cada mujer (p. 589)

fiat money *dinero fiat* Dinero que no se puede cambiar por nada de valor intrínseco; declarado dinero por decreto de gobierno (p. 497)

financial account *cuenta financiera* La porción del ajuste de pagos que da constancia a transacciones internacionales que tiene activos financieros, como acciones y bonos, y activos verdaderos, tal como fábricas y edificios de oficinas (p. 571)

financial capital *capital financiero* Dinero necesitado para comenzar o expandir un negocio (p. 229)

financial intermediaries *intermediarios financieros* Bancos y otras instituciones que sirven como intermediarios, aceptando fondos de ahorradores y prestandolos a los prestatarios (p. 295)

firm *empresa* Unidad de negocio o empresa formada por un empresario que busca beneficio el cual combina recursos para producir bienes y servicios (p. 63)

fixed cost *costo fijo* Cualquier costo de producción que es independiente de la producción de una empresa (p. 150)

fixed exchange rate *taza de cambio fija* Taza de cambio fija dentro de un estrecho rango de valores y mantenida por las continuas compras y ventas de la moneda de un banco central (p. 579)

flexible exchange rate *taza de cambio flexible* Taza de cambio determinada por las fuerzas de oferta y demanda sin que el gobierno intervenga (p. 579)

foreign aid *ayuda extranjera* Una beca internacional o un prestamo hecho en términos favorables para promover desarrollo económico (p. 599)

foreign exchange *cambio extranjero* Dinero extranjero necesitado para hacer transacciones internacionales (p. 575)

fractional reserve banking system *sistema bancario de reserva fraccional* Solo una porción de los depositos del banco se respalda por las reservas (p. 497)

frictional unemployment *desempleo friccional* Ocurre por el tiempo requerido de emparejar buscadores de trabajo calificados con puestos disponibles (p. 388)

full employment *empleo completo* Ocurre cuando no hay nada de desempleo cíclico; relativamente bajo desempleo (p. 388)

G

General Agreement on Tariffs and Trade (GATT) *Acuerdo general a tarifas y comercio* Un tratado internacional de reducción de tarifas adoptado en 1947 que resultó en una serie de "vueltas" negociadas con la meta a un comercio más libre (p. 561)

general partnership *sociedad colectiva general* Los socios comparten en la responsabilidad de mantener el negocio y en cualquier responsabilidad legal de su operación (p. 237)

good *bien* Algo que se puede ver, sentir y tocar que requiere recursos escasos y satisface deseos humanos (p. 8)

government budget *presupuesto del gobierno* Un plan para desembolsos e ingresos del gobierno por un periodo específico, usualmente un año (p. 440)

government purchases *compras de gobierno* Gastos por todos los niveles de gobierno por bienes y servicios; no incluye transferencia de pagos (p. 324)

gross domestic product (GDP) *producto interno bruto (PIB)* El valor del mercado de todos los bienes y servicios terminados y producidos en los Estados Unidos durante un periodo asignado, usualmente un año (p. 322)

Group of Seven (G-7) *el grupo de siete of G-7* Los siete mercados de economía industrial principales, incluyendo los Estados Unidos, el Reino Unido, Francia, Alemania, Italia, el Japón y el Canada (p. 368)

H

hostile takeovers *toma de poder hostil* Una empresa compra el control de otra empresa contra los deseos de la gerencia de la empresa que se compra; una estrategia común de fusión en los años de 1980 (p. 300)

household *hogar* El más importante determinador de decisiones económicas, consistiendo en todos aquellos que viven bajo un techo (p. 62)

human capital *capital humano* El conocimiento, habilidad, y experiencia de una fuerza de trabajo aculumado (p. 360)

human resources *recursos humanos* La amplia categoría de esfuerzos humanos, tanto físicos como mentales, usada para producir bienes y servicios (p. 7)

I

implementation lag *lapso de implementación* El tiempo necesitado para ejecutar un cambio en póliza (p. 473)

import substitution *sustitución de importaciones* Una estrategia de desarrollo que enfatiza fabricación doméstica de productos que actualmente son importados (p. 598)

income approach to GDP *método de ingresos al PIB* Un método de calcular PIB al sumar todos los pagos a los dueños de los recursos usados para producir productos durante el año (p. 323)

income-assistance programs *programas de asistencia de ingresos* Programas del gobierno que ofrecen dinero y ayuda en-especie a los pobres (p. 86)

income effect of a price change *el efecto de ingresos a un cambio de precio* Una caida en el precio de un bien aumenta los verdaderos ingresos de un consumidor, haciendo que los consumidores puedan comprar el bien; para bienes normales, la cantidad exigida aumenta (p. 103)

increase in demand *aumento en demanda* Los consumidores mucho más quieren y pueden comprar el producto a cualquier precio (p. 170)

increase in supply *aumento en oferta* Los productores mucho más quieren y pueden ofrecer el producto a cualquier precio (p. 172)

individual demand *demanda individual* La exigencia de un consumidor individual (p. 107)

industrial market countries *paises de mercado industrial* Los mercados de economías avanzados del Oeste de Europa, Norteamérica, Australia, Nueva Zelanda y el Japón; también se llaman paises desarrollados (pp. 367, 588)

industrial policy *póliza industrial* La vista que el gobierno usando impuestos, subsidios y regulaciones debe nutrir las industrias y tecnologías del futuro, al darle a las industrias domésticas una ventaja sobre la competencia extranjera (p. 378)

Industrial Revolution *Revolución Industrial* Desarrollo de producción de grande escala bajo un techo durante el siglo 18 (p. 64)

inflation *inflación* Un aumento en el nivel del precio general de la economía (p. 398)

initial public offering (IPO) *oferta inicial pública* La venta inicial de acciones de una corporación al público (p. 299)

innovation *innovación* El proceso de cambiar una invención a un producto comercializable (p. 229)

institutional investors *inversionistas institucionales* Bancos, compañías de seguros, fondos mutuales, y otros negocios que compran, venden y son dueños de valores (p. 300)

interest rate *índice de interés* Interés anual como porcentaje de la cantidad prestada o ahorrada (p. 289)

investment *inversión* La compra de nuevas plantas, nuevo equipo, nuevos edificios, nuevas residencias, y adiciones netas al inventario (p. 324)

L

labor *trabajo* El esfuerzo físico y mental usado para producir bienes y servicios (p. 7)

labor force *fuerza de trabajo* Aquellos en la población adulta que están trabajando o buscando empleo (p. 390)

labor productivity *productividad de trabajo* Producción por unidad de trabajo; medida como el total de producción dividido por las horas de trabajo empleadas para producir ese producto (p. 359)

labor union *sindicato de trabajo* Un grupo de trabajadores que se juntan para obtener más pago y mejores condiciones de trabajo al negociar un contrato de trabajo con sus empresarios (p. 273)

laissez-faire *laissez-faire (política de mínima interferencia)* La doctrina que el gobierno no debe intervenir en una economía de mercado más alla de

lo mínimo requerido para mantener paz y derechos de propiedad (p. 404)

law of comparative advantage *ley de ventaja comparativa* El trabajador, empresa, región, o país con el costo de oportunidad más bajo de producir un producto debe especializarse en ese producto (p. 51)

law of demand *la ley de demanda* La cantidad de un bien exigido por periodo se relaciona a la inversa con su precio, otras constantes (p. 102)

law of diminishing marginal utility *ley de utilidad marginal disminuida* Entre más consuma una persona un bien por periodo, el aumento en utilidad total por consumir otra unidad más será más pequeño, otras cosas constantes (p. 103)

law of diminishing returns *ley de rendimientos reducidos* Al añadir más de un recurso variable a una cantidad específica de unos recursos fijos, el producto marginal eventualmente declina y puede ser negativo (p. 148)

law of increasing opportunity cost *ley del aumento de la oportunidad del costo* Cada aumento adicional de un bien requiere que la economía abandone sucesivamente aumentos más grandes del otro bien (p. 44)

law of supply *ley de oferta* La cantidad de un bien ofrecido en un periodo específico es usualmente relacionado en directo a su precio, otras cosas constantes (p. 132)

leading economic indicators *indicadores principales de la economía* Medidas que usualmente predicen, o llevan a recesiones o expansiones (p. 339)

liability *responsabilidad legal* La obligación legal de pagar cualquier deuda que el negocio encuentre (p. 235)

liability *pasivo* Una cantidad que se debe (p. 520)

limited liability company (LLC) *compañía con responsabilidad legal limitada* Un negocio con responsabilidad legal limitada para algunos dueños, el sistema de impuestos sencillo de los ingresos de negocio, y no tiene restricciones de propietarios (p. 245)

limited liability partnership (LLP) *sociedad colectiva con responsabilidad legal limitada* Tal como una compañía con responsabilidad limitada pero más facilmente convertida de una sociedad colectiva que exista (p. 245)

limited partnership *sociedad colectiva limitada* Por lo menos un socio general dirige el negocio y carga con la responsabilidad legal personal sin limite; otros socios suministran capital financiero pero tienen responsabilidad legal limitada (p. 245)

line of credit *linea de crédito* Un arreglo con un banco por el cual un negocio puede prestar dinero necesitado rapidamente (p. 296)

liquidity *liquidez* La habilidad que cualquier propiedad se pueda cambiar por efectivo (p. 300)

long run *a largo plazo* Un periodo durante el cual todos los recursos se pueden variar (p. 148)

long-run average cost curve *curva de promedio de largo plazo* Una curva que indica el más mínimo promedio de costo de producción a cada índice de producción cuando el tamaño de una empresa se le permite variar (p. 154)

M

M1 *M1* La más estrecha definición del abastecimiento de dinero; consiste en moneda (lo que incluye monedas) que el público no bancario tiene, depositos veríficables, y cheques de viajero (p. 506)

M2 *M2* Una definición más ancha del abastecimiento de dinero que consiste del M1 más los depósitos de ahorros, depósitos de denominación de poco tiempo, y cuentas de fondo común de inversiones (p. 508)

marginal *marginal* Incremental, adicional o extra; se refiere a un cambio en un variable de la economía, un cambio en el statu quo (p. 13)

marginal cost *costo marginal* El cambio en costo total resultando de una unidad de cambio en la producción; el cambio del costo total divido por el cambio en producción (p. 152)

marginal product *producto marginal* El cambio en producto total resultando de un cambio de una unidad en un recurso en particular, otros recursos constantes (p. 148)

marginal revenue *ingreso marginal* El cambio en ingreso total al vender otra unidad de un bien (p. 152)

marginal tax rate *índice de impuesto marginal* El porcentaje de cada dólar adicional de ingresos que va a pagar el impuesto (p. 435)

marginal utility *utilidad marginal* El cambio en servicio total resultando en una unidad de cambio en el consumo de un bien (p. 103)

market *mercado* Los medios por los cuales la gente compra y vende algo (p. 15); un acuerdo que permite compradores y vendedores intercambiar cosas por un precio de mercado (p. 163)

market demand *demanda del mercado* La suma de las exigencias individuales de todos los consumidores en el mercado (p. 107)

market economics *economía de mercado* Estudio del comportamiento de la economía en mercados particulares, tal como el mercado de computadores o por trabajo no cualificado (p. 14)

market economy *economía de mercado* Describe el sistema de economía de los Estados Unidos, donde los mercados juegan un papel relativamente grande (p. 38)

market for loans *mercado para prestamos* El mercado que trae junto a los prestadores (los que exigen los prestamos) y los ahorradores (los que ofrecen los prestamos) para determinar el índice de interés del mercado (p. 291)

market power *poder del mercado* La habilidad de una empresa de subir su precio sin perder todos sus clientes a la competencia (p. 193)

market structure *estructura de mercado* Características importantes de un mercado tal como el número de compradores y vendedores, productos uniformes entre vendedores, facilidad de entrar al mercado, y formas de competencia (p. 192)

maximizing political support *maximizar apoyo político* Objetivo que guía el comportamiento de oficiales elegidos; comparable a maximizar un beneficio por empresas y maximizar servicios por hogar (p. 450)

mediator *mediador* Un observador imparcial que se lleva cuando las negociaciones de trabajo se quiebran, para sugerir como resolver las diferencias (p. 274)

medium of exchange *medio de intercambio* Cualquier cosa generalmente aceptada por todos los partidiarios a pago de bienes y servicios (p. 491)

merchandise trade balance *ajuste de mercancia de comercio* El valor de los bienes exportados por un país menos el valor de los bienes importados durante un perido asignado (p. 568)

merger *fusión* La combinación de dos o más empresas que forman una sola empresa (p. 209)

minimum wage law *ley de salario mínimo* Establece un precio mínimo que un empresario le puede pagar a un trabajador por una hora de trabajo (p. 270)

mixed economy *economía mixta* Sistemas económicos que mezclan planificación central con mercados competitivos (p. 37)

money *dinero* Cualquier cosa que todo el mundo está dispuesto a aceptar a cambio de bienes y servicios (p. 53)

money demand *demanda de dinero* La relación entre cuánto dinero la gente desea mantener y la taza de interés (p. 522)

money multiplier *multiplicador de dinero* El múltiple por el cual el abastecimiento de dinero aumenta como resultado de un aumento en las reservas de exceso en el sistema bancario (p. 522)

money supply *abastecimiento de dinero* La reserva de dinero disponible en la economía en un tiempo asignado (p. 527)

monopolistic competition *competencia monopolística* Una estructura de mercado sin obstáculos para entrar y muchas empresas vendiendo productos que son lo suficientemente diferentes que la curva de demanda de cada empresa se inclina hacia abajo (p. 202)

monopoly *monopolio* Un solo proveedor de un producto sin sustitutos cercanos (p. 193)

movement along a given demand curve *movimiento por una cierta curva de demanda* Cambio en cantidad exigida resultando de un cambio en el precio de un bien, otras cosas constantes (p. 122)

movement along a given supply curve *movimiento por una curva de oferta determinada* Cambio en cantidad ofrecida resultando de un cambio en el precio del bien, otras cosas constantes (p. 143)

multilateral aid *ayuda multilateral* Ayuda de desarrollo de una organización, tal como el Banco Mundial, que obtiene fondos de un grupo de paises (p. 600)

multinational corporation (MNC) *corporación multinacional* Una corporación grande que hace y vende sus productos en todo el mundo (p. 307)

multiplier effect *efecto multiplicador* Cualquier cambio en la póliza fiscal afecta la demanda total por más del cambio original en gastos o impuestos (p. 466)

mutual fund *fondo mutual* Una institución financiera que emite sus propias acciones y con sus ganancias compra un portofolio de valores (p. 300)

N

national economics *economía nacional* Estudio del comportamiento de la economía en su totalidad, especialmente la economía nacional (p. 14)

natural monopoly *monopolio natural* Una empresa que puede servir al mercado entero a un costo por unidad más bajo de lo que pueden dos o más empresas (p. 71)

natural rate of unemployment *desempleo a un índice natural* El índice de desempleo cuando la economía está produciendo su nivel potencial de producto (p. 462)

natural resources *recursos naturales* Llamados "regalos de la naturaleza", usados para producir bienes y servicios; incluye recursos renovables y agotables (p. 7)

negative externalities *externalidades negativas* Biproductos de producción o consumo que imponen costos a terceros participantes que no son ni compradores ni vendedores (p. 78)

net exports *exportación neta* El valor de las exportaciones de un país menos el valor de sus importaciones (p. 325)

net worth *valor neto* Activos menos pasivos; también llamado como el capital del dueño (p. 520)

nominal GDP *PIB nominal* PIB basado en precios que predominan en el momento de la transacción; PIB del dólar actual (p. 331)

nominal interest rate *índice de interés nominal* El índice de interés expresado en dólares actuales como porcentaje de la cantidad prestada; el índice de interés en el acuerdo del prestamo (p. 401)

not-for-profit organizations *organizaciones sin fin de lucro* Grupos que no persiguen beneficio como su objetivo; estos se dedican a actividades de caridad, educación, humanitarias, culturales, profesionales u otras con razón social (p. 246)

O

oligopoly *oligopolio* Una estructura de mercado con un pequeño número de empresas cuyo comportamiento es interdependiente (p. 203)

open-access good *bien con acceso abierto* Un bien que es un rival en el consumo pero costoso en la exclusión (p. 76)

open-market operations *operaciones de mercado abierto* Comprar y vender valores del gobierno de los Estados Unidos como forma de regular el abastecimiento de dinero (p. 502)

opportunity cost *costo de oportunidad* El valor de la mejor alternativa que se deja pasar por alguna actividad o algo elegida (p. 20)

P

partnership *sociedad colectiva* Dos o más personas acuerdan de contribuir recursos al negocio por una cantidad del beneficio (p. 236)

payroll taxes *impuestos de nómina* Impuestos deducidos de los sueldos para apoyar al Seguro Social y Medicare (p. 441)

perfect competition *competencia perfecta* Una estructura de mercado con muchos compradores y vendedores, bien informados, de un producto idéntico sin obstáculos para entrar (p. 192)

physical capital *capital físico* Las máquinas, los edificios, carreteras, aeropuertos, redes de comunicación, y otras creaciones fabricadas que se usan para producir bienes y servicios; también se llaman bienes capitales (p. 360)

physical infrastructure *infraestructura física* Transportación, comunicación, energía, agua, y sistemas de sanidad que el gobierno facilita y regula (p. 604)

positive externalities *externalidades positivas* Biproductos de consumo o producción que benefician a terceros participantes que no son ni compradores ni vendedores (p. 79)

potential output *producción potencial* La producción máxima de la economía sostenible a largo plazo (p. 462)

price *precio* Lo que se paga cuando se compra algo, y lo que se recibe cuando se vende (p. 164)

price ceiling *precio máximo* Un precio máximo legal alto del cual un producto no se puede vender; para tener impacto, un precio máximo debe fijarse abajo del precio de equilibrio (p. 180)

price floor *precio mínimo* Un precio mínimo legal más bajo del cual un producto no se puede vender; para tener impacto, un precio mínimo debe fijarse más alto del precio de equilibrio (p. 180)

price level *nivel del precio* Una medida de combinación que refleja los precios de los bienes y servicios de la economía en relación a precios en un año de base (p. 344)

prime rate *índice de interés preferencial* El interés que cobran los bancos por prestamos a sus más fiables prestatarios de negocio (p. 297)

private good *bien privado* Un bien con dos características: (1) la cantidad consumida por una persona no está disponible para otros y (2) los que no pagan pueden ser facilmente excluidos (p. 76)

private property rights *derechos de propiedad privada* Reclamo legal que le garantiza a un dueño el derecho de usar un recurso o de cobrarle a otros por su uso (p. 69)

privatization *privatización* El proceso de cambiar empresas públicas a empresas privadas (p. 607)

production possibilities frontier (PPF) *límites de posibilidades de producción* Muestra las posibles combinaciones de los dos tipos de bienes que se pueden producir cuando recursos disponibles se emplean completa y eficientemente (p. 42)

productive efficiency *eficiencia productiva* Se logra cuando una empresa produce al costo más mínimo posible por unidad (p. 179)

productive resources *recursos productivos* Materias primas o factores de producción, usados para producir los bienes y servicios que quiere la gente (p. 5)

productivity *productividad* El valor de producción por cada unidad adicional de un recurso (p. 257); la proporción de producción a una medida específica de producto; usualmente refleja un promedio, tal como medidas de áridos de grano por hectarea de terreno cultivado (p. 359)

progressive taxation *impuestos progresivos* El impuesto como porcentaje de ingresos aumenta al paso que los ingresos aumentan (p. 435)

proportional taxation *impuestos proporcionales* El impuesto como porcentaje de ingresos se mantiene constante al paso que los ingresos aumentan; también llamado un impuesto fijo (p. 435)

public good *bien público* Un bien que, al producirse, está disponible para que todos lo consuman, pero que el productor no puede excluir facilmente a los que no pagan (p. 76)

publicly traded corporation *corporación publicamente comercializada* Propiedad de varios accionistas; las acciones se pueden comprar y vender (p. 243)

pure centrally planned economy *economía pura planificada centralmente* Un sistema económico en el cual todos los recursos son del gobierno y la producción es coordinada por los planes centrales del gobierno (p. 37)

pure market economy *economía de mercado puro* Un sistema económico sin participación del gobierno para que las firmas privadas den cuenta de toda la producción (p. 37)

Q

quantity demanded *cantidad exigida* La cantidad exigida a un precio en particular (p. 106)

quasi-public good *bien cuasi-público* Un bien que, al producirse, está disponible para todos, pero los que no pagan son facilmente excluidos (p. 76)

quota *cuota* Un límite legal de la cantidad de un producto en particular que se puede importar (p. 560)

R

rational ignorance *ignorancia racional* Una postura adoptada por votadores cuando ellos encuentran que el costo de comprender y votar sobre un tema en particular excede el beneficio esperado de hacerlo (p. 451)

real GDP *verdadero PIB* El total producto de una economía medido en dólares de constante poder de compra; PIB medido en términos de bienes y servicios producidos (p. 331)

real interest rate *índice de interés real* El índice de interés expresado en dólares de poder constante de comprar como porcentaje de la cantidad prestada; el índice de interés nominal menos el índice de inflación (p. 401)

recession *recesión* Un descenso en producción total que dura por lo menos dos trimestres consecutivos, o por lo menos seis meses (p. 336)

recognition lag *lapso de reconocimiento* El tiempo necesitado para identificar un problema macroeconómico (p. 473)

regressive taxation *impuestos regresivos* El impuesto como porcentaje de ingresos reduce al paso que los ingresos aumentan (p. 435)

representative money *dinero representativo* Notas bancarias que se intercambian por un productor específico, tal como el oro (p. 497)

required reserve ratio *proporción de reserva requerida* Una regulación federal que dicta el mínimo porcentaje de depósitos que cada banco debe mantener en reserva (p. 520)

required reserves *reservas requeridas* El equivalente del dólar que debe mantenerse en reserva; depósitos verificables multiplicado por la proporción de la reserva requerida (p. 521)

reserves *reservas* Efectivo que bancos tienen a la mano en sus cámaras de seguridad o en deposito con la Reserva Federal (p. 500)

resource complements *complementos de recursos* Un recurso trabaja con el otro en producción; una reducción en el precio de uno aumenta la demanda por el otro (p. 260)

resource substitutes *sustitutos de recurso* Un recurso puede remplazar otro en producción; un aumento en el precio de un recurso aumenta la demanda por el otro (p. 260)

retained earnings *ganancias retenidas* La porción del beneficio de una corporación depués de impuestos que se reinvierte en la empresa (p. 299)

right-to-work law *ley de derecho de trabajo* Ley estatal que dice que un trabajador en una compañía con sindicato no tiene que unirse al sindicato o pagar cuotas del sindicato para tener un trabajo allí (p. 274)

rules of the game *reglas del juego* Las instituciones formales e informales que dan incentivos de producción y promueven actividad económica; tal como las leyes, costumbres y convenciones (p. 360)

S

scarcity *escasez* Una condición en todas las sociedades porque no hay suficientes recursos productivos para satisfacer los deseos ilimitados de la gente (p. 6)

S corporation *corporación S* Obligación legal limitada que se combina con el sistema de impuestos sencillo de los ingresos del negocio; no puede tener más de 75 accionistas sin accionistas extranjeros (p. 245)

seasonal unemployment *desempleo estacional* Ocurre por cambios en la demanda de trabajo de una estación durante el año (p. 388)

secondary markets *mercados secundarios* Mercados de valores donde acciones y bonos que ya se vendieron por la corporación se pueden intercambiar (p. 300)

secondhand securities *valores de segunda mano* Acciones y bonos que ya se han vendido por la corporación (p. 300)

securities *seguridades* Acciones y bonos de corporación (p. 299)

service *servicio* Algo no físico que requiere recursos escasos y satisface deseos humanos (p. 8)

shift of a demand curve *cambio de una curva de demanda* Aumento o reducción en demanda resultando de un cambio en uno de los determinantes de demanda fuera del precio del bien (p. 122)

shift of a supply curve *cambio en una curva de oferta* Aumento o rebaja en oferta resultando de un cambio en uno de los determinantes de oferta fuera del precio del bien (p. 144)

short run *a corto plazo* Un periodo durante el cual por lo menos uno de los recursos de la empresa es fijo (p. 148)

shortage *escasez* A un precio determinado, la cantidad por la cual la cantidad exigida excede la cantidad ofrecida; una escasez usualmente forza que el precio suba (p. 164)

social insurance *seguro social* Transferencias de efectivo para los retirados, los desempleados y otros con una historia de trabajo y un historial de contribuciones al programa (p. 86)

soft budget constraint *restricción de presupuesto temporal* En economías planeadas centralmente, la condición del presupuesto que se enfrenta por empresas estatales que son subvencionadas cuando pierden dinero (p. 607)

sole proprietorship *negocio propio* La más sencilla forma de organización de un negocio; una sola persona es dueña y dirige la empresa (p. 234)

specialization *especialización* Ocurre cuando trabajadores individuales enfocan en tasks individuales, permitiendo que cada uno sea más eficaz y productivo (p. 51)

stagflation *estanflación* Una caída o estancamiento, del producto de una nación acompañado por inflación en el nivel de precio (p. 407)

standard of living *nivel de vida* El nivel de una economía de prosperidad económica; mejor medida por el valor de bienes y servicios producidos por cápita (p. 359)

strike *huelga* El intento de un sindicato de trabajo de retener trabajo de una empresa (p. 274)

structural unemployment *desempleo estructural* Ocurre porque los que buscan trabajo no tienen las habilidades exigidas (p. 388)

substitution effect on a price change *el efecto de sustituir a un cambio de precio* Cuando el precio de un bien cae, los consumidores sustituyen ese bien por otros bienes, los cuales son ahora relativamente más caros (p. 103)

supply curve *curva de oferta* Una curva o linea que muestra las cantidades o un bien en particular ofrecido a varios precios durante un periodo específico, otras cosas constantes (p. 132)

supply of loans curve *curva de oferta de prestamos* Una curva con inclinación hacia arriba mostrando la relación positiva entre el índice de interés y la cantidad de prestamos ofrecidos, otras cosas constantes (p. 291)

supply *oferta* Una relación mostrando las cantidades de un bien que productores quieren y pueden vender a varios precios durante un periodo específico, otras cosas constantes (p. 132)

supply-side economics *economía de oferta de lado* Póliza de macroeconomía que enfoca en el cambio hacia la derecha de la curva de oferta total por medio de una reducción de impuesto u otros cambios que aumenten incentivos de producción (p. 408)

surplus *excedente* A un precio determinado, la cantidad por la cual la cantidad ofrecida excede la cantidad exigida; un excedente usualmente forza que el precio baje (p. 164)

T

tariff *trifa* Un impuesto a importaciones (p. 560)

tastes *gustos* Preferencias del consumidor; preferencias y aversiones en cosumo; se asume que son constantes por una cierta curva de demanda (p. 122)

tax incidence *incidencia de impuesto* Aquellos que soportan la carga del impuesto (p. 435)

total cost *costo total* Costo fijo más costo variable; el costo de todos los recursos usados por una empresa (p. 150)

total product *producto total* La producción total de una empresa (p. 148)

total revenue *ingresos totales* El precio multiplicado por la cantidad exigida a ese precio (p. 111)

trade deficit *déficit de comercio* La cantidad por la cual el valor de mercansias de importación excede el valor de mercancias de exportación durante un periodo asignado (p. 568)

trade surplus *exceso de comercio* La cantidad por la cual el valor de mercansias de exportación excede el valor de mercansias de importación durante un periodo asignado (p. 568)

traditional economy *economía tradicional* Sistema económico formado en su mayor parte por costumbre o religión (p. 40)

transaction cost *costo de transacción* El costo de tiempo e información requerido para realizar intercambio (p. 167)

transition economy *economía en transición* Sistema económico en proceso de cambio de planificación central a mercados competitivos (p. 39)

U

U.S. Agency for International Development (USAID) *Agencia de los Estados Unidos para Desarrollo Internacional* La agencia federal que coordina ayuda extranjera al mundo en desarrollo (p. 600)

underemployment *subempleo* Trabajadores están sobre calificados para sus trabajos o trabajan menos horas que lo que prefieren (p. 389)

unemployment benefits *beneficios de desempleo* Transferencias de dinero a trabajadores desempleados que buscan trabajo activamente y que llenan otros requisitos (p. 394)

unemployment rate *índice de desempleo* El número buscando trabajo dividido por el número en la fuerza de trabajo (p. 390)

Uruguay Round *La vuelta de Uruguay* La más reciente y la más completa de las ocho negociaciones de comercio multilaterales después de la guerra bajo GATT; creó la (WTO) Organización Mundial de Comercio (OMC) (p. 562)

utility *servicio* La satisfacción de consumo; sensación del bienestar (p. 63)

V

value added *valor adicional* A cada etapa de producción, el valor de un producto menos el costo de bienes intermediarios usado para producirlo (p. 326)

variable cost *costo variable* Cualquier costo de producción que cambia al paso que cambia la producción (p. 150)

vertical merger *fusión vertical* Una empresa combina con otra de la cual compra aportaciones o a la cual vende productos, tal como una fusión entre un productor de acero y un productor de autos (p. 305)

W

welfare reform *reforma de bienestar* Una revisión del sistema de bienestar en 1996 que impuso un límite de bienestar de por vida de cinco años por recipiente y otras condiciones (p. 416)

world price *pecio mundial* El precio al cual un bien se intercambia internacionalmente; determinado por la oferta mundial y la demanda mundial por el bien (p. 560)

World Trade Organization (WTO) *Organización Mundial de Comercio* La fundación legal e institucional del sistema multilateral de comercio que siguió a GATT en 1995 (p. 562)

Chapter 1 **p. 5**, In the News: The Gallup Business Monitor, "Many Americans have dreams of wealth," *Las Vegas Review Journal,* February 17, 2003, 1D **p. 8,** Span the Globe: Peter Hadfield, "Public Sold on Ugly, Wasteful Vending Machines," *South China Morning Post,* February 14, 2001; "Coke Testing Vending Unit That Can Hike Prices in Hot Weather," *New York Times,* October 28, 1999; "Sales Per Vending Machine Accelerates in Japan," *Beverage Digest,* August 29, 1999 **p. 10,** In the News: The Gallup Business Monitor, "As the Dow average goes, so goes Americans' economic confidence," *Las Vegas Review Journal,* October 28, 2002, 1D **p. 11,** E-conomics: May Wong, The Associated Press, "More businesses feeling right at home," *Las Vegas Review Journal,* June 24, 2002, 3D **p. 18,** Movers & Shakers: *USA Today Magazine,* www.randomhouse.com **p. 19,** In the News: Rebecca Gomez, The Associated Press, "Women continue moves into top jobs," *Las Vegas Review Journal,* November 19, 2002, 6D **p. 27,** Connect to History: Cotton, Lee. (July 15, 2002). The Virginia Company of London: Success or Failure? *Colonial National Historical Park, National Park Service, Jamestown Historic Briefs.* Retrieved February 7, 2003 from the World Wide Web: http://www.nps.gov/colo/Jthanout/VACompany.html; Fishwick, Marshall W. (1974) *Jamestown: First English Colony.* New York: American Heritage Publishing Company; Harrington, J.C. (1952) *Glassmaking at Jamestown.* Richmond: Dietz Press; Lieberman, Jethro K. (1999). *Companion to the Constitution: How the Supreme Court Has Ruled on Issues from Abortion to Zoning.* Los Angeles: University of California Press; Short, John. (February, 1994). *Glassmaking at Jamestown. Colonial National Historical Park, National Park Service, Jamestown Historic Briefs.* Retrieved February 7, 2003 from the World Wide Web: http://www.nps.gov/colo/Jthanout/Glassmak.html

Chapter 2 **p. 33,** In the News: Peter Landers, "Westerners Profit As Japan Opens Its Drug Market," *Wall Street Journal,* December 2, 2002, p.1 **p. 39,** Ethics in Action: Chris Jones, Gaming Wire, "COMDEX, 'Star Wars' creator pushes for better prevention of digital piracy," *Las Vegas Review Journal,* November 20, 2002, 4D **p. 41,** In the News: Joel Millman, "U.S. Chile to Meet for Final Round of Talks Over Free-Trade Pact," *The Wall Street Journal,* October 02, 2002, A2 **p. 44,** E-conomics: Jon Swartz, *USA Today,* November 18, 2002, 2C **p. 49,** Connect to History, Fishwick, Marshall W. (1974) *Jamestown:*

First English Colony. New York: American Heritage Publishing Company; Lieberman, Jethro K. (1999). *Companion to the Constitution: How the Supreme Court Has Ruled on Issues from Abortion to Zoning.* Los Angeles: University of California Press. Middletown, Arthur Pierce. (1953). *Tobacco Coast.* Newport News, Virginia: Mariners' Museum; Scharf, J. Thomas. (1967) *History of Maryland: From the Earliest Periods to the Present Day.* Hatboro, Pennsylvania: Tradition Press; *Tobacco News and Information.* (1998). A Brief History of Jamestown, Virginia. http://tobacco.org/History/Jamestown.html, February 10, 2003; *Tobacco News and Information.* (1998). Economic Aspects of Tobacco during the Colonial Period, 1612–1776; http://tobacco.org/History/Jamestown.html. February 10, 2003 **p. 50,** In the News: The Associated Press, "Heart patients do better with specialized outpatient care," *Las Vegas Review Journal,* November 21, 2002, 10B **p. 52,** Span the Globe: Julie Watson, The Associated Press, "Mexican inmates making furniture bound for Texas," *Las Vegas Review Journal,* December 2, 2002, 22A **p. 55,** Movers & Shakers: Interview via email; www.scripps.com/annrpt/99/nofrills/mess/mmain.html, and www.cablecenter.org/library/collections/oral_histories/history_detail.cfm?Selected History=183 (This is the Cable Center Library/Special Collections/Oral Histories)

Chapter 3 **p. 61,** In the News: Genaro C. Armas, The Associated Press, "Working parents finding more child care options," *Las Vegas Review Journal,* May 22, 2002, 1D **p. 65,** Span the Globe: Ted Anthony, The Associated Press, "China still trying to embrace global economy," *Las Vegas Review Journal,* December 11, 2002, 27A and *The New York Times,* April 28, 2003 **p. 68,** In the News: Neil King, Jr., "New Dumping Law Lines the Pockets of Manufacturers," *Wall Street Journal,* December 5, 2002, p. 1 **p. 69,** E-conomics: Bob Porterfield, The Associated Press, "Opening statements aired in copyright case," *Las Vegas Review Journal,* December 4, 2002, 8D and Electronic Frontier Foundation web site, http://www.eef.org/, "Jury Acquits Elcomsoft" press release **p. 74,** Movers & Shakers: *Reno Gazette-Journal:* www.rgj.com/news/stories/html/2003/01/09/31670.php, United States Hispanic Chamber of Commerce: www.ushcc.com **p. 75,** In the News: Sharon Theimer, The Associated Press, "Lobbyists push for new lawsuit limits," *Las Vegas Review Journal,* December 6, 2002, 24A **p. 79,** Ethics in Action: H. Josef Heber, The Associated Press,

"Support grows for arctic oil plan," *Las Vegas Review Journal,* March 13, 2003, 13A **p. 82,** In the News: Laura Meckler, The Associated Press, "encouraging statistics cited in new report," *Las Vegas Review Journal,* July 12, 2002, 5B **p. 91,** Connect to History: Hall, Kermit L. (Ed.). (1992). *The Oxford Companion to the Supreme Court of the United States.* New York: Oxford University Press; Lieberman, Jethro K. (1999). *Companion to the Constitution: How the Supreme Court Has Ruled on Issues from Abortion to Zoning.* Los Angles: University of California Press; Puth, Robert C. (1988). *American Economic History.* New York: The Dryden Press, Harcourt Brace Jovanovich College Publishers

Chapter 4 p. 101, In the News: Chris Jones, Gaming Wire, "HDTV coming slowly into view," *Las Vegas Review Journal,* April 11, 2003, p. D-1 **p. 106,** Ethics in Action: Pavel Rahman, The Associated Press, "Stampede for free clothes leaves at least 30 dead," *Las Vegas Review Journal,* December 2, 2002, p. 20A **p. 109,** In the News: Michelle Morgante, The Associated Press, "U.S. avocado capital cheers annual Super Bowl boost," *Las Vegas Review Journal,* Janurary 21, 2003, p. 10B **p. 111,** Span the Globe: Kenneth R. Weiss, Los Angeles Times, "Study finds industrial fleets have stripped oceans of big fish," *Las Vegas Review Journal,* May 15, 2003, p. 7-A **p. 117,** Movers & Shakers: Interview via email and www.awib.org **p. 118,** In the News: Scott McCartney, "Airlines Try Business-Fare Cuts, Find They Don't Lose Revenue," *The Wall Street Journal,* November 22, 2001, p. A-1 **p. 121,** E-conomics: Chris Jones, Gaming Wire, "Electronics experts tout power of women consumers," *Las Vegas Review Journal/Gaming Wire,* January 11, 2003, p. 3-D **p. 125,** Connect to History: *Gale Encyclopedia of U.S. History.* Thomas Carson & Mary Bonk, ed. Detroit, Gale Group. 1999; Michl, H.E. *The Textile Industries.* Washington, the Textile Foundation. 1938; *Oxford Companion to British History.* John Cannon, ed. New York, Oxford University Press. 1997; Puth, Robert C. American Economic History. New York, The Dryden Press. 1988; Watkins, James L. *King Cotton: A Historical and Statistical Review.* New York, Negro University Press. 1969

Chapter 5 p. 131, In the News: Yuki Noguchi, The Washington Post, "Wrong numbers: Dwindling profits kill off pay phones," *Las Vegas Review Journal,* January 1, 2003, p. 3D **p. 136,** Span the Globe: *Las Vegas Review Journal,* "Goats: Love for cashmere grows into affection for flock," February 3, 2003, pp. 1B and 7B; and http://www.bharattextile.com/newsitems/1974934 **p. 140,** In the News: The Office of International Information Programs, U.S. Department of State. http://usinfo.state.gov

p. 144, E-conomics: Shirley Leung and Ron Lieber, "The New Menu Option At McDonald's: Plastic," The *Wall Street Journal,* December 16, 2002, B1 **p. 146,** Movers and Shakers: http://www.pmqnews.com/papa_johns_quality_initiative.htm; http://louisville.bizjournals.com/louisville/stories/2001/11/26/story2.html; www.papajohns.com; http://www.louisville.com/voice/schnat113.shtml; http://www.forbes.com/finance/mktguideapps/personinfo/FromPersonIdPersonTearsheet/jhtml?passedPersonId=170010 **p. 147,** In the News: Sources: Joahn Tagliabue, "Now Playing Europe: Invasion of Multiplex," *The New York Times,* January 27, 2000; Bruce Orwall and Gregory Zuckerman, "After Joining the Megaplex Frenzy, Regal Gets the Box-Office Blues," *The Wall Street Journal,* September 27, 2000; Kenneth Gosselin, "State's Cinema Building Boom Fading to Black," *Hartford Courant,* October 26, 2000; and U.S. Census Bureau, *Statistical Abstract of the United States: 2000* **p. 155,** Ethics in Action: http://www.nytimes.com/2003/06/23/business/23COMP.html?th **p. 157,** Connect to History: *Gale Encyclopedia of U.S. History.* Thomas Carson & Mary Bonk, ed. Detroit, Gale Group. 1999; Michl, H.E. *The Textile Industries.* Washington, the Textile Foundation. 1938; Oxford Companion to British History. John Cannon, ed. New York, Oxford University Press. 1997; Puth, Robert C. *American Economic History.* New York, The Dryden Press. 1988; Watkins, James L. *King Cotton: A Historical and Statistical Review.* New York, Negro University Press. 1969

Chapter 6 p. 163, In the News: Raymond Gorman and James Kehr, "Fairness as a Constraint on Profit Seeking," *American Economic Review,* 82 (March, 1992), pp. 355–58, Joe Pereira, "Hasbro Trims 5% of Work Force," *The Wall Street Journal,* October 13, 2000. "Retailers Predict Hot Toys," Associated Press, October 17, 2000. The Toy Industry Association web site http://www.toy-tma.com/index.html and Pokemon World http:///www.pokemon.com/ **p. 166,** E-conomics: http://wifinetnews.com/ **p. 168,** Movers & Shakers: http://www.maryengelbreit.com; http://sbm.sbmin.com/asp/DisplayArticles.asp?ArticleId=827&CatId=78 **p. 169,** In the News: Thomas A. Fogarty, "Many consumers gasp at February gas bills," *USA Today,* March 12, 2003, p. B-1 **p. 174,** Ethics in Action: The Associated Press, "Price of Recordings Fixed, Judge Rules," June 28, 2002, http://www.nytimes.com **p. 178,** In the News: Amy Dockser Marcus, "Blood Supply Hits Lowest Level in Years; Surgeries Canceled," *The Wall Street Journal,* June 26, 2002 **p. 185,** Connect to History: Carlos, Ann M. *The North American Fur Trade, 1804–1821: A Study in the Life-Cycle of a Duopoly.* New York: Garland Publishing, Inc. 1986; Chittenden, Hiram Martin. *American Fur Trade of the Far West,* vol. 1 & 2. University of Nebraska. Press. 1987; Fuchs, Victor R.

The Economics of The Fur Industry. New York: Columbia University Press 1957; Lewis, Jon E. *The Mammoth Book of the West.* New York: Carrol & Graf Publishers, Inc.; 1996; *Oxford History of the American West.* Milner, Clyde A, O'Connor, Carol A., Sandweiss, Martha A., eds. New York: Oxford University Press. 1994

Chapter 7 p. 191, In the News: Bruce Stanley, The Associate Press, "War concerns push gold to six-year high," *Las Vegas Review Journal,* December 6, 2002, p. 2D **p. 194,** Span the Globe: Steve Frank, "Ebay's Stock Charges Ahead," *The Wall Street Journal,* July 8, 2001; Michelle Slatalla, "At a Virtual Garage Sale, It Frequently Pays to Wait," *The New York Times,* November 2, 2000; "The Heyday of the Auction," *Economist,* July 24, 1999 **p. 198,** Ethics in Action: The Associated Press, "States await court ruling on drug case," *Las Vegas Review Journal,* January 23, 2003, p. B-1 **p. 201,** In the News: Martha Brannigan, "Congress's Removal of 'Slots' Opens a Flood of New York Airports Gates," *The Wall Street Journal,* December 4, 2000; "Air Travel, Air Trouble," *Economist,* July 7, 2001; Rafer Guzman and Jane Costello, "Weather, La Guardia Flight Reductions Lift Airlines' On-Time Arrival Records," *The Wall Street Journal,* July 20, 2001; and Steven Morrison and Clifford Winston, *The Evolution of the Airline Industry* (Washington, D.C.: Brookings Institution, 1995) **p. 207,** Movers & Shakers: interview with Dwight Cooper **p. 208,** In the News: *The New York Times,* August 19, 21, and 23, 2003 **p. 211,** E-conomics: James Grimaldi, "Judge Orders Microsoft Split in 2," *Washington Post,* June 8, 2000; Ted Bridis, "Microsoft Ruling Sets High Standard for Proving Antitrust-Law Violations," *The Wall Street Journal,* July 2, 2001; Paul Krugman, "The Smell Test," *The New York Times,* July 1, 2001; John Wilke et al., "Ruling Sends Case to Lower Court, Denounces Judge Jackson's Findings," *The Wall Street Journal,* June 29, 2001; John Wilke and Ted Bridis, "Justice Department Says It Won't Seek Court-Ordered Breakup of Microsoft," *The Wall Street Journal,* September 7, 2001; Microsoft Announces Concessions on Licensing Deals with PC Makers, *The Wall Street Journal,* July 11, 2001; Steven Levy, Shooting with Live Ammo," *Newsweek,* August 13, 2001 and http://www.msnbc.com/news/COMJUSTICEVSMS_front.asp **p. 215,** Connect to History: Carlos, Ann M. *The North American Fur Trade, 1804–1821: A Study in the Life-Cycle of a Duopoly.* New York: Garland Publishing, Inc. 1986; Chittenden, Hiram Martin. *American Fur Trade of the Far West,* vol. 1 & 2. University of Nebraska. Press. 1987; Fuchs, Victor R. *The Economics of The Fur Industry.* New York: Columbia University Press 1957; Lewis, Jon E. *The Mammoth Book of the West.* New York: Carrol & Graf Publishers, Inc. 1996; *Oxford History of the American*

West. Milner, Clyde A, O'Connor, Carol A., Sandweiss, Martha A., eds. New York: Oxford University Press. 1994

Chapter 8 p. 225, In the News: Frappa Stout, *USA Weekend Magazine,* March 7, 2003, p. 17 **p. 230,** Span the Globe: *Fast Company,* January, 2003, p. 104 **p. 232,** Movers & Shakers: www.boomercareer.com/public/127_4.cfm?sd=41 "Roxanne Quimby Mines Her Own Beeswax for Millions" by Denise Lang; www.burtsbees.com **p. 233,** In the News: Tony Batt, Stephens Washington Bureau, "House votes 315-113 to toughen bankruptcy laws," *Las Vegas Review Journal,* February 23, 2003, p. 3B **p. 241,** In the News: James F. Peltz, Los Angeles times, "CEOs upset over reputations," *Las Vegas Review Journal,* July 19, 2003 **p. 244,** Ethics in Action: The Gallup Business Monitor, "Americans distrust corporate CEOs, poll shows," *Las Vegas Review Journal,* July 24, 2002, p. 7D and "Execs discuss ethics in U.S. businesses," *Las Vegas Review Journal,* March 17, 2003, p. 2D **p. 249,** Connect to History: Engerman, Stanley L. & Gallman, Robert E. *The Cambridge Economic History of the United States: The Long Nineteenth Century, volume II.* Cambridge, England: Cambridge University Press. 2000; Foner, Eric & Garraty, John A. eds. *The Readers Companion to American History.* New York: Houghton Mifflin. 1991; Heilbroner, Robert L. "Carnegie & Rockefeller" *A Sense of History: The Best Writing from the Pages of American Heritage.* New York: American Heritage. 1985; Puth, Robert C. *American Economic History.* Fort Worth: Dryden Press. 1988; Wall, J.F. *Andrew Carnegie.* New York: Oxford University Press. 1970; Warren, Kenneth. *Big Steel: The First Century of the United States Steel Corporation, 1901-2001.* University of Pittsburgh Press. 2001

Chapter 9 p. 255, In the News: Productivity and Costs report for second quarter 2003, revised, U.S. Department of Labor, Bureau of Labor Statistics, September 4, 2003 **p. 258,** Span the Globe: Frank Davies, Knight Ridder Newspapers, "Survey shows officials and the public at odds regarding immigration," *Las Vegas Review Journal,* February 18, 2002, p.18A **p. 265,** Movers & Shakers: interview with Dr. Tim Kremchek **p. 266,** In the News: Stefan Fatsis, "Thanks to Tiger's Roar, PGA Tour Signs Record TV Deal Through 2007," *The Wall Street Journal,* July 17, 2001. "Executive Pay," *Economist,* September 30, 2000. Robert H. Frank and Philip J. Cook, *The Winner-Take-All Society* (New York: Free Press, 1995). Barbara Whitaker, "Producers and Actors Reach Accord," *New York Times,* July 5, 2001. *Economic Report of the President,* January 2001, at http://w3.access.gpo.gov/eop/ **p. 270,** Ethics in Action: Genaro C. Armas, The Associated Press, "Census: Women still trail men at

671

highest salary levels," *Las Vegas Review Journal,* March 25, 2003, p. 9A **p. 273,** In the News: Troy Wolverton, "Labor pains," CNET News.com, January 16, 2001, http://www.news.com **p. 280,** E-conomics: John Miano, "Do High-Tech Firms Really Need Imported Workers?" *USA Today,* September 21, 2000. Scott Thurm, "Cisco Systems Helps to Train Union Workers in Web's Ways," *The Wall Street Journal,* July 3, 2001. Mark Boslet, "Lighting the Labor Fuse," *The Standard.com,* August 20, 2000. Steven Greenhouse, "Amazon Fights Union Activity," *New York Times,* November 29, 2000. Keith Ervin, "Microsoft Temps Group Joins Union," *Seattle Times,* June 4, 1999, and the CWA web site at http://www.cwa-union.org/

p. 281, Connect to History: Engerman, Stanley L. & Gallman, Robert E. *The Cambridge Economic History of the United States: The Long Nineteenth Century, volume II.* Cambridge, England: Cambridge University Press. 2000; Foner, Eric & Garraty, John A. eds. *The Readers Companion to American History.* New York: Houghton Mifflin. 1991; Puth, Robert C. American Economic History. Fort Worth: Dryden Press. 1988.

Chapter 10 p. 287, In the News: Paraphrase of actual pop-up ad for Mortgage Marketing On Line, September 11, 2003 and "Re-fi boom waning for mortgage lenders," *Milwaukee Business Journal,* September 11, 2003 **p. 292,** Ethics In Action: Christopher J. Gearon, "Tug of War Over Predatory Lending," *AARP Bulletin,* April 2003 **p. 294,** In the News: Stacy Forster, "Web Banks Seek Better Way to Take Customer Deposits," *The Wall Street Journal,* November 20, 2000. Pat Maio, "Wells Fargo CEO Sees Online Unit Profitable by April '02," Dow Jones Newswire, April 29, 2001. Juniper Bank's web address is http://www.juniper.com **p. 296,** E-conomics: Purva Patel, South Florida Sun-Sentinel, "Credit fraud cases growing nationally," *Las Vegas Review Journal,* December 18, 2003, p. 9D **p. 303,** In the News: "Banking Mergers," http:biggovernment.com/banking%20mergers.htm, April 15, 2003 **p. 307,** Span the Globe: James Hall and Nina Stechler Hayes, Dow Jones Newswires, "Krispy Kreme, Two Other Parties Plan to open 25 Stores in U.K.," *The Wall Street Journal,* November 20, 2002, p. B5D

p. 310, Movers & Shakers: Interview with Paul Gbodi, interview with franchise director at Jani-King, http://www.janiking.com **p. 311,** Connect to History: Engerman, Stanley L. & Gallman, Robert E. *The Cambridge Economic History of the United States: The Long Nineteenth Century, volume II.* Cambridge, England: Cambridge University Press. 2000. Foner, Eric & Garraty, John A. eds. *The Readers Companion to American History.* New York: Houghton Mifflin. 1991. Heilbroner, Robert L. "Carnegie & Rockefeller" *A Sense of History: The Best Writing from the Pages of American*

Heritage. New York: American Heritage. 1985. Puth, Robert C. *American Economic History.* Fort Worth: Dryden Press. 1988. Wall, J.F. *Andrew Carnegie.* New York: Oxford University Press. 1970. Warren, Kenneth. *Big Steel: The First Century of the United States Steel Corporation, 1901–2001.* University of Pittsburgh Press. 2001

Chapter 11 p. 321, In the News: "The U.S. Statistical System and a Rapidly Changing Economy," *Brookings Policy Brief,* no. 63 (July 2000): 2–8. Leonard Nakamura, "Is the U.S. Economy Really Growing Too Slowly? Maybe We're Measuring Growth Wrong," *Federal Reserve Bank of Philadelphia Business Review* (March–April 1997): 1–12 and Economic Report of the President, January 2001 **p. 325,** Span the Globe: Hans Greimel, The Associated Press, "Japan unveils reforms to stimulate economy," *Las Vegas Review Journal,* October 31, 2002, p. 24A **p. 328,** In the News: *Daily Policy Digest* article, National Center for Policy Analysis, June 27, 2001. D.A. Barber, "The 'New' Economy?," *Tucson Weekly,* January 8, 2003

p. 332, E-conomics: Gary McWilliams, "Dell Fine-Tunes Its PC Pricing to Gain an Edge in Slow Market," *The Wall Street Journal,* June 8, 2001. "Improved Estimates of the National Income and Product Accounts for 1959–95; Results of the Comprehensive Revision," *Survey of Current Business* 76 (January/February 1996); *Survey of Current Business* 81 (August 2001); and "From Investment Boom to Bust," *Economist,* March 1, 2001 **p. 335,** In the News: Jon E. Hilsenrath, "Real-Time Data Show Economy Reacting Positively to Iraq News," *The Wall Street Journal,* April 15, 2003, p. D-2 **p. 342,** Movers & Shakers: Interview with Norman Mayne; www.dorothylane.com and http://www.fastcompany.com/magazine/25/dorothy.html

p. 343, In the News: John D. McKinnon and Anne Marie Squeo, "Shaky Economic Times Limit Bang of New Defense Spending," *The Wall Street Journal,* April 15, 2003, p. A1 **p. 351,** Connect to History: Chernow, Ron. *The House of Morgan.* New York: Atlantic Monthly Press. 1990; Foner, Eric & Garraty, John A. ed. *The Readers Companion to American History.* Boston: Houghton Mifflin Company. 1991; Greider, William. *Secrets of the Temple: How the Federal Reserve Runs the Country.* New York: Simon and Schuster. 1987; Morris, Richard B. and Morris, Jeffrey B. *Encyclopedia of American History.* New York: Harper Collins. 1996; Parish, Peter J. ed. *Reader's Guide to American History.* Chicago: Fitzroy Dearborn Publishers. 1997; Puth, Robert C. *American Economic History.* New York: the Dryden Press, 1982

Chapter 12 p. 357, In the News: "China economic growth seen accelerating in 2004,"Reuters, September 25, 2003. Martin Crutsinger, Associated

Press, "2Q Economic Growth Revised Upward," September 26, 2003. World Bank (National GDP Totals for 2002). "German government casts doubt on own 2003, 2004 growth forecasts," *French Weekly Economic Report,* September 24, 2003 **p. 361,** Ethics in Action: BusinessWeek Online, http://biz.yahoo.com/bizwk/030812/ca200308120184_ca004_1.html

p. 365, Movers & Shakers: http://www.govtech.net/magazine/visions/feb99vision/yang/yang.phtml, http://docs.yahoo.com/info/misc/history.html

p. 366, In the News: Gordon M. Fisher, "The Development and History of the Poverty Thresholds," *Social Security Bulletin,* Vol. 55, No. 4, Winter 1992, pp. 3–14. U.S. Census Bureau Historical Poverty Tables. U. S. Census Bureau 2003 Poverty Guideline. World Bank report, "Two Years of Intifada, Closures and Palestinian Economic Crisis." *Lusaka Zambia Post,* August 28, 2003. Aneel Salman, "Breaking the cycle of poverty," *Talking Global News* **p. 372,** E-conomics, "Solving the Paradox," *Economist,* September 23, 2000; David Morgan, "Dot-Coms May Play Sleeper Role in U.S. Slowdown," Reuters, January 17, 2001; Leila Jason, "Software Lets Managers Watch Their Business from a Distance," *The Wall Street Journal,* August 30, 2001; Stephen Oliner and Daniel Sichel, "The Resurgence of Growth in the Late 1990s: Is Information Technology the Story?" Working Paper (May 2000), Federal Reserve Board **p. 374,** In the News: Center for Defense Information; Hon. Claude Bolton's (Assistant Secretary of the Army) keynote address to Conference on the Acquisition of Software Intensive Systems; "Spending on Homeland Security," Reuters, September 30, 2003; Department of Commerce figures on GDP/GNP

p. 378, Span the Globe: http://www.airbus.com/about/history.asp and William A. McEachern, *Economics: A Contemporary Introduction,* 6th edition, p. 463 **p. 381,** Connect to History: Bryant, Keith L. & Dethloff, Henry C. *A History of American Business.* Edgewood Cliffs: Prentice Hall. 1990; Chandler, Jr., A. *Giant Enterprise: Ford General Motors and the Automobile Industry.* New York: Harcourt, Brace, and World; Foner, Eric & Garraty, John A. ed. *The Readers Companion to American History.* Boston: Houghton Mifflin Company. 1991; Hurley, Daniel, *Cincinnati, the Queen City.* Cincinnati: The Cincinnati Historical Society. 1982; Kross, Herman E. and Gilbert, Charles. American Business History. Edgewood Cliffs: Prentice Hall, 1972; Morris, Richard B. and Morris, Jeffrey B. *Encyclopedia of American History.* New York: Harper Collins. 1996; Murdock, Eugene. *The Buckeye Empire: an Illustrated History of Ohio Enterprise.* Northbridge: Windsor Publications. 1988; Parish, Peter J. ed. *Reader's Guide to American History.* Chicago: Fitzroy Dearborn Publishers. 1997; Puth, Robert C. *American Economic History.* New York: The Dryden Press, 1982

Chapter 13   p. 387, In the News: "No picnic for millions this Labor Day," Associated Press story, August 30, 2003, http://www.cnn.com/2003/US/08/30/labor.day.ap/index.html; "Tarnished Gold," *Newsweek,* July 28, 2003, online archives http://archives.newsbank.com/ar-search/we/Archives?p_action=doc&p_docid=0FC9981EF35...; "Layoff Rose Sharply Last Month, Report Says," *New York Times,* September 5, 2003, http://www.nytimes.com/2003/09/05/business/05CND-JOBS.html?hp=&pagewanted=print&p... **p. 396,** Movers & Shakers: www.umassalumni.com/special_events/Bateman/taylor_bio.htm; www.pka.com/wjeff.html; www.monster.com **p. 397,** In the News: "The South Rises Again," *Economist,* March 7, 1998, p. 89, http://www.reelclassics.com/Articles/General/topten-article.htm Checked update on all-time box office champs NOT adjusted for inflation, from Exhibitor Relations Co., 9/2/03, published online at http://movieweb.com/movie/alltime.html **p. 400,** Ethics in Action: "Energy Dept. probes high gas prices," Associated Press story, http://www.cnn.com/2003/US/South/09/03/gas.price.probe.ap/index/html "Gasoline prices skyrocket in some parts of the country," CNN report, http://www.cnn.com/2001/US/09/12/gas.prices/index.html "Gregg calls for an investigation into gas price gouging," September 12, 2001, Indiana state government press release, http://www.state.in.us/legislative/hdpr/R45_09132001.html "Soaring Gas Prices in Missouri Under Investigation," September 12, 2001, Missouri Digital News, http://www.mdn.org/2001/STORIES/GAS1.HTM **p. 403,** In the News: http://www.umich.edu/news/Releases/2003/Feb03/r020303.html   http://www.post-gazette.com/localnews/20030408top50psychp8.asp **p. 409,** E-conomics: "The Onion: Funny site is no joke," from Business 2.0, http://www.cnn.com/2203/TECH/ptech/08/28/bus2.feat.onion.site/index.html

p. 411, Connect to History: Allen, Larry, *Encyclopedia of Money.* Santa Barbara: Checkmark Books, 2001; Engerman, Stanley L. & Gallman, Robert E. The *Cambridge Economic History of the United States: The Long Nineteenth Century, Volume II.* Cambridge, England: Cambridge: University Press. 2000; Foner, Eric & Garraty, John A. eds. *The Readers Companion to American History.* New York: Houghton Mifflin. 1991; Gordon, John Steele. "American Taxation," *American Heritage,* May/June, 1996; Puth, Robert C. *American Economic History.* Fort Worth: Dryden Press. 1988; Rosenbaum, Robert A., ed. *The Penguin Encyclopedia of American History.* New York: Penguin Reference, 2003; Engerman, Stanley L & Gallman, Robert E. The Cambridge History of the United States. New York: Cambridge University Press, 1996; Carson, Thomas, ed. Gale Encyclopedia of United States History. Detroit: Gale Group, 1999 **p. 412,** In the News: "The real face of homelessness," from TIME.COM, January 13, 2003, reprinted online at http://www.cnn.com/2003/ALLPOLITICS/01.13.timep.homelessness.tm/index.html "Census Bureau: U.S. poverty rate lowest in 20 years," CNN report, online http://www.cnn.com/2000/US/09/26/census.poverty.02/index.html 2003 *World Almanac and Book of Facts,* pp. 408–409

p. 417, Span the Globe: "Pro-Poor Tourism: Harnessing the World's Largest Industry for the World's Poor," International Institute for Environment and Development, May 2001. "Pro-poor Tourism: Opportunities for Sustainable Local Development," D&C Development and Cooperation (No. 5, September/October 2000, pp. 12–14), reprinted online at http://www.dse.de/zeitschr/de500-3.htm "Developing Tourism in Lower Mekong River Basin Countries," Asian Development Fund news release, December 12, 2002. http://www.adb.org/Documents/News/2002/nr2002250.asp

Chapter 14 p. 429, In the News: *Cavalier Daily,* September 18, 2003; United Press International Wire Story: "Nation called on to cut teen drinking," September 11, 2003 **p. 432,** E-conomics: "What Can Government Demand for Its Money?" *The Chronicle of Philanthropy,* July 24, 2003 **p. 437,** In the News: The Boston Globe, August 27, 2003; "On the Economy," *Industry Week,* August, 2003, p. 64; *The Washington Times,* July 21, 2003, Commentary: "Those tax cuts beginning to work," p. A20 **p. 444,** Span the Globe: Emily Parker, "Japan Needs an Exit Strategy," October 15, 2003, *Wall Street Journal* **p. 447,** In the News: "Medicare privatization language softens," United Press International, October 9, 2003; "Medicare Drugs: Fast-Moving Bill Gathers Special Interest Add-Ons," Newhouse News Service, June 20, 2003; "House Republicans fear weakened Medicare bill; Conservatives pledge to vote against measure that lacks reforms," *The Washington Times,* September 15, 2003 **p. 449,** Ethics in Action: "Oral arguments before U.S. Supreme Court," *Minnesota Daily,* September 16, 2003 **p. 453,** Movers & Shakers: http://www.usatoday.com/news/politicselections/2002-11-06-sebelius_x.htm http://www.ksgovernor.com/meetkathleen.php http://www.ksgovernor.org/cabinet.html

Chapter 15 p. 459, In the News: John Schwartz, "Social Security Checks to Rise 2.6%," *New York Times,* October 20, 2001; David Rosenbaum, "The President's Budget: Putting Faith in Discipline," *New York Times,* April 10, 2001; Charles Zwick and Peter Lewis, "Apocalypse Not: Social Security Crisis Is Overblown," *The Wall Street Journal,* April 11, 2001; "Status of the Social Security and Medicare Programs: A Summary of the 2001 Annual Report," Social Security and Medicare Boards of Trustees, March 19, 2001 **p. 463,** Span the

Globe: "laissez-faire," *Encyclopedia Britannica online,* http://search.eb.com/eb/print?eu=47953; "physiocrats," *Encyclopedia Britannica online,* http:search.eb.com/eb/print?eu=61379; "France," *Encyclopedia Britannica online,* http://search.eb.com/eb/print?eu=119330

p. 468, In the News: "Gramm-Rudman-Hollings," *Encyclopedia Britannica online,* http://search.eb.com/ebi/article?eu=335534&query=gramm-rudmann&ct= "Deficit-Focused Budget Reforms," http://www.house.gov/rules/jcoc2z.htm "The Budget Enforcement Act: Its Operation Under a Budget Surplus," CRS Report for Congress, http://www.house.gov/rules/98-97.htm; "BUDGET: Eliminating the National Debt is Priority #1," Fritz Hollings's Newsroom **p. 472,** E-conomics: "input-output analysis," *Encyclopedia Britannica online,* http://search.eb.com/eb/print?eu=43439; "economic forecasting," *Encyclopedia Britannica online,* http://search.eb.com/eb/article?query=economic+forecasting&ct=&eu=109000&tocid=25804 **p. 474,** Movers & Shakers: http://www.askmen.com/men/business_politics/29c_philip_knight.html www.nike.com http://www.stanfordalumni.org/news/magazine/1997/janfeb/articles/knight.html http://www.hoovers.com/free/co/factsheet.xhtml?COID=14254 **p. 475,** In the News: Department of Treasury Bureau of Public Debt, http://www.publicdebt.treas.gov/cgi-bin/cgiwrap/~www/opdpnhis.cgi http://www.publicdebt.treas.gov/opd/opdpenny.htm; "National Debt clock stops, despite trillions of dollars in red ink," CNN, online report, http://www.cnn.com/2000/US/09/07/debt.clock/index.html "Stopping the Clock: National Debt Clock to be Unplugged as Debt Shrinks," Associated Press story, reprinted on http://abcnews.go.com/sections/business/DailyNews/debtclock000515.html "National Debt Clock restarted," Associated Press story, reprinted on http://www.tallahassee.com/mld/tallahasee/business/3643411.htm?template=contentModule . . . and on http://abcnews.go.com/sections/business/DailyNews/debtclock020711.html **p. 481,** Ethics in Action, Robert J. Barro, "The Ricardian Approach to Budget Deficits," *Journal of Economic Perspectives* 3 (Spring 1989); Jay Mathews, "How High Is the Deficit, the Dow? Most in Survey Didn't Know," *Hartford Courant,* October 19, 1995, and David Rosenbaum, "Congress Agrees on Final Details of Tax-Cut Bill," *New York Times,* May 26, 2001 **p. 483,** Connect to History: *The American Heritage Encyclopedia of American History,* John Mack Faragher, ed., New York: Henry Holt and Company, 1998; Gordon, John Steele, Hamilton's Blessing, New York: Walker & Company, 1997; Gordon, John Steele, "The Founding Wizard" American Heritage, v. 41, no.5, July/August, 1990; Owens, Mackubin, "Alexander Hamilton," *The Founders Almanac*

Chapter 16 p. 489, In the News: *Knoxville News-*

Sentinel, June 22, 2003 **p. 494,** Ethics in Action: "Getting your life back; Locally based resource center supports victims of identity theft," *The San Diego Union-Tribune,* October 20, 2003 **p. 496,** In the News: "Gold could become Islamic euro," The Times (London), October 8, 2003 **p. 499,** E-conomics: "Review of Top US Online Banking Sites Finds Many Common Features, but Significant Gaps in Functionality and Usability," PR Newswire Association, Inc., October 6, 2003 **p. 504,** Connect to History: Allen, Larry. *Encyclopedia of Money.* New York: Checkmark Books, 2001; Carson, Thomas, ed. *Gale Encyclopedia of United States Economic History.* Detroit: Gale Group, 1999; *Economics and the Historian,* Berkeley & Los Angles: University of California Press, 1996; "Evolution of Money and Banking in the United States," *Business Review.* Federal Reserve Bank of Dallas (December, 1975); Faragher, John Mack, ed. *The American Heritage Encyclopedia of American History.* New York: Henry Holt and Company, 1998; Froner, Eric & Garraty, John A. The Reader's Companion to American History. Boston: Houghton Mifflin Company, 1991; Mokyr, Joel, ed. *The Oxford Encyclopedia of Economic History.* New York: Oxford University Press, 2003; Morris, Richard B. & Morris, Jeffery B., ed. Encyclopedia of American History. New York: Harper Collins, 1996; Parish, Peter J. ed. *Reader's Guide to American History.* Chicago: Fitzroy Dearborn Publishers, 1997; Puth, Robert C. *American Economic History.* New York: Harcourt Brace Jovanovich College Publishers, 1988; Rosenbaum, Robert A, ed. *The Penguin Encyclopedia of American History.* New York, Penguin Reference, 2003 **p. 505,** In the News: Copyright 2003, American Banker-Bond Buyer, a division of Thomson, CardLine, October 3, 2003 **p. 506,** Span the Globe: Board of Governors of the Federal Reserve System, October 17, 2003 report on M1; Cincinnati Post Online Service: In US They Trust, September 19, 2000, "U.S. Anti-Counterfeiting Efforts Effective, Says Treasury," U.S. Embassy Report, Tokyo, Japan 2003 **p. 512,** Movers & Shakers: E-mail correspondence with Tony Brown; www.cdfifund.gov; www.morethanabank.com/kimsHouseFY04testimony040903.doc

Chapter 17 p. 519, In the News: "U.S.: Saddam's family took $1 billion from bank," CNN report, reprinted on http://www.cnn.com/2003/WORLD/meast/05/06/sprj.irq.main/index.html; "Jesse James," *Encyclopedia Britannica online,* http://search.eb.com/ebi/print?eu=297080; "Bonnie and Clyde," *Encyclopedia Britannica online,* http://search.eb.com/eb/print?eu=13655 **p. 523,** E-conomics: "Online bank aimed at truck drivers debuts," *Computerworld,* August 15, 2000, reprinted on http://www.cnn.com/2000/TECH/computing/08/15/ebank.for.truckers.idg/index.html;

"credit unions," Encyclopedia Britannica online, http://search.eb.com/eb/print?eu=27263 **p. 525,** In the News: Greg Ip, "U.S. Federal Reserve Cuts Funds Rate by Half a Point to 40-Year Low Level," *The Wall Street Journal,* November 7, 2001; "How Low Can They Go?," *Economist,* October 6, 2001; "Minutes of the Federal Open Market Committee" and "FOMC Statement on Interest Rates," January 3, 2001, March 20, 2001, April 18, 2001, May 15, 2001, October 2, 2001, and November 6, 2001; "Fed cuts rates a quarter point," CNN report, http://www.cnn.com/2001/BUSINESS/12/11/fed.rate.cut/index.html; "U.S. Fed leaves rates on hold," CNN report, http://www.cnn.com/2002/BUSINESS/asia/09/24/US.fed.biz/index.html **p. 531,** Ethics in Action: "Enron Collapse stirs echoes of '80s Savings and loan woes," *St. Petersburg Times,* January 13, 2002. Reprinted on http://www.sptimes.com/2002/01/13/news_pf/Columns/Enron_collapse_stirs_shtml **p. 535,** Movers & Shakers: http://www.myprimetime.com/work/ge/schultzbio/index.shtml; www.starbucks.com; Howard Schultz, *Pour Your Heart Into It: How Starbucks Built a Company One Cup at a Time, Hyperion,* 1997 **p. 536,** In the News: Peter White, "The Power of Money," *National Geographic,* January 1993; Frederic Dannen and Ira Silverman, : "The Supernote," *New Yorker,* October 23, 1995; "Russia Official Nods to Money Boost," *New York Times,* September 30, 1998; Michael Bryan et al. "Who Is That Guy on the $10 Bill?" *Economic Commentary: Federal Reserve Bank of Cleveland,* July 2000 **p. 539,** Span the Globe: "Close race in Argentina election," CNN report, reprinted on http://www.cnn.com/2003/WORLD/americas/04/27/argentina.poll/index.html; "Germany," *Encyclopedia Britannica online,* http://search.eb.com/eb/article?eu=109160&tocid=58204&query=hyperinflation&ct=; "Bolivia," *Encyclopedia Britannica online,* http://search.eb.com/eb/article?eu=108670&tocid=218814&query=hyperinflation&ct= **p. 543,** Connect to History: Foner, Eric & Garraty, John A. ed. *The Readers Companion to American History.* Boston: Houghton Mifflin Company. 1991; Greider, William. *Secrets of the Temple: How the Federal Reserve Runs the Country.* New York: Simon and Schuster. 1987; Morris, Richard B. and Morris, Jeffrey B. *Encyclopedia of American History.* New York: Harper Collins. 1996; Parish, Peter J. ed. *Reader's Guide to American History.* Chicago: Fitzroy Dearborn Publishers. 1997; Puth, Robert C. *American Economic History.* New York: the Dryden Press, 1982

Chapter 18 p. 553, In the News: "Paying the price of free trade: Shattered dreams," *Edmonton Journal* (Alberta), August 31, 2003 **p. 555,** Ethics in Action: "FTAA Environmental Outlook Bleak, Experts Say," Inter Press Service, Inter Press Service, October

14, 2003; "Pollution Intensive Industry In Mexico Under Nafta: Model And Empirical Evidence," The Fletcher Journal of Development Studies VOLUME XV, 1999 **p. 559,** In the News: "Automotive Coalition Company Executives Travel to Washington to Urge Bush Administration to End Steel Tariffs," PR Newswire Association, Inc., October 8, 2003; "End the Steel Tariffs," *The Washington Post,* September 26, 2003, p. A26 **p. 563,** Span the Globe: "Free Trade Area Of The Americas: Big stumbling blocks remain," *The Atlanta Journal and Constitution,* October 30, 2003; "NAFTA and Workers' Rights and Jobs," Public Citizen; "North American Free Trade Agreement," Wikipedia, the free encyclopedia **p. 565,** Movers & Shakers, Information from Toyota's communications department. http://www.toyota.com/about/community/ education/mx_auto_training.html; http://archive. infoworld.com/articles/hn/xml/00/10/09/001009hn planettoyota.xml; http://www.jsonline.com/wheels/ peak/feb02/23136.asp **p. 567,** In the News: "Czech couple says they paid middlemen for Wal-Mart jobs," *The Tuscaloosa News* (Alabama), October 27, 2003; "Controversy surrounds employees on L-1 Visas," *The Dallas Morning News,* July 23, 2003 **p. 571,** E-conomics: "US Aid Agency-Backed Project To Develop E-Commerce In Uzbekistan,"BBC Monitoring International Reports, June 20, 2003; Council on Foreign Relations, Inc., Foreign Affairs, September 2003–October 2003; "Bush and Foreign Aid," Copyright 2003 Scripps Howard, Inc., Scripps Howard News Service; "U.S. stingy, says new index method," Scripps Howard News Service, June 13, 2003 **p. 574,** In the News: "Trade imbalance not China's choice," *China Daily,* August 25, 2003; The Main Wire, October 31, 2003; "U.S. Try FX Report Finds No FX Manipulation," AFX News Limited, October 26, 2003 **p. 581,** Connect to History: Carnes, Marc C. MacMillan Information Now Encyclopedia: U.S. History. New York. MacMillan Library Reference, 1996; Schwarz, Frederick D. "Abominations," *American Heritage* (November/ December, 2003)

Chapter 19 p. 587, In the News: "Okinawan Longevity: Demographic and Epidemiological Perspectives," a study by Drs. D. Craig Willcox and Bradley J. Willcox, http://www.oic-longevity.wwma. net/Abstracts/Drs._Willcox_willcox.html; "World's oldest turns 116 in Japan," Associated Press Story, September 17, 2003, http://www.cnn.com/2003/ WORLD/asiapcf/east/09/16/japan.oldster.ap/index.html; "World's oldest man dies at 114," Associated Press story, September 29, 2003, http://www.cnn.com/2003/ WORLD/asiapcf/east/09/28/japan.oldest.ap/index.html; "Living Longer: Study: Japanese, Australians Live Longest," ABC news story, http://abcnews.go.com/

sections/world/DailyNews/lifeexpectancy000604.html; "Life is short in Sierra Leone," BBC News story, June 5, 2000, http://news.bbc.co.uk/2/hi/africa/778027.stm **p. 592,** E-conomics: "Exporting Jobs Saves IT Money," from Computerworld magazine, March 23, 1999, http://www.cnn.com/TECH/computing/9903/23/ exportjobs.idg/index.html; "Finally a Productivity payoff from IT?," Fortune.Com, online version of Fortune Magazine, December 18, 2002, http://cnn.technology. printthis.clickability.com/pt/cpt?action=cpt&expire=- 1&urlID=489270…; "There's More to Consider than Cheap Labor," Computerworld magazine, April 28, 2003, http://www.computerworld.com/printthis/ 2003/0,4814,80662,00.html **p. 596,** Movers & Shakers: www.ebay.com; http://yahoo.businessweek. com:/print/bwdaily/dnflash/aug2003/nf20030818_ 1844_db049.htm?pi **p. 597,** In the News: Gina Chon, "Dropped Stitches," *Asiaweek,* December 22, 2000; Naomi Koppel, "Bush Policy May Break WTO Deadlock," Associate Pres, December 27, 2000; David Postman and Linda Mapes, "Why WTO Unified So Many Foes," *Seattle Times,* December 6, 1999; Leslie Kaufman and David Gonzalez, "Labor Standards Clash with Global Reality, New York Times, April 24, 2001; World Trade Organization web site, http://www.wto.org **p. 601,** Span the Globe: Michael Fletcher, "Fewer People Searched by Customers in Past Year," *Washington Post,* October 19, 2000; Alex Keto, "White House Watch: Bush Put on Notice on Trade," Dow Jones Newswire, August 2, 2001; Daniel Machulaba, "U.S. Ports Are Losing the Battle to Keep Up with Overseas Trade," *The Wall Street Journal,* July 9, 2001; Jim Yardley, "Truck-Choked Border City Fears Being Bypassed," *New York Times,* March 15, 2001; U.S. Customs Service home page, http://www.customs. treas.gov/; "China-Japan trade war worsens," CNN report 6/5/01, http://www.cnn.com/2001/BUSINESS/ asia/06/05/china.tradewar/index.html **p. 603,** In the News: "African Leaders Prepare for summit," IDG story, June 20, 2000, http://edition.cnn.com/2000/ TECH/computing/06/20/african.it.idg/; "Ghana tries to bridge computer-technology gap," *Computing* magazine, February 17, 1998, http://www.cnn.com/TECH/ computing/9802/17/ghana.internet/index.html **p. 606,** Ethics in Action: "Haiti: Growth and Structure of the Economy," Library of Congress information online, http://countrystudies.us/haiti/45.htm; "Jean-Claude Duvalier," Library of Congress information online, http://countrystudies.us/haiti/18.htm **p. 611,** Connect to History: Carnes, Marc C. *MacMillan Information Now Encyclopedia: U.S. History.* New York. MacMillan Library Reference, 1996; "The Past, Present and Future of the Multilateral Trading System," *WT Conference Daily,* September 10, 2003